Lecture Notes in Artificial Intelligence 2313

Subseries of Lecture Notes in Computer Science
Edited by J. G. Carbonell and J. Siekmann

Lecture Notes in Computer Science
Edited by G. Goos, J. Hartmanis, and J. van Leeuwen

Springer
Berlin
Heidelberg
New York
Barcelona
Hong Kong
London
Milan
Paris
Tokyo

Carlos A. Coello Coello
Alvaro de Albornoz
Luis Enrique Sucar
Osvaldo Cairó Battistutti (Eds.)

MICAI 2002: Advances in Artificial Intelligence

Second Mexican International Conference on Artificial Intelligence
Mérida, Yucatán, Mexico, April 22-26, 2002
Proceedings

Springer

Volume Editors

Carlos A. Coello Coello
CINVESTAV-IPN
Computer Science Section, Electrical Engineering Department
Av. IPN 2508, Col. San Pedro Zacatenco, Mexico, D.F. 07300, Mexico
E-mail: ccoello@cs.cinvestav.mx

Alvaro de Albornoz
ITESM-Mexico City, Computer Science Department
Calle del Puente 222, Tlalpan, Mexico, D.F. 14380, Mexico
E-mail: albornoz@campus.ccm.itesm.mx

Luis Enrique Sucar
ITESM-Cuernavaca, Computer Science Department
Reforma 182-A, Lomas de Cuernavaca, Temixco, Morelos 62589, Mexico
E-mail: esucar@campus.mor.itesm.mx

Osvaldo Cairó Battistutti
ITAM, Department of Computer Science
Rio Hondo 1, Progreso Tizapan, Mexico, D.F. 01000, Mexico
E-mail: cairo@itam.mx

Cataloging-in-Publication Data applied for

Die Deutsche Bibliothek - CIP-Einheitsaufnahme

Advances in arti□cial intelligence / MICAI 2002, Second Mexican International Conference on Arti□cial Intelligence, Mérida, Yucatán, Mexico, April 22 - 26, 2002. Carlos A. Coello Coello ... (ed.). - Berlin ; Heidelberg ; New York ; Barcelona ; Hong Kong ; London ; Milan ; Paris ; Tokyo : Springer, 2002
(Lecture notes in computer science ; Vol. 2313 : Lecture notes in arti□cial intelligence)
ISBN 3-540-43475-5

CR Subject Classi□cation (1998): I.2, I.4, F.4.1, F.1

ISSN 0302-9743
ISBN 3-540-43475-5 Springer-Verlag Berlin Heidelberg New York

Springer-Verlag Berlin Heidelberg New York
a member of BertelsmannSpringer Science+Business Media GmbH

http://www.springer.de

Printed in Germany

Typesetting: Camera-ready by author, data conversion by Olgun Computergra□k
Printed on acid-free paper SPIN 10846597 06/3142 5 4 3 2 1 0

Preface

Artificial Intelligence has failed to accomplish at least two highly significant predictions as we enter the new millennium. The English mathematician Alan Mathison Turing predicted that by the year 2000 we would have a machine that could pass the Turing test. The film "2001: A Space Odyssey", portrayed an intelligent computer named HAL which, among other things, was able to speak and understand English, and even read the lips of humans having a conversation. Such a machine would be created, according to Arthur C. Clarke, by the year 1997. We have reached the year 2002 and neither of these two predictions have been fulfilled. However, there have been many significant achievements in artificial intelligence and several new challenges are now on the horizon.

Two years ago, we held the first Mexican International Conference on Artificial Intelligence, MICAI 2000, which took place on April 11–14, 2000, in the city of Acapulco, México. After a first highly successful conference, we are pleased to introduce the second Mexican International Conference on Artificial Intelligence, MICAI 2002, which took place on April 22–26 in Mérida, Yucatán, México. The main aim of the conference was to promote research in AI, and cooperation among Mexican researchers and their peers worldwide.

As a historical note, it is worth mentioning that MICAI originated from the union of the Mexican National AI Conference (RNIA) and the International AI Symposium (ISA), organized annually by the Mexican Society for AI (SMIA, since 1984) and by the Monterrey Institute of Technology (ITESM, since 1988), respectively.

Over 85 papers (in English) from 17 different countries were submitted for consideration to MICAI 2002. After a thorough review process, MICAI's program committee and the program chairs accepted 56 high-quality papers which are included in these proceedings.

We would like to acknowledge the support of the American Association for Artificial Intelligence (AAAI), and the International Joint Conference on Artificial Intelligence (IJCAI). We are especially grateful for the warm hospitality and generosity offered by the Universidad Autónoma de Yucatán (UADY) and the Universidad Mesoamericana de San Agustín (UMSA).

A special word of thanks goes to the members of the advisory board, the members of the program committee, our sponsors, and our support staff.

Last but not least, we warmly thank all of the attendants to the conference for their participation.

April 2002

Carlos A. Coello Coello
Alvaro de Albornoz
Luis Enrique Sucar Succar
Osvaldo Cairo

Organization

MICAI 2002 was organized by the Mexican Society for Artificial Intelligence and the Universidad Autónoma de Yucatán (UADY), and the Universidad Mesoamericana de San Agustín (UMSA).

Conference Committee

Conference Chair:	L. Enrique Sucar (ITESM-Cuernavaca, Mexico)
	Osvaldo Cairo (ITAM, Mexico)
Program Chair:	Carlos A. Coello (CINVESTAV-IPN, Mexico)
	Alvaro de Albornoz (ITESM-CCM, Mexico)
Tutorials:	Gustavo Arroyo Figueroa (IIE, Mexico)
Workshops:	Humberto Sossa Azuela (CIC-IPN, Mexico)
Local Arrangements:	Francisco Madera (UADY, Mexico)
	Fernando Curi Quintal (UADY, Mexico)
	Pilar García Santos (UMSA, Mexico)

Advisory Committee

Felipe Bracho	Robert de Hoog	Pablo Noriega
Alan Bundy	Felipe Lara	Judea Pearl
Ofelia Cervantes	Christian Lemaître	Antonio Sánchez
Anthony Cohn	Jay Liebowitz	Xindong Wu
Francisco Garijo	Cristina Loyo	Wolfgang Wahlster
Randy Goebel	Donald Michie	Carlos Zozaya
Adolfo Guzmán	José Negrete	

Program Committee

David W. Aha	Carlos Brizuela	André de Carvalho
Juan M. Ahuactzin	Paul Brna	Argelio de la Cruz Rivera
Enrique Alba	Bill P. Buckles	Antonio D'Angelo
Matías Alvarado	Osvaldo Cairó	Thomas G. Dietterich
Alvaro de Albornoz	Francisco Cantú	Francisco J. Diez
James Allen	François E. Cellier	Jürgen Dix
Ronald Arkin	Jesús Cardeñosa	Bruce Draper
Gustavo Arroyo	Gabriela Cembrano	Wlodizislaw Duch
Gerardo Ayala	Carolina Chang	Vladimir Estivill Castro
Antonio Bahamonde	Carlos A. Coello Coello	Jesús Favela
Ricardo Beausoleil	Ulises Cortés	Joaquín Fdez-Valdivia
Ivan Bratko	Carlos Cotta-Porras	Robert Fisher

Juan J. Flores
Olac Fuentes
Pedro L. Galindo Riaño
José Antonio Gámez
Michael Gelfond
Alexander Gelbukh
Eduardo Gómez Ramírez
José Luis Gordillo
Silvia Guardati
Adolfo Guzmán Arenas
Arturo Hernández
Rafael M. Huber
Fernando Jiménez
Leo Joskowicz
Natalia Juristo
Henry Kautz
Nicolás Kemper Valverde
Ingrid Kirchsning
Mario Köppen
Angel Kuri Morales
Gerhard Lakemeyer
Pedro Larrañaga Mugica
Jean-Paul Laumond
Christian Lemaître
Bing Liu
R. López de Mántaras
Jacek Malec
Ana Ma. Martínez
Horacio Martínez
René V. Mayorga
Julian F. Miller
Maria Carolina Monard
Raúl Monroy
Guillermo Morales
Eduardo Morales
Francisco Mugica
Rafael Murrieta
Alexander Nari'yani
Juan A. Nolazco Flores
Gustavo Núñez Esquer
Konstantine M. Nyunkin
Gabriela Ochoa
Alberto Ochoa
Felipe Padilla Díaz
Andrés Pérez-Uribe
David Poole
Alessandro Provetti
María Cristina Riff
Carlos Ramírez
Patricia Rayón Villela
Jordi Riera Colomer
Katya Rodríguez
Raúl Rojas
Carlos Mariano Romero
Luis Alberto Pineda
Roger Z. Ríos
H. Rodríguez Hontoria
C. Rodríguez Lucatero
Alberto Sanfeliú Cortés
Eugene Santos Jr.
Leonid Sheremetov
Carles Sierra
Wolfgang Slany
Humberto Sossa
Rogelio Soto
Libor Spacek
Thomas Stützle
Enrique Sucar Succar
Ricardo Swain Oropeza
Demetri Terzopoulos
Miguel Tomasena
Carme Torras I Genis
Juan M. Torres Moreno
Edgar Vallejo Clemente
Johan van Horebeek
Maarten van Someren
Rineke Verbrugge
Felisa Verdejo
Toby Walsh
Alfredo Weitzenfeld
Franz Wotawa
Fritz Wysotzki
Shlomo Zilberstein
Carlos Zozaya

Collocated Conferences

TAINA – Workshops on AI

Sponsoring Institutions

The American Association for Artificial Intelligence
International Joint Conference on Artificial Intelligence
The Mexican Society for Computer Science

Supporting Institutions

CINVESTAV-IPN, UADY, UMSA, ITESM, ITAM, CIC-IPN, IIE, Universidad del Mayab, Estratel, FT Software.

We would like to thank Alberto Pastrana, Raúl Godoy Montañez, Luis Rodríguez Carvajal, Orlando Piña, the ACM student chapter at UADY, the Student Association at UADY, and the Student Council at UADY for their excellent organizational support. Special thanks go to Nareli Cruz Cortés and the Springer-Verlag staff for editing this volume.

Table of Contents

Robotics and Computer Vision

Heuristic Search and Optimization

Neural Networks

Machine Learning

Multiagent Systems

Uncertainty Management

AI Tools and Applications

Motion Planning for Car-Like Robots Using Lazy Probabilistic Roadmap Method

Abraham Sánchez L.[1], René Zapata[1], and J. Abraham Arenas B.[2]

[1] LIRMM, UMR5506 CNRS, 166 rue Ada 34392,
Montpellier Cedex 5, France
{asanchez, zapata}@lirmm.fr

[2] Facultad de Ciencias de la Computación, BUAP
Puebla, Pue., México
{aarenas}@cs.buap.mx

Abstract. In this paper we describe an approach to probabilistic roadmap method. Our algorithm builds initially a roadmap in the configuration space considering that all nodes and edges are collision-free, and searches the roadmap for the shortest path between start and goal nodes. If a collision with the obstacles occurs, the corresponding nodes and edges are removed from the roadmap or the planner updates the roadmap with new nodes and edges, and then searches for a shortest path. The procedure is repeated until a collision-free path is found. The goal of our approach is to minimize the number of collision checks and calls to the local method. Experimental results presented in this paper show that our approach is very efficient in practice.

1 Introduction and Motivation

We consider the basic problem, where there is one robot present in a static and known environment, and the task is to compute a collision-free path describing a motion that brings the robot from its current position to some desired goal position. The space where the robot and the obstacles are physically present is called the *workspace* $\mathcal{W}$. The planning is mostly performed in another space, the *configuration space* $\mathcal{CS}$. Each placement of the robot in $\mathcal{W}$ is mapped to a point in $\mathcal{CS}$. The portion of $\mathcal{CS}$ corresponding to collision-free placements of the robot is referred to as the *free-configuration space* $\mathcal{CS}_f$.

Automatic motion planning has applications in many areas such as robotics, virtual prototyping, graphic animation, medical surgery, and computational chemistry. Although many different motion planning methods have been proposed, most are not used in practice since they are computationally infeasible except for some restricted cases. Indeed, there is strong evidence that any complete planner requires time exponential in the number of degrees of freedom (dofs) of the robot. For this reason, attention has focused on randomized or probabilistic motion planning methods.

Probabilistic roadmap method (PRM) is a general planning scheme building probabilistic roadmaps by randomly selecting configurations from the free-configuration space and interconnecting certain pairs by simple feasible paths.

C.A. Coello Coello et al. (Eds.): MICAI 2002, LNAI 2313, pp. 1–10, 2002.

The method has been applied to a wide variety of robot motion planning problems with remarkable success [1], [2], [3], [4], [5].

There are two main classes of PRM planners [6]: *multi-query* and *single-query* planners. A multi-query planner pre-computes a roadmap and then uses it to process multiple queries [2], [3], [4], [5]. In general, the query configurations are not known in advance, so the roadmap must be distributed over the entire $\mathcal{CS}_f$. On the other hand, a single-query planner computes a new roadmap for each query [1], [6], [7]. Its only goal is to find a collision-free path between two query configurations. The less free space it explores before finding such a path, the better. Single query planners are more suitable in environments with frequent changes.

Since PRM planners perform relatively expensive pre-computation, they are most suitable for processing multiple queries in a static environment. However, of particular interest are planners that with little preprocessing can answer single queries very quickly. Such planners can be used to re-plan paths in applications where the configuration space obstacles could change. This occurs, for instance, when the robot changes tools, grasps an object, or a new obstacle enters the workspace.

In this paper we further develop probabilistic planning techniques in direction of achieving general and practical useful single query planners. We present a extended approach based upon a general scheme for lazy evaluation of the feasibility of the roadmap. Original version of lazy PRM was presented by Bohlin and Kavraki [8]. The scheme suggested for lazy evaluation of roadmaps is general and can be applied to any graph that needs to be explored. In addition to lazy PRM, other related algorithms, and variations of PRM, can benefit from this scheme and significantly increase performance.

This paper is organized as follows. Section 2 presents works related to nonholonomic motion planning. Section 3 deals with car-like robots and briefly presents the local method, Reeds & Shepp's paths. Our algorithm is described in detail in Section 4, and experimentally evaluated in Section 5. Section 6 discusses our results and presents future work.

2 Previous and Related Work

A first single-shot random planner for free-flying planar robots was described in [1] and subsequently expanded into a general learning approach for various robot types in [2]. Vallejo, Jones and Amato [7] propose an adaptive framework for single-shot motion planning. The author's strategy consists of adaptively select a planner whose strengths match the current situation, and then switch on-line to a different plannner. Experimental results show that this strategy solves queries that none of the planners could solve on their own; and is suitable for crowded environments in which the robot's free-configuration space has narrow corridors such as in maintainability studies in complex 3-D CAD models.

The lazy PRM presented by Bohlin and Kavraki [8] describes an algorithm, which minimize the number of collision checks performed during planning. In contrast with classic PRMs, the planner initially assumes that all nodes and edges in the roadmap are collision-free, and searches the roadmap at hand for a shortest path between the start and the goal node. The nodes and edges along the path are checked for collision. If a collision with the obstacles occurs, the corresponding nodes and edges are removed from the roadmap. Planner either finds a new shortest path, or first updates the roadmap with new nodes and edges, and searches for a shorter path. The process is repeated until a collision-free path is found. Experimental results show a six dof robot in a realistic industrial environment.

Another simple and efficient approach for solving single-query path planning problems is presented in [6] by Kuffner and Lavalle. The approach works by incrementally building two rapidly-exploring random trees (RRTs) rooted at the start and the goal configurations. The key idea is to bias the exploration towards unexplored portions of the space by sampling points in the state space, and incrementally "pulling" the search tree toward them. The drawbacks for this method are the choice of the a suitable metric, the construction of nearest-neighbors and the collision detection. Experimental results presented by the authors include planning problems that involve holonomic constraints for rigid and articulated bodies, manipulation, nonholonomic constraints, kinodynamic constraints, and kinematics closure constraints.

The planner presented by Sánchez and Latombe [9] uses a lazy collision-checking strategy (it postpones collision tests along connections in the roadmap until they are absolutely needed) with single-query bi-directional sampling techniques (it does not pre-compute a roadmap, but uses the two input query configurations to explore as little space as possible and searches the robot's free space by concurrently building a roadmap made of two trees rooted at the query configurations). Combining these techniques, the planner can solve path planning problems of practical interest (i.e. with realistic complexity) in times ranging from fractions of a second to a few seconds.

Planners based on lazy strategy [8] and [9] always use as local method the computing of the straight-line segment (Euclidean distance). Much research has been done on motion plannning for nonholonomic car-like robots (see [10] for a review). Švestka and Overmars [4] use the RTR paths as local method. An alternative is to use a local method that constructs the shortest path connecting the two configurations as was done in [11], [5], [12]. Another randomized strategy that has been used for non-holonomic planning is the RRT approach [6].

3 Model of a Car-Like Robot

With reference to Fig. 1, the coordinates x and y determine the position in the plane of the rear wheel axle mid-point of the car, while θ is the angle that the unit direction vector forms with the positive x axis. A *configuration* of the car is given by a triple $(x, y, \theta) \in \Re^2 \times S^1$, where S^1 is the unit circle in the plane. The point $(x, y) \in \Re^2$ will be referred to as the *position* of the car in the plane.

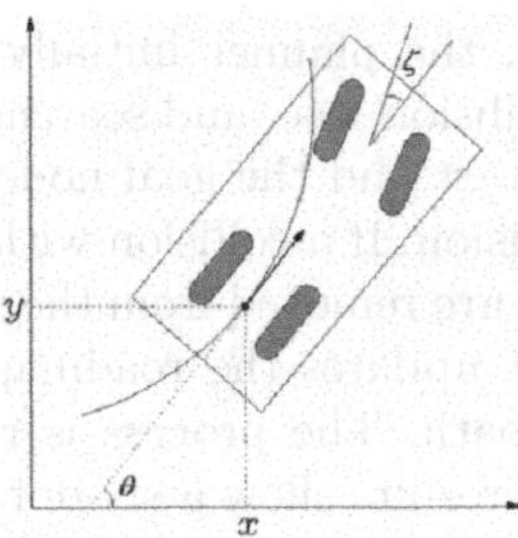

Fig. 1. A car-like robot

The proposed model corresponds to the motion in the plane of a particle subject to curvature constraints.

Distance computation plays a crucial role in robot motion planning. The distance from a robot configuration to an obstacle is the length of the shortest feasible path bringing the robot in contact with the obstacle. Car-like robots are non-holonomic systems. This means that any path in the configuration space is not necessarily feasible. As a consequence, the length of the shortest feasible paths induces a special distance, the so-called non-holonomic distance, that is not an Euclidean distance.

For an overview on geometric algorithms to compute obstacle distance for a point-wise car-like robot moving both forward and backward or only forward among polygonal obstacles, see [13].

3.1 Shortest Path without Obstacle

The study of the shortest path for a car-like robot has already an history. It has first been addressed without considering the presence of any obstacle. The pioneering result has been achieved by Dubins who characterized the shape of the shortest paths when the robot moves always forward [13]. Shortest paths are a finite sequence of at most 3 pieces consisting of straight line segments or arcs of a circle with radius 1. More recently, Reeds and Shepp have provided a sufficient family of 48 shor-test paths for the car-like robot moving both forward and backward [11]: optimal paths are constructed by a finite sequence of at most five elementary pieces which are either straight line segments or arcs of a circle of radius 1.

A comprehensive overview on optimal trajectories for mobile robots is presented in [14].

3.2 Shortest Paths in the Presence of Obstacles

The problem of computing the shortest path for a car-like robot in the presence of obstacles is a very difficult one. The existence of a shortest collision-free path for Reeds and Shepp's car is no more guaranteed. A shortest path may not exist [15]. The problem for Dubin's car has been recently proved to be NP-hard [16].

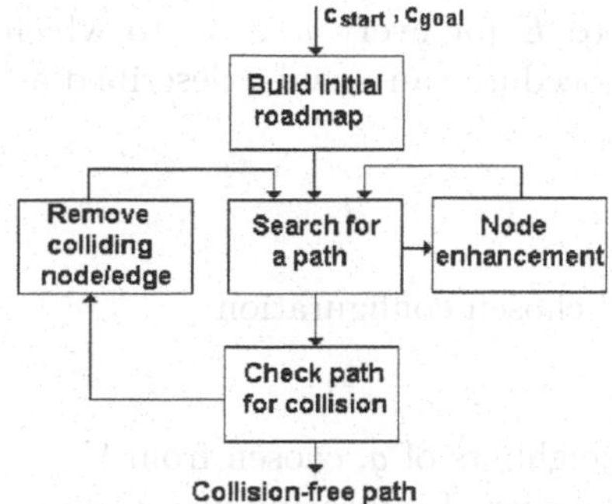

Fig. 2. High-level description of the algorithm

More recent results solve the problem of computing a shortest path when the obstacles are pairwise disjoint and when they are bounded by curves whose curvature is greater than 1 (i.e., the so-called moderate obstacles) [17].

4 The Algorithm for Lazy PRM

Classic PRMs computation is organized in two phases: the *learning phase* and the *query phase* [2], [3]. During the learning phase a probabilistic roadmap is constructed by repeatedly generating random free configurations of the robot and connecting these configurations using a simple, but very fast local motion planner. The flexibility of this approach lies on the fact that the properties of the paths computed in the query phase are induced by the paths computed by the local method. We use the Reeds & Shepp paths as local method [11].

Following the learning phase, multiple queries can be answered. In contrast with classic PRMs, our planner initially assumes that all nodes and edges in the roadmap are collision-free, and searches in the roadmap a shortest path between the start and goal configurations. If a collision occurs, the corresponding nodes and edges are removed. The planner finds a new path, or updates the roadmap with new nodes and edges. The procedure is repeated until a collision-free path is found. This procedure can terminate in either of two ways. If there exist feasible paths in the roadmap between q_{start} and q_{goal}. Otherwise, if there is no feasible path.

Fig. 2 shows a high-level description of the algorithm. The rest of this section explains the different steps of the algorithm in more detail. Our work is most closely parallels to the work of Bohlin and Kavraki [8].

4.1 Building the Initial Roadmap

The first step of the algorithm is to build a roadmap. The procedure is extremely simple. It builds up a graph $G = (V, E)$ by repeatedly generating a random configuration q, adding q to V, computing a set $V_c \in V$ (k's neighbors), and adding an edge (q, n) to E for every $n \in V_c$ to which the local method can connect from q. The procedure can now be described as follows:

$V \leftarrow q_{start}, q_{goal}$
$E \leftarrow \emptyset$
while $n_{nodes} < N$ do
    $q \leftarrow$ a 'randomly' chosen configuration
    if $q \in \mathcal{CS}$ then
        $V \leftarrow V \cup \{q\}$
        $V_c \leftarrow$ a set of neighbors of q, chosen from V
        forall $v \in V_c$, in order of increasing $d(v, q)$ do
            if $\neg$ connected$(q, v) \wedge L(q, v) \subset \mathcal{CS}$ then
                $E \leftarrow E \cup \{(q, v)\}$
end

4.2 Searching for a Path

The second procedure in the algorithm is to find a shortest path in G between q_{start} and q_{goal}, or to determine that no one exists. For this purpose we use the A^* algorithm. If the search procedure succeeds in finding a path, we need to check it for collision. Otherwise, if no path exists in the roadmap, we report failure, or go to node enhancement step to add more nodes to the roadmap and start searching again depending on the overall time allowed to solve the problem.

4.3 Checking Paths for Collision

When the A^* algorithm has found a shortest path between c_{start} and c_{goal}, we need to check the nodes and edges along the path for collision. Collision detection must be performed during the operation of the algorithm in order to determine when the process of subdivision has succeeded in a particular interval. It's should be noted that the detection of collision is performed for a certain pre-specified class of trajectories. In particular, for the car-like robot, the trajectories are composed of arcs of circles and straight line segments. Furthermore, arctangents need not be computed, since the ordering of possible intersections by angle can be done by comparing the sines and cosines of the angles, which can be computed from the cross and dot product of the appropriate vectors.

In this implementation, collision detection is performed by considering pairs of robot vertices and obstacles edges, and obstacle vertices and robot edges for each portion of a trajectory, we perform $O(mn)$ operations, where m and n are the number of robot vertices and obstacle vertices, respectively, but it seems clear that with some preprocessing we could reduce this complexity.

4.4 Node Enhancement

If the search procedure fails, so there does not exist a feasible path between q_{start} and q_{goal} in the roadmap and then it is necessary more new nodes to continue

Fig. 3. A planned path obtained in 0.67 sec

the search. In this step, we generate N_e new nodes. During the construction of the roadmap without taking into account the collisions with the obstacles, if there exist nodes that were not connected using the nodes addition strategy (k-nearest), the algorithm proceeds to execute during certain time the same strategy to try to connect them to the roadmap. In our experiments presented in the next section, we have not carried out the execution of the algorithm in scenes with narrow passages. An analysis of the different experiments shows that this step is executed sporadically. However, if this step is executed several times, it may cause problems with clustering of nodes. To avoid this phenomenon, we only use edges whose end-nodes are generated uniformly at random when selecting seeds.

5 Experimental Results

This section presents experimental results for car-like robots obtained by applying the algorithm described above to different scenes. The algorithm has been implemented in Java and the tests were performed on an Intel © Pentium III processor-based PC running at 866 Mhz with 128 Mb RAM.

After having executed our algorithm in different scenes, in the majority of the cases the motion planning problem is solved. The algorithm produces a first roadmap by sampling configuration spaces uniformly. It computes the shortest path in this roadmap between two query configurations and tests it for collision. If a collision is detected the node and/or edge where it occurs are removed, and a new shortest path is computed and tested; and so on.

Fig. 3 shows an example of a planned path for a car-like robot: the workspace is modeled by a grid of 250×150 pixels; the total running of the graph searching is 0.67 sec. Fig. 4 shows a parallel parking scenario (we used for this example 100 nodes and the path is computed in 0.22 sec). The third scene is shown in Fig. 5, we used for this example 150 nodes and the path is computed in 1.56 sec.

In Table 1 are shown the experimental results for the classic problem (Fig. 4). These results for basic PRM include the number of collision checks, the number

Fig. 4. The classic example: parking a car

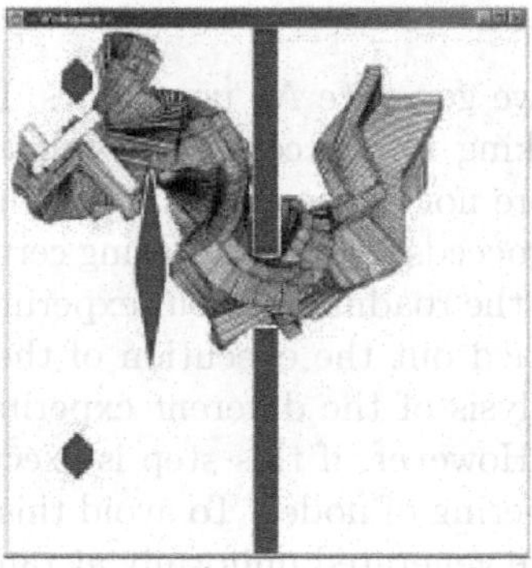

Fig. 5. A more complicated scene, the planned path is computed in 1.56 sec

of calls to local method; the running times are divided into two parts: firstly, graph building (learning phase), and finally the graph searching (query phase).

Experimental results for lazy PRM are given in Table 2, include the number of calls to local method during the graph searching and collision checks, and the running time for the solution path.

6 Discussion and Future Work

The aim of this approach is to minimize the number of collision checks and calls to the local method while searching the shortest feasible path in a roadmap. This is done on the expense of frequent graph search. However, if the robot and the obstacles have a very simple geometry, then the collision checking is very fast. We clearly see in Table 1 that collision checking represents the vast majority of the planning time, but also that the graph building takes a lot of time. Comparing the number of collision checks performed by Lazy PRM in Table 2 to the number of collision checks required to explore the entire initial roadmap in Table 1, we

Table 1. Performance data for Basic PRM for the classic problem: parking a car

Basic PRM	20 nodes	40 nodes	60 nodes	80 nodes	100 nodes
graph building	2.74	5.88	8.57	11.37	14.77
graph searching	0.275	0.600	0.600	0.110	0.280
calls to local method	43	183	447	720	941
coll. checking	17759	49808	96750	129998	176231
found feasible path	yes	yes	yes	yes	yes

Table 2. Performance data for Lazy PRM for the classic problem: parking a car

Lazy PRM	20 nodes	40 nodes	60 nodes	80 nodes	100 nodes
graph searching		0.570	0.500	0.460	0.220
calls to local method		85	91	97	101
coll. checking		9232	9905	10705	11206
found feasible path	no	yes	yes	yes	yes

see that Lazy PRM only explores a small fraction of the roadmap. Single queries are handled very quickly; indeed, no preprocessing is required[1]. The algorithm has one parameter that is critical for the performance: N, the initial number of nodes.

PRMs planners spend most of their time performing collision checks (often much more than 90%). Several approaches are possible to reduce the overall cost of collision checking:

- Developing faster collision-checking algorithms (in the case of 3-dimensional environments);
- Designing sampling strategies to obtain smaller roadmaps. For example, the method described in [5] keeps the number of nodes in the roadmap to a minimum. Candidate nodes are generated uniformly at random, one at time. A node is inserted to the roadmap only if it can be connected to at least two components of the roadmap, or if it does not see any other node;
- Postpone collision-checking operations until they are absolutely needed.

The advantages of our implementation is the capability of running on any platforms that support Java. One can notice that computing time depend on the platforms where the application is executed.

A lot of useful future research can be done in various directions, as in the generation of paths executable by real robots, automatic parameter choice (for instance, the number of nodes), sensor-based motion planning in partially unknown environments, motion planning in dynamic environments, an extension of the planner to represent 3-dimensional environments, and finally for solving nonholonomic motion planning problems for mobile manipulators.

[1] In our case, due to the strategy of node adding, the construction of the roadmap requires certain time that is proportional to the number of nodes.

References

1. Overmars, M. H.: A random approach to motion planning. Technical Report RUU-CS-92-32, Utrecht University (1992)
2. Overmars, M. H., Švestka, P.: A probabilistic learning approach to motion planning. Workshop on the Algorithmic Foundations of Robotics. A. K. Peters (1994) 19-37
3. Kavraki, L. E., Švestka, P., Latombe, J-C., Overmars, M. H.: Probabilistic roadmaps for path planning in high-dimensional configuration spaces. IEEE Transactions on Robotics and Automation. Vol 12, No. 4 (1996) 566-579
4. Švestka, P., Overmars, M. H.: Motion planning for car-like robots using a probabilistic learning approach. The International Journal of Robotics Research. Vol 16, No. 2 (1997) 119-143
5. Nissoux, C., Siméon, T., Laumond, J. P.: Visibility based probabilistic roadmaps. IEEE International Conference on Intelligent Robots and Systems (1999)
6. Kuffner, J. J., LaValle, S. M.: RRT-Connect: An efficient approach to single-query path planning. IEEE International Conference on Robotics and Automation (2000)
7. Vallejo, D., Jones, C., Amato, N. M.: An adaptive framework for 'single-shot' motion planning. Technical Report 99-024. Texas A&M University (1999)
8. Bohlin, R., Kavraki, L. E.: Path planning using lazy PRM. IEEE International Conference on Robotics and Automation (2000) 521-528
9. Sánchez, A. G., Latombe, J-C.: A single-query bi-directional probabilistic roadmap planner with lazy collision checking. Int. Symposium on Robotics Research (ISRR'01) (2001)
10. Laumond, J-P Ed.: Robot motion planning and control. Springer Verlag (1988)
11. Reeds, J. A., Shepp, R. A.: Optimal paths for a car that goes both forward and backwards. Pacific Journal of Mathematics. 145(2) (1990) 367-393
12. Sánchez, L. A., Arenas, B. J. A., Zapata, R.: Optimizing trajectories in non-holonomic motion planning. In 3er Encuentro Internacional de Ciencias de la Computación. INEGI (2001) 479-488
13. Vendittelli, M., Laumond, J. P., Nissoux, C.: Obstacle distance for car-like robots. IEEE Transactions on Robotics and Automation. Vol 15, No. 4 (1999) 678-691
14. Souères, P., Boissonnat, J-D.: Optimal trajectories for non-holonomic robots. In Robot motion planning and control, J. P. Laumond Ed. Vol 229, Springer Verlag (1998)
15. Desaulniers, G.: On shortest paths for a car-like robot maneuvering around obstacles. Robotics and Autonomous Systems. Vol 17 (1996) 139-148
16. Reif, J., Wang, H.: The complexity of the two dimensional curvature-constrained shortest-path problem. Robotics: The algorithmic perspective. P. K. Agarwal et al. Eds, A. K. Peters (1998)
17. Agarwal, P. K., Raghavan, P., Tamaki, H.: Motion planning for a steering-constrained robot through moderate obstacles. In ACM Symp. on Computational Geometry (1995)

A Vision System for Environment Representation: From Landscapes to Landmarks

Rafael Murrieta-Cid[1,*], Carlos Parra[2,**], Michel Devy[3], Benjamín Tovar[1], and Claudia Esteves[1]

[1] ITESM Campus Ciudad de México Calle del puente 222, Tlalpan, México D.F.
{rmurriet,betovar,cesteves}@campus.ccm.itesm.mx

[2] Pontificia Universidad Javeriana Cra 7 No 40-62 Bogotá D.C., Colombia
carlos.parra@javeriana.edu.co

[3] Laboratoire d'Analyse et d'Architecture des Systèmes (LAAS-CNRS)
7, Avenue du Colonel Roche, 31077 Toulouse Cedex 4, France
michel@laas.fr

Abstract. In this paper a complete strategy for scene modeling from sensory data acquired in a natural environment is defined. This strategy is applied to outdoor mobile robotics and goes from environment recognition to landmark extraction. In this work, environment is understood as a specific kind of landscape, for instance, a prairie, a forest, a desert, etc. A landmark is defined as a remarkable object in the environment. In the context of outdoor mobile robotics a landmark has to be useful to accomplish localization and navigation tasks.

1 Introduction

This paper deals with the perception functions required to accomplish the exploration of a natural environment with an autonomous robot. From a sequence of range and video images acquired during the motion, the robot must incrementally build a model, correct its situation estimate or execute some visual-based motion. The main contribution of this paper concerns the enhancement of our previous modeling methods [10,9,11,8,3,1,4] by including more semantic information. This work has shown through intensive experimentation that scene interpretation is a useful task in mobile robotics because it allows to have information of the environment nature and semantic. In this way, the robot will have the needed information to perform complex tasks. With this approach it becomes possible to command the robot with semantic instead of numerical vectors. For instance the command of going from (x_1, y_1) to (x_2, y_2) can be replaced with *"Go from the tree to the rock"*.

2 The General Approach

This work is related to the context of a Mars rover. The robot must first build some representations of the environment based on sensory data before exploiting

* This research was funded by CONACyT, México

** This research was funded by the PCP program (Colombia -COLCIENCIAS- and France) and by the ECOS Nord project number C00M01.

C.A. Coello Coello et al. (Eds.): MICAI 2002, LNAI 2313, pp. 11–20, 2002.

them. The proposed approach is suitable for environments in which (1) the terrain is mostly flat, but can be made by several surfaces with different orientations (i.e. different areas with a rather horizontal ground, and slopes to connect these areas) and (2) objects (bulges or little depressions) can be distinguished from the ground. Several experimentations on data acquired on such environments have been done. Our approach has been tested partially or totally in the EDEN site of the LAAS-CNRS [8,9], the GEROMS site of the CNES [11], and over data acquired in the Antarctica [16]. These sites have the characteristics for which this approach is suitable. The EDEN site is a prairie and the GEROMS site is a simulation of a Mars terrain. The robot used to carry out these experiments is the LAMA robot (figure 1).

Related work: The construction of a complete model of an outdoor natural environment, suitable for the navigation requirements of a mobile robot, is a quite difficult task. The complexity resides on several factors such as (1) the great variety of scenes that a robot could find in outdoor environments, (2) the fact that the scenes are not structured, then difficult to represent with simple geometric primitives, and (3) the variation of the current conditions in the analyzed scenes, for instance, illumination and sensor motion. Moreover, another strong constraint is the need of fast algorithm execution so that the robot can react appropriately in the real world.

Several types of partial models have been proposed to represent natural environments. Some of them are numerical dense models [5], other are probabilistic and based on grids [7]. There exist also topological models [6]. In general, it is possible to divide the type of information contained in an environment model in three levels (one given model can contain one or several levels) [2]: (1) geometric level: it contains the description of the geometry of the ground surface or some of its parts. (2) topological level: it represents the topological relationships among the areas in the environment. These areas have specific characteristics and are called "places". (3) semantic level: this is the most abstract representation, because it gives to every entity or object found in the scene, a label corresponding to a class where it belongs (tree, rock, grass...). The classification is based on *a priori* knowledge learnt off-line and given to the system. This knowledge consist on (1) a list of possible classes that the robot could identify in the environment, (2) attributes learnt from some samples of each class, (3) the kind of environment to be analyzed, etc.

2.1 The Navigation Modes

We propose here two navigation modes which can make profit of the same landmark-based model: trajectory-based navigation and sensor-based navigation.

The sensor-based navigation mode needs only a topological model of the environment. It is a graph, in which a node (a place) is defined both by the influence area of a set of landmarks and by a rather flat ground surface. Two landmarks are in the same area if the robot can execute a trajectory between

Fig. 1. LAMA robot

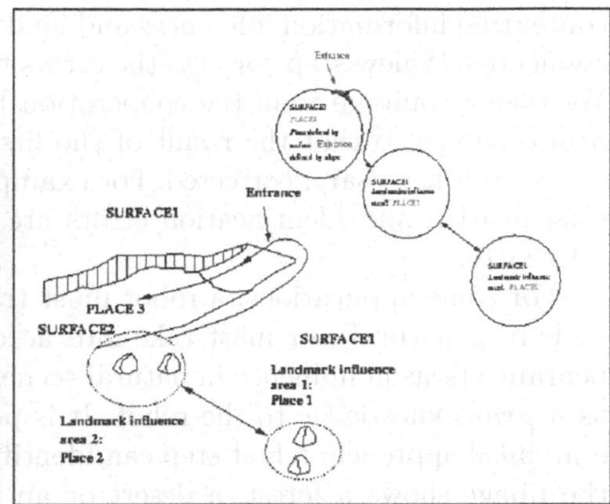

Fig. 2. Topological model

them, with landmarks of the same set always in the stereo-vision field of view (max range = 8m). Two nodes are connected by an edge if their ground surfaces have significantly different slopes, or if sensor-based motions can be executed to reach one place from the other. The boundary between two ground surfaces is included in the environment model by using B-Spline representing the area border [3]. These boundaries can be interpreted as "doors" towards other places. These entrances are characterized by their slope. A tilted surface becomes an entrance if the robot can navigate through it. An arc between two nodes corresponds either to a border line, or to a 2D landmark that the robot must reach in a sensor-based mode. In figure 2 a scheme representing the kind of environment where this approach is suitable and its representation with a graph are shown.

The trajectory-based navigation mode has an input provided by a geometrical planner which is selected inside a given landmark(s) influence area. The landmarks in this navigation mode must be perceived by 3D sensors because they are used to localize the robot (see figure 17). The sensor-based navigation mode can be simpler because it exploits the landmarks as sub-goals where the robot has to go. The landmark position in a 2D image is used to give the robot a direction for the motion (see figure 16). Actually, both of the navigation modes can be switched depending on (1) the environment condition, (2) whether there is 3D or 2D information and (3) the availability of a path planner. In this paper we present overall examples when 3D information is available.

3 Environment Modeling

In order to build this environment model, we developed an approach which consists in steps executed in sequence using different attributes in each one and profiting intensively by contextual information inferences. The steps are environment recognition, image segmentation, region characterization and classification, contextual information inferences and landmark selection. The steps are strongly connected. A new step corrects the errors that might arise on the previous ones. We take advantage from the cooperation between the segmentation and classification steps so that the result of the first step can be checked by the second one and, if necessary, corrected. For example, over-segmentation is corrected by classification and identification errors are corrected by contextual information inferences.

For some applications, a robot must traverse different types of environment (urban or natural), or must take into account changes in the environment appearance (season influence in natural scenes). All these variations could be given as *a priori* knowledge to the robot. It is possible to solve this problem by a hierarchical approach: a first step can identify the environment type (i.e., whether the image shows a forest, a desert or an urban zone) and the second one the elements in the scene. Global image classification is used as an environment recognition step where a single type of environment is determined (i.e., forest, desert or urban zones). In this way, an appropriate database is found making it easier to label the extracted regions by a reduced number of classes and allowing to make inferences from contextual information. Involving this information helps controlling the complexity of the decision-making process required to correctly identify natural objects and to describe natural scenes. Besides, some objects (such as a river, a hole, or a bridge) cannot be defined or recognized in an image without taking into account contextual information [15]. It also allows to detect incoherences such as a grass surrounded with sky or rocks over trees on a flat ground.

For several reasons, it is better to perform the interpretation of the scene in different steps by using different attributes in each one taking into account the system involved in the image acquisition. The attributes used to characterize environments must be different because they have different discriminative power according to the environment. For instance, in lunar-like environment color is not useful given that the entire environment has almost the same colors, but texture and 3D information are. In terrestrial natural areas the color is important because it changes drastically according to the class the object belongs to.

Now, let us describe the sensors used in our experiments. Our robot is equipped with a stereo-vision system composed by two black and white cameras. Additionally to this stereo-vision system a single color camera has been used to model scenes far away from the robot. We want to associate intensity attributes to an object extracted from the 3D image. This object creates a 2D region in the intensity image acquired at the same time than the 3D one. The 3D image is provided by a stereo-vision algorithm [11]. Image regions corresponding to areas which are closer to the sensors (max range 8m) are analyzed by using 3D and intensity attributes. In these areas, stereo-vision gives valid information. Regions corresponding to areas further from the sensors reliable range will be analyzed by using only color and texture attributes given that 3D information is not available or too noisy. For these areas, since color is a point-wise property of images and texture involves a notion of spatial extent (a single point has no texture), color segmentation gives a better compromise between precision of region borders and computation speed than texture segmentation, consequently, color is used in the segmentation step.

Environment recognition: Our environment recognition method is based on the metric known as the Earth Mover's Distance [12]. This metric is based on operations research theory and translates the image identification problem into a transportation problem to find the optimal work to move a set of ground piles to a set of holes. The ground piles and holes are represented by clusters on the images which map to a feature space and may be constructed by any attribute on the images (i.e. color spaces, textures, ...). These approaches are not able to identify the elements in the scene, but the whole image as an entity. We construct a 3-dimensional attribute space for the images comparison. Two axes map to $I_2 I_3$, the uncorrelated chrominance attributes obtained from the *Principal Components Analysis.* The other axis correspond to texture entropy feature computed from the sum and difference histograms.

For the environment recognition step we feed our system with six classes of environments: forest (Fig 3), Mars (Fig. 4), Moon (Fig. 5), prairie (Fig. 6), desert (Fig. 7) and a snowed forest (Fig. 8). Every class is constructed with a set of images. Our system finds the environment class where the test image (Fig. 9) belongs. The test image shows a *prairie.* Even thought the classes prairie and forest are similar the system assigns correctly the image test to the prairie class. It is also capable to differentiate *Moon* images from the *snowed forest* images although the colors are similar. In our tests the system was also capable of differentiate Mars from the desert, but the similarity was greater (the work to move a set of clusters to the other was smaller).

Segmentation: Image segmentation for region extraction: this segmentation is based on clustering and unsupervised classification. The image is segmented to obtain the main regions of the scene. This first step can be performed by the use of the color attribute on the 2D image or by the use of geometrical attributes on the 3D image [9,10].

Characterization: Each region of the scene is characterized by using several attributes computed from the color, texture or geometrical informations [14,13].

Classification: Our identification step is based on a supervised learning process, for this reason its good performance depends on the use of a database representative enough of the environment. It is important to remark that prototyping is done to build the learning samples set in order to get a representative enough database. Actually we are making two types of prototyping, one with the images by using image comparison and the other with the learning sampling set. Bayesian classification is used to associate every region in the image with a semantic label. This classification method has some drawbacks. It needs the computation of all the set or the previously defined attributes. Bayesian classification has been criticized arguing that it needs frequently a lot of knowledge

Fig. 3. Forest **Fig. 4.** Mars **Fig. 5.** Moon

Fig. 6. Prairie **Fig. 7.** Desert **Fig. 8.** Snowed Forest

Fig. 9. Test image **Fig. 10.** Original image **Fig. 11.** 3D segmentation

about the problem. It has also been pointed out that this approach has a lot of faults when representing and manipulating knowledge inside a complex inference system. In order to deal with these drawbacks, attribute selection has to be done in a pre-processing step (by using PCA and Fisher criteria) and inferences are added to the system by an independent process such as environment recognition and contextual information.

Contextual information inferences: The specific environment analyzed in this work consist in natural areas where ground is flat or with a smooth slope. By the use of some contextual characteristics of the environment the model consistency can be tested. Possible errors in the identification process could be detected and corrected by using simple contextual rules. A set of rules allow to find eventual errors introduced by the identification step [10]. The probability of belonging to a given class is used to decide whether the region should be re-labeled or not. If this probability is smaller than a given threshold the region is re-labeled.

To show the construction of the representation of the scene based on only 2D information, we present the process in a image. These regions were obtained from the color segmentation phase. Sometimes a real element is over-segmented, consequently a fusion phase becomes necessary. In this step, connected regions belonging to the same class are merged. Figure 12 shows the original image. Figure 13 shows the color image segmentation and the identification of the regions. The defined classes are a function of the environment type. Here, we have chosen 4 classes which correspond to the main elements in our environment: grass, sky, tree and rock. Labels in the images indicate the nature of the regions: (R) rock, (G) grass, (T) tree and (S) sky. The coherence of the model is tested by using the topological characteristics of the environment. The Region at the top right corner of the image was identified as grass, however this region has a relatively low probability (less than a given threshold) of belonging to this class, in this case the system can correct the mistake by using contextual information. This region is then relabeled as tree. Figure 14 shows the final model of this scene. Figure 15 shows the gray levels used to label the classes.

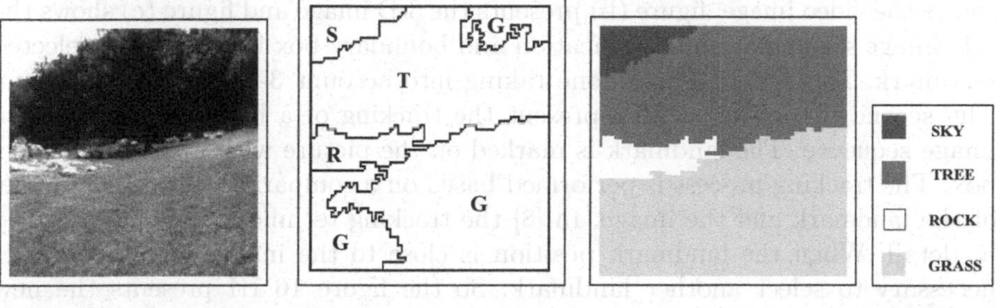

Fig. 12. Original image **Fig. 13.** Segmentation and Identification **Fig. 14.** Final model **Fig. 15.** Classes

3.1 Landmark Selection

Landmarks in indoor environments correspond to structured scene components, such as walls, corners, doors, etc. In outdoor natural scenes, landmarks are less structured. We have proposed several solutions like maxima of curvature on border lines [3], maxima of elevation on the terrain [4] or on extracted objects [1].

Based on our previous works a landmark is defined as a remarkable object [1], which should have some properties that will be exploited in the robot localization or in visual navigation task, but in this work the landmark is associated to a semantic label. The two main properties which we use to define a landmark are: **Discrimination:** A landmark should be easy to differentiate from other surrounding objects. **Accuracy:** A landmark must be accurate enough so that it can allow to reduce the uncertainty on the robot's situation, because it will be used for robot localization.

Depending on the kind of navigation performed (section 2) the landmarks have different meaning. In trajectory-based navigation landmarks are useful to localize the robot and of course the bigger number of landmarks in the environment the better. For topological navigation a sequence of different landmarks (or targets) is used as sub-goal the robot must successively reach [9]. For this last kind of navigation commutation of landmarks is an important issue. We are dealing with this task, based on the position of the landmark in the image (see section 4, image 16). The landmark change is automatic. It is based on the nature of the landmark and the distance between the robot and the target which represents the current sub-goal. When the robot attains the current target (or, more precisely, when the current target is close to the limit of the camera field of view), another one is dynamically selected in order to control the next motion [9].

4 Robot Navigation Based on the Landmark-Based Model

Robot visual navigation is done by using the proposed model. We illustrate this task with a experiment carried out with the mobile robot LAMA. Figure 16 (a) shows the video image, figure (b) presents the 3-D image and figure (c) shows the 3-D image segmentation, classification and boundary box including the selected landmark. The selection was done taking into account 3-D shape and nature. The second line of figure 16 represent the tracking of a landmark through an image sequence. The landmark is marked on the picture with a little boundary box. The tracking process is performed based on a comparison between a model of the landmark and the image. In [8] the tracking technique used is described in detail. When the landmark position is close to the image edge it becomes necessary to select another landmark. So the figure 16 III presents the new landmark selection based on image segmentation and classification. The next sequence of tracking is shown on the line IV of figure 16 and the next landmark commutation is presented on line V. Finally on the line VI the robot continue navigation task.

4.1 Experiments of Simultaneous Localization and Modeling (SLAM)

We illustrate this task with an experiment carried out in the EDEN site at LAAS-CNRS. In this work SLAM task is based on landmark extraction. The strategy to select the landmarks is the one presented on section 4. Left column of figure 17 shows 2-D images corresponding to left stereo-vision camera. On these images the rocks selected as target and the zone where the target is looking for are shown. The results obtained regarding environment modeling are shown on the second column. The maps of the environment and the localization of the robot are presented on the third column. On the row "I" the robot just takes one landmark as reference in order to localize itself. On the last row the robot uses 3 landmarks to perform localization task, the robot position estimation is shown by using rectangles. The current robot's situation and the numerical attributes of the

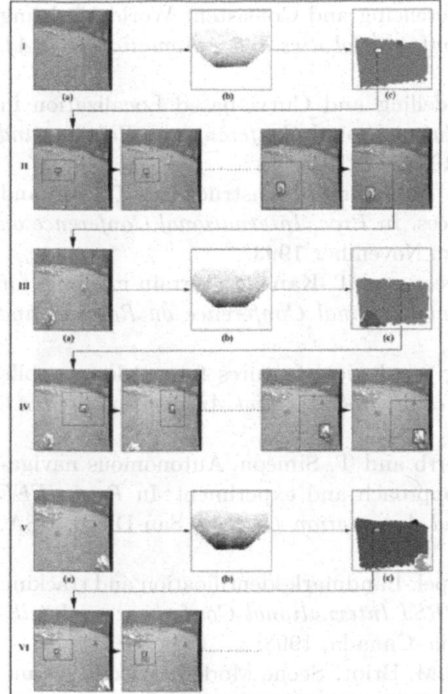

Fig. 16. Visual robot navigation

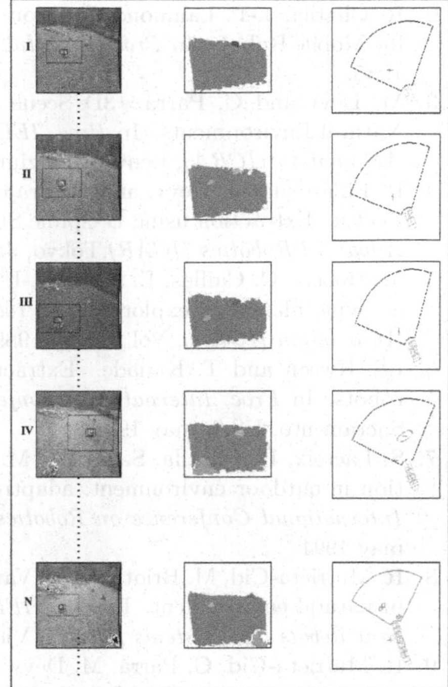

Fig. 17. Simultaneous localization and modeling (SLAM)

landmark features are updated by using an Extended Kalman Filter (EKF). The most important result here is that the robot position uncertainty does not grow thanks to the usage of landmarks. The landmarks allow to stop the incremental growing of the robot position uncertainty.

5 Conclusion

The work presented in this paper concerns the environment representation applied to outdoor mobile robotics. A model of the environment is constructed in several steps: environment recognition, region extraction, object characterization, object identification, landmarks selection. Robot navigation based on the landmark-based model is presented.

References

1. S. Betg-Brezetz, P. Hébert, R. Chatila, and M. Devy. Uncertain Map Making in Natural Environments. In *Proc. IEEE International Conference on Robotics and Automation (ICRA)*, Minneapolis, USA, April 1996.

2. R. Chatila, J.-P. Laumond, Position Referencing and Consistent World Modeling for Mobile Robots. In *Proc IEEE Int. Conf. on Robotics and Automation (ICRA)*, 1985.
3. M. Devy and C. Parra. 3D Scene Modelling and Curve-based Localization in Natural Environments. In *Proc. IEEE International Conference on Robotics and Automation (ICRA)*, Leuven, Belgium, 1998.
4. P. Fillatreau, M. Devy, and R. Prajoux. Modelling of Unstructured Terrain and Feature Extraction using B -spline Surfaces. In *Proc. International Conference on Advanced Robotics (ICAR)*,Tokyo, Japan, November 1993.
5. M. Hebert, C. Caillas, E. Krotkov, I. Kweon and T. Kanade. Terrain mapping for a roving planetary explorer. In *Proc. International Conference on Robotics and Automation (ICRA)*, Vol 2, may 1989.
6. I.S. Kweon and T. Kanade. Extracting topological features for outdoor mobile robots. In *Proc. International Conference on Robotics and Automation (ICRA)*, Sacramento, USA, may 1991.
7. S. Lacroix, R. Chatila, S. Fleury, M. Herrb and T. Simeon Autonomous navigation in outdoor environment: adaptive approach and experiment In *Proc. IEEE International Conference on Robotics and Automation (ICRA)*, San Diego, USA, may 1994.
8. R. Murrieta-Cid, M. Briot, and N. Vandapel. Landmark identification and tracking in natural environment. In *Proc. IEEE/RSJ International Conference on Intelligent Robots and Systems (IROS)*, Victoria, Canada, 1998.
9. R. Murrieta-Cid, C. Parra, M. Devy and M. Briot. Scene Modelling from 2D and 3D sensory data acquired from natural environments. In *Proc. IEEE International Conference on Advanced Robotics (ICAR)*, Budapest, Hungary, 2001.
10. R. Murrieta-Cid, C. Parra, M. Devy, B. Tovar and C. Esteves. Building multi-level models: From landscapes to landmarks. Submitted to *the IEEE International Conference on Robotics and Automation (ICRA2002)*.
11. C. Parra, R. Murrieta-Cid, M. Devy & M. Briot. 3-D modelling and robot localization from visual and range data in natural scenes.. In *Proc. International Conference on Vision Systems (ICVS)*, Las Palmas, Spain, January 1999.
12. Y. Rubner, C. Tomasi, and L. Guibas. A metric for distributions with applications to image databases. In *IEEE International Conference on Computer Vision*, Bombay, India, 1998.
13. T.S.C Tan and J. Kittler. Colour texture analysis using colour histogram. *I.E.E Proc.-Vis.Image Signal Process.*, 141(6):403–412, December 1994.
14. M. Unser. Sum and difference histograms for texture classification. *I.E.E.E. Transactions on Pattern Analysis and Machine Intelligence*, 1986.
15. Strat, T. and Fischler M. Context-Based Vision: Recognizing Objects Using Information from Both 2-D and 3-D Imagery. *I.E.E.E. Transactions on Pattern Analysis and Machine Intelligence, 1986 Vol13, Num10, pages 1050-1065, October, 1991.*
16. N. Vandapel, S. Moorehead, W. Whittaker, R. Chatila and R. Murrieta-Cid. Preliminary results on the use of stereo color cameras and laser sensors in Antarctica. In *Proc. 6th International Symposium on Experimental Robotics (ISER)*, Sydney Australia, 1999.

Adapting the Messy Genetic Algorithm for Path Planning in Redundant and Non-redundant Manipulators

Victor de la Cueva[1] and Fernando Ramos[2]

[1] ITESM Campus Veracruz, División de Profesional
Av. Eugenio Garza Sada 1, Ex Campo de Golf Ruiz Galindo
C.P. 94500, Córdoba, Ver., Mexico
Tel (271) 7-17-05-31; Fax (271) 7-17-05-41
vcueva@campus.ver.itesm.mx

[2] ITESM Campus Cuernavaca, División de Ingeniería y Ciencias
Av. Paseo de la Reforma 182-A, Col. Lomas de Cuernavaca
C.P. 62589, Cuernavaca, Mor., México
Tel. (777) 3-29-71-94; Fax (777) 3-29-71-96
framos@campus.mor.itesm.mx

Abstract. We are presenting in this work a method to calculatc collision free paths, for redundant and non redundant robots, through an adaptation of the Messy Genetic Algorithm with a fitness function weakly defined. The adaptation consists in replacing the two crossing operators (cut and splice) traditionally used by a mechanism similar to that one used in the simple genetic algorithm. Nevertheless, the mechanism presented in this work was designed to work with variable length strings. The main advantages of this method are: even though the fitness function is weakly defined good solutions can be obtained; it does not need a previous discretization of the work space; and it works directly within such space without needing any transformation as in the C-space method. In this work, the fitness function is defined as a linear combination of values which are easily calculated.

Key words: Genetic Algorithms, Path Planning, Obstacle Avoidance.

1 Introduction

One of the most important problems to be solved in robotics is to find collision free paths in a given world. This problem can be expressed as follows: to find a sequence of robotic configurations to go from an initial to a final one. A robotic configuration can be defined by the following vector:

$$RCi = [1, \ldots, n] \text{ for } i = 1, \ldots, m \quad (1)$$

where *i* is the angular value of the joint *i*. In this case, we say that the joint values are expressed in the joint space.

C.A. Coello Coello et al. (Eds.): MICAI 2002, LNAI 2313, pp. 21–30, 2002.

Each configuration is mapped into the user space (work space) as a vector representing position and orientation values of the end-effector in the user space. In this way, a path can be represented by a sequence of intermediate points that links an initial with a final point which are represented by position and orientation values. Figure 1 illustrates an example of a path, which is represented by a set of robotic configurations.

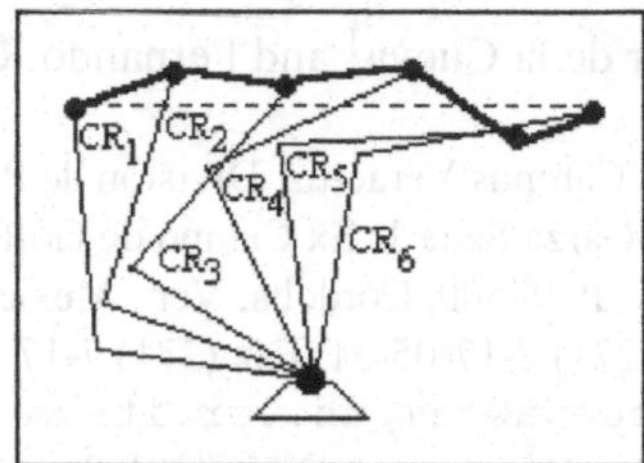

Fig. 1. A path represented by a 6 robotic configurations

Two main problems have to be solved when robotic paths have to be found. The first one concerns the number of points that compose a path in the work space which is infinite. The second one is related with the number of possible paths to go from a point to another one is also infinite.

These problems increase the computational complexity (PSPACE hard problem [1]) in methods based on search mechanisms which is due to the fact that the search space is huge. Based upon the problems described above, it is necessary to make simplifications, suppositions, and to set restrictions in the search space in order to make it easier to handle.

The methods to solve this problem can be classified in two major approaches [2]. Methods based on explicit programming, where the user defines all the manipulator motions needed to accomplish a task. The model based programming methods, where the set of control points is automatically found given the initial and the final point. The human intervention is reduced with the use of this method.

The following methods applied to the calculation of collision free paths have produced good results [1]: road maps (e.g. [3] and [4]), cell decomposition (e.g. [5] and [6]), potential fields (e.g. [7]).

These different approaches work in the configuration space (C-space) [8] moving in the free space to find the path to go from an initial to a final point without collisions.

This work can be considered as an extension of the work carried out for mobile robots in [9], and it aims to build paths without collisions for both redundant and non redundant robots. Genetic algorithms are optimization methods based on natural selection and evolution [10]. They have been used in robotics such as in [11] and [12]. We have adapted the messy genetic algorithm presented by Goldberg in [13] and revisited in [14] and [15]. Our method can be classified as a "model based programming" method. The definition of the problem and the complete procedure that has been used is described below.

2 Problem Definition

The problem can be defined as follows: a sequence of robotic configurations has to be found to reach a final point form an initial robotic configuration.. This sequence is composed of neighbor configurations. Two configurations are neighbors if the following condition is satisfied:

Def. Let C1 and C2 be two configurations, which are represented as follows: $C1=(\theta_{11},\theta_{12},...,\theta_{1n})$ and $C2=(\theta_{21},\theta_{22},...,\theta_{2n})$, and let ε be a range predefined by the user, and expressed in terms of angles. If, for all the pairs $\{(\theta_{11},\theta_{21}),(\theta_{12},\theta_{22}),...,(\theta_{1n},\theta_{2n})\}$, the condition $\theta_{1i}=\theta_{2i}$, is satisfied, except for only one pair $(\theta_{1k},\theta_{2k})$ in which $|\theta_{1k}-\theta_{2k}|=\varepsilon$, then C1 and C2 are neighbors, where k = 1, ... ,n; and θ_{ik} is the value of the joint k in the configuration i.

In order to get two neighbor configurations, we move just one joint at a time, in such a way that the movement satisfied the condition $|\theta_{1k} - \theta_{2k}| = \varepsilon$ described above. Where θ_{1k} is the current value of the joint k in the configuration 1, and θ_{2k} is the value obtained once the movement has been done. In [8] and [16] there is a similar method to obtain the space of configurations, because this method varies also only one joint at a time to obtain the approximation to the configuration space.

3 Procedure Description

A relevant characteristic of the problem treated in this work is that we do not know the length of the sequence of robotic configurations described above. This sequence represents a path. The length of this path should be related to the length of the individuals in the population. Given the fact that we will work with a set of paths with different sizes, then we can not predefine a fixed size of the desired path. The messy genetic algorithm (mGA), works with a population of individuals and different length, which can vary as the generation changes. We take advantage of this property to adapt the messy genetic algorithms to the changing nature of the length of the path being searched.

An original aspect of this work is that each individual in the population of the genetic algorithm represents a path of the robotic work space, then the genetic algorithm evolves a population of paths. This population converges to a set of optimal paths.

In our case, an optimal path has three characteristics:

1. To go from an initial to a final point given by the user. The closer the end-effector is to the desired final point the better the path will be.
2. To avoid the obstacles in the work space.
3. The path has to be as short as possible. The length of the path can be measured by counting the number of robotic configurations that builds the path.

Those characteristics described above define the fitness function of the genetic algorithm.

It is important to work with individuals with variable lengths due to the fact that the final path length is unknown. We describe below the way of specifying the fitness function as well as the method for encoding the robotic configuration in the string of an individual.

3.1 Coding

The conditions of coding are: The angular movement value of a joint is predefined, only movements between neighbor configurations are accepted, only one joint at a time could be modified, we can choose a joint and the sense of movement.

Two senses of movement are accepted Counter Clockwise (CCW) and Clockwise (CW). One bit can be used to specify the movement sense (CW or CCW). The joint to be moved is represented by a binary number of n bits. The expression 2^n serves to specify the maximum quantity of joints to be accepted by a chain.

3.2 Chain Size

The size of a gene (the minimal information unit) will be given by:

$$tg = na + 1 \tag{2}$$

where, *na* bits are required to represent a joint and one bit to indicate the sense of movement.

An individual *i*, that represents a complete path, will be composed of m_i genes, where this number is variable and also different for each individual. This number also represents the number of robotic configurations that composes a path. At the same time, this number changes as the process evolves. The size, which is specified in bits, of an individual *i* (tbi_i) will be given by m_i multiplied by the size of the gene *tg*, that is:

$$tbi_i = m_i * tg \tag{3}$$

3.3 An Example

By using a notation of lists in LISP language, the following example shows a chain that represents a path for a robot of three joints:

$$((1\ 0\ 0)\ (0\ 1\ 0)\ (1\ 1\ 1)\ (0\ 0\ 1)) \tag{4}$$

The expression above represents a path which contains four configurations. Each group of three bits represent a configuration. In general, when one joint is moved, then the rest of the joints remain without any change. Afterwards, a new configuration is obtained by moving a chosen joint while the rest of the joints remain unchanged. This means that only one joint can be moved at a time. Therefore, it is possible to represent a configuration only with the registration of this movement. The two most significant bits are used to represent a code for each joint (e.g. 00 for joint 1). The least significant bit represents the sense of movement: 0 for CW and 1 for CCW.

In order to interpret the string, it should be known: the initial values of the joint angles and the rotation that will perform the joint.

3.4 Crossing

The adaptation of the mGA consisted in replacing the two crossing operators (cut and splice) traditionally used, by a mechanism similar to that one used in the simple genetic algorithm. Nevertheless, the mechanism presented in this work was designed to work with variable length strings.

The cross operation between two individuals in any place if the string can give a non valid individual due to the fact that all of the individuals require to have a specific number of bits in accordance to the number of joints. This number should be a multiple of *tg* (the size in bits of the gene). The cross operation should be carried out between genes that represent configurations. This procedure is described below.

First, two individuals of the population are selected by using the tournament method, where the best individuals have the biggest probability to be selected.

A condition to have a valid path is to have a multiple of *tg* bits. For this reason, the crossing point should be placed between genes. Besides, a movement is the minimal information entity in the string (a gene). The crossing is carried out by a point obtained randomly in the string number one, and another randomly obtained point in the string number two. The crossing is performed in these points.

Both the current individuals and the new ones can have a different length. The length of the string is proportional to the length of the path. This length is represented by the cardinality of the sequence of the neighbor configurations that compose the path.

3.5 Fitness Function

The fitness function is composed of several functions that satisfy the three characteristics of an optimal path previously described.

A first goal to reach is to find a path to link the initial with the final configurations which are specified by the user. The first aspect to consider in the fitness function is how close is the end-effector to the desired final point. This distance is calculated by the formula between two points:

$$d(P1,P2) = \sqrt{(x_1 - x_2)^2 + (y_1 - y_2)^2} \tag{5}$$

Then the first function of the fitness function is given by

$$\text{Closeness}(P1, P2) = d(P1,P2) \tag{6}$$

We can observe that the smaller the distance the bigger the qualification obtained by a given point. P1 is the final position of the end-effector and P2 is the final point to be reached.

Once the population is able to link the initial with the final points, the length represented by the population should be optimized. The best paths are those ones with a shortest length. The shortest paths obtain a higher reward. The function to supply this worth is similar to that one used for the Shortest_distance function.

$$\text{Shortest\_distance(path)} = \text{length(path)} \tag{7}$$

where length(path) function obtains the length of the path to be evaluated and it is represented by the number of configurations that composed this path. The shorter the path the bigger the worth obtained.

Finally, it should be added to the fitness function a penalty for each collision between a configuration of the path being evaluated and an obstacle. A configuration that causes a collision is considered as a non valid configuration. A penalty is assigned which is proportional to the number of non valid configurations that are contained by the path.

$$\text{Non\_collision(path)} = K * \text{non\_valids(path)} \tag{8}$$

where the non_valids(path) function represents the number of the configurations of the path that are non-valid. K is a penalty constant, which increase the penalty value given by the number of non-valid configurations of the path. In this case, K = 100 was used, in order to eliminate the paths that contain at least a non-valid configuration.

In this way, the final fitness function is defined as:

$$\text{Fitness(path)} = \text{Closeness(PFT,PFU)} + \text{Shortest\_distance(path)} + \text{Non\_collision(path)} \tag{9}$$

if PFT (the final point of the path) is the same that PFU (the desired final point), or:

$$\text{Fitness(path)} = \text{Closeness(PFT,PFU)} + \text{Non\_collision(path)} \tag{10}$$

if the path being built does not still reach the desired point.

We consider that a path has reached a desired point if the position of the end-effector of the last configuration in the path is within a circle of radius *R*. This circle is defined around the desired final point (a neighborhood of the final point).

We can observe that the defined fitness is a linear combination of some values easily calculated. This is a fitness function that does not express in detail the relations between its terms. One of the advantages of using genetic algorithms is that we can obtain good results even if the fitness function is weakly defined as that one we used in this work.

4 Obtained Results

The method proposed was tested with robots represented by straight lines or polygons (rectangles) as links, and in 2D. Angular and prismatic movements are considered, and only one degree of freedom for each joint. Nevertheless, the extension to 3D is not complicated. The obstacles are represented by straight lines or polygons.

Table 1. A complete descriptions of the tests.

Test	Number of joints	Length of the links	Initial configuration	EE initial (x,y)	Obstacles	EE final (x,y)	Figure of the found path
1	2	(4,4)	(-30°,90°)	(5.46,1.46)	from (2,0.5) to (2,1.5) and from (3,0.5) to (3,1.5)	(2.5,1)	4
2	4	(2,2,2,2)	(0°,0°,0°,0°)	(8,0)	from (6,0.5) to (8,2)	(6,2)	6

We present two tests with a planar robot. The links are represented by straight lines and revolute joints. The global reference of the robot is in the coordinates (0,0). The movement of a joint is = 5, and the neighborhood of the final point is R = 0.4 units. We must remember that in 2D a robot with 3 or more joints is considered redundant. We present a complete description in Table 1 and the obtained paths are shown in Figures 2 and 3.

The test number 1 was repeated with links of a non-redundant robot represented by one unit wide rectangles. One obstacle was represented by a rectangle too. This obstacle was in: (4,2), (4,6), (6,6) and (6,2). The initial configuration was (0,0). The calculated path to go from (8,0) to (2,3) is shown in Figure 4.

There was a test number 3 with a two prismatic joints robot. Its links was represented by one wide rectangles. One joint moves parallel to the X axis and the other in the Y axis. The robot is fixed in (0,0). The initial point is (4,0) and the final point in (4,6).

There is a rectangular obstacle with vertex in (3,3), (7,3), (7,4) and (3,4). The calculated path and some of its positions are shown in Figure 5.

This method works correctly to calculate paths without collisions for redundant and non-redundant robots as we have shown in the test after running the genetic algorithm with a maximum of 100 generations. The genetic algorithm found a path by satisfying the three characteristics established before.

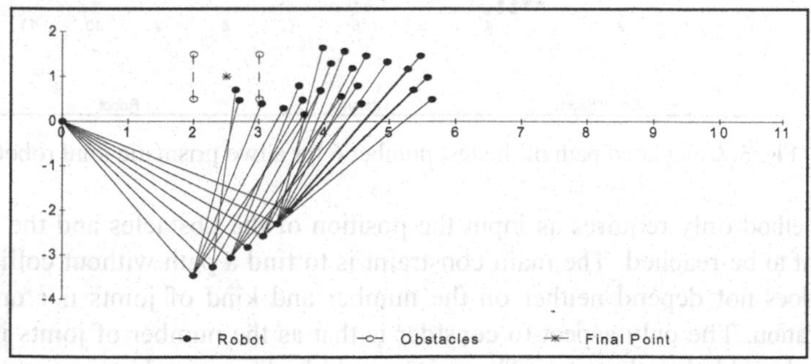

Fig. 2. Obtained path for the two joint robot (non redundant) for test 1

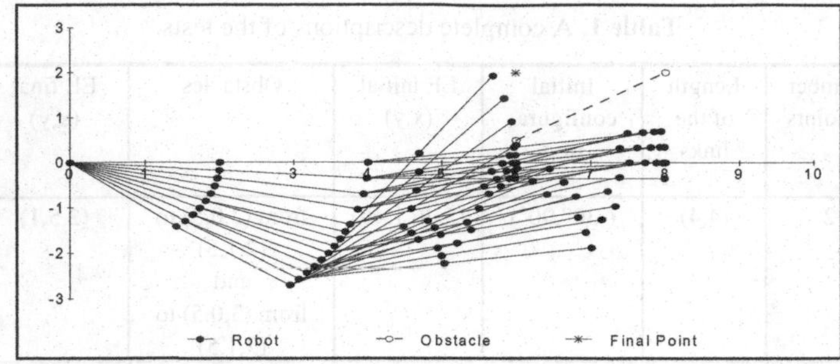

Fig. 3. Obtained path for the four joint robot (redundant) for test 2

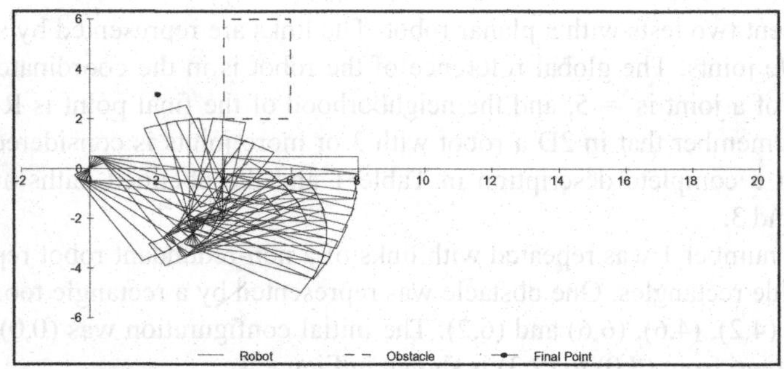

Fig. 4. Calculated path of the test 5 for a non-redundant rectangle link robot

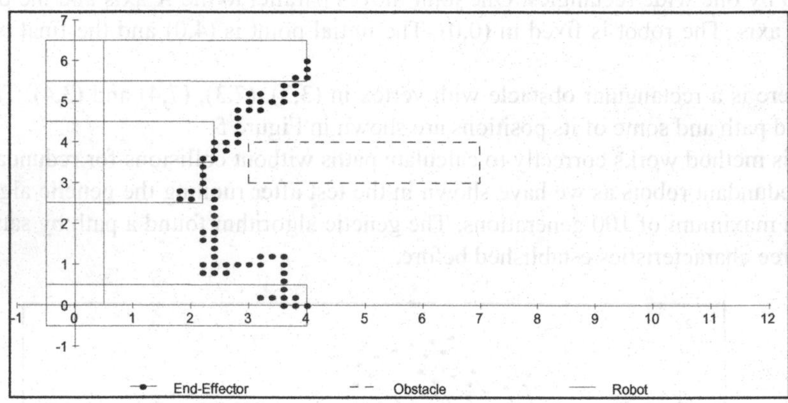

Fig. 5. Calculated path of the test number 6 for a two prismatic joint robot

The method only requires as input the position of the obstacles and the initial and final point to be reached. The main constraint is to find a path without collisions. The method does not depend neither on the number and kind of joints nor on the links representation. The only aspect to consider is that as the number of joints increases a bit could be added to the gene. The string could be longer and consequently the calculation time will increase. Nevertheless, we can represent a big number of joints with a relatively little number of bits.

5 Conclusions

In the robotic application we are presenting in this paper the genetic algorithm works only with direct kinematics. Then, the method does not depend on the complex calculation of the Inverse Jacobian matrix. Therefore, an advantage of this method is that the robots can be redundant or non-redundant and, also they can be situated in singular positions as we have shown by the results of the tests. Due to the fact that the method presented in this work does not depend on the previous model of the free space this method can be applicable in on-line operations.

The genetic algorithm is able to supply good results, even though the relationships between the terms that composed the fitness function are weakly defined. The evolutionary process of the genetic algorithm is robust under these conditions, however, a better definition of the fitness function could improve the performance and consequently the results. So far, the fitness function is only guided by the distance between the current and the final desired position and the obstacles to be avoided.

In the first exploration with genetic algorithms the robots are in 2D. An adaptation to 3D is being carried out. We point out that this adaptation process is being done without many complications. The obstacles will be represented as well in 3D.

References

1. J.C. Latombe, *Robot Motion Planning*, (Norwell: Kluwer Academic Publishers, 1990).
2. W.T. Park, "Minicomputer software organization for control of industrial robots", *Proc. Joint Automat. Contr. Conf.*, San Francisco, CA, 1977.
3. R. A. Brooks, "Solving The Find-Path Problem by Good Representation of Free Space", *IEEE Transacitions on System, Man, and Cybernetics*, 13(3), 1983, 190-197.
4. J.F. Canny and B.R. Donald, "Simplified Voronoi Diagram", *Discrete and Computational Geometry*, Springer-Verlag, 3, 1988, 219-236.
5. T. Llozano-Pérez, "Automatic Planning of Manipulator Transfer Movements", *IEEE Trans. on System, Man and Cybernetics*, SMC-11(10), 1981, 681-698.
6. J.T. Schuartz and M. Sharir, "On the piano movers' problem I: the case of a two-dimensional rigid polygonal body moving amidst polygonal barriers", *Communication on Pure and Applied Mathematics*, 36,1983, 345-398.
7. O. Khatib, "Real-Time Obstacle Avoidance for Manipulators and Movile Robots", *International Journal of Robotics Research*, 5(1), 1986, 90-98.
8. T. Lozano-Pérez, "An algorithm for planning collision free paths among polyhedral obstacles", *Communications ACM*, 1979, 22(10), 560-570.
9. V. de la Cueva y F. Ramos, "Cálculo de trayectorias libres de colisiones para un robot móvil mediente la utilización de un algoritmo genético", *Memorias del 1er. Encuentro de Computación,* Taller de Visión y Robótica, Querétaro, Qro., 1997, 1-6.
10. D. Goldberg. *Genetic Algorithms in Search, Optimization and Machine Learning.* (U.S.A.: Addisson Wesley, 1986).
11. Y. Davidor. *Genetic Algorithms and Robotics: A Heuristic Strategy for Optimization.* (Singapore: World Scientific Publishing, 1991).

12. Y. Davidor, "Genetic Algorithms in Robotics", *Dynamic, Genetic, and Chaotic Programming*, (New York: Jhon Wiley & Sons, Inc., 1992).
13. D. Goldberg, B. Korb, and K. Deb, "Messy Genetic Algorithms: Motivation, Analysis, and First Results", *Complex Systems*, 3(5), 1989, 493-530.
14. D. Goldberg, B. Korb, and K. Deb. "Messy Genetic Algorithm revisited: studies in mixed size and scale". *Complex Systems*, 4(4), 415-44, 1990.
15. D. Goldberg, K. Deb, Kargupta & Harik, "Rapid accurate optimization of difficult problems using fast messy genetic algorithms", *Proc. of the Fifth International Conference on Genetic Algorithms*, Morgan Kaufmann, 1993, 56-64.
16. T. Lozano-Pérez, M. Brady and J. Hollerbach, *Robot Motion: Planning and Control*, (Massachusetts: MIT Press, Series in Artificial Intelligence, 1983).

Navigation Advice from *pq-Histograms*

G. Gomez[1], L. Enrique Sucar[1], and Duncan F. Gillies[2]

[1] Dept. of Computing, ITESM-Morelos
A.P. 99-C, 62050, Morelos. México
{gegomez,esucar}@campus.mor.itesm.mx
[2] Dept. of Computing, Imperial College
180 Queen's Gate, London SW7 2BZ. England
dfg@doc.ic.ac.uk

Abstract. We propose a novel visual navigation clue based on summarising the local 3D information into a single structure, called *pq-histogram*. This structure is obtained by discretising the local orientation or $[p, q]$ of an image, and building a two dimensional histogram. This histogram gives a global view of the 3D shape of the world, therefore it could be used for navigation. The potential application of the *pq-histogram* is illustrated in two domains. Firstly, semi-automatic navigation of an endoscope inside the human colon. Secondly, mobile robot navigating in certain environments, such as corridors and mines. In both cases, the method was tested with real images with very good results.

1 Introduction

We propose a novel histogram for summarising the local 3D information or *pq* in a single structure, called *pq-histogram*. This histogram provides a reliable and fast clue for visual navigation. The *pq-histogram* is obtained by discretising the local orientation $[p, q]$ of an image in a logarithmic scale. This histogram gives a global view of the 3D shape of the world, thus it is useful for determining free space and avoiding walls.

Considering an indoor environment, the relative depth gives useful information, not only about the general shape of this surroundings, but also for navigation. However, the crude output of a shape from shading method is not enough for guiding an endoscope or a mobile robot.

The local shape information used by the *pq-histogram* structure is computed using a direct shape form shading (SFS) technique [12]. This particular SFS algorithm has the advantage that it is very fast (not iterative), hence it can be a reliable and fast clue for navigation.

Although there are several alternatives and more precise ways to obtain three dimensional shape of indoor environments, such as laser range sensors or sonars, these are not always applicable. For instance, inside the narrow and sensible area of a human colon. Moreover, these sensors have also problems with certain types of surfaces, thus more visual clues should be used as a complement to have a more robust system. We have developed a method that obtains useful information for navigation from the *pq-histogram*. As we shall see, it can be used

C.A. Coello Coello et al. (Eds.): MICAI 2002, LNAI 2313, pp. 31–40, 2002.

as a fast clue for navigation in certain restricted environments, in particular for tube-like scenarios, such as in endoscopy, mines, sewers and corridors.

We have applied the *pq-histogram* for navigation in two types of domains. In the first class, such as in endoscopy and sewers, there are possible movements in 2D (i.e. up, down, left, right). In this cases we use a 2D *pq-histogram*, and we have applied it for semi-automatic endoscope navigation. In the second type, it was applied to standard mobile robots, with movements on the plane (e.g. left, right). In this case we use a 1D *pq-histogram* discarting the q component, i.e. we do not expect up/down movements. We have applied this histogram as a useful clue for mobile robot navigation in corridors.

The remainder sections are organised as follows. First, we briefly describe the local shape from shading technique which is used to obtain the p, q information from the images. Then we develop the *pq-histogram*, and explain how it can be used for navigation, initially, in an ideal tube. The next two sections present real scenarios: endoscope navigation in endoscopy and mobile robot navigation in corridors. Finally, we conclude giving some directions for future work.

2 Shape from Shading

Shape from shading (see e.g. [6,11,12] and a recent survey [15]) recovers tridimensional information from a single image with no feature matching. Shape from shading techniques deal with the task of inferring 3D surfaces directly from the intensity map. Notice that intensity by itself is not enough to recover the 3D surface. Therefore, shape from shading approaches introduce some constraints such as picewise smoothness, uniform Lambertian reflectance, light source far away, orthographic projection, to name a few. However, recent developments encompass relaxing some assumptions [16] or overcoming excessive smoothing [4]. Almost all these algorithms are iterative, hence they are not suitable for real-time tasks such as navigation. Global SFS algorithms provide very good depth maps, but they are too costly computationally. Conversely, local SFS algorithms are faster, but provide noisy depth maps which are not good enough for certain domains.

Rashid [12] developed a local algorithm for the determination of shape from shading. He considers a point light source which is at the same point of the camera and near to the surface of the objects, which resemble the conditions inside a human colon and tube-like scenarios. His direct algorithm estimates the slope of small patches on the surface, it is quite efficient and appropriate to be implemented in parallel, hence it has a big potential as a fast clue for visual navigation.

This SFS algorithm is briefly described in the next section, for a more detailed description see the original reference [12].

2.1 Local Shape from Shading Algorithm

The image intensity, in general, depends on the surface orientation and its reflective characteristics. Considering a near point light source illumination, denoted by position vector S, the intensity varies according to the inverse square distance between the light source and the surface point, so the surface absolute position, Z, is another parameter. For a *near* point light source, the image intensity at x, y is given by:

$$E(x,y) = \frac{S_0 \rho(x,y) cos\theta_i}{r^2} \tag{1}$$

where S_0 is the light source intensity constant, $\rho(x,y)$ is the reflection coefficient or albedo, θ_i is the angle between the source direction and the surface normal, and r is the distance between the light source and the surface point. Considering a camera-centered coordinate system we have $r = S - P$, where $S = [T, U, V]$ is the point light source vector and $P = [X, Y, Z]$ is the surface position vector. Thus, we can write (1) in vector notation as:

$$E(x,y) = S_0 \rho(x,y) \frac{(S-P)\cdot n}{|n||S-P|^3} \tag{2}$$

where n is the surface normal vector, and is defined as $n = (p, q, -1)$, $p = \frac{\partial Z}{\partial X}$, and $q = \frac{\partial Z}{\partial Y}$. Rashid [12] considered the case of a single light source at the origin ($S = [0,0,0]$) and perspective projection.

$$E(x,y) = S_0 \rho(x,y) \frac{1 - xp - yp}{Z^2 \sqrt{(p^2+q^2+1)[1+x^2+y^2]^{\frac{3}{2}}}} \tag{3}$$

There are three unknowns p, q, and Z and only one equation. Rashid obtains further information by considering the directional derivatives in the x and y directions, which can be obtained from the partial derivatives of the image irradiance E. The total differential change in image irradiance at an image point can be evaluated as $dE = E_x dx + E_y dy$ where $E_x = \frac{\partial E}{\partial x}$ and $E_y = \frac{\partial E}{\partial y}$. By considering normalised derivatives, $R_x = \frac{E_x}{E}$ and $R_y = \frac{E_y}{E}$, and approximating Z by its Taylor series, we get two independent equations:

$$R_x = -3\left(\frac{p_0}{1 - p_0 x - q_0 y} + \frac{x}{1 + x^2 + y^2}\right) \tag{4}$$

$$R_y = -3\left(\frac{q_0}{1 - p_0 x - q_0 y} + \frac{y}{1 + x^2 + y^2}\right) \tag{5}$$

This is an important result in which we have two equations with two unknowns, p and q, and the absolute position (Z_0), average albedo (ρ_{av}), and light source (S_0) constant have been cancelled out. Equations (4) and (5) can be written as two linear equations with two unknowns, and can be directly solved to obtain the surface gradients p and q for each image point. We only need to know its intensity, E, and its gradient in two orthogonal directions, E_x and E_y, assuming a near and smooth surface in which the albedo varies slowly.

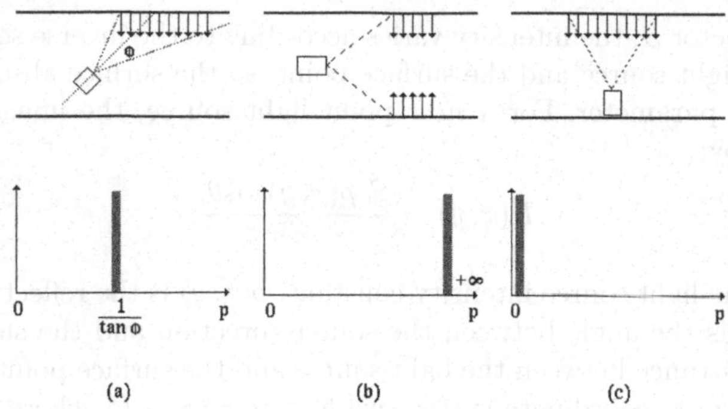

Fig. 1. Normal vectors and the corresponding *p-histogram*. Each case depicts different orientations of the camera with respect to the tube's main axis. In (a) we depict the general case with an angle ϕ. Cases (b) and (c) depict the two extremes, with $\phi = 0$ and $\phi = 90$, respectively.

3 The *pq-Histogram*

The local depth $[p, q]$ is perpendicular to the camera axis Z, and it gives the orientation with respect to two orthogonal axis (X, Y). This can be represented as the surface normal vector $n = [p, q, -1]$. The surface orientation can vary from perpendicular to the camera with p and q equal to zero, to parallel to the camera with p and q close to "infinity". If we assume an environment with a shape similar to a tube, a reasonable approximation of the position of free space will be a function of the direction in which the majority of the normal vectors are pointing to. This is clear if we consider an infinite ideal tube (figure 1) and take a cross section along the X axis, so we have only the p component of the normal vector.

If there is an angle ϕ between the camera axis, Z, and the tube's main axis (figure 1-a), then normal vectors in the cross section will have p values that correspond to this angle ϕ, i.e. $p = \frac{1}{tan\phi}$. We can illustrate this if we construct a *p-histogram* as shown in figure 1-a, that represents the number of p vectors for each slope. In this case, the histogram will have n entries for p such that $tan\phi = \frac{1}{p}$ and zero for all other values. There are two special cases that we have to take into account. One is if the camera is at the centre of the tube and parallel to its axis (figure 1-b), then all the normal vectors are parallel to the camera axis and $[p, q] \to \infty$. The other extreme is if the camera is close to the wall of the tube and pointing directly into it (figure 1-c), then the normal vectors are all nearly perpendicular to the camera axis and $[p, q] \approx 0$.

If we extend this analysis to the 3D surface of a tube, we shall have a distribution of $[p, q]$ which will not be a single slot in the histogram. The tube's curvature will produce different values for $[p, q]$, see figure 2-c for a real example. These values will be concentrated around the corresponding angle ϕ, which indicates the free space. So, from the $[p, q]$ distribution we can estimate ϕ, which gives the relative position of the free space of an ideal tube. We divide the space of possible values of $[p, q]$ into a small number of slots and we obtain a 2D histogram of this space (figure 2), which we denominate a *pq-histogram*. The size of the slots in p and q are in logarithmic scale (figure 2-a), that is, it increases exponentially from the origin to take into account the non–linear nature of the relation between $[p, q]$ and the angle (tangent function).

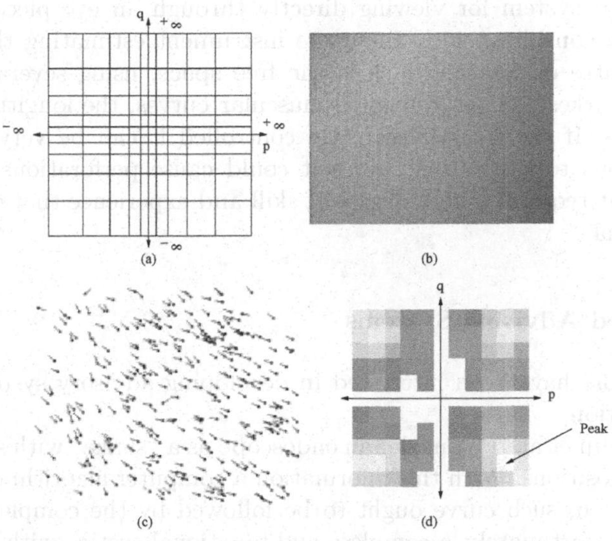

Fig. 2. An example. (a) A *pq-histogram* showing $[p, q]$ axis which are divided into a finite number of slots in logarithmic scale. Panel (b) depicts a section of a wall, vanishing to right, with a ceiling lamp. (c) show $[p, q]$ vectors computed with the shape from shading technique. Panel (d) depicts the *pq-histogram* for this scene, showing the corresponding peak or dominant orientation.

From this *pq-histogram*, we find the values of $[p, q]$ that occur more frequently, which correspond to the largest peak in the histogram, see figure 2-d. The position of this peak will give us a rough estimate of the free space; that is, there is a direct mapping between the location of a peak in the histogram and the angle of the free space in the image. For example, in figure 2-d the advising orientation (peak) corresponds to down/right.

Several real environments can be considered tube-like, such as the interior of the digestive system, sewers, mines, corridors, etc., and in these cases the *pq-histogram* can be applied as a fast navigation clue. It is a global approach, so it is quite robust, and it works in practice even if some of the assumptions are not fully satisfied, for instance a single point light source close to the camera, Lambertian surfaces, or ideal tube structure. This has been demonstrated in two applications, one for endoscopy and the other for mobile robots, which are described in the next two sections.

4 Endoscope Navigation

The endoscope is a flexible tube with viewing capability. It consists of a flexible shaft which has a manoeuvrable tip. The orientation of the tip can be controlled with pull wires that bend it in four orthogonal directions (*left/right, up/down*). It is connected to a cold light source for illumination of the internal organs and has an optical system for viewing directly through an eye piece or on a TV monitor. The consultant introduces the instrument estimating the position of the colon centre or *lumen*, which is the free space, using several visual clues such as the darkest region, the colon muscular curves, the longitudinal muscle, among others. If the tip is incorrectly controlled it can be very paintful and even dangerous to the patient, since it could cause perforations on the colon wall. Hence, it requires a high degree of skill and experience that only an *expert* endoscopist has.

4.1 Related Advising Systems

Several authors have been interested in developing advisory systems for endoscope navigation.

Buckingham et al. [1] consider an endoscope as a "snake" with sensors at predetermined positions. With this information a computer algorithm fits a smooth curve, and then, such curve ought to be followed by the complete endoscope. In practice, unfortunately, a complete and functional system with this approach is difficult to build. The mechanical join must be small enough, i.e. for describing smooth curves. This fact leads a hyper-redundant manipulator [2], with a not straightforward kinematics for a real-time application. However, other works following this approach [5,7,13], have shown its feasibility in a long term period.

A related work applied to sinus surgery is described in [14]. This graphical interface can show in real-time the full path followed by the endoscope, rigid in this case. Before that, a complete 3D view of the patient's head must be stored. In contrast to sinus surgery, in colonoscopy we cannot take a static view. The colon is not rigidly fixed, even its muscular contractions can change the panorama.

Okatani [10] et al. developed a shape-from-shading algorithm for estimating and tracking the position of the lumen. In their approach, a physician introduces the initial segmentation for the lumen. Moreover, there is a lens calibration step in order to retrieve good estimates. The resulting equations are approximated by a iterative minimisation method, which becomes too costly computationally. In contrast, we do not need in advance an initial segmentation nor calibration.

Deguchi [3] et al. have used a shape-from-motion approach. As it is well-known, rigidity is an inherent assumption of this technique, but a real human colon does not follow this constraint. Kim [9] et al. have relaxed the matching by introducing a small stereo system. However, the narrow baseline of two or three cameras fitted in a reduced area (like an endoscope tip) produces poor depth maps.

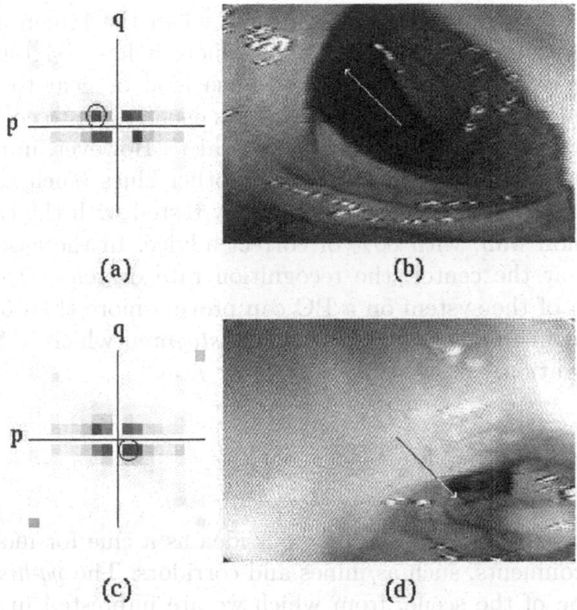

Fig. 3. Examples in colon images. Figures (a) and (c) depict *pq-histograms*, the selected directions are marked with circles. Figures (b) and (d) depict the suggested orientation superposed on the original image.

To summarise, the previous approaches require additional imaging, make unrealistic assumptions, initial segmentations, or are too expensive computationally, therefore they are not really useful for real–time endoscope navigation. In contrast, our approach only requires a single camera as in any standard endoscope, and it is very fast (not iterative) thus it can be used in real time.

4.2 The *pq-Histogram* in Endoscopy

In the case of colonoscopy, of course, we do not have an ideal tube. However, its basic shape is similar to a tube and the *pq-histogram* structure is applicable. Irregularities and some incorrect $[p, q]$ values due to image antifacts such as textures, edges and specularities, will distort the histogram. Nevertheless, we assume that these will be reflected as "noise" in the histogram, and the main cluster will still correspond to the direction of the lumen or free space. That is, an advantage of this technique is that it is a *global method*, therefore the local variations do not have a big effect on the overall result.

This method has been tested with real colonoscopy images taken from videotapes. Two examples, including their *pq-histograms* and suggested orientation, are shown in figure 3. Suggested orientations (peaks) are marked with circles, and their relative position to the axis coordinates indicate the corresponding left-right/up-down movement to follow. In practice, we have observed that this technique tends to give more reliable results when the lumen or free space is located towards the edge in the image, i.e. where it has a significant deviation from the centre of the colon. When the lumen is at or near to the centre, the distribution is more uniform and the peaks are usually due to colon walls irregularities, therefore there could appear "false peaks". However, in these situations is when the lumen is easier to obtain using other clues (such as the "dark region" [8]). The algorithm has been extensively tested with the camera pointing towards one colon wall, with 80% of correct advice. In the case of having the lumen roughly at the center, the recognition rate decreases to 60%-70%. An implementation of the system on a PC can process more than 5 images (256 x 256) per second including the SFS and *pq-histogram*, which is fast enough for endoscope navigation.

5 Robot Navigation

Interestingly, we can also use the previous idea as a clue for mobile navigation in certain environments, such as mines and corridors. The *pq-histogram* returns the global shape of the scene, from which we are interested in the free space. Complete advise of left/right and up/down is not necessary because we do not expect to move up/down our mobile robots[1]. Instead, we use only the voting over p vectors, in the sense of only deciding left/right.

It is not our claim to replace sonars or range finder sensors nor show a complete navigation system based on this clue, but contributing to the navigation task with a complementary and fast clue. Figure (4) depicts two distinct scenarios as an example of such a visual feedback.

Figure (4-b) depicts a corridor, where the wall in some sense is violating the assumption of smooth Lambertian surface. The *pq-histogram* accurately points out the free space, that is to say the peak in the histogram, figure (4-a). In this case there are two illumination sources, one above the robot and the another one a standard ceiling lamp. Needless to say, this is another violation to the initial assumptions, but it is a more realistic scenario. The second example, figure (4-d), depicts a scene with only one light source and a more smooth surface. Accordingly to the scene, the *pq-histogram*, figure (4-c), depicts the peak at the correct side. These examples show that, in spite of violating some assumptions, the resulting peak still corresponds to the free space. We have done a more comprehensive test of the technique in corridors, with a nearly perfect record (>95%) of correct advices.

Obviously, a mobile robot system must take into account more information than a left/right clue. However, this visual feedback is an interesting and reliable information for navigation. Even more, it does not require a full (and probably costly) reconstruction of the surroundings. Indeed, a global sketch is enough. It can be used in several real scenarios, such as in mines, sewers, pipes and corridors, as a fast way to avoid walls and as a clue for following the free space.

[1] Nomad 200 and SuperScout II.

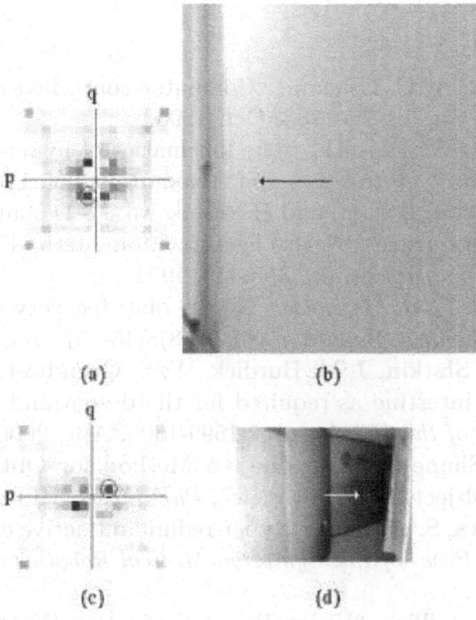

Fig. 4. Examples in corridors. Figures (a) and (c) depict *pq-histograms*, the selected directions are marked with circles. Figures (b) and (d) depict the suggested orientation on the original image.

6 Conclusions and Future Work

We have developed a structure for summarising local depth information in a *pq-histogram*. A *pq-histogram* allow us to integrate the local orientation data in a global structure, opening the door to more practical applications of shape from shading techniques. We have shown two domains in which the *pq-histogram* can be applied: endoscopy and robot navigation. The approximate position of the *lumen* or free space can be extracted from the peak of the *pq-histogram*. This was tested with real colon videotapes with promising results. We also have presented its application to mobile robots, where it can be used as a fast clue for certain indoor environments or as a complement to other sensors. An important feature of this structure is that, given its global nature, it is quite robust so it works in practice even if several of the initial assumptions are not fully satisfied. It is also a direct and very fast technique, thus it can be used for real–time applications. We plan to develop post–processing techniques for the *pq-histogram* to strength the final advice. We are also working in integrating this technique with other information sources.

Acknowledgments

One of the authors, G. Gomez, wishes to express his gratitude to the CGC programme of the ETH-Zürich for their support during this research project.

References

1. R. O. Buckingham, A. C. Graham, "Computer controlled redundant endoscopy", *Proc. of the SMC*, vol. 3:1779-1783, Oct. 1996.
2. G. S. Chirikjian, J. W. Burdick, "The kinematics of hyper-redundant robot locomotion", *IEEE Trans. on Robotics and Automation*, vol. 11(6):781-793, Dec. 1995.
3. K. Deguchi, T.Sasano, H.Arai, and H.Yoshikawa, "3-D shape reconstruction from endoscope image sequences by the Factorization Method", *IAPR Workshop on Machine Vision Applications*, pp. 455-459, 1994.
4. P. L. Worthington, E. R. Hancock, "Needle map recovery using robust regularizers", *Image and Vision Computing*, vol. 17(8):545-557, June 1999.
5. H. D. Hoeg, A. B. Slatkin, J. M. Burdick, W. S. Grundfest, "Biomechanical modeling of the small intestine as required for the design and operation of a robotic endoscope", *Proc. of the ICRA*, vol. 2:1599-1606, Apr. 2000.
6. B. K. P. Horn, "Shape from Shading: A Method for Obtaining the Shape of a Smooth Opaque Object from One View", *PhD thesis*, MIT AI TR-232, June 1970.
7. K. Ikuta, M. Nokota, S. Aritomi, "Hyper-redundant active endoscope for minimum invasive surgery", *Proc. of Int. Symp. on Medical Robotics and Computer Assisted Surgery*, 1994.
8. G. N. Khan, D. F. Gillies, "Vision-Based Navigation System for an Endoscope", *Image and Vision Computing*, vol. 14(10):763-772, Dec. 1996.
9. J. Kim, D. Hwang, H. Jeong, "Development of depth extraction algorithm for the stereo endoscopic image", *Proc. of the Intl. Conf. of the IEEE Engineering in Medicine and Biology Society*, vol. 2:884-887, 1998.
10. T. Okatani, K. Deguchi, "Shape reconstruction from an endoscope image by Shape from Shading technique for a point light source at the projection center", *CV&IU*, vol. 66(2):119-131, May 1997.
11. A. Pentland, "Local shading analysis", *IEEE Trans. on PAMI*, vol 6(2):170-187, March 1984.
12. H. U. Rashid, P. Burger, "Differential Algorithm for the Determination of Shape from Shading Using a Point Light Source", *Image and Vision Computing*, vol. 10(2):119-127, 1992.
13. A.B. Slatkin, J. Burdick , "The development of a robot endoscope", *Proc. of the IROS*, vol. 1:162-171, June 1995.
14. J. Yamashita, Y. Yamauchi, M. Mochimaru, Y. Fukui, K. Yokoyama, "Real-time 3-D model-based navigation system for endoscopic paranasal sinus surgery", *IEEE Trans. on Biomedical Eng.*, vol. 46(1):107-116, Jan. 1999.
15. R. Zhang, P.S. Tsai, J.E. Cryer, M. Shah, "Shape from Shading: a survey". *IEEE Trans. on PAMI*, vol. 21(8):690-706, Aug. 1999.
16. R. Zhang, M. Shah, "Shape from intensity gradient", *IEEE Trans. on SMC - A*, vol. 29(3):318-325, May 1999.

Path Planning Using a Single-Query Bi-directional Lazy Collision Checking Planner

Gildardo Sánchez-Ante

Dept. of Computer Science
ITESM Campus Guadalajara
Av. Gral. Ramon Corona 2514
Zapopan, Jalisco, 45140
MEXICO
gsanchez@campus.gda.itesm.mx

Abstract. Applications such as programming spot-welding stations require computing paths in high-dimensional spaces. Random sampling approaches, such as the Probabilistic Roadmaps (PRM) have shown great potential in solving path-planning problems in this kinds of environments. In this paper, we review the description of a new probabilistic roadmap planner, called SBL, which stands for Single-query, Bi-directional and Lazy Collision Checking, and we also add some new results that allow a better comparison of SBL against other similar planners. The combination of features offered by SBL reduces the planning time by large factors, making it possible to handle more difficult planning problems, including multi-robot problems in geometrically complex environments. Specifically, we show the results obtained using SBL in environments with as many as 36 degrees of freedom, and environments in which narrow passages are present.

1 Introduction

The problem of planning the motion of multiple robots sharing portions of their working spaces is considered as an extension of the "basic" problem of motion planning [1]. We have recently developed a new PRM planner that combines a single-query bi-directional sampling/search strategy with a lazy collision-checking strategy that postpones collision tests until they are absolutely necessary. This planner, called SBL (for Single-query, Bi-directional, Lazy collision-checking), is described in detail in [2]. It is significantly more efficient than previous PRM planners, which enables its application to problems involving multiple robots interacting in geometrically complex environments.

The remainder of this paper is structured as follows: Section 2 defines terms used throughout this paper. Section 3 provides a summary of the SBL algorithms. Section 4 presents experimental results on single-robot (6 dof) and multi-robot (up to 36 dofs) problems. The planner's code and movies illustrating its functioning can be downloaded from http://robotics.stanford.edu/~latombe/projects/.

C.A. Coello Coello et al. (Eds.): MICAI 2002, LNAI 2313, pp. 41–50, 2002.

2 Definitions

In what follows, $\mathcal{C}$ denotes the configuration space of a robot and $\mathcal{F} \subset \mathcal{C}$ its free space. No explicit geometric representation of $\mathcal{F}$ is computed. Instead, given any $q \in \mathcal{C}$, a collision checker returns whether $q \in \mathcal{F}$. A path τ in $\mathcal{C}$ is considered collision-free if a series of points on τ, such that every two successive points are closer than some ε, are all collision-free. A rigorous test (eliminating the need for ε) is possible by using a distance-computation algorithm instead of a pure collision checker [3, 4].

A query to a PRM planner is defined by two *query configurations*, q_i and q_g. If these configurations lie in the same component of $\mathcal{F}$, the planner should return a collision-free path between them; otherwise, it should indicate that no such path exists. There are two main classes of PRM planners: *multi-query* and *single-query*. A multi-query planner pre-computes a roadmap which it later uses to process multiple queries [5, 6]. To deal with any possible query, the roadmap must be distributed over the entire free space. Instead, a single-query planner computes a new roadmap for each query [4, 7, 8]. The less free space it explores to find a path between the two query configurations, the better. Single-query planners are more suitable in environments with frequent changes [7, 4, 9, 10].

A single-query planner either grows one tree of milestones from q_i or q_g, until a connection is found with the other query configuration (*single-directional* search), or grows two trees concurrently, respectively rooted at q_i and q_g until a connection is found between the two trees (*bi-directional* search) [4]. In both cases, milestones are iteratively added to the roadmap. Each new milestone m' is selected in a neighborhood of a milestone m already installed in a tree T, and is connected to m by a local path (hence, m' becomes a child of m in T). Bi-directional planners are usually more efficient than single-directional ones.

SBL is a single-query, bi-directional PRM planner. Unlike previous such planners, it does not immediately test the connections between milestones for collision. Therefore, rather than referring to the connection between two adjacent nodes in a roadmap tree as a *local path*, we call it a *segment*.

3 Description of the Planner

The planner iteratively builds two milestone trees, T_i and T_g, respectively rooted at q_i and q_g. Each loop performs two steps: EXPAND-TREE and CONNECT-TREES. EXPAND-TREE adds a milestone to one of the two trees. CONNECT-TREES tries to connect the two trees. The planner returns *failure* if it has not found a solution path after s iterations. If the planner returns *failure*, either no collision-free path exists between q_i and q_g, or the planner failed to find one.

Each expansion of the roadmap consists of adding a milestone to one of the two trees. The algorithm first selects the tree T to expand. Then, a milestone m is picked from T with probability inverse of $\eta(m)$ (a number that measures the current density of milestones of T around m) and a collision-free configuration q is picked at a distance less than ρ from m. This configuration q is the new milestone. The use of the probability distribution $\pi(m) \sim 1/\eta(m)$ was introduced in [7] to avoid over-sampling regions of $\mathcal{F}$. It guarantees that the distribution of milestones eventually diffuses through the subsets of $\mathcal{F}$ reachable from q_i and q_g. In [4, 7] this condition is required to prove that the planner will eventually find a path, if one exists. The alternation between the two trees prevents any tree from eventually growing much bigger than the other, as the advantages of bi-directional search would then be lost. The images in Fig. 1 illustrate the process.

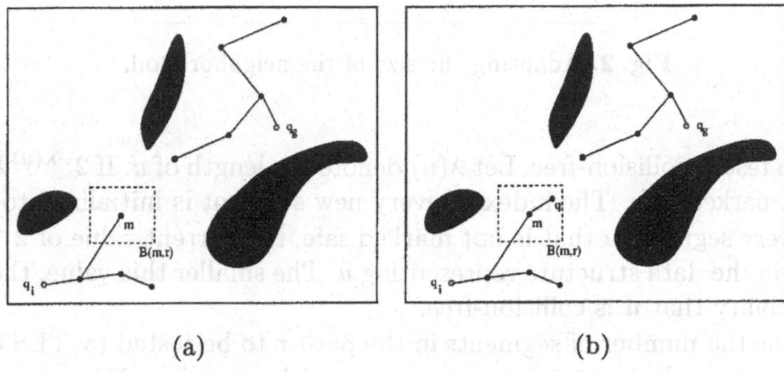

Fig. 1. Expanding the tree.

When expanding the tree, SBL applies an adaptive sampling strategy, by selecting a series of up to k milestone candidates, at random, from successively smaller neighborhoods of m, starting with a neighborhood of radius ρ. When a candidate q tests collision-free, it is retained as the new milestone. The segment from m to q is not checked here for collision. On the average, the jump from m to q is greater in wide-open regions of $\mathcal{F}$ than in narrow regions. This is illustrated in Fig. 2.

Let m now denote the milestone that was just added by EXPAND-TREE. Let m' be the closest milestone to m in the other tree. The two trees are connected by a segment, called a *bridge*, between m and m' if these two milestones are less than some ζ apart. The bridge creates a path τ joining q_i and q_g in the roadmap. The segments along τ, including the bridge, are now tested for collision. This is done by an algorithm called TEST-PATH, which returns *nil* if it detects a collision. The reader is referred to [11] for implementation details.

The planner associates a collision-check index $\kappa(u)$ with each segment u between milestones (including the bridge). This index takes an integer value indicating the resolution at which u has already been tested. If $\kappa(u) = 0$, then only the two endpoints of u (which are both milestones) have been tested collision-free. If $\kappa(u) = 1$, then the two endpoints and the midpoint of u have been tested collision-free. More generally, for any $\kappa(u)$, $2^{\kappa(u)} + 1$ equally distant points of u

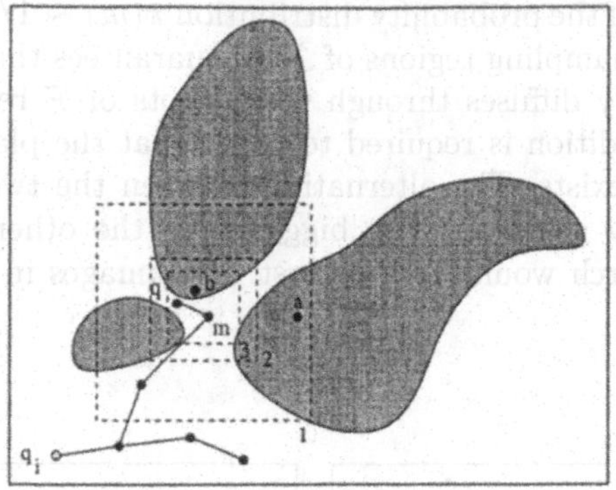

Fig. 2. Adapting the size of the neighborhood.

have been tested collision-free. Let $\lambda(u)$ denote the length of u. If $2^{-\kappa(u)}\lambda(u) < \varepsilon$, then u is marked safe. The index of every new segment is initialized to 0.

For every segment u that is not marked safe, the current value of $2^{-\kappa(u)}\lambda(u)$ is cached in the data structure representing u. The smaller this value, the greater the probability that u is collision-free.

Let p be the number of segments in the path τ to be tested by TEST-PATH, and $\{u_1, u_2, ..., u_p\}$ denote those segments, with u_1 originating at q_i and u_p ending at q_g. TEST-PATH(τ) maintains a priority queue U sorted in decreasing order of $2^{-\kappa(u)}\lambda(u)$ of all the segments $\{u_1, u_2, ..., u_p\}$ that are not marked *safe*.

TEST-PATH makes use of the algorithm TEST-SEGMENT, that tests the segments u_i for collision. Each loop of TEST-PATH results in increasing the index on the segment u that is in first position in U. This segment is removed from U. It is re-inserted in U if TEST-SEGMENT(u) neither detects a collision, nor marks u as *safe*. If u is re-inserted in U, it may not be in first position, since the quantity $2^{-\kappa(u)}\lambda(u)$ has been divided by 2. TEST-PATH terminates when a collision is detected – then the colliding segment is removed – or when all segments have been marked *safe* (i.e., U is empty) – then the path τ is returned.

The removal of a segment u disconnects the roadmap into two trees. If u is the bridge that CONNECT-TREES created to connect the two trees, the two trees return to their previous state. Otherwise, the removal of u results in a transfer of milestones from one tree to the other. No milestone is removed from the roadmap. The collision-checking work done along all segments, except the one that tested to collide, is saved in their indices.

4 Experimental Results

In Fig. 3 we show six environments in which the planner was tested. Fig. 3(a) shows the case of a PUMA robot with 6-dof transferring a piece of metal from a lathe to a press. Fig. 3(b) shows a FANUC robot transporting a metal sheet from the press to a table, while Fig. 3(c) through Fig. 3(e) illustrates artificial environments with several narrow passages. Finally, Fig. 3(f) shows six robots in an environment that emulates an automotive spot-welding station.

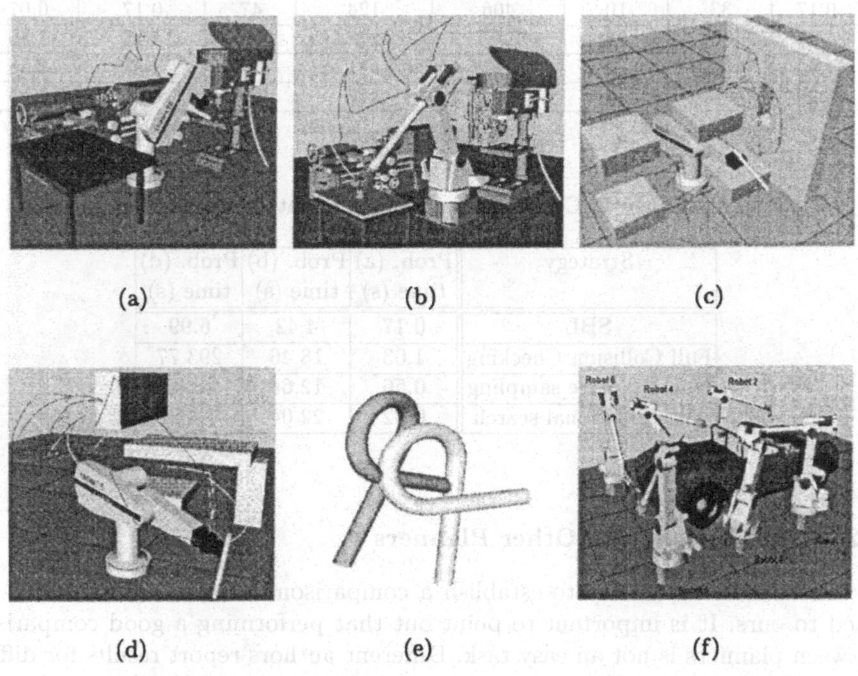

Fig. 3. Path planning environments.

SBL is written in C++. The running times reported below were obtained on an 1-GHz Pentium III processor and 1 Gb of main memory running Linux. The planner uses the PQP checker. The distance threshold ρ was set to 0.15 and the resolution ε was set to 0.012.

4.1 Basic Performance Evaluation

Table 1 gives averages over 100 runs of SBL on the first four environments of Fig. 3. In all reported cases, the planner found a path in reasonable time; there was no failure. The running times in Table 1 do not include path optimization, which in all cases took an additional 0.2 to 0.4s.

In order to better measure the relative influence of each one of the different strategies on the performance of SBL, we run a set of experiments enabling/disabling the lazy collision checking, the adaptive sampling and the bidirectional search. The results are presented in Table 2. It is clear that the biggest saving is due to the lazy collision checking strategy in most of the cases.

Table 1. Statistics for environments in Fig. 3.

	Total time (s)	Milest. in roadmap	Milest. in path	Total Nr. of Coll. Checks	Coll. Checks on the path	Samples tested	Time for Coll.Checks	Std. Dev. (s)
a	0.17	33	10	406	124	47	0.17	0.07
b	4.42	1405	24	7267	277	3769	4.17	1.86
c	4.45	1609	39	11211	411	7832	4.21	2.48
d	6.99	4160	44	12228	447	6990	6.30	3.55

Table 2. Contribution of the different strategies.

Strategy	Prob. (a) time (s)	Prob. (b) time (s)	Prob. (d) time (s)
SBL	0.17	4.42	6.99
Full Collision Checking	1.03	18.46	293.77
Non-adaptive sampling	0.56	12.65	33.65
Uni-directional search	0.32	22.04	72.39

4.2 Comparison with Other Planners

In this subsection, we try to establish a comparison between several works related to ours. It is important to point out that performing a good comparison between planners is not an easy task. Different authors report results for different problems, ran in different computers with different strategies for the planner, and sometimes with different implementations of the collision checker.

We will first consider a problem provided by Boris Yamrom, from the GE Corporate Research & Development Center. The problem – called "alpha puzzle"– contains a narrow passage and has been proposed as a benchmark for motion planning algorithms [12]. The puzzle consists of two tubes, each twisted into an alpha shape; one tube is the obstacle and the other the moving object (robot). The environment is illustrated in Fig. 3(e). The goal is to separate the intertwined tubes. Each tube consists of 1008 triangles. The models are given in world coordinates in which the robot and obstacle tubes are in an intertwined configuration.

There are several versions of this problem. Each one was obtained scaling the obstacle tube along the z-axis by a constant factor greater than 1, which had the effect of widening the gap between the two prongs of the alpha. Thus, the hardest version is the original problem (scale 1.0), and the easiest version is the 1.5 scaled version.

Another set of runs was carried out using the alpha puzzle as a benchmark to compare the performance of several planners [13], such as: Obstacle-Based Probabilistic Roadmaps (OBPRM) [12], Rapid Random Trees (RRT) [9] and Ariadne's Clew Algorithm (ACA) [14]. They also tested a single-shot version of the Ariadne's Clew Algorithm (S-ACA). The planners were ran on an HP

Convex 9000/V2200 with 16 PA-8200 processors, each running at 220 MHz with 4 GB of physical memory and 9 GB of swap. Our results for the SBL planner were obtained in a Pentium III PC with 2 processors, each running at 1 GHz and 1 GB of physical memory. Recall that our code does not take advantage of both processors. It uses only one of them at running time.

In Table 3 we reproduce the results reported in [13] for OBPRM, RRT and ACA. The results for SBL were obtained by Mitul Saha, from Stanford University.

Table 3. Comparison between planners running the alpha puzzle.

Problem	Planner	Running time (s)	Solution found?
α-1.5	OBPRM	3495	yes
	RRT	5555	no
	ACA	1699	yes
	SBL	1500	yes
α-1.2	OBPRM	94150	no
	RRT	49455	yes
	ACA	83934	no
	S-ACA	68934	yes
	SBL	10800	yes

On the other hand, we also tried to compare SBL against the planner described in [15]. As a matter of fact, the environment shown in Fig. 3(c) was created trying to reproduce one of the environments used in that work. The experiments reported were ran in a 400-MHz Pentium II processor with 512 MB RAM. The planner was implemented in C++ as a plug-in module to RobotStudio (Developed by ABB Digital Plant Technologies AB, Götemborg, Sweden).

More specifically, we ran the following queries:

- **Q1**: starting from home configuration, the robot picks a sheet of metal from the table.
- **Q2**: the robot puts the sheet of metal at the press.
- **Q3**: the robot returns to home.

Query **Q1** emulates the query (A $\rightarrow$ B) presented in Fig. 4 of [15], while query **Q2** resembles query (C $\rightarrow$ D). Query **Q3** is supposed to represent the one labeled as J $\rightarrow$ A in [15]. The results are summarized in Table 4.

A number of uniformly distributed points (nodes) is sampled, and connections (edges) are established between pairs of points being sufficiently close. Nodes and edges form a roadmap of paths assumed to be feasible. Then, the shortest path between the two query configurations is found and the nodes and edges on this path are checked for collision. In case that a collision if found, the corresponding node/edge is removed and the process is started again.

Table 4. Comparison between SBL and Lazy PRM [15].

Query	Planner	Running time (s)	Number of collision checks
Q1	Lazy PRM	12.7	92
	SBL	0.029	83
Q2	Lazy PRM	36.8	445
	SBL	0.17	320
Q3	Lazy PRM	18.2	142
	SBL	0.06	89

Table 5. Statistics on 9 multi-robot problems.

	Total time (s)	Milest. in roadmap	Milest. in path	Total Nr. of Coll. Checks	Coll. Checks on the path	Samples tested	Time for Coll.Checks	Std. Dev. (s)
PI-2	0.26	11	4	242	58	18	0.26	0.52
PII-2	0.25	11	5	248	76	13	0.25	0.17
PIII-2	2.44	191	17	2356	243	718	2.41	1.57
PI-4	3.97	62	7	1015	106	193	3.96	5.67
PII-4	3.94	56	10	968	166	112	3.93	2.4
PIII-4	30.82	841	32	8895	542	2945	3057	15.55
PI-6	28.91	322	14	3599	121	1083	28.82	28.91
PII-6	59.65	882	30	6891	533	1981	59.41	31.08
PIII-6	442.85	5648	91	47384	1525	24511	439.39	170.46

The numbers reported for Lazy PRM in Table 4 are the averages over 20 runs for each task. In order to have a better idea on how the time is distributed between the different phases, consider the following. For query **Q1**, 6.6 seconds were spent building the graph, while 6.1 seconds were used for collision checking. The time used for finding the path was negligible. In the case of query **Q2**, 0.8 seconds were required for graph building, 0.5 seconds for graph searching and 35.4 seconds for collision checking. In query **Q3**, the distribution was 6.6 seconds for graph building and 11.6 seconds for collision checking.

4.3 Multi-robot Examples

We ran SBL on several problems in the environment of Fig. 3(f), which represents a spot-welding station found in automotive body shops. This station contains 6 robots each with 6 dofs each. SBL treats them as if they formed a single robot with 36 dofs, hence builds a roadmap in a 36-D configuration space. To keep SBL general, we did not take advantage of specific properties of the environment. For example, SBL assumes that collisions may occur between any two bodies of any two robots, while many pairs of bodies cannot collide.

Table 5 gives averages over 100 runs of SBL on 9 problems. Fig. 4 shows the initial and final configurations for the problem named PIII-6 in Table 4. PIII-2 and PIII-4 are the same problem, but reduced to robots 1 and 2, and robots 1 through 4, respectively. The problems PI-2/4/6 and PII-2/4/6 are simpler, with either the initial or the goal configurations being the rest configuration of the robots.

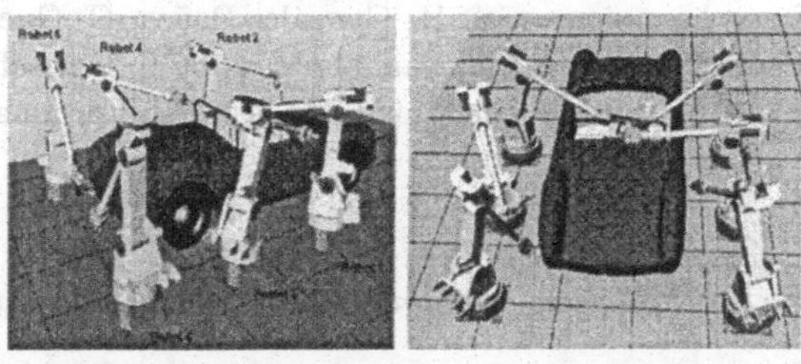

Fig. 4. Initial and goal configurations, problem III.

In all $100 \times 3 \times 3 = 900$ runs, SBL successfully returned a path in a satisfactory amount of time. In each run, the maximum number of milestones allowed to the planner was set to 10,000, but the maximum number of milestones actually generated by SBL was 6917 for a run of problem PIII-6. The increase in the running times when the number of robots goes from 2 to 4 to 6 is caused both by the quadratic growth in the number of pairs of bodies that are tested at each collision-checking operation and by the greater difficulty of the problems due to the constraints imposed by the additional robots upon the motions of the other robots. We created a specific version of SBL that tests only the pairs of bodies that can possibly collide. For the most complex problem (PIII-6), the average running time was reduced to 323 s.

5 Conclusion

This paper shows that a PRM planner combining a lazy collision-checking strategy with single-query bi-directional sampling techniques can solve path-planning problems of practical interest (i.e. with realistic complexity) in times ranging from fractions of a second to a few seconds for a single or few robots, and from seconds to a few minutes for multiple robots.

One interesting research topic is now to extend SBL to facilitate the programming of multi-robot spot-welding stations in automotive body shops. In particular, each robot must perform several welding operations, but the ordering of these operations is not fully specified. Hence, the planner will have to compute an optimized tour of the welding locations to be visited by each robot. This is a variant of the Traveling Salesman Problem, where the distance between two locations is not given and, instead, must be computed by SBL. Clearly, if there are r locations to visit, we do not want to invoke this planner $O(r^2)$ times; a better method must be found.

Acknowledgments This research was conducted in the C.S. Dept. at Stanford University under the direction of Prof. Jean-Claude Latombe. It was funded by grants from GM Research and ABB. G. Sánchez's stay at Stanford was partially supported by ITESM (Campus Guadalajara) and a fellowship from CONACyT. This paper has greatly benefited from discussions with H. González-Baños, C. Guestrin, D. Hsu, L. Kavraki, and F. Prinz. PQP was made available to us by S. Gottschalk, M. Lin, and D. Manocha from the C.S. Dept. at the University of North-Carolina in Chapel Hill.

References

1. J. C. Latombe. *Robot Motion Planning.* Kluwer Academic Publishers, Boston, MA, 1991.
2. G. Sánchez-Ante and J. C. Latombe. A single-query bi-directional probabilistic roadmap planner with lazy collision checking. In *Proc. 10th Int. Symp. of Robotics Research, ISRR'2001*, Lorne, Victoria, Australia, 2001.
3. J. Barraquand, L. E. Kavraki, J. C. Latombe, T. Y. Li, R. Motwani, and P. Raghavan. A random sampling scheme for path planning. *Int. J. of Robotics Research*, 16(6):759–774, 1997.
4. D. Hsu. *Randomized Single-Query Motion Planning in Expansive Spaces.* PhD thesis, Stanford University, Stanford, CA, USA, 2000.
5. L. E. Kavraki. *Random Networks in Configuration Space for Fast Path Planning.* PhD thesis, Stanford University, Stanford, CA, USA, 1994.
6. L. E. Kavraki, P. Švestka, J. C. Latombe, and M. H. Overmars. Probabilistic roadmaps for path planning in high-dimensional configuration spaces. *IEEE Trans. on Robotics and Automation*, 12(4):566–580, 1996.
7. D. Hsu, J. C. Latombe, and R. Motwani. Path planning in expansive configuration spaces. In *Proc. IEEE Int. Conf. Rob. & Autom.*, pages 2719–2726, 1997.
8. J.J. Kuffner, Jr. *Autonomous Agents for Real-Time Animation.* PhD thesis, Stanford University, Stanford, CA, USA, 1999.
9. J.J. Kuffner, Jr. and S. M. LaValle. RRT-connect: An efficient approach to single-query path planning. In *Proc. IEEE Int. Conf. Rob. & Autom.*, 2000.
10. S. M. LaValle and J.J. Kuffner, Jr. Randomized kinodynamic planning. *Int. J. on Robotics Research*, 20(5):378–400, 2001.
11. G. Sánchez-Ante and J. C. Latombe. A single-query bi-directional probabilistic roadmap planner with lazy collision checking. Manuscript submitted to *Int. J. on Robotics Research*, 2001.
12. N. M. Amato, O. B. Bayazit, L. K. Dale, C. Jones, and D. Vallejo. OBPRM: An obstacle-based PRM for 3D workspaces. In P. K. Agarwal et al., editor, *Robotics: The Algorithmic Perspective*, pages 155–168, 1998.
13. D. Vallejo, I. Remmler, and N. M. Amato. An adaptive framework for "single shot" motion planning: A self-tuning system for rigid and articulated robots. In *Proc. IEEE Int. Conf. Rob. & Autom.*, 2001.
14. E. Mazer, J. M. Ahuactzin, and P. Bessiere. The Ariadne's clew algorithm. *Journal of Artificial Intelligence Research*, 9:295–316, 1998.
15. R. Bohlin and L. E. Kavraki. Path planning using lazy PRM. In *Proc. IEEE Int. Conf. Rob. & Autom.*, pages 521–528, 2000.

An Exploration Approach for Indoor Mobile Robots Reducing Odometric Errors

Leonardo Romero, Eduardo F. Morales, and L. Enrique Sucar

ITESM, Campus Morelos, Temixco, Morelos, 62589, Mexico
lromero@zeus.ccu.umich.mx
{emorales,esucar}@campus.mor.itesm.mx

Abstract. To learn a map of an environment a mobile robot has to explore its workspace. This paper introduces a new exploration approach that minimizes movements of the robot to reach the nearest unexplored region of the environment. In contrast to other methods, this approach takes into account *rotations of the robot* as well as the distance traveled by the robot, to compute an optimal movement policy to reach the nearest unexplored region. The robot acquires a kind of *inertial mass* that decreases the number of movements that changes the orientation of the robot, and hence reduces odometric errors. This approach is tested using a mobile robot simulator with very good results.

1 Introduction

This paper presents an exploration approach for an indoor mobile robot using its sensors, to learn a *Probabilistic Grid-based Map* (PGM) [2,9,14] of an environment. A PGM is a two dimensional map where the environment is divided in square regions or cells of the same size that have occupancy probabilities associated to them. The map learned is commonly used by a mobile robot for navigation while it does a high level task.

During the exploration, the robot movements are typically measured by an odometer and other sensors can be used to reduce odometric errors (a *position tracking problem*). In order to build useful maps, odometric errors have to be reduced or corrected. However, given the perceptual limitations and accuracy of sensors, odometric errors not always can be reduced. In this work, the main idea is to minimize orientation changes of the robot during the exploration, reducing odometric errors. See [1] for calibration procedures to improve odometric accuracy and [1,3] for a review of position tracking systems.

Research on exploration strategies has developed two general approaches: *reactive* and *model based* [7]. By far the most widely–used exploration strategy in reactive robotics is *wall following*. Model based strategies vary with the type of model being used, but they are based on the same underlying idea: *go to the least–explored region*. Most model based exploration approaches direct the robot towards the nearest unexplored region, following a path with minimum distance or *cost* [5]. In [13] the cost for traversing a grid cell is determined by

C.A. Coello Coello et al. (Eds.): MICAI 2002, LNAI 2313, pp. 51–60, 2002.

its occupancy probability, while in [7,8] the cost is determined by the distance between cells.

This paper introduces a novel approach to explore a static indoor environment minimizing a *total distance* from the robot to the nearest unexplored cell. In contrast to other methods, this approach considers the movements that change the orientation of the robot besides the *linear distance* traveled by the robot.

In other words, the idea is to give to the robot a kind of *inertial mass* that reduces the number of changes of orientation during the exploration, and hence odometric errors are reduced.

This approach is an improved version of the exploration technique given in [12]. An heuristic to reduce orientation changes of the robot is described in [12], but that heuristic works while the goal cell (the nearest unexplored cell) remains the same. As soon as there is another goal cell in other direction, a new policy of movements is computed to reach the new goal. The problem is that the new policy does not take into account the actual orientation of the robot. The new version do considers the actual orientation of the robot and hence the robot try to hold its orientation.

The remainder of this paper is organized as follows. Section 2 describes the proposed exploration approach, a modified version of the *value iteration* algorithm to include the orientation of the robot as a new state. Section 3 presents experimental results using a mobile robot simulator. Finally, section 4 is devoted to the conclusions and future work.

2 Exploration Approach

The general idea for exploration is to move the robot on a minimum–cost path to the nearest unexplored grid cell. The minimum–cost path is computed using a modified version of *value iteration*, a popular dynamic programming algorithm.

2.1 Initial Considerations

This section reviews relevant issues of a previous version of the exploration approach, published in [12].

When the robot starts to build a map, all the cells have the same probability of occupancy $P(O) = 0.5$. A cell is considered *unexplored* when its occupancy probability is in an interval close to 0.5, defined by two constants $[Pe_{min}, Pe_{max}]$ ($Pe_{min} < 0.5 < Pe_{max}$), and *explored* otherwise.

Cells are defined as *free* or *occupied.* A cell is considered occupied when its $P(O)$ reaches a threshold value Po_{max} and continues to be occupied while its $P(O)$ does not fall below a threshold value Po_{min} (where $Po_{min} < Po_{max}$). It is considered *free* in other case. This mechanism prevents changes in the state of occupancy of a cell by small probability changes. We assume that $Pe_{max} < Po_{min}$, so an unexplored cell is also a free cell. In this way, the PGM becomes a binary map when cells are classified as occupied or free. This binary map will be called *occupied–free* map.

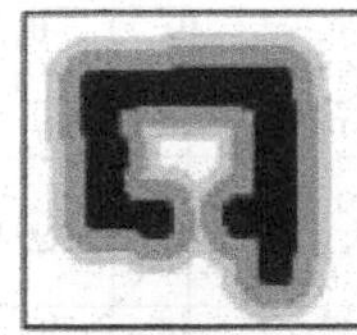

Fig. 1. A travel space due to multiple occupied cells. From darker to lighter: occupied cells (black), warning cells (dark gray), travel cells (light gray), and far cells (white)

In this work, a cylindrical (circular base) robot was used, so the configuration space (c–space) [6] can be computed by *dilating* the occupied cells by an amount equal to the robot's radius, and considering the robot as a point.

To guide the mobile robot by safe places, avoiding collisions with obstacles, the *travel space* concept is introduced in [12]. The travel space splits the cells of the occupied–free map in four categories (see Figure 1): *occupied cells,* after the dilation of real occupied cells; *warning cells*, cells close to an occupied cell; *travel cells*, cells close to a warning cell and *far cells*, any free cell that is not a warning or a travel cell. For simplicity, cells of type *warning*, *travel* or far, will be call *free* cells in the travel space.

The *travel space* can be computed incrementally after each change of state of a cell in the occupied–free map while the robot is exploring the environment. The idea is to associate costs to cells depending on its type. If warning cells and far cells have costs higher than travel cells, then a kind of *wall following* strategy for exploration is taken into account. If warning cells closer to occupied cells have higher costs, we get a kind of *repulsive force* between obstacles and the robot. This force avoids collisions with obstacles.

2.2 Movements of the Robot

In this work we consider that the robot can perform only 8 possible movements, one per cell in its vicinity, in the following way. As shown in Figure 2, if the robot executes movement m_i $(i = 0, ..., 7)$, it rotates first (if needed) to orientation θ_i, and then it moves forward, leaving the robot with orientation θ_i. If a movement m_i also can be denoted by (d_x, d_y), where dx is the change in x (pointing to the bottom) and dy is the change in y (pointing to the left), the set of valid movements is given by $M_v = \{(1,0),(1,1),(0,1),(-1,1),(-1,0),(-1,-1),(0,-1),(1,-1)\}$.

2.3 Global Search

A policy to move to the unexplored cells following minimum–cost paths is computed using the travel space and a modified version of *value iteration*. Previous approaches use a variable V associated to each cell of the map. $V(x,y)$ denotes the accumulated cost to travel from cell (x,y) to the nearest unexplored cell.

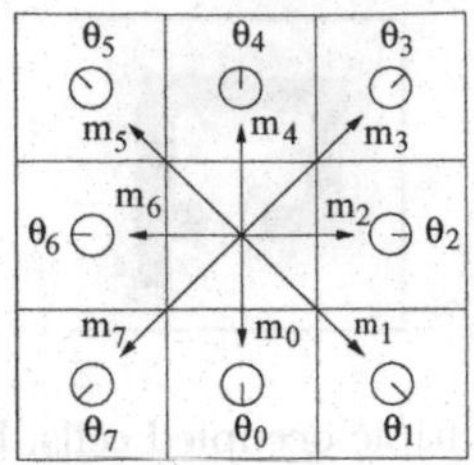

Fig. 2. If the robot executes movement m_i, it turns to orientation θ_i and then it moves forward

This approach introduces a variable V *per each possible movement of the robot.* Let $V_i(x,y)$ ($i = 0, ..., 7$) be the accumulated cost to travel from cell (x,y), when the robot has orientation θ_i, to the nearest unexplored cell. The new algorithm takes into account $V_i(x,y)$ and it has two steps:

1. Initialization.
   (a) Unexplored cells (x,y) are initialized with $V_i(x,y) = 0$, $i = 0, ..., 7$ (in other words, unexplored cells are the goals for the robot and they have null costs).
   (b) Explored cells that are free in the *travel space* are initialized with $V_i(x,y) = \infty$, $i = 0, ..., 7$. Only these cells can change their value in the next step.
2. Update. For all orientations of the explored free cells do:

$$V_i(x,y) \leftarrow \quad min_{(m_j=(d_x,d_y))\in M_v}\{V_j(x+d_x,y+d_y)+C_d((x,y),(d_x,d_y))+C_g(i,j)\} \tag{1}$$

   where C_g is a cost associated when the robot rotates from θ_i to θ_j. Term $C_d((x,y),(d_x,d_y))$ measures the cost of moving from the cell (x,y) to the cell $(x+dx, y+dy)$ and is given by:

$$C_d((x,y),(d_x,d_y)) = (1+C(x+d_x,y+d_y))Dist((x,y),(x+d_x,y+d_y)) \tag{2}$$

   $Dist(p_1,p_2)$ is the distance between cells p_1 and p_2 (e.g. 1 or $\sqrt{2}$). $C(x,y)$ represents the cost associated with cell (x,y) in the *travel space*, based on its type.
   This update rule is iterated until the values $V_i(x,y)$, $i = 0, ..., 7$ converge.

When the values of $V_i(x,y)$ converge, the robot should execute the best movement, given its position (x_r, y_r) and its orientation θ_r. The best movement $M(x_r, y_r, \theta_r)$ is given by:

$$M(x_r,y_r,\theta_r) \leftarrow$$

$$arg\_min_{(m_j=(d_x,d_y))\in M_v}\{V_j(x_r+d_x,y_r+d_y)+C_d((x_r,y_r),(d_x,d_y))+C_g(r,j)\} \tag{3}$$

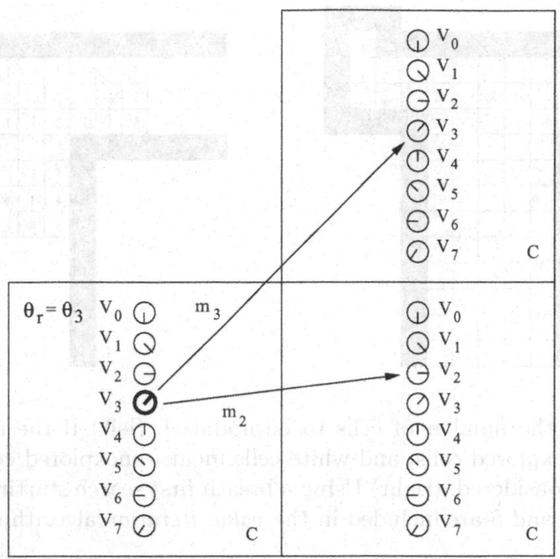

Fig. 3. Strategy to punish orientation changes

Exploration ends when $V_i(x, y) = \infty$ for the cell where the robot is placed, which means that there is no way to reach an unexplored cell.

Figure 3 illustrates this approach. The robot has orientation $\theta_r = \theta_3$ and movements m_2 and m_3 are considered. Movement m_2 takes into account value V_2 of the right cell and the robot has to rotate 45°. In a similar way, movement m_3 considers value V_3 of the other cell and the robot does not have to rotate.

2.4 Efficiency Considerations

To reduce the time to compute a policy of movements, two strategies are considered:

1. In the initialization of the *value iteration* algorithm we include only free cells between the robot position and the nearest unexplored cell (or cells). It does not make sense to include free cells that are far away from the robot position because they are not going to be useful for the robot. Instead of including all unexplored cells as goals, only include the unexplored cell (or cells) nearest to the robot (see Figure 4 (a)). We use a breadth first search, starting from the position of the robot, to define the free cells to include in the algorithm. If the nearest unexplored cells are in level n, in the search tree, only free cells in levels $1, 2, ..., n$ are included in the value iteration algorithm (an example is shown in Figure 4 (b)).
2. During the updating process of the value iteration algorithm we use a *bounding box* [13]. The idea is to update only cells inside a rectangle or box. In each iteration, the box is adjusted according to the position of cells that were updated in the previous iteration. Figure 5 shows an example.

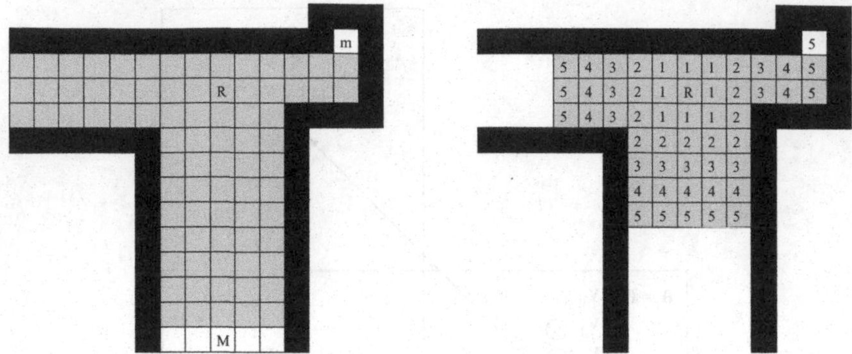

Fig. 4. Reducing the number of cells to be updated. (left) If the robot is in cell R, gray cells means explored cells, and white cells means unexplored cells, then only the nearest cell m is considered. (right) Using a breath first search starting from R, all cells of levels 1, 2, 3, 4 and 5 are included in the *value iteration* algorithm

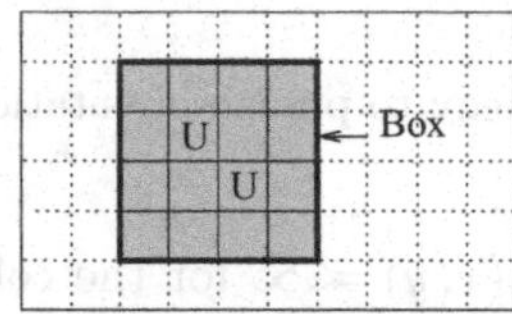

Fig. 5. Using a *bounding box* to update cells. If cells U were updated in a previous iteration, next time only gray cells inside the box are going to be considered

3 Experimental Results

We consider a differential drive robot [4] (see figure 6). The differential scheme consists of two wheels on a common axis, each wheel driven independently, and one or two caster wheels to ensure balance. The robot has the ability to drive straight, to turn in place, and to move in an arc.

The idea of these experiments was to build maps of a simulated environment and compare the *total distance*, d_T, traveled by the robot wheels, including rotations, for three different costs of making rotations of the robot. If d_L is the distance traveled when the robot moves forward and d_R is the distance traveled when the robot rotates, then the total distance is given by $d_T = d_L + d_R$. For a differential drive robot with distance D_r (the distance from a traction wheel to the center of the robot, as indicated in Figure 6), d_R is given by $d_R = \frac{\pi D_r}{8} g_u$, where g_u is the rotation of the robot (in units of 45°).

3.1 Context

In the simulations, the mobile robot have an odometer, ultrasonic and laser range sensors (implemented with a laser line generator and a camera). The system used

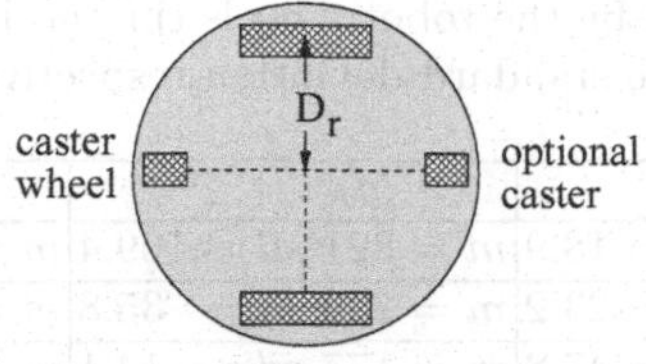

Fig. 6. Bottom view of a differential drive robot

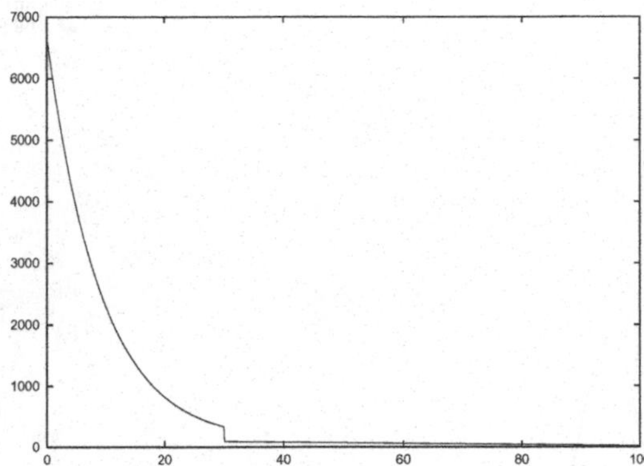

Fig. 7. Cost of warning cells depends on the distance (in *cm*) to the nearest occupied cell

to test this exploration approach follows the ideas described in [10,11] for sensor data fusion and position tracking.

The simulator introduces an uniform random error of ±3% on rotations and ±10% on displacements. When the robot moves forward, the path followed by the robot is not necessarily in the desired direction. The simulator introduces a uniform random variation of ±5°.

Cells in the *travel space* have a cost that depends on their type. Far cells have a cost $C_f = 600$ and travel cells have a cost $C_t = 1$. Figure 7 shows the cost of warning cells based on their distance to the nearest obstacles (up to 100 *cm*). This assignment for the warning cells builds a high *repulsive force* when the robot is very close to obstacles (30 *cm* or less). In these experiments we use a linear function to compute C_g (the cost of making rotations of the robot), given by $C_g = K_g g$, where K_g is a constant and g is the rotation (in units of 45°) required by the robot to move to an adjacent cell.

3.2 Results

Figure 9 shows the simulated environment of $12 \times 9\,m$ used to test the exploration approach. We build 10 maps for this simulated environment with the same value of K_g. Table 1 shows statistical results for d_L, d_R and d_T, for $K_g = 0, 50, 300$. These results show that higher K_g values decrease the number of movements

Table 1. Distances traveled by the robot wheels (in *cm*) for different values of K_g (m and sd are the mean and the standard deviation respectively)

K_g	d_L	d_R	d_T
0	$m = 2607$ $sd = 18.9$	$m = 821$ $sd = 109.4$	$m = 3428$ $sd = 123.6$
50	$m = 2547$ $sd = 23.2$	$m = 230$ $sd = 35.8$	$m = 2777$ $sd = 57.0$
100	$m = 2518$ $sd = 47.8$	$m = 177$ $sd = 14.1$	$m = 2696$ $sd = 46.9$

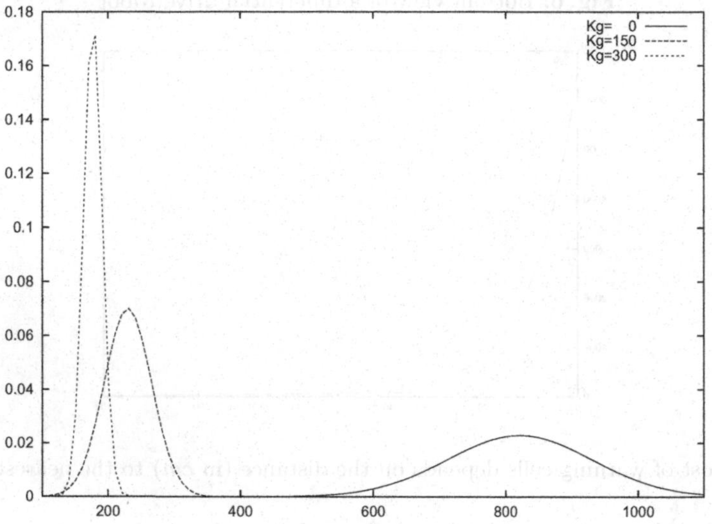

Fig. 8. Statistical results of d_R (in *cm*) for different K_g values

Table 2. Time (in *ms*) to compute a policy of movements with different values of K_g using a PC Pentium III, 733 Mhz. m is the mean and sd is the standard deviation of the measured data

Case	m	sd
t_1 with $K_g = 0$	80	40
t_2 with $K_g = 300$	457	80
t_2/t_1	5.3	1.2

that change the orientation of the robot (d_R), and hence the total distance (d_T). Figure 8 shows results for d_R assuming a normal distribution. It is evident the reduction for d_R when K_g increases.

Typical cases of the path followed by the robot for $K_g = 0$ and $K_g = 300$ are shown in Figure 9. When $K_g = 0$ there were 49 orientation changes of the robot (of 45°). When $K_g = 300$ there were 12 changes, a significant reduction. Statistical information about the time to compute policies of movements (one computation after each movement of the robot) in these two maps are shown in table 2. When $K_g = 0$ the algorithm only uses one V variable per cell, when $K_g > 0$ the algorithm uses the 8 values of V per cell. On average there were an

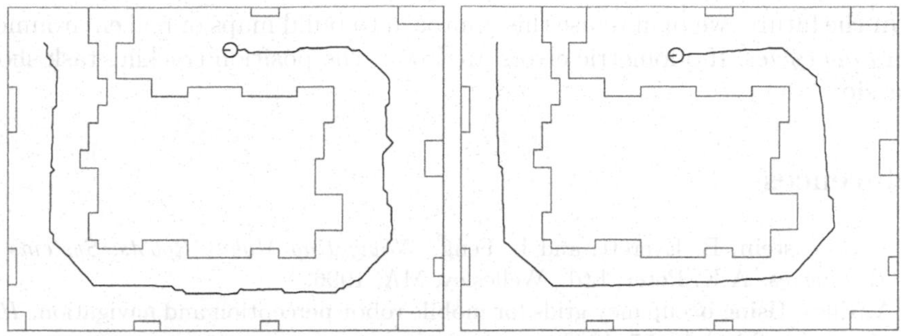

Fig. 9. Paths followed by the robot for $K_g = 0$ (left) and $K_g = 300$ (right)

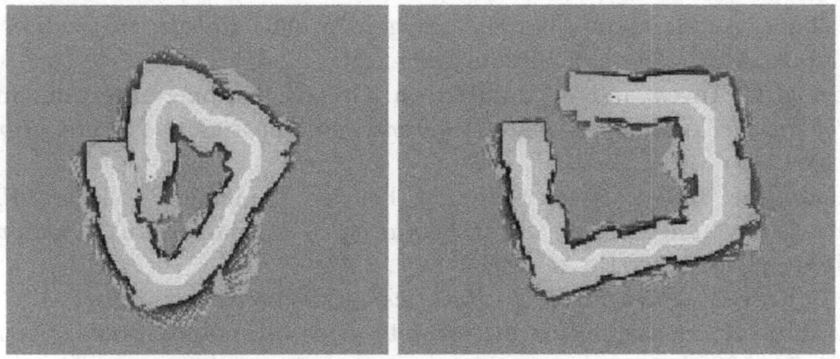

Fig. 10. Maps built without using odometric corrections with $K_g = 0$ (left) and $K_g = 300$ (right). Dark areas represent cells with occupancy probabilities near to 1

increment of about 5.3 times when K_g changed from 0 to 300. Finally, Figure 10 shows the PGMs built by the simulated robot without using the position tracking procedure. The grid cells are $10 \times 10\,cm^2$. The lighter trace on the map is given by the odometer and it shows the path followed by the robot. Note that the map is worse when $K_g = 0$ (the odometric error is higher).

4 Conclusions

A new approach for a mobile robot to explore an indoor environment that reduces rotations of the robot, and hence odometric errors, has been described.

As the experimental results confirm, K_g (the cost associated to rotations) is analog to the effect of a *inertial mass*: it tends to keep the orientation of the robot unchanged.

The increment of time to compute a policy of movements is about 5.3 times the amount used without punish rotations of the robot. However, with the reduction in the number of cells included in the algorithm and using the *bounding box* technique, the computation time is about half a second (on a PC Pentium III, 733 Mhz), a small enough time within the whole map building process.

In the future, we plan to use this approach to build maps of real environments with *long cycles*. If odometric errors are lower, the position tracking task should be easier.

References

1. J. Borenstein, B. Everett, and L. Feng. *Navigating Mobile Robots: Systems and Techniques*. A.K. Peter, Ltd., Wellesley, MA, 1996.
2. A. Elfes. Using occupancy grids for mobile robot perception and navigation. *IEEE Computer*, 22(6):46–57, 1989.
3. J.-S. Gutmann, W. Burgard, D. Fox, and K. Konolige. An experimental comparison of localization methods. In *Proc. International Conference on Intelligent Robots and Systems (IROS'98)*, 1998.
4. J. L. Jones, A. M. Flynn, and B.A. Seiger. *Mobile Robots: inspiration to implementation*. A. K. Peters, 2 edition, 1999.
5. S. Koenig, C. Tovey, and W. Halliburton. Greedy mapping of terrain. In *Proceedings of the IEEE International Conference on Robotics and Automation, ICRA*, May 2001.
6. J-C. Latombe. *Robot Motion Planning*. Kluwer Academic Publishers, 1991.
7. D. Lee. *The Map–Building and Exploration of a Simple Sonar–Equipped Robot*. Cambridge University Press, 1996.
8. P. J. McKerrow. *Introduction to Robotics*. Addison-Wesley, 1991.
9. H. P. Moravec. Sensor fusion in certainty grids on mobile robots. *AI Magazine*, 9(2):61–74, 1988.
10. L. Romero, E. Morales, and E. Sucar. Learning probabilistic grid–based maps for indoor mobile robots using ultrasonic and laser range sensors. In O. Cairo, E. Sucar, and F.J. Cantu, editors, *MICAI2000, Advances in Artificial Intelligence, LNAI 1793*, pages 389–398. Springer, 2000.
11. L. Romero, E. Morales, and E. Sucar. Buildings maps for indoor mobile robots using ultrasonic and laser range sensors. *Computación y Sistemas*, 2001. (to appear).
12. L. Romero, E. Morales, and E. Sucar. An exploration and navigation approach for indoor mobile robots considering sensor's perceptual limitations. In *Proceedings of the IEEE International Conference on Robotics and Automation, ICRA*, May 2001.
13. S. Thrun. Learning maps for indoor mobile robot navigation. *Artificial Intelligence*, 99(1):21–71, 1998.
14. S. Thrun, A. Bucken, W. Burgar, et al. Map learning and high-speed navigation in rhino. In D. Kortenkamp, R. P. Bonasso, and R Murphy, editors, *Artificial Intelligence and Mobile Robots*, pages 21–52. AAAI Press/The MIT Press, 1998.

Feature Matching Using Accumulation Spaces

Jesús A. Martínez Nuño and Juan Humberto Sossa Azuela

Centro de Investigación en Computación - IPN
Av. Juan de Dios Bátiz s/n, Esq. Miguel Othón de Mendizábal
UPALM-IPN Zacatenco, México. D.F.C.P. 07738
hsossa@cic.ipn.mx, jmartinezn@ipn.mx

Abstract. A new way to solve the matching problem between model and image features is described in this paper. Matches between features accumulate in a region of an abstract space; a space similar to the Hough space. In such a space, found clusters determine possible 2D rotations and scale changes of the object in the image. Finally the relative position between model and image features is verified in each cluster. The use of a space of accumulation drastically reduces the complexity of matching. The proposed approach has been tested with several images with very promising results.

1 Introduction

One of the main problems in Computer Vision when trying to match features is the high complexity of the algorithms used, exponential in many cases (see [2]). In these methods, features from a model are associated with features extracted from an image.

The Hough transform [4] has been used during many years to detect lines, circles, and others objects in images (see [5]). This technique uses a space where a matrix of accumulation contains the votes of possible poses. If an instance (of the model) in the image is found, then a point in the accumulation matrix will receive many votes. The main disadvantage when using this technique is that each degree of freedom introduces one dimension to the accumulation matrix. The extension to the 3D case is almost prohibitive.

The alignment techniques use subsets of image features and model features in order to determine the relative orientation of the image and the model. Any alignment based technique matches features of both subsets. Examples of these methods are those developed by Ayache and Faugeras [6] and Lowe [7].

The interpretation trees (see [1] and [2]), use two-dimensional models whose primitive are lines to find objects in images. The main disadvantage of this method is its exponential complexity, $O(m^n)$, where m is the number of model features and n is the corresponding number of features in the image.

In this paper we propose a new way to efficiently match features from model and features detected from an image. In a first step the angle and the ratio between pairs of features (one from the model and one form the image) are computed. Each couple (angle, ratio) then votes into the accumulation space. Once all possible couples have been calculated, the clusters with more votes are localized in the accumulation space. Finally, the correct association between pairs is verified.

C.A. Coello Coello et al. (Eds.): MICAI 2002, LNAI 2313, pp. 61–68, 2002.

1.1 Outline of the Paper

The remaining of the paper is organized as follows. In Section 2 the functioning of the proposed approach is presented. First a general description of it is given. A short explanation when the primitives used are lines and corners is then given also in this section. In Section 3 some preliminary results are presented, both for the case of synthetic and real images. In short, in section 4 the conclusions and directions for future research are finally presented.

2 Method

The central problem to solve is to determine which image primitives are part of an instance of the object of interest. The object is modeled using a set of primitives or features. A primitive can be any part or measurement computed directly from an image of the object: a line, a corner, a patch, and so on. In this approach each primitive is coded as a vector as follows:

$$\vec{p} = (type, orientation, size, position)$$

where:

type:	Is a character indicating the type of primitive.
orientation:	Is the angle of the primitive with regard to a reference axe in the image plane.
size:	Is the natural length of the primitive, and
position in the plane:	Are the coordinates (x,y) of a reference point in the primitive.

2.1 General Description of the Method

We begin by defining a double transformation between Cartesians products as

$$PI \times PM \rightarrow \Theta \times R \rightarrow PI \times PM \times \mathrm{N}$$

where *PM* and *PI* are respectively, the set of extracted primitives from the model and the set of extracted primitives from the image to be analyzed, $\Theta = [0, 2\pi)$, $R = (0, \infty)$ and N={1,2,3,…}. Interval Θ is discretized in steps of 2π/36, (each 10 degrees). Interval R is discretized adaptively as follows.

With each pair $(\vec{p}_i, \vec{p}_m) \in PI \times PM$ we compute the angle θ_{im} between *orientations* of theses two primitives and the ratio r_{im} between their *sizes*. Each computed pair $(\theta_{im}, r_{im}) \in \Theta \times R$ does contribute with a vote into the accumulation space $\theta - r$. This vote may be isolated or part of a cluster. Each cluster has a representative $(\bar{\theta}, \bar{r})$ (average of the cluster). The vote contributes to the cluster if $0.8\bar{r} \le r_{im} \le 1.2\bar{r}$. Each cluster defines a class. Each class is associated with the pairs $(\vec{p}_i, \vec{p}_m)$ that voted for the class. So we have the element $(\vec{p}_i, \vec{p}_m, class) \in PI \times PM \times \mathrm{N}$.

The elements $\vec{p}_i$ in a *class* may be part of a same instance of the modeled object. The values $(\overline{\theta}, \overline{r})$ of the class are related with a possible rotation and scale change of the instance with regard to the model.

Once the classes were build, we next verify the relative positions between primitives inside each *class*. In order to verify these relative positions between primitives, we suppose that $(\vec{p}_{i1}, \vec{p}_{m1})$ and $(\vec{p}_{i2}, \vec{p}_{m2})$ belong to the same *class* with $(\overline{\theta}, \overline{r})$ representing the *class*. Also we suppose that $\vec{p}_{i1}$ and $\vec{p}_{m1}$ is a correct matching (our reference match).

We now build two reference vectors $\vec{v}_1$ that goes from the *positions* of $\vec{p}_{i1}$ to $\vec{p}_{i2}$, and $\vec{v}_2$ going from the *positions* of $\vec{p}_{m1}$ to $\vec{p}_{m2}$ (Fig. 1). If $\vec{v}_1 \approx \overline{r} R_{\overline{\theta}}(\vec{v}_2)$ then $\vec{p}_{i2}$ and $\vec{p}_{m2}$ will be selected as a correct match too. Here $R_{\overline{\theta}}(\vec{v}_2)$ is the rotation of $\vec{v}_2$ at $\overline{\theta}$ degrees.

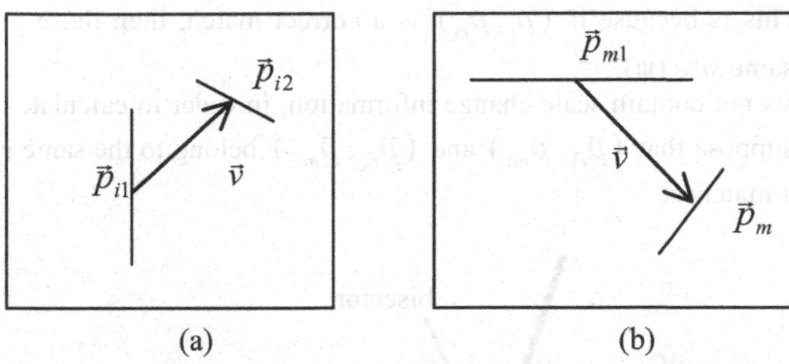

Fig. 1. Reference vectors (a) In the image, (b) In the model

When a new match must be verified, one can use any of the matches already verified as the next reference match. It is not necessary to verify this last match with all the already verified matches, since a transitive relationship is fulfilled. The reader can easily show this.

2.3 Regards when Primitives are Straight Lines

If the primitives used are lines (Fig. 2), the components of
$\vec{p} = (type, orientation, size, position)$
are:

type: 'L' for Line.
orientation: is the angle γ of the line with regard to x-axis in the image plane.
size: is the length of the line, and
position: are the coordinates (x,y) of the middle point of the line.

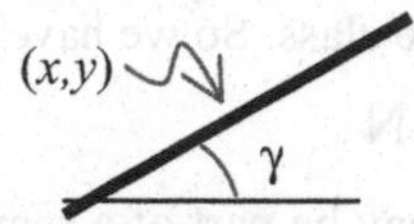

Fig. 2. Components of the primitive line

2.4 Regards when Primitives are Corners

The method can also use corners as the matching primitives. The method differs slightly. Here we explain the differences. In this case the components of $\vec{p} = (type, orientation, size, position)$ are (Fig. 3):

type:	'C' corner.
orientation:	is the angle γ between bisector and x-axis.
size:	is the angle ψ of the corner.
position:	are the coordinates of the vertices (x,y).

In this case only the *classes* whose representative $(\bar{\theta}, \bar{r})$ has $r \approx 1$ will be taken into account. This is because if $(\vec{p}_i, \vec{p}_m)$ is a correct match, then those primitives must have the same *size* (ψ).

Since $\bar{r}$ does not contain scale change information, in order to calculate the scale change, let us suppose that $(\vec{p}_{i1}, \vec{p}_{m1})$ and $(\vec{p}_{i2}, \vec{p}_{m2})$ belong to the same *class* and they are correct matches.

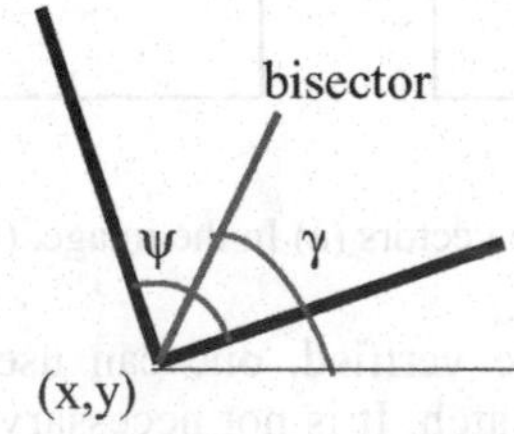

Fig. 3. Components of the primitive corner

If d_1 and d_2 are the distances between *positions* of [$\vec{p}_{i1}$ and $\vec{p}_{i2}$] and the *positions* of [$\vec{p}_{m1}$ and $\vec{p}_{m2}$] respectively, then the ratio d_1/d_2 will be the scale change.

Once computed the scale change, the general method continues with the verification of the relative positions between primitives.

3 Preliminary Results

In this section the preliminary results testing the performance of the proposed approach are presented. Only primitive lines are used. To extract lines we use the line detector described in Appendix A. This line detector is quite simple and acceptably quicker than the classic Hough's transform based line detector.

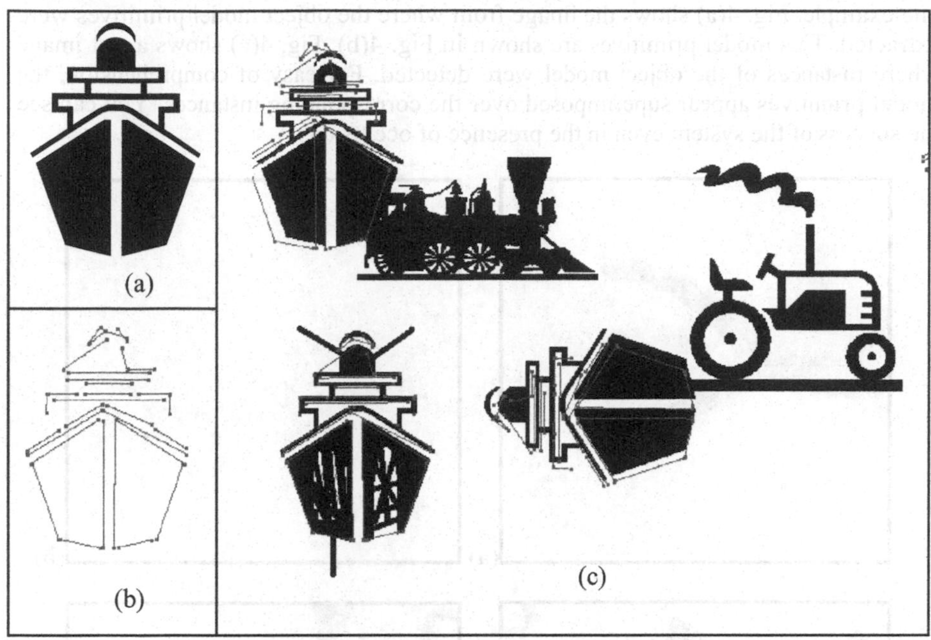

Fig. 4. a) Image of an object. b) Extracted primitives, c) Detected instances

Fig. 5. Localized instances of a 'T'

3.1 Results with Synthetic Images

Here the proposed approach was tested with several synthetic images. We show just one example. Fig. 4(a) shows the image from where the object model primitives were extracted. This model primitives are shown in Fig. 4(b). Fig. 4(c) shows a test image where instances of the object model were detected. For easy of comprehension, the model primitives appear superimposed over the corresponding instances. You can see the success of the system even in the presence of occlusions.

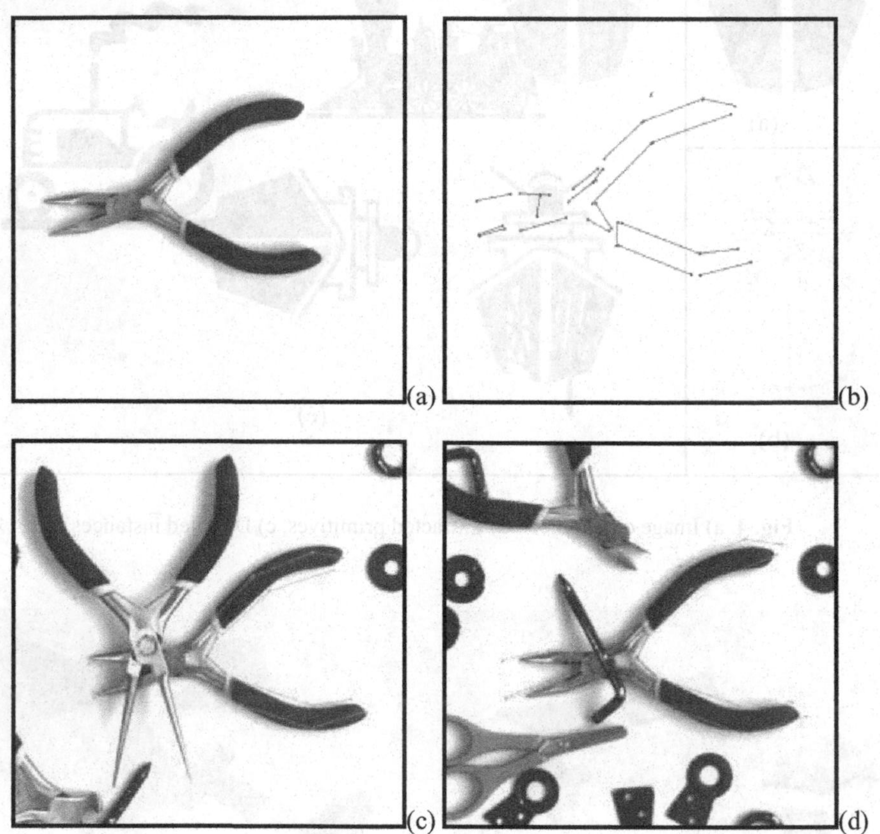

Fig. 6. (a) An object. (b) Its model. (c) and (d) Localized instances of the model

3.2 Results with Real Images

In this case, the system was tested with more realistic images. Here we show two examples. In the first case the model was to be searched is a 'T'. In Fig. 5 you can appreciate the success of the detection even in the presence of small affine transformations. Note how in Fig. 5(a), the system is not able to detect the right upper T. The system in this case did not detect enough image features to associate them with those belonging to the model.

In the second experiment the object to be detected was the one shown in Fig 6(a). Its model is shown in Fig. 6(b). Figs. 6(c) and 6(d) show two results. You can appreciate the efficiency of the proposed approach even in the presence of small occlusions.

In the presented examples, the required time for the detection was on average of 50 ms in a 350 Mhz Pentium II PC. We have used images of 532x516 pixels of 8 bits.

4 Conclusions and Directions for Further Research

We have presented a new approach for feature matching. In a first step, the accumulation of feature matches in the abstract space determines possible rotations in 2D and scale changes between a model and an instance of it in the image.

In a second step the relative position between model and image features is verified in each cluster. In other words we first collect primitives with the same possible rotation and scale change, then we verify the translations between model and instance implicitly.

The use of a space of accumulation allows to discard many incorrect matches of primitives and drastically reduces the computation. It can be easily verified that the complexity of our method is O(*mn*), where *m* is the number of primitives of the model and *n* it is the number of primitives extracted of the image.

Presently, we are extending the proposed approach to the case of more complex features such as corners and patches. This demands the use of efficient ways to integrate different kind of primitives. We are actually working also in this direction. We hope with this to obtain better results at the moment of detect object in an image.

Acknowledgments

The authors would like thank the reviewers for their pertinent comments and to CONACYT, under grant 34880-A and to CIC-IPN, Mexico for their economical support for the development of this research.

References

1. W. E. L. Grimson and T. Lozano-Perez. Localizing overlapping parts by searching the interpretation tree. IEEE Transactions on Pattern Analysis and Machine Intelligence. 9 (4): 469-482, 1987.
2. W. E. L. Grimson. The combinatorics of object recognition in cluttered environments using constrained search. Artificial Intelligence 44: 121-165, 1990.
3. T. Y. Zhang and C. Y. Suen. To Fast parallel Algorithm for Digital Thinning Patterns, Comm. ACM, 27(23): 236-239, 1984.
4. P. V. C. Hough. Methods and Means for Recognizing Complex Patterns. U.S. Patent 3,069,654. 1962.
5. D. H. Ballard and C. M. Brown Computer Vision. Prentice-Hall, 1982.

6. N. Ayache and O. Faugeras. HYPER: TO new approach for the recognition and positioning of two dimensional objects. IEEE Transactions on Pattern Analysis and Machine Intelligence, 8(1): 44-54, 1986.
7. D.G. Lowe. Three dimensional object recognition from singles two dimensional images. Artificial Inteligente, 31: 355-395, 1987.

Appendix A

Procedure to Extract Lines

We extract lines by following the next steps:

1. Detect edges (edges as 1 and background as 0).
2. Obtain the skeleton (edges of a pixel of wide).
3. Build lines from these thin edges.

To detect edges we use the following simple mask:

2	-1
-1	0

To obtain the skeleton we use the very well known method by Zhang and Suen [3].
To finally build lines we use the following steps:

1. Scan the image *g* until finding a pixel g(*x*,*y*)=1, initialize $(x_i,y_i)=(x,y)$ and make g(*x*,*y*)=0.
2. Look for a 8-neighbor of (*x*,*y*) with value 1 and initialize (x_f,y_f) with such a neighbor's coordinates, setting $g(x_f,y_f)=0$. If there is no such a pixel then go to step 8.
3. Build the unitary vector û in the direction of the vector (x_f-x_i,y_f-y_i).
4. Look for a pixel with value 1 in the following coordinates:
   $\gamma = (x_f,y_f)+\hat{u}$
   $\gamma = (x_f,y_f)+R(45^o)\hat{u}$
   $\gamma = (x_f,y_f)+R(-45^o)\hat{u}$
   $\gamma = (x_f,y_f)+2\hat{u}$
   $\gamma = (x_f,y_f)+3\hat{u}$
   where R(ω) is a rotation of ω degrees.
5. If a pixel is found, assign to (x_f,y_f) the value of the coordinates of the first pixel found in step 4 and make $g(x_f,y_f)=0$. If no such a pixel is found then go to step 7.
6. Return to step 3 if the distance of the point $((x_i+x_f)/2,(y_i+y_f)/2)$ to the centroid of the points located for the current line is smaller than a predetermined value.
7. The points (x_i,y_i) and (x_f,y_f) determine the last extracted line. In order to represent the line as a primitive we need to calculate:
   position: $(xm,ym)=((x_i+x_f)/2,(y_i+y_f)/2)$
   size: $L = ((x_f-x_i)2+(y_f-y_i)2)1/2$
   orientation: $\varphi = \cos\text{-}1((x_f-x_i)/L)$
8. In order to continue extracting more lines, return to step 1 and continue from the last point (*x*,*y*) found in step 1.
9. Repeat the procedure until processing the last image pixel.

On Selecting an Appropriate Colour Space for Skin Detection

G. Gomez[1], M. Sanchez[2], and L. Enrique Sucar[1]

[1] Dept. of Computing, ITESM-Morelos
A.P. 99-C, 62050, Morelos. México
{gegomez,esucar}@campus.mor.itesm.mx
[2] Faculty of Sciences, UAEM
Av. Universidad 1001, Cuernavaca, Morelos
minerva@servm.fc.uaem.mx

Abstract. We present a comprehensive and systematic approach for skin detection. We have evaluated each component of several colour models, and then we selected a suitable colour model for skin detection. Such approach is well-known in the machine learning community as *attribute selection.* After listing the top components, we exemplify that a mixure of colour components can discriminate very well skin in both indoor and outdoor scenes. The spawning space created by such componens is nearly convex, therefore it allow us to use even simple rules to discriminate skin to non-skin points. These simple rules can recognise 96% of skin points with just 11% of false positives. This is a data analysis approach that will help to many skin detection systems.

1 Introduction

Skin detection is a very important step in many vision systems like gestures, hand tracking, video indexing, region of interests, face detection, etc. (see e.g. [2,4,6,10,14,15,16,17] to name just a few) Pixel based skin detection can narrow the search space prior to high-level layers. However, this is not an easy task. Skin values can vary with ambient light, such as colour lamps acting as filters, specularities, shadows, daylight, etc. Moreover, different cameras returns different values for the same scene. Finally, other input devices, such as scanners do not follow closely the CIE standards. Hence, skin detection becomes a cumbersome step, therefore, it is usual to have systems where people wear artificial landmarks or devices.

Skin detection has a long tradition in computer vision, however, there has been a recent interest in using probilistic methods for skin detection. One popular choice are the Skin Probability Maps or SPMs for short [1,2,8]. Nevertheless, there is a lack of work addressing which components for the SPMs are more reliable. Hence, many SPMs work on raw RGB, HSV, YC_bC_r, though it is recognised that a fixed transformation from RGB values does not affect the overlap between skin and non-skin [8]. We show that *a mixure of colour components* do achieve a high recognition rate, whilst the overlap between skin and non-skin clusters is minimised.

C.A. Coello Coello et al. (Eds.): MICAI 2002, LNAI 2313, pp. 69–78, 2002.

2 Skin Detection

Although the RGB (Red,Green,Blue) space is quite sensitive to intensity variations, it is widely used [1,2,21]. A SPM is a lookup table where RGB values directly address a voting slot. Two 3D histograms, one for skin and one other for non-skin, are computed. After dividing every slot by the total count of elements, we get an associated probability on a $[r, g, b]$ index. Statistics are derived from these two 3D histograms. Then, the conditional probability of a pixel with RGB values to be skin or non-skin is:

$$P(rgb|skin) = \frac{Hist_{skin}[r, g, b]}{Total_{skin}}, \qquad P(rgb|{\sim}skin) = \frac{Hist_{non-skin}[r, g, b]}{Total_{non-skin}}$$

a new pixel can be labeled as skin if it satisfy a given threshold θ:

$$\frac{P(rgb|skin)}{P(rgb|{\sim}skin)} \geq \theta$$

where θ is obtained empirically. Thus, the recognition ratio is a tradeoff between reducing false positives, and increasing correct skin classification. It has been found, in a recent survey [1], that a 95% of skin detection accomplished 20% of false matches. This high error rate is perhaps a consequence of an initial assumption in the 3D histograms, that is, skin points will form a cluster in some colour model, in this case raw RGB space. However, the sparseness of skin points and the overlap in RGB space is considerable. We argue that there are more reliable axes, where the overlap is minimised. We can select different axis from different colour models, as we shall see in next sections.

3 An Appropriate Colour Space

As far as we know, there is no work addressing the selection of appropriate *colour components* for skin detection. Previous work evaluate a *single* and thus limited colour space [1,6,18,21], such as HSV, YC_rC_b, YUV, RGB, normalised RGB, etc. However, their limited performance would suggest that we are looking at the incorrect colour model. Therefore, we have changed the common methodology of having a *single* colour model. We *evaluated each component* of several colour models, and then we selected a set of appropriate colour components for skin detection.

We decomposed and analysed each component of the following colour models: HSV, YIQ, RGB-Y, Gaussian Colour Model [5], YES, YUV, CMY, CIE XYZ, RGB, normalised RGB, CIE L*a*b*, CIE L*u*v*, CIE xyY, CIE u'v'w', and YC_rC_b, as well as some non-linear relations: r/g, r/b, g/b, x/y, x/z, y/z, and $(\frac{r}{r+g+b} - \frac{1}{3})^2 + (\frac{g}{r+g+b} - \frac{1}{3})^2$. To the latter we shall refer it as Wr [17]. In addition, we have also included Chroma, Hue, and Luminance computed from CIE L*a*b*. All white references were set to 240,240,240. Hue from HSV was shifted into the range $-30 < h < 330$, so that the red range becomes continuous.

3.1 Datasets

We explored the performance of several colour components in two image types: (i) skin/non-skin indoor, (ii) skin/non-skin outdoor. We used several daylight and illumination conditions, as well as a number of input sources. These image sets cover more than 2000 people from different races and ages. These cover a wide range of illumination conditions, from Tungsten lamps (~3200K) to daylight (D_{65} or 5000K-5500K). We expected a shift to yellow in indoor scenes (Tungsten), and a little to blue in outdoor conditions (sun-shine). In the case of outdoor scenes, we use both direct sun-shine and shadows. A significant difference to [1,2,8] is that we do not use web skin images, because those are mainly scanned, and many scanners do not follow very closely the CIE standards. Moreover, there is also no control on filters and manipulations commonly used in photographic studios.

After having carefully labeled 33500 image[1] windows as skin and non-skin, we applied a statistical test, T-test at 95%, to decide whether or not indoor and outdoor skin data sets are different. This test shows that there is a significant difference (>5%). Nevertheless we shall see that, in practice, both data sets behave quite similar.

We took the *average of every image window* as the input to a classification system[2]. While it is usual to work with every pixel, we opt for averaging each sample window. Hence, many image antifacts were minimised, such as small spots, lumps, and freckles.

3.2 Selecting Variables

For every colour model we analysed each component independently. All colour components were analysed in view that we do not want to find the most discriminative components, but the complementarity among these. It is important to stress such a difference, because one might think in using a standard PCA technique. In PCA one can select variables corresponding to high eigen-values from the resulting eigen-vectors. This analysis does not show complementarity, that is, many "good" variables overlap and hence its individual contributions are minimal. Conversely, we wish to select a minimal set of complementary variables, maximising recognition and minimising errors.

Since a sparse distribution of skin points along a given colour component is not a promising signal, we select colour components with a compact range of skin. Further, two promising variables (with compact ranges in skin) will spawn a compact 2D space, and so forth. The basic idea is to select variables, from which we are interested in maximal coverage of skin points and minimal overlap to non-skin.

Therefore we start by selecting variables exhibiting a compact range for skin points, and with a minimal overlap to non-skin points. Several tools were applied

[1] A typical size of each window is 35x35 pixels. The dataset is freely available by contacting to any author.

[2] 80% for training, and 20% for testing.

to select variables, such as CN2 [3], C4.5 [12], and J48 [20]. Other tools, like χ^2, PCA, and 1-Rule [7], were also used to have a close treatment to certain variables.

Once we have selected one variable, we can focus on the dataset covered by its range. Then, using this reduced dataset we search the most discriminant variable again. In the case of indoor and outdoor scenes, the first selected variable was E of the YES colour model. This variable has a range where 96.98% of skin samples has been preserved, and this range introduces 22.41% of non-skin samples. These non-skin (false matches) will be reduced by adding a new variable. Roughly speaking we have applied the following three steps:

1. Using one promising variable from the poll, create a new dataset by applying its range. The dataset should have a good proportion of true positives, and a reduced number of false positives. The false positives will be reduced by looking for a new variable.
2. Compute new ranges on the remaining variables over the current dataset. Select the best variable which not only reduces false positives, but also covers the maximum number of skin points.
3. Is this new variable significantly enough for reducing false positives? If so, apply such a range, create a current dataset, and continue with step two. Otherwise, discard this variable, select the next one from the original poll, and restart from step one.

Notice that we are working at this stage with *window averages*, however, as we shall see, such results can be extrapolated to single pixels.

3.3 An Initial Two-Dimensional Space

After having founding E component of YES as the starting variable, we computed the next variable on the narrowed dataset. Our top components among all tests done are shown in table 1. Despite the big coverage of I, RY, and C_r, these are not complementary variables, and its combination only represents a marginal reward.

Table 1. Top variables among all test done.

Component	Colour space
E	YES
RY	RGBy
C_r	YC_rC_b
R/G	RGB
H	HSV
U	YUV
I	YIQ

Interestingly we found two complementary variables which achieve more than 95% of recognition with just 10% of false matches for indoor+outdoor samples.

Our initial hypothesis was oriented to find a three dimensional colour space, but nevertheless, we found that the spawning space of E and R/G permits to observe a cluttered zone for skin. Such cluster has a minimal overlap with non-skin, and skin points share a nearly convex area. Figure 1 depicts a section of this mixed colour map.

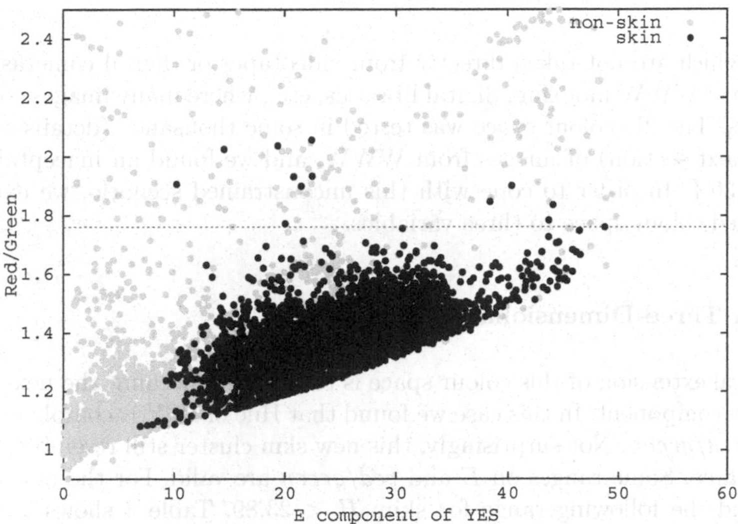

Fig. 1. A colour space for skin detection in indoor and outdoor scenes. In this space 95% of skin points share a nearly convex area with a minimal overlap to non-skin.

By using Machine Learning tools like CN2, C4.5, and J48, we compute a couple of rules for this convex area, from which we found that a single range in E and R/G are good enough to recognise more than 97% of skin with just 10.6% of false matches in indoor+outdoor images. Such ranges are easily appreciated in figure 1. Hence, a final recognition rule can be written as follows:

```
if (E > 13.4224) and (red/green < 1.7602) then
 label := skin
else
 label := non-skin
```

where E component is calculated [13] as: $E = \frac{1}{2}(red - green)$.

Although it is possible to compute a double range for the E or r/g components its overall contribution is marginal. Table 2 shows the resulting statistics. Notice the 96% of recognition with just 10.2% of false acceptances for both datasets, though a T-test does not show a similarity at 95%.

This recognition rate does not need to store two 3D SPMs, nor fitting undesirable thresholds. However, some skin detection systems need to recognise

Table 2. Results using $[E, red/green]$ colour space for skin detection.

Scenes	Recognition	Error
Indoor	97.95%	10.65%
Outdoor	93.74%	9.22%
Both	96.59%	10.20%

scenes which are not taken directly from videotapes or digital cameras. This is the case of WWW indexing, digital libraries, etc., where many images come from scanners. The 2D colour space was tested in some thousands (details are found in the next section) of images from WWW, and we found an inaceptable error rate of 30%. In order to cope with this unconstrained scenario, we extend the computed colour space to three variables.

3.4 A Three-Dimensional Space

A natural extension of this colour space is to take into account the next complementary component. In this case we found that Hue of HSV is complementary to E and $red/green$. Not surprisingly, this new skin cluster still resembles a nearly convex area. Same ranges on E and $red/green$ are valid. For the new variable, we found the following range for skin: $H < 23.89$. Table 3 shows recognition results for this new $[E, red/green, H]$ colour space. We exposed this new colour space to a more unconstrained data set. We labeled 5000 small *non-skin* images from WWW. The new data set includes many "noisy" images among the most difficult ones [8] for skin detectors, such as wood, flowers, and desert. We preserve our original amount of skin images. Then, the "challenge" set was indoor + outdoor + "noise". Figure 2 depicts a section of the challenge set, in which 95% of skin points are together, but nevertheless it is also more sparse and introduces 16.91% of false matches.

Table 3. Colour space $[E, red/green, H]$ for skin detection.

Scenes	Recognition	Error
Indoor	95.58%	8.76%
Outdoor	93.74%	8.72%
Challenge	95%	16.91%

Notice again that it is not necessary to store the SPMs for skin and non-skin, nor fitting empirical thresholds, and it is comparably fast since it take just some basic arithmetic and conditional statements. However, with this new axes we can compute SPMs, and we expect good results since the skin/non-skin is not as overlapped as in the case of raw RGB.

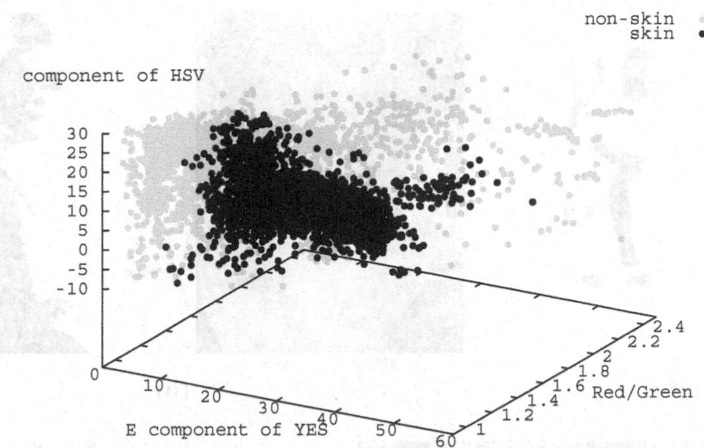

Fig. 2. A section of the $[E, red/green, H]$ colour space for skin detection. 95% of skin points share a nearly convex area with a minimal overlap to non-skin.

4 Final Comments

We can now summarise on the appropriateness of the synthetic colour space. The colour space was obtained after averaging thousands small windows of indoor and outdoor scenes. Despite this, we applied the same space to *all pixels* from the data-set. Before doing so, the ranges were fitted to cope with more variability. Due to the fact that E and $red/green$ are based on the same two axes (red and green), then, both components can be expressed as $20 + green < red < 1.7602 * green$, and it is in agreement to other works [11,19]. The component H now has a range $-17.4545 < H < 26.6666$. The final recognition rate was 96% of skin points, and 11% of false positives. This produces an overall recognition[3] rate of 95%. A 95% of recognition on 9.8 million pixels in 5.4 seconds[4] can be good enough for many applications in computer vision and robotics (e.g. gestures, tracking, face detection, etc.) where the primary source is a camera or videotape. Figure 3 shows several illumination conditions and its pixel-based segmentation using last values. Notice that the segmentation is not sparse, and it returns good results in both indoor and outdoor scenes.

Because of Hue is not the faster choice, we have explored another components. Preliminary results are shown in the figure 4, where we show faster alternatives to Hue. However the analysis of other possible colour spaces are far beyond the scope of this paper. Nevertheless, the inclusion of Hue is highly recommended as a trade-off between recognition rate and running-time.

Our findings should not be extrapolated to images from scanners or WWW sites, since it has been built to different purposes. Perhaps one should argue that this colour space does not mean a thing in terms of colour science, i.e. colloqui-

[3] True negatives and positives divided by the total number of points.

[4] A standard PC of 1 Ghz

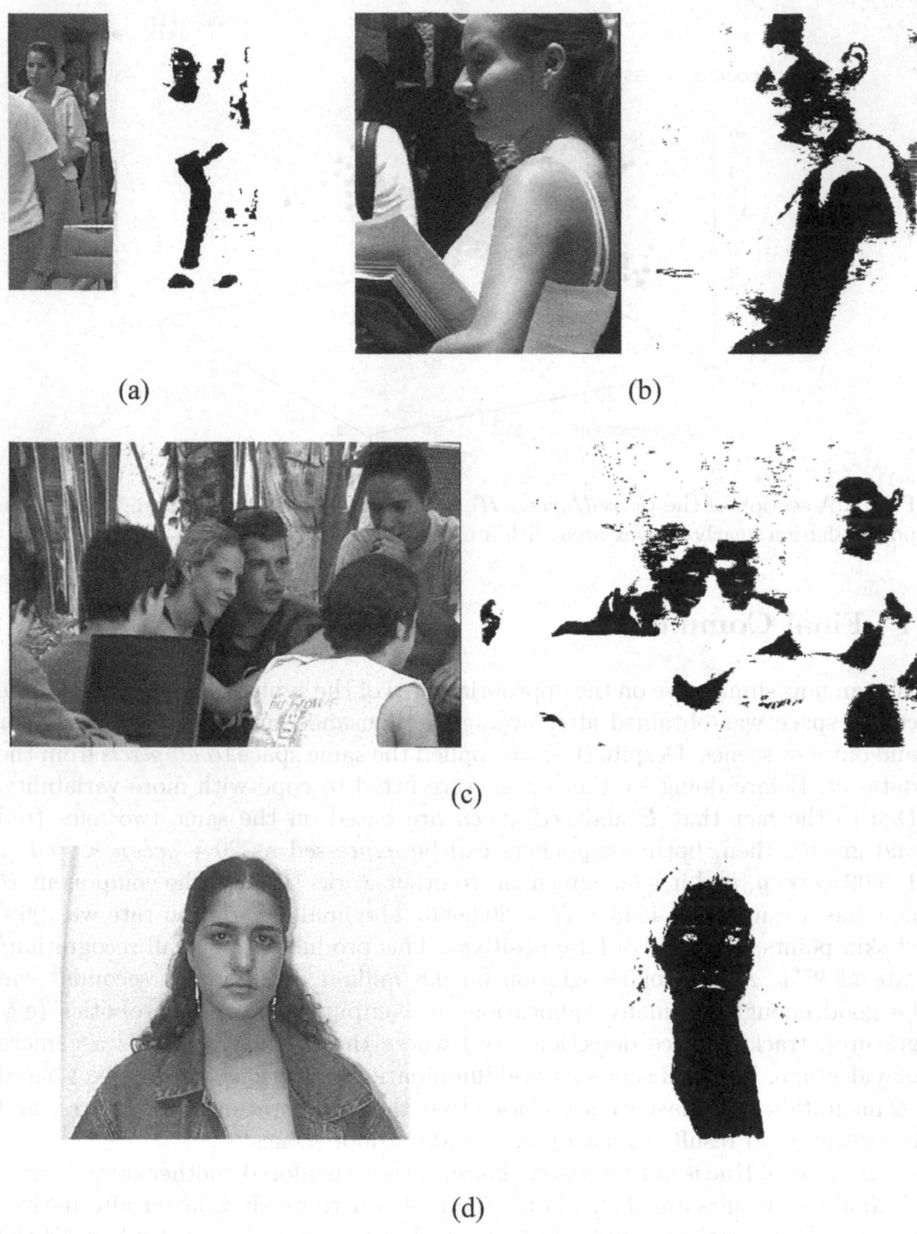

Fig. 3. Examples of skin detection. (a) Indoor with poor illumination. (b) Outdoor under sun shines, (c) Outdoor with daylight, and (d) Indoor with good illumination.

ally, nothing to say about perceptual stimulus. Nonetheless, we have shown a methodology which can be used to create better colour spaces for pattern recognition. Research involved in SPMs will also find useful this methodology, since

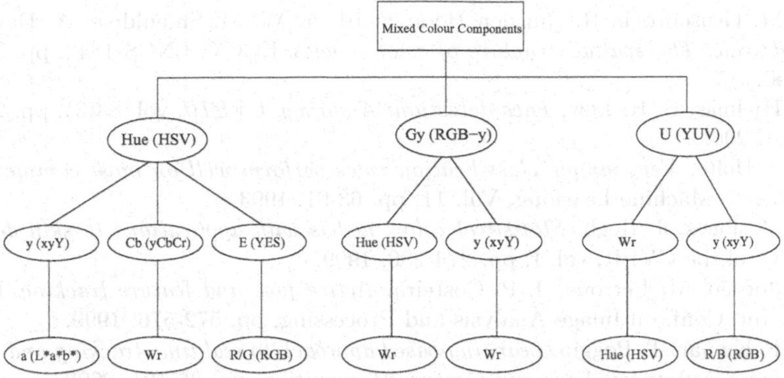

Fig. 4. Preliminary results show a more complete view of complementary variables.

it is not necessary to change the technique, but only the axes in the histograms. These colour components are just opening the door to far complex recognition procedures.

5 Conclusions and Future Work

We found that there is a seldom appropriate colour model for pixel based skin detection in indoor and outdoor scenes. Further, it has been argued [8] that there is no a fixed transformation, based on RGB, that outperform the original RGB space. Therefore, we explored a *mixure of colour components*, taking into account its complementarity. Such approach is well-known in the machine learning community as attribute selection. To exemplify, we have shown a reliable colour space for skin detection in indoor and outdoor images. This colour space has three axis: E of YES, the ratio red/green, and H from HSV. This space has shown a low susceptibility to noise from unconstrained sources, illumination conditions and cameras. We found an acceptable error, recognition rate, and running time which are quite competitive to any previous work in the area.

References

1. J. Brand, J. S. Mason, *A comparative assessment of three approaches to pixel-level human skin-detection.* Proc. of the ICPR, vol. I, pp. 1056-1059, 2000.
2. J. Brand, J. S. Mason, M. Roach, M. Pawlewski. *Enhancing face detection in colour images using a skin probability map.* Proc. of the Int. Conf. on Intelligent Multimedia, Video and Speech Processing, pp. 344-347, 2001.
3. P. Clark and R. Boswell. *Rule induction with CN2.* In Y. Kodratoff, ed., Machine Learning - EWSL-91, 151-163, Berlin, 1991. Springer-Verlag.
4. M. Fleck, D. A. Forsyth, C. Bregler. *Finding nacked people.* Proc. of the ECCV, vol. II, pp. 592-602, 1996.

5. J. M. Geusebroek, R. van den Boomgaard, A. W. M. Smeulders, A. Dev. *Color and scale: The spatial structure of color images.* ECCV, LNCS 1842, pp. 331-341, 2000.
6. E. Hjelmas, B. K. Low, *Face detection: A survey, CV&IU*, vol. 83(3), pp. 236-274, Sept. 2001.
7. R.C. Holte, *Very simple classification rules perform well on most commonly used datasets.* Machine Learning, Vol. 11, pp. 63-91, 1993.
8. M. J. Jones, J. Regh. *Statistical color models with applications to skin detection.* Proc. of the CVPR, vol. I, pp. 274-280, 1999.
9. L. Jordão, M. Perrone, J. P. Costeira. *Active face and feature tracking.* Proc. of the Int. Conf. on Image Analysis and Processing, pp. 572-576, 1999.
10. V. P. Kumar, T. Poggio. *Learning-based approach to real time tracking and analysis of faces.* Automatic Face and Gesture Recognition, pp. 96-101, 2000.
11. A. Ogihara, A. Shintani, S. Takamatsu, S. Igawa. *Speech recognition based on the fusion of visual and auditory information using full-frame color images.* IEICE Trans. on Fundamentals, pp. 1836-1840, 1996.
12. J.R. Quinlan, *C4.5: Programs for Machine Learning*, Morgan Kaufmann, San Mateo, CA, 1993.
13. E. Saber, A. M. Tekalp, R. Eschbach, K. Knox. *Automatic image annotation using adaptive color classification.* Graphical Models and Image Processing, vol. 58, pp. 115-126, 1996.
14. E. Saber, A. M. Telkap. *Frontal-view face detection and facial feature extraction using color, shape and symmetry based cost functions.* Pattern Recognition Letters, vol. 19, pp. 669-680, 1998.
15. L. Sigal, S. Sclaroff, V. Athitsos. *Estimation and Prediction of Evolving Color Distributions for Skin Segmentation under Varying Illumination.* Proc. of the CVPR, vol. II, pp. 152-159, 2000.
16. K. Sobottka, I. Pitas. *Segmentation and tracking of faces in color images.* Automatic face and gesture recognition, pp. 236-241, 1996.
17. M. Soriano, B. Martinkauppi, S. Huovinen, M. Laaksonen. *Skin Detection in Video Under Changing Illumination Conditions.* Proc. of the ICPR, vol I, pp. 839-842, 2000.
18. J.-C. Terrillon, M. Shirazit, H. Fukamachi, S. Akamatsu, *Comparative performance of different skin chrominance models and chrominance spaces for the automatic detection of human faces in color images, Automatic Face and Gesture Recognition*, pp. 54-61, 2000.
19. T. Wark, S. Sridharan. *A syntactic approach to automatic lip feature extraction for speaker identification.* ICASSP, pp. 3693, 1998.
20. I. H. Witten, E. Frank, *Data Mining*, Morgan Kaufmann, 1999.
21. B. Zarit, B. J. Super, F. K. H. Quek. *Comparison of Five Color Models in Skin Pixel Classification.* Workshop on Recognition, Analysis, and Tracking of Faces and Gestures in Real-Time Systems, pp. 58-63, 1999.

A Methodology for the Statistical Characterization of Genetic Algorithms

Angel Fernando Kuri-Morales

Instituto Tecnológico Autónomo de México
Río Hondo No. 1, México D.F.
akuri@rhon.itam.mx

Abstract. The inherent complexity of the Genetic Algorithms (GAs) has led to various theoretical an experimental approaches whose ultimate goal is to better understand the dynamics of such algorithms. Through such understanding, it is hoped, we will be able to improve their efficiency. Experiments, typically, explore the GA's behavior by testing them *versus* a set of functions with characteristics deemed adequate. In this paper we present a methodology which aims at achieving a solid relative evaluation of alternative GAs by resorting to statistical arguments. With it we may categorize any iterative optimization algorithm by statistically finding the basic parameters of the probability distribution of the GA's optimum values without resorting to *a priori* functions. We analyze the behavior of 6 algorithms (5 variations of a GA and a hill climber) which we characterize and compare. We make some remarks regarding the relation between statistical studies such as ours and the well known "No Free Lunch Theorem".

1 Introduction

The appeal of using GAs in optimization problems is largely dependent on the fact that they make very light demands on the characteristics of the functions to optimize. Their users, on the other hand, have to cope with the problem of choosing the right breed of GA. Theoretical studies [1], [2], [3], [4] shed some light on what to expect and [5], [6] and many others have tried to establish the reliability of a given GA experimentally. Here we focus on the experimental approach wherein, usually, conclusions are derived from selective and heuristically determined simulations. Rarely, if ever, these approaches may yield other than qualitative measures for two main reasons: a) The functions, usually determined "by hand" are limited in scope and range and b) The probability functions describing the algorithm's behavior are unknown and no bounds are, therefore, reachable. We propose a methodology where both problems are circumvented by a) Generating automatically the functions to optimize and b) Finding the parameters for the probability distributions of the best values from statistical theoretical considerations.

This paper is organized in 5 further sections. Section 2 describes the way in which unbiased functions are determined; section 3 succinctly describes the algorithms under study; section 4 describes the statistical method; in section 5 we present our results; finally, in section 6 we reach our conclusions and make some final remarks.

C.A. Coello Coello et al. (Eds.): MICAI 2002, LNAI 2313, pp. 79–88, 2002.

2 Automatic Generation of Unbiased Functions

To generate functions automatically we resort to Walsh functions $\psi_j(x)$ which form an orthogonal basis for real-valued functions defined on $(0,1)^l$, where x is a bit string and l is its length. By using such functions we allow for an easier cluster (schema) analysis of the results (not included in this paper). We restrict our study to the functions in $\Re^2$ and, hence, focus on functions of the form *y=f(x)* but the method is easily extendible to $\Re^n$ [7]. Henceforth, any function F(x) thusly defined can be written as a linear combination of the ψ_j 's (a Walsh polynomial).

$$F(x) = \sum_{j=0}^{2^l-1} \omega_j \psi_j(x) \tag{1}$$

where
$$\psi_j(x) = \begin{cases} +1 & \text{if } \pi(x \wedge j) = 0 \\ -1 & \text{if } \pi(x \wedge j) = 1 \end{cases} \tag{2}$$

$x \wedge j$ is the bitwise AND of x and j; $\pi(x)$ denotes the parity of x; and $\omega_j \in \Re$. Therefore, the index j and argument x of $\psi_j(x)$ must be expressed in comparable binary. We, therefore, used 48 bits to represent x in a fixed point format $\pm$ 23.24 (i.e. a sign bit; 23/24 bits for the integer/decimal parts of the number) and, consequently, also 48 bits for the index, i.e. $-2^{24} < x < +2^{24}$ and $0 \le j \le 2^{48} - 1$. For example, a) $\psi_{267,386,880}(7) = -1$ or b) $\psi_{\text{FF00000}}(7.5) = +1$. We set a similar range for the Walsh coefficients, i.e. $-2^{24} < \omega_j < +2^{24}$. Therefore, any Walsh monomial $\omega_j \psi_j$ is uniquely represented by a binary string of length 96. Finally, we allow at least one but no more than 48 non-zero terms in (1). Given this last condition, (1) is replaced by

$$\gamma(x) = \sum_{j=1}^{48} \alpha_j \omega_j \psi_j(x) \tag{3}$$

where
$$\alpha_j = \begin{cases} 1 & \textit{if the } j-th \textit{ term is present} \\ 0 & \textit{if the } j-th \textit{ term is not present} \end{cases}$$

Denoting with τ the number of non-zero terms in 3 we see that a full (τ=48) function's binary representation is 4,608 bits long. We denote the space of all possible functions defined by (3) with Ξ and its cardinality with ξ. It is easy to see that $\xi \approx \sum_{i=1}^{47} (2^{96})^i$ which is a very large number. Therefore, the method outlined above provides us with an unlimited reservoir of functions in $\Re^2$. Equally importantly, the random selection of a number τ and, thereafter, the further random selection of τ different indices and τ different ω_j's yields a uniquely identifiable function from such reservoir. It is also important to point out that, to make a fair comparison, a large (122,516) pool of Walsh functions was randomly generated. Then the $\gamma(x)$'s which the algorithms were required to minimize were all gotten from the same pool, thus allowing us to test the algorithms in a homogeneous functional environment.

3 Algorithms

We compared the following algorithms: a) A random mutation hill climber (RHC) described in [8], b) A simple (canonical) GA (CGA) described in [9] where, however, the best individual was externally preserved but did not participate in the genetic process, c) A simple eliTist (ETA) GA where the best individual was preserved and *did* participate in the genetic process, d) A statistical GA (SGA) described in [10] which does not rely on a population of individuals but, rather, on a unique statistical genome which captures the stochastic nature of the whole population, e) An eclectic GA (EGA) described in [11] which is actually a self-adaptive poli-algorithm (a GA with deterministic coupling/selection plus a RHC), f) A so-called Vasconcelos GA which is simply the EGA stripped of the RHC and self-adaptive mechanisms of the EGA. In what follows we refer to the algorithms in a) to f) as *A(i)*, *i=1,...,6*. The interested reader may see the references.

It should be pointed out that, for the purposes of this work, we are restricting the use of these algorithms to minimize the functions of Ξ and that the process of minimization is unconstrained, i.e. we search for the least value of the functions in (3) in a pre-defined number of generations with the parameters illustrated in table 1. We use the following: $P_c \equiv$ probability of crossover, $P_m \equiv$ probability of mutation, $N \equiv$ population's size, $T \equiv$ size of elite; "*" means the parameter is self-adaptive, "-" means the parameter is not applicable.

Table 1. Operational Parameters for Selected Algorithms

Algorithm	P_c	P_m	N	T
CGA	0.9	0.005	50	1
TGA	0.9	0.005	50	1
EGA	*	*	*	50
SGA	-	0.005	50	5
VGA	0.9	0.005	50	50
RHC	-	-	1	1

4 Statistical Methodology

We want to answer the following. *Q*: For any given algorithm *A(i)*, what is the probability that we find a certain minimum value (denoted by κ) for any $\gamma(x)$ given that *A(i)* is iterated *G* times?

Since one of our premises is that the $\gamma(x)$ be selected randomly from Ξ we do not know, a priori, anything about the probability distribution function of the κ's. To answer Q we rely on the following known theorems from statistical theory.

T1) Any sampling distribution of means (sdom) is distributed normally for a large enough sample size *n*.

Remark: This is true, theoretically, as $n \to \infty$. However, it is considered that any *n*>20 is satisfactory. We have chosen *n*=36.

T2) In a normal distribution (with mean μ_X and standard deviation σ_X) approximately 1/10 of the observations lie in the intervals: $\mu_X - 5\sigma_X$ to μ_X -1.29σ_X; μ_X - 1.29σ_X to μ_X–0.85σ_X; μ_X-0.85σ_X to μ_X–0.53σ_X; μ_X-0.53σ_X to μ_X– 0.26σ_X; μ_X-0.26σ_X to μ_X and the symmetrical μ_X to 0.26σ_X, etc.

Remark: These deciles divide, therefore, the area under the normal curve in 10 unequally spaced intervals. The expected number of observed events in each interval will, however, be equal.

T3) The relation between the population distribution's parameters [which we denote with μ (the mean) and σ (the standard deviation)] and the sdom's parameters (which we denote with μ_X and σ_X) is given by $\mu = \mu_X$ and $\sigma = \sqrt{n} \cdot \sigma_X$.

Remark: In our case $\sigma = 6\sigma_X$.

T4) The proportion of any distribution found within *k* standard deviations of the mean is, at least, $1\text{-}1/k^2$.

Remark: Chebyshev's bound generality makes it quite a loose one. Tighter bounds are achievable but they may depend on the characteristics of the distribution under study. We selected $k = 4$, which guarantees that our observations will occur with probability = 0.9375.

T5) For a set of *r* intervals, a number of O_i observed events in the *i*-th interval, a number of expected E_i events in the *i*-th interval, *p* distribution parameters and $\nu = r - p - 1$ degrees of freedom, the following equation holds.

$$P\left(Z \,\middle|\, \sum_{i=1}^{r} \frac{(O_i - E_i)^2}{E_i} > c_0 + c_1\nu + c_2\nu^2 + c_3\nu^3 + c_4\nu^4 \right) = 0.05 \qquad (4)$$

$c_0 \approx +1.98829512$

$c_1 \approx +2.06290867$

$c_2 \approx -0.06021040$

$c_3 \approx +0.00205163$

$c_4 \approx -0.00002637$

where $P(Z) \equiv$ probability that the distribution is normal.

Remarks: The summation on the left of (4) is the χ^2 statistic; the polynomial to the right of the inequality sign (call it $T(\nu)$) is a least squares Chebyshev polynomial approximation to the theoretical χ^2 for a 95% confidence level. In our case, $\nu = 7$ for which $T(\nu) \approx 14.0671$. Furthermore, if we choose the deciles as above, we know that $E_i = \eta/10 \; \forall i$, where η is a sample of size n. A further condition normally imposed on this goodness-of-fit test is that a minimum number of observations θ (usually between 3 and 5) be required in each interval. Thus, (4) is replaced by

$$P\left[Z \left| \left(\sum_{i=1}^{r} \frac{(O_i - E_i)^2}{E_i} > c_0 + c_1 v + c_2 v^2 + c_3 v^3 + c_4 v^4 \right) \vee (O_i < \theta \quad \forall i) \right] = 0.05 \right. \tag{5}$$

Making $\theta = 5$ and using the parameters' values described above, equation (5) finally takes the following form.

$$P\left[Z \left| \left(\frac{\sum_{i=1}^{10} O_i^2 - (\eta/5) \sum_{i=1}^{10} O_i + (\eta^2/10)}{\eta/10} \le 14.0671 \right) \& (O_i \ge 5) \right] = 0.95 \right. \tag{6}$$

4.1 Algorithm for the Determination of the Distribution's Parameters

In what follows we describe the algorithm which is an evident conclusion resulting from all the foregoing considerations. We describe it for the characterization of any minimization algorithm. The reader should keep in mind that this is one of *A(i)*.

1. Generate a random binary string as per (3); this is one possible $\gamma(x)$.
2. Minimize $\gamma(x)$ iterating *A(i)* for *G* generations.
3. Store the best value κ.
4. Repeat steps (1-3) 36 times.
5. Calculate the average best value κ.
6. Repeat steps (4-5) 50 times.
7. Calculate $\mu_{\bar{\kappa}}$ and $\sigma_{\bar{\kappa}}$.
8. Standardize the κ's.
9. Repeat steps 4-5,7-8 until $\chi^2 < 14.0671$ and $O_i \ge 5$.
10. The sdom's distribution is now known to be normal with *P(Z)=0.95*.
11. Calculate $\mu = \mu_{\bar{\kappa}}$ and $\sigma = 6\sigma_{\bar{\kappa}}$. We have extracted the expected best value of κ for this algorithm; we also know κ distribution's standard deviation.
12. In the absence of knowledge of the characteristics κ's probability distribution function we appeal to T4, from which we find:

$$P(\mu - 4\sigma \le \kappa \le \mu + 4\sigma) = 0.9375 \tag{7}$$

But now we can answer *Q*, for we know that $P(\kappa > \hat{\kappa}) \le 0.0625$ (where $\hat{\kappa} = \mu + 4\sigma$: the worst case $\hat{\kappa}$) or, equivalently, that $P(\kappa > \mu_{\bar{\kappa}} + 24\sigma_{\bar{\kappa}}) \le 0.0625$. We now know that the probability that the best (minimum) value found by *A(i)* when minimizing

$\gamma(x)$ (for any given x in Ξ) exceeds κ is statistically negligible. In other words, we have found a quantitative, unbiased measure of *A(i)*'s performance in $\Re^2$.

5 Results

The methodology just described was applied to all *A(i)* algorithms systematically increasing the number of generations *G(i)* such that *G(i)*=30,50,100,150 for *i*=1,2,3,4. We show the results for G(1-4) in tables 2-5. The column with heading "Relative" shows the performance relative to the best algorithm; "Samples" shows the number of κ's that were needed to calculate before normality was achieved; "Funcs" denotes the number of functions which were minimized during this experiment.

Table 2. Comparison of Algorithms for 30 Generations

	μ_κ	σ_κ	κ	Relative	Samples	Funcs
VGA	-68.817	4.862	47.871	1.000	86	3096
EGA	-64.585	4.717	48.623	1.016	66	2376
TGA	-65.316	4.778	49.356	1.031	81	2916
CGA	-67.716	4.974	51.660	1.079	89	3204
SGA	-68.755	5.122	54.173	1.132	98	3528
RHC	-49.133	5.549	84.043	1.756	1170	3510

RHC was iterated so as to force comparable computational costs in all algorithms. The values in columns 2, 3 and 4 are, for convenience, divided by 10^6.

Table 3. Comparison of Algorithms for 50 Generations

	μ_κ	σ_κ	κ	Relative	Samples	Funcs
VGA	-67.212	4.505	40.908	1.000	72	2592
EGA	-68.271	4.778	46.401	1.134	72	2592
TGA	-70.618	5.012	49.670	1.214	71	2556
CGA	-69.668	5.081	52.276	1.278	87	3132
SGA	-70.796	5.380	58.324	1.426	63	2268
RHC	-49.133	5.549	84.043	2.054	70	3500

Table 4. Comparison of Algorithms for 100 Generations

	μ_κ	σ_κ	κ	Relative	Samples	Funcs
EGA	-68.780	4.855	47.740	1.000	70	2592
VGA	-73.295	5.123	49.657	1.040	70	2520
SGA	-73.947	5.202	50.901	1.066	70	2520
TGA	-69.768	5.138	53.544	1.122	66	2376
CGA	-71.713	5.381	57.431	1.203	86	3096
RHC	-49.181	5.529	83.515	1.749	35	3500

Table 5. Comparison of Algorithms for 150 Generations

	$\mu_{\bar{\kappa}}$	$\sigma_{\bar{\kappa}}$	$\hat{\kappa}$	Relative	Samples	Funcs
VGA	-74.535	4.020	21.945	1.000	76	2736
EGA	-69.065	3.828	22.810	1.039	69	2484
TGA	-71.813	4.120	27.067	1.233	73	2628
SGA	-77.519	4.360	27.121	1.236	77	2772
CGA	-73.788	4.233	27.810	1.267	87	3132
RHC	-49.133	5.549	84.041	3.830	24	3600

Notice that the number of samples needed was not homogeneous. This is interesting in that the typical method of finding the estimators for the mean and variance the size of the sample remains fixed. Here it is seen that a variable sample size is needed and that its size is considerable.

On the other hand, the best GA (relative to $\hat{\kappa}$) does not remain constant, although in all cases VGA and EGA alternate the first and second places. Although EGA yields a poor $\hat{\kappa}$ for G(4), its low performance is offset by a lower (better) deviation. As expected, the RHC was worse than any of the GA variations.

When $\bar{\kappa}$ (and not $\hat{\kappa}$) is considered, however, the order of performance is significantly modified. SGA displays the best $\bar{\kappa}$ throughout, with VGA improving as generations increase. EGA, on the other hand, displays a more modest behavior. Also notable is the fact that performance improves markedly when the number of generations is increased.

In the following three graphs we show the performances for κ's upper bound ($\hat{\kappa}$), mean value ($\bar{\kappa}$) and standard deviation (σ), respectively. The horizontal axis displays *G(i)*; its scale is divided by 10. The vertical axis displays $\hat{\kappa}$, $\bar{\kappa}$ and σ, respectively; its scale is divided by 10^6.

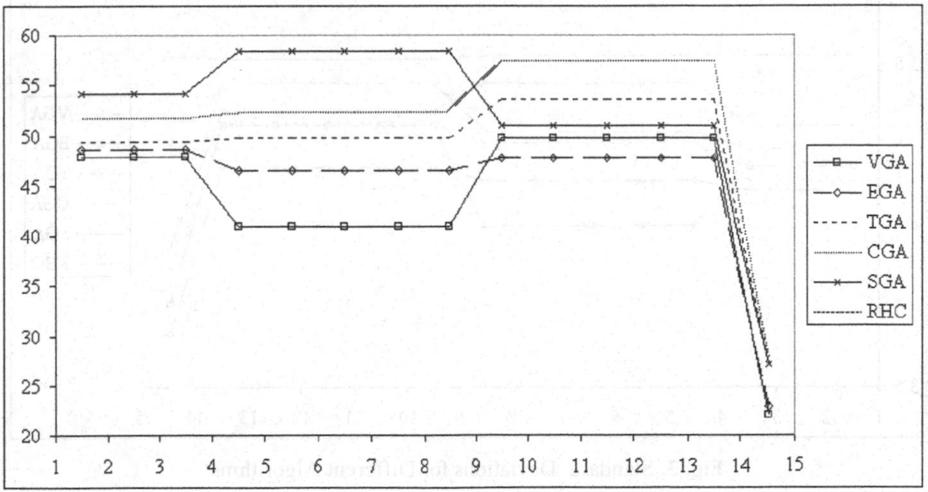

Fig. 1. Performance of Different GAs for $\hat{\kappa}$

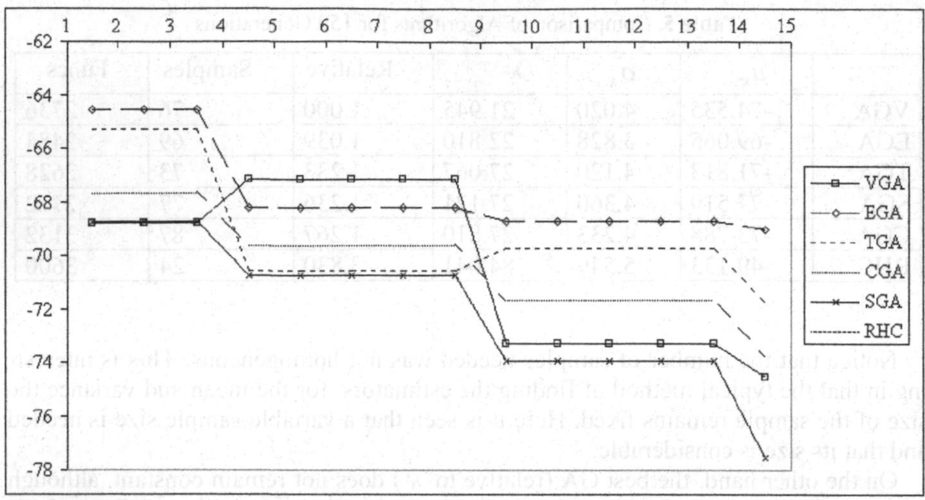

Fig. 2. Performance of Different GAs for κ

In figures 1 and 2 we have omitted the graph for RHC to allow for better reading of the other algorithm's performances.

In figure 3 we show how the standard deviations change with the number of generations. Of all algorithms EGA displays the most constant behavior. We may remark that this is so because of its self-adaptive nature.

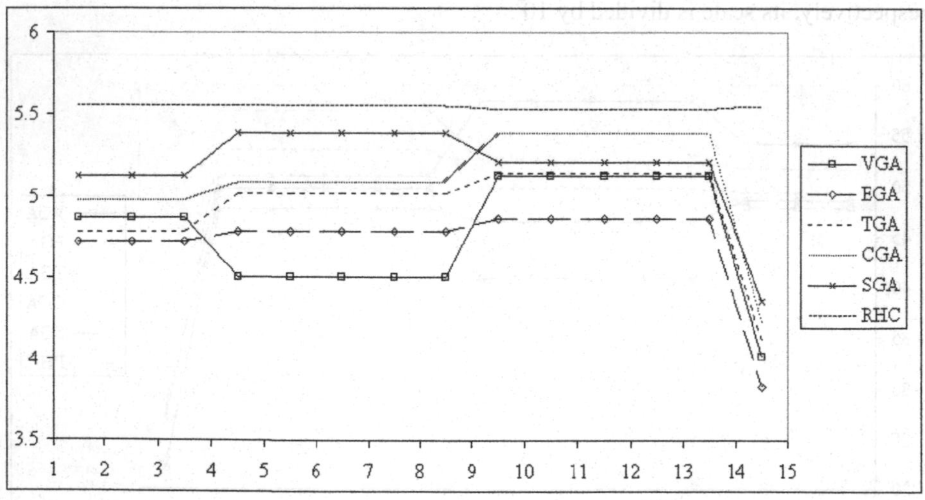

Fig. 3. Standard Deviations for Different Algorithms

6 Conclusions

We have shown that it is possible to characterize a set of algorithms and quantify their expected behavior. To do this it is necessary to invest a considerable amount of computer resources. In the experiments reported, a total of 69,154 functions were minimized. In exchange for this considerable effort we extracted solid values for κ and κ.

Analysis of the resulting data may be extended well beyond the comments above. We are unable to do this here for reasons of space, but hope to do this in a paper to appear soon. Nonetheless, we can, very generally, state that the conclusions that we arrive at are consistent with our expectations in most cases. For instance, self-adaptation yields "smoother" behavior; proportional selection is less good than ranked $(\mu+\lambda)$ schemes; uniform crossover favors convergence; hillclimbers are worse than GAs in general, etc. Moreover, we are not only able to validate our intuition, but to do so quantitatively. For example, not only do we know that VGA is better than CGA with *G(4)* generations, but *how much* better.

We are aware that statistical analysis of this kind do not highlight the particular cases which are often most interesting. However, they do allow us to affirm what we can expect from the algorithms *in general* with a high degree of confidence and, furthermore, establish bounds on the worse case expected performance of the said algorithms. If, as is our intent, we must select from a variety of possible algorithms in order to achieve efficiency, the proposed methodology yields reliable unbiased elements aimed at making the best choice.

Finally, we would like to comment as to how the results above relate to the No-Free-Lunch-Theorem (NFLT) [12] which, intuitively put, asserts that we should not expect any algorithm to be better than any other, in general. We are confronted here with an apparent contradiction, for we claim that the results above apply, in general. Clearly, the values for κ and κ in any of the algorithms allow for their categorization. But the apparent contradiction is easily dispensed with because our functions do not have the scope required by the NFLT. Although we have worked with a very large functional space, no matter how large, it does not encompass *all* the possible functions. For instance, multivariate and constrained functions are not included, to mention only two important kinds which have been left out. Therefore, what interest does it have, if any, to apply the proposed methodology? In the past, most of the experimental analysis have been biased, demonstrative and of limited scope, so that there is no way to determine whether some of the conclusions may have been incorrect. Within the realm of Ξ we are able to avoid biased and merely qualitative conclusions. In that sense the proposed method is an improvement over others generally employed.

References

1. Mitchell, M., "What Makes a Problem Hard for a Genetic Algorithm? Some Anomalous Results and Their Explanation", Machine Learning, 13, 285-319, 1993.
2. Back, T., "The Interaction of Mutation Rate, Selection and Self-Adaptation Within a Genetic Algorithm", R. Maumnler and B. Manderick, editors: Parallel Problem Solving from Nature, 2, 85-94, Elsevier, Amsterdam, 1992.

3. Fogel, D., Ghozeil, A., "Schema Processing under Proportional Selection in the Presence of Random Effects", IEEE Transactions on Evolutionary Computation, Vol. 1:4, 290-293, 1997.
4. Kuri, A., and Galaviz, J., "Towards a New Framework for the Analysis of Genetic Algorithms", International Computation Symposium, I.P.N., México, 1998.
5. De Jong, K., Sarma, J., "An Analysis of the Effects of Neighborhood Size and Shape on Local Selection Algorithms," Proc. of PPSN-96, the Second International Conference on Parallel Problem Solving from Nature, Springer-Verlag, 1996.
6. Mitchell, M., Forrest, S., and Holland, J., "The Royal Road for Genetic Algorithms: Fitness Landscapes and GA Performance", in F.J. Varela and P. Bourgine, eds., *Towards a Practice of Autonomous Systems: Proceedings of the First European Conference on Artificial Life*, MIT Press, 1992.
7. Schmitzberger, P., "Approximation and Interpolation of High Dimensional Functions by generalized Walsh Polynomials", in R. Trobec et al., eds., *Proceedings of the International Workshop Parallel Numerics '96*, Gozd Martuljek, Slovenia, 150-164, 1996.
8. Mitchell, M., *An Introduction to Genetic Algorithms*, 4:129, MIT Press, 1996.
9. Goldberg, D., *Genetic Algorithms in Search, Optimization and Machine Learning*, Addision- Wesley, 1989.
10. Kuri, A., "A Statistical Genetic Algorithm", National Computation Meeting, Hidalgo, México, 1999.
11. Kuri, A., and Villegas, C., "A Universal Genetic Algorithm for Constrained Optimization", 6th European Congress on Intelligent Techniques and Soft Computing, Aachen, Germany, 1998.
12. Wolpert, D., and Macready, W., "No Free Lunch Theorems for Optimization", IEEE Transactions on Evolutionary Computation, 1:67-82, 1997.

MPSA: A Methodology to Parallelize Simulated Annealing and Its Application to the Traveling Salesman Problem

Héctor Sanvicente-Sánchez[1] and Juan Frausto-Solís[2]

1 IMTA, Paseo Cuauhnáhuac 8532, Col Progreso, C.P. 62550, Jiutepec, Morelos, México
hsanvice@tlaloc.imta.mx

[2] ITESM Campus Cuernavaca, Reforma 182-A, Col. Lomas de Cuernavacca, A.P. 99-C, Cuernavaca, Morelos, México
jfrausto@campus.mor.itesm.mx

Abstract. The Methodology to Parallelize Simulated Annealing (MPSA) leads to massive parallelization by executing each temperature cycle of the Simulated Annealing (SA) algorithm in parallel. The initial solution for each internal cycle is set through a Monte Carlo random sampling to adjust the Boltzmann distribution at the cycle beginning. MPSA uses an asynchronous communication scheme and any implementation of MPSA leads to a parallel Simulated Annealing algorithm that is in general faster than its sequential implementation version while the precision is held. This paper illustrates the advantages of the MPSA scheme by parallelizing a SA algorithm for the Traveling Salesman Problem.

Keywords: Simulated Annealing, Combinatorial Optimization, Parallel Algorithms, and Traveling Salesman Problem.

1 Introduction

The Simulated Annealing (SA) algorithm is a simple and effective optimization method to find near optimal solutions to NP-hard problems [1, 2]. Through a SA state of the art review [3, 4] it is found that the most important SA investigation line is how SA become more efficient. Parallelization is recognized like a powerful strategy to increase algorithms efficiency; however, SA Parallelization is a hard task because it is essentially a sequential process. Recently we developed a Methodology to Parallelize Simulated Annealing (MPSA)[5]. Through MPSA, we can get a parallel Simulated Annealing algorithm.

The Traveling Salesman Problem is an NP-hard combinatorial optimization problem [6] and it is one of the most widely used benchmark problems to evaluate the performance of heuristic random search algorithms.

2 Simulated Annealing Algorithm and the Traveling Salesman Problem

The SA algorithm [1, 2] uses the Metropolis criteria to accept o reject successive random modifications from an actual solution S_i, in a problem, until a near optimal

C.A. Coello Coello et al. (Eds.): MICAI 2002, LNAI 2313, pp. 89–97, 2002.

solution. The process is controlled by the temperature parameter *c*, which initially is set at a high value, and over time, it is decreased until the frozen. The SA algorithm is implemented as follow:

```
Procedure SIMULATED ANNEALING
Begin
   INITIALIZE(Si=actual_solution, c=initial_temperature)
   k = 0
   Repeat
        Repeat
             Sj = PERTURBATION(Si)
             METROPOLIS_CRITERIA(COST(Sj), COST(Si))
        Until thermal equilibrium
        k = k + 1
        c = COOLING(c)
   Until stopcriterio
End
```

The Traveling Salesman Problem consists to find the shortest distance tour through a set of n cities, traversing every city exactly once. It assumes that always there is a path joining two towns directly. Traveling Salesman Problems are classified in [7]: Symmetric Traveling Salesman Problem (TSP), Hamiltonian Cycle Problem (HCP), Asymmetric Traveling Salesman Problem (ATSP), Sequential Ordering Problem (SOP) and Capacitated Vehicle Routing Problem (CVRP). TSP establishes that the distance from town *i* to *j* is equal to the distance from *j* to *i*, while in ATSP, it may be different. SOP is an ATSP problem with precedence constraints. CVRP consists to find the minimal length of the route that satisfies the node demands without violating the capacity constraints. This paper focused on TSP.

3 Parallel Simulated Annealing Algorithms

Works that done a parallel design of SA algorithm can be clustered into two approaches:

- Pseudo-parallel SA algorithms: Sequential SA algorithms are running on different processors at the same time or the data domain is assigned to different processors where a sequential SA is running. The principal methods are Data Configuration Partition (DCP) [8, 9, 10], Parallel Independent Annealing (PIA) [2, 9] and Parallel Markov Chains (PMC) [2, 9, 10].
- Parallel SA algorithms: SA algorithm is divided into tasks, which are distributed among several processors. Parallel Markov Chains (PMC) [2, 9, 10], Parallel Markov Trials (PMT) [2, 8, 9, 10], Adaptive Parallel Simulated Annealing (APSA) [2, 10], Speculative Trees [8, 11] and Systolic [8] are parallel SA algorithms.

In general, the parallel designs of SA perform poorly. DCP has a big communication overhead to checking the border condition. PIA has the same executing time than the sequential SA. PMC performs in a good way just at high temperatures and few processors. PMT performs well only for low temperatures and has a big communication overhead. APSA combines PMC and PMT and has a big communication overhead. However, Diekmann *et al.* [10] report a speedup of 85 on 121 processors solving the TSP on a parallel computer with 320 Transputers processors (OCCAM-2). They take advantages of the four high-speed communication channel of each Transputer. Speculative trees usually have a huge communication overhead and systolic algorithm works with few processors and reduce the SA efficacy.

Some algorithms combine SA with genetic algorithms and neuronal networks and use the intrinsic parallelism of these methods [2, 12]. However, they are not pure parallel SA algorithms.

Recently, we have proposed MPSA [5], which is a methodology that leads to massive parallelism of the SA algorithm. Any parallel SA algorithm derived through MPSA has an executing time that in the best case takes only the last temperature cycle and a little communication overhead. However, in the worst case, it takes the same time than the sequential SA algorithm. In general, the executing time will be shorter than the sequential version, while the precision will be almost the same. Section 5 shows experimental results that confirm these statements.

4 Methodology to Parallelize Simulated Annealing

4.1 MPSA's Kernel

Analyzing the SA algorithm (see section 2 and Fig. 1), it can be noted that two nested cycles form it. The external cycle establishes a descendent sequence of the control parameter from the initial temperature, c_1, until the frozen, c_f, and the internal cycle does a random walk on the solution space $\mathbf{S} = \{S_i\}$. The random walk is done, at fixed temperature, until the equilibrium is gotten, i.e., a Markov Chain (MC) is built until the stationary distribution is reached at step L_i.

MPSA [5] does an external cycle parallelization of the SA algorithm. The external cycle parallelization implies that several processors build their own MC, each one at different temperature. That is, instead of a new MC at temperature c_{k+1} being started at the end of the MC at temperature c_k all the MC's in the SA algorithm are started at the same time (see Fig. 2). Ideally, it lets a massive parallelization under the SA asymptotic convergence. The cooling scheme parameters must be known and can be taken from literature works. MPSA establishes that any parallel SA algorithm must have the same cooling scheme than the sequential SA algorithm.

A strong problem is that the initial solution for each MC is the final solution of the MC generated in the previous temperature. However, from the Statistics Mechanics it is known that thermal equilibrium is given by the Boltzmann distribution function (BDF). The BDF, $q(c_i)$, is a parametric family curves. Each curve establishes the probability distribution function (pdf) for the system's states at temperature c_i.

In every MC, pdf will pass from $q(c_i)$ to $q(c_j)$, both defined according to BDF. For high temperatures, when $c_i \rightarrow \infty$, $q(c_i)$ is an homogeneous distribution function over all the solution space, **S**. Then, through BDF family curves the pdf can be known at the beginning and at the end of each internal cycle of the SA algorithm (see Fig. 2).

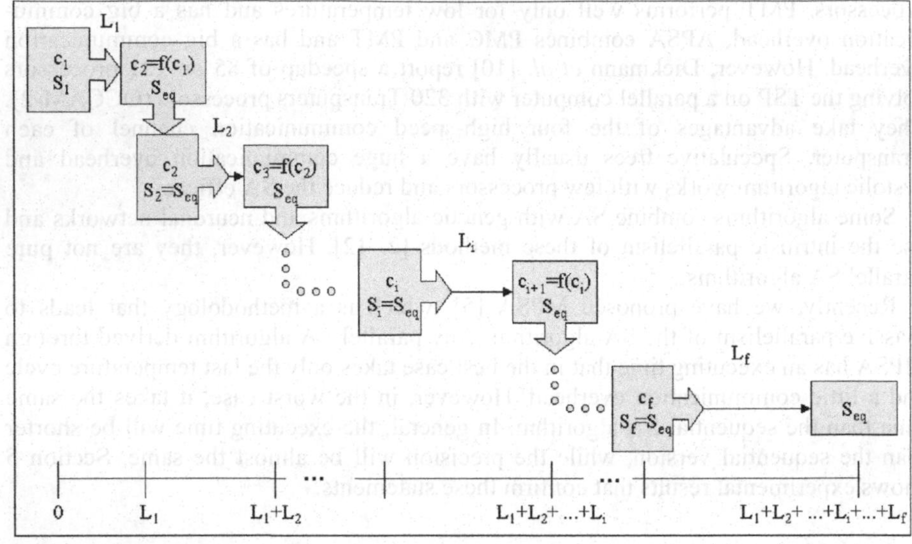

Fig. 1. Sequential SA algorithm schematization

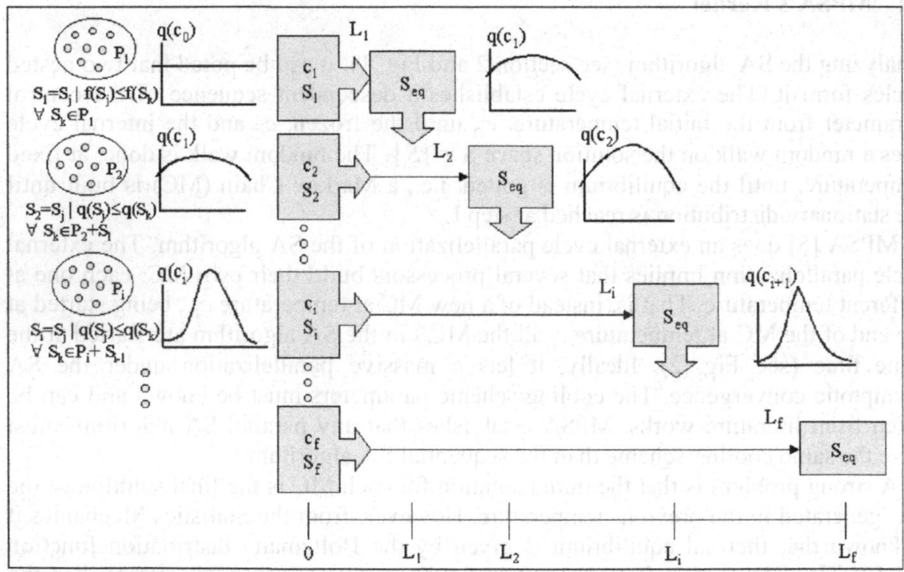

Fig. 2. Schematization for the external cycle parallelization in the SA algorithm

The pdf at the beginning of the internal cycle at temperature c_{k+1} is given by the pdf at the end of the internal cycle for the previous temperature c_k, in the descendent sequence $\{c_i\}$. This knowledge is used by MPSA taking independent and off line Monte Carlo random samplings, one for each temperature, to adjust the initial pdf through a population of points (see Fig. 2). So the initial solution for each temperature is established like the best one through two criteria. The first one establishes that the solution with the highest Boltzmann probability will be taken as the initial solution, and the second criteria sets the initial solution like the configuration with minimum cost for homogeneous or quasi-homogeneous pdf's.

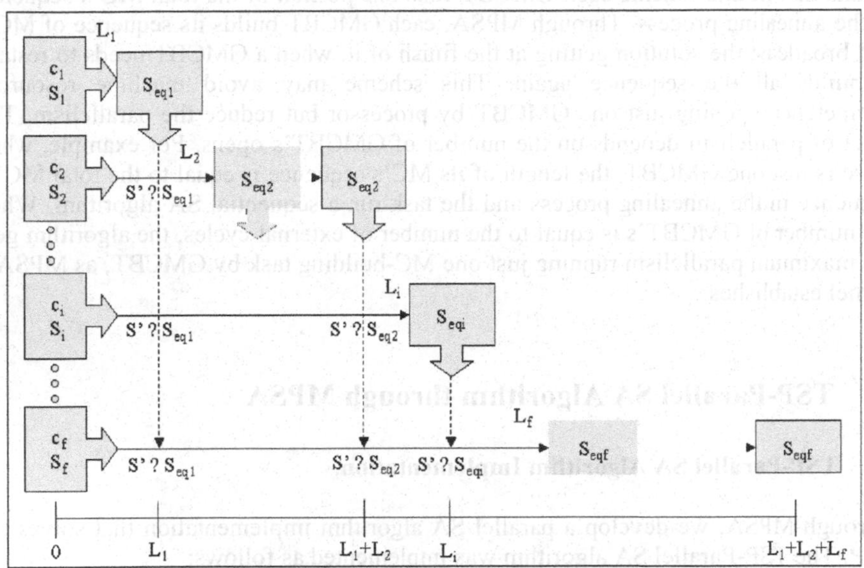

Fig. 3. MPSA asynchronous communication scheme

MPSA uses an asynchronous communication scheme and each processor broadcasts its final solution to all the processors working at lower temperature than it does. When a processor receives a solution, it checks if it is better than its actual solution. If it is, the processor will restart its MC with this new solution, else, it continues working in a normal way (see Fig. 3). The first criterion to check a better solution is the highest Boltzmann distribution probability and the second one is the cost value.

4.2 Virtual Parallelization and Levels of Parallelism

MPSA's kernel establishes that each processor executes just one task and that it generates an homogeneous MC at the temperature c_i assigned to it (this task will be named MC-building task). Like, MPSA lets a massive parallelization, if we do not have enough processors it must be implemented in a virtual way. This is, each processor executes more than one MC-building task.

A virtual parallelization reduces efficiency because tasks running in one processor compete by resources. Besides, a virtual parallelization into a LAN needs to take into account LAN-communication speed and network load. If one process T can be divided into two parallel tasks (T1, T2) and if they are running at the same time in just one processor. The executing time of T1 and T2 is equal to the executing time of sequential T process, more a little Operating System handled and communication time. The efficiency decreases even more if the number of parallel tasks grows up and just one processor runs all of them.

For MPSA, a solution is getting levels of parallelism. It is done clustering MC-building tasks into just one task named Group of MC-building tasks (GMCBT). That means that in this scheme each GMCBT runs one portion of the total MC's-sequence in the annealing process. Through MPSA, each GMCBT builds its sequence of MC's and broadcast the solution getting at the finish of it, when a GMCBT needs to restart, it builds all the sequence again. This scheme may avoid machine resources competence opening just one GMCBT by processor but reduce the parallelism. The level of parallelism depends on the number of GMCBT's opens. For example, when there is just one GMCBT, the length of its MC's sequence is equal to the total MC's-sequence in the annealing process and the task run a sequential SA algorithm. When the number of GMCBT's is equal to the number of external cycles, the algorithm gets the maximum parallelism running just one MC-building task by GMCBT, as MPSA's kernel establishes.

5 TSP-Parallel SA Algorithm through MPSA

5.1 TSP-Parallel SA Algorithm Implementation.

Through MPSA, we develop a parallel SA algorithm implementation that solves the TSP. The TSP-Parallel SA algorithm was implemented as follows:

- Let n be the number of cities and $\mathbf{D} = [d_{i,j}]$ be the distance matrix whose elements $d_{i,j}$ denote the distance between cities i and j.
- The solution space $\mathbf{S} = \{S_k\}$ is represented by the set of all cyclic permutations $S_k = (\pi(1), ..., \pi(n))$, where $\pi(i)$, $i = 1, ..., n$, denotes the successor city of city i in the tour represented by S_k. Then, the solution space cardinality is $|\mathbf{S}| = (n-1)!$.
- The cost function is:

$$f(S_k) = \sum_{i=1}^{n} d_{i,\pi(i)} \quad (1)$$

- A modified solution S_j is generated from S_i, by randomly choose two cities p and q and reversing the sequence in which the cities in between cities p and q are traversed, i.e. the 2-change generation mechanism.
- The cost difference between two solutions (S_i, S_j) is calculated incrementally from the following expression:

$$\Delta f = -d_{p,\pi(p)} - d_{\pi^{-1}(q),q} + d_{p,\pi^{-1}(q)} + d_{\pi(p),q} \quad (2)$$

where $\pi^{-1}(q)$ denotes the antecessor city of city q.
- The thermal equilibrium is reached in an asymptotic way. However, literature reported that quasi-equilibrium is getting after $2|\mathbf{N}|$ or $3|\mathbf{N}|$ iterations [2], where $|\mathbf{N}|$ is the neigborhood size for an actual solution. For the 2-change generation mechanism $|\mathbf{N}| = n^2$.

- The initial temperature or temperature for the first internal cycle, c_1, is established through a tuning procedure.
- The intermediate temperatures are establishes through the cooling function $c_{k+1} = \alpha\, c_k$, where α is the coefficient of decrement of temperature and c_k is the temperature for the *k* internal cycle.
- The final temperature, c_f, is defined through a threshold parameter close to zero.

5.2 TSP-Parallel SA Algorithm Test

The TSP-Parallel SA algorithm was tested running it on an homogeneous parallel virtual machine (HPVM) to avoid differences among speed processors. The HPVM was implemented through PVM library with two Silicon Graphics workstations O2-R10000 at 200 Mhz that was connected into a dedicated LAN through a workgroup hub for 8 machines.

To measure the parallel efficiency we take into account the follow:

- For MPSA, all the GMCBT's start at the same time and the GMCBT working with the last portion of the total MC-sequence in the annealing process is the end task. If we measure the effective executing time for this last GMCBT, we have the executing time for all the parallel process.
- For ANSI C/C++, the *clock()* function measure the effective CPU time for one task. It is, the effective number of *clock's* assigned by the operating system to execute the task (this is true for the Silicon Graphics Operating System IRIX 6.3).

The second fact let us run a massive parallelism through a virtual parallelization with just a few machines and measure the parallel efficiency for different levels of parallelism.

TSP-Parallel SA algorithm performance was test on two TSP instances taken from the TSPLIB [7]. The TSP instances used were the gr120 and the si1032 of 120 and 1032 towns, respectively. They were selected because the distances between cities are in integer values, they have an explicit distance matrix and their optimum value is reported on the TSPLIB [7].

We did 10 runs for 10 different levels of parallelism on 2 cooling schemes for the gr120 TSP instance, and 10 runs for 9 different levels of parallelism on one cooling scheme for the si1032 TSP instance. The levels of parallelism are expressed through the number of opening tasks. We opened 1, 2, 3, 5, 9, 11, 21, 51, 100 and 111 tasks. The two cooling schemes, for the gr120 TSP instance, take only a different coefficient of decrement of temperature ($\alpha = 0.85$, $\alpha = 0.95$). The SA algorithm gets better solutions or closes the solutions' variation range when $\alpha \rightarrow 1$, but increases its executing time. The others cooling scheme parameters were defined as follow: $c_1 = 3114252$, $c_f \leq 0.05$ and MC length $L = 2|N| = 28800$. For the Si1032 TSP instance the SA parameters were $c_1 = 511171$, $c_f \leq 0.05$, $\alpha = 0.85$ and $L = 2130048$.

Figure 4 shows the test results. It shows that the TSP-Parallel SA algorithm-executing time decreases fastly at the firsts levels of parallelism and, after time, the executing time decrement is slowly. This behavior done that the parallel efficiency decreases when the number of GMCBT increases. However, the precision just decreases a little bit when the level of parallelism is increased. The average solution quality is held at the same level of the sequential SA algorithm.

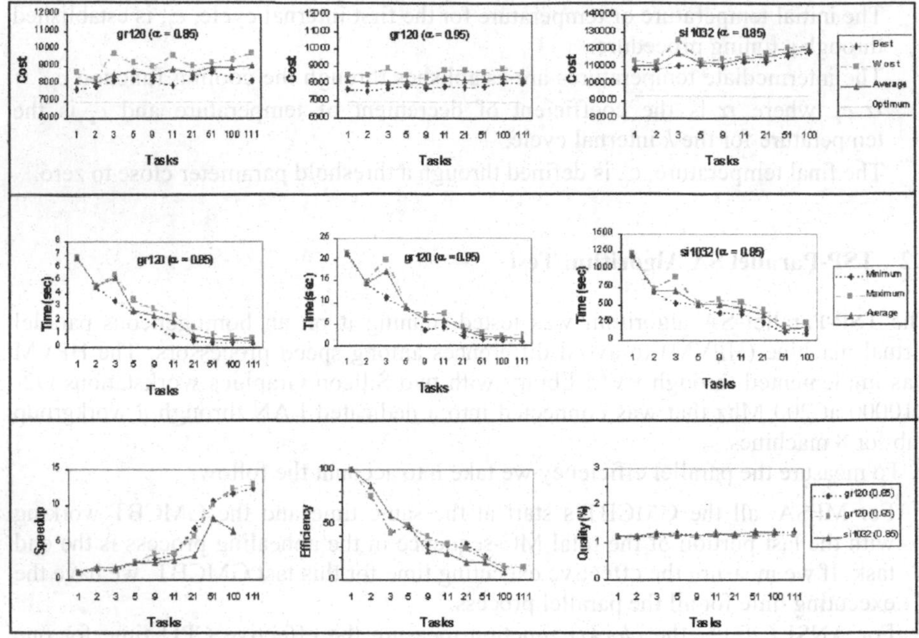

Fig. 4. TSP-Parallel SA algorithm performance

The solution quality is measured dividing the TSP-Parallel SA algorithm solution by the optimal solution and the parallel efficiency is measured dividing the speedup by the number of tasks (GMCBT's) that were opened.

The sequential SA algorithm performance is reported in the point with just one task.

It must be noted that for the gr120 TSP instance with cooling scheme with $\alpha = 0.85$ and for the si1032 TSP instance the number of SA-external cycles are 111 and 100, respectively. Then for these cooling schemes we got the maximum level of parallelism.

From figure 4, we can say that a balance among speedup, parallel efficiency and resources must be done, but in general, any TSP-Parallel SA algorithm derived through MPSA is faster than the SA sequential version.

6 Conclusions

MPSA, methodology ideally lets a massive parallelization of the implemented parallel SA algorithm through the parallelization of the temperature cycle. Although in reality, it must be done in a virtual way. Through MPSA a TSP-Parallel SA algorithm implementation is in general faster than the sequential SA algorithm and the precision is held.

Like MPSA parallelize the temperature cycle and almost all the parallel SA algorithm parallelize the internal cycle it can be combined with other parallel SA algorithm to increase the speedup and the efficiency.

The sampling overhead in MPSA is avoided by an off line sampling. Therefore, it is considered part of the tuning process of the parallel SA algorithm. MPSA uses an asynchronous communication scheme that reduces the communication overhead. As was shown in the paper, the overhead by resources competition in a virtual parallelism may be balanced through a scheme of parallelism levels.

References

1. Kirkpatrik, S., Gelatt Jr., C.D. and Vecchi, M.P., 1983. Optimization by simulated annealing. Science, Vol. 220, No. 4598, pp. 671 - 220.
2. Aarts, E. and Korst, J., 1989. Simulated annealing and Boltzmann machines: A stochastic approach to combinatorial optimization and neural computing. John Wiley & Sons, Great Britain, 272pp.
3. Sanvicente-Sánchez, H., 1997. Recocido simulado: optimización combinatoria. Estado del arte. Instituto Tecnológico y de Estudios Superiores de Monterrey (campus Morelos), México. 72 pp.
4. Sanvicente-Sanchez, H., 1998. Recocido simulado paralelo. Propuesta de Tesis Doctoral. Instituto Tecnológico y de Estudios Superiores de Monterrey (Campus Morelos), México, 38 pp.
5. Sanvicente-Sánchez, H. and Frausto-Solís, J., 2000. A methodology to parallel the temperature cycle in simulated annealing. In: O.Cairo, L.E. Sucar and F.J. Cantu (Editors): MICAI 2000, LNAI 1793, Springer-Verlang, Germany, pp. 63 – 74.
6. Papadimitriou, C.H., 1994. Computational complexity. Addiso-Wesley Publishing Company, USA, 523 pp.
7. Reinelt, G., 1995. TSPLIB95. http://softlib.rice.edu/softlib/tsplib.
8. Greening, D.R, 1990.Parallel simulated annealing techniques. Physica D., Vol. 2, pp.293 – 306.
9. Azencott, R., 1992. Simulated Annealing: Parallelization techniques. R. Azencott (Editor). John Wiley & Son, USA, 200pp.
10. Diekmann, R., Lüling, R. and Simon, J., 1993. Problem independent distributed simulated annealing and its applications. Tech. Report No. TR-003-93. Department of Mathematics and computer Science, University of Paderborn, Germany, 23 pp.
11. Sohn, A. 1995. Parallel N-ary speculative computation of simulated annealing. IEEE Transactions on Parallel and Distributed systems, Vol. 6, No. 10, pp 997 – 1005.
12. Chen, H., Flann, N.S. and Watson, D.W., 1998. Parallel genetic simulated annealing: a massively parallel SIMD algorithm. IEEE Trans on Parallel and Distributed Systems, Vol. 9, No. 2, pp. 126 – 136.

A Cultural Algorithm for Constrained Optimization

Carlos A. Coello Coello and Ricardo Landa Becerra

CINVESTAV-IPN
Departamento de Ingeniería Eléctrica
Sección de Computación
Av. Instituto Politécnico Nacional No. 2508
Col. San Pedro Zacatenco
México, D.F. 07300, Mexico
ccoello@cs.cinvestav.mx
rlanda@computacion.cs.cinvestav.mx

Abstract. In this paper, we propose a technique that exploits knowledge extracted during the search to improve the performance of an evolutionary algorithm used for global optimization. The approach is based on a cultural algorithm combined with evolutionary programming and we show that produces highly competitive results at a relatively low computational cost.

1 Introduction

Evolutionary Computation (EC) techniques have become increasingly popular in the last few years. This popularity is mainly due to the fact that EC techniques have been able to successfully solve a wide variety of complex problems [7].

However, EC techniques are normally used as "blind heuristics" in the sense that no specific domain knowledge is used or required. However, several researchers have proposed different mechanisms to extract knowledge (or certain design patterns) from an evolutionary algorithm to improve convergence of another one (e.g., [20]).

In this paper, we propose the use of a biological metaphor called "cultural algorithm" as a global optimization technique. Cultural algorithms are based on the following notion: in advanced societies, the improvement of individuals occurs beyond natural selection; besides the information that an individual posseses within his genetic code (inherited from his ancestors) there is another component called "culture". Culture can be seen as a sort of repository where individuals place the information acquired after years of experience. When a new individual has access to this library of information, it can learn things even when it has not experienced them directly. Humankind as a whole has reached its current degree of progress mainly due to culture.

C.A. Coello Coello et al. (Eds.): MICAI 2002, LNAI 2313, pp. 98–107, 2002.

2 Notions of Cultural Algorithms

Some social researchers have suggested that culture might be symbolically encoded and transmitted within and between populations, as another inheritance mechanism [5,16]. Using this idea, Reynolds [17] developed a computational model in which cultural evolution is seen as an inheritance process that operates at two levels: the micro-evolutionary and the macro-evolutionary levels[1].

At the micro-evolutionary level, individuals are described in terms of "behavioral traits" (which could be socially acceptable or unacceptable). These behavioral traits are passed from generation to generation using several socially motivated operators. At the macro-evolutionary level, individuals are able to generate "mappa" [16], or generalized descriptions of their experiences. Individual mappa can be merged and modified to form "group mappa" using a set of generic or problem specific operators. Both levels share a communication link. Reynolds [17] proposed the use of genetic algorithms to model the micro-evolutionary process, and Version Spaces [15] to model the macro-evolutionary process of a cultural algorithm.

The main idea behind this approach is to preserve beliefs that are socially accepted and discard (or prune) unacceptable beliefs. Therefore, if we apply a cultural algorithm for global optimization, then acceptable beliefs can be seen as constraints that direct the population at the micro-evolutionary level [12].

3 Previous Work

Reynolds et al. [18] and Chung & Reynolds [2] have explored the use of cultural algorithms for global optimization with very encouraging results. Chung and Reynolds [2] use a hybrid of evolutionary programming and GENOCOP [13] in which they incorporate an interval constraint-network [3] to represent the constraints of the problem at hand. An individual is considered as "acceptable" when it satisfies all the constraints of the problem. When that does not happen, then the belief space, *i.e.*, the intervals associated with the constraints, is adjusted. This approach is really a more sophisticated version of a repair algorithm in which an infeasible solution is made feasible by replacing its genes by a different value between its lower and upper bounds. Since GENOCOP assumes a convex search space, it is relatively easy to design operators that can exploit a search direction towards the boundary between the feasible and infeasible regions.

In more recent work, Jin and Reynolds [8] proposed an n-dimensional regional-based schema, called *belief-cell*, as an explicit mechanism that supports the acquisition, storage and integration of knowledge about non-linear constraints in a cultural algorithm. This *belief-cell* can be used to guide the search of an EC technique (evolutionary programming in this case) by pruning the instances of infeasible individuals and promoting the exploration of promising regions of the search space. The key aspect of this work is precisely how to represent and save

[1] Note that other researchers have also proposed the idea of using culture to improve the performance of an evolutionary algorithm (see for example [19]).

the knowledge about the problem constraints in the belief space of the cultural algorithm.

The idea of Jin and Reynolds' approach is to build a map of the search space similar to the "Divide-and-Label" approaches used for robot motion planning [10]. This map is built using information derived from evaluating the constraints of each individual in the population of the EC technique. The map is formed by dividing the search space in sub-areas called *cells*. Each cell can be classified as: feasible (if it lies completely on a feasible region), infeasible (if it lies completely on an infeasible region), semi-feasible (if it occupies part of the feasible and part of the infeasible regions), or unknown (if that region has not been explored yet). This map is used to derive rules about how to guide the search of the EA (avoiding infeasible regions and promoting the exploration of feasible regions).

4 Constrained Optimization

In this paper, we use cultural algorithms with evolutionary programming (CAEP) [2]. The basic idea is to "influence" the mutation operator (the only operator in evolutionary programming) so that current knowledge about the properties of the search space can be properly exploited.

In a cultural algorithm there are two main spaces: the normal population adopted with evolutionary programming and the belief space. The shared acquired knowledge is stored in the belief space during the evolution of the population. The interactions between these two spaces are described as follows [2]:

1. Select an initial population of p candidate solutions, from a uniform distribution within the given domain for each parameter from 1 to n.
2. Assess the performance score of each parent solution by a given objective function f.
3. Initialize the belief space with the given problem domain and candidate solutions.
4. Generate p new offspring solutions by applying a variation operator, V as modified by the influence function, *Influence*. Now there are $2p$ solutions in the population.
5. Assess the performance score of each offspring solutions by the given objective function f.
6. For each individual, select c competitors at random from the population of size $2p$. Conduct pairwise competitions between the individual and the competitors.
7. Select the p solutions that have the greatest number of wins to be parents for the next generation.
8. Update the belief space by accepting individuals using the acceptance function.
9. Go back to step 4 unless the available execution time is exhausted or an acceptable solution has been discovered.

Most of the steps previously described are the same as in evolutionary programming [6]. The acceptance function accepts those individuals that can contribute with their knowledge to the belief space. The update function creates the new belief space with the beliefs of the accepted individuals. The idea is to add to the current knowledge the new knowledge acquired by the accepted individuals.

The function to generate offspring used in evolutionary programming is modified so that it includes the influence of the knowledge space in the generation of offspring. Evolutionary programming uses only mutation and the influence function indicates the most promising mutation direction. The remaining steps are the same used in evolutionary programming.

For unconstrained problems, Chung [1] proposes the use of two types of knowledge: (1) situational, which provides the exact point where the best individual of each generation was found; and (2) normative, which stores intervals for the decision variables of the problem, in the regions where good results were found.

5 Beliefs as Constraints

As we mentioned before, Jin and Reynolds [8] modified Chung's proposal as to include in the belief space information about feasibility of the solutions. We will explain next the changes performed in more detail, since our current proposal is an extension of Jin & Reynolds' algorithm.

First, Jin and Reynolds eliminated the situational knowledge and added constraints knowledge. Taking advantage of the intervals of good solutions that are stored in the normative portion of the belief space, they created what they called "belief cells". These belief cells are a subdivision of the intervals of good solutions, such that feasibility of the cells can be determined. When the intervals of the variables are modified, the cells are also modified. As indicated before, there are 4 types of cells (see Figure 1)[2]: (1) feasible, (2) infeasible, (3) semi-feasible (contain part of both areas) and (4) unknown.

The influence that the belief space has on the generation of offspring consists of moving individuals that lie on infeasible cells towards feasible cells. Actually, in this process, semi-feasible cells are given preference because in most difficult constrained problems, the optimum lies on the boundary between the feasible and infeasible regions. However, Jin & Reynolds [8] do not modify the rules used to update the normative part of the belief space proposed by Chung [1]: the intervals are expanded if the accepted individuals do not fit within them; conversely, they are tightened only if the accepted individuals have a better fitness. This may reduce the intervals towards infeasible regions in which the objective function values are higher.

[2] Other authors have also proposed the use of a map of the feasible region. See, for example, [11].

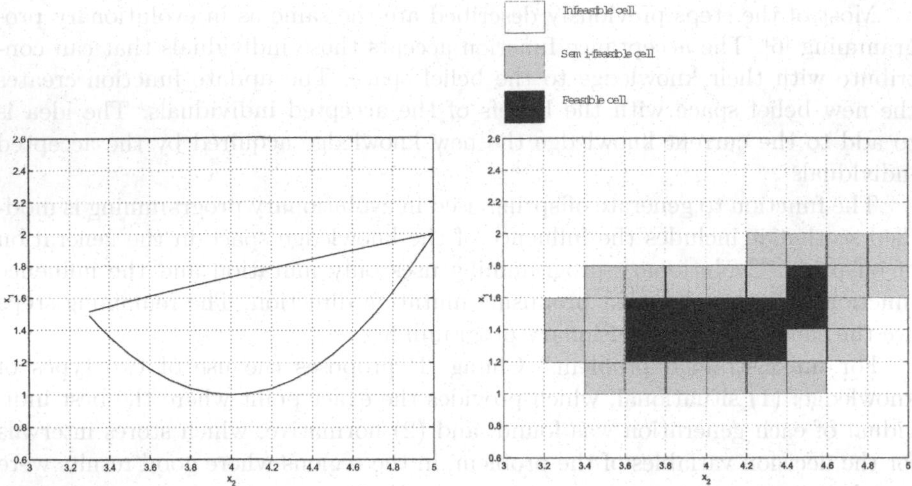

Fig. 1. The figure at the left illustrates the feasible region of a problem. In this case, the lines represent the boundary between the feasible and infeasible regions. The figure at the right illustrates the representation of the constraints part of the belief space for the search space of the same problem.

6 Proposed Approach

The approach proposed here is a variation of Jin & Reynolds' technique [8]. Next we will describe the main differences between traditional evolutionary programming and our approach.

6.1 Initialization of the Belief Space

The lower and upper boundaries (called l and u, respectively) of the promising intervals for each variable are stored in the normative part of the belief space, together with the fitness for each extreme of the interval (called L and U, respectively). This part is initialized putting in the boundaries of the variables the values given in the input data of the problem. The initial fitnesses in all cases are $+\infty$[3].

Regarding the constraints of the problem, the interval given in the normative part is subdivided into s subintervals such that a portion of the search space is divided in hypercubes. The following information of each hypercube is stored: number of feasible individuals (within that cell), number of infeasible individuals (within that cell), and the type of region. The type of region depends on the feasibility of the individuals within. Four types are defined:

- **if** $feasible\ individuals = 0$ **and** $infeasible\ individuals = 0$, **then** *cell type* = *unknown*

[3] This is assuming a minimization problem.

– **if** *feasible individuals* > 0 **and** *infeasible individuals* $= 0$, **then** *cell type* $=$ *feasible*
– **if** *feasible individuals* $= 0$ **and** *infeasible individuals* > 0, **then** *cell type* $=$ *infeasible*
– **if** *feasible individuals* > 0 **and** *infeasible individuals* > 0, **then** *cell type* $=$ *semi* $-$ *feasible*

To initialize this part, all counters are set to zero and the cell type is initialized to "unknown" (other values could be used in this case, but that would obviously affect the performance of the algorithm).

6.2 Updating the Belief Space

The constraints part of the belief space is updated at each generation, whereas the normative part is updated every k generations. The update of the constraints part consists only of adding any new individuals that fall into each region to the counter of feasible individuals. The update of the normative part is more complex (that is the reason why it is not performed at every generation). When the interval of each variable is updated, the cells or hypercubes of the restrictions part are changed and the counters of feasible and infeasible individuals are reinitialized. Furthermore, this update is done taking into consideration only a portion of the population. Such a portion is selected by the function *accept()*, taking as a parameter (given by the user) the percentage of the total population size to be used.

In the approach proposed in this paper, the conditions to reduce the intervals are stronger: an interval is reduced only if the accepted individual has a better fitness AND it is feasible. In order to make this mechanism work, it is necessary to modify the acceptance function so that feasible individuals are preferred and fitness is adopted as a secondary criterion. If this is not done, then the condition for interval reduction will not hold most of the time because the accepted individuals are more likely to be infeasible.

6.3 Influence of Beliefs in the Mutation Operator

Mutation takes place for each variable of each individual, with the influence of the belief space and in accordance with the following rules:

– If the variable j of the parent is outside the interval given by the normative part of the constraints, then we attempt to move within such interval through the use of a random variable.
– If the variable is within a feasible, a semi-feasible or an unknown hypercube, the perturbation is done trying to place it within the same hypercube or very close to it.
– Finally, if the variable is in an infeasible cell, we try to move it first to the closest semi-feasible cell. However, if none is found, we try to move it to the feasible or unknown closest cell. If that does not work either, then we move it to a random position within the interval defined by the normative part.

6.4 Tournament Selection

The rules for updating the belief space may produce that knowledge becomes specialized at a slower rate. To improve the speed of the algorithm, we take advantage of the rules for performing tournament selection. After performing mutation, we will have a population of size $2p$ (p parents generate p children). Tournament is performed considering the entire population (i.e., we use $(\mu + \lambda)$ selection). Tournaments consist of c confrontations per individual, with the c opponents randomly chosen from the entire population. When the tournaments finish, the p individuals with the larger number of victories are selected to form the following generation. The tournament rules adopted for the current proposal are very similar to those adopted by Deb in his penalty approach based on feasibility [4]. However, unlike Deb's approach, in our case, we never add violated constraints (as normally done with penalty-based approaches).

The new tournament rules adopted by our approach are the following:

1. If both individuals are feasible, or both are infeasible, then the individual with the best fitness value wins.
2. Otherwise, the feasible individual always wins.

7 Comparison of Results

To validate our approach, we have used the well-known benchmark proposed in [14] which has been often used in the literature to validate new constraint-handling techniques. The specific test functions used are the following:

1. **g04**:
   Minimize:
   $$f(\boldsymbol{x}) = 5.3578547x_3^2 + 0.8356891x_1x_5 + 37.293239x_1 - 40792.141 \quad (1)$$
   subject to:
   $$\begin{aligned} g_1(\boldsymbol{x}) &= 85.334407 + 0.0056858x_2x_5 + 0.0006262x_1x_4 - 0.0022053x_3x_5 - 92 \le 0 \\ g_2(\boldsymbol{x}) &= -85.334407 - 0.0056858x_2x_5 - 0.0006262x_1x_4 + 0.0022053x_3x_5 \le 0 \\ g_3(\boldsymbol{x}) &= 80.51249 + 0.0071317x_2x_5 + 0.0029955x_1x_2 + 0.0021813x_3^2 - 110 \le 0 \\ g_4(\boldsymbol{x}) &= -80.51249 - 0.0071317x_2x_5 - 0.0029955x_1x_2 - 0.0021813x_3^2 + 90 \le 0 \\ g_5(\boldsymbol{x}) &= 9.300961 + 0.0047026x_3x_5 + 0.0012547x_1x_3 + 0.0019085x_3x_4 - 25 \le 0 \\ g_6(\boldsymbol{x}) &= -9.300961 - 0.0047026x_3x_5 - 0.0012547x_1x_3 - 0.0019085x_3x_4 + 20 \le 0 \end{aligned}$$
   where: $78 \le x_1 \le 102$, $33 \le x_2 \le 45$, $27 \le x_i \le 45$ ($i = 3, 4, 5$).
2. **g08**
   Minimize:
   $$f(\boldsymbol{x}) = \frac{\sin^3(2\pi x_1)\sin(2\pi x_2)}{x_1^3(x_1 + x_2)} \quad (2)$$

Table 1. Comparison of the results for the test functions selected from [14].

TF	optimal	Best Result		Mean Result		Worst Result	
		CAEP	KM	CAEP	KM	CAEP	KM
g04	-30665.539	-30664.8	-30664.5	-30611.1	-30655.3	-30466.8	-30645.9
g08	-0.095825	-0.095825	-0.095825	-0.09525552	-0.0891568	-0.0901302	-0.0291438
g11	0.750	0.7402695	0.75	0.79299844	0.75	0.8380483	0.75
g12	1.000	1.000	0.999999857	0.99725459	0.999134613	0.9863316	0.991950498

subject to:

$$g_1(\boldsymbol{x}) = x_1^2 - x_2 + 1 \leq 0$$
$$g_2(\boldsymbol{x}) = 1 - x_1 + (x_2 - 4)^2 \leq 0$$

where $0 \leq x_1 \leq 10$, $0 \leq x_2 \leq 10$.

3. **g11**
   Minimize:

$$f(\boldsymbol{x}) = x_1^2 + (x_2 - 1)^2 \tag{3}$$

subject to:

$$h(\boldsymbol{x}) = x_2 - x_1^2 = 0$$

where: $-1 \leq x_1 \leq 1$, $-1 \leq x_2 \leq 1$.

4. **g12**
   Maximize:

$$f(\boldsymbol{x}) = (100 - (x_1 - 5)^2 - (x_2 - 5)^2 - (x_3 - 5)^2)/100 \tag{4}$$

subject to:

$$g(\boldsymbol{x}) = (x_1 - p)^2 + (x_2 - q)^2 + (x_3 - r)^2 - 0.0625 \leq 0$$

where: $0 \leq x_1 \leq 10$ $(i = 1, 2, 3)$, and $p, q, r = 1, 2, \ldots, 9$. The feasible region of the search space consists of 9^3 disjointed spheres. A point (x_1, x_2, x_3) is feasible if and only if there exist p, q, r such that the above inequality holds.

The parameters used by our approach are the following: population size = 20, maximum number of generations = 2500, the belief space is updated at every 20 generations, tournaments consist of 10 encounters by individual (half the population size). These parameters were derived empirically after numerous experiments.

Our results are compared to the homomorphous maps of Koziel & Michalewicz [9] (one of the best current constraint-handling techniques for evolutionary algorithms) in Table 1. The results of Koziel and Michalewicz were obtained with 1,400,000 fitness function evaluations, whereas our approach required only 50,020 fitness function evaluations.

As can be seen in Table 1, our approach produces very good results with respect to the homomorphous maps (which is considerably more difficult to implement) at a fraction of its computational cost. The main reason for this cost reduction is that the belief cells are used to guide the search of the evolutionary algorithm very efficiently, avoiding that it moves to unpromising regions of the search space.

8 Conclusions and Future Work

We have presented an approach based on cultural algorithms and evolutionary programming for constrained optimization. The approach has provided good results at a relatively low computational cost. This suggests that the proper use of domain knowledge may certainly improve the performance of an evolutionary algorithm when this is properly done. Also, it suggests that such domain knowledge may be extracted during the evolutionary process in which we aim to reach the global optimum of a problem. This contrasts with the more conventional approach of using domain knowledge extracted from previous runs of an evolutionary algorithm.

The proposed technique is relatively simple to implement, but it still requires some further implementation refinements. Some of our future work precisely involves the use of spatial data structures to store the belief cells. This should lower the memory usage of the approach which is currently its main drawback.

Acknowledgements

The first author acknowledges support from CONACyT through project No. 32999-A. The second author acknowledges support from CONACyT through a scholarship to pursue graduate studies at CINVESTAV-IPN.

References

1. Chan-Jin Chung. *Knowledge-Based Approaches to Self-Adaptation in Cultural Algorithms.* PhD thesis, Wayne State University, Detroit, Michigan, 1997.
2. Chan-Jin Chung and Robert G. Reynolds. A Testbed for Solving Optimization Problems using Cultural Algorithms. In Lawrence J. Fogel, Peter J. Angeline, and Thomas Bäck, editors, *Evolutionary Programming V: Proceedings of the Fifth Annual Conference on Evolutionary Programming*, Cambridge, Massachusetts, 1996. MIT Press.
3. Ernest Davis. Constraint propagation with interval labels. *Artificial Intelligence*, 32:281–331, 1987.
4. Kalyanmoy Deb. An Efficient Constraint Handling Method for Genetic Algorithms. *Computer Methods in Applied Mechanics and Engineering*, 186(2/4):311–338, 2000.
5. W. H. Durham. *Co-evolution: Genes, Culture, and Human Diversity.* Stanford University Press, Stanford, California, 1994.
6. Lawrence J. Fogel. *Artificial Intelligence through Simulated Evolution. Forty Years of Evolutionary Programming.* John Wiley & Sons, Inc., New York, 1999.
7. David E. Goldberg. *Genetic Algorithms in Search, Optimization and Machine Learning.* Addison-Wesley Publishing Company, Reading, Massachusetts, 1989.

8. Xidong Jin and Robert G. Reynolds. Using Knowledge-Based Evolutionary Computation to Solve Nonlinear Constraint Optimization Problems: a Cultural Algorithm Approach. In *1999 Congress on Evolutionary Computation*, pages 1672–1678, Washington, D.C., July 1999. IEEE Service Center.
9. Slawomir Koziel and Zbigniew Michalewicz. Evolutionary Algorithms, Homomorphous Mappings, and Constrained Parameter Optimization. *Evolutionary Computation*, 7(1):19–44, 1999.
10. Jean-Claude Latombe. *Robot Motion Planning*. Kluwer Academic Publishers, Norwell, Massachusetts, 1993.
11. Carlos E. Mariano and Eduardo F. Morales. Distributed Reinforcement Learning for Multiple Objective Optimization Problems. In *2000 Congress on Evolutionary Computation*, volume 1, pages 188–195, Piscataway, New Jersey, July 2000. IEEE Service Center.
12. Zbigniew Michalewicz. A Survey of Constraint Handling Techniques in Evolutionary Computation Methods. In J. R. McDonnell, R. G. Reynolds, and D. B. Fogel, editors, *Proceedings of the 4th Annual Conference on Evolutionary Programming*, pages 135–155. The MIT Press, Cambridge, Massachusetts, 1995.
13. Zbigniew Michalewicz and Cezary Z. Janikow. Handling Constraints in Genetic Algorithms. In R. K. Belew and L. B. Booker, editors, *Proceedings of the Fourth International Conference on Genetic Algorithms*, pages 151–157, San Mateo, California, 1991. Morgan Kaufmann Publishers.
14. Zbigniew Michalewicz and Marc Schoenauer. Evolutionary Algorithms for Constrained Parameter Optimization Problems. *Evolutionary Computation*, 4(1):1–32, 1996.
15. Tom Mitchell. *Version Spaces: An Approach to Concept Learning.* PhD thesis, Computer Science Department, Stanford University, Stanford, California, 1978.
16. A. C. Renfrew. Dynamic Modeling in Archaeology: What, When, and Where? In S. E. van der Leeuw, editor, *Dynamical Modeling and the Study of Change in Archaelogy*. Edinburgh University Press, Edinburgh, Scotland, 1994.
17. Robert G. Reynolds. An Introduction to Cultural Algorithms. In A. V. Sebald and L. J. Fogel, editors, *Proceedings of the Third Annual Conference on Evolutionary Programming*, pages 131–139. World Scientific, River Edge, New Jersey, 1994.
18. Robert G. Reynolds, Zbigniew Michalewicz, and M. Cavaretta. Using cultural algorithms for constraint handling in GENOCOP. In J. R. McDonnell, R. G. Reynolds, and D. B. Fogel, editors, *Proceedings of the Fourth Annual Conference on Evolutionary Programming*, pages 298–305. MIT Press, Cambridge, Massachusetts, 1995.
19. Lee Spector and Sean Luke. Cultural Transmission of Information in Genetic Programming. In John R. Koza, David E. Goldberg, David B. Fogel, and Rick L. Riolo, editors, *Genetic Programming 1996: Proceedings of the First Annual Conference*, pages 209–214, Stanford University, CA, USA, 28–31 July 1996. MIT Press.
20. Zhiming Zhang and T. Warren Liao. Combining Case-Based Reasoning with Genetic Algorithms. In Scott Brave and Annie S. Wu, editors, *Late Breaking Papers at the 1999 Genetic and Evolutionary Computation Conference*, pages 305–310, Orlando, Florida, 1999.

Penalty Function Methods for Constrained Optimization with Genetic Algorithms: A Statistical Analysis

Angel Fernando Kuri-Morales[1] and Jesús Gutiérrez-García[2]

[1] Instituto Tecnológico Autónomo de México
Río Hondo No. 1, México D.F.
akuri@rhon.itam.mx

[2] Centro de Investigación en Computación
Instituto Politécnico Nacional, México D.F.
jgg@cic.ipn.mx

Abstract. Genetic algorithms (GAs) have been successfully applied to numerical optimization problems. Since GAs are usually designed for unconstrained optimization, they have to be adapted to tackle the constrained cases, i.e. those in which not all representable solutions are valid. In this work we experimentally compare 5 ways to attain such adaptation. Our analysis relies on the usual method of selecting an arbitrary suite of test functions (25 of these) albeit applying a methodology which allows us to determine which method is better within statistical certainty limits. In order to do this we have selected 5 penalty function strategies; for each of these we have further selected 3 particular GAs. The behavior of each strategy and the associated GAs is then established by extensively sampling the function suite and finding the worst case best values from Chebyshev's theorem. We have found some counter-intuitive results which we discuss and try to explain.

1 Introduction

Constrained optimization problems are interesting because they arise naturally in engineering, science, operations research, etc. In general, a constrained numerical optimization problem is defined as:

$$\begin{array}{lll} \text{Minimize} & f(\bar{x}) & \bar{x} \in \Re^n \\ \text{Subject to} & h_i(\bar{x}) = 0 & i = 1,...m \\ & g_i(\bar{x}) \leq 0 & i = m+1,...p \end{array} \quad (1)$$

Without loss of generality we may transform any optimization problem to one of minimization and we, therefore, develop our discussion in such terms. Constraints define the feasible region, meaning that if the vector $\vec{x}$ complies with all constraints $h_i(\bar{x}) = 0$ and $g_i(\bar{x}) \leq 0$ then it belongs to the feasible region. Traditional methods relying on calculus demand that the functions and constraints have very particular characteristics (continuity, differentiability, second order derivability, etc.); those based on GAs have not such limitations. For this reason, among others, it is of practical interest to be able to ascertain which of the many proposed constraint handling strategies is best.

C.A. Coello Coello et al. (Eds.): MICAI 2002, LNAI 2313, pp. 108–117, 2002.

This paper is organized in 4 further sections. Section 2 succinctly describes the methods under analysis; in section 3 we describe the experiments performed; in sections 4 and 5, finally, we present our results and conclusions.

2 Strategies

The strategies we selected are variations of what is the most popular approach to constrained optimization: the application of penalty functions [1]. In this approach, a constrained problem is transformed into a non-constrained one. The function under consideration is transformed as follows:

$$F(\vec{x}) = \begin{cases} f(\vec{x}) & \vec{x} \in \textit{feasible region} \\ f(\vec{x}) + \textit{penalty}(\vec{x}) & \vec{x} \notin \textit{feasible region} \end{cases} \tag{2}$$

and the problem described in (1) turns into the one of minimizing (2) if a proper selection of the penalty function is achieved. We now describe the way in which this penalty function (denoted by $P(\vec{x})$) has been tackled in the strategies we selected. In what follows we denote Homaiffar's, Joines & Houck's, Schoenauer & Xanthaki's, Powell & Skolnick's and Kuri's methods as methods H, J, S, P and K, respectively.

2.1 Method H

This strategy was originally described in [2]. It defines l penalty levels depending on the magnitude of the violation of the constraints. To define such levels it demands to define intervals for each of the violations and a penalty value for every interval.

$$P(\vec{x}) = \begin{cases} 0 & \vec{x} \in M \\ \sum_{i=1}^{m} R_{i,j} H_i^2(\vec{x}) & \vec{x} \notin M \end{cases} \tag{3}$$

M is the set all feasible individuals; index *i* refers both to constraints of inequality and equations (g_i and h_i respectively); the function H is defined as the maximum value between 0 and g_i for $i=1,...m$ and the absolute value of h for $i = m+1, ..., p$. Constant *R* is defined as follows:

$$R_{ij} = \begin{cases} R_{i,1} & \text{if } a_{0,i} < H_i(\vec{x}) < a_{1,i} \\ R_{i,2} & \text{if } a_{1,i} < H_i(\vec{x}) < a_{2,i} \\ & \dots \\ R_{i,l} & \text{if } a_{l-1,i} < H_i(\vec{x}) < a_{l,i} \end{cases} \tag{4}$$

This method requires the definition of $m(2l+1)$ parameters which remain constant throughout. Hence, this is a *static penalty method.*

In our experiments it was impossible to consider special values for R_{ij} in every function and, hence, we decided to utilize 4 penalty levels with R = 100, 200, 500,

1000 (instead of 50, 60 and 90 as reported in [1]) and intervals of (0-10), (10-100), (100-1000) and (1000- ∞).

2.2 Method J

The original description of this method may be found in [3]. In it a dynamic (non-stationary) penalty function is defined. That is, the penalty, function changes as the GA proceeds. The definition is as follows:

$$P(\vec{x},\alpha,\beta) = \rho_k^{\alpha} \times SVC(\beta,\vec{x}) \tag{5}$$
$$\rho_k = C \times k \quad k = \#\,generation$$
$$SVC(\beta,\vec{x}) = \sum_{i=1}^{p} f_i^{\beta}(\vec{x}) \quad \beta = 1,2,...$$

where α, β and C are parameters of the method and k is the number of generation under consideration. The values we used to test the method were $C = 0.5$, $\alpha = 2$ and $\beta = 2$.

2.3 Method S

Shoenauer and Xanthakis's method, originally described in [4], does not only define a penalty function; it resorts to an algorithm to find feasible individuals from the evaluation of the constraints as fitness functions and eliminating those individuals which do not comply with the constraints. The algorithm is as follows:

- Start with a random population (which, in general, holds both feasible and unfeasible individuals)
- Set $j = 1$ (j is a constraint counter)
- Evolve this population to minimize the violation to the *j-th* constraint until a percentage (ϕ) of the population is feasible for this constraint. Then:

$$F(\vec{x}) = g_j(\vec{x}) \tag{6}$$

- $j \leftarrow j+1$
- The present population is the starting point for the next phase of evolution, which consists of the minimization of the *j-th* constraint. During this phase those points which do not comply with the 1, 2, ..., *j-th* constraint are eliminated from the population.
- Stop if a percentage (ϕ) of the population which complies with the *j-th* constraint is reached.
- If $j<m$, the last two steps are repeated, otherwise ($j = m$) function f is minimized, rejecting all unfeasible individuals.

To implement this method it was deemed necessary to establish full elitism [5] since, otherwise, the number of individuals in the population decreased importantly for every new generation. In keeping the best N individuals (where N denotes the size of the population) we guarantee that even if there is no new individual satisfying the *j-th* constraint we can always count with all individuals of the previous generation. This insures that the size of the population remains constant even when eliminating those individuals which violate the constraints.

2.4 Method P

This method was developed circa 1993 [6] and includes a heuristic to single out non-feasible points: "Any feasible solution is better than a non-feasible one". The penalty function is defined as follows:

$$P(\vec{x}) = r\sum_{j=1}^{p} f_j(\vec{x}) + \rho(\vec{x},t) \qquad \vec{x} \notin M \tag{7}$$

$$\rho(\vec{x},t) = max\left\{0, \max_{x\in M}\{f(\vec{x})\} - \min_{x\notin M}\{f(\vec{x})\} + \sum_{j=1}^{p} f_j(\vec{x})\right\}$$

where r is a constant. The value set for r in our experiments is 2.

2.5 Method K

This is the simplest of all the methods considered and it consists of defining the penalty function as follows: [7]

$$P(\vec{x}) = \begin{cases} \left[K - \sum_{i=1}^{s} \frac{K}{p}\right] - f(\vec{x}) & s \neq p \\ 0 & otherwise \end{cases} \tag{8}$$

where K is a large constant [$O(10^9)$], p is the number of constraints and s is the number of these which have been satisfied. K's only restriction is that it should be large enough to insure that any non-feasible individual is graded much more poorly than any feasible one. Here the algorithm receives information as to how many constraints have been satisfied but is not otherwise affected by the strategy. Notice, however, that in this method the penalty is not *added* to $f(\vec{x})$ as in (2) but, rather, it *replaces* $f(\vec{x})$ $\left(F(\vec{x}) = K - \sum_{i=1}^{s} \frac{K}{p}\right)$ when any of the constraints is not met. This subtle difference does, indeed, seem to make a difference (as discussed in the sequel).

3 Experiments

We designed three different algorithms to test the behavior of each of the methods. The intent is to explore whether the particular GA determines significant performance differences. For instance, see if Homaiffar's method is better than Joines' for a given algorithm but with a different one the opposite is true.

All individuals were Gray encoded with a fixed point format with 14 bits for the integer part and 20 bits for the decimal part, thus yielding an effective range of $-2^{15} < x < +2^{15}$ for any number x. The algorithms for the experiments were set as follows ($p_c \equiv$ crossover probability; $p_m \equiv$ mutation probability; $N \equiv$ population size; $G \equiv$ number of generations):

G1: $p_c = 0.9$, $p_m = 0.05$, $N = 100$, $G = 100$; proportional selection; 1-point crossover; the best individual was preserved (simple elitism).

G2: $p_c = 0.9$, $p_m = 0.07$, $N = 50$, $G = 100$; proportional selection; 1-point crossover; the best 25 individuals were preserved.

G3: $p_c = 0.9$, $p_m = 0.07$, $N = 50$, $G = 100$; deterministic (Vasconcelos' [5]) selection; 1-point crossover; the best N individuals were preserved (full elitism).

The combinations in G1, G2 and G3 are arbitrary and, indeed, reflect no intention on our part but to determine whether there is a qualitative difference in the methods such that when applied to a problem with different algorithm *the method* (as opposed to the algorithm) yields significantly different results. In the analysis that follows we emphasize this goal.

To analyze the behavior of every method we selected a suite of 25 functions, (which we cannot discuss because of space), but they range from the relatively simple to solve to the very difficult to solve. Our method, as described in what follows, requires the knowledge of the solution to the problem and we were, in that sense, somewhat limited in our choice of functions. Thereafter, we executed algorithms G1, G2 and G3 and measured their behavior. Every method was tried exhaustively for every algorithm. We refer to the corresponding experiments as $G\alpha A$: for instance, G1H refers to the using algorithm G1 and Homaiffar's method; G2P singles out algorithm G2 and Powell's method. We use the letters H, J, K, P or S to refer to the different methods. To find a quantitative measure of relative performance we follow the next procedure.

3.1 Statistical Evaluation of an Algorithm

It is common to run a set of experiments to establish a comparison between proposed methods, algorithms and the like. Any such attempt is lacking since generality may not be reached from a finite set of experiments. Here we follow a similar methodology but extract hard numerical bounds because we are able to find the mean and standard deviation of the unknown distributions of all the $G\alpha A$ experiments.

3.1.1 Extracting the Distribution's Parameters

It is possible, indeed, to try to approximate the population's basic parameters (μ and σ) from the estimators $\bar{x}$ and s. The key issue is the adequate determination of the size of the sample. In this case we know nothing about the distribution under study (i.e. the probability that the best value from $G\alpha A$ exceeds a certain value). Hence, to find the basic parameters (which are usually calculated from $\bar{x} = \frac{1}{N}\sum_{i=1}^{N} x_i$ and

$s = \sqrt{\frac{1}{N-1}\sum_{i=1}^{N}(x_i - \bar{x})^2}$) we, first, rely on the fact that any sampling population of means (for a sufficiently large sample) is normally distributed. We perform enough simulations to insure that, indeed, the measured means are thusly distributed. This we ascertain by complying with a χ^2 goodness-of-fit test with a 99% level of confidence which allows us to find $\mu_{\bar{X}}$ and $\sigma_{\bar{X}}$. Second, we know that $\overline{f(\bar{x})}$ for $G\alpha A$ is given by $P(\overline{f(\bar{x})} < \mu_{\bar{X}} + 1.96\sigma_{\bar{X}}) \geq 0.95$ (since this distribution is gaussian). Third, for the non-gaussian distribution of $f(\bar{x})$ we further know (from Chebyshev's theorem) that $P(f(\bar{x}) < \mu_{\bar{X}} + 4 \cdot [6\sigma_{\bar{X}}]) \geq 0.9375$. These bounds, on the other hand, are pertinent only for the $G\alpha A$'s. The point is, nonetheless, that the calculated values are absolute within statistical certainty limits and the foregoing conclusions, within these limits, are uncontestable.

3.1.2 The Statistical Algorithm

1. $\alpha \leftarrow 1$ (determine the parameter set)
2. $\beta \leftarrow 1$; (determine the method)
   $A \leftarrow M(\beta)$ (*where* $M(i) = H, J, K, P, S$ *for* $i = 1, ..., 5$)
3. $i \leftarrow 1$ (count the number of samples)
4. $j \leftarrow 1$ (count the elements of a sample)
5. A function is selected randomly from the suite.
6. Experiment $G\alpha A$ is performed with this function and a) the best value and b) the number of satisfied constraints are stored.
7. $j \leftarrow j+1$
8. If $j \leq 36$, go to step 5 (a sample size of 36 guarantees normality).
9. The average $\bar{x}_i = \frac{1}{N}\sum_j f_j(\bar{x})$ of the best fitness' values is calculated.
10. $i \leftarrow i+1$
11. If $i \leq 50$, go to step 4
12. According to the central limit theorem, the $\bar{x}_i$ distribute normally. We, therefore, define 10 intervals which are expected to hold 1/10 of the samples assuming a normal distribution: i.e., the intervals are standardized. If the samples are indeed normally distributed the following 2 conditions should hold.

    a) At least 5 observations should be found in each of the 10 intervals (which explains why we test for 50 in step 11).

    b) The values of a χ^2 goodness of fit test should be complied with (which we demand to be in the 99% confidence level).

    We, therefore, check for conditions (a) and (b) above. If they have not been reached, go to step 4.
13. Once we are assured (with probability = 0.99) that the $\bar{x}_i$'s are normally distributed, we calculate the mean $\mu_{\bar{X}}$ and standard deviation $\sigma_{\bar{X}}$ of the sampling distribution of the measured mean values of the best fitnesses for this experiment.

Moreover, we may calculate the mean μ and the standard deviation σ of the distribution of the best values (rather than the means) from $\mu = \mu_X ; \sigma = 6\sigma_X$. Notice that, therefore, we characterize the statistical behavior of experiment $G\alpha A$ *quantitatively*.
14. $\beta \leftarrow \beta + 1$. If $\beta < 5$, go to step 3.
15. $\alpha \leftarrow \alpha + 1$. If $\alpha < 3$, go to step 2.
16. End.
□

In step 5 of the algorithm a function is randomly selected and the fitnesses of the various functions thusly chosen are averaged. However, for this to be mathematically consistent we need to normalize the results in a way such that all functions have a comparable best case. We achieve this by dividing the best measured value by the known best value (which is why we stated, above, that our choice of functions is somewhat curtailed). Therefore, the best possible (normalized) value is always 1. Furthermore, the GAs are not guaranteed to find feasible solutions in all cases. But we must normalize even those solutions corresponding to unfeasible individuals; we did this by multiplying the number of unfulfilled constraints times the largest penalty assigned to a given individual in generation 100 of each experiment. This explains the large values reported for μ_X and σ_X in the tables which follow.

4 Results

In table 1 we show the sampling of means average values and standard deviations for each tested method. We point out that Schoenauer's method was only simulated with G3 because it requires full elitism.

Table 1. Values of $\mu_{\bar{x}}, \sigma_{\bar{x}}$ for the experiments performed

Experiment	$\mu_{\bar{x}}$	$\sigma_{\bar{x}}$
G1K	1.47155E281	2.20060E280
G1H	2.27267E281	3.54317E280
G1J	2.32140E281	2.35599E280
G1P	2.13868E281	2.22789E280
G2K	1.66157E281	2.05705E280
G2H	2.40939E281	2.14969E280
G2J	2.29502E281	2.41732E280
G2P	2.07283E281	2.34106E280
G3K	1.61322E281	2.00831E280
G3H	2.37554E281	2.58420E280
G3J	2.14620E281	2.59664E280
G3P	1.90579E281	2.39071E280
G3S	1.92934E281	2.40484E280

Since, from Chebyshev's theorem, we know that the proportion of any distribution found within k standard deviations of the mean is, at least, $1-1/k^2$ (k is any positive number greater than 1) we decided to set k=4 and, therefore, a probability certainty of 0.9375. Then we calculated the upper bound (worst case minimum value) for the experiments. These are shown in table 2, where the $G\alpha A$ are ordered according to this bound, from best to worst.

Table 2. Upper Bound for Best Values of $G\alpha A$ with P=0.975 (/E281)

Experiment	μ_X	σ_X	Upper Bound	Relative Performance
G3K	1.6132	0.2008	6.4332	1.0000
G2K	1.6616	0.2057	6.5985	1.0257
G1K	1.4716	0.2201	6.7530	1.0497
G1P	2.1387	0.2228	7.4856	1.1636
G2H	2.4094	0.2150	7.5686	1.1765
G3P	1.9058	0.2391	7.6435	1.1881
G2P	2.0728	0.2341	7.6914	1.1956
G3S	1.9293	0.2405	7.7010	1.1971
G1J	2.3214	0.2356	7.9758	1.2398
G2J	2.2950	0.2417	8.0966	1.2586
G3J	2.1462	0.2597	8.3781	1.3023
G3H	2.3755	0.2584	8.5776	1.3333
G1H	2.2727	0.3543	10.7763	1.6751

The table above shows that the algorithms have not had decisive influence on the results with the exception of G2H; the method is the key element to be considered when measuring the performance of the procedures. Surprisingly, method K has turned out to be better than the rest for all methods. Also surprising are the relative performances. Relative to G3K (the best overall) the ratios for $G\alpha K$ are 1:1.02:1.05; the ones of $G\alpha P$ are 1.16:1.19:1.20; the one of $G\alpha S$ is 1.20 (recall that method S was only tried with G3); the ones of $G\alpha J$ are 1.24:1.26:1.30; and those of $G\alpha H$ are 1.17:1.33:1.67: with the exception of $G\alpha H$ all methods are closely clustered and seem to be insensitive to the algorithm. Also noteworthy is the fact that the relative difference between the best and worst performances is 67%.

5 Conclusions

From the previous results it follows that method K has yielded the best of all those we analyzed. This seems to contradict the reported experience regarding the mentioned methods. For example, in [8] the following is concluded:

"Penalties which are functions of the distance from feasibility are better performers than those which are merely functions of the number of violated constraints..."

Likewise, in [1], [9], [10] and [11] it is assumed that, as seems intuitively satisfying, those methods which take advantage of greater information are the most adequate to establish penalty functions. Interestingly, in none of these the validity of this intuitive dictum is proven either theoretically and/or experimentally. In [1], in fact, the conclusions (for only three functions) are contradictory; something which, in light of our results, is to be expected. Hence it is valid to ask whether this expectation is not satisfiable in general and, in fact, the results we found seem to experimentally refute the previously mentioned intuition. However, assuming that the intuitive assertion were correct, some possible explanations for the apparent anomaly are the following.

a) In this comparative analysis the same parameters for the penalty method were applied to all functions. Would it be more adequate, perhaps, to adjust the parameters particularly for every function?

b) It is possible that the combination of full elitism and the algorithm implemented in *GαK* maintain a varied population and this favors the efficiency of the method and that this accelerates, in general, the identification of the best value.

c) It is also possible that method K (in those cases where none of the method reaches the feasible region) does find points which satisfy a larger number of constraints in 100 generations while other methods are "closer" to satisfying all constraints.

This last hypothesis is illustrated in figure 1.

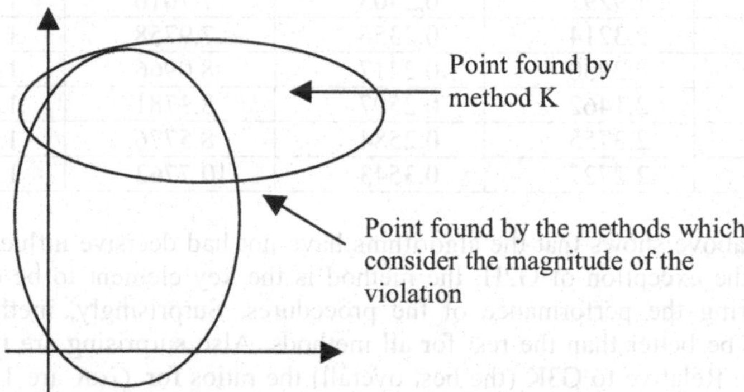

Fig. 1. The point found by the methods which consider the size of the violation does not satisfy any constraint, whereas method K complies with one of them

If this were the situation we could conclude that method K finds the feasible points "trying" to satisfy the constraints one at a time and the methods which consider the magnitude of the constraint (as in three of the remaining methods) "try" to find the solution considering all constraints simultaneously.

d) It is possible that these results hold only for this suite of functions and that the suite displays this atypical behavior coincidentally. In this regard we must mention that we tested the calculated bounds with functions outside the suite and, as expected, the values are consistent with our study.

e) Finally, we may consider that method K is better because the suite consists (or is considered to consist) of "simple" functions. This argument depends on what we mean by a "simple" function. Although some of the functions in the suite would generally be considered to be in this category, some others certainly do not. At any rate, we may point out that if method K is better in those not-so-especially-difficult functions (those which we find on a day-to-day basis) then one possible conclusion is that it should be applied by default, resorting to some of the other methods only in case of a specifically complex or anomalous function.

There is much work still to be done. We plan to extend the study to a set of functions generated automatically in such a way that the possible bias in the suite is eliminated. In a mechanized set we also expect to make the difficulty inherent to the functions in the set more homogeneous.

References

1. Coello, C., "Theoretical and Numerical Constraint-Handling Techniques used with Evolutionary Algorithms: A Survey of the State of the Art", Computer Methods in Applied Mechanics and Engineering, 2001 (to be published).
2. Homaiffar A., Qi C. & Lai S., "Constrained Optimization Via Genetic Algorithms". Simulation, 62:4, pp. 242-254, 1994.
3. Joines, J and Houck, C., "On the Use of Non-Stationary Penalty Functions to Solve Nonlinear Constrained Optimization Problems with GA's". Proceedings of first IEEE Conference on Evolutionary Computation, pp. 579-584, 1994.
4. Shoenauer, M. and Xanthakis, S., "Constrained GA Optimization". Proceedings of the Fifth International Conference on Genetic Algorithms, pp. 573-580, 1993.
5. Kuri, A., *A Comprehensive Approach to Genetic Algorithms in Optimization and Learning. Theory and Applications*, Vol. 1. Instituto Politécnico Nacional, pp 270, 1999.
6. Powell, D. and Skolnick, M., "Using Genetic Algorithms in Engineering Design Optimization with Non-linear Constraints". Proceedings of the Fifth International Conference on Genetic Algorithms. pp. 424-430, 1993.
7. Kuri, A., "A universal Eclectic Genetic Algorithm for Constrained Optimization". Proceedings 6th European Congress on Intelligent Techniques & Soft Computing, EUFIT'98, pp. 518-522, 1998.
8. Richardson J., Palmer M., Liepins G. & Hilliard M., "Some Guidelines for Genetic Algorithms with Penalty Functions". Proceedings of the IEEE International Conference on Evolutionary Computation, pp.191-197, 1989.
9. Back, T., *Evolutionary Algorithms in Theory and Practice*, Oxford University Press, New York, 1996.
10. Coello, C.,"Use of a Self-Adaptive Penalty Approach for Engineering Optimization Problems", Computers in Industry, 41(2):113-127, 2000.
11. Fogel, D., *Evolutionary Computation. Toward a New Philosophy of Machine Intelligence*, the Institute of Electrical and Electronic Engineers, New York, 1999.

Automatic Generation of Control Parameters for the Threshold Accepting Algorithm

Joaquín Pérez[1,2], Rodolfo Pazos[2], Laura Velez[3], and Guillermo Rodríguez[1]

[1] Instituto de Investigaciones Eléctricas
jperez@iie.org.mx, gro@iie.org.mx
[2] Centro Nacional de Investigación y Desarrollo Tecnológico
pazos@sd-cenidet.com.mx
[3] Instituto Tecnológico de Cd. Madero
lvelez@itcm.edu.mx

Abstract. In this article a new method to obtain the control parameters values for the Threshold Accepting algorithm is presented, which is independent of the problem domain and size. This approach differs from the traditional methods that require knowing first the problem domain, and then knowing how to select the parameters values to solve specific problem instances. The proposed method is based on a sample of problem instances, whose solution allows us to characterize the problem and to define the parameters. To test the method the combinatorial optimization model called DFAR was solved using the Threshold Accepting algorithm. The experimental results show that it is feasible to automatically obtain the parameters for a heuristic algorithm, which will produce satisfactory results, even though the kind of problem to solve is not known. We consider that the proposed method principles can be applied to the definition of control parameters for other heuristic algorithms.

1 Introduction

The Threshold Accepting (TA) algorithm, which is a variant of the Simulated Annealing algorithm, is a general-purpose heuristic technique that allows solving combinatorial optimization problems, and obtains better quality solutions than Simulated Annealing [3] and consumes less processing time [7].

The TA implementation is simple, it requires (like in Simulated Annealing) among other things, the selection of a cooling method, which is the specification of an initial temperature, the strategy for thermal equilibrium, the temperature reduction factor, and the algorithm halting conditions. Nevertheless, it is a difficult task to propose an effective cooling plan that obtains a balance between quality and processing time [3]. It requires plenty of knowledge of the nature of the problem to be solved, which is not usually trivial [5].

Traditionally the cooling plan has been obtained by trial and error, this is why it is interesting to study in deep the algorithm to analytically obtain its parameters.

In the following sections, the strategies used to automatically generate a cooling plan are explained. The plan is prepared by gathering partial statistical data of an actual experiment, to obtain one step to come close to a new problem. Particularly these strategies are applied to the solution of the distribution design problem in distributed databases modeled by DFAR [9].

C.A. Coello Coello et al. (Eds.): MICAI 2002, LNAI 2313, pp. 118–127, 2002.

2 The Mathematical Model

To determine the storage units and their location to process queries with minimum time and cost in a distributed database is a non-trivial problem, which is called the distribution design problem.

This problem has been partially solved with different models and techniques [2, 6], and all of them solve it in two sequential phases: fragment definition and fragment allocation in the different sites. The mathematical model DFAR constitutes an innovative approach by integrating both phases in one.

2.1 Objective Function

In this optimization model, the decision to store an attribute m in site j is represented by the binary variable x_{mj}. If $x_{mj} = 1$ attribute m is stored in site j, and $x_{mj} = 0$ otherwise.

The objective function models the transmission costs and data access using four terms: transmission, access to fragments, fragment storage, and fragment migration. With these four terms the dynamic nature of distributed databases is considered.

$$\min z=\sum_k \sum_i f_{ki} \sum_m \sum_j q_{km} l_{km} c_{ij} x_{mj} + \sum_i \sum_k \sum_j c_1 f_{ki} y_{kj} + \sum_j c_2 w_j + \sum_m \sum_i \sum_j a_{mi} c_{ij} d_m x_{mj} \quad (1)$$

where

f_{ki} = emission frequency of query k from site i;

q_{km} = usage parameter, $q_{km} = 1$ if query k uses attribute m, otherwise $q_{km} = 0$;

l_{km} = number of communication packets for transporting attribute m for query k = $(p_m s_k)/PA$;

where

p_m = size in bytes of attribute m;

s_k = selectivity of query k (number of tuples returned when query k is executed);

PA = communication packet size in bytes;

c_{ij} = communication cost between sites i and j;

c_1 = cost for accessing several fragments to satisfy a query; e.g., the processing cost of a join in a query that accesses two or more fragments;

y_{kj} = decision variable, $y_{ki} = 1$ if query k accesses one or more attributes located at site j, and $y_{kj} = 0$ otherwise;

c_2 = cost for allocating a fragment to a site; e.g., the cost incurred for having a copy of the key in each fragment;

w_j = decision variable, $w_i = 1$ if there exist one or more attributes at site j, and $w_i = 0$ otherwise;

a_{mi} = indicator of previous allocation, $a_{mi} = 1$ if attribute m is currently located at site i, otherwise $a_{mi} = 0$;

d_m = number of communication packets required to move attribute m to another site if necessary; = $(p_m * CA)/PA$

where

CA = cardinality of the relation.

2.2 Intrinsic Constraints of the Problem

Since replication of attributes is not considered, these constraints specify that each attribute is going to be allocated to only one site. Additionally, each attribute must be allocated to a site that executes at least one query involving the attribute. These constraints are expressed as follows:

$$\sum_j x_{mj} = 1 \quad \forall m$$ each attribute must be stored in only one site; (2)

$$x_{mi} \le \sum_k q_{km} \varphi_{ki} \quad \forall m, i$$ where (3)

$$\varphi_{kt} = \begin{cases} 1, & \text{if } f_{ki} > 0 \\ 0, & \text{if } f_{ki} = 0 \end{cases}$$

each attribute m must be allocated to a site i that executes at least one query involving the attribute;

$$t\, w_j - \sum_m x_{mj} \ge 0 \quad \forall j$$ this constraint forces the value of w_i to 1 when any x_{mi} equals 1, and induces w_i to 0 otherwise; (4)

where

t = number of attributes;

$$t\, y_{kj} - \sum_m q_{km} x_{mj} \ge 0 \quad \forall k, j$$ this constraint forces y_{ki} to 1 when any $q_{km}x_{mi}$ equals 1, and induces y_{kj} to 0 otherwise; (5)

$$\sum_m x_{mj}\, p_m CA \le cs_j \quad \forall j$$ The space occupied by all attributes stored in site j must not exceed the site capacity; (6)

where

cs_j = capacity of site j.

3 Method of Solution

Because the general problem of distribution belongs to the class of problems *NP*-Hard and the DFAR modeling belongs to the class *NP*-complete, the space of possible solutions is very large, even for small problems. This justifies approaching the solution by using the same means than the heuristic method of the Threshold Accepting algorithm.

3.1 The Simulated Annealing and Threshold Accepting Algorithms

The Simulated Annealing algorithm proposed in [5] is an improved version of the local optimization algorithms. This heuristic method implements the Metropolis algorithm [1] to simulate the process of physical metal annealing.

The algorithm begins with the best feasible solution $x \in N$ and $N \subset X$ (where X is the set of all feasible solutions) and a control parameter T (called *temperature* due to the analogy with statistical mechanics) initialized with a suitably high value. A neighboring solution $y \in H(x)$ is generated, where $H(x) \subset X$; if $\Delta z = z(y) - z(x) \le 0$, then y is accepted as the new next solution; otherwise, the probability that the new configuration is accepted is $P(\Delta z) = \exp(-\Delta z/T)$, which is compared with a uniformly distributed random number in the interval (0, 1). This process is repeated until an *equilibrium* condition is reached, in which case, in order to reduce the temperature, this is multiplied by *a reduction factor* and the process is repeated again. The algorithm stops when the system no longer produces significant improvement, which is called *freezing*. Note that the possibility of accepting a solution that increases the cost, tends to diminish as the temperature T does it.

```
begin
   real T, μ
   integer i, S, L
   x = the best solution of a set L of
         feasible solutions.
   T = high initial value of temperature
   S = set size
   repeat
      repeat
         for i = 1 to S
            y = neighboring solution
            if z(y) - z(x) < T then
               x = y
            else
               the new solution is not accepted
            end_if
            i = i + 1
         end_for
      until thermal equilibrium is reached
         T = μT
   until freezing is reached
end
```

Fig. 1. Threshold Accepting Algorithm

The Threshold Accepting (TA) heuristic method is a variant of Simulated Annealing (SA), and the main difference between these two methods is in the acceptance criteria for worse solutions in the energy value. In both algorithms the acceptance of worse configurations depends on the temperature; nevertheless, whereas in the SA technique the temperature is a factor affected by the statistical distribution, in TA the same parameter represents the upper limit for the acceptance of a worse configuration. In TA the temperature alone represents the acceptance threshold and it is not necessary to compute probabilities, or to make random decisions [3, 7]. The TA algorithm is shown in Figure 1.

3.2 Review of Previous Work

The Simulated Annealing algorithm has been implemented as a solution method for diverse combinatorial optimization problems [5]; nevertheless, few articles specify all the control parameters of the algorithm [5]. While some present methods for parameter selection and no experimental results, others only show results but not the selection approach.

The definition of the control parameters is an important factor that can significantly affect the algorithm performance [3]. A brief summary of how other researchers have defined these parameters follows.

3.2.1 Initial Temperature

In SA as in TA, an initial very high temperature leads to a diversified search; i.e., the algorithm will spend a long time since it allows any solution to be accepted. If one begins with a very low temperature, the system will not be able to explore sufficiently enough the solution space and possibly it will stall in a local minimum.

The following are proposed strategies by other researchers:

- The initial temperature provided is a sufficiently high constant value, to allow that 100% of trials is accepted [5].
- The initial temperature is obtained with the following formula: $T_0 = (-\Delta z/\ln(F_0))$ [4].
- The initial temperature is obtained by multiplying the worst solution of the first generation by 100 [8].

3.2.2 Equilibrium

In order to determine when a system is in equilibrium, the following strategies have been proposed:

- Keep a record of accepted and rejected solutions. If the number obtained reaches a given threshold, then the equilibrium has been reached [5].
- A maximum number of iterations for the temperature is established [4].

3.2.3 Temperature Attenuation Procedure

This procedure defines how the temperature will be reduced whenever equilibrium is achieved. Some of the proposed procedures are as follows:

- The exponential cooling procedure [5], defined as $T_n = (T_1/T_0)^n T_0$, where $(T_1/T_0) = 0.9$.
- The geometric series cooling procedure [5], defined as $T = \mu T$, where μ is a small constant.

3.2.4 Freezing

This parameter defines the algorithm halting criteria. Some proposed halting criteria in the literature are the following:

- When the present temperature takes a specified constant value.
- When a determined number of iterations is reached [7, 10].
- When the percentage of accepted solutions exceeds a limit [5].

4 Implementation

Traditionally, to devise a cooling plan, the researcher experiments with different combinations and chooses that one that he considers more suitable. To this end, it is necessary to provide certain constant values so that they serve as control parameters; these are difficult to specify specially if one does not know the nature of the problem domain in depth.

The method proposed by us allows to almost totally automate the determination of the algorithm parameters, providing a means to know more about the problem and contributing with a frame of reference for later experimentation.

4.1 Problem Mapping

In order to show the implementation viability of the TA algorithm and the proposed cooling plan, the distribution design problem in distributed databases modeled with DFAR was solved.

Specifically in the solution of the DFAR model, x is a one-dimensional vector of integer numbers, where the subscripts represent the attributes of the relation (table) and the array elements represent the sites where the fragments will be allocated.

The neighborhood $H(x)$ is defined as the set of all feasible solutions that satisfy the model constraints. It can be obtained by changing randomly the location of an attribute from one site to another.

4.2 Preliminary Experiments

In order to improve the performance of the Threshold Accepting method, the original algorithm was modified in three different ways. In these strategies, unlike the traditional method in which the seed temperature for an iteration solution is taken from the previous iteration temperature, now the best global seed is selected; i.e., it can be the previous seed or the seed for the best solution of a set S of previous solutions.

For each one of the strategies, trials conducted using six samples of different sizes (generated with the method described in section 4.4) and cooling factors of 0.70, 0.75, 0.80 and 0.85. It was observed that the traditional and best global strategies provide the best results with a cooling factor of 0.85. Therefore, it was decided to continue with the traditional method.

4.3 The Proposed Cooling Plan

Initial temperature *T*. The strategies reported in [9] were initially taken. It was observed that when the initial T was too high, it significantly affected the processing time of large problems. In order to establish an appropriate initial value for T according to the size of the problem, the following criterion was used: the initial temperature is a control parameter that uses the same units as the cost function [5], and is set so that 40% of the solutions generated in a size n sample are rejected. This is implemented in the following way: a sample of 100 random feasible neighboring solutions is generated. The result obtained from the difference of the pair of solutions

x_i and x_{i+1} is recorded in d_i, for $i = 1, 2, ..., 99$. Vector d is then sorted in decreasing order and the value of the 41st element of the vector is assigned to T, so that 40% of the rejected solutions are discarded.

Equilibrium. In the process of physical annealing, for any given temperature, there is a maximum size of the crystals that form the metal; at this point there is a balance between the internal force that drives the growth of crystals and the metallic structure rigidity. Similar to this effect is the strategy for the heuristic Threshold Accepting technique that follows [9]: equilibrium is reached when the average values of the present set $z^*(x)$ and the previous set $z^*(y)$, satisfy the expression $z^*(y) - z^*(x) < 0.001z^*(y)$ or when the minimum values of two consecutive sets satisfy expression $z_{min}(y) - z_{min}(x) < 0{,}001\ z_{min}(y)$.

Cooling factor or temperature reduction factor μ. Currently, experiments with some strategies that allow automating this parameter are under way. At the moment, the geometric series cooling procedure with a factor of 0.85 was selected, since better results are obtained as discussed in section 4.2.

Freezing. As the temperature drops the possibility of moving to worse solutions is practically null; therefore, the process can be stopped before the temperature value reaches 0. Initially, freezing was assumed when ten consecutive temperatures without improvement occurred [9], at present, cooling is assumed when for the current temperature T, there exist three consecutive sets where all solutions are rejected, that is, freezing is reached when the following condition is satisfied:

$$z(y) - z(x) \geq T, \quad \forall y \in L_i, L_{i-1}, L_{i-2}. \tag{7}$$

4.4 Large Test Cases Generation with Well-Known Solutions

In order to validate the Threshold Accepting algorithm, it is required to generate large test cases of problems whose optimal solution is well known, to this end the next three steps are followed:

- A small problem is generated whose solution can be obtained through any commercial combinatorial optimization software. We refer to it as basic problem M_b.
- In order to generate a new problem M_n, two basic disjoint problems are combined. Thus, by the independence property, the value of the solution for the new problem is the sum of the values of the solutions for each basic problem.
- Each new problem M_n, can be considered as a new basic problem M_b with well-known solution, which can in turn be combined with another problem.

4.5 Experimental Results

The Threshold Accepting algorithm was coded in Borland C; the experiments were executed in a workstation PC Pentium at 133 MHz with the Windows NT operating system.

Table 1. Test cases

Prob	Attrib	Sites	Cons	Size (bytes)
P1	10	4	8	660
P2	10	20	15	3640
P3	15	18	14	3412
P4	35	10	16	3684
P5	25	10	32	5268
P6	37	40	46	21228
P7	98	26	27	17112
P8	72	29	42	21212
P9	80	36	42	25644
P10	85	20	82	37148
P11	94	47	91	61484
P12	86	52	121	79008
P13	98	68	95	83032
P14	112	61	111	93300
P15	95	89	94	102380

Table 1 shows the main parameters of 15 randomly generated test cases, each problem was run 30 times. Table 2 shows the results obtained using the proposed strategies of this article and the traditional methods to determine the initial temperature and the freezing criterion on the basis of the definition of arbitrarily selected constant values.

Table 2. Proposed strategy and traditional methods with constant limits

	Proposal		T_{INI} = 500000		T_{INI} = 500	
Prob.	Best Sol.	Time	Best Sol.	Time	Best Sol.	Time
P1	5377.40	0.01	5377.40	0.06	5377.00	0.00
P2	211767.98	0.26	227598.78	0.32	211767.98	0.14
P3	361994.50	0.26	453464.81	0.26	361994.50	0.14
P4	630494.00	0.34	630494.00	0.63	630494.00	0.18
P5	293245.62	0.20	294633.62	0.35	293245.62	0.20
P6	4958823.00	3.40	4932984.00	4.74	4989253.50	3.13
P7	7079232.00	4.09	7081352.00	4.66	7095350.00	3.68
P8	8078685.00	4.52	8076882.00	5.84	8174192.00	3.70
P9	8998638.00	5.79	9028670.00	6.04	9060626.00	4.93
P10	13867769.00	6.75	13873975.00	6.96	13867298.00	5.95
P11	75777264.00	24.86	75838672.00	28.54	75825568.00	22.49
P12	97647824.00	34.21	97450192.00	41.16	98352784.00	30.28
P13	118199792.00	43.14	118288784.00	48.32	118464416.00	40.12
P14	126946656.00	48.50	126363160.00	56.33	127016392.00	47.42
P15	166402688.00	62.32	165170464.00	69.67	165932416.00	61.32

Table 2. (Horizontal Continuation)

	Accept = 40		Accept = 2	
Prob.	Best Sol.	Time	Best Sol.	Time
P1	5377.40	0.01	5377.40	0.02
P2	212484.78	0.12	211784.00	0.28
P3	364414.50	0.16	361994.50	0.30
P4	643381.00	0.16	630494.00	0.37
P5	293245.62	0.20	293245.00	0.27
P6	5156602.00	2.67	4966426.50	3.84
P7	7384091.00	2.34	7056755.00	4.47
P8	8319554.00	2.92	8086501.00	5.03
P9	9302163.00	3.54	9047942.00	5.96
P10	14061334.00	3.45	13872730.00	7.07
P11	79629104.00	16.35	75856304.00	26.63
P12	103860472.00	22.92	97298928.00	36.68
P13	124942704.00	31.42	118232064.00	45.98
P14	134261952.00	33.98	126755480.00	53.57
P15	178560064.00	50.09	164870752.00	69.32

5 Conclusions and Future Work

In this article the feasibility to solve the mathematical model DFAR was presented. Using a Threshold Accepting heuristic method, which is a variant of the Simulated Annealing algorithm, and based on statistics, a new mechanism to automate the cooling plan was designed. The proposed automatic approach to generate parameters for the algorithm is very useful and helps users to decide which values to use for the cooling plan. This type of techniques is a tool that relieves users from the task of setting the values, since they affect either positive or negatively the performance of the system. The results are encouraging from the point of view of quality, however the response times of the proposed approach can be refined in order to improve the algorithm, and to include all of the parameters.

This article contributes to the field of automatic generation of control parameters, which deals with the regulation of algorithm performance, promoting a framework to evaluate other cooling methods and to expand the knowledge about the nature of the problems domain.

Finally, it was shown that it is feasible to solve large problems found in real applications and it is perceived the potential of the algorithm to solve these problems in reasonable time.

References

1. Metropolis, N., Rosenbluth, A.W., Rosenbluth, M.N., Teller, A.H., and Teller, E.: Equation of State Calculations by Fasting Computing Machines. J. Chemical Phys., Vol. 21, (1953).

2. Ceri, S., Pelagatti, G.: Distributed Databases: Principles & Systems. McGraw-Hill, New York (1984).
3. Dueck, G., Scheuer, T.: Threshold Accepting: a General Purpose Optimization Algorithm Appearing Superior to Simulated Annealing. Journal of Computational Physics, Vol. 90 (1990) 161-175.
4. Beasley, J.F., Dowsland, K., Glover, F., Laguna, M.: Modern Heuristic Techniques for Combinatorial Problems. Colin R. Reeves, New York (1993).
5. Kirkpatrick, S., Gelatt, C.D., Vecchi, M.P.: Optimization by Simulated Annealing. Science 220 (1983) 671-680.
6. March, S.T., Rho, S.: Allocating Data and Operations to Nodes in Distributed Database Design. Transactions on Knowledge and Data Engineering, Vol. 7, No. 2 (1995).
7. Morales, L., Garduño, R., Romero, D.: The Multiple-Minima Problem in Small Peptides Revisited: the Threshold Accepting Approach. Journal of Biomolecular Structure & Dynamics, Vol. 9, No. 5 (1992) 951-957.
8. Adler, D.: Genetic Algorithms and Simulated Annealing: a Marriage Proposal. IEEE International Conference on Neural Networks (1993) 1104-1109.
9. Pérez, J., Pazos, R., Frausto, J., Ramírez, S., Reyes, F.: Dynamic Allocation of Vertical Fragments in Distributed Databases Using the Threshold Accepting Algorithm. Proceedings of 10th IASTED International Conference on Parallel and Distributed Computing and Systems, Las Vegas (1998) 210-213.
10. Telley, H., Liebling, Th.M., Mocellin, A.: Reconstruction of Polycrystalline Structures: a New Application of Combinatorial Optimization. Journal Computing, Vol. 38 (1987) 1-11.

Genetic Algorithms and Case-Based Reasoning as a Discovery and Learning Machine in the Optimization of Combinational Logic Circuits

E. Islas Pérez[1], Carlos A. Coello Coello[2], Arturo Hernández-Aguirre[3], and Alejandro Villavicencio Ramírez[1]

[1] Instituto de Investigaciones Eléctricas
Av. Reforma 113, Col. Palmira, 62490 Temixco Morelos, México
eislas@iie.org.mx, avila@iie.org.mx

[2] CINVESTAV-IPN; Depto. de Ingeniería Eléctrica, Sección de Computación,
Av. IPN No. 2508, Col. San Pedro Zacatenco, México, D.F. 07300, México,
ccoello@cs.cinvestav.mx

[3] CIMAT, Depto. de Computación, Guanajuato, Gto. 36240, México
artha@cimat.mx

Abstract. In this paper we show how case-based reasoning techniques can be used to extract and reuse solutions previously found by a heuristic (a genetic algorithm in our case) used to solve problems in a specific domain (MSI and SSI combinational circuit design). This reuse of partially built solutions allows us to improve convergence time of our heuristic since the building blocks of the "good" solutions in design space are incorporated earlier in the search process. Our system is illustrated with the design of a full adder circuit being this circuit the solution of two interconnected half-adder. Furthermore, with the analysis of the obtained results we are able to rediscover several of the traditional Boolean rules used for circuit simplification and we are also able to find a new and interesting simplification rule.

1 Introduction

The focus of this paper is to show how Case-Based Reasoning (CBR) techniques can be used to extract and reuse design patterns that emerge from the evolutionary process of a Genetic Algorithm (GA) used to design combinational circuits. We build a database of solutions previously found (to certain circuits) which we consider having some (potentially) useful information. Then, using CBR techniques, we retrieve this information when solving similar circuits, aiming to improve convergence time of the GA used.

2 Related Work

Apparently, the first attempt to combine CBR and GAs was done by Louis et al. [5]. In this paper, the authors use CBR-principles to explain solutions found by a GA.

C.A. Coello Coello et al. (Eds.): MICAI 2002, LNAI 2313, pp. 128–137, 2002.

These ideas were further developed by Louis & Johnson [4]. Although Louis & Johnson [4] used a few examples from circuit design (mainly parity checkers) to illustrate their principles, they did not focus their work specifically on the design of combinational circuits as in our case. Nevertheless, our current proposal has been influenced by this prior work. Several other researchers have proposed approaches that combine CBR and GAs (see for example [8]). However, the emphasis of these papers has been to illustrate the benefits of this sort of hybrid scheme rather than emphasizing a certain application domain like in our case. Also, some researchers in evolvable hardware have pointed out the potential benefits of using GAs as a discovery engine capable of producing novel and even inspirational designs. Miller et al. [6], for example, showed that through the evolution of a hierarchical series of examples, it was possible to rediscover the well-known ripple-carry principle for building adder circuits of any size. Recently, Thomson [9] explored the potential of evolving larger systems more quickly via a method of visualizing the subcomponents of the final solution when they appear.

3 Case-Based Reasoning

CBR is a problem-solving paradigm that in many respects is fundamentally different from other major AI approaches [2]. Instead of relying solely on general knowledge of a problem domain, or making associations along generalized relationships between problem descriptors and conclusions, CBR is able to utilize the specific knowledge of previously experienced, concrete problem situations (cases). A CBR system can be divided in the following main stages:

1. *Identifying the new problem:* The system receives the input case (new problem) and analyses its most important attributes and characteristics in order to search amongst the cases that are most similar to the cases in the case base. The attributes used to measure the similarities between the cases are called indexes.

2. *Finding cases with similarities to the new case:* The following step is to find the cases that have more attributes in common with the attributes of the new case using the indexes found in the previous step. Sometimes it is necessary to reduce the subset in order to find the most relevant cases. The algorithm should be fast and efficient due to the fact that cases retrieval is a critical and important aspect when the case base is sufficiently large.

3. *Arriving at the Solution:* Once we have the most similar cases, the system starts the adaptation process, which consists of the combination and modification of the most similar cases to form a new solution, and additionally an interpretation or an explanation depending on the application of the system.

4. *Evaluating the solution:* The solution obtained in the previous stage is a tentative or potential solution. It is necessary to do an evaluation of the proposed solution before giving it to the final user.

5. *Assignment and storing of the new case:* Once the solution has been created and evaluated, it is given to the user and then it is possible to create a new case. This new

case is formed from the solution found and the original case (problem). Indexes are assigned to the new case and it is stored in the case base.

6. *Explaining, repairing and testing:* If the solution fails, it is important that the system obtains and analyses the information in order to avoid making the same mistakes. If something unusual happens, the system should try to explain it.

4 Statement of the Problem

We will extract knowledge at two stages of the evolutionary process: at the end of a run and during a run. In the first case, the knowledge to be extracted will be the Boolean laws used by the evolutionary algorithm to design a circuit. These laws will be obtained after comparing the results produced from two or more runs of the GA (with different parameters) with the solution produced by a human designer. In the second case, the knowledge extracted will be the building blocks that the circuit structurally maintains during its evolutionary process. When some individuals arrive at a certain threshold (given by the circuit when all the outputs are accomplished) in their fitness value during the evolutionary process, it means that these circuits have evolved long enough to contain good building blocks and we can then extract the knowledge that they contain and store it in a case base for further use. Our approach consists of storing solutions that were previously generated by the same GA and use them as a memory of "past experiences". Then, we can use a mechanism to detect cases similar to the one being solved and retrieve from this "memory" some solutions that can be useful to solve the problem at hand.

In this work we use a matrix encoding (encoded as fixed-length linear chromosomes) that we have adopted in previous work [1] combined with tournament selection, one-point crossover and uniform mutation. For reasons of simplicity we used only five type of gates (AND, OR, NOT, XOR, WIRE [1]). In order to evaluate the fitness value of each circuit we counted the number of WIRES (absence of gates) in the matrix encoding.

5 Proposed System

The proposed system that combines a GA with CBR is depicted in Fig. 1.

The process of extracting knowledge in the two situations previously mentioned can be described as follows:

1. *At the end of the evolutionary process:* In this case, we perform complete runs of a GA solving a certain circuit. Once a solution is found, a new case is formed with such a solution and the original problem. The original problem will be considered as the attributes in the case base and the solution will be the output of the case. As a future work we will include in the system other attributes, in order to have indexes that help to retrieve the most similar cases in a more efficient way.

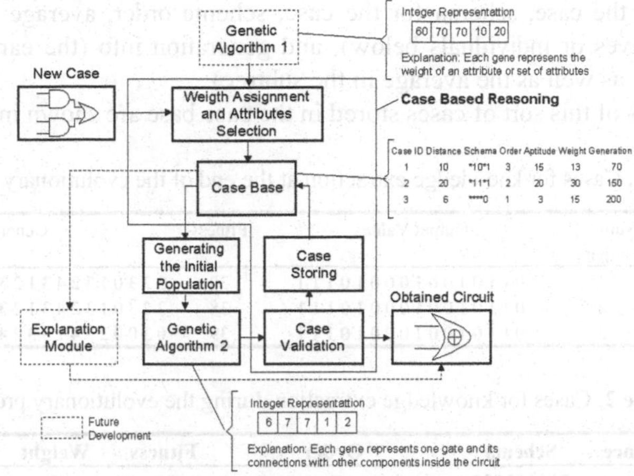

Fig. 1. Proposed system to optimize combinational logic circuits using GAs and CBR

2. *During the evolutionary process:* In this case, our work is inspired on the research of Louis [3]. The GA records data for each individual in the population as it is created and evaluated. Such data includes a fitness measure, the genotype and chronological data, as well as some information on the individual's parents. This collection of data is the initial case data. Though normally discarded by the time an individual is replaced, all of the case data collected is usually contained in the GA's population at some point and it is easy to extract. When a sufficient number of individuals have been created over a number of generations, the initial case data is sent to a clustering program. A hierarchical clustering program clusters the individuals according to both, the fitness and the alleles of the genotype. This clustering constructs a binary tree in which each leaf includes the data of a specific individual. The binary tree structure provides an index for the initial case base. The numbers at the leaves of the tree correspond to the case number (an identification number) of an individual created by the GA.

5.1 Representing Circuits in the Case Base

Depending on the stage at which knowledge is extracted, the representation adopted to store it in the case base can vary:

1. *At the end of the evolutionary process:* The cases will be stored from problems that have been solved previously and they will be used for seeding the initial population of a GA. The attributes contained in this part of the case base are the following: case ID, number of inputs, number of outputs, output values, fitness, and genotype.
Some examples of this sort of cases stored in the case base are shown in Table 1.

2. *During the evolutionary process:* The best individuals are recognized during early generations of the evolutionary process. Afterwards they are stored as cases in the case base and retrieved in later generations. Some of the attributes that are contained in this part of the case base are the following [3]: case ID, distance from the root of the tree

to the level of the case, schema for the case, scheme order, average fitness, weight (number of leaves or individuals below), and generation info (the earliest and latest leaf occurrence as well as the average in the subtree).
Some examples of this sort of cases stored in the case base are shown in Table 2.

Table 1. Cases for knowledge extraction at the end of the evolutionary process

Case ID	Num. Inputs	Num. Outputs	Output Values	Fitness	Genotype
1	3	2	0 1 1 0 1 0 0 1 0 0 0 1 0 1 1 1	39	3 2 3 0 1 3 2 4 3 1 2 3 2 1 3 4 1 0 3 2 3 1
2	3	2	0 1 1 0 1 0 0 1 0 0 0 1 0 1 1 1	38	3 2 3 0 1 3 2 4 3 1 2 3 2 1 4 4 1 3 3 2 0 4
3	3	2	0 1 1 0 1 0 0 1 0 0 0 1 0 1 1 1	39	0 2 0 0 2 3 4 1 3 3 2 4 1 4 3 1 2 3 1 1 3 0

Table 2. Cases for knowledge extraction during the evolutionary process

Case ID	**Distance**	**Schema**	**Order**	**Fitness**	**Weight**	**Generation**
1	5	710*13*2*	6	30	6	50
2	2	**4*50*2*	4	60	8	30
3	8	350610*7*	7	65	4	32

Additionally, we also performed some analysis by hand to understand the way in which the GA performs the simplification of a circuit. As we will show in some of the examples presented next, the GA was able to rediscover several of the simplification rules commonly used in Boolean algebra and, furthermore, it was able to discover "new" simplification laws that are stored in the case base and can also be used by human designers.

6 An Example

Next, we will provide an example of how is the knowledge extracted both at the end and during the evolutionary process of a GA with integer representation used to design combinational logic circuits at the gate-level.

We want to find the Boolean expression that corresponds to the circuit whose outputs must have exactly the same behaviour as the truth table shown in Table 3. We will start by providing the steps followed to extract knowledge at the end of the evolutionary process. First, we performed 10 runs using integer representation and the following parameters: population size=600, maximum number of generations = 200, crossover rate = 0.6, mutation rate = 0.001. The best solution found from these runs has 9 gates and its corresponding Boolean expression is shown (under "GA Setup 1") in Table 4. This Boolean expression is not better than the best solution found by a Human Designer using Karnaugh maps (this solution has 6 gates). However, we additionally performed 10 more runs using a population size of 3000 and a maximum number of generations of 120. The best solution found from these runs has 4 gates (it is better than the solution produced by a human expert) and its corresponding Boolean expression is shown (under "GA Setup 2") in Table 4. In order to say that a solution is better than other it is important to say that in the logic circuit field simplicity depends on the means of measurement that we use. One possibility is the number of gates, which measures circuit area.

Table 3. Truth table for the circuit of the example (a parity checker)

A	B	C	D	X
0	0	0	0	1
0	0	0	1	0
0	0	1	0	0
0	0	1	1	1
0	1	0	0	0
0	1	0	1	1
0	1	1	0	1
0	1	1	1	0
1	0	0	0	0
1	0	0	1	1
1	0	1	0	1
1	0	1	1	0
1	1	0	0	1
1	1	0	1	0
1	1	1	0	0
1	1	1	1	1

Table 4. Comparison of results between a human designer and two setups of our GA

Human Designer
X = ((A ⊕ B)' ⊕ (C⊕D)') '
6 gates
3 NOT, 3 XOR
GA Setup 1
X = ((A⊕C) ⊕ B) '⊕ ((B'B) + D')'
9 gates
1 AND, 1 OR,3 XOR, 4 NOT
GA Setup 2
X = ((A ⊕ B) ⊕ (C⊕D)) '
4 gates
1 NOT, 3 XOR

Analysis. The next step was to analyse (by hand) the solutions produced by our GA with respect to those generated by the human designer:

$$X = ((A \oplus B)' \oplus (C \oplus D)')' = ((A \oplus B) \oplus (C \oplus D)') \quad (1)$$

We have discovered a "new" theorem for XOR gates of the type:

$$(S' \oplus T)' = S \oplus T = S' \oplus T' \quad (2)$$

A case stored in the case base as a product of the analysis at the end of the evolutionary process is shown in Table 5. Using other circuits, we were able to produce several other cases and we were able to rediscover several simplification laws from Boolean algebra and even discover some new ones. For example, we discovered some non-trivial simplifications, such as (A + (A ⊕ B)) ⊕ (A ⊕ B) = AB. All these cases were stored in the case base with the aim of reusing this knowledge with other circuits.

Table 5. Case stored in the case base at the end of the evolutionary process for the circuitwhose truth table is shown in Table 3

Original case	Solution	Description	Number of gates eliminated
(S' ⊕ T)'	S ⊕ T	"New" theorem applied to XOR gates obtained from the comparison between the solution found by the second run of the GA and the solution obtained by a human designer.	3 - 1 = 2

Then, we performed an analysis during the evolutionary process, trying to detect the basic building blocks used by the evolutionary algorithm to generate the best solutions produced. Fig. 2 shows several snapshots of the solutions produced by our GA (the wiring is omitted for reasons of clarity) with the second set of parameters previously described (population size = 3000, maximum number of generations = 120). From these pictures, we can see that the circuit has a fitness value of 17 at generation 9 and we were able to recognize the building blocks used by the GA (such building blocks are indicated with a shadowed box). At generation 67, the maximum fitness has increased, reaching 27, and we can observe that the building blocks previously mentioned have moved to a different position. Finally, when reaching generation 101, we have a fitness of 37 (i.e., a feasible circuit with only 4 gates). Although the building blocks are in a different position, the circuit has the same behavior as in the circuits in earlier stages. For this reason we proceed to store it in our case base. This same process was applied to several other circuits, including a subtractor, a 2-bit magnitude comparator, a half-adder and a full adder. The details of these experiments are available at [7].

6.1 A Case Study: Use of CBR to Design a 2x2 Bit Full Adder

To provide an insight into some of the possible applications of our work, we chose a second example in which we want to illustrate how can we use previously acquired knowledge (derived from the design of a 2x2 bit half adder) to produce a 2x2 bit full adder. We were interested in analysing different possibilities regarding the use of CBR to improve the performance of the GA. Therefore, we decided to perform three experiments:

First Experiment: Only previous solutions to the full adder circuit with different fitness values were stored in a case base and some of these individuals were retrieved to seed a percentage of the initial population of a GA before running it. The individuals were taken from different generations with different fitness values in a previous set of runs for the full adder circuit. The initial population was a mixture of previous solutions (10%) and random solutions (90%). This mixture is necessary to avoid an excessive selection pressure that would cause premature convergence. However, the issue of finding the proper number of cases to be injected in the population of a GA is still an open research area [4]. The best-known solution to this circuit has a fitness of 36 (i.e., a feasible circuit with 5 gates), and we stored solutions with a fitness value of up to 22. This also intends to reduce selection pressure in the GA.

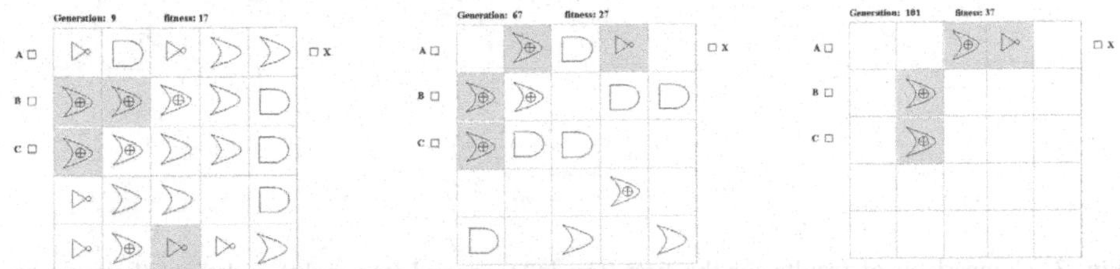

Fig. 2. Solutions obtained by our GA at generations 9 (top left), 67 (top right), and 101 (bottom) for the circuit whose truth table is shown in Table 3

Second Experiment: Some solutions to different logic circuits including the full adder, the half-adder, the comparator and other circuits were stored in the case base. The most similar cases would then be used to seed a portion of the initial population of a GA before running it. The same mixture of individuals as before was adopted in this case.

Third Experiment: Some solutions to different logic circuits including all the circuits as in the previous experiment, but without including the full adder circuit were stored in the case base. The most similar cases would then seed a part of the initial population of a GA were retrieved before running it. The same mixture of individuals as before was adopted in this case.

The results produced from the three experiments are shown in Fig. 3. As we expected, when previous knowledge is used, the GA arrives more rapidly to the best-known solution to this circuit. In the first experiment, our GA converges, on average, at generation 87, whereas the GA without knowledge required almost 100 generations to converge (on average). In the second experiment, the GA performed the same as in the first experiment. The interesting issue to analyse here is that our system decided to extract from the case base the previous solution to the full adder (with fitness of 22), instead of the solution to the half adder. This is explained by the fact that the full adder presents a greater resemblance with the circuit being designed. The experiment showed us the capability of our system to discriminate correctly among several circuits. In our third experiment, we can observe that the GA begins to evolve from a fitness value of 14 in generation one, analogously to the GA with its initial population randomly generated. However, the circuit evolves in a completely different way after that, due to the fact that the system retrieves as the most similar case the previous solution found for the half-adder circuit. In this case, the GA that uses the case base finds a valid circuit at generation 34, whereas the conventional GA finds a valid circuit at generation 45. This illustrates how the use of case base reasoning can actually help the GA to explore the search space in a more efficient way. As an important conclusion we can say that our approach was able to find the solution more rapidly although in the case base only existed a similar solution.

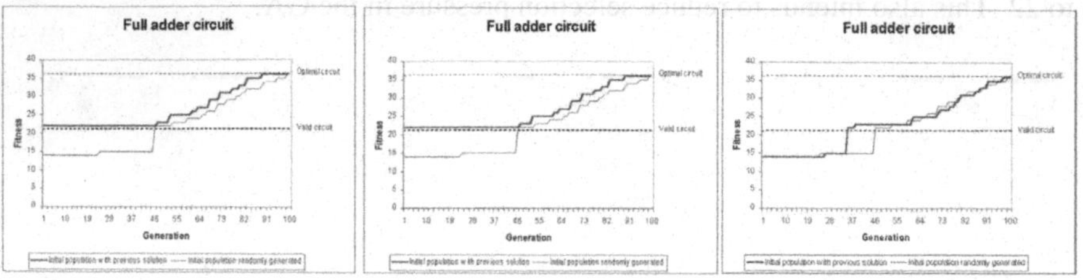

Fig. 3. Comparison of results for the first (top left), second (top right) and third (bottom) experiments. The label "experiment" indicates the runs in which we used cases previously generated by other runs of our GA (i.e., use of the case base)

7 Conclusions and Future Work

We have illustrated the potential of combining CBR with a GA to improve performance. The introduction of domain-specific knowledge within a GA is not straightforward, and care must be taken of not biasing the search too strongly as to produce premature convergence. The mixture of individuals proposed in this work (10% of the population were taken from the case base and 90% were randomly generated) seems to be a good choice, at least for the small and medium size circuits used in our experiments [7] (many details were excluded due to space limitations). However, more experimentation in this direction is still necessary. Our approach extends some of the previous efforts to extract design patterns from a GA used to design circuits [6, 9], since we show not only how these patterns can be extracted, but also how can they be reused by a GA to design more complex circuits using as building blocks the circuits previously solved. Furthermore we have put forward the view that the analysis of evolutionary algorithms results can be regarded as a discovery engine of well-known laws or theorems, and new principles or theorems. We studied this idea in the context of digital logic. We suggested that new principles can be discovered by examining a series of evolved designs, in our case, for some arithmetic logic circuits. We examined the concept of the space of all circuit representations, but we feel that similar ideas may be well carried over the general field of design.

Acknowledgements

The first author acknowledges to some students in the UAEM for doing some of the analysis shown in this paper. The second author acknowledges partial support from CINVESTAV through project JIRA'2001/08, and from CONACyT through the NSF-

CONACyT project No. 32999-A. The third author acknowledges partial support for this work by grant No. 01-02-202-111 from Consejo de Ciencia y Tecnología del Estado de Guanajuato (CONCyTEG).

References

1. C.A. Coello Coello, A.D. Christiansen, and A. Hernández Aguirre. Use of Evolutionary Techniques to Automate the Design of Combinational Circuits. *International Journal of Smart Engineering System Design*, 2(4):299-314, (June 2000).
2. V. Kolodner. *Case Based Reasoning*. Morgan Kaufmann Publishers, San Mateo, California, (1993).
3. S.J. Louis. *Genetic Algorithms as a Computational Tool for Design*. PhD thesis, Department of Computer Science, Indiana University, (August 1993).
4. S.J. Louis and J. Johnson. Solving Similar Problems using Genetic Algorithms Case-Based Memory. In Thomas Bäck, editor, *Proceedings of the Seventh International Conference on Genetic Algorithms*, pages 283-290, San Francisco, California, (1997). Morgan Kaufmann Publishers.
5. S.J. Louis, G. McGraw, and R. Wycko. Case-based reasoning assisted explanation of genetic algorithm results. *Journal of Experimental and Theoretical Artificial Intelligence*, 5:21-37, (1993).
6. J. Miller, T. Kalganova, N. Lipnitskaya, and D. Job. The Genetic Algorithm as a Discovery Engine: Strange Circuits and New Principles. In *Proceedings of the AISB Symposium on Creative Evolutionary Systems* (CES'99), Edinburgh, UK, (1999).
7. E. Islas Pérez. *Development of a Learning Platform using Case Based Reasoning and Genetic Algorithms. Case Study: Optimization of Combinational Logic Circuits*. Master's thesis, Maestría en Inteligencia Artificial, Facultad de Física e Inteligencia Artificial, Universidad Veracruzana, November (2000).
8. C. L. Ramsey and J.J. Grefenstette. Case-Based Initialization of Genetic Algorithms. In Stephanie Forrest, editor, *Proceedings of the Fifth International Conference on Genetic Algorithms*, pages 84-91, San Mateo, California, (1993). Morgan Kauffman Publishers.
9. P. Thomson. Circuit Evolution and Visualisation. In Julian Miller, Adrian Thompson, Peter Thomson, and Terence C. Fogarty, editors, *Evolvable Systems: From Biology to Hardware*, pages 229-240. Springer-Verlag, Edinburgh, Scotland, (April 2000).

Time-Domain Segmentation and Labelling of Speech with Fuzzy-Logic Post-Correction Rules

O. Mayora-Ibarra[1] and F. Curatelli[2]

[1] ITESM, Campus Cuernavaca, Av. Paseo de la Reforma 182-A, Lomas de Cuernavaca Temixco, Mor. C.P. 62589, México
[2] DIBE, Universitá di Genova, Via Opera Pia 11A, 16145 Genova, Italy

Abstract. In speech recognition, the procurement of accurate patterns that describe an input signal is a crucial task. Frequency-domain processing provides with rich information for such signal descriptions. However a first interpretation of the time-domain characteristics of the speech utterances may be enough for obtaining important information contained in the signal in a faster way. This paper shows that segmentation and labelling of speech may be performed using only time-domain information in an exact and accurate way. The method obtains syllable and phoneme level segmentation in two stages. The first identifies sonority decrease intervals for estimating transitions between syllables. The second, refines the placement of boundaries using a set of fuzzy-rules that compared current time-marks with previously computed syllable-transition values. The system was tested using an Italian language digit database. The reported results show that the accuracy of the inter-syllabic boundary placements get improved when using the fuzzy-correction method.

1 Introduction

Traditionally, manual speech segmentation has been considered a time consuming, tedious and prone to human-error task [1]. The development of new techniques that enable automatic segmentation and labelling of speech are therefore highly useful and sought-after by speech technology researchers. The main role that automatic speech segmentation has in speech recognition developments consists in simplifying the process of word matching, that will be unfeasible in large vocabulary applications, to a more realistic syllable or phone-based matching. In this sense, the reference patterns will be reduced to a few syllable or phoneme level representations, capable of reconstructing any possible word in the vocabulary. Such approach will reduce memory requirements and minimise the computational complexity in large vocabulary developments.

The use of segmentation and labelling technologies has founded applications in two main areas of speech processing. The first one is related to speech recognition. In that case, segmentation is used for training and testing of continuous speech input as a sequence of spoken utterances. Segmentation of speech is usually performed first for

C.A. Coello Coello et al. (Eds.): MICAI 2002, LNAI 2313, pp. 138–145, 2002.

constructing user models during a training phase and then during the speech recognition stages. The second area where segmentation and labelling is of relevant use, refers to speech synthesis where quick adaptations in Text-To-Speech (TTS) systems are required to model a specific user's voice. In both applications it is necessary to create prosodic models for defining specific speakers.

The speech segmentation and labelling method proposed here is based on a complementary time-domain and fuzzy-logic approach. The selection of temporal parameters rather than frequency-domain features was motivated by the less computational complexity required for processing the speech signal with such kind of information processing [2] [3]. This consideration may be of relevance specially if we consider that some on-chip implementations are based on such approach [4]. The use of fuzzy-logic technology was motivated by the successful performance of such systems in speech segmentation applications [5] [6] [7], and especially in boundary post-correction developments [8]. In this work, we proposed a set of fuzzy-logic rules to reduce the erroneous estimations of the phone boundaries by comparing time-domain information and statistic historic boundary values. The rest of the paper is organised as follows. Section 2 introduces a general overview of syllable-based segmentation technology. In Section 3 the time-domain segmentation method and the fuzzy-logic correction technique are described. Section 4 outlines the experiment design and presents detailed results for boundary estimation before and after the fuzzy-logic correction. Some examples of syllable and phone labelling results are also presented in the same section. Finally, Section 5 presents some concluding remarks and outlines future work.

2 Syllable Based Segmentation

The use of syllables as the basis of speech recognition developments, provides a higher level of coarticulation for constructing words than phone-based systems. In consequence, the generation of synthesised speech can also be improved with such kind of approaches. The previous is due to the high influence that prosodic parameters (like pitch, stress, time) have for representing syllable segment models. However, syllable-based segmentation still focus the problem of managing large syllabic databases and efficiently handling the coarticulation effects by improving the articulation between adjacent segments. Some studies [9], have proposed the creation of different syllable categories to lower this last difficulty. An example of this can be seen by defining special types of syllables like "L" or "R" segments (left or right syllables) that are used to identify the first or last syllables of words respectively (therefore there is expected a specific kind of information before and after them).

One of the principal parameters used for time-domain segmentation of speech is the *sonority decrease*. This feature is related to the attenuation of the acoustic intensity of speech that occurs between the transition of adjacent syllables. It is commonly used to perform an analysis of an acoustic intensity function of the speech signal in the time domain in order to identify the interval in which that function assumes minimum values. These intervals correspond to the time frames in which the transition from one syllable to the next may occur.

3 System Overview

The segmentation method proposed in this work is performed in two different stages. The first one obtains time-domain segments by means of zero-crossing computations during the sonority-decrease intervals. The zero-crossing information is used to estimate the transition interval and to set preliminary boundary marks between syllables. The second phase refines the time marks obtained in the previous stage by comparing them with statistical boundary levels by means of a set of fuzzy logic rules. An overview of this system is shown in figure 1.

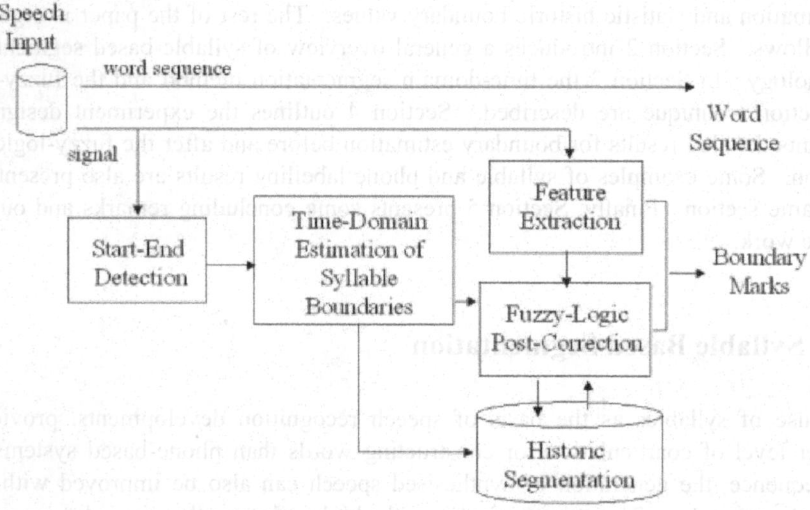

Fig. 1. Segmentation System Overview

3.1 Time Domain Segmentation

The first stage of the proposed syllable-bounding method refers to time-domain segmentation. The aim at this stage is to obtain an accurate identification of word-boundaries and to select a rough placement of syllable/phone time marks. First, the starting and ending points of the speech signal were obtained using a modified version of Rabiner's [10] well-known algorithm for isolated utterances The modified algorithm obtained starting and ending points in a semi-continuous speech stream. The next phase of the method was then to process the bounded speech signal in order to obtain the zero-crossings above an empirically selected offset value (higher than the threshold level used for obtaining the starting and ending points in Rabiner's work). An adequate selection of the offset level allows obtaining time intervals with only few peaks or not peaks at all and therefore, to identify sonority decrease intervals where the boundaries should be positioned.

In order to eliminate non-significant instants within the sonority decrease interval (the time between one syllable and the next) it was required to set inferior limits to the duration of both, the sonority decrease and to the syllable intervals. In this way, the sonority decrease starting and ending points were compacted in one single value in order to estimate the transition from one syllable and the next. An experimental value that provide adequate results was that of selecting the transition value 20 milliseconds before the left boundary of the sonority decrease intervals as shown in figure 2.

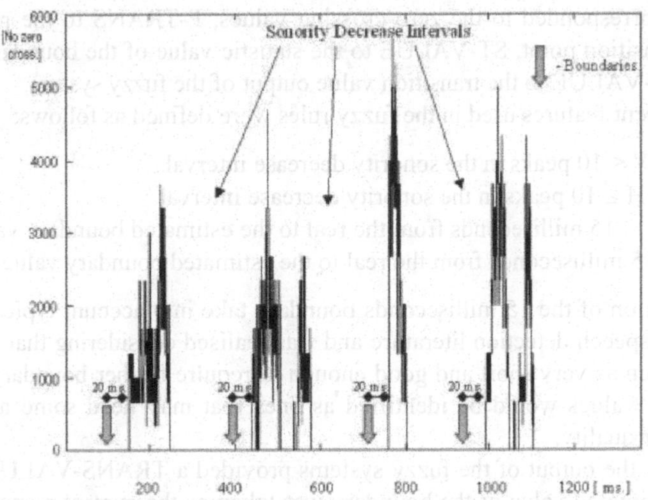

Fig. 2. Boundary Selection within Sonority-Decrease Interval

The method as far as this point didn't used any information about the content of the input speech signal. However, the use of previously defined words and phrases for training the speech recognition system, suggested to use the a-priori knowledge of the content of training speech in order to obtain two main advantages:

- Segmentation corrections in case the algorithm finds more or less syllables than expected.
- Use statistics from previous segmentation tests together with fuzzy logic rules to refine the boundary placement.

3.2 Fuzzy-Logic Refinement of Time Marks

The second step of the segmentation method, proposed a comparison of the previous boundary estimations with a historic file containing transition values associated to previously recorded utterances. These comparisons were used to correct the position of boundaries according to some fuzzy-logic rules criteria. The main motivation of using fuzzy rules for this task was that fuzzy logic provides a very coherent way of introducing human knowledge (that is fuzzy by nature) in computer-oriented systems. The knowledge introduced in this case was the initial boundary computations and the statistical transition values contained in the historic file. The proposed fuzzy rules are listed below:

IF (ZC is LOW => P-TRANS is HIGH)
IF (ZC is HIGH => P-TRANS is LOW)

IF ((P-TRANS is HIGH) and (ST-VALUE is CLOSE) => TRANS-VALUE=OK)
IF ((P-TRANS is HIGH) and (ST-VALUE is FAR) => TRANS-VALUE=VERIFY-1)
IF ((P-TRANS is LOW) and (ST-VALUE is CLOSE) => TRANS-VALUE=VERIFY-2)
IF ((P-TRANS is LOW) and (ST-VALUE is FAR) => TRANS-VALUE=REJECT)

where ZC corresponded to the zero-crossing values, P-TRANS to the probability of having a transition point, ST-VALUE to the statistic value of the boundary placement and TRANS-VALUE to the transition value output of the fuzzy system.

The different features used in the fuzzy rules were defined as follows:

- ZC-LOW < 10 peaks in the sonority decrease interval
- ZC-HIGH ≥ 10 peaks in the sonority decrease interval
- CLOSE < 15 milliseconds from the real to the estimated boundary value.
- FAR ≥ 15 milliseconds from the real to the estimated boundary value.

The selection of the 15 milliseconds boundary take into account typical time intervals used in speech detection literature and was realised considering that lower values should be seen as very short and good enough to require further boundary corrections while longer values would be identified as ones that may need some adjustment to increase their quality.

Whenever the output of the fuzzy systems provided a TRANS-VALUE=OK statement, the estimated value of the boundary was taken as the current response. In case that the system output a VERIFY attribute, a correction function computed the mean value between the estimated and the statistic data and then entered it as the proposed boundary. REJECTED estimations are treated by the method in a similar way than the "VERIFY" estimations with the only difference that the mean value criteria is applied twice instead of only one time (i.e. first the mean value between the statistic value and the original estimation and then between the same statistic value and the new estimation).

4 Results

The proposed method was tested using the SPK-IRST digit database for the Italian language [11]. The system was trained using repetitions of isolated occurrences of each digit. The trained samples were taken from the input of various speakers and were associated manually to construct several patterns for segmentation purposes composed by:

- Number of syllables in the word
- Number of phones in each syllable
- Length average of each syllable within the word
- Length average of each phone within the syllable

The system was tested using input from different speakers in a semi-continuous way (with short pauses between one word and the next). The identification of the starting and ending segments of each word as well as the intermediate syllables were compared to the graphically observed real values. The first stage output, therefore the first estimation values of the boundaries (before the fuzzy correction), show that the preliminary boundary setting was performed adequately (for a 15 ms. error interval) in 87% of the cases. The remaining 13% fell in the VERIFY 1 and 2 cases and were adjusted with the mean value criteria. The boundary placement after the fuzzy-rules correction was improved as shown in Table 1.

Table 1. Boundary placements for error margin < 15 ms

Fuzzy System Output	Before Correction	After Correction
OK	87%	95%
VERIFY-1	8%	3%
VERIFY-2	5%	2%
REJECT	0%	0%

A detailed listing of the syllable labelling for 8 samples of the word "zero" (correspondent in Italian to the digit "0") are shown in Table 2. The results presented in this table were obtained after the fuzzy-logic correction.

Table 2. Syllable labelling for the digit "zero" (expressed in milliseconds)

Samples ZERO	Type of Segmentation	ZE Start-End	RO Start-End
Sample 1 ZERO	Autom.-Seg.	164-435	435-596
	Manual-Seg.	155-427	427-600
Sample 2 ZERO	Autom.-Seg.	126-420	420-616
	Manual-Seg	126-418	418-617
Sample 3 ZERO	Autom.-Seg.	154-443	443-599
	Manual-Seg.	151-429	429-604
Sample 4 ZERO	Autom.-Seg.	139-405	405-517
	Manual-Seg	148-403	403-519
Sample 5 ZERO	Autom.-Seg.	187-478	478-648
	Manual-Seg.	181-472	472-659
Sample 6 ZERO	Autom.-Seg.	86-355	355-506
	Manual-Seg	82-346	346-514
Sample 7 ZERO	Autom.-Seg.	213-508	508-660
	Manual-Seg.	207-497	497-664
Sample 8 ZERO	Autom.-Seg.	179-451	451-606
	Manual-Seg	174-446	446-611

Table 3 shows an extension of the previous results when expanded from syllable to phone labelling. In this case, the attribute levels of the fuzzy rules were re-tuned to appropriate values for phone matching. In both cases, syllable and phone labelling, the results were compared to the segmentation values obtained manually from the displayed waveform. For every phone unit there has been reported the initial and final time expressed in milliseconds.

Table 3. Extension to phone labelling for the digit "zero" (expressed in ms.)

Samples ZERO	Type of Segmentation	Z Start-End	E Start-End	R Start-End	O Start-End
Sample 1	Autom.-Seg.	164-232	232-435	435-472	472-596
ZERO	Manual-Seg.	155-223	223-427	427-469	469-600
Sample 2	Autom.-Seg.	126-200	200-420	420-465	465-616
ZERO	Manual-Seg	126-194	194-418	418-458	458-617
Sample 3	Autom.-Seg.	154-226	226-443	443-479	479-599
ZERO	Manual-Seg.	151-212	212-429	429-472	472-604
Sample 4	Autom.-Seg.	139-206	206-405	405-447	447-517
ZERO	Manual-Seg	148-198	198-403	403-452	452-519
Sample 5	Autom.-Seg.	187-260	260-478	478-517	517-648
ZERO	Manual-Seg.	181-257	257-472	472-517	517-659
Sample 6	Autom.-Seg.	86-153	153-355	355-390	390-506
ZERO	Manual-Seg	82-148	148-346	346-387	387-514
Sample 7	Autom.-Seg.	213-287	287-508	508-543	543-660
ZERO	Manual-Seg.	207-278	278-497	497-537	537-664
Sample 8	Autom.-Seg.	179-247	247-451	451-487	487-606
ZERO	Manual-Seg	174-242	242-446	446-488	488-611

5 Conclusions

In this paper it was introduced a two-stage algorithm for performing automatic segmentation and labelling of speech. The first stage identified sonority decrease intervals from incoming speech and performs an initial estimation of boundary transitions between syllables. The second part of the method, consisted in refining the placement of the original boundaries by using a set of fuzzy-logic rules that compared the time-marks obtained in the first stage with a historic file that contained previously stored-transition values. The experiments were done using an Italian language database consistent in a series of digits spoken by different users. The proposed segmentation and correction-methods demonstrated to perform with high accuracy for boundary placement and for labelling purposes within the 15 ms. error margin proposed in this work. The selection of this error margin was done considering the time-distance between manually set boundaries and the output given by our method. Good results within this error margin range were also reported when extended the segmentation from syllable to phones. Future work will consist in exploring other parameters given by the time-domain method (i.e. the pitch and other formant information) and updating the fuzzy-logic rules with such information.

References

1. A. Ljolje and M. D. Riley, "Automatic Segmentation and Labelling of Speech", Proc. IC-ASSP 91, (1991) pp. 473-476..
2. J. W. Pitton, K Wang and B Juang, ``Time-frequency analysis and auditory modeling for automatic recognition of speech", Proceedings of the IEEE, Vol. 84, No. 9, Sep. (1996), pp.1199-1214.
3. J. Saunders, "Real-time discrimination of broadcast speech/music," in Proc. Int. Conf. Acoustic, Speech, and Signal Processing (ICASSP-96), vol. 2, Atlanta, GA, May 7-10, (1996), pp. 993-996.
4. N. Kumar, W. Himmelbauer, G. Cauwenberghs and A. Andreou, "An Analog VLSI Chip with Asynchronous Interface for Auditory Feature Extraction," IEEE Trans. Circuits and Systems II: Analog and Digital Signal Processing, 45 (5), (1998), pp 600--606,.
5. S. Raptis and G. Carayannis, "Fuzzy Logic for Rule-Based Formant Speech Synthesis", Proc. EUROSPEECH 97, (1997), pp. 1599-1602..
6. C. T. Hsieh, M.C. Su, E. Lai and C.H. Hsu., "A Segmentation Method for Continuous Speech Utilizing Hybrid Neuro-Fuzzy Network" Journal of Information Science and Engineering. Vol 15 (1999), pp. 615-628,.
7. C. T. Hsieh and S. C. Chien, "Speech segmentation and clustering problem based on fuzzy rules and transition states," Twelfth International Association of Science and Technology for Development International Conference on Applied Information, (1994), pp.291-294..
8. D. Torre Toledano, M. A. Rodríguez Crespo, J. G. Escalada Sardina "Trying to Mimic Human Segmentation of Speech Using HMM and Fuzzy Logic Post-correction Rules" Proceedings of third ESCA/COSCOSDA International Workshop on Speech Synthesis. November (1998)
9. I. Kopecek. "Automatic Segmentation into Syllable Segments", Proceedings of First International Conference on Language Resources and Evaluation, May (1998), pp. 1275-1279.
10. L. R. Rabiner and M. R. Sambur, "An algorithm for determinig the endpoints of isolated utterances," The Bell System Technical Journal, Vol. 54, No. 2, (1975), pp. 297-315.
11. SPK Isolated Digit Database (in Italian language), ITC-IRST, ELRA-S0049.

IL MT System. Evaluation for Spanish-English Pronominal Anaphora Generation*

Jesús Peral and Antonio Ferrández

Departamento de Lenguajes y Sistemas Informáticos
Universidad de Alicante. Alicante, Spain
{jperal,antonio}@dlsi.ua.es

Abstract. In this paper the pronominal anaphora generation module of a complete interlingua Machine Translation (MT) approach is presented. The approach named AGIR (*Anaphora Generation with an Interlingua Representation*) allows the generation of anaphoric expressions into the target language from the interlingua representation of the source text. AGIR uses different kinds of knowledge (lexical, syntactic, morphological and semantic information) to solve the Natural Language Processing (NLP) problems of the source text. The paper presents the evaluation of the generation of English and Spanish (including zero pronouns) third person personal pronouns into the target language. The following results have been obtained: a precision of 80.39% and 84.77% in the generation of Spanish and English pronominal anaphora respectively.

1 Introduction

The problem of anaphoric expressions is one of the most difficult to solve in Natural Language Processing (NLP). This problem must be treated as two different processes: resolution and generation. The first one searches for the discourse entity to which the anaphor refers to. On the other hand, the process of generation consists on the creation of references over a discourse entity.

In the context of Machine Translation (MT) the resolution of anaphoric expressions is of crucial importance in order to translate/generate them correctly into the target language. After evaluating many commercial and experimental MT systems we observe that one of the main problems of them is that they do not carry out a correct pronominal anaphora generation. Solving the anaphora and extracting the antecedent are key issues in a correct generation into the target language. Unfortunately, the majority of MT systems do not deal with anaphora resolution and their successful operation usually does not go beyond the sentence level. This paper presents a complete approach that allows pronoun resolution and generation into the target language.

AGIR (*Anaphora Generation with an Interlingua Representation*) system works on unrestricted texts unlike other systems, the KANT interlingua system [10], the Météo system [3], the Candide system [2], etc. that are designed

* This paper has been partially supported by the Spanish Government (CICYT) project number TIC2000-0664-C02-02.

C.A. Coello Coello et al. (Eds.): MICAI 2002, LNAI 2313, pp. 146–155, 2002.

for well-defined domains. Although full parsing of these texts could be applied, we have used partial parsing of the texts due to the unavoidable incompleteness of the grammar. This is a main difference with the majority of the interlingua systems such as the DLT system based on a modification of Esperanto [17], the Rosetta system which is experimenting with Montague semantics as the basis for an interlingua [1], the KANT system, etc. as they use full parsing of the text.

After the parsing and solving pronominal anaphora, an interlingua representation of the whole text is obtained. From this interlingua representation, the generation of anaphora (including intersentential anaphora), the detection of coreference chains of the whole text and the generation of Spanish zero-pronouns into English have been carried out, issues that are hardly considered by other systems. Furthermore, this approach can be used for other different applications, e.g. Information Retrieval, Summarization, etc.

In the following section (section 2), the complete approach that includes Analysis and Generation modules will be described. These modules will be explained in detail in the next two sections. In section 5, the Generation module has been evaluated in order to measure the efficiency of our proposal. Finally, the conclusions of this work will be presented.

2 AGIR Architecture

AGIR system architecture (figure 1) is based on the general architecture of a MT system which uses an interlingua strategy. Translation is carried out in two stages: from the source language to the interlingua, and from the interlingua into the target language. Modules for analysis are independent from modules for generation. In this paper, although we have only studied the Spanish and English languages, our approach is easily extended to other languages, i.e. multilingual system, in the sense that any analysis module can be linked to any generation module. As can be observed in figure 1, there are two independent modules in the process of generation: Analysis and Generation modules.

3 AGIR's Analysis Module

In AGIR, the analysis is carried out by means of SUPAR (*Slot Unification Parser for Anaphora resolution*) system [5]. SUPAR is a computational system focused on anaphora resolution. It can deal with several kinds of anaphora, such as pronominal anaphora, one-anaphora, surface-count anaphora and definite descriptions. In this paper, we focus on pronominal anaphora resolution and generation into the target language. The input of SUPAR is a grammar defined by means of the grammatical formalism SUG (*Slot Unification Grammar*). A translator that transforms SUG rules into Prolog clauses has been developed. This translator will provide a Prolog program that will parse each sentence. SUPAR allows to carry out either a full or a partial parsing of the text, with the same parser and grammar. Here, partial parsing techniques have been used due to the

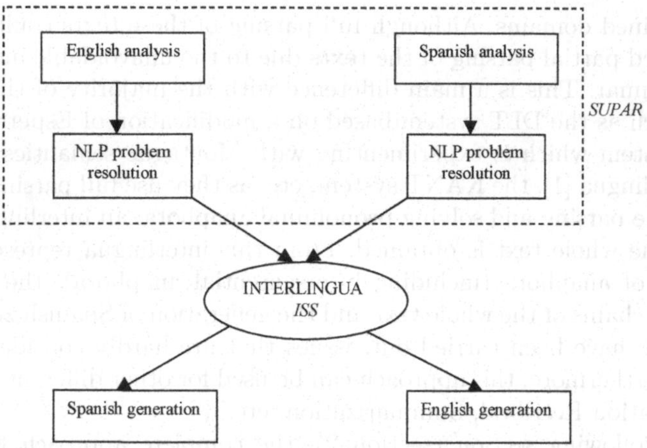

Fig. 1. AGIR architecture

unavoidable incompleteness of the grammar and the use of unrestricted texts (corpora) as inputs.

The analysis of the source text is carried out in several stages. The first stage of the analysis module is the lexical and morphological analysis of the input text. Due to the use of unrestricted texts as input, the system obtains the lexical and morphological information of the text's lexical units from the output of a part-of-speech (POS) tagger. The word, as it appears in the corpus, its lemma and its POS tag (with morphological information) is supplied for each lexical unit in the corpus.

The next stage is the parsing of the text (it includes the lexical and morphological information extracted in the previous stage). The corpus is split into sentences before applying the parsing. The output will be the Slot Structure (SS) that stores the necessary information[1] for NLP problem resolution.

In the third stage a module of Word Sense Disambiguation (WSD) is used to obtain a single sense for the different text's lexical units. The lexical resources WordNet [9] and EurowordNet [16] have been used in this stage.

The SS enriched with the information of previous stages will be the input for the following stage in which NLP problems (anaphora, extraposition, ellipsis, etc.) will be treated and solved.

After the anaphora resolution stage, a new Slot Structure (SS') is obtained. In this new structure the correct antecedent (chosen from the possible candidates after applying a method based on restrictions and preferences [5]) for each anaphoric expression will be stored together with its morphological and semantic

[1] The SS stores for each constituent the following information: constituent name (NP, PP, etc.), semantic and morphological information, discourse marker (identifier of the entity or discourse object) and the SS of its subconstituents.

information. The new structure SS' will be the input for the last stage of the Analysis module.

In the last stage AGIR generates the interlingua representation of the whole text. This is the main difference between AGIR and the rest of MT systems that carry out a processing of the input text sentence by sentence. The interlingua representation will allow the correct generation of the intrasentential and intersentential pronominal anaphora into the target language. Moreover, AGIR allows the identification of coreference chains of the text and their subsequent generation into the target language.

The interlingua representation of the input text is based on the clause as main unit of this representation. Once the text has been split into clauses, AGIR uses a complex feature structure for each clause. It is composed of semantic roles and features extracted from the SS of the clause. Semantic roles that have been used in this approach are the following: ACTION, AGENT, THEME and MODIFIER that correspond to verb, subject, object and prepositional phrases of the clause respectively. The notation we have used is based on the representation used in KANT interlingua. To identify these semantic roles when partial parsing has been carried out and no semantic knowledge is used, the following heuristic has been applied:

H_1 Let us assume that the NP parsed before the verb is the agent of the clause. In the same way, the NP parsed after the verb is the theme of the clause. Finally, all the PP found in the clause are its modifiers.

It is important to emphasize that the interlingua lexical unit has been represented in AGIR using the word and its correct sense in WordNet. After accessing to the ILI (Inter-Lingual-Index) module of EuroWordNet, we will be able to generate the lexical unit into the target language.

Once the semantic roles have been identified, the interlingua representation will store the clauses with their features, the different entities that have appeared in the text and the relations between them (such as anaphoric relations). This representation will be the input for the generation module. More details about the interlingua representation in AGIR have been presented in [15,13].

4 AGIR's Generation Module

The interlingua representation of the source text is taken as input of the Generation module. The output of this module is the target text, that is, the representation of the source text's meaning with words of the target language. In this paper we are only describing the generation of third person personal pronouns into the target language, so we have only focused on the differences (syntactic and morphological) between the Spanish and English languages in the generation of the pronoun. These differences are what we have named discrepancies (a detailed study of Spanish-English-Spanish discrepancies is shown in [15,13]).

4.1 Syntactic Discrepancies

Elliptical Zero-Subject Constructions (Zero-Pronouns). The Spanish language allows to omit the pronominal subject of the sentences. These omitted pronouns are usually named zero pronouns. While in other languages, zero pronouns may appear in either the subject's or the object's grammatical position, (e.g. Japanese), in Spanish texts, zero pronouns only appear in the position of the subject. In [14,6] the processing of Spanish zero pronouns in AGIR is presented. Basically, in order to generate Spanish zero pronouns into English, they must first be located in the text (ellipsis detection), and then resolved (anaphora resolution). At the ellipsis detection stage, information about the zero pronoun (e.g. person, gender, and number) must first be obtained from the verb of the clause and then used to identify the antecedent of the pronoun (resolution stage).

Pleonastic Pronouns. Sometimes pronouns can be used in a non-referential construction, that is, appear due to some requirement in the grammar of the language. These pronouns are usually named pleonastic. In AGIR, the pleonastic use of pronoun *it* has been detected before the anaphora resolution stage and thereby will not be resolved. These pronouns will appear marked like pleonastics in the interlingua representation, they will not have antecedent and they will not be generated into Spanish. In order to detect pleonastic *it* pronouns in AGIR, a set of rules, based on pattern recognition, that allows the identification of this kind of pronouns is constructed. These rules are based on the study developed by other authors [8,11] that faced with this problem in a similar way.

4.2 Morphological Discrepancies

Number Discrepancies. This problem is generated by the discrepancy between words of different languages that express the same concept. These words can be referred to a singular pronoun in the source language and to a plural pronoun in the target language. In order to take into account number discrepancies in the generation of the pronoun into English or Spanish a set of morphological (number) rules is constructed. The left-hand side of the number rule contains the interlingua representation of the pronoun and the right-hand side contains the pronoun in the target language.

Gender Discrepancies. Gender discrepancies came from the existing morphological differences between different languages. For instance, English has less morphological information than Spanish. The English plural personal pronoun *they* can be translated into the Spanish pronouns *ellos* (masculine) or *ellas* (feminine), the singular personal pronoun *it* can be translated into *él/éste* (masculine) or *ella/ésta* (feminine), etc. In order to take into account gender discrepancies in the generation of the pronoun into English or Spanish a set of morphological (gender) rules is constructed.

5 Evaluation of Generation Module

The generation module takes the interlingua representation as input. Previously, pleonastic *it* pronouns have been detected (with a **P**recision[2] of 88.75%), Spanish zero pronouns have been detected (89.20% **P**) and resolved (81.38% **P**), and anaphoric third person personal pronouns have been resolved in English and Spanish (80.25% **P** and 82.19% **P** respectively).

Once the interlingua representation has been obtained, the method proposed for pronominal anaphora generation into the target language is based on the treatment of number and gender discrepancies.

5.1 Pronominal Anaphora Generation into Spanish

In this experiment the generation of English third person personal pronouns into the Spanish ones has been evaluated.

We have tested the method on both literary and manual texts. In the first instance, we used a portion of the SemCor collection (presented in [7]) that contains a set of 11 documents (23,788 words) where all content words are annotated with the most appropriate WordNet sense. SemCor corpus contains literary texts about different topics (laws, sports, religion, nature, etc.) and by different authors. In the second instance, the method was tested on a portion of MTI[3] corpus that contains 7 documents (101,843 words). MTI corpus contains Computer Science manuals about different topics (commercial programs, word processing applications, device instructions, etc.).

We randomly selected a subset of the SemCor corpus (three documents –6,473 words–) and another subset of the MTI corpus (two documents –24,264 words–) as training corpus. The training corpus was used for improving the number and gender rules. The remaining fragments of the corpus were reserved for test data.

We conducted a blind test over the entire test corpus applying the number and gender rules. The obtained results appear in table 1.

Table 1 shows the anaphoric pronouns of each document classified by semantic roles: AGENT, THEME and MODIFIER. The last three columns represent the number of pronouns successfully resolved, the total number of pronouns resolved and the obtained **P**recision, respectively. For instance, the a13 document of the SemCor corpus contains 17 pronouns with semantic role of AGENT, 2 pronouns with semantic role of THEME and 3 pronouns with semantic role of MODIFIER. The **P**recision obtained in this document was of 95.45% (21/22).

[2] By **P**recision we mean the number of pronouns successfully resolved divided by the total number of pronouns resolved in the text. A detailed study of the evaluation of the different tasks carried out in order to obtain the interlingua representation in AGIR can be found in [12].

[3] This corpus has been provided by the Computational Linguistics Research Group of the School of Humanities, Languages and Social Studies –University of Wolverhampton, England–. The corpus is anaphorically annotated indicating the anaphors and their correct antecedents.

Discussion. In the generation of English third person personal pronouns into the Spanish ones an overall **P**recision of 80.39% (582/724) has been obtained. Specifically, 90.16% **P** and 75.11% **P** were obtained in SemCor and MTI corpus respectively.

Table 1. Generation of pronominal anaphora into Spanish. Evaluation phase

Corpus		Subject	Complement		Correct	Total	P (%)
		AGENT	THEME	MODIF.			
SEMCOR	a02	21	5	1	23	27	85,19
	a11	10	5	0	14	15	93,33
	a13	17	2	3	21	22	95,45
	a14	40	10	1	48	51	94,12
	a15	32	5	4	34	41	82,93
	d02	14	2	3	18	19	94,74
	d03	13	0	1	12	14	85,71
	d04	50	6	9	59	65	90,77
	SEMCOR TOTAL	**197**	**35**	**22**	**229**	**254**	**90,16**
MTI	CDROM	38	24	7	47	69	68,12
	PSW	24	36	2	52	62	83,87
	WINDOWS	16	19	2	30	37	81,08
	SCANWORX	95	87	11	142	193	73,58
	GIMP	66	33	10	82	109	75,23
	MTI TOTAL	**239**	**199**	**32**	**353**	**470**	**75,11**
	TOTAL	**436**	**234**	**54**	**582**	**724**	**80,39**

From these results we have extracted the following conclusions:

- In SemCor corpus all the instances of the English pronouns *he*, *she*, *him* and *her* have been correctly generated into Spanish. It is justified by two reasons:
  - The semantic roles of these pronouns have been correctly identified in all the cases.
  - These pronouns contain the necessary grammatical information (gender an number) that allows the correct generation into Spanish, independently of the antecedent proposed as solution by the AGIR system.

  The errors in the generation of pronouns *it*, *they* and *them* have been originated by different causes:

  - Mistakes in the anaphora resolution stage, i.e., the antecedent proposed by the system is not the correct one (44.44% of the global mistakes).This causes an incorrect generation into Spanish mainly due to the proposed antecedent and the correct one have different grammatical gender.

    - Mistakes in the identification of the semantic role of the pronouns that cause the application of an incorrect morphological rule (44.44%). These mistakes are mainly originated by an incorrect process of clause splitting.
    - Mistakes originated by the electronic dictionary from English to Spanish (11.12%). Two circumstances can occur: (a) the word does not appear in the dictionary; and (b) the word's gender in the dictionary is different to the real word's gender due to the word has different meanings.
- In MTI corpus, nearly all the pronouns are instances of the pronouns *it*, *they* and *them* (96.25% of the total pronouns). The errors in the generation of these pronouns are originated by the same causes than in SemCor corpus but with different percentages:
    - Mistakes in the anaphora resolution stage (22.86% of the mistakes).
    - Mistakes in the identification of the pronouns' semantic role (62.86%).
    - Mistakes originated by the English-Spanish dictionary (14.28%).

5.2 Pronominal Anaphora Generation into English

In this experiment the generation of Spanish third person personal pronouns (including zero pronouns) into the English ones has been evaluated.

We have tested the method on literary texts. We used a portion of the Lexesp corpus that contains a set of 31 documents (38,999 words). Lexesp corpus contains literary texts about different topics (politics, sports, etc.) from different genres and by different authors.

We randomly selected a subset of the Lexesp corpus (three documents –6,457 words–) as training corpus. The remaining fragments of the corpus were reserved for test data.

We conducted a blind test over the entire test corpus applying the number and gender rules. The obtained results appear in table 2.

Discussion. In the generation of Spanish third person personal pronouns into the English ones an overall **P**recision of 84.77% (657/775) has been obtained. From these results we have extracted the following conclusions:

- All the instances of the Spanish plural pronouns (*ellos*, *ellas*, *les*, *los*, *las* and zero pronouns in plural) have been correctly generated into English. It is justified by two reasons:
    - The semantic roles of these pronouns have been correctly identified in all the cases.
    - The equivalent English pronouns (*they* and *them*) lack gender information, i.e., are valid for masculine and feminine, then the antecedent's gender does not influence the generation of these pronouns.
- The errors occurred in the generation of the Spanish singular pronouns (*él*, *ella*, *le*, *lo*, *la* and zero pronouns in singular). They have been originated by different causes:
    - Mistakes in the anaphora resolution stage (79.66%).
    - Mistakes in the application of the heuristic used to identify the antecedent's semantic type (20.34%). This fact involves the application of an incorrect morphological rule.

Conclusion

In this paper the pronominal anaphora generation module of a complete interlingua MT approach (for Spanish and English languages) is presented and evaluated. The interlingua representation of the whole text is one of the main advantages of our system due to several problems, that are hardly solved by the majority of MT systems, can be treated and solved. These problems are the generation of intersentential anaphora, the detection of coreference chains and the generation of Spanish zero-pronouns into English. In the evaluation, the following results have been obtained: a Precision of 80.39% and 84.77% in the generation of English and Spanish personal pronouns (including zero pronouns) into the target language respectively.

Table 2. Generation of pronominal anaphora into English. Evaluation phase

Corpus		Subject	Complement		Correct	Total	P (%)
		AGENT	THEME	MODIF.			
LEXESP	txt1	19	3	1	21	23	91,30
	txt2	35	7	1	33	43	76,74
	txt3	21	4	1	19	26	73,08
	txt4	13	4	1	15	18	83,33
	txt5	13	4	1	14	18	77,78
	txt6	17	1	0	16	18	88,89
	txt7	22	3	4	28	29	96,55
	txt8	10	0	0	9	10	90
	txt9	9	3	1	8	13	61,54
	txt10	17	2	1	19	20	95
	txt11	7	0	1	7	8	87,5
	txt12	25	4	0	29	29	100
	txt13	16	0	0	12	16	75
	txt14	11	0	0	10	11	90,91
	txt15	16	3	5	18	24	75
	txt16	11	1	2	13	14	92,86
	txt17	14	1	0	11	15	73,33
	txt18	9	4	0	10	13	76,92
	txt19	7	0	1	7	8	87,5
	txt20	17	3	1	13	21	61,90
	txt21	4	2	0	6	6	100
	txt22	12	1	2	15	15	100
	txt23	15	4	2	19	21	90,48
	txt24	21	7	2	25	30	83,33
	txt25	92	11	5	100	108	92,59
	txt26	132	16	11	129	159	81,13
	txt27	24	6	1	27	31	87,10
	txt28	21	5	2	24	28	85,71
	TOTAL	**630**	**99**	**46**	**657**	**775**	**84,77**

References

1. L. Appelo and J. Landsbergen. The machine translation project Rosetta. In T.C. Gerhardt, editor, *I. International Conference on the State of the Art in Machine Translation in America, Asia and Europe: Proceedings of IAI-MT86, IAI/EUROTRA-D*, pages 34–51, Saarbrucken (Germany), 1986.
2. A. Berger, P. Brown, S.D. Pietra, V.D. Pietra, J. Gillett, J. Lafferty, R.L. Mercer, H. Printz, and L. Ures. The Candide system for Machine Translation. In *Proceedings of the ARPA Workshop on Speech and Natural Language*, pages 157–163, Morgan Kaufman Publishers, 1994.
3. J. Chandioux. MÉTÉO: un système opérationnel pour la traduction automatique des bulletins météreologiques destinés au grand public. *META*, 21:127–133, 1976.
4. R. Dale. *Generating referring expresions: constructing descriptions in a domain of objects and processes.* MIT Press, Cambridge, Mass, 1992.
5. A. Ferrández, M. Palomar, and L. Moreno. An empirical approach to Spanish anaphora resolution. *Machine Translation*, 14(3/4):191–216, 1999.
6. A. Ferrández and J. Peral. A computational approach to zero-pronouns in Spanish. In *Proceedings of the 38th Annual Meeting of the Association for Computational Linguistics (ACL'2000)*, pages 166–172, Hong Kong (China), 2000.
7. S. Landes, C. Leacock, and R. Tengi. Building semantic concordances. In C. Fellbaum, editor, *WordNet: An Electronic Lexical Database*, pages 199–216. MIT Press, Cambridge, Mass, 1998.
8. S. Lappin and H.J. Leass. An algorithm for pronominal anaphora resolution. *Computational Linguistics*, 20(4):535–561, 1994.
9. G. Miller, R. Beckwith, C. Fellbaum, D. Gross, and K. Miller. WordNet: An on-line lexical database. *International journal of lexicography*, 3(4):235–244, 1990.
10. T. Mitamura, E. Nyberg, and J. Carbonell. An efficient interlingua translation system for multi-lingual document production. In *Proceedings of Machine Translation Summit III*, Washington, DC (USA), 1991.
11. C.D. Paice and G.D. Husk. Towards the automatic recognition of anaphoric features in English text: the impersonal pronoun "it". *Computer Speech and Language*, 2:109–132, 1987.
12. J. Peral. *Resolución y generación de la anáfora pronominal en español e inglés en un sistema interlingua de Traducción Automática.* PhD thesis, University of Alicante, 2001.
13. J. Peral and A. Ferrández. An application of the Interlingua System ISS for Spanish-English pronominal anaphora generation. In *Proceedings of the Third AMTA/SIG-IL Workshop on Applied Interlinguas: Practical Applications of Interlingual Approaches to NLP (ANLP/NAACL'2000)*, pages 42–51, Seattle, Washington (USA), 2000.
14. J. Peral and A. Ferrández. Generation of Spanish zero-pronouns into English. In D.N. Christodoulakis, editor, *Natural Language Processing - NLP'2000*, volume 1835 of *Lecture Notes in Artificial Intelligence*, pages 252–260, Patras (Greece), 2000. Springer-Verlag.
15. J. Peral, M. Palomar, and A. Ferrández. Coreference-oriented Interlingual Slot Structure and Machine Translation. In *Proceedings of the ACL Workshop Coreference and its Applications*, pages 69–76, College Park, Maryland (USA), 1999.
16. P. Vossen. EuroWordNet: Building a Multilingual Database with WordNets for European Languages. *The ELRA Newsletter*, 3(1):7–12, 1998.
17. A.P.M. Witkam. *Distributed language translation: feasibility study of multilingual facility for videotex information networks.* BSO, Utrecht, 1983.

Out-of-Vocabulary Word Modeling and Rejection for Spanish Keyword Spotting Systems

Heriberto Cuayáhuitl and Ben Serridge

SpeechWorks International Inc.
KM 5.6 Lateral Recta Cholula, Fraccionamiento Villa Futura,
Lote 10, Piso 2, San Andrés Cholula, Puebla, Mexico 72820
{heriberto,ben}@speechworks.com
www.speechworks.com

Abstract. This paper presents a combination of out-of-vocabulary (OOV) word modeling and rejection techniques in an attempt to accept utterances embedding a keyword and reject utterances with non-keywords. The goal of this research is to develop a robust, task-independent Spanish keyword spotter and to develop a method for optimizing confidence thresholds for a particular context. To model OOV words, we employed both word and sub-word units as fillers, combined with n-gram language models. We also introduce a methodology for optimizing confidence thresholds to control the tradeoffs between acceptance, confirmation, and rejection of utterances. Our experiments are based on a Mexican Spanish auto-attendant system using the SpeechWorks recognizer release 6.5 Second Edition, in which we achieved a reduction in error of 8.9% as compared to the baseline system. Most of the error reduction is attributed to better keyword detection in utterances that contain both keywords and OOV words.

1 Introduction

In directed-dialog systems deployed in Mexico, we have observed a high percentage of out-of-vocabulary speech, especially immediately following deployment. Most of the out-of-vocabulary (OOV) data are due to noise in the environment and to speech artifacts such as partial words. It is clearly important to improve the performance of such systems on OOV utterances in order to identify when a recognizer's hypothesis is correct and when it may be an error. In the past, three methods have been proposed for attacking the OOV problem: word spotting, confidence scoring and rejection. In the first method, some of the word spotters proposed were HHM-based [1, 5] continuous speech recognition systems, while other investigations were segment-based [2, 3, 4]. In these systems, a variety of units have been investigated for the purpose of modeling out-of-vocabulary speech, ranging from phonemes to syllables to entire words. N-gram language models for the transitions between keywords and filler models were used to constrain the OOV model.

C.A. Coello Coello et al. (Eds.): MICAI 2002, LNAI 2313, pp. 156–165, 2002.

Confidence scoring techniques have been developed to identify potentially misrecognized words from a set of confidence features extracted from the recognition process, in which sub-word and word units of the hypothesized words were used to compute scores [4, 6]. Finally, several post-processing rejection methods have been proposed to classify the hypothetical output of the recognizer as correct or incorrect based on filler models with thresholds setting [7, 8].

In this research, we have experimented with word spotting using several different filler units, including phonemes, syllables, full words, and combinations of the above, in an attempt to deal robustly with utterances that include keywords embedded within unconstrained speech. Unlike many word-spotting systems in which the goal is to detect a limited number of keywords in otherwise unconstrained speech, a directed dialog system must be able to handle a large vocabulary of keywords while at the same time dealing robustly with utterances that contain non-keywords. In addition, in this work we have explored the optimization of confidence thresholds in an attempt to accept, confirm and reject utterances within unconstrained speech. Our experiments, using the SpeechWorks segment-based recognizer, are based on data collected from an auto-attendant application (CONMAT) deployed in Mexico, with a vocabulary of 2,288 keywords (names of people and places, including synonyms). Results are given in terms of a novel evaluation criterion that takes into account acceptance, confirmation, and rejection confidence measures. This new evaluation criterion was developed because previous works have not treated the possibility of confirmation. This measure also permits the optimization of the confidence thresholds that control the use of confirmation.

In the remainder of the paper we first provide an overview of the OOV problem in section 2. We then describe the proposed techniques for modeling OOV words and for optimizing confidence thresholds in section 3 and 4. In section 5, we describe the methodology used for evaluating our experiments. Finally, in section 6 we describe the experimental framework and discuss the results of the experiments in the CONMAT domain.

2 The OOV Problem

Even with the effort of many researchers in recent decades, today's speech recognition technology is far from perfect. There are two primary deficiencies in a typical recognizer [4]. First, the models used in a recognition process may be inadequate, for any number of reasons. Second, recognizers are typically developed for *closed set* recognition (predefined vocabulary), when in real environments unknown words, partial words, and non-speech noises cause problems associated with *open set* recognition. To address this problem, we propose a classification of kinds of speech that a recognizer can receive as input, shown in figure 1. Ideally, a recognizer should accept the terminal nodes T1, T2 and T6-T9, while rejecting T3, T4 and T5. Table 3 shows the evaluation corpus according to this classification and reveals that an important number of utterances contain keywords together with OOV words while others contain only OOV words.

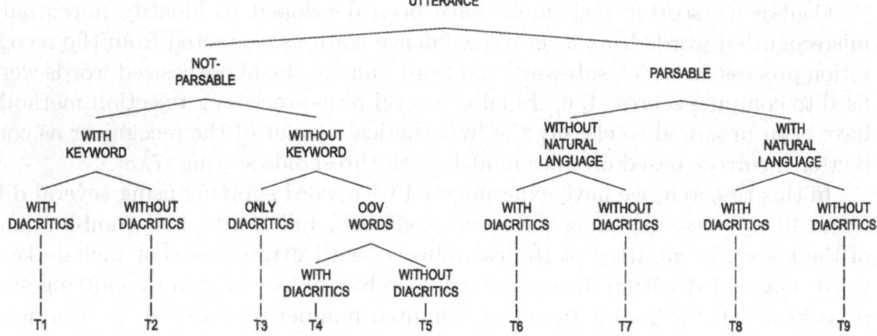

Fig. 1. Classification of kinds of speech in spoken dialog systems. Diacritics refer to the presence of non-speech sounds.

3 OOV Word Modeling

There are two common approaches for modeling OOV words. The first approach consists in augmenting the keyword models with "filler" or garbage models, which are trained to account for non-keywords and background noise. The second approach uses a large vocabulary continuous speech recognition system (LVCSR) to produce a word string and then look for the keywords in that string.

Previous studies [2] have suggested that the latter approach yields higher performance, but it requires costly computation and extensive training data for each domain. In this research we use a set of task-independent filler models, which can be used in any system in Spanish. The word spotters described here are based on the configuration proposed by [3], and work with several filler units, including phonemes, syllables and full words. The recognition network for a word spotter is shown in figure 2, where F_i represents the generic word model based on filler units and W_i represents the search network for the word recognizer. Any transition between keywords and fillers is allowed, as well as self-transitions for both keywords and fillers. Although this configuration allows multiple instances of a keyword within the same utterance, in this work we restrain the network to allow at most one keyword in each utterance.

3.1 Phonemic Filler Models

One approach for modeling non-keywords in continuous speech recognition is to use phonemes, which can represent the acoustics of all non-keywords in a given language. This approach offers at least two advantages: first, it allows phrases with flexible vocabularies, so that all non-keywords can be modeled through the same set of fundamental units; and second, it simplifies the difficult task of predicting all non-keywords for a new system. In this work, we have defined the following set of 23 phonemes for Spanish: */a/*, */e/*, */i/*, */o/*, */u/*, */ch/*, */d/*, */f/*, */g/*, */k/*, */l/*, */ll/*, */m/*, */n/*, */ñ/*, */p/*, */r/*, */rr/*, */s/*, */t/*, */v/*, */x/*, */w/*.

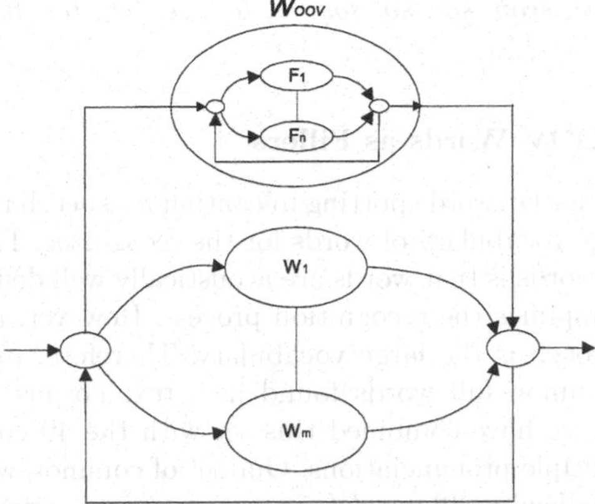

Fig. 2. Recognition network for a generic word spotting system. $F_1 ... F_n$ are "filler" models for OOV speech, and $W_1 ... W_n$ are keywords in the vocabulary.

3.2 Syllabic Filler Models

The main constraint in continuous speech recognition is the co-articulation effect present in fluent speech. Thus, the phonemes as basic sounds suffer variations because a phoneme is influenced by its contiguous phonemes. Therefore, recognition at the phoneme level is a difficult task. Phonologic evidences suggest that the syllable unit plays an important role in spoken language processing, particularly under adverse acoustic situations [9]. The syllabic division process explained in [11] yielded the set of syllables defined for this approach. We found 860 different syllables in the text corpus described in 3.4. Although this number is only a subset of the total number of syllables possible in Spanish, we believe that our set can form most of the words in Spanish.

In word spotting systems, the use of a high number of filler models is a disadvantage because it requires costly computation. In order to obtain better performance using syllables as fillers, we defined a second set. That set groups syllables according to the articulation place, allowing classes of syllables that sound acoustically similar. According to this grouping, we obtained a set of 344 broad-class syllables. Unfortunately, with this set we still have significant computational cost. So we classified the set of syllables as common and uncommon. A syllable is considered *common* when its relative frequency is equal or higher than the arithmetic mean of broad-class syllables frequencies. The remaining broad-class syllables are considered *uncommon.* Thus, our new set of syllables consists of 49 common broad-class syllables. In an effort to improve the modeling of common syllables, we allowed our new set of syllables to have multiple pronunciations based on the syllables that sound acoustically similar. Our syllabic set of fillers for Spanish is composed of the following: *a, al, da, de, des, do, dos, e, el, en, es, la, las, le, lo, los, na, nas, ne, nen, nes, no, nos, o, on, ra, re, ro, sa, se, sea, sen, seo, seon, ser, so, sos, ta, tan, te, ten, ter, to, ton, tor, tos, tra, tre, tro.*

3.3 Common OOV Words as Fillers

Another approach for keyword spotting in continuous speech recognition consists in designing a large vocabulary of words for the recognizer. The main advantage of using complete words is that words are acoustically well defined. Thus, the use of whole words simplifies the recognition process. However, a big disadvantage of using this approach is the large vocabulary. Therefore, in this approach we used the most common full words found in a text corpus. For modeling the rest of the words, we have combined this set with the 49 common broad-class syllables using multiple pronunciations. Our set of common words for spanish is composed of the following fillers: *del, una, para, como, esta, son, pero, donde, tambien, hasta, entre, todo, tambien, desde, fue, sobre, hay, solo, puede, asi, cuando, todos, parte, gran, otros, hacia, tiempo, tiene, estos, cada.*

3.4 Language Models

In order to reduce computational cost in the word spotting systems, we trained the networks of each word spotter with bigram language models. Our training set for filler models consists of a text file with 92,009 words in Spanish, including a variety of topics such as health, education, politics, and literature.

4 Confidence Thresholds

An efficient post-processing rejection procedure is necessary to reject utterances with non-keywords and to accept or confirm utterances embedding keywords. The aim of post-processing is to decide if for a given utterance, the recognized sequence of words should be accepted, confirmed, or rejected. When the SpeechWorks recognizer hypothesizes an utterance, it also provides a recognition confidence score from 0 to 999. Two pre-defined confidence thresholds, the low threshold (LT) and the high threshold (HT), divide the confidence score range into three regions: the *rejection region*, covering scores in the range of 0-LT, in which utterances are rejected without confirmation; the *confirmation region* (scores in the range LT-HT), in which utterances are confirmed before making any final decision; and finally, the *acceptance region* (scores in the range HT-999), in which the recognition result is accepted without confirmation. Note that, during the threshold-setting process, if we increase HT, some utterances that used to be accepted will now be confirmed, while on the other hand, if we increase LT, some utterances that used to be confirmed will now be rejected. Furthermore, optimal confidence thresholds vary from one recognition context to another.

Our method for setting confidence thresholds is based on the metric proposed in this work called *DER* (Discriminative Error Rate). The *DER* metric, shown in equation 2, weights the number of occurrences of each type of error β_i

Table 1. Possible outcomes of a recognition event

Result	Description	Recognition	Rejection
ca_iv	Correct Acceptance IV	Correct	Accepted
cc_iv	Correct Confirmation IV	Correct	Confirmed
fa_iv	False Acceptance IV	Incorrect	Accepted
fr_iv	False Rejection IV	Unknown	Rejected
fc_iv	False Confirmation IV	Incorrect	Confirmed
cr_oov	Correct Rejection OOV	N/A	Rejected
fa_oov	False Acceptance OOV	N/A	Accepted
fc_oov	False Confirmation OOV	N/A	Confirmed

Table 2. Penalty values associated with different possible errors

Priority	Measure(s)	Cost(α_i)
Extremely Important	*fa_iv, fa_oov*	1.00
Very Important	*fc_iv*	0.75
Important	*fr_iv*	0.50
More o Less Important	*fc_oov*	0.25
Less Important	*cc_iv*	0.10

(*cc_in, fa_iv, fr_in, fc_in, fa_oov and fr_oov*) with its corresponding penalty α_i. N is the total number of utterances. The formula for optimizing the confidence thresholds (calculating CT_{op}) consists in minimizing the DER for all the possible combinations of LH and HT, as shown in equation 1. We optimized two sets of confidence thresholds. The first set was optimized in utterances with only keywords and the second set was optimized with utterances that contain kewords and OOV words. In the case of a recognition result containing only fillers (no keyword) the utterance is rejected without considering the confidence measure.

$$CT_{op} = \min\left[DER\right], \forall HT > LT. \tag{1}$$

$$DER = \left(\sum_i \alpha_i \beta_i\right) /N. \tag{2}$$

5 Evaluation Criteria

The evaluation of each technique is made according to recognition accuracy and computational cost. Recognition accuracy is computed using the DER (Discriminative Error Rate) metric defined by the equation 2. Computational cost is computed by the cost per second of speech (CSS), defined by the equation 3, where SDUR is the average duration (in seconds) of each utterance and RESP is the average amount of time (in seconds) the recognizer required for processing each utterance.

$$CSS = (RESP/SDUR) \tag{3}$$

Table 3. Evaluation corpus

Terminal Node	Test Set
T1	61
T2	376
T3	1442
T4	149
T5	879
T6	207
T7	3393
T8	70
T9	727
TOTAL	7304

6 Experiments and Results

6.1 Experimental Setup

Our experiments used the SpeechWorks segment-based speech recognition engine, based on the SUMMIT speech recognition system [10]. All the experiments in this paper are based on an auto attendant system (CONMAT) deployed at the Universidad de las Américas (UDLA-P) in Mexico. The domain includes people names, department names and places inside the university. This system was used in this work because it is working in a real environment, because the speech data during early deployment showed a high number of utterances containing OOV words, and because speech data were available for training and testing. The word lexicon used in our experiments consists of a total of 2,288 words. The text used to train language models consists of 92,009 words. The training set for optimizing confidence thresholds consist of 3,352 utterances (2,894 for only keywords and 458 for keywords with OOV words). Table 3 shows the test set classified according to kind of speech (terminal nodes illustrated in figure 1).

6.2 Results

We summarize the results of experiments with three different types of filler models in table 4. Our main goal here was to demonstrate whether OOV word modeling and rejection can detect OOV words without significantly affecting the accuracy for IV utterances. These results show that before optimizing the confidence thresholds (LT and HT), the baseline system (no fillers) and the word spotter using phonemes achieved the lowest error rates (ER). After optimizing the thresholds, the word spotter using syllables achieves the lowest ER, paying the price in computational cost.

Detailed information of our experiments is shown in figures 3 and 4. According to the classification of kinds of speech described in figure 1, all the word spotters show significant improvements in the terminal nodes that contain both keywords and OOV words, especially the syllabic word spotter. The baseline

Table 4. Results of experiments in the test set (* results with optimized thresholds)

Experiment	DER	DER*	CSS
Baseline - Predefined Grammar	0.132	0.101	0.46
Word spotter using phonemes	0.134	0.101	0.58
Word spotter using syllables	0.142	0.092	1.73
Word spotter using common words	0.186	0.093	2.00

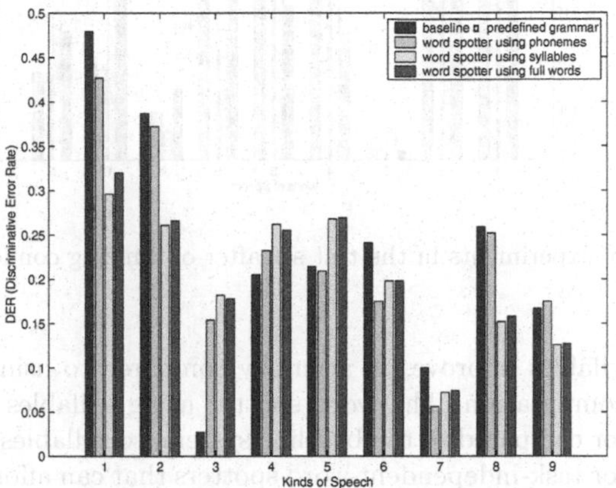

Fig. 3. Results of experiments in the test set before optimizing confidence thresholds.

system shows better rejection in the three terminal nodes (T3-T5), principally in the node that contrains only dicritics (T3).

After the optimization of thresholds, in figure 4 we can observe that again all the word spotters present better keyword detection compared to the baseline system, especially the syllabic word spotter. In the utterances that contain only OOV words, the baseline system achieved the lowest ER in the terminals T3-T5, and all the word spotters show significant improvements in utterances containing only with diacritics (T3).

7 Conclusions and Future Work

The final results showed that the use of fillers helped significantly when the keyword is embedded in utterances with OOV words (T1, T2, T6-T9). The rejection of utterances recognized as only fillers helped to avoid false acceptances of utterances containing no speech at all. We found that the use of fillers increased false acceptances in utterances with OOV speech but no keywords (T4 and T5). This is due to measuring confidence on the fillers and using that confidence to make the acceptance decision, instead of using only the confidence releated to the keyword itself. (The use of other techniques such as slot-based confidence scoring could help here significantly.) Our results also showed that the word

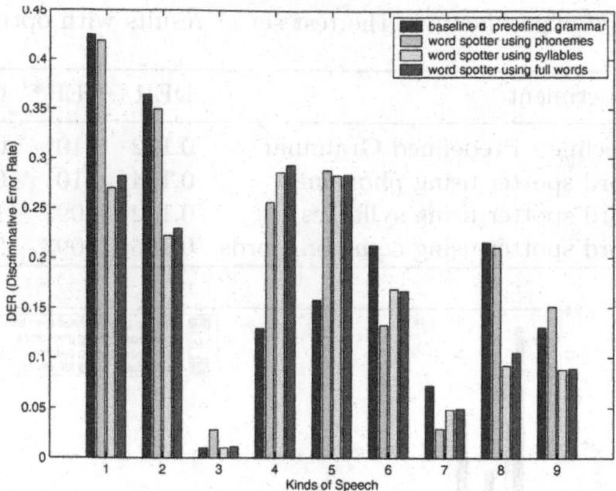

Fig. 4. Results of experiments in the test set after optimizing confidence thresholds.

spotter using syllables improves in accuracy compared to using phonemes, but requires more computation. The word spotter using syllables achieved a 8.9% reduction in error compared to the baseline system, so syllables as fillers seem to be a good unit for task-independent word spotters that can afford computational overhead. The classification of kinds of speech proposed in this work was useful to see the areas improved and the areas to be improved. Finally, the DER (Discriminative Error Rate) metric proposed in this work was very useful in order to summarize the results of each experiment with only one value, which considers all the confidence measures used by the SpeechWorks recognizer, allowing direct comparison between experiments.

In future, we will continue research in the application of slot-based confidence scoring, as well as in the optimization of search parameters. We also plan to investigate techniques for adaptive rejection and perform experiments using morphemes as filler units. Finally, we will perform experiments using our techniques in other domains, including numeric domains and domains with several keywords.

References

1. Lleida, J. B., Salavedra, J., Bonafonte, A., Monte, E., Martinez, A.: Out-Of-Vocabulary Word Modeling and Rejection for Keyword Spotting. In Proc. EUROSPEECH, pp. 1265-1268, 1993.
2. Manos, A.: A Study on Out-Of-Vocabulary Word Modeling for a Segment-Based Keyword Spotting System. Master Thesis, Massachusetts Institute of Technology, Cambridge, MA, USA, April 1996.
3. Bazzi, I., Glass, J.: Learning Units for Domain-Independent Out-of-Vocabulary Word Modeling. In Proc. EUROSPEECH, Aalborg, Denmark, September 2001.

4. Hazen, J. T., Bazzi, I.: A Comparison and Combination of Methods for OOV Detection and Word Confidence Scoring. In Proc. ICASSP, Salt Lake City, USA, May 2001.
5. Qing, G., Yonghong, Y., Zhiwei, L, Baosshen, Y., Quingwei, Z., Juian, L.: Keyword Spotting in Auto-Attendant System. In Proc. ICSLP, Beijing, China, October 2000.
6. Benitez, C. M., Rubio, A., Garcia, P., Verdejo, D. J.: Word Verification Using Confidence Measures in Speech Recognition. In Proc. ICASSP, Istanbul, Turkey, June 2000.
7. Jouvet, D., Bartkova, K. Mercier, G.: Hypothesis Dependent Threshold Setting for Improved Out-Of-Vocabulary Data Rejection. In Proc. ICASSP, Phoenix, Arizona, USA, March 1999.
8. Bouwman, G., Sturm, J., Boves, L.: Effect of OOV rates on Keyphrase Rejection Schemes. In Proc. EUROSPEECH, Aalborg, Denmark, September 2001.
9. Zhilong, H., Schalkwyk, J., Barnard, E., Cole, R.: Speech Recognition Using Syllable-Like Units. In Proc. ICSLP, Philadelphia, USA, October 1996.
10. Zue, V., Glass, J., Phillips, M., Sennef, S.: The SUMMIT Speech Recognition System: Phonological Modeling and Lexical Access. In Proc. ICASSP, pp. 49-52, 1990.
11. Cuayáhuitl, H.: Técnicas para Mejorar el Reconocimiento de Voz en Presencia de Habla Fuera del Vocabulario. Master Thesis, Universidad de las Américas Puebla, Cholula, Puebla, Mexico, May 2000.

The *DIME* Project*

L.A. Pineda, A. Massé, I. Meza, M. Salas, E. Schwarz,
E. Uraga, and L. Villaseñor

Department of Computer Science
Institute for Applied Mathematics and Systems (IIMAS), UNAM

Abstract. In this paper a general description and current state of the project *Diálogos Multimodales Inteligentes en Español (DIME) -Intelligent Multimodal Dialogs in Spanish-* is presented. The purpose of the project is to develop a multimodal conversational agent with spoken input and output facilities in Spanish in a design oriented domain: kitchen design. In this paper, the state of the project, current results, an overview of the prototype system and future work are presented.

1 Introduction

In this paper, the current state of the project *DIME: Diálogos Multimodales Inteligentes en Español -Intelligent Multimodal Dialogs in Spanish-* is presented. The purpose of the project is to develop a multimodal conversational agent with spoken input and output facilities in Spanish in a design oriented domain: kitchen design.

Here, we focus on the three main current tasks of the project: the first consists in the compilation, transcription and tagging of a multimodal *corpus* in a design domain; the second is the development of a Spanish speech recognition system specialized in the language employed in the application domain; the third is the definition of a Spanish grammar and parser for Spanish, comprehensive enough to interpret the lexicon and grammar observed in the *DIME* corpus. In this paper the results of these three modules are presented, and also a brief description of the current state of the prototype system.

This project is developed in a collaboration between the Department of Computer Science, at the Institute for Applied Mathematics and Systems (IIMAS) of the National University of Mexico (UNAM), the ITESM, Campus Morelos, and the Department of Computer Science of the University of Rochester, with the support of the bilateral program between the United States and Mexico NSF/CONACyT for the development of computer science.

2 The *DIME Corpus*

The first task of the project was the collection of a corpus on the application domain: The *DIME* corpus. We required an application domain that, on the one

* A previous version of this paper in Spanish was present at the SLPLT2 workshop that was held in Jaén, Spain, in September, 2001.

C.A. Coello Coello et al. (Eds.): MICAI 2002, LNAI 2313, pp. 166–175, 2002.

hand, was general enough to be accessible and potentially interesting to many people, meriting the use of natural language and, on the other, simple enough to be modelled with current computational technology. In addition, in order to study multimodal communication, it was required to have a domain in which the use of spatial references, either supported by explicit gestures or not, were abundant. Also, we intended to study intentions or speech acts that were expressed through gestures, as commonly happens in multimodal communication, supporting the case for a domain in which it was natural to use an interactive graphics interface. An application domain meeting these requirements seemed to be kitchen design. This is a simple and intuitive task that can be performed by many people, and yet, there are a number of design rules, known by expert designers, that can help to improve the quality and functionality of the designs, and the presence of a design assistant can be justified for this task. In summary, kitchen design was thought to be a kind of task that can be assisted through intelligent multimodal agents, and it was chosen for the project.

As first step we proceeded to develop the *DIME* corpus. It was collected with the help of a Wizard of Oz scenario [12]. In our experiment, subjects were not under the illusion that they were interacting with a real system, but the restrictions placed on the interface had an influence on the language used and the kind of gestures performed by both the wizard and the subject. The wizard, in addition, was instructed to limit his expressivity, and to take the initiative and provide help only in case he noted that some constraints or kitchen design rules were violated or ignored by the user, resembling better the expected behavior of a real system.

To carry on with the experiment, a laboratory with two small chambers was built. This environment allowed the subject and the wizard to solve kitchen design tasks in a collaborative way, yet avoiding visual contact. The task was supported by specialized hardware and software through which all events, both graphical and linguistic, were recorded. This is illustrated in Figure 1.

The graphical interface used in the experiments is shown in Figure 2. For the construction of this environment, a commercial product was used [3]. Further references about this setting can be found in [12].

Each session consisted in an explanation given to the user, a system demonstration and the solution of two tasks; the first was designed mainly to familiarize the user with the environment, and the second was a more comprehensive design task. The experiment was applied to 16 different subjects, in addition to some complementary sessions. From this effort, we obtained 31 dialogs, with a total of 27,459 token words, with an average of 886 words per dialog, 5779 utterance (185 per dialog), 3606 turns (115 per dialog) and 7:10 hours of recordings (14 minutes per dialogue).

The linguistic data obtained through the experiments is used to develop the language models of the speech recognition system, to guide the development of the Spanish lexicon and grammar, and to identify and model the speech acts that occur in the application domain, which will be used in the construction of the pragmatics interpretation and dialogue manager modules of the system.

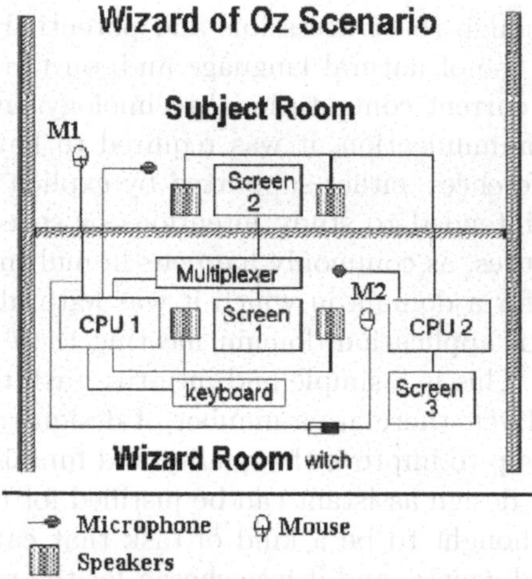

Fig. 1. Setting for the Wizard of Oz experiment

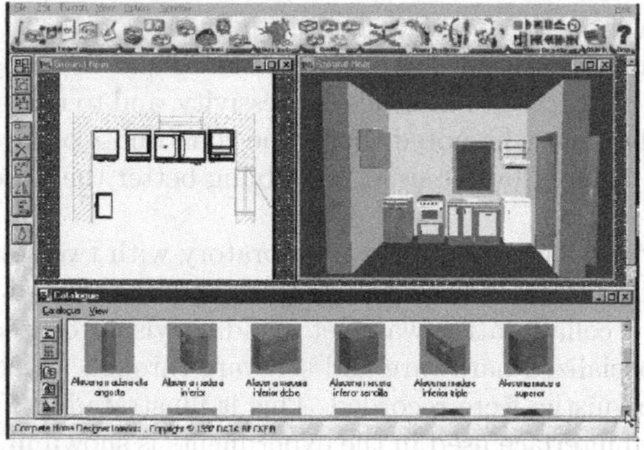

Fig. 2. Wizard of Oz interface

The dialogues were first segmented and transcribed ortographically; however, as the purpose of the project is to build a system for continuous, but not spontaneous speech, the dialogues were simplified eliminating interjections, noises, long pauses, stutters, speech-repairs, simultaneous speech, interruptions, etc. As a result of this process, two versions of the corpus are available: for spontaneous and continuous speech. The corpus is available for the research community [12].

3 Speech Recognition

In the context of the project, a module for speech recognition in Spanish focused on the application domain is being developed. In particular, we are developing acoustic-phonetic models, pronunciation dictionaries and language models for the ASR system using the *CSLU Toolkit* [5] and the *HTK* [6] system. With the purpose to create the pronunciation dictionaries, a phonetic alphabet for Mexican Spanish, *Mexbet,* was defined [9]. A set of rules for grapheme to morpheme conversion, including allophonic variation, for automating the process of phonetic transcription and the creation of pronunciation dictionaries, was also defined.

As an initial stage, a set of acoustic models based on neural nets and hidden Markov models was developed. These models were trained with three different architectures, the first two with the CSLU Toolkit and the last with HTK; the first architecture employed a neural net only, the second a hybrid model in which the output nodes of a neural network were initialized with the help of a set of hidden Markov models, and the third was based on hidden Markov models exclusively. As a language model a finite state grammar including word sequences normally found in telephone transfer calls was used. This domain was used to evaluate the first set of models. The performance of these models for a continuous, multilocutor speech, with a vocabulary of 107 words, was satisfactory, as the recognition level for the three architectures were 96.79%, 92.55% and 91.09% respectively.

The acoustic models were later used to recognize speech in the kitchen design domain. For this purpose, the models were evaluated with the *DIME* corpus. In this evaluation, a bigram based language model, trained with the *DIME* corpus for both continuous and spontaneous speech, was used. However, as the *DIME* corpus contains a number of allophonic variation not considered in the original acoustic models, the results of this evaluation were poor. For this reason, a new set of acoustic models was trained using the HTK toolkit and the Tlatoa corpus [8]. The results of the new evaluation were 25.21% and 20.82% of recognition at the word level for the continuous and spontaneous speech respectively. Currently, and with the aim to improve the recognition levels in our system, a new phonetically rich and balanced corpus is being developed; with this new corpus, it will be possible to create acoustic models for the 625 context dependent phonetic combinations (i.e., each phone has a left and right context) that we have identified in Mexican Spanish.

4 Spanish Grammar and Parser

One of the main objectives in the *DIME* project is to create a Spanish grammar and a parser robust enough to deal with the grammatical phenomena and lexica that appear in the continuous version of the *DIME* corpus. As a theoretical framework for developing this grammar *Head-driven Phrase Structure Grammar* (HPSG) [16] and its associated developing environment LKB [2] were adopted.

Independently of the similarities between English and Spanish, there are several syntactic phenomena particular to Spanish that pose interesting challenges to computational syntactic theories. In particular, the Spanish clitic pronoun system has no direct counterpart in English; also, although the auxiliary verb systems of Spanish and English are similar in several respects, they are by no means identical, and there are a number of subtle properties of the Spanish grammar that give rise to ambiguities that do not occur in English, but have to be dealt with in computational applications. In addition, Spanish's verb morphology is richer than English, allowing the omission of subjects, a phenomena that does not occur in English. Also the linear word-order of English is much more strict than the word-order of Spanish, making the interpretation of Spanish a very hard task. For all these reasons, the definition of a Spanish grammar and parser was thought to be one of the main objectives of this project.

Currently we have focused on two of these phenomena: the auxiliary verb system and the clitic system. The Spanish auxiliaries pose a number of interesting challenges: *puedes mostrar* (can show) is a verbal phrase formed by an auxiliary verb (*poder*) and an infinitive, where the subject of the auxiliary verb indicates the agent of the non-personal form; however and unlike English, where auxiliary verbs have almost been deprived of their original lexical meanings, in Spanish some forms are still used in their original sense, in addition to their grammatical roles as auxiliaries, producing a number of interesting ambiguities. For instance, in *puedes con las matemáticas (you are able to do mathematics)* the verb *poder (to be able to)* preserves its original meaning of capacity, unlike English where the form *be able to* is preferred to in this latter sense, and it is not an auxiliary, as shown by our analysis [13].

The clitic system is also very important the Spanish language. In general, clitics are atonic grammatical units, mostly function words, that are attracted by tonic units, usually words with semantic content, forming a single lexical unit. An important kind of clitics occur in conjunction with pronouns; for instance, *me* in the word *mostrarme,* is an enclitic pronoun attached to the infinitive form of the verb *mostrar*. These kind of words occur often in periphrastic constructions in conjunction with auxiliary verbs as in *¿puedes mostrarme el catálogo?* (*can you show me the catalog?*). Here, the natural intuition for Spanish speakers, which is reflected in the orthography, is that these two lexical items, of different syntactic categories, form a single word, whose grammatical category is a verbal phrase in which one of the verbal arguments, the indirect object *me*, is already included. However, in the equivalent sentence *¿me puedes mostrar el catálogo?*, the pronoun occurs before the verbal phrase as an independent lexical form. Here, the distance of the proclitic pronoun *me* to the periphrasis is much larger than the one in the enclitic case and it is perceived as an independent lexical unit, as reflected by the Spanish orthography.

In our analysis both sentences receive a similar syntactic and semantic analysis. In the enclitic case, the periphrasis takes the verbal phrase *mostrarme el catálogo* as a complement of *puedes*. In this case it is possible the reading in which *poder* is an auxiliary verb and indicates the possibility of performing the action of showing. Additionally, our analysis permits also the reading in which *poder* has the sense of capacity and it is not an auxiliary; in these latter case *puedes* requires an agent, the one who has the capability of showing.

In the proclitic case, *puedes* takes as its complement the verbal phrase *mostrar el catátogo*. In this phrase the verb *mostrar* needs its indirect object, which is represented by the clitic *me*. However, the verb *mostrar* can not take the clitic as its complement, because it is not behind the verb, but in front of the whole periphrasis. Therefore, it is the verb *puedes* which takes the clitic and shares it with *mostrar*. In this latter case both readings, capacity and possibility, are also possible.

Within the context of the *DIME* project, we have developed a systematic analysis for these problems [13,14], and the interaction of these two grammatical systems, currently being developed, will permit the interpretation of a large number of sentences of the *DIME* corpus.

5 Speech Act Analysis

The first level of multimodal interpretation outputs the semantic representation of the natural language expressions input by the user, and the output of the graphical parser which interprets the graphical events expressed by the user through the interface. This information is passed to the semantic interpretation process which is responsible for reference resolution, both anaphoric and indexical, and also for determining the intentions expressed by the user; intensions can be simple and can be expressed by a single utterance, or can be complex requiring several utterances, and even several turns, to be expressed and understood along the conversational process. The literal interpretation of *¿me puedes mostrar el catálogo?* is a question asking whether the system has the possibility or the ability to show the catalog, but in the context of our application domain, it is rather an imperative statement commanding the system to show the catalog. To make this inference is part of the job of the pragmatic interpretation component of the system.

One important assumption in the development of this kind of systems is that the set of intentions that can be expressed during task oriented dialogues is finite and small, and can be characterized through a task analysis. In kitchen design, for instance, users can express the intention of including an object in a particular design, change the properties or relations of a number of objects, or simply to remove an object from the design; however, these simple intentions are normally expressed in the context of more complex intentional structures. In our dialogues, for instance, it is common to observe that when a user asks for the inclusion of a piece of furniture, the assistant requires to clarify the desired position before the action takes place; these two intentions form intentional units. The identification of such intentional structures is the purpose of the task analysis, and the result of this process is the *intentional structure* of the application domain. In *DIME*, the intentional structure is specified as the representation of the primitive intentions of the domain with their structural relations; the identification of such primitives and structural relations are obtained empirically out of the corpus.

With the purpose to analyze and characterize the intentional structure of our application domain, the tagging scheme for task oriented dialogs *DAMSL* was adopted [15]. In this scheme, speech acts are analyzed in four orthogonal dimensions, namely, the communication level, the information level, and the

Table 1. Corpus segment

Forward	Backward	U#	S	Utterance (Spanish)	Utterance (English)
info-req		29	u:	¿me puedes mostrar el catálogo?	can you show me the catalog?
commit	accept ack	30	s:	ok	ok
assert	answer	31	s:	graphical action	
reassert	answer	32	s:	hay un catálogo de alacenas, uno de estantes, uno de estufas y extractores, uno de fregaderos y máquinas lavatrates	there is a catalog of cupboards, one of shelves, one of stoves, one of extractors and one of sinks and washing machines
info-request		33	u:	¿me puedes mostrar el catálogo de fregaderos y máquinas lavatrates?	can you show me the catalog of sinks and washing machines?
commit	accept ack	34	s:	ok	ok
assert	answer	35	s:	graphical action	
reassert	answer	36	s:	éste es el catálogo de fregaderos y máquinas lavatrastes	this is the catalog of sinks and washing machines
info-request		37	s:	¿quieres alguno en particular?	do you want a particular one?
info-request	hold	38	u:	¿a ver cuál es la diferencia entre el tercero y el cuarto?	let's see, what is the difference between the third and the fourth one?
check	accept-part	39	s:	¿entre éste y éste?	between this and this?
assert	answer	40	u:	si	yes
assert	answer	41	s:	éste tiene una superficie más larga que sale del mueble y éste abarca solamente hasta donde llega la máquina lavatrastes	this has a surface that gets off the furniture and this only covers up to where the dish washing machine gets to
action-dir		42	u:	¿me puedes poner el tercero junto a la estufa?	can you place the third one next to the stove?
check	accept-part	43	s:	¿éste junto a la estufa?	this one next to the stove?
assert	answer	44	u:	si por favor	yes please
commit	accept ack	45	s:	ok	ok
assert		46	s:	graphical action	
check		47	s:	¿así está bien?	is it all right?
assert	answer	48	u:	sí	yes

forward and backward relations of each expression. However, as the continuous version of the *DIME* corpus is used for this task, it is assumed that there are not communication problems and different information levels; consequently, the analysis for only the last two dimensions of DAMSL was required. Also, the scheme was modified and extended to deal with the peculiarities of the domain, and the multimodal aspect of the project. The analysis of a small segment of the corpus for just one conversational turn, with the forward and backward relations of the user and system utterances, is shown in Table 1.

In the context of the project, some graphical actions are performed with the purpose to express an intention and hence are considered speech acts. For this reason, *DAMSL* was extended considering that graphical actions performed by the system with a communicative intent, as a response to intentions expressed by users, are considered speech acts. In Table 1, for instance, utt29 expresses a forward *information request* speech act that needs to be attended to by the system. In utt30, the system establishes two backward and one forward functions; the *accept* and *acknowledgment* backwards speech acts take notice and accept the user request, and the forward *commit* speech acts is a charge to the discourse model that needs to be discharged before the intentional cycle is terminated. The *answer* speech act in the backward function of utt31 discharge the commit of *utt30,* and the *assert* forward function, which is realized graphically, satisfied the information request initiating the intentional transaction. In the example at hand, the system chose to strengthen its response by providing a *reassert* speech act, showing the information requested also in a textual form. This last expression closes the intentional cycle. The dialogue is modelled as a sequence of conversational cycles of this kind, as shown in the rest of Table 1. A formal model for this kind of interaction is currently being developed.

In order to test the adequacy of the tagging scheme, the *Kappa* coefficients [1] that measure the agreement of different taggers working on the same corpus, were used in a pilot test. According to the first results, the tagging definitions and procedures in *DAMSL* manual [15] were modified, and a new version, similar to the one reported in Chiba [4], but one in which graphical speech acts were contemplated, was defined.

In our current proposal, dialogues are also analyzed at three levels of granularity: the micro, messo and macro level. Table 1 shows the micro level in which the dialogue is segmented into speaker turns and utterance tokens within turns. The messo level consists in a dialogue structure in which so-called common ground units (CGU) are identified. A CGU contains all and only the tokens needed to add some bit of content to the common ground between the conversational participants. CGUs require some initiating material by one participant presenting new content and some feedback or acknowledgment by the other participant. If a token adds new content and there is no accessible ungrounded CGU whose contents could be acknowledged with the current token, then a new CGU is created, and the token is included in it. However, if there is an accessible CGU for which the current token acknowledges the content, repairs the content, cancels the CGU, continues the content in such a way that all content could be

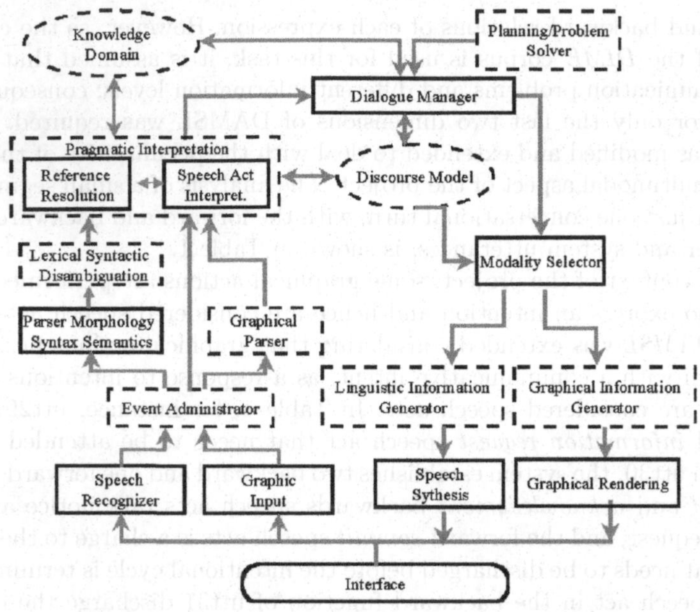

Fig. 3. Architecture of the prototype system

grounded together, then this content is added to the current CGU. To carry on with the dialogue, all CGUs must eventually be grounded. Finally, the macro level consists in a level in which the dialogue is organized in terms of informational and/or intentional units. In this level, the main intentions expressed by the user during the conversation are represented, and to carry on with the conversation, units at this level of representation need to be completed also.

6 The Prototype System

For the implementation of the project's prototype we are using *Open Agent Architecture* (*OAA*) [7]. This is a development environment for distributed systems which offers several advantages over competing technologies like *CORBA* and Microsoft *DCOM*, due, mainly, to its flexibility for handling multimodal asynchronous events. This flexibility permits to develop the prototype system incrementally, adding new modules and enriching the existing ones. The architecture of the *DIME* prototype is shown in Figure 3, where continuous lines indicate the modules that have been partially implemented, and the dashed lines indicate the modules that will be addressed in the future.

For the multimodal reference resolution the model proposed in Pineda and Garza [11] will be used, and for the rest of the system strategies similar to those followed in *TRIPS* [10] will be employed.

Acknowledgments

We gratefully thank James Allen and his group at Rochester University; also to Enrique Sucar, to Eduard Hovy and to the anonymous reviewers of this paper. This project is being developed within the context of the bilateral initiative for the development of computer science between USA and Mexico, NSF/CONACyT with the support of CONACyT grant C092A; we also acknowledge the support of CONACyT grants 27948-A and 31128A.

References

1. J. Carletta. Assessing agreement on classification tasks: The kappa statistics. *Computational Linguistics*, 22(2):249–254, 1996.
2. A. Copestake. The LKB system. Technical report, Stanford University, 2001. http://www-csli.stanford.edu/~aac/lkb.html.
3. Alpha Software Corporation and Data Becker GmbH & Co KG. *Complete Home Designer Interiors, Users Guide 1998*. 1998.
4. M. Core et. al. 3rd. workshop of the discourse resource initiative. Technical report, Dept. of Cognitive and Information Sciences. Chiba University. Japan, 1999. No. 3 (CC-TR-99-1).
5. S. Sutton et. al. Universal speech tools: the CSLU toolkit. In *Proc. of the I'ntl Conf. on Spoken Language Processing (ICSLP)*, ICSLP Conferences, pages 3221–3224, Sidney, Australia, November 1998.
6. S. Young et. al. *The HTK Book*. Entropic Cambridge Research Laboratory, Cambridge University, England, 1997.
7. L. D. Martin. *The Open Agent Architecture: A framework for building distributed software systems*. http://www.ai.sri.com/~oaa/, 1999.
8. Grupo Tlatoa. *Speech Technology Research Group: TLATOA*. http://info.pue.udlap.mx/~sistemas/ tlatoa/, 2001.
9. E. Uraga. *Mexbet: Conjunto de símbolos fonéticos para el español*. IIMAS-UNAM, México, http://cic2.iimas.unam.mx/multimod/dime/doctos/espectrogramas/ tablafonemas.html, 2001.
10. J. Allen; G. Ferguson y A. Stent. An architecture for more realistic conversational systems. In *Proceedings of IUI-2001*, pages 1–8, Santa Fe, NM, January 2001.
11. L. A. Pineda y G. Garza. A model for multimodal reference resolution. *Computational Linguistics*, 26(2):139–194, June 2000.
12. L. Villaseor; A. Massé y L. A. Pineda. The DIME corpus. In *ENC01, 3er Encuentro Internacional de Ciencias de la Computacin*, Aguascalientes, México, 2001. SMCCINEGI.
13. Ivan Meza y Luis A. Pineda. The spanish auxiliary verb system in HPSG. In *Proceedings of CICLing-2002*. Springer-Verlag, LNCS (to be published), 2002.
14. Ivan Meza; Erik Schwarz y Luis Pineda. The clitic pronoun system in HPSG. to appear.
15. J. Allen y M. Core. Draft of DAMSL: Dialog act markup in several layers. Technical report, U. of Rochester, 1997.
16. I. Sag y T. Wasow. *Syntactic Theory: A Formal Introduction*. CSLI Publications, Stanford, 1999.

Detecting Deviations in Text Collections: An Approach Using Conceptual Graphs

M. Montes-y-Gómez[1,2], A. Gelbukh[1], and A. López-López[2]

[1] Center for Computing Research (CIC-IPN), México.
mmontesg@susu.inaoep.mx, gelbukh@cic.ipn.mx
[2] Instituto Nacional de Astrofísica, Optica y Electrónica (INAOE), México.
allopez@inaoep.mx

Abstract. Deviation detection is an important problem of both data and text mining. In this paper we consider the detection of deviations in a set of texts represented as conceptual graphs. In contrast with statistical and distance-based approaches, the method we propose is based on the concept of generalization and regularity. Among its main characteristics are the detection of rare patterns (that attempt to give a generalized description of rare texts) and the ability to discover local deviations (deviations at different contexts and generalization levels). The method is illustrated with the analysis of a set of computer science papers.

Keywords: natural language processing, deviation detection, text mining, conceptual graphs, regularity.

1 Introduction

For our civilization, knowledge is the most valuable treasure. Most of this knowledge exists in the form of natural language as books, journals, reports, etc. Therefore, the real possession of all this knowledge depends on our capabilities for doing different tasks with texts, for instance: search for interesting texts, compare different texts, or summarize them.

Text mining, the new research area of text processing, is focused in this kind of tasks. Mainly, it is concerned with the discovery of interesting patterns, such as clusters, associations, *deviations*, similarities and differences from text collections (Feldman, 1999; Mladenic, 2000; Ciravegna *et al.*, 2001).

Currently, most methods of text mining use simple and shallow representations of the texts. On one hand, such representations are easily extracted from texts and easily analyzed, but on the other hand, they usually restrict the discovered patterns to the topic level.

To make text mining more useful, richer representations than just keywords, i.e., representations with more types of textual elements, must be used. On the basis of this idea, we are designing a method for doing text mining at detail level (Montes-y-Gómez, 2002). This method uses *conceptual graphs* (Sowa, 1999) for representing

C.A. Coello Coello et al. (Eds.): MICAI 2002, LNAI 2313, pp. 176–184, 2002.

the texts content, and considers different tasks, such as: clustering generation, association discovery and deviation detection.

This paper focuses on the detection of rare patterns – also called deviations – among a set of conceptual graphs representing document details. Basically, it presents a method that detects deviations based on the concept of *regularity* – instead of distance – and that allows detecting local deviations and deviations at different levels of generalization.

The paper is organized as follows. Section 2 describes some previous work on deviation detection. Section 3 introduces conceptual graphs and their clustering. Section 4 presents a method for detecting deviations in a set of conceptual graphs. Then Section 5 shows some experimental results from the analysis of a set of computer science papers. Finally, section 6 draws some preliminary conclusions.

2 Related Work

Traditional statistical methods consider deviations as a source of noise, and try to reduce their effects. On the contrary, recent data mining methods consider the deviations a especially interesting hidden knowledge about data. These methods are mainly of two kinds: methods that use additional information about the data (e.g. Guzmán, 1996), and methods that take advantage of the data's own redundancy (Han and Kamber, 2001). Among the latter we distinguish the following two approaches:

- *The statistical approach* assumes a distribution model for the data, and then identifies deviations with respect to the model using a discordancy test. The application of this test requires knowledge about the data (such as the data distribution) and knowledge about the distribution parameters (such as mean and variance). This approach is presented in (Barnett and Lewis, 1994).
- *The distance-based approach* considers that an object *o* in a data set *S* is a deviation with parameters *p* and *d*, if at least a fraction *p* of the objets in *S* lie at a distance greater than *d* from *o*. The application of this approach requires a distance measure between the objects of the problem and some parameters, such as the number of neighbors of a given object in order to be not considered as a deviation (Knorr and Ng, 1998).

In text mining two different approaches are used for detecting deviations. The first approach focuses on detecting rare texts in a given collection (Alexandrov *et al.*, 2000). The second allows detecting rare topics in a collection (Feldman and Dagan, 1995; Allan *et al.*, 1998).

3 Background

3.1 Conceptual Graphs

A conceptual graph is a bipartite graph (Sowa, 1999) with two different kinds of nodes: concepts and relations.

- *Concepts* represent entities, actions, and attributes. Concept nodes have two attributes: type and referent. Type indicates the class of the element represented by the concept. Referent indicates the specific instance of the class referred to by the node. Referents may be generic or individual.
- *Relations* show the inter-relationships among the concept nodes. Relation nodes also have two attributes: valence and type. Valence indicates the number of concepts involved in the relation, while the type expresses its semantic role.

For instance, the graph

[cat:Tom]←(agt)←[chase]→(ptn)→[mouse]→(atr)→[brown]

represents the phrase "*Tom is chasing a brown mouse*". It has three concepts and three relations. The concept [cat: Tom] is an individual concept of the type *cat* (a specific cat Tom), while the concepts [chase] and [mouse] are generic concepts. All relations in this graph are binary. For instance, the relation (attr) for *attribute* indicates that the mouse has brown color. The other two relations stand for *agent* and *patient* of the action [chase].

3.2 Conceptual Clustering

In some previous work, we presented a method for *conceptual clustering* of conceptual graphs (Montes-y-Gómez *et al.*, 2001). There, we argued that the resulting conceptual hierarchy expresses the hidden organization (structure) of the collection of graphs, but also constitutes an abstract or *index* of the collection that facilitate the discovery of other hidden patterns, e.g. the contextual deviations. Following, we briefly explain the main characteristics about this conceptual hierarchy.

Conceptual clustering –unlike the traditional cluster analysis techniques– allows not only to divide the set of graphs into several groups, but also to associate a description to each group and to organize them into a hierarchy. The resulting hierarchy *H* is not necessarily a tree or lattice, but a set of trees (a forest). This hierarchy is a kind of inheritance network, where those nodes close to the bottom indicate specialized regularities and those close to the top suggest generalized regularities[1]. In section 5, we show part of a cluster hierarchy built from a set of computer science papers.

Formally, each node $h_i \in H$ is represented by a triplet ($cov(h_i)$, $desc(h_i)$, $coh(h_i)$). Here $cov(h_i)$, the coverage of h_i, is the set of graphs covered by the regularity h_i; $desc(h_i)$, the description of h_i, consists of the common elements of the graphs of $cov(h_i)$; $coh(h_i)$, the cohesion of h_i, indicates the least similarity among any two graphs of $cov(h_i)$.

Also, the node h_i is an antecessor of the node h_j if: $cov(h_j) \subset cov(h_i)$, $desc(h_j) < desc(h_i)$ and $coh(h_j) \geq coh(h_i)$.

---

[1] The construction of the conceptual hierarchy is a knowledge-based procedure (Montes-y-Gómez *et al.*, 2001). Basically, a concept hierarchy (defined by the user in accordance with his interests) handles the generalization/specialization of the graphs when the conceptual hierarchy is constructed.

4 Conceptual Graph Deviations

4.1 Basic Considerations

Our method, different to the statistical and distance-based approaches, is based on the concept of *regularity*. Basically, it defines any object (graph or text in our case) without a representative characteristic –a characteristic that is common to a great number of its "neighbors"– as a rare object, and consequently as a possible deviation. This approach is similar to that proposed by Arning *et al.* (1996), who define a deviation as those elements that increase the variance of the complete set of objets.

The detection of deviations in a set of conceptual graphs is supported on the following ideas. Given a set of conceptual graphs, $C=\{G_i\}$:

- A *representative characteristic* is any common generalization g_c of more than m conceptual graphs of the set, where m is a given threshold. Let denote by F the set of representative characteristics of C.
- A *rare conceptual graph* is a graph that has no representative characteristic[2]. Thus, the set of rare graphs is defined as: $R=\{G_r \in C | \nexists g_c \in F : G_r < g_c\}$.
- A deviation d is a pattern that describes one or more of the rare graphs. In other words, a deviation is a generalization of some rare graphs of C. Thus, given a deviation d the following conditions are satisfied:

  1. $\exists G_r \in R : G_r < d$.
  2. $\nexists G \in C, \nexists g \in F : G < g \wedge G < d$.

Therefore, given a set of conceptual graphs C, a *contextual deviation* is an expression of the form: $g_i : g_j\,(r,s)$. In this expression g_i is the context and g_j is the description of the rare graphs (a *m*-deviation); r is the rarity of the deviation on the context, and s is the support of the context with respect to the whole set. For instance, the following deviation indicates that just 4% of the graphs about animals (of some imaginary set) mention a bird of prey, while 32% of the graphs of the entire set are about animals: [animal]: [bird]→ (kind)→[prey] (4%,32%).

4.2 Method for Detecting the Deviations

Detecting deviations in a given set of graphs is defined as the problem of finding all $g_i : g_j\,(r,s)$ expressions according with the user defined threshold m.

The process of detection of the deviations in a set of conceptual graphs C is based on the existance of a conceptual clustering H. Each node h_i of this hierarchy represents a different context (related subset) of C, groups the graphs of $cov(h_i)$ and is described by the conceptual graph $desc(h_i)$.

For each context (node of the hierarchy), we detect deviations based on the following definitions:

[2] If there is no representative characteristic, then it is not possible to detect any deviation.

```
Procedure Detect_Deviations in H

Parameters m
for each node hi of the hierarchy H
   set NOT_RARE ← Ø
   for each son-node hs of hi
     if |cov(hs)| ≥ m X |cov(hi)|
        Insert in NOT_RARE the graphs covered by hs
   for each son-node hs of hi
     if |cov(hs)| < m X |cov(hi)|
       if the node hs does not cover any graph of NO_RARE
          Define rarity r ← |cov(hs)|/|cov(hi)|
          Define support s ← |cov(hi)|/|C|
          Build deviation hi : hs (r, s).
       else
          Maximal_Deviations of hi considering hs
Procedure Maximal_Deviation of hi considering hk

Parameters hi, hj, NOT_RARE of hi
for each son-nodo hs of hk
   if hk does not cover any graph of NO_RARE
     Define rarity r ← |cov(hk)|/|cov(hi)|
     Define support s ← |cov(hi)|/|C|
     Build deviation hi : hk (r, s).
   else
     Maximal_Deviation of hi considering hk
```

Fig. 1. Deviation detection algorithm

Representative characteristic: The description $desc(h_j)$ of the node $h_j < h_i$ is a *representative characteristic* for the context h_i if $\left|cov(h_j)\right| \geq m \times \left|cov(h_i)\right|$.

Rare conceptual graph: The graph $G_i \in cov(h_i)$ is a *rare graph* for the context h_i if there is no representative characteristic $desc(h_j)$ of context h_i such that $G_i \in cov(h_j)$. The set of rare conceptual graphs of the context h_i is denoted by $R(h_i)$.

Contextual deviation: The description $desc(h_k)$ of the node $h_k < h_i$ is a *contextual deviation* of the context h_i if $\forall G_i \in cov(h_k)$ it holds $G_i \in R(h_i)$. In this case, the contextual deviation is expressed as:

$$desc(h_i) : desc(h_k)\left(r = \frac{|cov(h_k)|}{|cov(h_i)|}, s = \frac{|cov(h_k)|}{|C|}\right)$$

These definitions allow finding *all* contextual deviations for a given set of graphs, and also for a given m. Many of these deviations are redundant. For instance, if the graphs that mention birds are rare then the graphs about birds of prey are also rare. Thus, it is necessary to eliminate the redundant deviations.

Redundant deviation: The contextual deviation $g_i : g_k(\alpha, \beta)$ is *redundant* if there is another contextual deviation $g_i : g_j(\gamma, \beta)$ such that $g_k < g_j$.

Logical Analysis of Programs

The first part of the paper is devoted to techniques for the automatic generation of invariants. The second part provides criteria for using the invariants to check simultaneously for correctness (including termination) or incorrectness. A third part examines the implications of the approach for the automatic diagnosis and correction of logical errors.

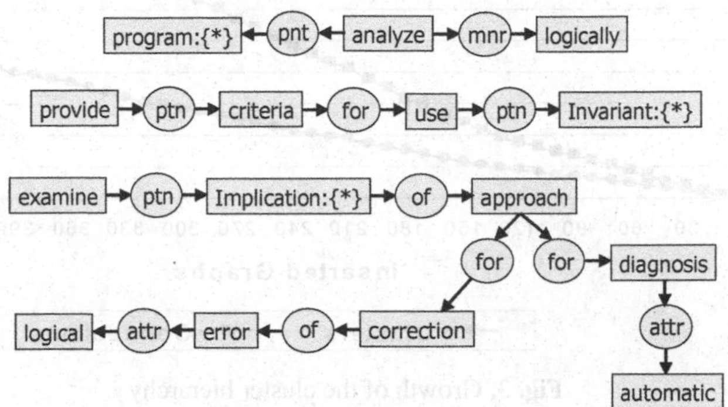

Fig. 2. A scientific paper and it conceptual graph

The basic algorithm for detecting deviations in a set of conceptual graphs – in their conceptual hierarchy – works as follows. It traverses all the hierarchy (using a *bottom-up* approach) and for each node h_i (a context) defines the set of representative characteristics and rare elements. Then, it detects the nodes $h_j < h_i$ whose descriptions $desc(h_j)$ represent a contextual deviation for the given context h_i. The algorithm is described in figure 1.

5 Experimental Results

This section describes the analysis of a set of conceptual graphs that represents the content of 495 paper surrogates of computer science. Figure 2 shows a paper surrogate and its corresponding conceptual graph. The method to extract and build the graphs is described in (Tapia-Melchor and López-López, 1998; Montes-y-Gómez, 1999).

In order to detect the deviations in the given set of graphs, we first built it conceptual clustering. The experiments demonstrate that this kind of clustering, when the graphs represent text details, is practical. For instance, figure 3 shows an almost linear growth in the number of clusters and connections of the conceptual hierarchy. Also, this clustering is rich enough for discovering patterns, since it maintains most conceptual and relational information. The figure 4 shows a small part of the resulting hierarchy.

For the experiments we use $0.1 \leq m \leq 0.5$. The best case was obtained with $m = 0.25$. We detected 23 deviations; two examples are showed in Figure 5. They indicate that the papers are focused on the description of different *procedures*, being the *data division* the procedure less studied. Also, some papers consider the *solution of equations*, but just very few study the solution of *polynomial equations by the Barstow-Hitchcock method.*

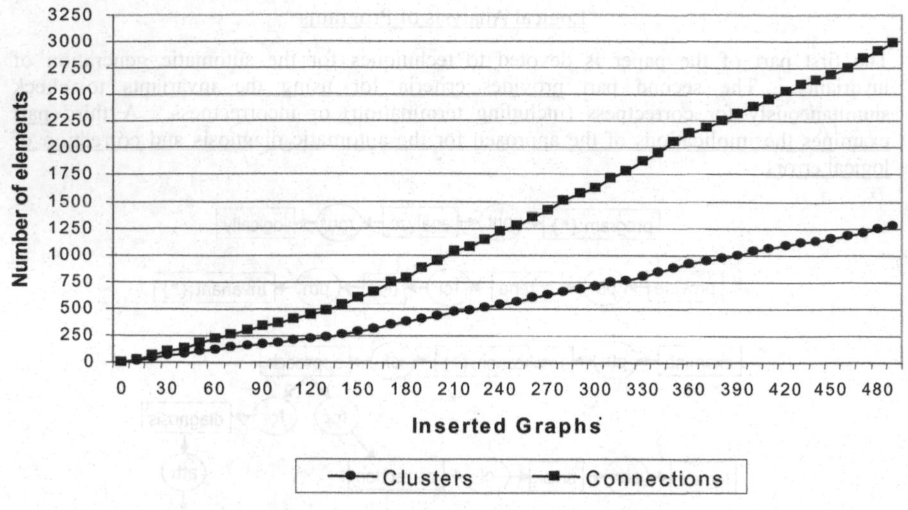
Number of elements
Inserted Graphs
Clusters
Connections

Fig. 3. Growth of the cluster hierarchy

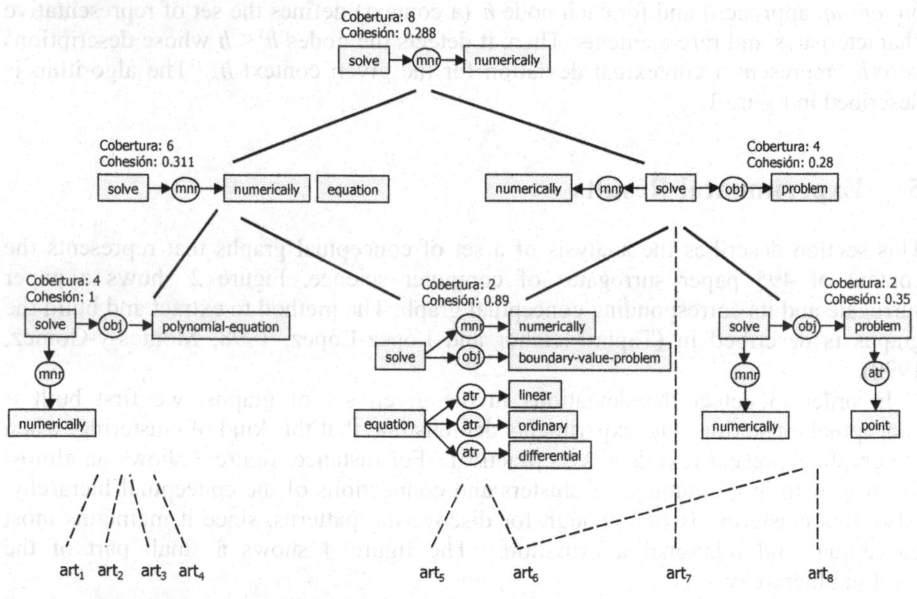
Cobertura: 8
Cohesión: 0.288
solve
mnr
numerically
Cobertura: 6
Cohesión: 0.311
equation
Cobertura: 4
Cohesión: 0.28
obj
problem
Cobertura: 4
Cohesión: 1
polynomial-equation
Cobertura: 2
Cohesión: 0.89
boundary-value-problem
atr
linear
ordinary
differential
Cobertura: 2
Cohesión: 0.35
point
art1 art2 art3 art4 art5 art6 art7 art8
art1 a art4 – ...(numerical solution of the polynomial equation)...
art5 – ...(the numerical solution of boundary value problems for linear ordinary differential equations)...
art6 – ...(the numerical solution of an n-point boundary value problem for linear ordinary differential equations)...
art7 - ...(the numerical solution of a thin plate heat transfer problem)...
art8 - ...(the numerical solution of nonlinear two-point boundary problems by finite difference methods)...

Fig. 4. A part of the cluster hierarchy

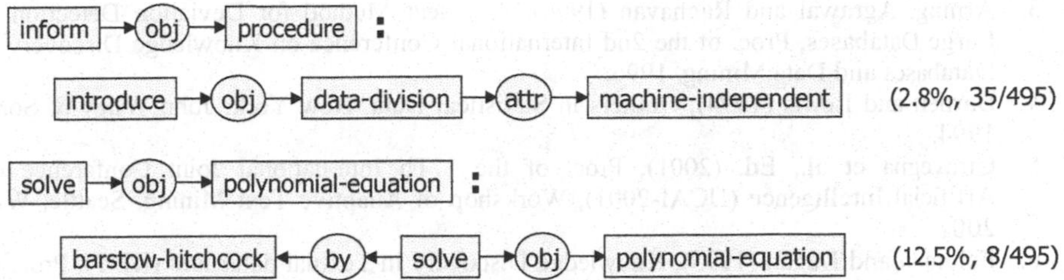

Fig. 5. Two deviations of the set of computer science papers.

6 Conclusions

Current methods of text mining use simple and shallow representation of texts, for instance, a list of keywords. On one hand, such representations are easily extracted from texts and easily analyzed, but on the other hand, they usually restrict the expressiveness and diversity of the discoveries.

Our research is focused on this problem. Basically, we proposed to use conceptual graphs for representing the text content, and developed some methods to analyze this kind of representations and discover detail patterns among texts.

In this paper we present a method for detecting rare patterns –deviations– in a given set of conceptual graphs. This method is different from traditional statistical and distance-based approaches, because it detects the deviations based on the concept of regularity. Some important characteristics of this method are:

- Detects not only rare graphs but also patterns about them. These patterns summarize the content of the rare graphs.
- Uses the conceptual clustering of the graphs as an index of the collection. This strategy facilitates the detection of local deviations.
- Identifies deviations for different contexts of the set of graphs (local deviations), and thus allows visualizing the deviations from different perspectives and at different levels of generalization.

Acknowledgements

This work was done under partial support of CONACyT, CGEPI-IPN, and SNI, Mexico.

References

1. Alexandrov, M., A. Gelbukh, and P. Makagonov (2000), On Metrics for Keyword-Based Document Selection and Classification, Proc. of the Conference on Intelligent Text Processing and Computational Linguistics CICLing-2000, Mexico City, Mexico, February 2000.
2. Allan, Papka and Lavrenko (1998), On-line new Event Detection and Tracking, Proc. of the 21st ACM-SIGIR International Conference on Research and Developement in Information Retrieval, August 1998.

3. Arning, Agrawal and Raghavan (1996), A Linear Method for Deviation Detection in Large Databases, Proc. of the 2nd International Conference on Knowledge Discovery in Databases and Data Mining, 1996.
4. Barnett and Lewis (1994), Outliers in Statistical Data, New York: John Wiley & Sons, 1994.
5. Ciravegna et al., Ed. (2001), Proc. of the 17Th International Joint Conference on Artificial Intelligence (IJCAI-2001), Workshop of Adaptive Text Mining, Seattle, WA, 2001.
6. Feldman and Dagan (1995), Knowledge Discovery in Textual databases (KDT), Proc. of the 1st International Conference on Knowledge discovery (KDD_95), pp.112-117, Montreal, 1995.
7. Feldman, Ed. (1999), Proc. of The 16th International Joint Conference on Artificial Intelligence (IJCAI-1999), Workshop on Text Mining: Foundations, Techniques and Applications, Stockholm, Sweden, 1999.
8. Guzmán (1996), Uso y Diseño de Mineros de Datos, J. Soluciones Avanzadas, Num. 34, 1996.
9. Han and Kamber (2001), Data Mining: Concepts and Techniques, Morgan Kaufmann Publishers, 2001.
10. Knorr and Ng (1998), Algorithms for Mining Distance-based Outliers in Large Datasets, Proc. of the International Conference on Very Large Data Bases (VLDB'98), Newport Beach, CA, 1997.
11. Mladenic, Ed. (2000), Proc. of the Sixth International Conference on Knowledge Discovery and Data Mining, Workshop on Text Mining, Boston, MA, 2000.
12. Montes-y-Gómez, Gelbukh, López-López (1999), Document intentions expressed in titles. Extraction, representation, and possible use, Selected Works 1997-1998, Center for Computing Research (CIC-IPN), 1999.
13. Montes-y-Gómez, Gelbukh, López-López, Baeza-Yates (2001), Un Método de Agrupamiento de Grafos Conceptuales para Minería de Texto, J. Procesamiento de Lenguaje Natural, Vol. 27, Septiembre 2001.
14. Montes-y-Gómez (2002), Minería de texto usando la semejanza entre estructuras semánticas, Ph.D. thesis, Center for Computing Research (CIC-IPN), Mexico, 2002.
15. Tapia-Melchor and López-López (1998), Automatic Information Extraction from Documents in WWW, Séptimo Congreso Internacional de Electrónica, Comunicaciones y Computadoras, CONIELECOMP 98, Febrero, 1998.
16. Sowa (1999), Knowledge Representation: Logical, Philosophical and Computational Foundations, 1st edition, Thomson Learning, 1999.

Using Long Queries in a Passage Retrieval System*

Fernando Llopis, Antonio Ferrández, and José Luis Vicedo

Departamento de Lenguajes y Sistemas Informáticos
University of Alicante
Alicante, Spain
{llopis,antonio,vicedo}@dlsi.ua.es

Abstract. Previous works in Information Retrieval show that using pieces of text obtain better results than using the whole document as the basic unit to compare with the user's query. This kind of IR systems is usually called *Passage Retrieval (PR)*. However, there is not a general agreement about how one should define those pieces of text (also known as *passages*), in order to obtain an optimum performance. This paper proposes a PR system based on a novel selection of variable size passages. It presents an evaluation that shows better results than a standard IR system and several well-known PR systems. Also, the influence of short queries with reference to long queries is evaluated.

1 Introduction

Information Retrieval (IR) systems are defined as tools capable of extracting a ranked list of relevant documents from a user's query. These systems are based on measuring the similarity between each document and the query, by means of several formulas that typically use the frequency of query terms in the documents. This way of measuring causes larger documents to have a greater frequency of chances to be considered as being relevant., because of their higher number of terms that coincide with those of the query.

In order to solve this problem, some IR systems measure the similarity in accordance with the relevance of the pieces of adjoining text that form the documents, where these pieces of text are called *passages*. This kinds of IR systems, which are usually called *Passage Retrieval (PR)*, allows that the similarity measure is not affected by the size of the document. Moreover, PR systems obtain better accuracy than IR systems, and they also return the precise piece of text in answer to the query, a fact that is especially important when large documents are returned.

PR systems are more complex than IR systems, since the number of textual units to be compared is higher (each document is formed by several passages) and the number of modules is higher (above all when the passage splitting is accomplished after processing each query as it is proposed in [4]). Nevertheless, the higher complexity of PR gives better results. For example, in [1] the improvement reaching a 20%, and in [4] an high as 50%.

* This paper has been partially supported by the Spanish Government (CICYT) projects numbers TIC2000-0664-C02-02 and TIC2001-3530-C02-02

C.A. Coello Coello et al. (Eds.): MICAI 2002, LNAI 2313, pp. 185–193, 2002.

The PR system presented in this paper is called *IR-n*. It defines a novel passage selection model, which forms the passages from sentences in the document. IR-n has been used in the last Cross-Language Evaluation Forum (CLEF-2001) and in the last Text REtrieval Conference (TREC-2001) in the Question Answering track. Moreover, it has been compared with two standard IR systems, the first one based on cosine similarity measure by Salton [8], and the second the well-known IR system called Z/Prise [12]. The test has been conducted on the same set of documents and questions. Furthermore, our system is compared with other PR systems.

The following section presents the backgrounds in PR. Section 3 describes the architecture of our proposed PR system. In section 4, we give a detailed account of the test, experiments and obtained results. Finally, we present the conclusions of this work.

2 Backgrounds in Passage Retrieval

The most frequent similarity measures between documents and queries are cosine [8], the pivoted cosine [10] and the okapi system [11]. These models are mainly based on counting the number of terms that documents and queries are share and applying a normalization process.

The main differences between different PR systems are the way they select the passages, that is to say, what they consider a passage and the size of it. According to the taxonomy proposed in [1], the following PR systems can be found: *discourse-based model, semantic model* and *window model*. The first one uses the structural properties of the documents, such as sentences or paragraphs (e.g. the one proposed in [7], [9]) in order to define the passages. The second one divides each document in semantic pieces, according to the different topics in the document (e.g. those in [2]). The last one uses windows with a fixed size to form the passages [1], [3].

On the one hand, it looks obvious that discourse-based models are more effective since they are using the structure of the document itself. However, the main problem with them is that the results could depend on the writing style of the document's author. On the other hand, window models have the advantage that they are simpler to use, since the passages have a previously known size, whereas the remaining models have to bear in mind the variable size of each passage. Nevertheless, discourse-based and semantic models have the advantage that they return logical and coherent fragments of the document, which is quite important if these IR systems are used for other applications such as Question Answering. Finally, it should be mentioned that semantic and window models can partially or fully overlap pieces of the same text each other in order to fine-tune the results.

The passage extraction model that we are proposing allows us to benefit from the advantages of discourse-based models, since logical information units of the text, such as sentences, form the passages. Moreover, another novel proposal in our PR system is the relevance measure, which unlike other discourse-based models is not calculated from the number of passage terms, but from the fixed number of passage sentences. It allows a simpler calculation of this measure unlike other discourse-based or semantic models. Although we are using a fixed number of sentences for each passage, we consider that our proposal differs from the window models since our passages do not have fixed sizes (i.e. a fixed number of words) because they are using sentences with a variable size.

3 Overview of the System

In this section, we are briefly describing the architecture of the proposed PR system, namely IR-n. We are focusing on its two main modules: the indexation and the document-extracting modules.

3.1 Indexation Module

The main aim of this module is to generate the dictionaries that contain all the required information for the document-extracting module. It requires the following information for each term:

- The number of documents that contain the term.
- For each document:
  - The number of times that the term appears in the document.
  - Position of the term in the document: the number of sentences and position in the sentence.

Where we are considering as terms, the stems produced by the "Porter stemmer" on those words that do not appear in a list of stop-words, a list that is similar to those used in IR systems. For the query, the terms are also extracted in the same way, that is to say, their stems and positions in the query are query words that do not appear in the list of stop-words. In principle, it supposes that we need more information than for standard IR systems. But, as it will be shown the results showed benefits that exceed this storage increase.

3.2 Document-Extracting Module

This module extracts the documents according to thier similarity with the user's query. The scheme in this process is as follows:

1. Query terms are sorted according to the number of documents in which they appear, where the terms that appear in fewer documents are processed firstly.
2. The documents that contain some query term are extracted.
3. The following similarity measure is calculated for each passage *p* with the query *q*:

$$\text{Similarity\_measure}(p, q) = \sum_{t \in p \wedge q} W_{p,t} * W_{q,t}$$

   Where:
   $W_{p,t} = \log_e(f_{p,t} + 1)$.
   $f_{p,t}$ is the number of times that the term *t* appears in the passage *p*.
   $W_{q,t} = \log_e(f_{q,t} + 1) * \text{idf}$.
   $f_{q,t}$ is the number of times that the term *t* appears in the query *q*.
   $idf = \log_e(N / f_t + 1)$.
   N is the number of documents in the collection.
   f_t is the number of documents that contain the term *t*.

4. Each document is assigned the highest similarity measure from its passages.
5. The documents are sorted by their similarity measure.
6. The documents are presented according to their similarity measure.

As it will be noted, the similarity measure is similar to the cosine measure presented in [8]. The only difference is that the size of each passage (the number of terms) is not used to normalise the results. This difference makes the calculation simpler than other discourse-based PR systems or IR systems, since the normalization is accomplished according to a fixed number of sentences per passage. Another important detail to notice is that we are using *N* as the number of documents in the collection, instead of the number of passages. That is because in [4] it is not considered relevant for the final results.

Table 1. Precision results obtained on *Los Angeles Times* collection with different number of sentences per passage

	Precision IR-n					
Recall	5 Sent.	10 Sent.	15 Sent.	20 Sent.	25 Sent.	30 Sent.
0.00	0.6378	0.6508	0.6950	*0.7343*	0.6759	0.6823
0.10	0.5253	0.5490	0.5441	*0.5516*	0.5287	0.5269
0.20	0.4204	0.4583	0.4696	*0.4891*	0.4566	0.4431
0.30	0.3372	0.3694	0.3848	*0.3964*	0.3522	0.3591
0.40	0.2751	0.3017	0.2992	*0.2970*	0.2766	0.2827
0.50	0.2564	0.2837	0.2678	*0.2633*	0.2466	0.2515
0.60	0.1836	0.1934	0.1809	*0.1880*	0.1949	0.1882
0.70	0.1496	0.1597	0.1517	*0.1498*	0.1517	0.1517
0.80	0.1213	0.1201	0.1218	*0.1254*	0.1229	0.1279
0.90	0.0844	0.0878	0.0909	*0.0880*	0.0874	0.0904
1.00	0.0728	0.0722	0.0785	*0.0755*	0.0721	0.0711

The optimum number of sentences to consider per passage is experimentally obtained. It can depend on the genre of the documents, or even on the type of the query as it is suggested in [3]. We have experimentally considered a fixed number of 20 sentences for the collection of documents in which we are going to work [6]. Table 1 presents the experiment where the 20 sentences per passage obtained the best results.

As it is commented in section 2, the proposed PR system can be classified into discourse-based models since it is using variable-size passages that are based on a fixed number of sentences (but different number of terms per passage). The passages overlap each other, that is to say, let us suppose that the size of the passage is *N* sentences, then the first passage will be formed by the sentences from 1 to N, the second one from 2 to N+1, and so on. We have decided to overlap just sentences based on the following experiment, where several numbers of overlapping sentences have been tested. In this experiment, Table 2, it will be observed that only one overlapping sentence obtained the best results.

4 Evaluation

In this section, the evaluation is presented, in which the obtained results show the improvement that introduce our proposal.

Table 2. Experiments with a different number of overlapping sentences

Recall	IR-n with 1 overlap.	IR-n with 5 overlap.	IR-n 10 overlap.
0.00	*0.7729*	0.7211	0.7244
0.10	*0.7299*	0.6707	0.6541
0.20	*0.6770*	0.6072	0.6143
0.30	*0.5835*	0.5173	0.5225
0.40	*0.4832*	0.4144	0.4215
0.50	*0.4284*	0.3704	0.3758
0.60	*0.3115*	0.2743	0.2759
0.70	*0.2546*	0.2252	0.2240
0.80	*0.2176*	0.1914	0.1918
0.90	*0.1748*	0.1504	0.1485
1.00	*0.1046*	0.0890	0.0886
Medium	*0.4150*	0.3635	0.3648

4.1 Experiments

Some experiments have been carried out to measure the improvement of our proposal. These experiments have been run on a TREC collection: *Los Angeles Times*. This collection is formed by 113.005 documents, where the medium number of words per sentence is about 29, and the average number of terms per sentence is about nine. However, it should be noticed that this collection has a heterogeneous format and size, where the longest document has 807 sentences, and the smaller just 1 sentence.

A set of 47 queries has been used for the evaluation. These queries have been previously used in the last Cross-Language Evaluation Forum (CLEF) in which the authors participated . In CLEF conference, all the 47 test queries were formulated in three different ways: title, description and narrative. Title queries are usually formed by between 2 and 4 words (after discarding stop-words). Description queries are quite similar to title queries, whereas narrative queries are longer, since they are usually formed by several sentences. The following example shows the differences between them:

Title query: “Pesticides in Baby Food”.

Description query: “Find reports on pesticides in baby food”.

Narrative query: “Relevant documents give information on the discovery of pesticides in baby food. They report on different brands, supermarkets, and companies selling baby food which contains pesticides. They also discuss measures against the contamination of baby food by pesticides”.

It should be remarked that description and narrative queries include terms that are not relevant for the query (e.g. *relevant documents* or *find reports*), which should be filtered. Two experiments have been carried out, one with title queries (short query), and the second one with narrative queries (long queries), whose results are shown in the following two sub-sections.

The evaluation measures in this paper are those used in TREC conferences, namely recall and precision:

$$\text{Recall} = \frac{\text{Number of relevant documents extracted}}{\text{Number of relevant texts in the collection}}$$

$$\text{Precision} = \frac{\text{Number of relevant documents extracted}}{\text{Number of extracted documents}}$$

In order to compare our proposal, IR-n, with other proposals, two IR systems have been run on the same set of documents and queries. The first one is the vectorial standard model defined in [8]. The second one is the Z/Prise system [12].

4.2 Results Obtained in Short Queries

Table 3 presents the interpolated precision for standard levels of recall. The second column in this table presents the results obtained by the vectorial model [8], the third by Z/Prise [12], the last column shows our system, IR-n.

From Table 3, it can be observed that our proposal obtains better precision results than the vectorial model for all the different passage size. For 20 sentences length and recall 0.20, the benefit reaches 25%. With reference to Z/Prise, similar results are obtained, although it should be mentioned that Z/Prise uses query expansion, and we do not, moreover we are using *title* form for the queries, that suppose a medium of 3 words. Besides, IR-n obtains better results than Z/Prise average (0.4270 and 0.4208 respectively).

Table 4 presents the results obtained when 5, 10, 15, 20, 30 and 200 documents are extracted. Again, the results show that IR-n is quite superior to the vectorial model, and quite similar to Z/Prise, although in this case, our system is superior to Z/Prise when fewer documents are extracted, in spite of not using query expansion techniques as idoes Z/Prise.

Table 3. Obtained results on *Los Angeles Times* collection and 47 CLEF title-queries

	Precision		
Recall	Vectorial model	Z/Prise	IR-n
0.00	0.5668	0.7583	0.7816
0.10	0.5049	0.7278	0.7354
0.20	0.4394	0.6476	0.6927
0.30	0.3889	0.5632	0.5898
0.40	0.3547	0.4904	0.4864
0.50	0.3182	0.4389	0.4376
0.60	0.2678	0.3315	0.3290
0.70	0.2157	0.2825	0.2724
0.80	0.1765	0.2343	0.2385
0.90	0.1567	0.1925	0.2002
1.00	0.1205	0.1317	0.1339
Medium	0.3028	0.4208	0.4270

Table 4. Precision obtained with different number of extracted documents

Precision	Vectorial model	Z/Prise	IR-n
At 5 docs	0.3021	0.4638	0.4851
At 10 docs	0.2766	0.3872	0.4000
At 15 docs	0.2582	0.3135	0.3376
At 20 docs	0.2426	0.2851	0.2904
At 30 docs	0.2014	0.2383	0.2468
At 100 docs	0.1089	0.1215	0.1189
At 200 docs	0.0662	0.0705	0.0699
At 500 docs	0.0311	0.0318	0.0319
At 1000 docs	0.0164	0.0167	0.0164
R-Precision	0.2749	0.4009	0.4113

4.3 Results Obtained in Long Queries

In this experiment, we have tried to examin the benefits of using long queries (narrative form presented in section 4.1), with reference to short queries. In this case, the same systems are tested: vectorial model and our system, namely IR-n. Moreover, we have proposed two novel ways to calculate the measure with these long queries: *M1* and *M2*. Both measures divide the query into sentences and run the search process in an individual way for each sentence. The difference between both is that *M1* assigns to each document the average of the similarity measure obtained by each sentence of the query, whereas *M2* assigns the maximum measure.

In Table 5 and Table 6, the obtained results are presented. From these results, we can deduce the following conclusions. On the one hand, IR-n obtains again better results than the vectorial model, although the differences are not as high as those obtained with short queries. On the other hand, the two novel measures that we are proposing, M1 and M2, do not obtain the expected improvement since similar results to IR-n are presented, although we expect that they would work better with a different passage length. Anyway, it will be tested in future works.

Table 5. Precision vs. Recall with long queries

	Precision					
Recall	Vectorial model	Vectorial model M1	Vectorial model M2	IR-n	IR-n M1	IR-n M2
0.00	0.7772	0.7639	0.6766	0.8235	0.7966	0.7351
0.10	0.6981	0.6929	0.5949	0.7754	0.7757	0.6903
0.20	0.6373	0.6201	0.5079	0.7143	0.7120	0.6168
0.30	0.6049	0.5796	0.4536	0.6482	0.6340	0.5361
0.40	0.5592	0.5360	0.4205	0.5807	0.5593	0.4710
0.50	0.5176	0.5067	0.3993	0.5255	0.5169	0.4431
0.60	0.4245	0.4030	0.3386	0.4428	0.4416	0.3867
0.70	0.3657	0.3289	0.2883	0.3977	0.3933	0.3421
0.80	0.3143	0.2915	0.2548	0.3267	0.3216	0.2770
0.90	0.2766	0.2574	0.2105	0.2518	0.2600	0.2079
1.00	0.2256	0.2170	0.1783	0.1849	0.1836	0.1702
Medium	0.4773	0.4563	0.3776	0.5040	0.4965	0.4265

Table 6. Obtained results with long queries

Precision	Vectorial model. Completa	Vectorial model. Medium	Vectorial model. Maximum	IR-n. Completa	IR-Medium	IR-n Maximum
At 5 docs	0.4681	0.4468	0.3957	0.5234	0.5191	0.4596
At 10	0.3894	0.3766	0.3404	0.4340	0.4340	0.3681
At 15	0.3390	0.3277	0.2908	0.3759	0.3702	0.3177
At 20	0.3000	0.2926	0.2521	0.3255	0.3277	0.2766
At 30	0.2504	0.2426	0.2113	0.2589	0.2631	0.2319
At 100	0.1211	0.1196	0.1072	0.1236	0.1253	0.1106
At 200	0.0740	0.0721	0.0649	0.0730	0.0731	0.0662
At 500	0.0328	0.0321	0.0296	0.0319	0.0320	0.0300
At 1000	0.0173	0.0165	0.0162	0.0172	0.0170	0.0158
R-Precis.	0.4644	0.4287	0.3454	0.4739	0.4758	0.4172

Table 7. Comparison between short and long queries

	Precision	%Difference
Short queries		
Vectorial model	0.3028	+0.00
Z/Prise	0.4208	+38.96
IR-n	0.4270	+41.01
Long Queries		
Vectorial model	0.4773	+0.00
Vectorial model (M1)	0.4563	-4.39
Vectorial model (M2)	0.3776	-20.88
IR-n	0.5040	5.59
IR-n (M1)	0.4965	4.02
IR-n (M2)	0.4265	-10.64

5 Conclusions and Future Works

In this paper, a novel passage extraction model has been presented. This model can be included in the discourse-based models since it is using the sentences as logical units to divide the document into passages. The passages are formed by a fixed number of sentences, which does not mean that it could be included in the window models, since our passages do not have a fixed number of words. In this paper, a similarity measure is also proposed, which allows us to calculate the similarity between documents and queries in a simpler way than other discourse-based models. Finally, the proposed system, namely IR-n, has been evaluated and compared with other IR and PR-systems: vectorial model, Z/Prise and window models, where IR-n obtains better precision, in spite of not using query expansion techniques as does Z/Prise.

Moreover, we have tried to check the benefit of using long queries with reference to short queries. It can be observed that IR-n obtains better results than the vectorial model, although the differences are not as high as with short queries.

As future works, we intend to work in several topics about PR. For example, we intend a greater study the influence of the passage length with reference to different set of documents and different queries. Moreover, we intend to incorporate in IR-n system several query expansion techniques in order to set a real comparison with other IR systems as Z/Prise.

References

1. Callan, J. *Passage-Level Evidence in Document Retrieval.* In Proceedings of the 17 th Annual ACM SIGIR Conference on Research and Development in Information Retrieval, Dublin, Ireland, 1994, pp. 302-310.
2. Hearst, M. and Plaunt, C. *Subtopic structuring for full-length document access.* Proceedings of the Sixteenth Annual International ACM SIGIR Conference on Research and Development in Information Retrieval, June 1993, Pittsburgh, PA, pp 59-68
3. Kaskiel, M. and Zobel, J. *Passage Retrieval Revisited* SIGIR '97: Proceedings of the 20th Annual International ACM July, 1997, Philadelphia, PA, USA, pp 27-31
4. KaszKiel, M. and Zobel, J. *Effective Ranking with Arbitrary Passages.* Journal of the American Society for Information Science (JASIS), Vol 52, No. 4, February 2001, pp 344-364.
5. Kaszkiel, M.; Zobel, J. and. Sacks-Davis, R.. *Efficient Passage Ranking for Document Databases.* ACM transactions on Information Systems, Vol 17, Nº 4, October 1999, pp 406-439
6. Llopis, F. and Vicedo, J. *Ir-n system, a passage retrieval system at CLEF 2001* Working Notes for the Clef 2001 Darmstdt, Germany , pp 115-120
7. Namba, I *Fujitsu Laboratories TREC9 Report.* Proceedings of the Tenth Text REtrieval Conference, TREC-10. Gaithersburg,USA. November 2001, pp 203-208
8. Salton G. *Automatic Text Processing: The Transformation, Analysis, and Retrieval of Information by Computer,* Addison Wesley Publishing, New York. 1989
9. Salton, G.; Allan, J. Buckley *Approaches to passage retrieval in full text information systems.* In R Korfhage, E Rasmussen & P Willet (Eds.) Prodeedings of the 16 th annual international ACM-SIGIR conference on research and development in information retrieval. Pittsburgh PA, pp 49-58
10. Singhal, A.; Buckley, C. and Mitra, M. *Pivoted document length normalization.* Proceedings of the 19th annual international ACM-SIGIR conference on research and development in information retrieval, 1996.
11. Venner, G. and Walker, S. *Okapi '84: 'Best match' system.* Microcomputer networking in libraries II. Vine, 48,1983, pp 22-26.
12. Zprise developed by Darrin Dimmick (NIST) Available on demand at http://itl.nist.gov./iaui/894.02/works/papers/zp2/zp2.html

Object-Oriented Constraint Programming with J.CP

Georg Ringwelski

Fraunhofer FIRST, Kekuléstrasse 7, 12489 Berlin, Germany
georg.ringwelski@first.fraunhofer.de

Abstract. We give a short introduction to Asynchronous Constraint Solving (ACS), which is a new execution model to solve constraint satisfaction problems through constraint propagation and search. Propagation is based on the theory of chaotic iteration and search is implemented with explicit constraint retraction. ACS is designed for the object-oriented development of distributed or strongly interactive applications. Our implementation **J.CP** makes use of this new execution model. **J.CP** is a Java package, which combines the declarativity of constraint programming with the features of the object-oriented programming language Java. Constraints are autonomous objects that can be posted and retracted in concurrently running solvers that communicate via common constraint variables.

1 Introduction

Constraint programming has reached many application areas of Artificial Intelligence since it was introduced in the early 1980's. Based on the sound theoretical basis of constraint logic programming (in short CLP)[11, 10] or concurrent constraint programming [15], it was integrated in many programming languages, most of them being Prolog implementations such as clp(R) [11] or SICStus Prolog [4]. The interest in the integration of constraint processing into non-logic programming languages has grown together with the acceptance of constraint-based methods in the software community. Thus some systems have been implemented to integrate constraints into object-oriented programming languages such as C++ [12], Java [5, 16] or Oz/Mozart [6]. Beeing further developments of CLP all of these, however, have some drawbacks in object-oriented and distributed programms as we will discuss throughout the paper.

The success of **constraint programming** (CP) is a consequence of its declarativity. The "holy grail of programming" is getting close with constraint programming: "the user states the problem, the computer solves it"[1]. Many constraint satisfaction problems (CSP) can be solved by domain specific solvers. These solvers infer the solution of NP-hard problems by search in a massively reduced search space. The reduction is achieved by constraint propagation, which is an iterative reduction of the domains of the variables that are to be instantiated as a solution of the CSP. This algorithm has shown to be very efficient in many application areas.

[1] citation: E.C. Freuder, CONSTRAINTS, April 1997

C.A. Coello Coello et al. (Eds.): MICAI 2002, LNAI 2313, pp. 194–203, 2002.

Object-Oriented Programming (OOP) and the programming language **Java** have emerged the best choice for many professional software developers. Although Java is known to execute slower than other languages, its platform-independency and the large amount of APIs for almost any state-of-the-art application are convincing. Consequently, the **combination of CP and Java** seams to be a very promising approach to find new application areas for constraint programming. The use of a concurrent object-oriented implementation of variables, constraints and solvers together with Java's capabilities opens up application areas like

- the use of parallel or distributed running solvers, that cooperatively solve large CSPs. The necessary communication is performed by the common variable objects [3],
- the use of known, efficient problem solving algorithms, i.e. constraint propagation, in pure Java applications,
- the integration of constraints into the development-process of large object-oriented systems. I.e. constraints, variables and solvers can not only be integrated in them implementation, but also into analysis and design,
- the integration of constraint processing into the imperative programming paradigm through explicit constraint retraction. Software-developer can write constraint-based programs without having to understand the execution model of CLP,
- the use of Java's manyfold possibilities for user-interaction such as applets in constraint-based applications.

2 Asynchronous Constraint Solving

A constraint-based application with an Asynchronous Constraint Solver (ACS), consists of five main classes as presented in Figure 1. We will describe these components throughout this paper. A formal introduction to the execution model of ACS can be found in [14]

In contrast to very popular existing constraint solvers, ACS allows incremental constraint posting (the commercially very successful ILOG Solver [12] and the newly availible ILOG JSolver does not) and constraint retraction (CLP does not; e.g. SICStus [4] and ECL^{i}PS^e [17]). These two features support the development of highly **interactive applications**.

Constraint-based methods can be integrated into professional **software-development processes** because everything is implemented in regular objects. Most modern development tools and concepts are designed for the creation of object-oriented software written in imperative languages. Composition of constraint systems [2] is performed in a generic way, using the type system of the programming languages. Finally, the analysis and design of constraint-based programs can be done with software-engineering tools, making use of established methods for software development, such as design patterns or UML.

ACS is well suited for solving CSPs in **distributed applications**, i.e. DCSPs, because no global information is used by any component [13]. Search is

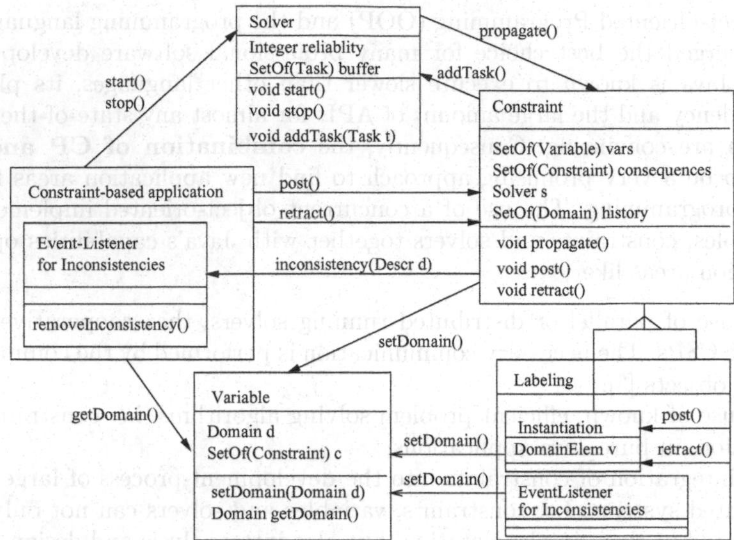

Fig. 1. Architecture of an application using ACS

implemented in an encapsulated component sending non-blocking messages to constraints and solvers. We can use (fast) non-blocking message passing because due to the asynchronous execution of constraint postings and retractions solvers can handle this. In difference to all solvers known to us we do not need to wait for the completion of constraint propagation after posting a constraint before we can continue program execution. This allows us to just send a message to a constraint-object to re-execute its propagation tasks or to execute its retraction-task some time later. In difference to Mozart/Oz [6] we thus have full propagation of domain restrictions across process borders.

2.1 Components of an ACS

Constraint variables are associated with a representation of their current domain. This representation is given as a vector of features (properties) non-ambiguously defining a set. For example a finite interval of integers can be represented by its minimum and maximum value leading to the representation $(min : int, max : int)$. If such a feature is changed, constraints depending on it must be reposted (propagation) in order to approximate arc-consistency in the constraint network.

Definition 1 (Constraint Variable). *A (constraint-) variable $v = (\overline{p}, C)$ of a domain D is given by*

1. *a vector $\overline{p} \in P = P_1 \times P_2 \times \ldots \times P_n$ of properties of the domain D of v, such that a mapping* $\mathsf{dom} : P \rightarrow \mathcal{P}ow(D)$ *exists*
2. *a family $C = (C_p)_{p \in \{P_1,\ldots,P_n\}}$ of sequences of constraints C_p*

Every constraint holds information on its variables and the solver it was posted in. Furthermore, the consequences and the history of the constraint are stored, providing necessary information for constraint retraction. The consequences are constraints that were reposted within the propagation of the constraint and thus have to be reversed for constraint retraction. The history is a snapshot of the current domains of the variables of the constraint which is restored when the constraint is retracted or before it is reposted during the retraction of another constraint.

Definition 2 (Constraint). *A constraint* $c = (\overline{v}, T, s, E, H)$ *is given by*

1. *a vector* $\overline{v}$ *of its variables*
2. *a set* $T = \{(i_1, p_1), ..., (i_n, p_n)\}$ *of propagation tasks where* i_j *are constraint implementations (constraint programs without solver or variable definitions) and* $p_j \in \{0, 1, ..., \top\}$ *are their associated priority values.*
3. *its solver* s
4. *a set* E *of constraints called c's consequences/entailed constraints*
5. *a* $\overline{v}$*-indexed family of domain descriptions (Def. 1, 1.)* $H = (h_{v_i})_{v_i \in \varepsilon(\overline{v})}$ *called c's history*

Remark: With ε we denote a mapping of vectors on sets, such that all components of the argument elements of the result: $\varepsilon(\overline{x}) = \varepsilon((x_1, ..., x_n)) := \{x_1, ..., x_n\}$.

The execution of the propagation tasks given with every constraint is organized by a constraint solver that in our approach runs concurrently to the application. The solver can be considered a (slightly extended) scheduler for the constraints' tasks. The solver always provides information on the progress of the current constraint propagation, which may be used by clients to decide when variable domains are read for further evaluations or output. This is expressed in the reliability value of the solver which is increased if a task (i.e. a propagation task or a constraint retraction) has been finished and is decreased if new tasks were stored due to a constraint posting or retraction. The reliability will reach $\top$, if no tasks are left to be evaluated. Furthermore the reliability is related to the priority of the solver-tasks such that the programmer can be sure that all tasks with priority x are finished once the reliability is higher than x.

Definition 3 (Asynchronous Constraint Solver). *An asynchronous constraint solver* $s = (B, r)$ *is given by a reliability value* $r \in \{0, 1, ..., \top\}$ *and a task buffer* $B = (T, next)$ *consisting of a set* $T = \{\langle post, c, p\rangle, \langle retract, c\rangle \mid$ *c is Constraint with solver s*$\}$ *of solver-tasks and a scheduling* $next : T$. *c must define a propagation task with priority* $p \in \{0, 1, ..., \top\}$.

3 Constraint Satisfaction with ACS

Given an ACS and implementations of the used constraints, any CSP can be formulated in an imperative program by defining variables and posting the respective constraints over them in declared solvers.

Definition 4 (Constraint Program). *A constraint program is an imperative program using the primitives 1 - 7, where v is a variable,* $\overline{p}$ *describes its domain d* ($\mathsf{dom}(\overline{p}) = d$) *and c is a constraint.*

1. *solver definitions* $s = newSolver()$
2. *variable definitions* $v = newVar(\overline{p})$
3. *domain queries* $\overline{p} = v.getDomain()$
4. *constraint definitions* $c = newConstr((\overline{v}, T, s, \emptyset, \emptyset))$
5. *constraint postings* $c.post()$
6. *constraint retractions* $c.retract()$
7. *wait statements* $s.awaitReliability(val)$ *that suspend the application-thread until* $val \leq r$ *for* $s = (B, r)$.

3.1 Constraint Propagation

The operational semantics of the primitives given in Definition 4 is described in detail in [14].

With the creation of a constraint solver object a concurrently running thread is started that waits for solver-tasks to be processed. Such tasks define method-calls that perform constraint propagation or retract previously posted constraints (Def. 3). If a constraint is posted or retracted in the constraint program or another constraint or if it is reposted by a variable (propagation), a corresponding task is created and buffered by the solver. A constraint may define several tasks that are associated to priority-values. These serve the solver-thread to schedule the tasks from the buffer for execution. If all tasks have been executed, the reliability-value of the solver is set to $\top$, signalizing that all possible propagation has been performed. The application, however, can continue before $\top$-reliability is reached. The priorities of the solver tasks are associated to reliability values such that if a certain reliability is reached it is assured that certain tasks have been successfully finished.

Constraints are implemented as objects that hold all necessary information for constraint retraction and provide one or more propagation tasks. These tasks may post other constraints or restrict the domains of the constraints' variables. If a variable domain is restricted, other constraints, that depend on it are reposted in order to reach the farest possible restrictions of all domains. The magnitude of such restrictions is implemented in the constraints. In difference to solvers without task-priorities we can also use inefficient or ineffective algorithms here because they will only be executed if the solver has some spare time to do so. In [1] K. Apt showed, that such a propagation process (a so-called chaotic iteration) will result in a stable state where no further domain reductions can be deduced from the posted constraints. This state is uniquely determined such that the order of the constraint execution is irrelevant for the result and can be varied by a task scheduler like we use it in ACS. We showed in [14] that the execution model of ACS is sound and complete wrt. chaotic iteration. This means that the invocation of propagation tasks will lead to the correct result and that retraction does not interfere with this property.

Constraint retraction creates a system state, where all relevant changes that resulted from the posting of a constraint are taken back. Such changes are domain restrictions of the constraint's variables and all variables that are reached through propagation. Furthermore the thus reduced domains are used by constraints that were posted after the retracted constraint. The retraction is performed by rebuilding former variable domains from the history stored in the constraints that were affected and by reposting all these constraints. Our algorithm is an adaption of retraction in CLP(FD) [8] where we abandon the use of a centralized history management by storing consequences of constraints locally (similar to [18]).

3.2 Search in ACS

In ACS non-deterministic search is implemented as a global constraint over all variables to be labeled. This labeling-constraint posts and retracts variable-instantiation constraints until a solution of the implemented CSP is found. These actions can be taken in any order such that any search algorithm that is based on evolving and restoring states can be implemented. Currently we investigate different refinement-based algorithms and test out the possibilities to integrate local search into ACS. All used search-algorithms are encapsuled in their corresponding constraint-objects. Encapsuled search is an important prerequisite for distributed constraint satisfaction [9].

In this paper we give a brief presentation of our implementation of chronological backtracking (CBT). As shown in Figure 1 CBT is implemented as a constraint (named Labeling), that defines an order on all variables to be labeled. The CBT constraint defines an agent for the first variable that posts an instantiation constraint over its variable and a selected value out of the variable's domain. After that the agent creates a similar agent for the next variable. The agents are implemented as constraints with very low priority such that the propagation of the instantiation will be finished, before the next agent starts. When every agent has posted an instantiation, a solution is found. If during this process an inconsistency occurs, i.e. an agent cannot find a value to instantiate its variable's domain, backtracking is called in the previous agent. This backtracking-method retracts the last instantiation and tries to find another (unused) value in the domain of the respective variable. A new instantiation is posted with this new value and the next agent is re-posted.

4 The Java Constraints Package J.CP

A prototypical solver for finite domain constraints that uses the asynchronous constraint-solving paradigm has been implemented (as shown in Figure 1). It is a regular Java package called **J.CP** that can be used by any Java application and runs on almost any hardware. Constraints are implemented in classes, which means that new constraints can easily be integrated into the system. Every new constraint is a specialization of a given class that provides all necessary methods for the execution in the ACS scheme. Thus only propagation algorithms (i.e. tasks) and their priority have to be defined with each new constraint that inherits all other properties from the prototype-class. The system is even extendable with other constraint systems by using the strict typing of Java. The combination of constraint systems [2] can be performed by defining constraints over variables of different systems. For example a less-or-equal constraint over a finite domain integer variable x and a real-number variable y can be implemented by: $x.setDomain(min(x), (int)\lceil max(y)\rceil)$; $y.setDomain((float)min(x), max(y))$.

Solvers extend the class `java.lang.Thread` and run concurrently to the application. The handling of inconsistencies is implemented with Java's asynchronous event-model. A solver holds references of all objects that implement an event-listener for inconsistency-events. These events implement the `java.util.EventObject` class and can thus be handled by the corresponding specialization of a `java.util.EventListener`. Furthermore in the event-objects all available information about the reasons for the failure are stored so that the listener can deduce the right action to resolve the inconsistency from the information given with the event.

Distribution in **J.CP** is based on the `java.rmi` package which allows method invocation in any object that is exported from another Java virtual machine (JVM) reachable via some network. In our implementation we use the standard RMI communication protocols and thus get the Internet as platform for the implementation of constraint networks.

4.1 Performance Results and Evaluation

In Table 1, we show some results of runtime experiments with **J.CP** using synchronous and asynchronous constraint execution. In the first, the propagation algorithm of every posted or reposted constraint is executed immediately, whereas in the second case constraints are executed asynchronously, as described in the previous sections. In the third column, we present the results of SICStus Prolog [4] with its Java-interface jasper. However, the results cannot really be compared because SICStus is implemented in C-code and can thus be expected to execute faster than a pure Java program like **J.CP** . As soon as possible we will compare **J.CP** with the newly availible ILOG JSOlver which is a pure java solver.

In all benchmarks no search is performed because propagation leads to a solution. The `order n`-benchmark can be described as follows $\forall x_i \in \{x_1, x_2, ..., x_{\mathtt{n}}\}$: $x_i \in \{1, 2, ..., \mathtt{n}\} \wedge x_{i-1} < x_i$ The only solution is thus $x_i = i$ for all $i \in \{1, 2, ..., \mathtt{n}\}$. In `reorder n`, we retract the constraint $x_{n/2-1} < x_{n/2}$ after the execution of `order` so that every x_i has a domain containing $n/2$ elements. In SICStus, retraction is simulated by backtracking to the named constraint and reposting all constraints that were subsequently called. All shown results are the average values of 10 tests.

The speedup of the asynchronous approach is due to the differing order of execution of the propagation algorithms. By executing the constraint retraction before the propagation of all other constraints is finished, we were even able to achieve a speedup of **J.CP** to jasper in the `reorder 1000` benchmark. Since the

Table 1. Comparison of **J.CP** with and without asynchronous constraint solving and SICStus v3.8.5 on a dual Pentium III Linux PC. Numbers represent milliseconds.

	J.CP synchronous	**J.CP** asynchronous	SICStus/jasper
`order 2`	28	329	712
`order 100`	398	699	790
`order 200`	1183	1253	932
`order 500`	6232	5340	2075
`order 1000`	23194	14344	6812
`reorder 100`	446	697	814
`reorder 200`	1392	949	992
`reorder 500`	7752	2834	2181
`reorder 1000`	28213	7108	7374

constraints are buffered, it is possible that due to the scheduling-algorithm a constraint c_1 that was posted or reposted after another constraint c_2 is executed first. We demonstrate the possible speedup achieved by this for `order 4` in Table 2.

Table 2. Comparison between optimal and normal (e.g. [10]) execution order of the `order 4` problem.

normal	optimal
$x_1 \in 1..4, x_2 \in 1..4, x_3 \in 1..4, x_4 \in 1..4$	$x_1 \in 1..4, x_2 \in 1..4, x_3 \in 1..4, x_4 \in 1..4$
$x_1 < x_2$ (from buffer) $x_1 \in 1..3, x_2 \in 2..4, x_3 \in 1..4, x_4 \in 1..4$	$x_1 < x_2$ (from buffer) $x_1 \in 1..3, x_2 \in 2..4, x_3 \in 1..4, x_4 \in 1..4$
$x_2 < x_3$ (from buffer) $x_1 \in 1..3, x_2 \in 2..3, x_3 \in 3..4, x_4 \in 1..4$	$x_2 < x_3$ (from buffer) $x_1 \in 1..3, x_2 \in 2..3, x_3 \in 3..4, x_4 \in 1..4$
$x_1 < x_2$ (propagation) $x_1 \in 1..2, x_2 \in 2..3, x_3 \in 3..4, x_4 \in 1..4$	$x_3 < x_4$ (from buffer) $x_1 \in 1..3, x_2 \in 2..3, x_3 = 3, x_4 = 4$
$x_3 < x_4$ (from buffer) $x_1 \in 1..2, x_2 \in 2..3, x_3 = 3, x_4 = 4$	$x_2 < x_3$ (propagation) $x_1 \in 1..3, x_2 = 2, x_3 = 3, x_4 = 4$
$x_2 < x_3$ (propagation) $x_1 \in 1..2, x_2 = 2, x_3 = 3, x_4 = 4$	$x_1 < x_2$ (propagation) $x_1 = 1, x_2 = 2, x_3 = 3, x_4 = 4$
$x_1 < x_2$ (propagation) $x_1 = 1, x_2 = 2, x_3 = 3, x_4 = 4$	

5 Case Study: Distributed Meeting Scheduling

As a first real-life application we implement a distributed meeting scheduling system (similar to [7]). The application has been developed using standard SWE tools and methods (UML) and is purely object-oriented. During the developent process we found the OO-scheme very adequate also for the analysis and design of the constraint-based components. As shown in Figure 2 every user has an agent running locally that is used as a private appointment calendar.

The meetings are modeled with some constraint variables that are the only shared information, such that the maximum privacy is kept for all users. Every

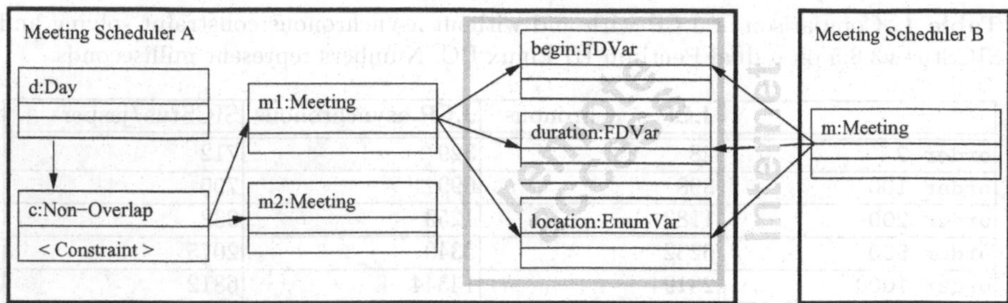

Fig. 2. The distributed meeting scheduler. Boxes describe software components, lines describe, which constraint object is posted by which other component.

user can propose meetings with any other users (which will also be synchronized with additional calendars of the user herself) by creating constraint variables and posting certain constraints on them. The attendees of the meeting will then receive a message that can be answered by posting new constraints on the meeting or just by rejecting the proposal. At some (defined) later time the meeting will be fixed wrt. time, duration and location which means that the constraint variables describing the meeting are instantiated. In difference to other such systems we can dynamically re-schedule meetings, because we can use search in the system. If a meeting has to be postponed, because another meeting is newly planned, this can be done automatically by the system by just retracting the instantiation(-constraint) and finding new values for the variables such that all constraints are satisfied. This can be done at any time and with any delay (communication time) because constraint posting and retraction can be performed asynchronously. This automatic rescheduling is organized with priority values that every user can associate to its meetings, unimportant meetings may be re-scheduled more often.

6 Concluding Remarks

We have presented the possibilities arising in the development of constraint-based software with the use of asynchronous constraint solvers. The expressiveness of ACS is not restricted wrt. CLP, so that known algorithms for constraint satisfaction problems can be fitted into the new paradigm. Our prototype implementation **J.CP** is designed for the use in the development of large software-packages that make use of constraint-based methods. Furthermore, the use in concurrent or distributed systems is supported, because no global information is used in the solving algorithm. **J.CP** is implemented in pure Java code, so that all features of the Internet programming language such as platform-independency are present for constraint-based software.

The relatively slow execution of Java programs is absorbed by the speedup achieved through the asynchronous execution. Other constraint-based application or the user can interfere at anytime with the propagation such that newly obtained information can be used immediately. In ACS, every constraint is scheduled according to its priority, which allows the execution of "important" constraints first. Here, expert knowledge on constraint solving such as "first propagate, then search" is applied in an adaptive manner.

References

[1] Krzysztof R. Apt. The essence of constraint propagation. *Theoretical Computer Science*, 221(1-2):179–210, 1998.

[2] Franz Baader and Klaus U. Schulz. Combination of constraint solvers for free and quasi-free structures. *Theoretical Computer Science*, 192:107–161, 1998.

[3] P. Berlandier and B. Neveu. Problem partitition and solvers coordination in distributed constraint satisfaction. In *Proc. PPAI95*, 1995.

[4] Mats Carlsson, Greger Ottosson, and Björn Carlson. An open-ended finite domain constraint solver. In *Proc. PLILP97*, volume 1292 of *LNCS*, 1997.

[5] Andy Hon Wai Chun. Constraint programming in java with jsolver. In *Proc. Practical Applications of Constraint Logic Programming PACLP99*, 1999.

[6] The Mozart Consortium. http://www.mozart-oz.org.

[7] Leonardo Garrido and Katia Sycara. Multi-agent meeting scheduling: Prelimenary experimental results. In *Proc. ICMAS96*, 1996.

[8] Yan Georget, Philippe Codognet, and Francesca Rossi. Constraint retraction in CLP(FD): Formal framework and performance results. *Constraints*, 4(1):5–42, February 1999. ISSN 1383-7133.

[9] Seif Haridi, Peter van Roy, Per Brand, and Christian Schulte. Programming languages for distributed applications. *New Generation Computing*, 16(3), 1998. Invited Paper.

[10] P. Van Hentenryck. *Constraint Satisfaction in Logic Programming.* MIT Press, 1989.

[11] J. Jaffar and J.L. Lassez. Constraint logic programming. In *Proceedings of the 14th ACM Symposium on Principles of Programming Languages POPL-87*, 1987.

[12] J.-F. Puget. A c++ implementation of clp. Technical report, ILOG, 1994. In Ilog Solver Collected papers.

[13] Georg Ringwelski. Distributed constraint satisfaction with cooperating asynchronous solvers. In Springer, editor, *Proceedings CP'01*, number 2239 in LNCS, page 777, 2001.

[14] Georg Ringwelski. A new execution model for constraint processing in object-oriented software. In *Proc. International Workshop on Functional and (Constraint) Logic Programming comprising the 10th International Workshop on Functional and Logic Programming and 16th Workshop on Logic Programming (WFLP01)*, 2001.

[15] V.A. Saraswat. *Concurrent Constraint Programming.* MIT Press, 1993.

[16] M. Torrens, R. Weigl, and B. Faltings. Java constraint library: Bringing constraint technology to the internet. In *Working notes of the Workshop on Constraints and Agents*, 1997.

[17] M. Wallace, S. Novello, and J. Schimpf. ECL^{i}PS^e: A platform for Constraint Logic Programming. Technical report, IC-Parc, Imperial College, London, UK, 1997.

[18] Armin Wolf, Thomas Gruenhagen, and Ulrich Geske. On incremental adaption of constraint handling rule derivation after constraint deletions. *Journal of Applied Artificial Intelligence, Special Issue on Constraint Handling Rules*, 2000.

A Hybrid Treatment of Evolutionary Sets

Bernhard Heinemann

Fachbereich Informatik, FernUniversität Hagen
PO Box 940, D–58084 Hagen, Germany
Phone: +49-2331-987-2714, Fax: +49-2331-987-319
E-mail: Bernhard.Heinemann@fernuni-hagen.de

Abstract. This paper is about a synthesis of two quite different modal reasoning formalisms: the logic of subset spaces, and hybrid logic. Going beyond commonly considered languages we introduce names of objects involving sets and corresponding satisfaction operators, thus increase the expressive power to a large extent. The motivation for our approach is to logically model some general notions from topology like closeness, separation, and linearity, which are of fundamental relevance to spatial or temporal frameworks; in other words, since these notions represent basic properties of space and time we want them to be available to corresponding formal reasoning. We are interested in complete axiomatizations and effectivity properties of the associated logical systems, in particular.

Keywords: topological reasoning, temporal reasoning, modal logic, hybrid logic, reasoning about knowledge

1 Introduction

Modal logic is indisputably one of the well–established and frequently applied logics in AI. In order to fit the qualitative and quantitative modelling requirements of AI a host of suitable modal systems has been developed. Vice versa, research into modal logic has always influenced advances in AI. Recently, a particularly important development of modal logic has attracted quite some attention of people working on logical aspects of computer science, AI, and computational linguistics: *hybrid logic.* In the paper [3] convincing reasons were given for the thesis that the advantages of modal and predicate calculi can be taken up with corresponding hybrid systems. The striking applicability of hybrid languages to *temporal reasoning* and *knowledge representation* was demonstrated there, in particular. Concerning the fundamentals of hybrid logic presupposed in this paper see [4], 7.3. Following the *sorting strategy* issued in [3], we propose below a hybridization of the 'two–sorted' modal logic of subset spaces, [7]. The latter system connects the notion of knowledge, [8], with certain concepts from general topology, [6], and is aimed at supplying an appropriate apparatus for *formal topological reasoning,* among other things.

Why is topological reasoning significant for AI? First, because of its connection with the logic of knowledge as explained in [7]. To say it suggestively, topological reasoning is nothing but reasoning about knowledge acquisition. Second, topology provides the solid mathematical framework for geometric notions.

C.A. Coello Coello et al. (Eds.): MICAI 2002, LNAI 2313, pp. 204–213, 2002.

Spatial objects and their mutual relationsships like closeness, separation or connection, are modelled adequately by topological means. Over and above this, there is yet another quite different idea inherent in topolgy: approximation. Approximating objects is topologically realized as a shrinking procedure applied to certain sets, the *neighbourhoods* of the points of the given topological space. Considering more special topological structures like *trees* or *chains* of neighbourhoods shows that a basis for modelling *temporal* phenomena is supported by topology as well. Now, when someone wants to deal *formally* with geometric or temporal data, this should be done on a formal ground specified unequivocally. Thus, from the point of view of a theorist, reasoning about topology should be the first objective in the development of spatial and temporal reasoning formalisms.

So far we have indicated a second area of application of the modal logic of subset spaces mentioned above and a further motivation to deal with it. In the present paper we extend the means of expression of this system considerably. While only closeness could be captured so far the treatment of separation and linearity becomes available now, among other things.

The paper consists of two parts. In the first one we enrich the modal language by *nominals,* i.e. names of states, and the new concept of naming *sets* of states as well. Moreover, we introduce corresponding hybrid *satisfaction operators.* Afterwards we present several examples of what can be expressed. These examples show that the language is actually powerful enough to do the job we have imposed on it. In the second part of the paper we define a different hybrid language going even better with subset spaces because names of *neighbourhood situations* are involved in it; that is, the loci are addressed directly now where formulas are evaluated. We treat the corresponding hybrid logic of *linear* subset spaces as an example showing how the new approach works. Above all, however, we study the distinguished class of structures with that by means of which temporally evolving sets can be modelled. Examples of such sets we have in mind are the actual knowledge state of an agent, and point sets representing geometric objects which change in the course of time. A Hilbert–style proof system is given, of which semantic completeness is shown. This result (Theorem 1 below) answers an open question of the modal treatment of subset spaces in a way, viz how the theory of gradually decreasing sets can be axiomatized. We also argue for decidability and determine the complexity of the logic. The corresponding Theorem 2 below shows that the system offers reasonable preconditions for practical applications as it satisfies the 'optimal' complexity bound. Concluding the paper we remark on further–reaching extensions of the language.

Due to the lack of space all proofs are omitted in this paper. They are contained in the technical report [11].

2 A First Modelling Attempt

Let PROP, NOM and SETN be three mutually disjoint sets of symbols called *propositional variables, nominals,* and *set names,* respectively. We usually denote propositional variables p, q, r, nominals i, j, k, and set names A, B, C. We define the set WFF of *well-formed formulas* of a hybrid bimodal language of subset spaces over PROP, NOM and SETN by

$$\mathrm{WFF} ::= p \mid i \mid A \mid \neg\alpha \mid \alpha \wedge \alpha \mid K\alpha \mid \Box\alpha \mid \epsilon_A\alpha.$$

In particular, we designate formulas by lower case Greek letters. The missing boolean connectives $\top, \bot, \vee, \rightarrow, \leftrightarrow$ are treated as abbreviations, if need be. The one–place modalities K and $\Box$ are familiar from the logic of subset spaces. The corresponding dual operators are written L and $\Diamond$ respectively.

Hybrid logic deals with nominals as names of states and *satisfaction operators* $@_i$, where $i \in \mathrm{NOM}$, among other things. The operators $@_i$ do not appear in the definition of the syntax above because they can be defined; see below. We will use them as abbreviations in this section. We have introduced a counterpart to nominals and satisfaction operators with regard to sets: set names and corresponding operators ϵ_A, where $A \in \mathrm{SETN}$. The dual of ϵ_A is written $\langle\epsilon_A\rangle$; accordingly, the dual of $@_i$ is designated $\langle @_i\rangle$. It should be noted that we do not consider hybrid binders like the $\downarrow$–operator in the technical part of this paper.

We will next give meaning to formulas. First, we have to agree upon the relevant structures. To this end we remind the reader of the semantic domains of the logic of subset spaces: these are pairs $(X, \mathcal{O})$ consisting of a non–empty set X and a system $\mathcal{O}$ of subsets of X, which carry a point–dependent only valuation $V : \mathrm{PROP} \longrightarrow \mathcal{P}(X)$; $\mathcal{P}(\cdot)$ designates the powerset here and below. Presently, the valuation has to be extended to $\mathrm{NOM} \cup \mathrm{SETN}$.

Definition 1 (Subset frames; hybrid subset spaces).

1. *Let X be a non–empty set and $\mathcal{O} \subseteq \mathcal{P}(X)$ a system of non–empty subsets of X such that $X \in \mathcal{O}$. Then the pair $(X, \mathcal{O})$ is called a* subset frame.
2. *A* hybrid subset space *is a triple $(X, \mathcal{O}, V)$, where $(X, \mathcal{O})$ is a subset frame and V a* hybrid valuation, *i.e., a mapping $V : \mathrm{PROP} \cup \mathrm{NOM} \cup \mathrm{SETN} \longrightarrow \mathcal{P}(X)$ such that*
   (a) $V(i)$ is a singleton subset of $\mathcal{P}(X)$ for all $i \in \mathrm{NOM}$, and
   (b) $V(A) \in \mathcal{O}$ for all $A \in \mathrm{SETN}$;
   $\mathcal{M} := (X, \mathcal{O}, V)$ is said to be based on *$(X, \mathcal{O})$.*

In subset space logics, satisfaction is defined with respect to *neighbourhood situations.* The set of neighbourhood situations of a given subset frame $(X, \mathcal{O})$ is defined as follows: $\mathcal{N} := \{x, U \mid (x, U) \in X \times \mathcal{O} \text{ and } x \in U\}$; notice that neighbourhood situations are written without brackets. In the subsequent definition of the relation $\models$ only the clauses for the non–standard connectives are included.

Definition 2 (Satisfaction and validity). *Let be given a hybrid subset space $\mathcal{M} := (X, \mathcal{O}, V)$ and a neighbourhood situation $x, U \in X \times \mathcal{O}$. We define*

$$\begin{array}{lll}
x, U \models_{\mathcal{M}} p & :\Longleftrightarrow & x \in V(p) \\
x, U \models_{\mathcal{M}} i & :\Longleftrightarrow & V(i) = \{x\} \\
x, U \models_{\mathcal{M}} A & :\Longleftrightarrow & V(A) = U \\
x, U \models_{\mathcal{M}} K\alpha & :\Longleftrightarrow & y, U \models_{\mathcal{M}} \alpha \text{ for all } y \in U \\
x, U \models_{\mathcal{M}} \Box\alpha & :\Longleftrightarrow & x, U' \models_{\mathcal{M}} \alpha \text{ for all } U' \in \mathcal{O} \text{ such that } x \in U' \subseteq U \\
x, U \models_{\mathcal{M}} \epsilon_A\alpha & :\Longleftrightarrow & \text{if } x \in V(A), \text{ then } x, V(A) \models_{\mathcal{M}} \alpha,
\end{array}$$

for all $p \in$ PROP, $i \in$ NOM, $A \in$ SETN, *and* $\alpha, \beta \in$ WFF. *In case* $x, U \models_{\mathcal{M}} \alpha$ *is true we say that* α holds in $\mathcal{M}$ at *the neighbourhood situation* x, U. *The formula* α *is called* valid in $\mathcal{M}$, *iff it holds in* $\mathcal{M}$ *at every neighbourhood situation. The notion of validity is extended to subset frames* $\mathcal{S}$ *by quantifying over all hybrid subset spaces based on* $\mathcal{S}$. *(Occasionally we write* $\mathcal{S} \models \alpha$ *if* α *is valid in* $\mathcal{S}$.*)*

The intended meaning of the satisfaction operator $@_i$ corresponding to the nominal i is given by $x, U \models_{\mathcal{M}} @_i\alpha :\iff$ if $V(i) = \{y\} \subseteq U$, then $y, U \models_{\mathcal{M}} \alpha$. Notice that the right–hand side is true iff $x, U \models_{\mathcal{M}} K(i \to \alpha)$. Thus $@_i$ can be defined, as was mentioned above already.

The question comes up naturally whether ϵ_A can be defined as well. Actually, this is not the case because one can 'leave' the actual neighbourhood with the aid of the connective ϵ_A, which is neither possible by means of K nor $\Box$.

A striking correspondence between modal and first–order definability of many classes of frames is known from ordinary modal logic. For example, the class of Kripke frames (W, R) satisfying $\forall x, y, z \in W : (x\,R\,y \wedge y\,R\,z \Rightarrow x\,R\,z)$ (i.e., R is transitive) coincides with the class of frames where the schema $\Box\alpha \to \Box\Box\alpha$ of modal formulas is valid. Hybridization improves the possibilities to define frames in this way; cf [2]. For instance, the class of *irreflexive* frames can be captured hybridly, but not modally as is well–known.

We are now interested in defining special classes of subset frames which are related to the areas of application mentioned above. The following properties of the set inclusion relation $\subseteq$ on $\mathcal{O}$ are considered, among others: *Reflexivity, Transitivity, Antisymmetry, Linearity.* Notice that only the first two of these properties are definable in usual modal logic, but *all* of them in hybrid logic. In [2] it was shown that one can even use *pure* formulas for this purpose, i.e., formulas without propositional variables. The formulas occurring in the subsequent proposition are subset space analogues to those. It should be remarked that pure formulas are crucial to hybrid completeness; we will make use of this fact in the next section.

Reflexivity and transitivity along with antisymmetry express that the structure $(\mathcal{O}, \subseteq)$ is a partial order. The property $\forall U, U' \in \mathcal{O} : (U \subseteq U' \vee U' \subseteq U)$ is valid in every linear frame, by definition. For a while we consider a somewhat weaker requirement on $\mathcal{O}$ saying that 'connected' members of $\mathcal{O}$ form a *chain* with respect to inclusion: $\forall U, U' \in \mathcal{O} : (U \cap U' \neq \emptyset \Rightarrow U \subseteq U' \vee U' \subseteq U)$. The subset space logic of this class of *treelike* frames was investigated in [9].

Proposition 1 (Defining properties of $\subseteq$). *Let* $\mathcal{S} = (X, \mathcal{O})$ *be a subset frame and* $A, B \in$ SETN *set names.*

1. *The following hybrid formulas are valid in* $\mathcal{S}$:
   (a) $A \to \Diamond A$ *(b)* $\Diamond\Diamond A \to \Diamond A$ *(c)* $A \to \Box(\Diamond A \to A)$
2. *The relation* $\subseteq$ *on* $\mathcal{O}$ *is treelike, iff* $\epsilon_A \Diamond B \vee \epsilon_B \Diamond A$ *is valid in* $\mathcal{S}$.

The class of spaces occurring in the first part of the next definition is frequently encountered in topology.

Definition 3 (Properties of $\mathcal{O}$). *Let* $\mathcal{S} = (X, \mathcal{O})$ *be a subset frame.*

1. *$\mathcal{S}$ is called a* local filter base, *iff for all $U, U_1, U_2 \in \mathcal{O}$:*

$$U_1, U_2 \subseteq U \wedge U_1 \cap U_2 \neq \emptyset \Rightarrow \exists \tilde{U} \in \mathcal{O} : \tilde{U} \subseteq U_1 \cap U_2.$$

2. *$\mathcal{S}$ is called a* locally linear frame, *iff for all $U, U_1, U_2 \in \mathcal{O}$:*

$$U_1, U_2 \subseteq U \Rightarrow U_1 \subseteq U_2 \vee U_2 \subseteq U_1.$$

Compared with Proposition 1, the K–operator now joins the formulas involved in defining these properties.

Proposition 2 (Defining properties of $\mathcal{O}$). *Let $\mathcal{S} = (X, \mathcal{O})$ be a subset frame and $A, B \in$ SETN set names.*

1. *$\mathcal{S}$ is a local filter base, iff $\Diamond A \wedge \Diamond B \rightarrow L\Diamond K(\langle \epsilon_A \rangle \top \wedge \langle \epsilon_B \rangle \top)$ is valid in $\mathcal{S}$.*
2. *$\mathcal{S}$ is a locally linear subset frame, iff $L\Diamond A \wedge L\Diamond B \rightarrow K\epsilon_A \langle \epsilon_B \rangle \top \vee K\epsilon_B \langle \epsilon_A \rangle \top$ is valid in $\mathcal{S}$.*

The notion introduced in Definition 3.1 is borrowed from general topology; cf [6]. Actually, local filter bases are usual filter bases and vice versa, because of the fact that X is contained in $\mathcal{O}$; cf Definition 1.1. For the same reason the two classes of locally linear and linear subset frames coincide. However, the local notions better fit in with the semantics of our language.

By the way, it should be remarked that the modal theory of linear subset frames has not been characterized up to now; concerning such frames in a *temporal* setting, cf [10]. Furthermore, axiomatizing the subset space logic of filter bases was left as an open problem in [7]. This problem has recently been solved; cf the thesis [15]. Interestingly enough the axiomatization given there is essentially infinite (but still recursive).

We now proceed to *separation properties*. We focus on the weakest one discussed in general topology, which is known as the separation axiom (T 0). This axiom plays an important part in modern theory of effectivity; cf eg [14].

Definition 4 (T 0–property). *Let be given a subset frame $\mathcal{S} = (X, \mathcal{O})$. Then $\mathcal{S}$ is called a* local T 0–space, *iff for all $x, x' \in X$ and $U \in \mathcal{O}$:*

$$x \neq x' \wedge x, x' \in U \Rightarrow \exists U_1, U_2 \in \mathcal{O} : ((x \in U_1 \wedge x' \notin U_1) \vee (x' \in U_2 \wedge x \notin U_2)).$$

Notice that again the classes of local and usual structures coincide. Proposing a corresponding hybrid formula, nominals come into play at this point.

Proposition 3 (Defining T 0–spaces). *Assume that $\mathcal{S} = (X, \mathcal{O})$ is a subset frame and $i, j \in$ NOM are state names. Then $\mathcal{S}$ is a local T 0–space, iff*

$$\mathcal{S} \models i \wedge L(j \wedge \neg i) \rightarrow \Diamond K \neg j \vee @_j \Diamond K \neg i.$$

For a corresponding characterization of the familiar class of *Hausdorff spaces* one simply has to replace $\vee$ by $\wedge$ in the above formula.

3 Naming Neighbourhood Situations

Though powerful, the language of the previous section does not fit in quite well with the modal and hybrid approach respectively. Since names are always interpreted with respect to the actual neighbourhood situation, unrestricted jumps as in hybrid logic are not allowed there. We get rid of this deficiency now by introducing symbols denoting neighbourhood situations instead of nominals and set names respectively. We utilize that it is true that subset space logics are *two–sorted* as mentioned in the introduction, but also *one–dimensional* in a sense; concerning modal logics of higher dimension cf [13].

Thus, we replace NOM and SETN by a set NNS of *names of neighbourhood situations* with typical elements $\mathfrak{n}, \mathfrak{m}$. We also remove the connectives ϵ_A from the definition of the set WWF of well–formed formulas ($A \in$ SETN) and insert the satisfaction operator corresponding to $\mathfrak{n} \in$ NNS for all $\mathfrak{n} \in$ NNS; this operator is designated $@_{\mathfrak{n}}$, and its dual is labelled by $\langle\,\rangle$–bracketing, as above.

Hybrid valuations are modified accordingly. In particular, $V(\mathfrak{n})$ consists of a single neighbourhood situation, for all $\mathfrak{n} \in$ NNS.

Concerning the satisfaction relation $\models$ we have to delete the three clauses involving nominals and set names and add the following ones:

Definition 5 (Semantics of $\mathfrak{n}$ and $@_{\mathfrak{n}}$). *Let be given a hybrid subset space $\mathcal{M} := (X, \mathcal{O}, V)$ and a neighbourhood situation $x, U \in \mathcal{N}$. Then we let*

$$\begin{aligned} x, U \models_{\mathcal{M}} \mathfrak{n} \quad &:\Longleftrightarrow V(\mathfrak{n}) = x, U \\ x, U \models_{\mathcal{M}} @_{\mathfrak{n}}\alpha &:\Longleftrightarrow V(\mathfrak{n}) \models_{\mathcal{M}} \alpha. \end{aligned}$$

Examples of correspondences à la Section 2 are implicitly included below. They are not treated in detail because we put the main emphasis on different subjects here. In the subsequent part of the paper we present the hybrid logic of linear subset spaces based on the language just defined. (Linear frames were introduced immediately before Proposition 1 above.) Theorem 1 below yields a 'hybrid solution' to the problem of axiomatizing the modal theory of these structures; see the corresponding remarks in the introduction and between Proposition 2 and Definition 4 above.

The axiomatization given in the following will be rounded off along with the requirements of the completeness proof, of which we sketch the main ideas for the expert reader. To begin with, we recall the modal axioms for general subset spaces:

1. All WFF–instances of propositional tautologies
2. $(p \to \Box p) \wedge (\neg p \to \Box \neg p)$
3. $K(\alpha \to \beta) \to (K\alpha \to K\beta)$
4. $K\alpha \to (\alpha \wedge KK\alpha)$
5. $L\alpha \to KL\alpha$
6. $\Box(\alpha \to \beta) \to (\Box\alpha \to \Box\beta)$
7. $\Box\alpha \to (\alpha \wedge \Box\Box\alpha)$
8. $K\Box\alpha \to \Box K\alpha$,

where $p \in \mathrm{PROP}$ and $\alpha, \beta \in \mathrm{WFF}$. This list is taken from [7].

The first thing that has to be done is to replace the schemata 4–5 and 7–8 by pure formulas doing the same job, in order to utilize later on the power of hybrid techniques as it was done in Theorem 7.29 of [4]. (Pure formulas were already considered in Section 2.) We get sound analogues to the formulas occurring in Proposition 1.1, among others:

4'. $(\mathfrak{n} \rightarrow L\mathfrak{n}) \wedge (LL\mathfrak{n} \rightarrow L\mathfrak{n})$
5'. $L\mathfrak{n} \rightarrow KL\mathfrak{n}$
7'. $(\mathfrak{n} \rightarrow \Diamond\mathfrak{n}) \wedge (\Diamond\Diamond\mathfrak{n} \rightarrow \Diamond\mathfrak{n})$
8'. $\Diamond L\mathfrak{n} \rightarrow L\Diamond\mathfrak{n}$,

for all $\mathfrak{n} \in \mathrm{NNS}$. Going beyond the modal abilities, the axiom of antisymmetry extends this list (cf Proposition 1.1(c)):

9. $\mathfrak{n} \rightarrow \Box(\Diamond\mathfrak{n} \rightarrow \mathfrak{n})$

We now list the bulk of the Hilbert–style axiomatization of hybrid logic given in [4], p 438 ff, which originates from [5] and serves as our second starting point:

10. $@_\mathfrak{n}(\alpha \rightarrow \beta) \rightarrow (@_\mathfrak{n}\alpha \rightarrow @_\mathfrak{n}\beta)$
11. $\langle @_\mathfrak{n} \rangle \alpha \leftrightarrow @_\mathfrak{n}\alpha$
12. $\mathfrak{n} \wedge \alpha \rightarrow @_\mathfrak{n}\alpha$
13. $@_\mathfrak{n}\mathfrak{n}$
14. $@_\mathfrak{n}\mathfrak{m} \wedge @_\mathfrak{m}\alpha \rightarrow @_\mathfrak{n}\alpha$
15. $@_\mathfrak{n}\mathfrak{m} \leftrightarrow @_\mathfrak{m}\mathfrak{n}$
16. $@_\mathfrak{m}@_\mathfrak{n}\alpha \leftrightarrow @_\mathfrak{n}\alpha$,

where $\mathfrak{n}, \mathfrak{m} \in \mathrm{NNS}$ and $\alpha, \beta \in \mathrm{WFF}$. Let Γ be a maximal consistent set and $\mathfrak{n}$ a name of a neighbourhood situation. We can derive from Γ the set $\Delta_\mathfrak{n} := \{\alpha \mid @_\mathfrak{n}\alpha \in \Gamma\} \subseteq \mathrm{WFF}$ then, which represents a natural candidate for realizing formulas of the type $@_\mathfrak{n}\alpha$ contained in Γ. The required properties of $\Delta_\mathfrak{n}$ can in fact be proved with the aid of the above axioms and the familiar derivation rules *modus ponens* and *necessitation,* as in hybrid logic; cf [4], 7.24. In particular, $\Delta_\mathfrak{n}$ is a uniquely determined maximal consistent set containing $\mathfrak{n}$.

The axiom schema called (*back*) in [4] occurs twice here because we have to take into account both modalities, K and $\Box$:

17. $L@_\mathfrak{n}\alpha \rightarrow @_\mathfrak{n}\alpha$
18. $\Diamond@_\mathfrak{n}\alpha \rightarrow @_\mathfrak{n}\alpha$

The same is true for the rule (PASTE) so that we have three additional rules:

$$\text{(NAME)}\ \frac{\mathfrak{m} \rightarrow \beta}{\beta} \qquad \text{(PASTE)}_K\ \frac{@_\mathfrak{n}L\mathfrak{m} \wedge @_\mathfrak{m}\alpha \rightarrow \beta}{@_\mathfrak{n}L\alpha \rightarrow \beta}$$

$$\text{(PASTE)}_\Box\ \frac{@_\mathfrak{n}\Diamond\mathfrak{m} \wedge @_\mathfrak{m}\alpha \rightarrow \beta}{@_\mathfrak{n}\Diamond\alpha \rightarrow \beta},$$

where $\mathfrak{m}$ is 'new' each time.

The axioms and rules stated so far enable us to perform the naming and pasting techniques of hybrid logic, respectively, in the present case as well; cf [4], p 441 ff. That is, we obtain a hybrid model $\mathcal{M}$ satisfying the following properties:

- $\mathcal{M}$ is yielded (in the sense of [4], Definition 7.26) by a maximal consistent set Γ containing a given non–derivable formula α. In particular, every point of $\mathcal{M}$ is some $\Delta_{\mathfrak{n}}$, where $\mathfrak{n}$ is taken from some suitably extended set of names of neighbourhood situations. ('$\mathcal{M}$ is named'.)
- The modalities K and $\Box$ induce accessibility relations $\xrightarrow{L}$ and $\xrightarrow{\Diamond}$ on $\mathcal{M}$, respectively, in the usual way.
- The *Existence Lemma* holds for $\xrightarrow{L}$ and $\xrightarrow{\Diamond}$; i.e., if s is a point containing $L\alpha$, then there exists a point t such that $s \xrightarrow{L} t$ and $\alpha \in t$ (and for $\Diamond\alpha$ and $\xrightarrow{\Diamond}$ correspondingly). ('$\mathcal{M}$ is pasted'.)
- The relation $\xrightarrow{L}$ is an equivalence relation.
- The relation $\xrightarrow{\Diamond}$ is reflexive, transitive and antisymmetrical.
- For all propositional symbols $p \in \mathrm{PROP}$ and all points s, t of $\mathcal{M}$: if $s \xrightarrow{\Diamond} t$, then $p \in s$ iff $p \in t$.
- The following *cross property* holds for $\mathcal{M}$:

  for all points s, t, u such that $s \xrightarrow{\Diamond} t \xrightarrow{L} u$ there exists a point v such that $s \xrightarrow{L} v \xrightarrow{\Diamond} u$.

  (This property is typical of the modal logic of subset spaces.)
- The *Truth Lemma* holds for $\mathcal{M}$; in particular, $\mathcal{M}$ falsifies α at Γ.

Our aim is to construct a linear subset space with the aid of $\mathcal{M}$ that falsifies α as well. Many of the properties we need for this purpose are already present in $\mathcal{M}$. The following is the decisive one and still missing:

> Whenever there are three $\xrightarrow{L}$–equivalence classes $[s], [t], [u]$ such that $[s]$ precedes $[t]$ with respect to $\xrightarrow{\Diamond}$ (i.e., there are $s' \in [s]$ and $t' \in [t]$ such that $s' \xrightarrow{\Diamond} t'$) and $[t]$ precedes $[u]$, then it is true that every $s' \in [s]$ having a $\xrightarrow{\Diamond}$–prolongation to $[u]$ also has such a prolongation to $[t]$.

This property causing all the problems we get in the modal case can be established by an appropriate hybrid axiom, which is the first one of the subsequent penultimate block of schemata. The other ones represent mutual exclusion of the relations $\xrightarrow{\Diamond}$ and $\xrightarrow{L}$ (unless the points coincide), weak connectedness of the relation $\xrightarrow{\Diamond}$, and dichotomy of the composite relation $\xrightarrow{L} \circ \xrightarrow{\Diamond}$:

19. $\Diamond\mathfrak{m} \wedge L\Diamond(\mathfrak{n} \wedge \Diamond\mathfrak{m}) \rightarrow \Diamond L\mathfrak{n}$
20. $\mathfrak{n} \wedge L(\mathfrak{m} \wedge \neg\mathfrak{n}) \rightarrow \neg\Diamond\mathfrak{m}$
21. $\Diamond\mathfrak{n} \wedge \Diamond\mathfrak{m} \rightarrow \Diamond\left((\mathfrak{n} \wedge \Diamond\mathfrak{m}) \vee (\mathfrak{m} \wedge \Diamond\mathfrak{n})\right)$
22. $@_{\mathfrak{m}} L\Diamond\mathfrak{n} \vee @_{\mathfrak{n}} L\Diamond\mathfrak{m}$

Now let Γ be as above, $s_0 := \Gamma$, t a further point of $\mathcal{M}$, and assume that the $\xrightarrow{L}$–equivalence class $[s_0]$ precedes $[t]$. Define

$$U_t := \{s \in [s_0] \mid s \text{ has a prolongation to } [t]\} \text{ and } \mathcal{O} := \{U_t \mid [s_0] \text{ precedes } [t]\}.$$

Then the pair $([s_0], \mathcal{O})$ is a linear frame because of the properties of $\mathcal{M}$ stated above. Furthermore, a hybrid valuation V can be induced 'faithfully' on $[s_0]$ by the valuation of $\mathcal{M}$, if the following final couple of axioms is added:

23. $\neg\mathfrak{n} \wedge \Diamond\mathfrak{m} \rightarrow K(\mathfrak{n} \rightarrow \Box\neg\mathfrak{m})$
24. $\Diamond\mathfrak{n} \wedge K\Diamond L\mathfrak{n} \rightarrow \mathfrak{n}$

The resulting hybrid subset space $\mathcal{M}' := ([s_0], \mathcal{O}, V)$ satisfies for all $\beta \in$ WFF, $s \in [s_0]$, and points t belonging to $\mathcal{M}$ such that s has a prolongation to $[t]$,

$$s, U_t \models_{\mathcal{M}'} \beta \iff \beta \in t_s,$$

where t_s is the (uniquely determined) element of $[t]$ such that $s \stackrel{\Diamond}{\longrightarrow} t$. This gives us the following completeness result.

Theorem 1 (Completeness). *The logical system* **S** *determined by the above axiom schemata and rules is sound and complete for the class of linear hybrid subset spaces.*

We briefly turn to the question of *decidability* of our logic. The method of decomposing models due to Georgatos, cf [9], can be suited appropriately to the case of linear frames; cf [12]. In this way decidability can be proved, and even more: since adding nominals and corresponding satisfaction operators does not increase the complexity of the base logic, cf [1], the satisfiability problem of the system **S** turns out to be 'only' complete in NP. Thus we obtain:

Theorem 2 (Decidability). *The set of all* **S***–theorems is co–*NP*–complete.*

4 Remarks on Extensions and Summary

In this final section we indicate a couple of ways how to modify and extend the above system. The most obvious thing to do is the investigation based on the language of the previous section of other classes of subset frames which are relevant to concrete modelling tasks. In particular, this approach should shed some new light on the classes of topological and treelike spaces respectively, which represent important frameworks for modelling knowledge acquisition. We believe that completeness can be obtained easier in the hybrid framework than in the modal one, among other things.

The question of integrating state variables and the $\downarrow$–binder (cf [5]) into our language is equally natural. Concerning this we suspect a positive answer, since these additional facilities do neither affect subsets nor support any jumps. Thus, the techniques of [5] can be applied to the present case as well. Not surprisingly, the resulting version of the hybrid logic of subset spaces expands the abilities of topological reasoning. For example, the Hausdorff property can now be expressed by

$$\downarrow \mathbf{x} K \downarrow \mathbf{y}(\neg\mathbf{x} \rightarrow \Diamond K\neg\mathbf{x} \wedge @_{\mathbf{x}}\Diamond K\neg\mathbf{y}).$$

However, decidability of the logic gets lost; see [1].

Let us now summarize: This paper is the beginning of a *hybrid logic of subset spaces,* a synthesis of hybrid logic and the modal logic of subset spaces promoting formal topological and, more specially, temporal reasoning. We have proposed a corresponding language and given examples of its expressiveness. Furthermore, we have proved completeness and decidability for the hybrid logic of linear subset spaces. This system describes logically the temporal evolution of sets like the actual knowledge state of an agent or a shrinking geometric object.

The detailed treatment of both richer languages and more concrete examples (going beyond mere mode of expression) are topics of future research. The development of different calculi like tableaux is a demanding challenge as well, especially in view of practical applications; cf [3] for a closer justification.

References

1. Carlos Areces, Patrick Blackburn, and Maarten Marx. A Road-Map on Complexity for Hybrid Logics. In J. Flum and M. Rodríguez-Artalejo, editors, *Computer Science Logic, CSL'99,* volume 1683 of *Lecture Notes in Computer Science*, pages 307–321, Berlin, 1999. Springer.
2. Patrick Blackburn. Internalizing Labelled Deduction. *Journal of Logic and Computation*, 10:137–168, 2000.
3. Patrick Blackburn. Representation, Reasoning, and Relational Structures: a Hybrid Logic Manifesto. *Logic Journal of the IGPL*, 8:339–365, 2000.
4. Patrick Blackburn, Maarten de Rijke, and Yde Venema. *Modal Logic*, volume 53 of *Cambridge Track in Theoretical Computer Science.* Cambridge University Press, Cambridge, 2001.
5. Patrick Blackburn and Miroslava Tzakova. Hybrid Languages and Temporal Logic. *Logic Journal of the IGPL*, 7(1):27–54, 1999.
6. Nicolas Bourbaki. *General Topology, Part 1.* Hermann, Paris, 1966.
7. Andrew Dabrowski, Lawrence S. Moss, and Rohit Parikh. Topological Reasoning and The Logic of Knowledge. *Annals of Pure and Applied Logic*, 78:73–110, 1996.
8. Ronald Fagin, Joseph Y. Halpern, Yoram Moses, and Moshe Y. Vardi. *Reasoning about Knowledge.* MIT Press, Cambridge, MA, 1995.
9. Konstantinos Georgatos. Knowledge on Treelike Spaces. *Studia Logica*, 59:271–301, 1997.
10. Bernhard Heinemann. About the Temporal Decrease of Sets. In C. Bettini and A. Montanari, editors, *Temporal Representation and Reasoning, 8th International Workshop, TIME-01*, pages 234–239, Los Alamitos, CA, 2001. IEEE Computer Society Press.
11. Bernhard Heinemann. Hybrid Languages for Subset Spaces. Informatik Berichte 290, FernUniversität, Hagen, October 2001.
12. Bernhard Heinemann. Linear Tense Logics of Increasing Sets. *Journal of Logic and Computation*, 12, 2002. To appear.
13. Maarten Marx and Yde Venema. *Multi-Dimensional Modal Logic*, volume 4 of *Applied Logic Series.* Kluwer Academic Publishers, Dordrecht, 1997.
14. Klaus Weihrauch. *Computable Analysis.* Springer, Berlin, 2000.
15. M. Angela Weiss. *Completeness of Certain Bimodal Logics for Subset Spaces.* Ph.D. thesis, The City University of New York, New York, 1999.

Games and Logics of Knowledge for Multi-agent Systems

Ahti Pietarinen

Department of Philosophy, University of Helsinki
P.O. Box 9, FIN-00014 University of Helsinki
pietarin@cc.helsinki.fi

Abstract. New types of knowledge constructions in epistemic logic are defined, whose semantics is given by a combination of game-theoretic notions and modal semantics. A new notion of knowledge introduced in this framework is focussed knowledge, which arises from the game-theoretic phenomenon of imperfect information in quantified versions of epistemic logics. This notion is shown to be useful in knowledge representation of multi-agent systems with uncertainty. In general, imperfect information gives rise to partialised versions of these logics.

1 Combining Games and Knowledge

Classical logic is a logic of perfect information transmission. This holds true of extensional propositional and predicate logics, and it also holds true of intensional modal logics and logics of epistemic notions (such as knowledge and belief). By perfect information transmission we mean that in the associated games, players transmitting semantic information from one logical component to another never lose this information.

Here it is shown that once we adopt semantics that is suitable not only for logics with perfect information but also for imperfect information ones, we are able to produce new logics with new expressive resources that are able to capture a variety of different notions of knowledge. Such notions are argued to be needed in an adequate representation of knowledge arising in certain multi-agent systems.

More precisely, the distinction between perfect and imperfect information transmission in relation to logic can be made rigorous within the framework of game-theoretic semantics (GTS, [5]), which implements a semantic game between two teams of players, the team of Verifiers (V, ∃loise) and the team of Falsifiers (F, ∀belard). These semantic games provide an evaluation method that can then be defined for a variety of logics.

If games are ones of perfect information, players are informed of all the past choices. If games are ones of imperfect information, at least some semantic information concerning past choices is hidden or lost during the game. New logics ensue when information flow is restricted in this very game-theoretic sense.

Research in epistemic logic and reasoning about knowledge has played an important role in artificial intelligence community for more than two decades.

C.A. Coello Coello et al. (Eds.): MICAI 2002, LNAI 2313, pp. 214–223, 2002.

On the other side, uncertainty has been a major topic even longer. The purpose of this paper is to combine the two. That is, we shall see how logics of knowledge can represent certain sense of uncertainty in multi-agent systems. In general, the unifying semantics based on games can be defined for a wide variety of other notions of knowledge as well, but we refrain from doing so in this paper.

The general feature of logics of knowledge with imperfect information is that these logics are partial, that is, there are sentences which do not have the truth-value TRUE and which do not have the truth-value FALSE. Partiality itself can be viewed as being derived from game-theoretic sources, however: if the associated semantic games are non-determined, all attempts of players trying to verify or trying to falsify a given sentence can be defeated. In contrast to partial modal logics that have existed in the literature [6], games can give rise to partiality at the level of complex formulas even if the underlying models are complete, that is, the language is completely interpreted.

Although the main purpose of this paper is purely a conceptual one, new multi-agent logics of knowledge that need games for their interpretation will be introduced. Far from being a purely technical enterprise, we motivate such languages by giving examples of knowledge representation schemes in multi-agent systems that virtually necessitate the introduction of such new types of epistemic logics. This is because the central concept that is seen to arise, the notion of focussed knowledge, involves an inherent notion of uncertainty and is argued to play an indispensable role in adequately representing knowledge in multi-agent systems where agents, such as communicating processors, do not always know the content of a message that has been sent to them. In particular, we show that there are simple systems with two or more agents whose knowledge can be naturally captured in the kind of epistemic logics advocated here.

2 Basic Epistemic Logic

What is knowledge? According to the Greeks, it meant "true, justified belief". Hintikka [3] proposes that it is "truth in epistemic alternatives". Many names can be given to these epistemic alternatives: they can be possible worlds, alternative states, scenarios, points in time or space, and so on. The key insight is that an agent i knows a proposition p in the world or state w, if and only if p is true in all of i's epistemic alternatives of w.

This analysis has led to a proliferation of notions of knowledge in logic, philosophy, computer science and artificial intelligence: nowadays we find notions of common, shared, distributed and mutual knowledge and belief. Furthermore, the distinction between *de dicto* versus *de re* in quantified epistemic logics is widely spread in the philosophy of language.

In brief, the well-formed formulas of ordinary propositional epistemic logic $\mathcal{L}$ are

$$\phi ::= p \mid \varphi \vee \psi \mid \neg\varphi \mid K_i\varphi \, .$$

$K_i\,\varphi$ is read "an agent i knows φ".

The semantics based on possible worlds is as follows. Let φ, ψ be formulas of ordinary propositional epistemic logic $\mathcal{L}$. A model is a triple $M = \langle \mathcal{W}, R, g \rangle$, where g is a total valuation function $g \colon \mathcal{W} \to (\Phi \to \{\mathsf{True}, \mathsf{False}\})$, assigning to each proposition letter $p \in \Phi$ a subset of a set of possible worlds $\mathcal{W} = \{w_0 \ldots w_n\}$ for which $\{w_i \mid g(w)(p) = \mathsf{True}, w \in \mathcal{W}\}$. $R = \{\rho_1 \ldots \rho_n\}$ is a set of accessibility relations for each agent $i = 1 \ldots n$, $\rho_i \subseteq \mathcal{W} \times \mathcal{W}$. Let us write $w_1 \in [w_0]_{\rho_i}$ to denote that a possible world w_1 is i-accessible from w_0, that is, w_1 belongs to the set of i's epistemic alternatives.

$$
\begin{array}{ll}
\langle M, w \rangle \models p & \text{iff } \{w \mid g(w)(p) = \mathsf{True}\}, p \in \Phi \, . \\
\langle M, w \rangle \models \neg\varphi & \text{iff } \langle M, w \rangle \not\models \varphi \, . \\
\langle M, w \rangle \models \varphi \vee \psi & \text{iff } \langle M, w \rangle \models \varphi \text{ or } \langle M, w \rangle \models \psi \, . \\
\langle M, w \rangle \models K_i \varphi & \text{iff } \langle M, w' \rangle \models \varphi, \text{ for all } w' \in [w]_{\rho_i} \, .
\end{array}
$$

The following section illustrates why this basic format may be inadequate, and what would be needed for multi-agent systems instead.

3 From Perfect to Imperfect Information: Knowledge in Multi-agent Systems

As noted, classical logic is a logic of perfect information transmission: within the game-theoretic framework to be given below this means that each evaluation step in truth-clauses is revealed to the next level. The same holds for classical epistemic and other modal logics. The assumption of perfect information is, however, inadequate for multi-agent systems, where information is often uncertain and hidden from other parties.

One manifestation of imperfect information is concurrent information processing. For example, the logic of concurrent processing may involve branching (aka Henkin or partially ordered) quantifiers [2]:

$$M \models \begin{matrix} \forall x \, \exists y \\ \forall z \, \exists w \end{matrix} \, Sxyzw \quad \text{iff} \quad \exists f \exists g \forall x \forall z \, Sxf(x)zg(z) \, . \tag{1}$$

For example, de Alfaro et al. [1] show that synchronous single-step control modules with static and fixed typing gives rise to similar Henkin quantifiers.

In the field of knowledge representation, there are two important outcomes. First, understanding knowledge of communicating multi-agent system benefits from this kind of concurrent notions. Second, we often need to move from propositional logics to first-order ones. To see the importance of these, suppose that a process U_2 sends a message x to U_1. We ought to report this by saying that "U_2 knows what x is", and "U_1 knows that *it* has been sent" (U_1 might knows this, say, because the communication channel is open). This is already a rich situation involving all kinds of knowledge. However, the knowledge involved in this two-agent system cannot be symbolised in ordinary first-order epistemic logic.

In this system, two clauses need to be represented "U_2 knows what has been sent", and "U_1 knows that something has been sent". The former includes what historically is known as *de re* knowledge and the latter *de dicto* knowledge.

However, what is not involved is the clause "U_1 knows that U_2 knows", nor the clause "U_2 knows that U_1 knows".

So the question is, how do we combine these clauses? It is easy to see that attempts such as the following three

$\exists x K_{U_2} \mathsf{Message}(x) \land K_{U_1} \exists y \mathsf{Message}(y)$
$K_{U_1} \exists x(\mathsf{Message}(x) \land K_{U_2} \mathsf{Message}(x))$
$\exists x(K_{U_2} \mathsf{Message}(x) \land K_{U_1} \exists y \mathsf{Message}(y) \land x \simeq y)$

all fail. So does an attempt that tries to use two variables and distinguishes between a message whose content is known ("$\mathsf{Content}(x)$"), and a message that has been sent ("$\mathsf{Sent}(y)$"):

$\exists x \exists y((K_{U_1} \mathsf{Content}(x) \simeq y) \land K_{U_2} \mathsf{Sent}(x))$.

This does not work because now U_2 comes to know what has been sent, which is clearly too strong.

What we need is information hiding alias branching, which hides the information about the choices for certain possible worlds:

$$\begin{matrix} \exists x & K_{U_2} \\ K_{U_1} \exists y & \end{matrix} (\mathsf{Message}(x) \land x \simeq y) \,. \tag{2}$$

Hence, when we have concurrent processing in quantified epistemic logics, and when there are two or more agents involved, a novel type of knowledge arises. Let us call this notion focussed knowledge, and it can be generalised to n agents.

Next, let us consider the question of what we mean by focussed knowledge. But for this we need to first define semantic games for formulas similar to those of (2).

4 Game-Theoretic Semantics for Epistemic Logic

4.1 Language and Its Partialisation

Let $K_j \psi$ be an $\mathcal{L}$-formula, and let $A = \{K_1 \ldots K_n\}, K_i \in A, i \in \{1 \ldots n\}$, such that $K_j \psi$ is in the scope of $K_1 \ldots K_n$. Now, if $B \subseteq A$, then $(K_j/B)\,\psi \in \mathcal{L}^*, K_j \notin B$.

For example, $K_1(K_2/K_1)\,\varphi$ and $K_1(\varphi \land (K_2/K_1)\,\psi)$ are wffs of $\mathcal{L}^*$. $K_1(K_2/K_1)\,\varphi$ can be read as "K_1 and K_2 know that φ", which is different from the multiplied reading "K_1 knows that φ and K_2 knows that φ".

Let us then look at GTS for $\mathcal{L}^*$. Every $\mathcal{L}^*$-formula φ defines a game $\mathcal{G}(\varphi, w, M)$ on a model M between two teams of players, the team of falsifiers $F = \{F_1 \ldots F_k\}$ and the team of verifiers $V = \{V_1 \ldots V_m\}$, where w is a state and g is an assignment to the propositional letters. The game $\mathcal{G}(\varphi, w, M)$ is defined by the following rules.

(G.¬) If $\varphi = \neg\psi$, V and F change roles, and the next choice is in $\mathcal{G}(\psi, w, M)$.
(G.∨) If $\varphi = (\psi \lor \theta)$, V chooses Left or Right, and the next choice is in $\mathcal{G}(\psi, w, M)$ if Left and $\mathcal{G}(\theta, w, M)$ if Right.

(G.K_i) If $\varphi = K_i\,\psi$, and the game has reached w, $F_j \in F$ chooses a possible world $w_1 \in [w]_{\rho_i}$, and the next choice is in $\mathcal{G}(\psi, w_1, M)$.

(G.(K_i/B)) If $\varphi = (K_i/B)\,\psi$, $K_i \notin B$, and the game has reached w, then $F_l \in F$ chooses a possible world $w_1 \in \mathcal{W}$ 'independently' of the choices made for the elements in B, and the next choice is in $\mathcal{G}(\psi, w_1, M)$.

(G.atom) If φ is atomic, the game ends, and V wins if φ is true, and F wins if φ is false.

The formulas $(K_i/B)\,\psi$ mean that there is imperfect information: a player choosing for K_i on the left-hand side of the slash is not informed about the choices made for the elements in B earlier in the game. Nothing is said about the accessibility relation in these cases, since we want to leave the interpretation of these modalities open.

The purpose of V is to show that φ is true in M (that is, $\langle M, w\rangle \models^+ \varphi$), and the purpose of F is to show that φ is false in M (that is, $\langle M, w\rangle \models^- \varphi$). If $\langle M, w\rangle \models^+ \varphi$, V wins, and if $\langle M, w\rangle \models^- \varphi$, F wins. A strategy for a player in a game $\mathcal{G}(\varphi, w, M)$ is a function assigning to each non-atomic subformula of φ a member of a team V or F, outputting an application of each rule, which is a possible world in $\mathcal{W}$, a value in $\{\mathsf{Left}, \mathsf{Right}\}$ (the connective information), or an instruction to change roles (negation). A winning strategy is a strategy by which a player can make operational choices such that every play results in a win for him or her, no matter how the opponent chooses.

Let φ be an $\mathcal{L}^*$-formula. We define that for any model M and $w \in \mathcal{W}$, $\langle M, w\rangle \models^+ \varphi$ if and only if a strategy exists which is winning for V in $\mathcal{G}(\varphi, w, M)$, and $\langle M, w\rangle \models^- \varphi$ if and only if a strategy exists which is winning for F in $\mathcal{G}(\varphi, w, M)$.

A game $\mathcal{G}$ is determined, if and only if for every play on φ, a winning strategy exists for V in $\mathcal{G}$ or a winning strategy exists for F in it. It is easy to see that games for $\mathcal{L}^*$ are not determined.

From non-determinacy it follows that the law of the excluded middle $\varphi \vee \neg\varphi$ fails in $\mathcal{L}^*$. This is a common thing to happen in logics with imperfect information. What is more, the phenomenon of non-determinacy is closely related to that of partiality, and can of course be generalised to logics with quantified notions.

To see the relation, observe that a partial model is a triple $M = \langle \mathcal{W}, R, g'\rangle$, where g' is a partial valuation function $g' \colon \mathcal{W} \to (\Phi \to \{\mathsf{True}, \mathsf{False}\})$, assigning to some proposition letters in Φ a subset $g'(\Phi)$ of a set of possible worlds $\mathcal{W} = \{w_0 \dots w_n\}$ for which p is true. Partiality then means that

$$\langle M, w\rangle \models^+ K_i\varphi \text{ iff } \langle M, w'\rangle \models^+ \varphi \text{ for all } w' \in \mathcal{W}, w' \in [w]_{\rho_i}\,.$$

$$\langle M, w\rangle \models^- K_i\varphi \text{ iff } \langle M, w'\rangle \models^- \varphi \text{ for some } w' \in \mathcal{W}, w' \in [w]_{\rho_i}\,.$$

Similarly for the dual modality $\neg K_i \neg\varphi$.

However, an illuminating alternative way of looking at the phenomenon of partiality in epistemic logics is through the lens of GTS, where the games are taken to be ones of imperfect information rather than perfect information. As seen above, such games can be applied to both propositional and first-order systems. This time partiality arises at the level of complex formulas, and does not need partial models. This is because partiality is a result of assumptions concerning information transmission between players.

One consequence is that semantic games allow us to study partiality in complete models, generalising the received approaches to partial modal logics in [6].

4.2 Focussed Knowledge and Extensive Forms of Games

There are important non-technical motivations as to why one should be interested in combining games with various modalities. We already briefly considered multi-agent systems that benefit from such a combination. In general, the combination in question gives rise to the new type of knowledge in multi-agent logics, termed focussed knowledge. Let us explain next what is meant by the notion of focus that arises in the quantified epistemic logics of imperfect information.

Language and Semantics. Let the syntax for first-order epistemic logic $\mathcal{L}_{\omega\omega}$ consist of a signature τ, a logical vocabulary, and rules for building up formulas:

$$\phi ::= P \mid K_i\varphi \mid \forall x\varphi \mid \exists x\varphi \mid \varphi \vee \psi \mid \neg\varphi \mid x \simeq y \,.$$

Let $Q\psi, Q \in \{\forall x_j, \exists y_j, K_i\}$ be an $\mathcal{L}_{\omega\omega}$-formula in syntactic scope of the elements in $A = \{K_1 \dots K_n, \forall x_k, \exists y_k\}$ (for finite integers $i, j, k, n; j \neq k$). Then $\mathcal{L}^*_{\omega\omega}$ consists of wffs of $\mathcal{L}_{\omega\omega}$ together with: if $B \subseteq A$, then $(Q/B)\,\psi$ is an $\mathcal{L}^*_{\omega\omega}$-formula, $Q \notin B$.

By means of this notation one can linearise the branching prefix in (2) while preserving its informational constraints:

$$K_{U_1}\exists y(\exists x/K_{U_1}y)(K_{U_2}/K_{U_1}y)\,(\mathsf{Message}(x) \wedge x \simeq y)\,. \tag{3}$$

Briefly, this formula hides the information about the choices for K_{U_1} and y when $\exists x$ has been reached, and choices for K_{U_1} and y when K_{U_2} has been reached.

A model M for $\mathcal{L}^*_{\omega\omega}$ is now a tuple $\langle \mathfrak{A}, \mathfrak{I}\rangle$, where $\mathfrak{A}$ is a τ-structure $\langle \mathcal{W}, D_{w_j}\rangle$ of a signature τ of a non-empty set of possible worlds $\mathcal{W}$ and a non-empty world-relative domain D_{w_j} of individuals. $\mathfrak{I}$ is an interpretation $\langle \pi, R\rangle$, where π attaches to each possible world a τ-structure together with a valuation from terms to the domain. Hence $P^{\pi(w_i)}$ means that the predicate P is interpreted in the world w_i.

We then need a valuation $g\colon X \to D_{w_i}$, which assigns individual variables in X to elements in D_{w_i}. Let us extend this to $g^{\pi(w_i)}\colon \mathcal{T} \to D_{w_i}$ which maps terms to the domains of individuals such that every n-ary function symbol f^n has a denotation of an n-ary (possible partial) operation in a domain D_{w_i}, every variable $x \in X$ has a denotation $g^{\pi(w_i)}(x) = x^{\pi(w_i)}$, every constant symbol $c \in C$ has a denotation $g^{\pi(w_i)}(c) = c^{\pi(w_i)}$, and every m-ary predicate symbol in P has a denotation of an m-ary predicate (or relation) in a domain D_{w_i}. Every term $t = f(t_1 \dots t_m)$ can now be recursively defined as $g^{\pi(w_i)}(t) = f^{\pi(w_i)}(g^{\pi(w_i)}(t_1) \dots g^{\pi(w_i)}(t_m))$. In addition to a relational τ-structure, π now attaches to each possible world a valuation $g^{\pi(w_i)}\colon \mathcal{T} \to D_{w_i}$.

We go on to enrich the semantics with a finite number of identifying functions (world lines) in M, extending the valuation g to a (partial) mapping from worlds to individuals, that is, to $g\colon X \to D_{w_i}^{\mathcal{W}}$, such that if $w \in \mathcal{W}$ and g is an identifying function, then $g(w) \in D_w$. These functions imply that individuals have only local aspects or manifestations of themselves in any particular world (cf. [4]). Two such functions may also meet at some world, and then part company.

The interpretation of the equality sign $\simeq$ (identifying functional) now is

$$\langle M, w_0, g\rangle \models x \simeq y \text{ iff for some } w_i, w_j \in \mathcal{W}, \exists f \exists h \text{ such that } f(w_i) = h(w_j)\,.$$

That is, two individuals are identical iff there are world lines f and h that pick the same individuals in w_i and in w_j. World lines can meet at some world but then pick different individuals in other worlds; the two-place identifying functional operation spells out when they meet. Individuals within a domain of a possible world are local and need to be cross-identified in order to be global and specific.

Interpretation of Focus. In order to understand quantified epistemic logic with imperfect information, what does the notion of focus mean in sentences like (2)? An important thing to note is that what is involved here is certain non-compositionality, which is the reason why we use games to give semantics for $\mathcal{L}^*$ and $\mathcal{L}^*_{\omega\omega}$.

The informal game rules now are:

(G.$\exists x \ldots K_i$**)** When K_i is in the scope of $\exists x$ (or they belong to different rows in the branching quantifier), and the game has reached w, the individual picked for x by a verifying player V has to be defined and exist in all worlds accessible from the current one.

This rule is motivated by the fact that the course of the play reached at a certain point in the game is unbeknownst to F choosing for K_i. This approach leads to the notion of specific focus on individuals in the sense of extensive games (see below).

The other game rule is

(G.$K_i \ldots \exists x$**)** When $\exists x$ is in the scope of K_i, the individual picked for x has to be defined and exist in the world chosen for K_i.

This rule leads to the notion of non-specific focus.

Finally, the rule for the hidden information says that:

(G.Q/B**)** If $\varphi = (Q/B)\psi, Q \in \{\forall x, K_i\}$, and the game has reached w, then if $Q = \forall x, F_1 \in F$ chooses an individual from the domain D_{w_1}, where w_1 is the world from which the first world chosen for the first modal operator in B departed from. The next choice is in $\mathcal{G}(\psi, w, g, M)$. If $Q = K_1$ then $F_1 \in F$ chooses a world $w_1 \in \mathcal{W}$ in the model M 'independently' of the choices made for the elements in B, and the next choice is in $\mathcal{G}(\psi, w_1, g, M)$. Likewise for $V_1 \in V$.

The notion of choosing 'independently' is explained below. Other game rules for $\mathcal{L}^*_{\omega\omega}$ are classical.

Extensive Forms of Games. Independent modalities mean that the player choosing for K_i is not informed about the choices made for $K_j, j \neq i$ in other rows of a branching quantifier prefix. In the linear notation, independence means that K_i's are exempted from the scope of K_j. Likewise for quantifiers.

This can be illustrated by taking hints from the theory of games. We shall apply a partitional information structure $(I_i)_{i \in N}$ in the corresponding extensive-form games, which partitions sequences of actions (histories) $h \in H$ into equivalence classes (information sets) $\{S^i_j \mid S^i_j \in (I_i)_{i \in N}, h \sim_i h' \in S^i_j, h, h' \in H, j = 1 \dots k,\ k = |V| = |F|\}$. The purpose of equivalence classes is to denote which histories are indistinguishable to players. The histories within an equivalence class are not known to a player i whose equivalence class is in question[1].

Uniformity of Strategies. Payoff functions $u_i(h)$ associate a pair of truth-values in $\{1, -1\}$ to terminal histories $h \in H$. Strategies are functions $f_i\colon P^{-1}(\{i\}) \to A$ from histories where players move to sequences of actions in A. If player i is planning his decisions within the equivalence class S^i_j annotated for him, player's strategies are further required to be uniform on indistinguishable histories $h, h' \in S^i_j$. In this case $f_i(h) = f_i(h'), i \in N$.

This leads to the following informal observation: *Tracing uniform strategies along the game histories reveals in which worlds the specific focus is located.* To see this, it suffices to correlate information sets of an extensive game for (3) with world lines of a suitable model M. To see an example, look at the extensive game for a linearised version of (2) given in Fig.1 (for brevity, the connective choice is not depicted here).

We can now see that the clause 'choosing independently' that appeared in the above game rules means that players' strategies have to be uniform on indistinguishable histories, that is, on worlds that they cannot distinguish.

The uniformity requirement agrees with the requirement that within non-trivial information sets, players' actions have to be the same. For example, the strategies in (2) for the members of V (for the action part only, ignoring the player function) include the two uniform functions

$f_{V_2}\colon \{(w'_1, a), (w'_1, b), (w'_2, a), (w'_2, b)\} \to \{a, b\}$
$g_{V_2}\colon \{(w'_1, a), (w'_1, b), (w'_2, a), (w'_2, b)\} \to \{w_1, w_2\}$

where f_{V_2} is $\{w'_1, w'_2\}$-uniform:

$$f_{V_2}(w'_1, a) = f_{V_2}(w'_2, a) \text{ and } f_{V_2}(w'_1, b) = f_{V_2}(w'_2, b)\ .$$

Likewise, g_{V_2} is $\{a, b\}$-uniform:

$$g_{V_2}(w'_1, a) = g_{V_2}(w'_2, a) \text{ and } g_{V_2}(w'_1, b) = g_{V_2}(w'_2, b)\ .$$

Similar uniform functions exist for the team F.

[1] By annotating equivalence classes with players we in fact generalise the traditional way of representing player's information in the theory of games, since they are no longer required to move at histories within their equivalence classes. See [7] for a more detailed exposition of extensive games in logic.

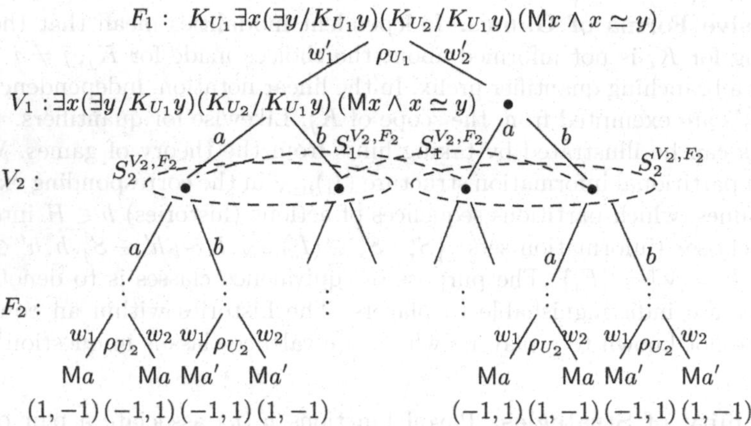

Fig. 1. An extensive imperfect information game for (2), with four information sets $S_1^{V_2}, S_1^{F_2}, S_2^{V_2}$ and $S_2^{F_2}$.

Two remarks are in order. First, the notion of uniformity puts some inevitable constraints on allowable models. In particular, at any modal depth d (defined in a standard way) there have to be the same number of departing worlds. In addition, if we assume that players can observe the set of available choices, the uniformity of strategies requires that the departing worlds have to in fact coincide for all indistinguishable worlds. In quantified contexts, this means that the domains have to coincide for any two worlds at the same depth d that are members of the same information set in the sense of extensive games.

Second, K_i's in different rows can either refer to (simultaneous) accessible worlds from the current one, or to detached submodels of M. In the latter case we evaluate formulas in

$$\langle M, (w_0^1, w_0^2 \dots w_0^n), g\rangle .$$

Hence the models can break into submodels, whence the designated worlds in each submodel would be independent by definition. It needs to be noted that in that case there can nonetheless be world lines that span across different submodels.

5 Applications and Conclusions

We have argued that certain multi-agent knowledge representation tasks call for expressive quantified epistemic logics that capture the notion of focussed knowledge, a notion difficult to be captured in classical perfect information logics.

A number of applications can be anticipated, although they cannot be surveyed here. The following list suggests some potential fields in computer science and artificial intelligence where some of these new epistemic logics with imperfect information together with the associated GTS may turn out to be useful.

– New epistemic logics can be helpful in understanding uncertainty in artificial intelligence and in distributed systems, and in exploring intensional dimensions of knowledge representation arising in inter-operation.
– Games can be used in unifying verification languages for multi-agent systems. This is possible because games implement notions of intention, planning, preference, memory, team playing, probabilities, bounded rationality and so on, all of which are relevant in research on multi-agent systems. The need for such unifying verification languages has been pointed out in [8].
– Reasoning about secure information flow carries the idea of what can be revealed to the opponent. In this sense, the notion of 'world-hiding' interlocks with the notion of 'key-hiding'. The cognate notions of the strategic meaning of programs, modularity and information dependencies may can receive increased game-theoretic importance.

Combining games with the semantics of epistemic logics is useful in delivering meanings for sentences possessing non-compositional information hiding. A quantified version of imperfect-information epistemic logic is helpful also in the conceptual representation of various forms of knowledge in multi-agent systems. One key notion that can be put to work in this respect is focussed knowledge. The general perspective is that games provide a unifying semantic foundation when combined with modalities, and that their imperfect information versions can partialise various epistemic logics so that partiality arises is maintained at the level of complex formulas.

References

1. de Alfaro, L., Henzinger, T.A., Mang, F.Y.C.: The control of synchronous systems. Proceedings of the 11th International Conference on Concurrency Theory, Lecture Notes in Computer Science **1877**. Springer-Verlag (2000) 458–473
2. Henkin, L.: Some remarks on infinitely long formulas. In: (no editor given) Infinistic Methods. Proceedings of the Symposium on Foundations of Mathematics, Warsaw, Panstwowe (2–9 September 1959). Pergamon Press, New York (1961) 167–183
3. Hintikka, J.: Knowledge and Belief. Cornell University Press, Ithaca (1962)
4. Hintikka, J.: On the logic of perception. In: Models for Modalities. Reidel, Dordrecht (1969) 151–183
5. Hintikka, J., Sandu, G.: Game-theoretical semantics. In: van Benthem, J., ter Meulen, A. (eds): Handbook of Logic and Language. Elsevier, Amsterdam (1997) 361–410
6. Jaspars, J., Thijsse, E.: Fundamentals of partial modal logic. In: Doherty, P. (ed.): Partiality, Modality, and Nonmonotonicity. Stanford, CSLI (1996) 111–141
7. Sandu, G., Pietarinen, A.: Informationally independent connectives. In: Muskens, R., van Loon, I., Mints, G. (eds): Logic, Language and Computation **9**. Stanford, CSLI (2002)
8. Wooldridge, M.: Semantic issues in the verification of agent communication languages. Journal of Autonomous Agents and Multi-Agent Systems **3**. (2000) 9–31

Modelling Learners of a Control Task with Inductive Logic Programming: A Case Study

Ma. Guadalupe Quintana[1] and Rafael Morales[2]

[1] Instituto Tecnológico de Zacatepec, Zacatepec, Mor., Mexico
55086mgq@iie.org.mx
[2] Instituto de Investigaciones Eléctricas, Temixco, Mor., Mexico
rmorales@iie.org.mx

Abstract. We present results of using inductive logic programming (ILP) to produce learner models by behavioural cloning. Models obtained using a program for supervised induction of production rules (RIPPER) are compared to models generated using a well-known program for ILP (FOIL). It is shown that the models produced by FOIL are either too specific or too general, depending on whether or not auxiliary relations are applied. Three possible explanations for these results are: (1) there is no way of specifying to FOIL the minimum number of cases each clause must cover; (2) FOIL requires that all auxiliary relations be defined extensionally; and (3) the application domain (control of a pole on a cart) has continuous attributes. In spite of FOIL's limitations, the models it produced using auxiliary relations meet one of the goals of our exploration: to obtain more structured learner models which are easier to comprehend.

1 Introduction

Learner modelling is the activity that characterises intelligent tutoring systems [17] by which they build computational representations of learners on the basis of learner behaviour and knowledge the system has about the subject matter. Although learner models can work as "black boxes," useful only to the systems that build them, there are a number of good reasons for making the models inspectable, and even modifiable by people like system designers, teachers, authorities, parents and learners [12,18].

The idea of building learner models constrained to be easily understandable and modifiable by the learners was explored in PACMOD [10], based on work done on *behavioural cloning* [2,8] to automatically acquire expert knowledge from expert behaviour. PACMOD uses RIPPER [4], a program for supervised induction of production rules, to build models of people learning to control a computer-based simulation of a pole hinged to a cart as an inverted pendulum while the cart runs on a straight track of finite length (Figure 1). The task itself is a classical problem in control theory [5] (using a force of variable magnitude)

C.A. Coello Coello et al. (Eds.): MICAI 2002, LNAI 2313, pp. 224–233, 2002.

which has also been used frequently for testing algorithms for machine learning [1,9,14] (usually with a force of constant magnitude). PACMOD does not use machine learning for acquiring knowledge to solve the problem but rather for building an explanation for the behaviour of individual learners. A similar work has been done by Subramanian and others for the task of piloting an autonomous underwater vehicle [6,19], but focused on the accuracy of the learner models rather than on their comprehensibility.

The learner models that PACMOD builds using RIPPER are sets of production rules. The preconditions of the rules are expressed as ranges for the variables that define the state of the pole and cart device – position and velocity of the cart; angle and angular velocity of the pole. The action part of each rule corresponds to one of the actions available to the learner, either pushing to the left or pushing to the right[1]. Evaluations of the system have shown that learners can get an overall understanding of their models, yet they also suggest that a big obstacle to a better understanding is the shallow structure of the models [13].

In this paper we present preliminary results of our exploration into using inductive logic programming (ILP) to provide more structure to the learner models built by PACMOD. Although the motivation of our work is to attain learner models which are easier to understand, this paper deals with a more basic issue: the accuracy of the models. The evaluation of the learner models is done in terms of their predictive power alone, although some other approaches to evaluating them are discussed in Section 5.

The tool used was Quinlan's FOIL [15,16]. Our work is different from previous research on using ILP for learner modelling [3] in the dynamic and continuous nature of the application domain and data.

The task of controlling the pole and cart is described in the next section. Section 3 is devoted to explaining how data was selected and prepared for RIPPER and FOIL. The main properties of the resulting learner models are described in Section 4, and illustrated with some examples. Section 5 contains a discussion of the results, and the paper ends with some conclusions and directions for future work.

2 The Task

The application domain of PACMOD is the task of controlling a simulation of a device composed of two parts: a cart running on a straight rail of finite length, and a pole hinged to the top of the cart as an inverted pendulum with its movement constrained to the vertical plane defined by the rail (Figure 1). Control of the device must be achieved by pushing the cart either to the left or to the right, using a force of fixed magnitude. The learner interacts with PACMOD using the arrow keys on the keyboard to command any of three actions: starting a new control trial (↑), pushing the cart to the left (←) or pushing it to the right (→). A control trial fails and ends whenever the pole falls over the cart or the cart reaches the end of the rail.

[1] A default rule with the action *wait* is chosen for all cases where no other rule applies.

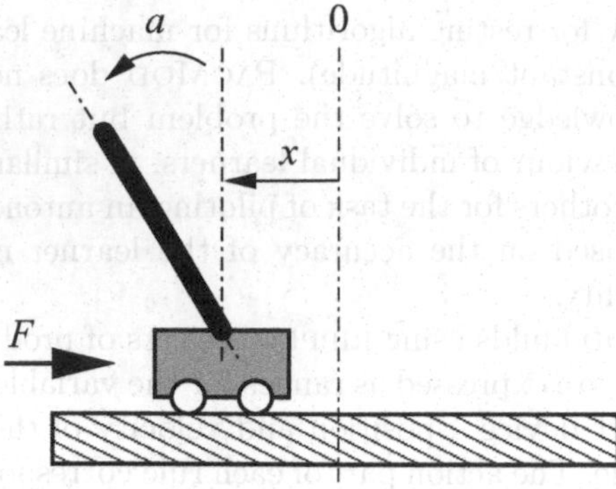

Parameter	Value
Mass of the cart	1 kg
Mass of the pole	0.1 kg
Length of the pole	1 m
Magnitude of the force	10 N
Length of the track	4.8 m

Fig. 1. The pole and cart problem. The physical parameters for the problem are shown in the table.

3 Selection and Preparation of Data

Data used for testing was obtained from traces of behaviour from three learners attempting to control the simulation of the pole and cart device. The first learner had a few hours of previous practice in the task, and his behaviour was recorded in two sessions of five minutes each: (a) one in which the initial conditions for every control trial were selected randomly from a set of only two opposite conditions, both with the cart departing a medium speed from the centre of the rail and the pole falling at medium speed in the same direction the cart moves ($x = \pm 0.4915\,\text{m}$, $\dot{x} = \pm 0.7150\,\text{m/s}$, $a = \pm 0.1054\,\text{rad}$ y $\dot{a} = \pm 0.2968\,\text{rad/s}$, all values chosen with the same sign[2]), and (b) another in which the initial conditions for every control trial were built by choosing randomly from a predefined range a value for each variable. Data from previous experiments with PacMod was used for the other two learners [10]. Both learners have had minimum experience at the task, and the learner models built by PacMod for them were among the most and least predictive, respectively.

The trace of behaviour for every learner is a series of records of the form (*device state*, *learner action*), recorded with time lags of 100 ms. Before building the learner models, the records were adjusted for taking into account the symmetry of the domain and possible delays due to reaction time. Cases with identical device state but different learner action were then eliminated. The results of the process were four files containing records of the form ($\dot{a}, a, \dot{x}, x,$ *action*), where $\dot{a}$, a, $\dot{x}$ and x are real numbers and *action* takes the value of either *left*, *inertia* or *right*, which corresponds to the learner actions of pushing the cart to the left, waiting and pushing the cart to the right, respectively. Finally, each file was divided into training data (corresponding to the first four minutes of the control

[2] Hereafter x stands for the cart position from the centre of the rail, and $\dot{x}$ denotes its velocity; a stands for the angle of the pole to the vertical, and $\dot{a}$ denotes its angular velocity.

Table 1. Summary of training and testing data from each one of the learners.

Learner	Cases					
	Training (4 minutes)			Testing (1 minutes)		
	left	*inertia*	*right*	*left*	*inertia*	*right*
1a	508	886	508	66	92	128
1b	636	732	636	93	103	54
2	725	766	725	47	137	44
3	1248	266	1248	174	49	156

session) and testing data (corresponding to the last minute of the session). The end result of the whole data preparing process is summarised in Table 1.

4 Model Induction

4.1 RIPPER

Besides the files containing the training and testing data, RIPPER [4] also requires an additional file with a list of the classes to be considered and a list of the attributes used to define the cases, and their types. Three classes were specified – *left*, *inertia* and *right* – and four continuous attributes were used – corresponding to the state variables of the pole and cart.

PACMOD instructs RIPPER to separate each class from the rest (using RIPPER's option `-aunordered`), to generate production rules that cover at least one percent of the training data each (option `-F`), and to give priority to avoiding false negatives over avoiding false positives (option `-L`). As a result, RIPPER produces a set of production rules containing rules for each class, and the final step in the modelling process is to make *inertia* the default class by substituting a default rule for all the rules corresponding to this class [10].

4.2 FOIL

FOIL was used to generate two models per learner: one without using auxiliary relations (hereafter called a *propositional* or *zeroth-order* model) and another one using auxiliary relations (hereafter called a *first-order* model). The input data to FOIL consists of one or several relations defined in extensional form, one of which is the relation that FOIL will try to define in intensional form (target relation). In other words, the input file contains positive and negative examples for the target relation, as well as positive examples for each one of the auxiliary relations. From these examples FOIL induces a definition of the target relation in terms of this and other relations, using Horn clauses.

In order to define the auxiliary relations, the reports written by the participants in previous experiments with PACMOD [10,13] describing strategies that they followed to try to control the pole on the cart were taken as a reference. The descriptions make use of composed concepts, constructed from the state

Table 2. Confusion matrix.

Data	Model		
	left	*inertia*	*right*
left	ll	li	lr
inertia	il	ii	ir
right	rl	ri	rr

variables of position, angle or speed; concepts such as "falling over", ' raising", "leaving" and "coming back to centre." Consequently, we chose to produce the first-order models using the extensional definitions of the following auxiliary relations, defined here in intensional form:

falling_right($\dot{A}$,A,$\dot{X}$,X) :- $A > 0$, $\dot{A} > 0$.
falling_left($\dot{A}$,A,$\dot{X}$,X) :- $A < 0$, $\dot{A} < 0$.
raising_right($\dot{A}$,A,$\dot{X}$,X) :- $A > 0$, $\dot{A} < 0$.
raising_left($\dot{A}$,A,$\dot{X}$,X) :- $A < 0$, $\dot{A} > 0$.
leaving_right($\dot{A}$,A,$\dot{X}$,X) :- $X > 0$, $\dot{X} > 0$.
leaving_left($\dot{A}$,A,$\dot{X}$,X) :- $X < 0$, $\dot{X} < 0$.
coming_right($\dot{A}$,A,$\dot{X}$,X) :- $X > 0$, $\dot{X} < 0$.
coming_left($\dot{A}$,A,$\dot{X}$,X) :- $X < 0$, $\dot{X} < 0$.

The cases (all positive) were taken from the corresponding training set, which means a different extensional definition of the auxiliary relations for each student. Nevertheless, the extensional definitions used by FOIL to produce the initial set of clauses were replaced by the corresponding intensional definitions – this time the same ones for all the learners – to filter the clauses with too small coverage and to evaluate the models.

Since the learner models had to contain relations for both the action to push towards the left and the action to push towards the right – that is, there were two target relations – it was necessary to execute FOIL twice to induce each one of the models. Additionally, due to the fact that FOIL does not allow the establishment of a minimum number of cases that each clause must cover, the models were filtered to eliminate all those clauses with coverage less than one percent of the training cases.

4.3 The Models

Table 3 summarises the results obtained when executing RIPPER and FOIL in the conditions described in the previous section. The evaluation of the models is made in terms of the classic measures of error, recall, precision and fallout, but with some adjustments that make them more suitable for our application, taking the so called *confusion matrix* as reference (Table 2).

Error is the percentage of all actions (cases in the classes *right* and *left*) and no actions (cases in the class *inertia* which the model classifies incorrectly:

$$\text{error} = 100 \times \frac{\textit{total of cases} - ll - ii - rr}{\textit{total of cases}}.$$

Table 3. Summary of the induction of the learner models using RIPPER and FOIL

Characteristics	Models											
	RIPPER				FOIL (zeroth order)				FOIL (first order)			
	1a	1b	2	3	1a	1b	2	3	1a	1b	2	3
Number of rules or clauses	8	9	9	7	22	36	43	42	8	10	8	8
Training (%):												
Error	28.86	28.24	26.81	12.45	30.23	24.70	23.47	8.83	54.36	43.21	47.56	16.65
Recall	76.97	87.97	81.10	93.75	43.41	61.08	64.21	90.26	85.43	89.47	80.14	92.23
Precision	69.76	71.87	75.05	90.07	100.00	100.00	99.89	99.96	45.64	56.79	52.44	83.35
Fallout	12.16	16.01	13.11	8.52	0.00	0.00	0.03	0.03	37.09	31.65	35.35	15.19
Testing (%):												
Error	22.73	26.80	39.47	14.51	25.17	28.40	36.84	14.25	35.31	44.80	68.86	20.84
Recall	90.21	84.35	52.75	94.55	71.65	59.18	15.38	87.27	95.36	93.88	78.02	90.91
Precision	78.83	72.51	50.00	87.64	89.10	86.14	66.67	93.51	64.69	55.20	31.14	79.16
Fallout	12.43	13.31	13.15	10.28	4.50	3.97	1.92	4.67	26.72	31.73	43.01	18.46

Recall is the percentage of all actions of the learner (cases in the classes *right* and *left*) classified correctly by the model:

$$\text{recall} = 100 \times \frac{ll + rr}{l* + r*}.$$

Precision is the percentage of all predictions of actions which are correctly done by the model (correct classifications of cases in the classes *left* and *right*):

$$\text{precision} = 100 \times \frac{ll + rr}{*l + *r}.$$

Fallout represents the percentage of no actions (cases in the class *inertia*) classified as actions plus actions (cases in the classes *left* and *right*) classified incorrectly as another action:

$$\text{fallout} = \frac{il + ir + rl + lr}{2(i*) + l* + r*}.$$

As an example of the models produced by RIPPER consider the following model of learner 1b:

right 253 38 IF $A \geq 0.173138$.
left 294 55 IF $A \leq -0.151901$.
left 80 17 IF $X \leq -0.187572$ $A \leq -0.089885$.
left 299 70 IF $A \leq -0.002631$ $\dot{A} \leq -0.218002$.
left 277 75 IF $A \leq 0.030254$ $\dot{A} \leq -0.291134$.
right 388 111 IF $A \geq 0.106096$.
right 355 112 IF $A \geq 0.023316$ $\dot{A} \geq 0.027685$.
left 383 127 IF $A \leq -0.030280$ $\dot{A} \leq 0.055225$.
right 350 130 IF $A \geq -0.054295$ $\dot{A} \geq 0.195421$.

The two integers between the action (class) and the keyword IF of each production rule correspond to the number of positives and false positives for the rule. The production rules are sorted in decreasing order according to the following measure of importance:

$$\frac{P}{P+N+2}.$$

The ten most important clauses of the propositional model produced by FOIL for the same learner are

right($\dot{A}$,A,$\dot{X}$,X) :- $\dot{X} > -0.942933$, $A > 0.326612$.
left($\dot{A}$,A,$\dot{X}$,X) :- $\dot{X} \leq 0.774837$, $A \leq -0.329387$.
right($\dot{A}$,A,$\dot{X}$,X) :- $A > 0.065941$, $\dot{A} > 0.155182$, $\dot{X} > -0.197856$, $X > -2.08424$.
left($\dot{A}$,A,$\dot{X}$,X) :- $A \leq -0.066824$, $\dot{A} \leq -0.155214$, $\dot{X} \leq 0.195398$, $X \leq 2.07357$.
right($\dot{A}$,A,$\dot{X}$,X) :- $A > 0.19414$, $X > -1.4208$, $\dot{X} > -1.30349$.
right($\dot{A}$,A,$\dot{X}$,X) :- $A > 0.002232$, $\dot{A} > 0.342165$, $\dot{X} > -0.385953$.
left($\dot{A}$,A,$\dot{X}$,X) :- $A \leq -0.002631$, $\dot{A} \leq -0.346481$, $\dot{X} \leq 0.383759$.
right($\dot{A}$,A,$\dot{X}$,X) :- $X > -1.35021$, $\dot{A} > -0.314095$, $\dot{X} > -0.540126$, $A > 0.150744$.
left($\dot{A}$,A,$\dot{X}$,X) :- $X \leq 1.33878$, $\dot{A} \leq 0.266279$, $\dot{X} \leq 0.539706$, $A \leq -0.151489$.
right($\dot{A}$,A,$\dot{X}$,X) :- $A > 0.13658$, $\dot{X} > 1.26678$, $\dot{A} > -0.761059$, $\dot{A} \leq -0.10900$.

Finally, the first-order model produced by FOIL for the same learner is the following (the last two clauses are superfluous, because there are previous clauses with the same antecedents):

right($\dot{A}$,A,$\dot{X}$,X) :- falling_right($\dot{A}$,A,$\dot{X}$,X).
left($\dot{A}$,A,$\dot{X}$,X) :- falling_left($\dot{A}$,A,$\dot{X}$,X).
right($\dot{A}$,A,$\dot{X}$,X) :- raising_right($\dot{A}$,A,$\dot{X}$,X).
left($\dot{A}$,A,$\dot{X}$,X) :- raising_left($\dot{A}$,A,$\dot{X}$,X).
right($\dot{A}$,A,$\dot{X}$,X) :- leaving_right($\dot{A}$,A,$\dot{X}$,X).
left($\dot{A}$,A,$\dot{X}$,X) :- leaving_left($\dot{A}$,A,$\dot{X}$,X).
right($\dot{A}$,A,$\dot{X}$,X) *:- raising_left*($\dot{A}$,A,$\dot{X}$,X).
left($\dot{A}$,A,$\dot{X}$,X) *:- raising_right*($\dot{A}$,A,$\dot{X}$,X).

5 Discussion

The data gathered from the learners of the task of controlling the pole on the cart (described in Section 2) has two very important properties.

1. The attributes used to describe the cases are not discrete but continuous.

2. The data seems to be very noisy. This property can be explained in terms of the fact that we have learners, not experts in the task. Another factor adding noise to the data is a variable delay in the learners' reaction to changes in the state of the device (for example, in some cases it is easier to predict a future state of the device than in others, and hence to plan an action in advance).

The combination of these properties with the characteristics of each learning algorithm and its implementation produced some interesting results.

- The option to establish a minimum number of cases to be covered by a rule allows RIPPER to deal with the noise in the data with greater tolerance, and to produce relatively small models containing somewhat imprecise rules. On the contrary, FOIL does not offer this option, which makes it much less tolerant to noise in data. In consequence, FOIL tends to produce models of zeroth order with a great amount of very specific and precise clauses, many of them covering less than 1% of the total number of cases.
- The propositional models generated by FOIL are of high accuracy and little contamination, even after eliminating the clauses that cover less than 1% of the training cases. Nevertheless, the elimination of the most specific clauses results in a considerable reduction in recall. In other words, these models predict accurately less actions than the first-order models produced by FOIL and the models generated by RIPPER.
- Each first-order model generated by FOIL is more intuitive and easier to comprehend than the corresponding propositional model and the model produced by RIPPER. Unfortunately, FOIL takes the extensional definitions of the auxiliary relations as exact and complete, which on the contrary are rather incomplete because the task is continuous by nature. FOIL uses the apparent precision of the extensional definitions to avoid false positives; but when the extensional definitions are replaced by the intensional ones, the first-order models turn out to be too general, with little precision and much fallout. Even if the extensional definitions of the auxiliary relations were improved by introducing more examples – in addition to the examples produced by the learner in turn – they would still be incomplete due to the continuous nature of the domain. A more natural approach would be to use a machine learning algorithm designed specifically to deal with continuous attributes, such as *first order regression* [7].

The predictive power of the learner models was estimated assuming that all actions are equally important. This is clearly a simplification, because there are situations in which any action from the user will have little effect on the following states of the device, whereas there are other situations in which the opportune selection of a proper action by the user would have a decisive effect on what follows thereafter (at least in the short term). It could be the case that our learner models are worse at predicting critical actions than at predicting less relevant ones.

A way to overcome this limitation in our evaluation procedure is to compare the performance of the task by each learner and his model. This has been done for PACMOD using RIPPER [11] and the outcome was consistent with related research on behavioural cloning: similar or better performance of the models in a narrow range of situations but worse performance in general.

Probably a better approach would weigh actions according to their importance for controlling the device in the given situation. This approach requires either more knowledge about the dynamics of the pole and cart, or more data about different ways of controlling the device from which the relative importance of each action could be inferred (e.g. by measuring the amount of information provided by each action).

6 Conclusions

In this paper we have compared the learner models for the task of controlling a pole on a cart produced by using two different programs for machine learning, RIPPER and FOIL; the first, a program for supervised induction of production rules and the second, a program for inductive logic programming. Compared to the learner models produced by RIPPER, the propositional models generated by FOIL are too specific, whereas the first-order models also produced by FOIL are too general. The first result derives from the fact that FOIL does not provide a way of specifying the minimum number of cases each clause must cover; a limitation that makes FOIL very sensitive to noise in the data. The second result stems from the necessity to define the auxiliary relations applied by FOIL in an extensional form, even though the application domain is of a continuous nature.

Despite the limitations of FOIL, the first-order models it produced look simpler and easier to comprehend than the others – yet a proper evaluation of these properties needs to be carried out. Other tools for inductive logic programming, particularly those designed for continuous domains and those accepting extensional definitions of auxiliary relations, may produce better first-order models which could be equally simple and easy to understand.

References

1. Barto A.G., Sutton R.S., Anderson C.W.: Neuronlike adaptive elements that can solve difficult learning control problems. IEEE Transactions on Systems, Man and Cybernetics **SMC-13** (1983) 834–846
2. Bratko I., Urbančič T., Sammut C.: Behavioural cloning of control skill. In: Michalski R.S., Bratko I., Kubat M. (eds.), Machine Learning and Data Mining: Methods and Applications. John Wiley & Sons (1997) 335–351
3. Chiu B.C., Webb G.I., Kuzmycz M.: A comparison of first-order and zeroth-order induction for Input-Output Agent Modelling. In: Jameson A., Paris C., Tasso C. (eds.), User Modeling: Proceedings of the Sixth International Conference, UM97. Springer Wien New York (1997) 347–358

4. Cohen W.W.: Fast effective rule induction. In: Prieditis A., Russell S. (eds.), Machine Learning: Proceedings of the Twelfth International Conference. Morgan Kaufmann (1995) Available as a WWW document from `http://www.research.att.com/ wcohen/ripperd.html`
5. Eastwood E.: Control theory and the engineer. Proceedings of the Institution of Electrical Engineers **115** (1968) 203–211
6. Gordon D.F., Subramanian D.: Cognitive modeling of action selection learning. In: Cottrell G.W. (ed.), Proceedings of the Eighteenth Annual Conference of the Cognitive Science Society. Lawrence Erlbaum Associates (1996)
7. Karalic A., Bratko I.: First order regression. Machine Learning **26** (1997) 147–176
8. Michie D., Bain M., Hayes-Michie J.: Cognitive models from subcognitive skills. In: McGhee J., Grimble M.J., Mowforth P. (eds.), Knowledge-Based Systems for Industrial Control. Peter Peregrinus, London (1990) 71–99
9. Michie D., Chambers R.A.: BOXES: An experiment in adaptive control. In: Dale E., Michie D. (eds.), Machine Intelligence, vol. 2. Oliver and Boyd, Edinburgh (1968) 137–152
10. Morales R.: Exploring Participative Learner Modelling and Its Effects on Learner Behaviour. Ph.D. thesis, University of Edinburgh, Department of Artificial Intelligence (2000)
11. Morales R., Pain H.: Modelling of novices' control skills with machine learning. In: Kay J. (ed.), UM99 User Modeling: Proceedings of the Seventh International Conference. No. 407 in CISM Courses and Lectures, Springer Wien New York (1999) 159–168
12. Morales R., Pain H., Bull S., Kay J. (eds.): Proceedings of the Workshop on Open, Interactive, and Other Overt Approaches to Learner Modelling. AI-ED'99, Le Mans, France (1999).
13. Morales R., Pain H., Conlon T.: Understandable learner models for a sensorimotor control task. In: Gauthier G., Frasson C., VanLehn K. (eds.), Intelligent Tutoring Systems: Fifth International Conference, ITS'2000. No. 1839 in Lecture Notes in Computer Science, Springer Verlag (2000) 222–231
14. Moriarty D.E., Miikkulainen R.: Efficient reinforcement learning through symbiotic evolution. Machine Learning **22** (1996) 11–32
15. Quinlan J.R.: Learning logical definitions from relations. Machine Learning **5** (1990) 239–266
16. Quinlan J.R., Cameron-Jones M.: FOIL: A midterm report. In: Brazdil P.B. (ed.), Proceedings of the European Conference on Machine Learning. No. 667 in Lecture Notes in Computer Science, Springer Verlag (1993) 3–20
17. Self J.: The defining characteristics of intelligent tutoring systems research: ITSs care, precisely. International Journal of Artificial Intelligence in Education **10** (1999) 350–364
18. Self J.: Open sesame?: fifteen variations on the theme of openness in learning environments (aied'99 invited talk). AIED Resources **10** (1999) 1020–1029. WWW document at `http: //cbl.leeds.ac.uk/ijaied/abstracts/Vol_10/self.html`
19. Subramanian D.: Inducing hybrid models of task learning from visualmotor data. In: Gleitman L.R., Joshi A.K. (eds.), Proceedings of the Twenty Second Annual Conference of the Cognitive Science Society. Lawrence Erlbaum Associates (2000)

Simple Epistemic Logic for Relational Database

Guillermo Morales-Luna

Programa de Ingeniería Molecular, Instituto Mexicano del Petróleo,
on leave of absence from Computer Science Section, CINVESTAV-IPN,
Av. I. P. N. 2508, 07300 Mexico City, Mexico
gmorales@cs.cinvestav.mx

Abstract. We use a simple epistemic logic to pose problems related to relational database design. We use the notion of attribute dependencies, which is weaker than the notion of functional dependencies, to perform design tasks since it satisfies Armstrong axioms. We discuss also the application of the simple epistemic logic to privacy protection and to statistical disclosure.

Keywords: Epistemic logic, database design, privacy protection, statistical disclosure.

1 Introduction

Several methods have been introduced to analyze security protocols, regarding cryptographic, authentication and privacy aspects, and it is at present time an area of intense research [4]. The methods based on formal methods of logic have played an important role, for specification and for automatic verification of protocols. Here we extend an epistemic logic introduced in [3], originally thought to model privacy protection. This logic can be formulated in a wider scope to formalize deductive aspects of relational databases. Formulated in a very weak form as logics without equality, these logics can describe certain purely logical dependencies between attributes in relational schemes and their corresponding notions of database normal forms.

The organization of this paper is as follows: In section 2 we introduce the simple epistemic logic, its syntax and its semantics. For a given database we construct a proper simple epistemic logic and several interpretations of the logic by considering coverings on the universe of the given database. Each such covering gives a general knowledge and for each element in the universe an own individual knowledge. We will construct a cover refinement procedure that is monotone with respect to general knowledges. In this section we will refer also to subsets of attributes and we will distinguish key and non-key sets of attributes aiming to the notions of normal forms. In section 3 we will discuss three applications of the built logics: The first one is related to database design. The logical dependencies satisfy proper versions of Armstrong's axioms for functional dependencies. Thus, the common procedures of database normalization can be carried on within the framework of the epistemic logics. The second application is related to privacy

C.A. Coello Coello et al. (Eds.): MICAI 2002, LNAI 2313, pp. 234–241, 2002.

protection as was done in [3]. The last potential application is related to statistical disclosure in large databases. The resulting disclosure problems pose counting versions of decidability problems in the epistemic logics. Hence, in spite that they can be formalized within the study of such logics, they are intractable in most cases.

2 Basic Definitions

In the following two subsections we introduce the syntactic and semantic notions of an epistemic logic and we discuss the complexity of the most basic decidability procedures in this logic.

2.1 Simple Epistemic Logic

Let P_0 be a given finite set of so called *atoms*. The *Boolean formulae*, $P_1 = \mathcal{B}(P_0)$, over the set P_0, is defined recursively by the following two rules:

- $[\phi \in P_0 \;\Rightarrow\; \phi \in P_1]$, in other words, $P_0 \subset P_1$, and
- $[\phi_1, \phi_2 \in P_1 \;\Rightarrow\; \neg\phi_1, \phi_1 \vee \phi_2, \phi_1 \wedge \phi_2 \in P_1]$

Any Boolean formula of the form $\neg\phi_1 \vee \phi_2$ will be written equivalently in an implicational way: $\phi_1 \rightarrow \phi_2$. Let K stand for a modal operator, read as "it is known that". Let $P_2 = K\mathcal{B}(P_0)$ be the set of formulae defined by the following rule:

- $[\phi \in P_1 \;\Rightarrow\; K\phi \in P_2]$.

The *simple epistemic logic*, or *information descriptive logic*, with atoms in P_0 is

$$SEL(P_0) = P_1 \cup P_2 = (nil + K)\mathcal{B}(P_0).$$

In this simple logic, the modal operator acts at most once in any well formed formula.

2.2 SEL-Structures

In the Kripke's style of "possible worlds" semantics for modal logics, for a given logic $\mathcal{L} = SEL(P_0)$, let us consider structures of the form $M = (W, R, \nu)$ where

- W is a finite set of *worlds*,
- $R \subset W \times W$ is an equivalence relation between worlds. R is called the *accesibility* relation, and
- $\nu : W \times P_0 \rightarrow Three = \{0, \uparrow, 1\}$ is a truth assignment.

The truth value "$\uparrow$" corresponds to the value "unknown". For each world $w \in W$ let $\nu_w : P_0 \rightarrow Three$, $\phi \mapsto \nu_w(\phi) = \nu(w, \phi)$ be the section function of ν at w. M is said to be a *SEL-structure*.

Let $Two = \{0, 1\}$ be the set of classical Boolean truth values. For any (partial) assignment $\sigma \in Two^{P_0}$, we say that σ is *compatible* with ν in a world $w \in W$ if

$$\forall \phi \in P_0 : \quad \phi \in \mathrm{dom}(\sigma) \;\&\; \nu_w(\phi) \neq \uparrow \Rightarrow \sigma(\phi) = \nu_w(\phi), \tag{1}$$

in other words, σ is compatible with ν in w if σ extends the section function ν_w. In this case we will write $\sigma \succeq \nu_w$. Obviously, any assignment $\sigma \in Two^{P_0}$ extends naturally to an assignment $\sigma \in Two^{\mathcal{B}(P_0)}$:

$$\begin{aligned} \sigma(\neg\phi) = 1 &\Leftrightarrow \sigma(\phi) = 0 \\ \sigma(\phi_1 \vee \phi_2) = 0 &\Leftrightarrow \sigma(\phi_1) = 0 \;\&\; \sigma(\phi_2) = 0 \\ \sigma(\phi_1 \wedge \phi_2) = 1 &\Leftrightarrow \sigma(\phi_1) = 1 \;\&\; \sigma(\phi_2) = 1 \end{aligned} \tag{2}$$

In this case, the assignment $\sigma \in Two^{\mathcal{B}(P_0)}$ is the *Boolean propagation* of the atomic assignment $\sigma \in Two^{P_0}$. Conversely, an *assignment* $\sigma \in Three^{\mathcal{B}(P_0)}$ is said to be *B-consistent* (*B* stands for *Boolean*) if the following rules, "dual" to equations (2), hold:

- $[\sigma(\neg\phi) \neq \uparrow \Rightarrow \{\sigma(\phi), \sigma(\neg\phi)\} = Two]$
- $[\sigma(\phi_1 \vee \phi_2) \neq 0 \Rightarrow \sigma(\phi_1) \neq 0 \text{ or } \sigma(\phi_1) \neq 0]$
- $[\sigma(\phi_1 \wedge \phi_2) \neq 1 \Rightarrow \sigma(\phi_1) \neq 1 \text{ or } \sigma(\phi_1) \neq 1]$
- $[\sigma(\phi_1 \Box \phi_2) = \uparrow \Rightarrow \sigma(\phi_1) = \uparrow \text{ or } \sigma(\phi_2) = \uparrow]$ where $\Box \in \{\vee, \wedge\}$.

The Boolean propagation of any atomic assignment is, indeed, *B*-consistent. From now on, we will consider just *B*-consistent assignments $\sigma \in Three^{\mathcal{B}(P_0)}$. For any Boolean formula $\phi \in \mathcal{B}(P_0)$, it is written $\sigma \models \phi$ if $\sigma(\phi) = 1$.

Let $\mathcal{C} \subset Two^{P_0}$ be a collection of assignments and let $M = (W, R, \nu)$ be a *SEL*-structure. For any world $w \in W$ and any Boolean formula $\phi \in \mathcal{B}(P_0)$ let us define

- $w \models_{\mathcal{C}} \phi$ if $\forall \sigma \in \mathcal{C}\, [\sigma \succeq \nu_w \Rightarrow \sigma \models \phi]$.
- $w \models_{\mathcal{C}} K\phi$ if $\forall v \in W\, [vRw \Rightarrow v \models_{\mathcal{C}} \phi]$.

Then for any $\mathcal{C} \subset Two^{P_0}$ and $M = (W, R, \nu)$, the following relations hold strightforwardly:

1. For any assignment $\sigma \in Three^{\mathcal{B}(P_0)}$ and any Boolean formula $\phi \in \mathcal{B}(P_0)$ the relation $\sigma \models \phi$ can be decided in time $t_{B,P_0}(\phi)$, which is indeed proportional to $k_0 + k_\phi$ where k_0 is the number of atoms in P_0 and k_ϕ is the number of Boolean connectives appearing in ϕ.
2. For any world $w \in W$ and any Boolean formula $\phi \in \mathcal{B}(P_0)$ the relation $w \models_{\mathcal{C}} \phi$ can be decided in time $t_{W,P_0}(\phi)$ proportional to $k_{\mathcal{C}} \cdot t_{B,P_0}(\phi)$ where $k_{\mathcal{C}}$ is the number of assignments in $\mathcal{C}$.
3. If there is an atom ϕ_0 and two assignments $\sigma_1, \sigma_2 \in \mathcal{C}$ giving to the atom ϕ_0 distinct truth values, i. e. $\sigma_1(\phi_0) \neq \sigma_2(\phi_0)$, then for any world $w \in W$, if $\nu_w(\phi_0) \neq \uparrow$ just one of the predicates $\sigma_1 \succeq \nu_w$ and $\sigma_2 \succeq \nu_w$ may hold. Let $W_i = \{w \in W | \sigma_i \succeq \nu_w\}$, $i = 1, 2$. The collection $\{W_1, W_2\}$ is a partition of W. Let w be a world. By re-enumerating if necessary, let us suppose $w \in W_1$. Thus, if $w \models_{\mathcal{C}} \phi$, where $\phi \in \mathcal{B}(P_0)$, then the substitution $\phi(\phi_0 | \nu_w(\phi_0))$ will produce a simpler Boolean formula that does not contain the atom ϕ_0.

4. For any world $w \in W$ and any Boolean formula $\phi \in \mathcal{B}(P_0)$ the relation $w \models_C K\phi$ can be decided in time $t_{K,W,P_0}(\phi)$ proportional to $k_{R(w)} \cdot t_{W,P_0}(\phi)$ where $k_{R(w)}$ is the number of worlds equivalent to w according to R.

2.3 Relational Schemes

Let $V \neq \emptyset$ be an *universe*, let A be a set of *attributes* and, for each $a \in A$, let $V_a \neq \emptyset$ be a *valuation* set and let $\pi_a : V \to V_a$ be a *projection* function. In such a case, for each *individual* $v \in V$ and each subset of attributes $B \subset A$, the sequence $\Pi_B(v) = (\pi_b(v))_{b\in B}$ is the *B-register* of individual v. Usually the A-register of any individual shall determine v univocally, i.e. $\Pi_A : V \to \prod_{a\in A} V_a$ is a one-to-one function. If a subset of attributes $B \subset A$ is such that Π_B is one-to-one then B is called a *superkey* in A. The triplet $T = (V, A, \Pi_A)$ is a *relational table in the A-database* defined over the universe V with *relational scheme* A.

For any $B \subset A$, the *relational table* corresponding to B is the matrix $M_B = (\pi_b(v))_{b\in B}^{v\in V}$: M_B has as columns the B-registers of the individuals in the universe. M_B can be regarded as a *horizontal cut* of the whole table, or matrix, M_A. Similarly, if $U \subset V$ is a subset of individuals, the submatrix consisting of columns corresponding to individuals in B is a *vertical cut* of the whole table.

2.4 Surrounding Functions

Let $T = (V, A, \Pi_A)$ be an A-table. A *surrounding function* on the universe V is a function $f : V \to 2^V = \mathcal{P}(V)$ such that for all individual $v \in V$: $v \in f(v)$. Let $\mathcal{S}(V) = \{f \in \mathcal{P}(V)^V | \forall v \in V : v \in f(v)\}$ be the class of surrounding functions. Let us introduce the relation $\preceq_r$ in $\mathcal{S}(V)$:

$$f \preceq_r g \;\Leftrightarrow\; \forall v \in V : f(v) \subseteq g(v). \tag{3}$$

$\preceq_r$ is an ordering in $\mathcal{S}(V)$. The *coarse* function $C : v \mapsto V$ is the greatest element in $\mathcal{S}(V)$ and the *embedding* function $I : v \mapsto \{v\}$ is the smallest element. Indeed, with this ordering, $\mathcal{S}(V)$ is a lattice: for any $f, g \in \mathcal{S}(V)$ their *join* and *meet* elements are respectively

$$\begin{array}{l} f \vee_{\mathcal{S}(V)} g : v \mapsto f(v) \cup g(v) \\ f \wedge_{\mathcal{S}(V)} g : v \mapsto f(v) \cap g(v) \end{array} \tag{4}$$

Any surrounding function $f \in \mathcal{S}(V)$ is a *covering* of the universe V, namely $V = \bigcup_{v\in V} f(v)$. The function f is a *partition* if "its values are pairwise disjoint":

$$\forall v, w \in W[\; f(v) \neq f(w) \;\Rightarrow\; f(v) \cap f(w) = \emptyset \;].$$

Thus, if $f_1, f_2 \in \mathcal{S}(V)$ are partitions and $f_1 \preceq_r f_2$ then f_1 is a refinement of f_2.

Let $\mathcal{L} = SEL(P_0)$ be the logic whose set of atoms is

$$P_0 = \{(a, \alpha) | a \in A \;\&\; \alpha \in \mathcal{P}(V_a) - \{\emptyset\}\}.$$

Any atom (a,α) can be read as "the value of attribute a falls into set α". If there are m attributes, $m = \mathrm{card}(A)$, and for each $a_i \in A$ there are n_i elements in the valuation set V_{a_i}, then the number of atoms is $\mathrm{card}(P_0) = \sum_{i=1}^{m} (2^{n_i} - 1)$. Let $\mathcal{C}_0$ be the collection of (classical) assignments over the set of atoms that distinguish just one element in each valuation set and are also monotonic, i.e. $\forall \sigma \in Two^{P_0}$: $\sigma \in \mathcal{C}_0$ if and only if the following two conditions are satisfied:

$$\forall a \in A\, \exists v' \in V_a[\, \sigma(a,\{v'\}) = 1 \,\&\, \forall w' \in V_a - \{v'\} : \sigma(a,\{v'\}) = 0\,] \tag{5}$$
$$\forall a \in A,\ \alpha_1,\alpha_2 \in \mathcal{P}(V_a) - \{\emptyset\}[\, \alpha_1 \subset \alpha_2 \,\&\, \sigma(a,\alpha_1) = 1 \ \Rightarrow\ \sigma(a,\alpha_2) = 1\,]. \tag{6}$$

Let $\mathcal{C}$ be the Boolean subalgebra spanned by $\mathcal{C}_0$ in Two^{P_0}.

Any function $f \in \mathcal{S}(V)$ determines a *SEL*-structure $M_f = (V, R_f, \nu_f)$, namely

- $\forall v,w \in V[\, v\, R_f\, w \ \Leftrightarrow\ f(v) = f(w)\,]$.
- $\nu_f : (w,(a,\alpha)) \mapsto \nu_f(w,a,\alpha) = \begin{cases} 1 & \text{if } \forall v \in V[\, v \in f(w) \ \Rightarrow\ \pi_a(v) \in \alpha\,] \\ 0 & \text{if } \forall v \in V[\, v \in f(w) \ \Rightarrow\ \pi_a(v) \notin \alpha\,] \\ \uparrow & \text{otherwise.} \end{cases}$

In this structure, the *individual knowledge about* an object $v \in V$ is the set of formulae that are provably known for v: $IK_f(v) = \{\phi \in SEL(P_0) | v \models_{M_f,\mathcal{C}} K\phi\}$. Two individuals $u,v \in V$ are *indescernible* if "the same is known about each of them": $IK_f(u) = IK_f(v)$. The *general knowledge* is the set of formulae that provably hold for every individual: $GK_f = \{\phi \in SEL(P_0) | \forall v \in V : v \models_{M_f,\mathcal{C}} \phi\}$.

Let $f,g \in \mathcal{S}(V)$ be two surrounding functions defined on V. Let us say that *g is at least as informative as f* if $GK_f \subset GK_g$ and in this case let us write $f \preceq_i g$.

For two functions $f,g \in \mathcal{S}(V)$ such that $f \preceq_r g$ and for any two worlds $u,v \in V$ the following relations hold:

1. $uR_f v \Rightarrow f(u) \subset g(v)$.
2. $\nu_{g,v} \succeq \nu_{f,v}$. Indeed, let $(a,\alpha) \in P_0$ be an atom. Since $f(v) \subset g(v)$ we have $\nu_{f,v}(a,\alpha) = \nu_{g,v}(a,\alpha)$.
3. For any $\phi \in \mathcal{B}(P_0)$:
   (a) If $v \models_{M_f,\mathcal{C}} \phi$ then $v \models_{M_g,\mathcal{C}} \phi$. Indeed, suppose that σ is an assignment such that $\sigma \succeq \nu_{g,v}$. Then $\sigma \succeq \nu_{f,v}$ and therefore $\sigma \models \phi$.
   (b) If $v \models_{M_f,\mathcal{C}} K\phi$ then for each $u \in V$ with $uR_f v$: $v \models_{M_g,\mathcal{C}} \phi$.

Statement 3.(b) above is weaker than asserting that the individual knowledge is monotonic with respect to the surrounding functions. However, next proposition holds:

Proposition 1. *If f is a refinement of g then g is at least as informative as f. In symbols: $\forall f,g \in \mathcal{S}(V)[\, f \preceq_r g \Rightarrow f \preceq_i g\,]$.*

Proof. Let $\phi \in GK_f$. Then $\forall v \in V$: $v \models_{M_f,\mathcal{C}} \phi$. From relation 3.(a) above: $v \models_{M_g,\mathcal{C}} \phi$. Hence $\phi \in GK_g$.

Now, let $B \subset A$ be a set of attributes. Let $V_B = \prod_{b \in B} V_b$ be the Cartesian product of valuation sets corresponding to attributes in B. Naturally, there is a map $\omega_B : \mathcal{P}(V) \to \mathcal{P}(V_B)$:

$$\forall U \subset V : \; \mathbf{b} \in \omega_B(U) \;\Leftrightarrow\; \exists u \in U : \mathbf{b} = (\pi_b(u))_{b \in B} .$$

Let $\Phi_B : \mathcal{S}(V) \to \mathcal{S}(V_B)$ be defined as follows: $\forall f \in \mathcal{S}(V)\ \forall\, \mathbf{b}', \mathbf{b} \in V_B$

$$\mathbf{b}' \in \Phi_B(f)(\mathbf{b}) \;\Leftrightarrow\; \exists v', v \in V : v' \in f(v) \;\&\; \mathbf{b}' = \Pi_B(v') \;\&\; \mathbf{b} = \Pi_B(v).$$

Then for any partition $f \in \mathcal{S}(V)$ the following diagram commutes:

$$\begin{array}{ccc} V & \xrightarrow{f} & \mathcal{P}(V) \\ \Pi_B \downarrow & & \downarrow \omega_B \\ V_B & \xrightarrow{\Phi_B(f)} & \mathcal{P}(V_B) \end{array} \tag{7}$$

(if f is not a partition but just a cover then only one inclusion may hold: $\forall v \in V$ $\omega_B \circ f(v) \subset \Phi_B(f) \circ \Pi_B(v)$). As before, any $f_B \in \mathcal{S}(V_B)$ determines a *SEL*-structure $M_{f_B} = (V_B, R_{f_B}, \nu_{f_B})$:

– $\forall \mathbf{b}_1, \mathbf{b}_2 \in V_B[\, \mathbf{b}_1 \; R_{f_B} \; \mathbf{b}_2 \;\Leftrightarrow\; f_B(\mathbf{b}_1) = f_B(\mathbf{b}_2) \,]$.
– $\forall (\mathbf{b}, a, \alpha)$

$$\nu_{f_B}(\mathbf{b}, a, \alpha) = \begin{cases} 1 & \text{if } a \in B \;\&\; \forall \mathbf{b}_1 \in V_B[\, \mathbf{b}_1 \in f_B(\mathbf{b}) \;\Rightarrow\; \pi_a(\mathbf{b}_1) \in \alpha \,] \\ 0 & \text{if } a \in B \;\&\; \forall \mathbf{b}_1 \in V_B[\, \mathbf{b}_1 \in f_B(\mathbf{b}) \;\Rightarrow\; \pi_a(\mathbf{b}_1) \notin \alpha \,] \\ \uparrow & \text{otherwise.} \end{cases}$$

Similarly, the *individual knowledge about* a tuple $\mathbf{b} \in V_B$ is the set of formulae that are provably known for $\mathbf{b}$: $IK_{f_B}(\mathbf{b}) = \{\phi \in SEL(P_0) | \mathbf{b} \models_{M_{f_B}, C} K\phi\}$. The *general knowledge* is the set of formulae that provably hold for every individual: $GK_{f_B} = \{\phi \in SEL(P_0) | \forall \mathbf{b} \in V_B : \mathbf{b} \models_{M_{f_B}, C} \phi\}$.

Since $\Pi_A : V \to V_A$ is a one-to-one function, V can be realized as a subset of V_A and $\mathcal{S}(V)$ as a subset of $\mathcal{S}(V_A)$. Thus, any validity proof on a *SEL*-structure $M_f = (V, R_f, \nu_f)$ can be translated into a validity proof on $M_{f_A} = (V, R_{f_A}, \nu_{f_A})$, where $f_A = \Phi_A(f)$.

3 Applications

3.1 Database Design

In the design of databases [2,6,7], an important problem is the normalization of the database and this involves the stating and proving of relationships between the formalized entities of the database. The typical relationships are the so called *functional dependencies.*

Let $T = (V, A, \Pi_A)$ be an A-table and let $B, C \subset A$ be two sets of attributes. The *functional dependency* $B \to C$ *holds* in T if

$$\forall u, v \in V : \; \Pi_B(u) = \Pi_B(v) \;\Rightarrow\; \Pi_C(u) = \Pi_C(v).$$

As there is no necessarily an equality notion in the constructed epistemic logics, let us introduce a weaker notion of functional dependency based on logical subsumption. Let $B, C \subset A$ be two sets of attributes. For any surrounding functions $f_{B\cup C} \in \mathcal{S}(B \cup C)$ and $f_B \in \mathcal{S}(B)$ let us relate them: $f_{B\cup C}$ *Pr* f_B if $f_B \circ \Pi_B = f_{B\cup C}$. For each $f \in \mathcal{S}(B \cup C)$ let us define:

$$B \overset{f}{\leadsto} C \Leftrightarrow \forall f_B \in \mathcal{S}(B)\,[f\ Pr\ f_B \Rightarrow GK_{M_{B\cup C},f} = GK_{M_B,f_B}] \tag{8}$$

This relation fulfills special forms of the Armstrong's axioms:

$$\begin{aligned} B \subset C \Rightarrow \forall f:\ B \overset{f}{\leadsto} C \quad &: \text{reflexivity} \\ B \overset{f}{\leadsto} C \Rightarrow B_0 B \overset{i_{B_0}\oplus f}{\leadsto} B_0 C \quad &: \text{augmentation} \\ f\ Pr\ g\ \&\ B \overset{f}{\leadsto} C\ \&\ C \overset{g}{\leadsto} D \Rightarrow B \overset{f}{\leadsto} D \quad &: \text{transitivity} \end{aligned}$$

where $i_{B_0} : \mathbf{b} \mapsto \{\mathbf{b}\}$ is the embedding surrounding function in V_{B_0}.

In this way, all current notions of dependencies closure, for both functional dependencies and sets of attributes, as well as the typical normalization procedures can be translated verbatim. The introduced *SEL*-logic is a tool to identify the functional dependencies. These should not be given in advance, but shall be proven within the *SEL*-logic. Of course this problem shall be extremmely difficult. Indeed, just the problem to recognize functional dependencies is a rather complex problem (more specifically, the problem to decide whether an attribute is prime, i.e. whether it belongs to a superkey, is NP-complete).

3.2 Privacy Protection

In [3], Hsu and Liau introduce a *SEL*-logic to model privacy protection. Given an A-table $T = (V, A, \Pi_A)$ let $P_0 = \{(a, \alpha) | a \in A\ \&\ \alpha \in \mathcal{P}(V_a) - \{\emptyset\}\}$ be the set of atoms. For each individual $v \in V$ let $\mathit{Cfd}(v) \subset \mathcal{B}(P_0)$ be the set of *confidential* information related to individual v. *Cfd* is thus a map $V \to \mathcal{P}(\mathcal{B}(P_0))$.

Given a set of attributes $B \subset A$ and a surrounding function $f \in \mathcal{S}(V_B)$ let us say:

- f is *safe* for $v \in V$ if $IK_f(v) \cap \mathit{Cfd}(v) = \emptyset$, i.e. no confidential data of v can be known from the information provided by $\Pi_B(V)$.
- f is *safe*, in general, if it is safe for each individual $v \in V$.

Then, given the map *Cfd* and a set of attributes $B \subset A$, in order to maintain the most information available as well as the safety of the database, it is necessary to calculate the minimal elements in the lattice $\mathcal{S}(V_B)$ that are safe. Let

$$MSF_B = \{f \in \mathcal{S}(V_B) | f \text{ is safe } \ \&\, \forall g \in \mathcal{S}(V_B)\ (g \text{ safe } \&\ g \preceq f\ \Rightarrow\ g = f)\}\,.$$

Then the goal of any privacy administrator is to find an element in MSF_B for a given $B \subset A$. Indeed, in practice not all of A is involved, but just a subset $P \subset A$ of *public* attributes.

This problem differs in difficulty depending on whether the set B contains or not prime attributes.

Hall's theorem [5] on graph theory (stating that there is matching in a graph whenever the Hall's condition is fulfilled) can be used to test the safety of surrounding functions (see [3]). If there is an unsafe function, say f, then it can be enlarged by taking $f \vee_{\mathcal{S}(V_B)} g$ where g is a function of the form $v \mapsto \bigcup_{u \in U_a} \pi_a^{-1}(u)$ for sets U_a such that $\pi_a(v) \in U_a \subset V_a$ and appropriate attributes $a \in A$ (usually those realizing the unsafety of f).

3.3 Statistical Disclosure

Given a large database, the administrators may be interested in providing reliable statistical information, mostly in aggregate form, as sums, averages, momenta, regression coefficients estimates or cardinalities, whilst particular information of individuals should be mantained inaccesible for most users in the database [1]. Attackers to the database may try to infer confidential information about an individual data subject. Several approaches have been used in order to maximize legitimate data access while keeping the risk of disclosure below an acceptable level. For instance, under *Query Size Restriction* (QSR) control, a response is denied when the cardinality of the query set (or its complement) is less than or equal to a specified integer.

The treatment of statistical disclosure problems with *SEL*-logics pose counting versions of decidability problems. Up to the construction introduced here, such problems are not treated *inside* the logic themselves. The counting versions shall, in general, be more difficult than their decidability counterparts.

References

1. N. R. Adam, J.C. Wortmann, Security-Control Methods for Statistical Databases: A Comparative Study, *ACM Computing Surveys*, 21, 4, 515-556, 1989.
2. C. Date, R. Fagin, Simple conditions for guaranteeing higher normal forms in relational database, *ACM Trans. on Database System*, vol. 17, no. 3, Sept. 1992.
3. Tsan-sheng Hsu, Churn-Jung Liau. A logical model for privacy protection. *Lecture Notes in Computer Science*, 2200: 110–124, 2001.
4. C. Meadows, Open issues in formal methods for cryptographic protocol analysis, In *Proceedings of DISCEX 2000*, pages 237–250. *IEEE Comp. Society Press*, 2000.
5. O.Ore, R.J.Wilson, *Graphs and their uses*, MAA, New Math Library, 1990.
6. E. Ozkarahan, *Database management: Concepts, design and practice*, Prentice Hall, 1990.
7. J. D. Ullman, *Principles of database and knowledge-base systems*, Computer Science Press, 1988.

Solving Optimal Location of Traffic Counting Points at Urban Intersections in CLP(FD)

Ana Paula Tomás

DCC-FC & LIACC, Faculdade de Ciências, Universidade do Porto,
R. do Campo Alegre, 823, 4150-180 Porto, Portugal
apt@ncc.up.pt

Abstract. We present an application of Constraint Logic Programming (CLP) for finding the minimum number and location of count-posts at urban roundabouts so as to obtain origin-destination data at minimum cost. By finding nice mathematical properties, we were able to model this problem as a constraint satisfaction problem in finite domains, and use CLP(FD) systems to solve it, with almost no implementation effort and very quickly.

1 Motivation and Introduction

Traffic studies require origin-destination (OD) data whose acquisition is difficult and expensive. Important, but often insufficient data is collected by counting vehicles that pass at specific points of the traffic network, either manually or automatically. In the past two decades, there has been a considerable amount of research on the difficult problem of OD matrix estimation from (link) traffic counts. Two recent publications [3,13] address the optimization of the number and location of traffic count-posts for traffic networks. In [3], a model and heuristic based algorithms are given for solving the minimum-cost Sensor Location Problem (SLP). This problem is that of finding the minimum number and location of count-posts in order to obtain the complete set of traffic flows on a transport network at minimum cost. Traffic studies for urban intersections are far less complex but still of prime importance in traffic engineering. In order to obtain OD data, it is typically necessary to carry out OD surveys, such as by manually recording registration numbers or making roadside video surveys. In this work, we present results from our research on the problem of finding the minimal number of exits and entries where OD surveys must be made, when some user-defined subset of traffic counts can be obtained at a relatively negligible cost (e.g., by direct observation in site). This can be viewed as a variant of the minimum-cost SLP. The model we propose is that of a constraint satisfaction problem in finite domains (CSP). No prior knowledge of turning movement coefficients is assumed or used in our work, which makes the problem clearly distinct from that in [3], so that we needed another approach.

This paper appears as a complement to previous work [14,15], which involved an exhaustive case analysis of all hypothetical roundabouts with n legs

C.A. Coello Coello et al. (Eds.): MICAI 2002, LNAI 2313, pp. 242–251, 2002.

(i.e., where n roads/streets meet), for increasing values of n, in computer. In it all strings $R_1R_2 \ldots R_n \in \{\mathrm{E}, \mathrm{D}, \mathrm{S}\}^\star$ were seen as possible roundabouts, with $R_i \in \{\mathrm{E}, \mathrm{D}, \mathrm{S}\}$ indicating whether road i is just an entry (E), just an exit (S) or both an entry and exit (D) road. In this way, we did not care whether some of these strings would ever represent real-world roundabouts. Both E and S refer to one-way streets, whereas D means double-way. Computer programs were developed (in C) to enumerate minimal subsets of OD flows that, when counted and used together with total counts at entries, exits and cross-sections, allow to deduce the complete OD matrix (q_{ij}) for a given time period. The focus was on the search for patterns for optimal cost solutions, that could eventually be used as practical rules by traffic engineers. To the best of our knowledge, no such a systematic study had been reported before. A major conclusion of [14] is that if a cost $c(q_{ij})$ is assigned to measuring q_{ij}, for each q_{ij}, the overall cost is minimized if the OD flows that should not be measured are selected in non-decreasing order of cost to form an independent set. In fact, in this case the problem is an instance of that of computing a maximum weight independent subset in a linear matroid which may always be solved by a Greedy Algorithm (see e.g. [4]). Therefore, it is solvable by a polynomial algorithm. Actually, that independence is the linear independence of the columns of the constraints matrix that are associated to the selected OD flows. It can be checked in polynomial time, for instance, by Gaussian elimination. Another important contribution of [14] was the development of a rather simple method to test for linear independence, for this specific problem, which involves only exact operations. By further exploiting its mathematical properties, in [15] it is shown the existence of an exact characterization of the optimal cost for the SLP when the OD flows $q_{i\,i+1}$'s are the ones of reduced measuring cost.

New Contributions. The work we now present is motivated by the claim [1] that the cost criteria should be more flexible to encompass specific features of the particular roundabout in study. By contrast to [14], the idea is no longer that of looking for patterns of optimal solutions but rather to solve the minimum-cost SLP for any given real-world roundabout, the relevant data being input by the end-user of the application. The problem structure is further exploited, putting some effort on the formulation of a fairly clean mathematical model of the problem so that, in the end, CLP(FD) systems could be used to solve it. For space reasons, we shall not include experimental results, but just say that problems are solved in fractions of a second. The use of Constraint Programming (CP) not only has led to a drastic reduction in the implementation effort but allows to easily extend the model to cater for other constraints that may be useful in practice. Although this work seems at first sight too focused, its methodology is of wider interest. The proposed solution for encoding the non-trivial constraint (4) (see section 3) represents a compromise between generate-and-test and constrain-and-generate techniques. It is an example of the tradeoff between efficiency and declarativeness. Significant pruning is achieved by extracting global, though incomplete, information. Furthermore, our approach clearly shows the advantage of exploiting affinities to well-known problems when facing a new one.

In the following section, we give a formal description of the problem and some of its mathematical properties. Then, in section 3, the CSP model and aspects of its implementation in CLP(FD) systems are discussed.

2 The Problem and Some Background

If we number the n meeting roads in the way traffic circulates, the roundabout is perfectly identified by a string $R_1R_2 \ldots R_n \in \{\mathrm{E}, \mathrm{D}, \mathrm{S}\}^\star$, as defined before. Let $\mathcal{O} = \{\imath_1, \ldots, \imath_e\}$ and $\mathcal{D} = \{\jmath_1, \ldots, \jmath_s\}$ be the ordered sets of origins and destinations, and $e = |\mathcal{O}|$ and $s = |\mathcal{D}|$ be their cardinalities. The traffic flow from the entry i to the exit j is denoted by q_{ij}, for $i \in \mathcal{O}$ and $j \in \mathcal{D}$. These flows are related to the total volumes at entries, exits and passing through the cross-sections of the circulatory roadway in frontal alignment with the meeting roads (respectively, O_i's, D_j's and F_k's) by (1)–(3).

$$\sum_{j \in \mathcal{D}} q_{ij} = O_i, \text{ for } i \in \mathcal{O} \tag{1}$$

$$\sum_{i \in \mathcal{O}} q_{ij} = D_j, \text{ for } j \in \mathcal{D} \tag{2}$$

$$\sum_{i \in \mathcal{O} \setminus \{k\}} \quad \sum_{j \in \mathcal{D},\, k \prec j \preceq i} q_{ij} = F_k, \text{ for } 1 \leq k \leq n \tag{3}$$

In (3), $j \in \mathcal{D}$, $k \prec j \preceq i$ stands for the exits between road k and road i, with k excluded. Vehicles are assumed to exit the roundabout and, in addition, loops are disallowed (i.e., vehicles do not pass their destination). Other cross-sections could be considered, as those that stand strictly between two consecutive roads, but the indeterminacy of (1)–(3) would not be reduced. For instance, the traffic volume I_k that passes between roads k and $k+1$ equals $F_k + O_k$. We also assume that counting O_i's, D_j's, F_k's and I_k's is of negligible cost when compared to other measuring tasks. So, a maximal independent set of such counts should be used, but it does not matter which one. At most $e + s$ total counts are globally non-redundant [14]. In fact, the matrix of the system (1)–(3), in the variables q_{ij}'s, has rank $e + s$ if and only if none of equations in (3) is of the form $F_k = 0$. Otherwise, the rank is $e + s - 1$, and the roundabout is identifiable by a string $R_1R_2 \ldots R_n$ of the language described by the regular expression $\mathrm{S}^\star(\mathrm{D}+\mathrm{SE})\mathrm{E}^\star$. We consider that traffic counts are error-free, an usually accepted condition [3,13]. Thus, if some flows in (1)–(3) are replaced by traffic counts, the resulting system is consistent. Then, by standard results of systems of linear equations (e.g. [11]), it is equivalent to any of its subsystems that consist of equations (1)–(2) and one of (3), say that of F_k, to which our analysis shall be confined.

Notation. Let $\mathbf{P}'$ be the matrix of such subsystem, and $\mathbf{p}'_{ij}$ be the column of q_{ij}. Let $\mathbf{P}$ be the matrix of (1)–(2) and $\mathbf{p}_{ij}$ be the column of q_{ij}. Clearly, $\mathbf{p}'_{ij}$

has just one more element than $\mathbf{p}_{ij}$, namely the coefficient, say σ_{ij}, of q_{ij} in the equation that defines F_k. In the sequel, we always refer to the case $k = 1$.

Provided that $es - rank(\mathbf{P}')$ of the q_{ij}'s are known (i.e., counted), the subsystem has a unique solution for the remaining $rank(\mathbf{P}')$ variables if and only if the related columns of $\mathbf{P}'$ are linearly independent. Let us take for example the roundabout SSEDE, where $\mathcal{O} = \{3,4,5\}$, $\mathcal{D} = \{1,2,4\}$. In this case, (1)–(3) may be written in solved form, for instance, as follows.

$$\begin{cases} q_{31}+q_{32}+q_{34}=O_3 \\ q_{41}+q_{42}+q_{44}=O_4 \\ q_{51}+q_{52}+q_{54}=O_5 \\ q_{31}+q_{41}+q_{51}=D_1 \\ q_{32}+q_{42}+q_{52}=D_2 \\ q_{34}+q_{44}+q_{54}=D_4 \\ q_{32}+q_{42}+q_{44}+q_{52}+q_{54}=F_1 \end{cases} \Leftrightarrow \begin{cases} q_{31} = q_{42} + q_{52} + F_1 - O_4 + D_1 - D_2 \\ q_{32} = -q_{42} - q_{52} + D_2 \\ q_{34} = O_5 - F_1 + O_4 - D_1 + O_3 \\ q_{41} = -q_{42} - q_{51} - q_{52} + D_2 + O_5 - F_1 + O_4 \\ q_{44} = q_{51} + q_{52} + F_1 - D_2 - O_5 \\ q_{54} = -q_{51} - q_{52} + O_5 \end{cases}$$

If the values of q_{42}, q_{52} and q_{51} are known (as well as O_3, O_4, O_5, D_1, D_2 and F_1) then the system has a unique solution for the remaining q_{ij}'s. The set $\mathcal{B}' = \{\mathbf{p}'_{31}, \mathbf{p}'_{32}, \mathbf{p}'_{34}, \mathbf{p}'_{41}, \mathbf{p}'_{44}, \mathbf{p}'_{54}\}$ is a basis (i.e., maximal independent set) of the linear subspace spanned by the columns of $\mathbf{P}'$. It is interesting to note that $\mathbf{p}'_{42} = \mathbf{p}'_{41} - \mathbf{p}'_{31} + \mathbf{p}'_{32}$, $\mathbf{p}'_{51} = \mathbf{p}'_{54} - \mathbf{p}'_{44} + \mathbf{p}'_{51}$ and $\mathbf{p}'_{52} = \mathbf{p}'_{54} - \mathbf{p}'_{44} + \mathbf{p}'_{41} - \mathbf{p}'_{31} + \mathbf{p}'_{32}$.

Our Problem. To find a basis $\mathcal{B}'$ formed of $rank(\mathbf{P}')$ independent columns of $\mathbf{P}'$, such that to measure the OD flows q_{ij}'s for the $\mathbf{p}'_{ij}$'s not in $\mathcal{B}'$, surveys are undertaken at a minimum number of exits and entries. Without further assumptions, it is not difficult to show that the optimal cost would be, in general, $(|\mathcal{O}| - 1) + (|\mathcal{D}| - 1)$, which means that the registration should take place at all the entries but one and at all the exits but one. We want to study whether this cost may be reduced by having some of the q_{ij}'s counted by other means, which are supposed to be less expensive, whatever that may mean.

Praça da República at Porto is a roundabout of type SEESDSE, for which a realistic scenario is as shown below, on the left, as claimed in [1].

$\mathcal{O}\backslash\mathcal{D}$	1	4	5	6
2		$\star$	$\star$	
3		$\star$	$\star$	
5				
7	$\star$			

	1	4	5	6
2	•	$\star$	$\star$	•
3	•	$\star$	?	
5	•	•		
7	$\star$	•	•	•

The OD flows that are cheap to obtain are marked with $\star$'s in the table on the left. In this particular case, by cheap we mean that they can be fully obtained by direct observation in site. An observer, standing at entry 2, can count q_{24} and q_{25}. The same applies to the pair q_{34} and q_{35}, and to q_{71}. By contrast, for instance, the geometry of the roundabout makes it too difficult to obtain q_{56} by direct observation, although roads 5 and 6 are consecutive. The solution on the right is one of the eight optimal solutions found by our prototype implementations of the following model in SICStus Prolog [12,2] and ECLiPSe [5]. It minimizes the number of locations where recording is done: at two entries (3 and 5) and two exits (5 and 6). The flows q_{ij}'s that would not be counted are marked with •'s, implying that these $\mathbf{p}'_{ij}$'s belong to $\mathcal{B}'$. The ones that should be obtained by direct observation are marked with $\star$'s. The symbol ? indicates that there are two alternatives to get q_{35}, either by recording or by direct observation.

3 Modeling the Minimum-Cost SLP as a CSP

Given the string $R_1R_2\ldots R_n$ that identifies the roundabout, let $\mathcal{O} = \{\imath_1, \ldots, \imath_e\}$ and $\mathcal{D} = \{\jmath_1, \ldots, \jmath_s\}$, as above. Suppose that Γ is the set of OD flows that may be obtained by some means that the user, possibly an engineer, finds preferable to recording, say $\Gamma = \{(i,j) \mid q_{\imath_i\jmath_j}$ may be collected by direct observation$\}$. Let $\Theta = \{i \mid (i,j) \in \Gamma$ for some $j\}$ define the table rows that have $\star$'s. In the sequel, *sensor* refers to recording means (e.g., somebody that is registering number-plates or a video that is recording image).

The Decision Variables:

$E_i \in \{0,1\}$ is 1 iff a sensor is located at entry $\imath_i$, with $1 \leq i \leq e$.
$S_j \in \{0,1\}$ is 1 iff a sensor is located at exit $\jmath_j$, with $1 \leq j \leq s$.
$V_i \in \{0,1\}$ is 1 iff an observer stands at entry $\imath_i$, with $i \in \Theta$.
$P_{ij} \in \{0,1\}$ is 1 iff $\mathbf{p}'_{\imath_i\jmath_j}$ would be in $\mathcal{B}'$, with $1 \leq i \leq e$, $1 \leq j \leq s$.
$X_{ij} \in \{0,1,-1\}$ if $(i,j) \in \Gamma$. Otherwise, $X_{ij} \in \{0,1\}$, for all i, j.

$$X_{ij} = \begin{cases} 1 \text{ iff } q_{\imath_i\jmath_j} \text{ is collected by a sensor} \\ -1 \text{ iff } (i,j) \in \Gamma \text{ and } q_{\imath_i\jmath_j} \text{ is directly collected at entry } i \\ 0 \text{ iff } q_{\imath_i\jmath_j} \text{ is not collected} \end{cases}$$

The model we propose is biased to allow effective propagation of values and constraints, when applying consistency techniques. This is one of the reasons why we have chosen $\{0,1,-1\}$ as domain of X_{ij} when $(i,j) \in \Gamma$.

The objective: To minimize $\sum_{i=1}^{e} e_i E_i + \sum_{j=1}^{s} s_j S_j + \sum_{i\in\Theta} o_i V_i$, where e_i, s_j, and o_i denote the defined costs for sensors and observers, the latter being assumed relatively insignificant.

The constraints: For all $1 \leq i \leq e$ and $1 \leq j \leq s$,

- To record the flow $q_{\imath_i\jmath_j}$, sensors must be located at entry $\imath_i$ and exit $\jmath_j$, that is $E_i + S_j \geq 2X_{ij}$. Notice that, if $E_i + S_j \in \{0,1\}$ then $X_{ij} \in \{0,-1\}$.
- To obtain $q_{\imath_i\jmath_j}$ by direct observation, there must be an observer at entry $\imath_i$, that is $V_i \geq -X_{ij}$.
- If $q_{\imath_i\jmath_j}$ is not explicitly collected then $\mathbf{p}'_{\imath_i\jmath_j} \in \mathcal{B}'$. Thus, $X_{ij} = 0 \Leftrightarrow P_{ij} = 1$ or equivalently, $X_{ij} + P_{ij} = 1$, for all $(i,j) \notin \Gamma$ and $X_{ij}P_{ij} = 0 \wedge X_{ij} + P_{ij} \neq 0$ for all $(i,j) \in \Gamma$.
- The set $\mathcal{B}' = \{\mathbf{p}'_{\imath_i\jmath_j} \mid P_{ij} = 1\}$ must be a basis to $\mathbf{P}'$. Equivalently, $\mathcal{B}'$ has cardinality $rank(\mathbf{P}')$, so $\sum_{i=1}^{e}\sum_{j=1}^{s} P_{ij} = rank(\mathbf{P}')$, and $\mathcal{B}'$ is a free set (i.e.

its elements are linearly independent), which is translated by (4), where the variables $\beta_{ij} \in \mathbb{R}$.

$$\sum_{\mathbf{p}'_{\imath_i \jmath_j} \in \mathcal{B}'} \beta_{ij} \mathbf{p}'_{\imath_i \jmath_j} = \mathbf{0} \Rightarrow \beta_{ij} = 0, \text{ for all } \beta_{ij} \tag{4}$$

– Although redundant, these are useful constraints during the search. An observer is placed at entry $\imath_i$ only if it has to count some $q_{\imath_i \jmath_j}$, with $(i,j) \in \Gamma$.

$$V_i = 1 \Rightarrow \exists_{(i,j) \in \Gamma} \; X_{ij} = -1 \tag{5}$$

A sensor is located at entry $\imath_i$ only if some OD flow $q_{\imath_i \jmath_j}$, with $(i,j) \notin \Gamma$, has to be counted. The same holds for sensors at exits.

$$\sum_{j=1,(i,j)\notin \Gamma}^{s} X_{ij} \geq E_i \quad \text{and} \quad \sum_{i=1,(i,j)\notin \Gamma}^{e} X_{ij} \geq S_j$$

Anyone with basic background on CLP(FD) may see that, with the exception of (4) and (5), these constraints can be straightforwardly encoded in CLP(FD). But, (5) may be implemented by *cardinality* operators — in SICStus Prolog, as `count(-1,XiStr,#>=,Vi)`, where `XiStr` is the list of X_{ij} with $(i,j) \in \Gamma$ — and, in ECLiPSe, as `#(Vi,CtrXi,NSti)`, where `CtrXi` is a list of constraints $X_{ij} = -1$ and `NSti` its length, for $(i,j) \in \Gamma$. Encoding (4) is certainly more tricky and challenging. Firstly, (4) renders the model of MIP (mixed integer programming) type rather than a CSP, so that we would have to combine two different constraint solvers. Secondly, $\mathcal{B}'$ is in fact a variable, which means that a constraint as the builtin `element/3` would be of use to link the variables. Furthermore, (4) is too sophisticated to be too often touched during optimization, unless we keep some track of no-goods. Because of that, in [14], we have not used CP. Rather we computed $\mathcal{B}'$ by a completion procedure that implemented depth-first search with chronological backtracking. Gaussian elimination was used to test for freeness in an incremental way, which also allowed to implement intelligent backtracking. Conflicts due to choices made near the root of the search tree were detected during search. When some $\mathbf{p}'_{ij}$ was found dependent on a subset of the columns already in $\mathcal{B}'$, such information was propagated upwards along the search tree. A careful analysis of the program output gave us a deeper insight on the problem structure. An important result of [14] is that in (4), $\beta_{ij} \in \mathbb{R}$ may be replaced by $\beta_{ij} \in \{0, 1, -1\}$, meaning that the problem is actually a CSP in finite domains. Since (1)–(2) are the constraints of a Linear Transportation Problem, $\mathbf{P}$ has well-known nice properties (e.g., [8,9]). From them, it follows that if a given $\mathbf{p}'_{ij} \notin \mathcal{B}'$ is a combination of the elements in a free subset $\mathcal{B}'$ of $\mathbf{P}'$, the unique linear combination giving $\mathbf{p}'_{ij}$ may be written as (6). Note that $\mathbf{p}'_{ij} = \mathbf{e}_i + \mathbf{e}_{e+j} + \sigma_{ij}\mathbf{e}_{e+s+1}$, for the unit vectors $\mathbf{e}_1, \ldots, \mathbf{e}_{e+s+1}$ of $\mathbb{R}^{e+s+1}$.

$$\mathbf{p}'_{ij} = \mathbf{p}'_{ij_1} - \mathbf{p}'_{i_1 j_1} + \mathbf{p}'_{i_1 j_2} - \cdots - \mathbf{p}'_{i_k j_k} + \mathbf{p}'_{i_k j} \tag{6}$$

In fact, the combination must mimic the one that defines $\mathbf{p}_{ij}$ in terms of the corresponding columns of $\mathbf{P}$. In SSEDE, $\mathbf{p}'_{52} = \mathbf{p}'_{54} - \mathbf{p}'_{44} + \mathbf{p}'_{41} - \mathbf{p}'_{31} + \mathbf{p}'_{32}$, because $\mathbf{p}_{52} = \mathbf{p}_{54} - \mathbf{p}_{44} + \mathbf{p}_{41} - \mathbf{p}_{31} + \mathbf{p}_{32}$ and $\sigma_{52} = \sigma_{54} - \sigma_{44} + \sigma_{41} - \sigma_{31} + \sigma_{32}$.

Given $\mathcal{B}'$, let $\mathcal{B} = \{\mathbf{p}_{ij} \mid \mathbf{p}'_{ij} \in \mathcal{B}'\}$. If $\mathcal{B}$ is not free, then $\mathcal{B}'$ is free if and only if there exists $\mathbf{p}_{ij} \in \mathcal{B}$ such that $\mathcal{B} \setminus \{\mathbf{p}_{ij}\}$ is free and the equality that gives $\mathbf{p}_{ij}$ as a combination of the columns in $\mathcal{B} \setminus \{\mathbf{p}_{ij}\}$ does not hold for the corresponding ones in $\mathcal{B}'$, because $\sigma_{ij} \neq \sigma_{ij_1} - \sigma_{i_1 j_1} + \sigma_{i_1 j_2} - \cdots - \sigma_{i_k j_k} + \sigma_{i_k j}$, as shown in [14].

Now, (6) has an interesting graphic interpretation. If we represent the elements of $\mathbf{P}$ in a table and link the ones that occur consecutively in (6) by edges, a simple cycle is defined, as we exemplify below.

	1	2	4
3	$\mathbf{p}_{31}$	$\mathbf{p}_{32}$	$\mathbf{p}_{34}$
4	$\mathbf{p}_{41}$	$\mathbf{p}_{42}$	$\mathbf{p}_{44}$
5	$\mathbf{p}_{51}$	$\mathbf{p}_{52}$	$\mathbf{p}_{54}$

σ_{ij}	1	2	4
3	**0** −	**1**	0
4	**0** −	+ −	**1**
5	0	**1** −	**1**

	1	4	5	6
2	$\mathbf{p}_{21}$	$\mathbf{p}_{24}$	$\mathbf{p}_{25}$	$\mathbf{p}_{26}$
3	$\mathbf{p}_{31}$	$\mathbf{p}_{34}$	$\mathbf{p}_{35}$	$\mathbf{p}_{36}$
5	$\mathbf{p}_{51}$	$\mathbf{p}_{54}$	$\mathbf{p}_{55}$	$\mathbf{p}_{56}$
7	$\mathbf{p}_{71}$	$\mathbf{p}_{74}$	$\mathbf{p}_{75}$	$\mathbf{p}_{76}$

σ_{ij}	1	4	5	6
2	**0** −	**0**	0	0
3	**0** −	**0**	0	0
5	0	1	**1** −	**0**
7	0	1	**1** −	**1**

These cycles show that $\mathbf{p}'_{52} = \mathbf{p}'_{54} - \mathbf{p}'_{44} + \mathbf{p}'_{41} - \mathbf{p}'_{31} + \mathbf{p}'_{32}$ in SSEDE, and exemplify a problematic square $\mathbf{p}'_{21} = \mathbf{p}'_{24} - \mathbf{p}'_{34} + \mathbf{p}'_{31}$ and an unproblematic square $\mathbf{p}'_{55} \neq \mathbf{p}'_{56} - \mathbf{p}'_{76} + \mathbf{p}'_{75}$ in SEESDSE. By our hypothesis that no vehicle passes its destination and the definition of F_1, it follows that the coefficient σ_{ij} (wrt F_1) is given by $\sigma_{ij} = 0$ if and only if $j = 1$ or $j > i$.

A subset $\mathcal{B}$ of the columns of $\mathbf{P}$ is free if and only if the graph $G_{\mathcal{B}}$ built in the following way is acyclic. Its vertices are the elements of $\mathcal{B}$, and each edge links a vertex in a given row (respectively, column) to the closest vertex in the same row (respectively, column), if there are at least two vertices in that line.

A subset $\mathcal{B}$ is a basis of the subspace spanned by the columns of $\mathbf{P}$ if and only if $G_{\mathcal{B}}$ is a tree and contains at least a vertex in each column and in each row of the table (e.g., [8,9]). This result supports our definition of `basis/5`, below.

In order to profit from consistency-based approaches to solving CSPs [10], we would like to replace (4) by other constraints that, although being incomplete, may be used to prune the search space in a more active and effective way. Moreover, we did not really want to spend much time tuning the implementation, but rather take advantage of CP as "one of the closest approaches computer science has yet made to the Holy Grail of programming: the user states the problem, the computer solves it" [7]. Three necessary conditions on $\mathcal{B}'$ are deduced from the properties that $G_{\mathcal{B}}$ must satisfy: $\sum_{j=1}^{s} P_{ij} \geq 1$ for all i, $\sum_{i=1}^{e} P_{ij} \geq 1$ for all j, and what we call *the Square-Free Property* (SQF, for short), which aims at getting rid of cycles that have a square shape. SQF states that,

$$\text{if } \sigma_{ij} - \sigma_{ij'} + \sigma_{i'j'} - \sigma_{i'j} = 0 \text{ then } P_{ij} + P_{ij'} + P_{i'j'} + P_{i'j} < 4 \tag{7}$$

and if in addition, none of these four positions (in a square) contains a $\star$ (i.e., if $\{(i,j),(i,j'),(i',j'),(i',j)\} \cap \Gamma = \emptyset$), then $E_i + E_{i'} \geq 1$ and $S_j + S_{j'} \geq 1$. Though the latter are binary constraints and arc-consistency techniques may be employed, we can achieve at least the same pruning while possibly defining fewer and more global constraints. Let us refer back to SEESDSE. Suppose there are no $\star$'s and that the entries with $\bullet$'s are of $\mathbf{p}'_{ij}$'s in $\mathcal{B}'$. Then, in both the following examples, $\mathcal{B}'$ would not be a basis since the graph $G_{\mathcal{B}}$ has problematic cycles.

	1	4	5	6
2	0	0	0	0
3	0	0	0	0
5	0	1	1	0
7	0	1	1	1

Two global constraints, $S_1 + S_2 + S_3 + S_4 \geq 3$ and $E_1 + E_2 + E_3 + E_4 \geq 3$, are deduced from these chains, and thus the optimal cost is $6 = (e-1)+(s-1)$. SQF may be insufficient to ensure that the computed set is a basis. It fails to prune cycles as the one shown below on the right, for SSEDE with $\Gamma = \{(1,3),(3,1)\}$.

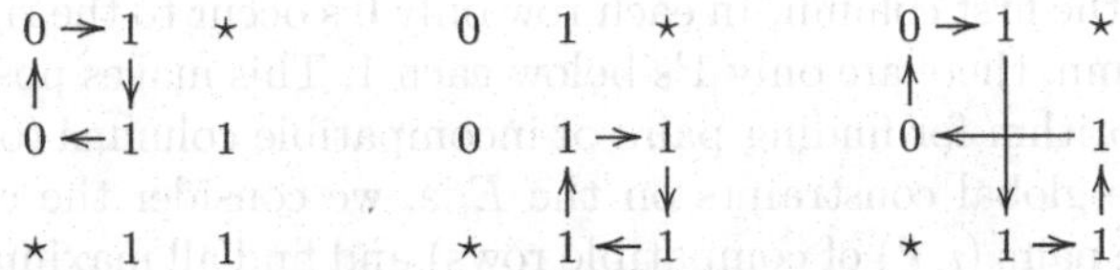

However, by enforcing the constraints given by SQF, relevant propagation and pruning is often achieved. So, we decided to firstly label P, guarded by such incomplete constraints, and then to check that P defines a basis. In SICStus, we do `minimize(solution(Vars,P,Rank,Ne,Ns,Sigmas),Cost)` with `solution/6` defined as follows, where `Vars` is the list of all the decision variables except the X_{ij}'s (so, we had previously a `?` in the solution), with the P_{ij}'s in its tail.

```
solution(Vars,P,Rank,Ne,Ns,Sigmas) :-
   labeling([],Vars),
   basis(P,Rank,Ne,Ns,Sigmas).
```

In real-life, we cannot usually expect an observer to be able to count more than three OD flows even if their destinations are in sight. An extensive simulation for randomly generated roundabouts, with $4 \leq n \leq 10$ and less than four $\star$'s per row, has shown that no-good solutions (i.e., for which `basis/5` fails) were found just in less than 5% of the cases.

When SQF is applied to two given rows i and i', it splits the columns that do not have $\star$'s in rows i and i', in two sets, say $\mathcal{A}_{(i,i')}$ and $\mathcal{B}_{(i,i')}$, according to whether or not they would be incompatible with the first one if the table had no $\star$'s (j and j' are *incompatible* if and only if $S_j + S_{j'} \geq 1$ must hold). All the columns in the same set are pairwise and globally incompatible.

	$E_1 + E_2 \geq 1$	$S_1 + S_2 + S_3 + S_4 \geq 3$	$\mathcal{A}_{(1,2)} = \{1,2,3,4\}, \mathcal{B}_{(1,2)} = \emptyset$
0 0 0 0	$E_1 + E_3 \geq 1$	$S_1 + S_4 \geq 1,\ S_2 + S_3 \geq 1$	$\mathcal{A}_{(1,3)} = \{1,4\}, \mathcal{B}_{(1,3)} = \{2,3\}$
0 0 0 0	$E_1 + E_4 \geq 1$	$S_2 + S_3 + S_4 \geq 2$	$\mathcal{A}_{(1,4)} = \{1\}, \mathcal{B}_{(1,4)} = \{2,3,4\}$
0 1 1 0	$E_2 + E_3 \geq 1$	$S_1 + S_4 \geq 1,\ S_2 + S_3 \geq 1$	$\mathcal{A}_{(2,3)} = \{1,4\}, \mathcal{B}_{(2,3)} = \{2,3\}$
0 1 1 1	$E_2 + E_4 \geq 1$	$S_2 + S_3 + S_4 \geq 2$	$\mathcal{A}_{(2,4)} = \{1\}, \mathcal{B}_{(2,4)} = \{2,3,4\}$
	$E_3 + E_4 \geq 1$	$S_1 + S_2 + S_3 \geq 2$	$\mathcal{A}_{(3,4)} = \{1,2,3\}, \mathcal{B}_{(3,4)} = \{4\}$

The constraints $E_i + E_{i'} \geq 1$, for all i and i', would be replaced by a single global constraint $E_1 + E_2 + E_3 + E_4 \geq 3$, which the program obtains by computing the *maximal independent sets in a graph*, as we explain below. And, similarly, for $S_1 + S_2 + S_3 + S_4 \geq 3$. As for Praça da República, SQF yields the following,

$$
\begin{array}{c|cccc}
 & & & & \\
\hline
 & 0 & \star & \star & 0 \\
 & 0 & \star & \star & 0 \\
 & 0 & 1 & 1 & 0 \\
 & \star & 1 & 1 & 1
\end{array}
\qquad
\begin{array}{ll}
E_1 + E_2 \geq 1 & S_1 + S_4 \geq 1 \\
E_1 + E_3 \geq 1 & S_1 + S_4 \geq 1 \\
 & \\
E_2 + E_3 \geq 1 & S_1 + S_4 \geq 1 \\
 & \\
E_3 + E_4 \geq 1 & S_2 + S_3 \geq 1
\end{array}
\quad\Bigg|\quad
\begin{array}{l}
\mathcal{A}_{(1,2)} = \{1, 4\},\ \mathcal{B}^{(1,2)} = \emptyset \\
\mathcal{A}_{(1,3)} = \{1, 4\},\ \mathcal{B}_{(1,3)} = \emptyset \\
\mathcal{A}_{(1,4)} = \{1\},\ \mathcal{B}_{(1,4)} = \{4\} \\
\mathcal{A}_{(2,3)} = \{1, 4\},\ \mathcal{B}_{(2,3)} = \emptyset \\
\mathcal{A}_{(2,4)} = \{1\},\ \mathcal{B}_{(2,4)} = \{4\} \\
\mathcal{A}_{(3,4)} = \{2, 3\},\ \mathcal{B}_{(3,4)} = \{4\}
\end{array}
$$

so that, $E_1 + E_2 + E_3 \geq 2$ (a clique). If $R_1 \in \{\mathrm{S}, \mathrm{D}\}$, any table of σ_{ij}'s (wrt F_1) has only 0's in the first column. In each row only 0's occur to the right of a second 0. In each column, there are only 1's below each 1. This makes possible to design an elegant algorithm for finding pairs of incompatible columns (or rows). Then, to obtain more global constraints on the E_i's, we consider the complementary relation (of the pairs (i, i') of compatible rows) and find all maximal independent sets with at least two elements in its undirected graph. This is not efficient in general, since finding *all* such sets is an NP-complete problem (e.g. [6]), but it works quite well in our specific case, as the graphs are either small or sparse. In SICStus, we use builtin predicates, `findall(Set,independent_set(UGraph,2,Set), LSets)`, to obtain such sets for a given `UGraph`. To compute the compatibility relations, the program starts from a complete graph with vertices `1..s`, from which it subsequently removes edges that link incompatible columns, while it constructs the graph of the compatibility relation for the rows and imposes (7).

We now look at `basis/5` and see how it may be defined in a declarative way. Let $\mathcal{B}' = \{\mathbf{p}'_{\imath_i \jmath_j} \mid P_{ij} \text{ is labelled to } 1\}$ and let $\mathcal{N}_{\mathcal{B}'} = \{(i, j) \mid \mathbf{p}'_{\imath_i \jmath_j} \in \mathcal{B}'\}$. The main idea is to obtain the largest subset $\mathcal{S} \subseteq \mathcal{B}'$ such that the graph $G_{\mathcal{S}}$ is a tree. Notice that if $\mathcal{B}'$ is a basis then either $\mathcal{S} = \mathcal{B}' \backslash \{\mathbf{p}'_{\imath_o \jmath_d}\}$, for one $\mathbf{p}'_{\imath_o \jmath_d} \in \mathcal{B}'$, or `Rank` is $e + s - 1$ and $\mathcal{S} = \mathcal{B}'$. Moreover, $\mathcal{S}$ can be found by a deterministic completion procedure, in which the possible resulting $\mathbf{p}'_{\imath_o \jmath_d}$ is the first node found to violate the tree-shape. It can be done iteratively — at iteration i, we try to link the chain of the nodes $(i, j) \in \mathcal{N}_{\mathcal{B}'}$ that were selected in row i, adopting a similar idea as that of the Kruskal's Algorithm for minimum spanning trees (e.g. [6]).

```
forest([],Trees,Trees,_,[]).
forest([I-NodesI|Nds],Trees,Treesf,LPod,[I-BasisI|Basis]) :-
 deleting(NodesI,Trees,RTrs,LTrees,I,LPod,BasisI),
 flatten(LTrees,NewTr),forest(Nds,[NewTr|RTrs],Treesf,LPod,Basis).
```

In calls to `forest/5`, `LPod` is bounded to `[]` or `[Pod]`, depending on `Rank`, `Trees` is `[[1],[2],...,[Ns]]`, with `Ns`$=s$, `Treesf` is `[[1,...,Ns]]` and `NodesI` is a list of terms `n(J,SigmaIJ)` that are the selections in row `I`. As suggested by its name, `deleting/7` implements deletion to pick up the tree where each node in `NodesI` is to be linked, gathering these trees (i.e., their vertices) in `LTrees`. It is deterministic. The node `n(J,SigmaIJ)` picks up the tree that contains `J`, and `deleting/7` fails when two nodes in `NodesI` are to be linked to the same tree in `Trees`, since such tree is removed when the first node is found. If `forest/5` succeeds then, when `Rank` is $e+s$, we still have to check that $\mathbf{p}'_{\imath_o \jmath_d}$ (in `Pod`) is not a linear combination of the elements in $\mathcal{S}$ (in the last argument of `forest/5`). This is dealt by a predicate that trivially succeeds if `LPod=[]`. If `LPod=[Pod]`, it solves $\sum_{\mathbf{p}'_{\imath_i \jmath_j} \in \mathcal{S}} \beta_{ij} \mathbf{p}_{\imath_i \jmath_j} = \mathbf{p}_{\imath_o \jmath_d}$, in $e+s-1$ variables $\beta_{ij} \in \{0, 1, -1\}$ and succeeds if and only if $\sum_{\mathbf{p}'_{\imath_i \jmath_j} \in \mathcal{S}} \beta_{ij} \sigma_{ij} \neq \sigma_{\imath_o \jmath_d}$, for the computed β_{ij}'s. This CSP in finite domains has a unique solution and it is easily definable since $\mathbf{p}_{ij} = \mathbf{e}_i + \mathbf{e}_{e+j}$, where $\mathbf{e}_i$ and $\mathbf{e}_{e+j}$ are unit vectors of the real space $\mathbb{R}^{e+s}$.

Further Work. An application of CLP(FD) to solve a real world problem was described, which illustrates how an adequate usage of problem-specific knowledge, namely to deduce global constraints, helps reduce the computational effort. We are now studying whether Constraint Programming may be successfully applied to sensor location problems for Transportation Networks.

Thanks. To anonymous referees for helpful comments. This work was partially supported by funds granted to LIACC through the *Programa de Financiamento Plurianual, Fundação para a Ciência e Tecnologia* and *Programa POSI*.

References

1. Andrade M.: *Métodos e Técnicas de Recolha de Dados de Tráfego – Algoritmo para a Definição da Matriz Origem-Destino.* Msc. Thesis, Faculty of Engineering, University of Porto, Portugal, 2000.
2. Carlsson M., Ottosson G., Carlson B.: An Open-Ended Finite Domain Constraint Solver. In *Proceedings of PLILP'97*, LNCS 1292, 191-206, Springer-Verlag, 1997.
3. Bianco L., Confessore G., and Reverberi P.: A Network Based Model for Traffic Sensor Location with Implications on O/D Matrix Estimates. *J. Transportation Science*, 35(1), 50–60, 2001.
4. Cook W., Cunningham W., Pulleyblank W., and Schrijver A.: *Combinatorial Optimization.* John Wiley & Sons, 1998, Chapter 8.
5. ECLiPSe User Manual Version 5.1.2, IC-PARC, Inperial College, London, 2001.
6. Cormen H., Leiserson C., Rivest R.: *Introduction to Algorithms*, MIT Press, 1990.
7. Freuder E.: In Pursuit of the Holy Grail, *Constraints*, 2(1), 57–62, 1997.
8. Hadley G.: *Linear Programming.* Addison-Wesley, 1969.
9. Hillier S. H., Lieberman G. J.: *Introduction to Operations Research.* McGraw-Hill, 6th Ed, 1995.
10. Marriott K., and Stuckey P.: *Programming with Constraints – An Introduction*, The MIT Press, 1998.
11. Mansfield L. E.: *Linear Algebra with Geometric Applications*, Marcel Dekker, 1976.
12. SICStus Prolog User Manual Release 3.8.6, SICS, Sweden, 2001.
13. Yang H., and Zhou J.: Optimal Traffic Counting Locations for Origin-Destination Matrix Estimation. *J. Transportation Research*, 32B(2), 109–126, 1998.
14. Tomás A. P., Andrade M., and Pires da Costa A.: Obtaining OD Data at Optimal Cost at Urban Roundabouts, Internal Report DCC-2-2001, DCC-FC & LIACC, University of Porto, 2001. `www.ncc.up.pt/fcup/DCC/Pubs/treports.html`. Presented at CSOR'01 Workshop (part of EPIA'01), Porto, December 2001.
15. Tomás A. P.: A Note on Sensor Location for Traffic Counting at Roundabouts – Solutions for a Particular Cost Function, Internal Report DCC-3-2001, DCC-FC & LIACC, University of Porto, 2001.

Flexible Agent Programming in Linear Logic

José Juan Palacios

Facultad de Ciencias de la Computación
B. Universidad Autónoma de Puebla, MÉXICO
jpalacio@aleteya.cs.buap.mx
http://www.cs.buap.mx/~jpalacio/

Abstract. We describe our work in progress on μACL, a light implementation of the language ACL *(Asynchronous Communications in Linear Logic)* for concurrent and distributed linear logic programming. Our description for computing elements (*Agents*) is inspired by the Actor model of concurrent computation. The essential requirements for Agent programming (communication, concurrency, actions, state update, modularity and code migration) are naturally expressed in μACL. Also, we describe some considerations towards the implementation of a distributed virtual machine for efficient execution of μACL programs.

Keywords: Agent Oriented Programming, Linear Logic, Multi-Agent Systems.

1 Introduction

Our main motivation behind this work is the declarative programming of Multi-Agent Systems (MAS), involving issues such as distributed planning, coordination and cooperation activities, etc. Girard's Linear Logic is very attractive for expressing distributed computation, in particular, founded in the *computation as proof search* paradigm. The inherent resource consciousness in Linear Logic, often expressed as *formulae as resources* conception, makes this formalism very attractive for planning, as shown for example in [KY93b,MTV93,Whi96].

We chose the ACL framework (*Asynchronous Communications in Linear Logic*) [KY94a,KY93a] as the main vehicle for experimentation. In ACL each formula is a process or a message; concurrent processes interact by means of asynchronous message passing. Messages in ACL capture both *channel* based communication and a kind of implicit broadcasting or selective communication based on message patterns. Each inference rule in the ACL proof system has an exact correspondence to some concurrent operation and the non-determinism in the proof search is associated with messages arrival order [KY93a]. The non-determinism in the clause activation for process reduction is essentially the same as that associated to messages arrival order, hence simplifying the operational model. Additionally, ACL can directly express the Actor model, asynchronous CCS and Linda-like communication [KY93a].

Therefore, our goals towards defining a light implementation of ACL are as follows:

C.A. Coello Coello et al. (Eds.): MICAI 2002, LNAI 2313, pp. 252–261, 2002.

1. to define a simple, easy to use and understand, Agents specification language based on ACL
2. to develop an efficient distributed implementation (virtual machine) for the above mentioned language.

The plan of this paper is as follows: after a short overview of ACL, we describe our simplification μACL, by means of an example we show the operation of agent programs as well as the expressiveness of this language. In the last section we describe some considerations towards a distributed implementation of a virtual machine for executing μACL programs.

2 Brief review of *ACL*

Each formula in ACL represents a *process* or a *message*, each *sequent* (multiset of formulae) $\vdash \Gamma$ corresponds in turn to some state of the system being modelled, i.e. a configuration of *processes and messages* (any resource in general). *Bottom-up* proof construction for a given sequent $\vdash \Gamma$ corresponds to the description of a computation starting at an initial configuration Γ. The syntax for ACL is defined as follows: given a set of *process predicate names* $\mathcal{A}_p$ and a set of *message predicate names* $\mathcal{A}_m$, the well formed formulae are:

$Cl ::= \forall \boldsymbol{X}.(A_p \circ\!- G)$ - Clause
$G ::= \bot | \top | A_m | ?A_m | A_p | G \parr G | G \& G | R | \forall \boldsymbol{X}.G$ - Goal
$R ::= \exists \boldsymbol{X}.(M \otimes G) | R \oplus R$ - message reception
$M ::= A_m^{\perp} | M \otimes M$ - multiset of messages to be received

where X ranges on terms, $A_p \in \mathcal{A}_p$, $A_m \in \mathcal{A}_m$.

The existential first order quantifier is characterized for *value passing*, while universal quantifier is used for *identifier creation*, identifiers work as *pointers to access resources* such as processes and messages [KY93a], allowing in principle that both messages and processes be considered as *first class objects.*

1. In the clause definition, $\forall \boldsymbol{X}(A_p \circ\!- G)$ means universal quantification for all free occurrence of variables in $A_p \circ\!- G$, and $V_F(A_p) \subseteq V_F(G)$ where $V_F(\boldsymbol{X})$ is the set of free variables in $\boldsymbol{X}$.
2. In the definition of R, $\exists \boldsymbol{X}(M \otimes G)$ represents existential quantification for all variables that occurs free in $M \otimes G$ and $V_F(M) \subseteq V_F(G)$.

The inference rules for this system, named ACL_1 are shown in fig. 1.

Par ($\parr$) describes both concurrent computation as well as asynchronous message sending, *Fork* (&) specifies a subprocess executing in parallel. Messages prefixed with ? can be read any number of times. *Tensor* ($\otimes$) in combination with linear negation ($.^{\perp}$) specifies synchronized (lazy) message reception. Non-deterministic choice (on availability) is described by *Plus* ($\oplus$), as well as joining clauses implicitly in $\mathcal{P}$. Method activation is similar as in concurrent logic languages (process reduction) involving a unification between the actual parameters of the selected process and the variables of the clause.

Concurrent composition:	*Fork:*
$\dfrac{!\mathcal{P} \vdash \Gamma, G_1, G_2}{!\mathcal{P} \vdash \Gamma, G_1 \parr G_2}[\parr]$	$\dfrac{!\mathcal{P} \vdash \Gamma, G_1 \quad !\mathcal{P} \vdash \Gamma, G_2}{!\mathcal{P} \vdash \Gamma, G_1 \& G_2}[\&]\ (fork)$
Message sending:	*Clause (method) activation:*
$\dfrac{!\mathcal{P} \vdash \Gamma, A_m, B}{!\mathcal{P} \vdash \Gamma, A_m \parr B}[C_1]$	$\dfrac{!\mathcal{P} \vdash \Gamma, G\theta}{!\mathcal{P} \vdash \Gamma, A_p\theta}[\circ\!-]$ where $(A_p \circ\!- G) \in \mathcal{P}$ θ denotes a substitution of free variables
Normal message reception:	
$\dfrac{!\mathcal{P} \vdash G_j[\boldsymbol{u}/\boldsymbol{X}], \Gamma}{!\mathcal{P} \vdash \oplus_{i=1,n}(\exists \boldsymbol{X}(m_{i1}(\boldsymbol{s_{i1}})^{\perp} \otimes ... \otimes m_{ik}(\boldsymbol{s_{ik}})^{\perp} \otimes G_i)), m_j(\boldsymbol{t_j}), \Gamma}[C_2]$	
Modal message reception:	
$\dfrac{!\mathcal{P} \vdash G_j[\boldsymbol{u}/\boldsymbol{X}], \Gamma, ?m_j(\boldsymbol{t_j})}{!\mathcal{P} \vdash \oplus_{i=1,n}(\exists \boldsymbol{X}(m_{i1}(\boldsymbol{s_{i1}})^{\perp} \otimes ... \otimes m_{ik}(\boldsymbol{s_{ik}})^{\perp} \otimes G_i)), ?m_j(\boldsymbol{t_j}), \Gamma}[C_3]$	
Identifier Rule:	*Rewriting Rule:*
$\dfrac{!\mathcal{P} \vdash A(id), \Gamma}{\vdash \forall \boldsymbol{X}.A(\boldsymbol{X}), \Gamma}[ID_1]$	$\dfrac{!\mathcal{P} \vdash p(t), \Gamma}{!\mathcal{P} \vdash p(s), \Gamma}[RW_1]$ if $s \longrightarrow t \in Rs$

Fig. 1. ACL_1 inference rules, $\mathcal{P}$ denotes a set of clauses (program), the ! means that clauses can be used *ad libitum*.

For the Rewriting rule ($[RW_1]$), Rs is a *rewriting system* ($s \longrightarrow t$ means 's becomes t under Rs'). In general, Rs can be any programming language *whose output is uniquely determined.* Hence, ACL with a rewriting system Rs can be considered an extension of Rs to a concurrent language with asynchronous communication facilities [KY93a]:

$$\text{ACL} = \text{Rs} + \textit{asynch. comm. facilities} \quad (1)$$

Example 1. A simple encoding for producer and consumer is shown:

$$prod \circ\!- m(a) \parr (ack(a)^{\perp} \otimes prod)$$
$$cons \circ\!- m(x)^{\perp} \otimes (ack(x) \parr cons)$$

in an endless loop, producer drops a message $m(a)$ and then awaits for acknowledgment in order to continue. Consumer acts dually. A proof tree describing the interaction among *prod* and *cons* is shown in fig. 2.

Note that it is not necessary to define an explicit communication channel between involved processes, in principle any other process could consume any given message if the process is waiting for it. ACL allows a kind of competition for consumption of messages.

Example 2. An encoding for Dijkstra's *dining philosophers* is shown:

$$\cfrac{\cfrac{\cfrac{\cfrac{\vdots}{!\mathcal{P} \vdash cons, prod}[C_2]}{!\mathcal{P} \vdash ack(a) \parr cons, ack(a)^{\perp} \otimes prod}[\parr, C_2]}{!\mathcal{P} \vdash m(a), ack(a)^{\perp} \otimes prod, m(x)^{\perp} \otimes ack(x) \parr cons}[C_2]}{!\mathcal{P} \vdash prod \parr cons}[\circ\!-prod, cons]$$

Fig. 2. Initial segment for the proof tree for example 1.

$philo(x) \circ\!- thinking(x) \parr fork(x)$ `/* philosopher ready */`
$thinking(x) \circ\!- hungry(x)$
$hungry(x) \circ\!- fork(x)^{\perp} \otimes fork(x-1)^{\perp} \otimes eat(x)$ `/* try to get forks */`
$eat(x) \circ\!- fork(x) \parr fork(x-1) \parr thinking(x)$ `/* return forks */`

Because messages (forks in this case) are linear, two neighbor philosophers compete with each other, only one of them may get a shared fork: synchronization is implicit in the clause *hungry*.

However, ACL can support communication based on explicit channels:

Example 3. A definition for a process that receives a list of processes and connects them in a linear topology is shown (from [KY94b]):

$linear\ ([], l, r) \circ\!- \perp$ `/* inaction - dies */`
$linear\ ([Pr], l, r) \circ\!- Pr(l, r)$ `/* sends message to Pr */`
$linear\ ([Pr|Ps], l, r) \circ\!-$
$\quad \forall x.(Pr(l, x) \parr linear(Ps, x, r))$ `/* recursive connection */`

Each process in the list receives the address (i.e, a channel) of left and right neighbors. When there are several processes in the list the connection and recursive reduction is performed concurrently. Note that a new channel is created dynamically in the third clause. A round-robin topology can be defined as follows:

$$ring(Pr) \circ\!- \forall x.(linear(Pr, x, x))$$

Processes, as well as messages, can be sent through a message (channel)[KY94b].

3 μACL

μACL is a subset of ACL, the intended purpose is to specify societies of *Agents*. The kind of agents we are considering is inspired in the Actor model[Agh90], as well as in the SELF language[US91]. We define an agent as a structure of *resource place holders* named *slots*. An agent is identified by its *name*, this name implicitly refers to the agent's *mailbox* which is a bounded buffer for incoming communications. A slot in turn is characterized by a unique *name* which can be bound to a *value*. Some of the slots could be classical (i.e. can be used any number of times), or could be linear, and some of them can be used to perform complex actions: these kind of slots are the *clauses* (or methods definition).

Clauses have a head (left-hand side) composed by a multiset of *messages patterns* (named *selectors list*) and a clause's body (right-hand side), which is composed of a multiset of *goals*. The behavior of an agent is *triggered by communication*: arriving messages that match a message pattern (selector) bind clause's variables and execute the goals (i.e a non-deterministic *pattern* → *action* performance). The execution of goals can also be performed in parallel, and multiple clauses can be *fired* at a given time.

From our equation (1) the chosen rewriting system for μACL is *LispkitLisp* [Hen80]:

μACL= Lispkit+ AGT module (ACL asynch. comm. facilities)

Lispkit syntax is shown in fig. 3.

x	variable	(EQ e_1 e_2)	relational expressions
(QUOTE s)	constant	(LEQ e_1 e_2)	
(ADD e_1 e_2)	arithmetic expressions	(CAR e)	structural expressions
(SUB e_1 e_2)		(CDR e)	
(MUL e_1 e_2)		(CONS e_1 e_2)	
(DIV e_1 e_2)		(ATOM e)	
(REM e_1 e_2)			

(IF e_1 e_2 e_3)	conditional form
(LAMBDA ($x_1 ... x_k$) e)	lambda expression
(e $e_1 ... e_n$)	function application
(LET ($x_1.e_1$)...($x_k.e_k$) e)	simple block
(LETREC ($x_1.e_1$)...($x_k.e_k$) e)	recursive block

Fig. 3. Well formed expressions for Lispkit programs: $x, x_1, ...x_k$ are atoms and $e, e_1, ...e_n$ are nested well formed expressions. s denotes any S-expression.

Our extension of Lispkit towards μACL is given by the following considerations

1. a *skeleton* for the definition of agents,
2. the description of agent's behavior (or life cycle)
3. a number of additional special primitives.

An agent is defined by means of a skeleton, which has the structure shown in fig 4.

The primitive AGT (agent block) defines the slots block for an agent (like a LETREC) identified by *name* (agent's class) and the slots themselves. Classical or static slots can be defined by LET, LETREC, and dynamic (persistent) slots by means of SLOT. Slots are initialized/updated only by means of a message SLF.

Clauses are composed by two parts: ((Head) ○– Body)

1. Head: which is composed in turn by a list of *message patterns* (selectors), implicitly joined by ⊗. Each message pattern has the form *(message-name args)*.

```
( AGT name
     /* -local definitions:-
        static -LET, LETREC-, dynamic -SLOT-*/
     ( SLOT n1..nk )
     :
     /* -operative part of agent- list of clauses: */
     ( /* begin clause */
     (  (m1a1) ... (mkak) ) /* clause head */
          G1 ... Gn /* clause body */
     ) /* end of clause */
     : /* other clauses */
)    /* end of AGT */
```

Fig. 4. Skeleton for agents: $n_1..n_k$ denote *slot names*, $\boldsymbol{a_i} = a_{i,1}, a_{i,2}, ...a_{i,n_i}$ denote arguments of messages and m_k denote message names or selectors. $G_1...G_n$ denote goal formulae. Indeed, everything is an S-expression.

2. Body: composed by a multiset of goal formulae implicitly joined by ⅋ . Each goal formulae describes an action, and can be one of the following:
   (a) inaction: *null*,
   (b) successful agent's termination: special message (TOP),
   (c) sending a message: *(To list-of-messages)* where *To* denotes the receptor of the message, and each message is described as a tuple *(message-name args)*. There are two main classes of receptors of messages:
      – Agent's Mailbox: a reference to an agent's mailbox is specified in a message (i.e., a point-point communication). The special name SLF is used when sender is the same as receiver. If *message-name* matches a slot, the result is a (logical) update for the slot's value. If *message-name* is a selector, the message is simply enqueued in the mailbox and eventually tried to match against the head of a clause (if any).
      – Global shared pool: when the message is simply dropped on the pool of messages, and (in principle) any agent can pick it up, this is specified by means of the (channel) name DROP.
   (d) applying a function (sequential computation): *(f args)* where *f* is bound to a LAMBDA value.

Clauses are implicitly joined by ⊕, hence involving non-deterministic (committed) choice. Note that message sending is structurally similar to function application.

Agents work as follows: after creation, it selects a the head of a clause that matches with incoming messages, then binds variables involved (on the side of the agent exclusively, different from usual Prolog unification) and executes (reduces) in turn the goals specified in the body of the selected clause. The agent performs in this way inside an endless loop (until explicit termination operation is executed, if any).

The remainder primitives incorporated to Lispkit are:

1. NEW: (function)- creates an agent (slot space and mailbox) and returns a reference to this new agent's mailbox.
   (selector)- the newly created agent receives this message selector with its arguments (if any), and performs the goals involved on right-hand side. Multiple NEW selectors (clauses) can be defined, involving different arguments for avoiding ambiguity. Indeed, this message can only be received once immediately after creation.
2. CLON: (function)- creates an exact copy of a running agent given as argument, and returns a new reference (mailbox). Also, this primitive can be applied on slots, the result is an S-exp that can be sent as a message, CLON can be used in combination with SLF for a kind of native code migration:

```
:   /* I'm sending to X a copy of myself! */
( ( (get_code X) ) (X (CLON SLF)))
```

Example 4. An encoding for example 1 is shown[1]:

<table>
<tr><td rowspan="2"><pre>(AGT prod
    (((NEW))
    (DROP (m a)) /* drops an item */
)
    (((ack x)) /* consumes ack */
    /* do nothing */
)
)</pre></td><td><pre>(AGT cons
        (((m x)) /* waits for item */
        (DROP (ack x)) /* consumes it
        and drops ack */
)
)</pre></td></tr>
<tr><td><pre>/*   interaction goal: */
        (NEW prod) (NEW cons)</pre></td></tr>
</table>

As another example, let us consider a group of agents that form a double linked list:

```
(AGT pp
    (SLOT i l r) /* number, left and right neighbors */
    (( (NEW x) )  (SLF (i x))) /* set my number -alias-*/
    (( (p (- i 1) X) (p (+ i 1) Y))  /* identify neighbors */
        (SLF (l X) (r Y)) )/* set neighbors as acquaintances */
    /* now, I can communicate directly with neighbors */
    .. (l (QUOTE Hello, how are you doing?)) ..
)

/* creation: inside a loop, j is the counter*/
.. (DROP (p j (NEW (pp j)))) ..
```

There is no necessity for a global coordinator in this example: after creation, each agent finds[2] and sets its two neighbors.

Please, note the importance of messages to SLF for logical update of knowledge: a message to *self* updates the contents of a slot with the name of selector,

[1] Although the syntax described is very simple, we will offer a *user's language* (following [Hen80]) in such a way that programs are more readable for humans.

[2] We are considering effective ways to express tests for matching as guards in the head of a clause.

but also it allows creation of a new slot (a new acquaintance, a fact, a rule, etc.). This type of logical update is strictly similar to that of Lolli[Hod92]: reducing a goal $\Gamma \vdash A \multimap B$ means to prove B with A in the premises: $\Gamma, A \vdash B$. In our interpretation, this means to incorporate the message A as a slot in the body of the Agent.

4 A distributed virtual machine for μACL

We sketch some considerations towards defining a distributed virtual machine (DVM) for μACL:

Data structures indeed, the basic data structure is a linked list (S-expression), the memory space is managed as a heap. Each agent is essentially an instance of SECD[Hen80], where the enviroment has more structure (i.e. the slots) in order to allow for dynamic aggregation, i.e. new resources can be incorporated to the slots (acquaintances, facts, clauses, etc.).

Communication mechanisms the DVM has a unique public port (*socket*) which is known to other DVMs (i.e. external communication). Through this port the broadcasting and dropped messages are received. In addition, each agent can activate any number of sockets for private communication (point-to-point), both for intra-DVM and inter-DVM. Unification and matching occurs on one side: from received message values to selected clause.

Threads involved for an agent each agent hast at least two threads of execution:

1. Mailbox (hidden): responsible for the (physical) messages buffer, this thread manages the incomming messages and also participates in the forum competing for linear messages in a pattern based search. When a message arrives to the global messages space (forum), the supervisor sends a message to each Agent for enquiring recollection; if this is the case (i.e. the agent has a selector that matches that message), each agent sends back a number for applying the *Bakery algorithm* of Lamport[Har98].Only one agent can consume that kind of message. When a classical ? message is sent, it is propagated to all agents, and a copy is allocated in each DVM togheter with a time stamp (for allocation purposes).
2. Executor (manifest): mailbox thread wakes up an executor thread for reducing the goals (body) of a selected clause. If no messages are available, executor sleeps.

Scheduler and supervisor each DVM periodically communicates to the others DVMs their load (a metric for weighting agents), so if neccesary could migrate agents for load balancing. Security issues are being considered. Domain names tables are organized and periodically updated.

Plan librarian and Knowledge Base these are special purpose agents provided by the system: a Plan librarian and KB. These agents can be incorporated as part of an individual Agent, but also these Agents can be shared among a community of agents. Indeed, plans are encoded uniformly as μACL clauses (but including 'free' metavariables to be instantiated in the execution of the plan), a KB has special operations (use/update) uniformly encoded as messages.

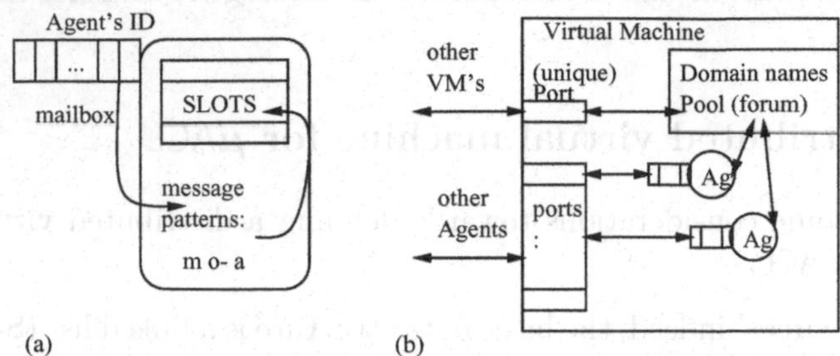

Fig. 5. (a) A μACL agent. (b) sketch of the virtual machine.

5 Related Work

A number of logic programming languages have been proposed according to the paradigm *proof search as computing*: LO [AP90] was one of the early languages involving concurrent logical objects with inter-built inheritance. Lolli [Hod92], a representative of the intuitionistic fragment, provides a right balance between expressivity and usability as a programming language. Several techniques for *efficient resource management* have been applied in the development of a compiler and abstract machine for a fragment of Lolli: LLP[TK96]. A fragment of Forum has been used to define $\mathcal{E}_{hhf}$ which is an executable linear logic language for modeling concurrent object-oriented logic programming [Del97], which is close to HACL[KY94b].

In [Ami99] Lygon is used for Agent programming. The Agent model described there is also inspired in the Actor model, but in ACL we have uniformity in representation: everything is a resource (messages, events, knowledge units, etc.) and the computation is always a kind of communication. Also, in ACL we can express reflexivity and reactivity in a natural way, hence we believe our approach is less complex than the above using Lygon.

6 Conclusion

We have presented μACL and its advantages for specification of communication-driven agents. μACL extends the applicative language Lispkit by adding just 6 primitives which are very easy to use. Concurrency, modularity, logical state update and inference (based on message passing) are the most important capabilities of μACL for Agent programming. Currently, we are implementing a translator for the user's language to μACL, and the compiler for μACL programs to the virtual machine byte codes. The translator and compiler are being implemented in ANSI C and the virtual machine is being developed in Java.

References

[Agh90] Gul Agha. Concurrent Object-Oriented Programming. *Communications of the ACM*, 33(9), September 1990.

[Ami99] Abdullah-Al Amin. Agent-Oriented Programming in Linear Logic. Master's thesis, RMIT University, Melbourne Australia, 1999.

[AP90] Jean-Marc Andreoli and Remo Pareschi. LO and behold! Concurrent structured processes. In *Proceedings of OOPSLA'90*, pages 44–56, Ottawa, Canada, October 1990. Published as ACM SIGPLAN Notices, vol.25, no.10.

[Del97] Giorgio Delzanno. *Logic and Object-Oriented Programming in Linear Logic.* PhD thesis, Universitá di Pisa-Genova-Udine, 1997.

[Har98] Stephen J. Hartley. *Concurrent Programming: the Java Programming Language.* Oxford Univ. Press., 1998.

[Hen80] Peter Henderson. *Functional Programming: Application and Implementation.* Prentice/Hall International, 1980.

[Hod92] Joshua S. Hodas. Lolli: An extension of λprolog with linear context management. In D. Miller, editor, *Workshop on the λProlog Programming Language*, pages 159–168, Philadelphia, Pennsylvania, August 1992.

[KY93a] Naoki Kobayashi and Akinori Yonezawa. ACL — a concurrent linear logic programming paradigm. In D. Miller, editor, *Proceedings of the 1993 International Logic Programming Symposium*, pages 279–294, Vancouver, Canada, October 1993. MIT Press.

[KY93b] Naoki Kobayashi and Akinori Yonezawa. Reasoning on actions and change in linear logic programming. Technical Report 23, University of Tokyo, 1993.

[KY94a] Naoki Kobayashi and Akinori Yonezawa. Asynchronous communication model based on linear logic. *Formal Aspects of Computing*, 3:279–294, 1994.

[KY94b] Naoki Kobayashi and Akinori Yonezawa. Higher-order concurrent linear logic programming. In *Proceedings of Theory and Practice of Parallel Programming (TPPP'94), Sendai, Japan*, Lecture Notes in Computer Science, 1994.

[MTV93] M. Masseron, C. Tollu, and J. Vauzeilles. Generating plans in Linear Logic I: Actions and proofs. *Theoretical Computer Science*, 113(2):349–371, 1993.

[TK96] Naoyuki Tamura and Yuko Kaneda. Extension of WAM for a linear logic programming language. In T. Ida, A. Ohori, and M. Takeichi, editors, *Second Fuji International Workshop on Functional and Logic Programming*, pages 33–50. World Scientific, Nov. 1996.

[US91] David Ungar and Randall B. Smith. SELF: the Power of Simplicity. *Lisp and Symbolic Computation*, 1991.

[Whi96] G. Graham White. The Design of a Situation-Based Lygon Metainterpreter: I. Simple Changes and Persistence. Technical Report 729, Department of Computer Science, Queen Mary and Westfield College, University of London, 1996.

Sample Complexity for Function Learning Tasks through Linear Neural Networks

Arturo Hernández-Aguirre[1,2], Cris Koutsougeras[2], and Bill P. Buckles[2]

Centro de Investigación en Matemáticas (CIMAT), Departamento de Computación
Guanajuato, Gto. 36240, Mexico
artha@cimat.mx
Department of Electrical Engineering and Computer Science,
Tulane University New Orleans, LA, 70118, Usa
hernanda,ck,buckles@eecs.tulane.edu

Abstract. We find new sample complexity bounds for real function learning tasks in the uniform distribution. These bounds, tighter than the distribution-free ones reported elsewhere in the literature, are applicable to simple functional link networks and radial basis neural networks.

1 Introduction

In the function learning problem the basic components interact as follows: 1) a process or phenomena P that is hard to describe by a set of equations is only known through a set of examples $\{(x, y)\}$. This is the *training set*, it only conveys partial information $\{t : x \rightarrow y\}$ about the overall input-output mapping $\{T : x \rightarrow y\}$ performed by P. Thus function T describes process P, but T can only be approximated by t. 2) A neural network is trained and issues a function f that approximates or mimics the *target function* t, thus the training process stops when $|t(x) - f(x)|$ is smaller than some error named *training error*. The function f is one of the infinite number of functions that the network can generate by changing its parameters (weights). 3) Once trained the network performance is estimated using new samples from P. This is *network generalization*, the most cherished property since now f becomes a description for T. The difference $|T(x) - f(x)|$ is called *generalization error* and it is expected to be upper-bounded by some ϵ for most of the new examples.

In that scenario a small training error does not guarantee small generalization error, thus there is often a trade-off between the training error and the confidence assigned to the training error as a predictor of the generalization error (training error is only a good predictor when the training set size is sufficiently large). The determining factor for this confidence is the network capacity, a measure directly related to the network size. Hence, for a set of m examples there exists a network of capacity C that provides the optimal generalization. In this paper we use PAC (Probably Approximately Correct) learning theory to estimate the relationship between network capacity, generalization and training set size. In PAC learning the network capacity is measured through the Vapnik-Chervonenkis dimension,

C.A. Coello Coello et al. (Eds.): MICAI 2002, LNAI 2313, pp. 262–271, 2002.

VC_{dim}. This is a powerful concept that denotes the finiteness of the classification capacity of a neural network. For instance, in an input space of dimension d the Perceptron generates 2^{d+1} dichotomies, thus only up to $d+1$ points can be correctly classified. The exponent is called the VC dimension. In other words, in spite of the infinite number of decision regions that a Perceptron can generate, its capacity is finite and just sufficient to accurately classify $d+1$ samples in two classes. Using these concepts PAC learning estimates the number of samples m that guarantee with some confidence level a bounded error in the generalization of a neural network whose capacity is VC_{dim}.

Much of the work on PAC learning has been done for distribution-free data, either for classification or function approximation problems. The search for tighter bounds has promoted the study of data with some fixed but possibly unknown distribution [6,3]. In this paper we address the function learning problem in the uniform distribution, and we improve and give explicit sample complexity bounds for two linear neural networks: simple functional link networks (SFLNNs), and radial basis function neural networks (RBFNNs) [7].

The organization of this article is the following. First we introduce PAC learning and necessary concepts around the framework. Next we prove sample complexity bounds for SFLNNs and RBFNNs, and give conclusion and final remarks in the last section.

2 Preliminaries

We use PAC theory to study the function learning problem in the uniform distribution. Some definitions of the basic concepts over which we later develop proofs for sample complexity bounds are given in this section.

Definition 1. (Training set) *Assume* $X \in \Re^d$ *any arbitrary set. A family of functions* $\mathcal{F}$ *is defined as a set of measurable functions.* $\forall f \in \mathcal{F}$, $f : X \to [0,1]$. *There is nothing special about the interval. A set of training data* $Z_d = \{(x_i, t(x_i))\}_{i=1}^m$ *whose elements are independent identically distributed according to some probability measure* P *on* X *is available.*

Notice that one of functions in $\mathcal{F}$ is issued by the network as an approximation to t. In PAC learning the size of the training set is called *sample complexity*.

Definition 2. (Linear neural network) *A linear neural network (LNN) is a connectionist network with one input layer of* u *neurons and a summation node as the only element of the output layer. The node transfer functions are elements of a set* Φ *of fixed, typically nonlinear* basis functions.

The LNN performs the mapping $f(\mathbf{X^d}, \omega) \to [\mathbf{0}, \mathbf{1}]$, where $\omega \in \Omega$ are adjustable parameters of the network (weights), $f = \sum_{i=1}^{u} \omega_i \phi_i + \omega_0$, and $\phi_i \in \Phi$. Φ is a family of functions such as radial basis functions or polynomials.

We are to estimate the approximation of $f \in \mathcal{F}$ to a "target" function t that we only know through its examples. We assume that the family of functions can approximate the unknown function. The similarity between two functions is measured as follows.

Definition 3. (Distance between two functions) *Given two measurable functions $f, g : X \longrightarrow [0, 1]$ and a uniform probability measure P on $[0, 1]$, the expected value of the difference $|f(x) - g(x)|$ is the following pseudo metric:*

$$d_P(f, g) = \int_X |f(x) - g(x)| P(dx)$$

This measure is the expected value of the difference of the two functions. Therefore, for highly similar functions f and g, $d_P(f, g)$ approaches zero. The *function learning problem* is to find the function $f \in \mathcal{F}$ that best approximates the "target" function g which we only know through examples. That is, the expected error $d_P(f, g)$ is "minimized". If we bound the difference or error by ϵ we can tell whether for a set of examples the functions are at a distance "ϵ-close" . In the following we call "hypothesis" any f produced by $\mathcal{F}$ as an approximation to the target function t.

Definition 4. ϵ-error generator example *A sample set $\mathbf{x} = [x_1, x_2, \ldots, x_m]$ is an ϵ-error generator example if $d_P[h(\mathbf{x}), t] > \epsilon$, thus the hypothesis h differs from t by more than ϵ.*

We will call the set of these points the *ϵ-error generator set of examples* or $r(m, \epsilon) = P^m\{\mathbf{x} \in X^m : d_P[h(\mathbf{x}), t] > \epsilon\}$

The Vapnik-Chervonenkis dimension is a measure of the capacity of a machine to partition some input space in two classes.

Definition 5. (VC-dimension) *A set of functions $f(x, \omega) \in \mathcal{F}$ has VC-dimension d_{vc} if there exists d_{vc} samples in X that can be shattered by this set of functions but there do not exist $d_{vc} + 1$ samples that can be shattered. Thus, d_{vc} is the cardinality of the largest set that can be shattered into all $2^{d_{vc}}$ partitions of two classes. If "large" arbitrary finite sets are shattered by $\mathcal{F}$ then the VC-dimension is said to be infinite (VC-dimension will be represented by $d_{vc}(\mathcal{F})$.*

For the two network models studied in this paper the VC dimension is well known [17]. The VC dimension of a LNN is $u + 1$, where u is the number of nodes (see Definition 2)

Definition 6. PAC algorithm *An algorithm A_m is said to be* **Probably Approximately Correct (PAC)** *if $r(m, \epsilon) \rightarrow 0$ as $m \rightarrow \infty$ for each $\epsilon > 0$.*

If an algorithm is PAC, then for each $\epsilon, \delta > 0$, there exists m_0 such that

$$P^m\{\mathbf{x} \in X^m : d_P[h(\mathbf{x}), g] > \epsilon\} < \delta \ \ \forall m > m_0$$

In other words, using a set of examples of size at least m_0 drawn with fixed probability distribution P^m, the hypothesis returned by the algorithm will have error less than ϵ with confidence at least $1 - \delta$. For a learning algorithm to be PAC, it is necessary the VC dimension of a network to be finite. By using the PAC learning framework it is easy to derive a lower bound to the sample complexity for the function learning problem. This has been shown elsewhere in the literature [17,16,4,2,1,14] but given the clarity of his exposition we prefer the one by Natarajan [9]. This is a distribution-free bound for function learning. Using an example set whose size is

$$m > \frac{8}{\epsilon}\{8d_{vc}\ln\frac{64}{\epsilon} + \ln\frac{2}{\delta}\} \qquad (1)$$

another example drawn with the same probability of distribution will have error at most ϵ with confidence at least $1-\delta$.

The distance between two functions is central in the next definition. We approach the function learning problem from the ϵ-cover perspective in a function space.

Definition 7. (ϵ-cover) *An ϵ-cover for $\mathcal{F}$ is the set of functions $\{d_i\}_{i=1}^{k} \in \mathcal{F}$ such that for any $f \in \mathcal{F}$, there is a d_i such that $d_P(f, d_i) < \epsilon$. An ϵ-cover with minimal size is called minimal ϵ-cover, and its size is denoted as $N(\epsilon, \mathcal{F}, d_P)$.*

Then an ϵ-cover is a subset of all functions $\{f_1, f_2, \cdots, f_n\}$ that can be generated by $\mathcal{F}$. At least one element of the ϵ-cover is guaranteed to be ϵ-close to *any* $f \in \mathcal{F}$. Therefore, the ability of $\mathcal{F}$ to generate ϵ-covers of pertinent size is essential for our goal. If the target function is one of $\{f_1, f_2, \cdots, f_\infty\}$ then at least one function in the ϵ-cover would be a valid approximation, and ultimately our solution. Thus, the learning problem can be seen as the generation of an ϵ-cover. Error minimization algorithms (like backpropagation) have been proved able to generate the minimum cover, therefore neural networks with finite VC dimension and trained by backpropagation will produce a hypothesis ϵ-close to the target hypothesis.

The following definition is a theorem proved in [18] (page 169). This theorem links the size of the example set for which there is an ϵ-cover of functions to the ϵ-error generator set of examples.

Definition 8. (Empirical risk minimization is PAC) *The minimal empirical risk algorithm (backpropagation) is PAC to accuracy ϵ for any fixed distribution whenever:*

$$r(m,\epsilon) \leq k \cdot e^{(-m\epsilon^2/8)} \qquad k : \textit{size of } \epsilon - \textit{cover}$$

Bounding the probabilistic factor $r(m, \epsilon)$ by the confidence δ, we can immediately derive the bound on the sample complexity that makes true the PAC-learning expression $Pr\{d_P(f,g) > \epsilon)\} \leq \delta$. This is:

$$m \geq \frac{8}{\epsilon^2}\ln\frac{k}{\delta}$$

The parameter k indicates the size of the $\epsilon/2$-cover (covering number). If the $e/2$-cover is minimal, k can be replaced by its estimation: $N(\epsilon/2, \mathcal{F}, d_P)$. An upper bound on the size of the $e/2$-cover (proved by Kolmogorov [10]) is

$$N(\epsilon, \mathcal{F}, d_P) \leq 2^{\left[\frac{L(\beta-\alpha)}{\epsilon}\right]^d}$$

for all $f \in \mathcal{F}, f : [\alpha, \beta]^d \to \mathcal{R}$, L is the Lipschitz constant of $\mathcal{F}$, and d_P is measured in the uniform distribution. It is worthy to see in the expression above how the number of representatives (functions) in the set cover depends "only" on the size of the Lipschitz constant (since we can consider *alpha*, *beta*, d, and ϵ as known parameters of the problem). The constant is an indicator of the *richness* or capacity of $\mathcal{F}$ to produce the ϵ-cover that contains the solution. The formula above is valid in the *infinite* norm (N_∞).

Definition 9. (Lipschitz condition) *Let f be a continuous function in $[a, b]$. If there is a finite constant $L \geq 0$ such that*

$$|f(x_1) - f(x_2)| \leq L|x_1 - x_2| \quad (x_1, x_2 \in [a, b]), \ f(0) = 0,$$

then we say that f satisfies the Lipschitz condition or f is a Lipschitz continuous function.

The constant is defined in the norm N_2. The following expression states the relationship between measures in the norms N_2 and N_∞ in a d dimensional space: $N_2(\boldsymbol{x}, \boldsymbol{y}) \leq \sqrt{d} \cdot N_\infty(\boldsymbol{x}, \boldsymbol{y})$

In the following we calculate the new bounds for sample complexity by constructing on the estimation of the Lipschitz constant.

3 Function Learning with SFLNNs

The first problem we want to consider is the estimation of the sample complexity of simple functional link neural network for function learning. Higher order neural networks are perhaps the most common representative. A simple functional link network implements a linear mapping by means of polynomials of one variable [13].

Lemma 1. (Lipschitz constant of a family of polynomials) *The Lipschitz constant L of a family $\mathcal{Q}$ of polynomials of the form $Q_n(x) = \sum_{i=1}^{n} a_i \cdot x^i + a_0$, of order n and coefficients $|a_i| \leq A$, is upper bounded as follows: $L \leq A(n^2 + n)/2$*

Proof. By definition of Lipschitz constant

$$\frac{|f(x) - f(y)|}{\|x - y\|_2}_{x,y \in [\alpha,\beta]^d} \leq L \leq sup_{\psi \in [\alpha,\beta]^d} \|\nabla f(\psi)\|$$

For a family of polynomials $\mathcal{Q}$ of the form $Q_n(x) = \sum_{i=1}^{n} a_i \cdot x^i(x) \ + a_0$, the gradient becomes

$$\frac{\partial\, Q_n(x)}{\partial(x)} = \sum_{i=2}^{n} i \cdot a_i x^{i-1} \ + a_1$$

On the interval I $[-1, 1]$, thus by making $\alpha = -1$ and $\beta = 1$, and assuming A is the maximum value of the coefficient, the series becomes

$$\frac{\partial\, Q_n(x)}{\partial(x)} = A(1 + 2x + 3x^2 + 4x^3 + 5x^4 ...)$$

The series attains its maximum value when $x = 1$. The expression becomes the addition of n natural numbers for which the cumulative can be bounded as follows:

$$A(1+2x+3x^2+4x^3+5x^4...) = A(1+2+3+4+5+\ldots) \leq \frac{An(n+1)}{2}, \quad \forall\, |x| \leq 1$$

Therefore, L (in norm N_2) is upper bounded as follows:

$$L \leq A(n^2+n)/2 \quad \forall\, x \in [-1,1]^d$$

Both sides of the inequality are expressed in N_2. With some abuse of the notation, the subindex in the Lipschitz constant denotes the norm of the environment where L is defined. It should clarify the further simplification (see Definition 7).

$$L_2 = \frac{L_\infty}{\sqrt{d}} \leq \sqrt{d}A(n^2+n)/2$$

$$L_\infty \leq \frac{Ad(n^2+n)}{2}$$

Now the main theorem on sample complexity for SFLNN. Assume the network uses as basis functions the family of polynomials whose Lipschitz constant was just found.

Theorem 1. (Sample Complexity for PAC-learning functions by means of SFLNN) *For a family of functions $\mathcal{Q} \in [-1,1]^d$ with minimal $\epsilon/2$-cover, the empirical risk minimization algorithm finds an approximation $f \in \mathcal{Q}$ to the target function g with accuracy and confidence parameters ϵ and δ whenever the sample complexity is*

$$m \geq \frac{8}{\epsilon^2} \ln \frac{Ad((n^2+n)/2)}{\delta}$$

The family of polynomials admits only one-dimensional input spaces, therefore $d = 1$. Thus,

$$m \geq \frac{8}{\epsilon^2} \ln \frac{A((n^2+n)/2)}{\delta}$$

Proof. Substituting the bound for the Lipschitz constant into **Theorem 1**, the result follows.

A simple example. Assume we wish a SFLNN to learn an approximation to a target function, one from the entire repertory of functions in $\mathcal{F}$. What is the sample complexity for the following required (expected) behavior? Parameters: Max error $\epsilon = 0.1$, confidence $\delta = 0.90$, size of the learning machine $n = 5$ ($u = 4$, see Definition 2), largest coefficient $A = 5$. Evaluating the sample complexity expression we get $m > 3538$ *samples*

In Table 1 we show the sample complexity bounds for two network size in the uniform distribution, and in the distribution free environment (Equation 1).

Table 1. Sample complexity estimation for PAC-learning functions with SFLNNs

VC-dim	Uniform Distr.	Distr. Free
5	3538	20740
10	4578	41417

4 Function Learning with RBFNNs

Radial basis functions neural networks (RBFNNs) have two virtues: They are built as the summation of linearly independent basis functions, commonly Gaussians, and they are capable of universal approximation [15]. We are to derive a lower bound on the sample complexity required by a *RBF* neural network for function learning in the PAC framework. The VC dimension is equal to the number of nodes for as long as the basis functions remain fixed [5]. This is to say the only adaptable parameters are the "weights" thus defining properties of the basis functions are fixed. Holden and Rayner [8] discuss this issue although their bound remains rather general. Niyogi and Girosi [11] also working on statistical procedures derived an upper bound to the approximation error in the norm L_2. They also derived a loose bound to the approximation error by constructing on the PAC formalism and the covering numbers. In [12] the PAC formalism is applied to networks with wavelets as node function. Our procedure yields a tighter bound and it is expressed in terms of practical network properties (as the number of nodes).

The typical radial basis function, centered at c_j and with radius r_j, is the Gaussian

$$\phi_j(x) = \exp(-\frac{(x-c_j)^2}{r_j^2})$$

Theorem 2. (Lipschitz constant of a family of Gaussian functions) *The Lipschitz constant L of a family $\mathcal{G}$ of Gaussian functions of the form $G_n(x) = \sum_{i=1}^n a_i \cdot \phi_i(x)$, $\phi_i(x) = e^{\frac{-(x-c_i)^2}{r_i^2}}$ with $r_i = r$ and coefficients $|a_i| \le A$, is upper bounded as follows: $L \le \sqrt{(\frac{2}{\epsilon})} \cdot \frac{nA}{r}$*

Proof. By definition of Lipschitz constant

$$\frac{|f(x)-f(y)|}{|x-y|}_{x,y\in[\alpha,\beta]} \le L \le sup_{\psi\in[\alpha,\beta]}|\nabla f(\psi)|$$

For a family of Gaussians $\mathcal{G}$ of the form $G_n(x) = \sum_{i=1}^n a_i \cdot e^{\frac{-(x-c_i)^2}{r_i^2}}$, the gradient becomes

$$\frac{\partial G_n(x)}{\partial(x)} = \sum_{i=1}^{n} -2 \cdot a_i \frac{x-c_i}{r_i^2} \cdot e^{\frac{-(x-c_i)^2}{r_i^2}}$$

Calculate the derivative, make the expression equal to zero, and writing for x we get its expression for a maximum (or minimum):

$$x = \frac{r_i}{\sqrt{2}} + c_i$$

We continue with the estimation of a bound to the gradient of the Gaussian function. We will substitute $x = \frac{r}{\sqrt{2}} + c$ (that maximizes the gradient) into the gradient equation and solve it for our primary goal $\frac{\partial G_n(x)}{\partial(x)}$

$$Solve \quad \frac{\partial G_n(x)}{\partial(x)} = \sum_{i=1}^{n} -2 \cdot a_i \frac{x - c_i}{r_i^2} \cdot e^{\frac{-(x-c_i)^2}{r_i^2}} \qquad for\ x = \frac{r_i}{\sqrt{2}} + c_i$$

Taking derivatives we get:

$$\frac{\partial G_n(x)}{\partial(x)} = \sum_{i=1}^{n} \frac{-\sqrt{2}}{r_i} \cdot e^{-1/2}$$

Assuming the coefficients are bounded as $|a_i| \leq A$, and that all the Gaussian functions of the network have the same radius, and for n terms of the series, the summation yields:

$$\frac{\partial G_n(x)}{\partial(x)} \leq \sqrt{\frac{2}{e}} \cdot \frac{nA}{r}$$

Which in consequence is an upper bound to the Lipschitz constant of the family of Gaussian functions:

$$L \leq \sqrt{\frac{2}{e}} \cdot \frac{nA}{r}$$

Again, both sides of the inequality are expressed in N_2 which we can transform into N_∞. We obtain:

$$L_\infty \leq \sqrt{\frac{2}{e}} \cdot \frac{ndA}{r}$$

We have now the possibility to enunciate the main theorem on sample complexity of RBFNNs. Assume the network uses as basis functions the family of Gaussians whose Lipschitz constant was just found.

Lemma 2. (Sample Complexity for PAC-learning functions by means of Radial Basis Functions) *For a family of functions $\mathcal{G}$ with minimal $\epsilon/2$-cover of the form $G_n(x) = \sum_{i=1}^{n} a_i \cdot \phi_i(x)$, $\phi_i(x) = e^{\frac{-(x-c_i)^2}{r_i^2}}$ with $r_i = r$ and coefficients $|a_i| \leq A$, the empirical risk minimization algorithm finds an approximation $f \in \mathcal{G}$ to the target function t with accuracy and confidence parameters ϵ and δ whenever the sample complexity is*

$$m \geq \frac{8}{\epsilon^2} \ln \frac{\sqrt{\frac{2}{e}} \cdot \frac{ndA}{r}}{\delta}$$

Table 2. Sample complexity estimation for PAC-learning functions with RBFNNs

VC-dim	Uniform Distr.	Distr. Free
5	2537	20740
10	3092	41417

Proof. Substituting the bound for the Lipschitz constant into **Theorem 2**, the result follows.

A simple example. Assume we wish a RBFNN to learn an approximation to a target function, one from the entire repertory of Gaussian functions in $\mathcal{F}$. What is the sample complexity for the following expected behavior? Parameters: Max error $\epsilon = 0.1$, confidence $\delta = 0.90$, size of the learning machine $n = 5$ ($u = 4$, see Definition 2), radius $r = 1.0$, input space $d = 1$, largest coefficient $A = 5$. The evaluation of the sample complexity formula yields: $m > 2537$ *samples*

In Table 2 we show the sample complexity bounds for two network size in the uniform distribution, and in the distribution free environment (Equation 1).

A comparison of the estimated sample complexity required by SFLNNs and RBFNNs (see Tables 1 and 2) is thought-provoking since it seems to indicate *easier function learn-ability* with RBFNNs.

5 Conclusions

The bounds known so far in PAC-learning assume distribution-free data so they are quite loose. It is natural to expect tighter bounds for specific probability distributions but it is certainly worth to mention that they are smaller in around one order of magnitude. A very interesting result on the bound to the sample complexity for function learning using radial basis functions is that it is independent of the position of the centers, c_i. This means that a training algorithm to find weights and position of the centers can be computationally expensive, but that will not reduce the sample complexity.

Acknowledgments

The first author acknowledges partial support for this work from Consejo de Ciencia y Tecnología del Estado de Guanajuato (CONCyTEG) by grant No. 01-02-202-111.

References

1. M. Anthony and P. Bartlett. *Neural Network Learning: theoretical foundations.* Cambridge University Press, Cambridge, England, 1992.
2. M. Anthony and N. Biggs. *Computational Learning Theory.* Cambridge University Press, Cambridge, England, 1992.

3. Gyora M. Benedek and Alon Itai. Learnability with respect to fixed distributions. *Theoretical Computer Science*, 86:377–389, 1991.
4. Anselm Blumer, Andrzej Ehrenfeucht, David Haussler, and Manfred K. Warmuth. Learnability and the Vapnik-Chervonenkis Dimension. *Journal of the ACM*, 36(4):929–965, October 1989.
5. Vladimir S. Cherkassky and Filip M. Mulier. *Learning from Data. Concepts, Theory, and Methods.* John Wiley and Sons, Inc., New York, 1998.
6. F. Denis and R. Gilleron. Pac learning under helpful distributions. In M. Li and A. Maruoka, editors, *Algorithmic Learning Theory, ALT97.* Springer-Verlag, 1997.
7. Arturo Hernández-Aguirre. *Sample Complexity and Generalization in Feedforward Neural Networks.* PhD thesis, Department of Electrical Engineering and Computer Science, Tulane University, 2000.
8. S.B. Holden and P.J.W. Rayner. Generalization and PAC Learning: Some New Results for the Class of Generalized Single-layer Networks. *IEEE Transactions of Neural Networks*, 6(2):368–380, March 1995.
9. Natarajan B. K. *Machine Learning. A theoretical approach.* Morgan Kaufmann Publishers, San Mateo, California, 1991.
10. Kolmogorov A. N. and V. M. Tihomirov. ϵ-entropy and ϵ-capacity of sets in functional space. *Americal Mathematical Society Translations*, 17:277–364, 1961.
11. P. Niyogi and F. Girosi. On the relationship between generalization error, hypothesis complexity, and sample complexity for radial basis functions. A.I. Memo 1467, Massachusetts Institute of Technology, AI Lab, February 1994.
12. H. Qia, N. Rao, and V. Protopopescu. Pac learning using nadaraya-watson estimator based on orthonormal systems. In M. Li and A. Maruoka, editors, *Algorithmic Learning Theory, ALT97.* Springer-Verlag, 1997.
13. A. Sierra, J. Macias, and F. Corbacho. Evolution of Functional Link Networks. *IEEE Transactions on Neural Networks*, 5(1):54–65, February 2001.
14. J. Takeuchi. Some improved sample complexity bounds in the probabilistic pac learning model. In S. Doshida and K. Furukawa, editors, *Algorithmic Learning Theory, Third Workshop ALT92.* Springer-Verlag, 1993.
15. Poggio Tomaso and Federico Girosi. A theory of networks for approximation and learning. A.I. Memo No. 1140, Massachusetts Institute of Technology. Artificial Intelligence Laboratory, July 1989.
16. Vladimir Naumovich Vapnik. *The Nature of Statistical Learning Theory.* Springer-Verlag, New York, 1995.
17. Vladimir Naumovich Vapnik. *Statistical Learning Theory.* Wiley, New York, 1996.
18. M. Vidyasagar. *A theory of learning and generalization: with applications to neural networks and control systems.* Springer-Verlag, London, 1997.

Extracting Knowledge from Artificial Neural Networks: An Empirical Comparison of Trepan and Symbolic Learning Algorithms

Claudia Regina Milaré, André Carlos Ponce Leon Ferreira de Carvalho, and Maria Carolina Monard

University of São Paulo - USP
Institute of Mathematics and Computer Science - ICMC
Department of Computer Science and Statistics - SCE
Laboratory of Computational Intelligence - LABIC
P. O. Box 668, 13560-970 - São Carlos, SP, Brazil
{claudia,andre,mcmonard}@icmc.sc.usp.br

Abstract. Extracting meaningful knowledge from Artificial Neural Networks (ANNs) is a current issue since, for several applications, the ability to explain the decisions taken by ANNs is even more important than their classification performance. Although some techniques have been suggested to solve this problem, a large number of these techniques can only be applied to some specific ANNs models. This paper proposes and investigates the use of symbolic learning algorithms, such as C.45, C4.5rules [13], and CN2 [4], to extract meaningful symbolic representations from trained ANNs. The main difference of this approach with other techniques previously proposed is that it can be applied to any supervised ANN model. The approach proposed is in some way similar to the one used by the Trepan algorithm [5], which extracts a symbolic representation, expressed as a decision tree, from a trained ANN. Experimental results are presented and discussed in order to compare the knowledge extracted from several ANNs using the proposed approach and the Trepan approach. Results are compared regarding two aspects: fidelity and comprehensibility. The results obtained show that our approach, using C4.5, C4.5rules and CN2 as symbolic learning algorithms, produces in general better comprehensible symbolic representation than Trepan for the trained ANNs considered in the experiments.

1 Introduction

Artificial Neural Networks (ANNs) have been successfully applied to a large number of problems in several domain applications. For several of these domains the understanding of how ANNs arrive to their decisions is a very important issue. The knowledge acquired by ANNs is usually represented through a set of numerical values associated to their connections. Usually this representation is not easily comprehensible to humans. The lack of comprehensibility of the ANNs' decision making process is one of the main barriers to their widespread use in various practical problems.

C.A. Coello Coello et al. (Eds.): MICAI 2002, LNAI 2313, pp. 272–281, 2002.

Several techniques to extract knowledge from ANNs have been proposed to overcome the incomprehensibility of the representation learned by ANNs [1,22]. However, these techniques suffer from some limitations. Aiming to extract meaningful knowledge from ANNs, this work proposes a general approach to extract symbolic representation from trained supervised ANNs [10]. In this approach, symbolic learning algorithms, commonly used by the Machine Learning community, such as C4.5, C4.5rules [13], and CN2 [4], are used. The knowledge extracted by these algorithms (decision trees and rule sets) are usually more comprehensible to humans than the knowledge extracted by ANNs. The proposed approach is similar to the one used by the Trepan algorithm [5].

This paper is organized as follows: Section 2 briefly describes some techniques to extract knowledge from ANNs and, in particular, the Trepan algorithm, which is used in this work; Section 3 discusses the proposed approach; Section 4 shows the experiments performed in order to compare our approach with Trepan. Finally, Section 5 presents some conclusions from this work.

2 Extraction of Knowledge from ANNs

Several criterions have been proposed to classify knowledge extraction techniques according to the degree of influence of the network internal structure on the knowledge extraction process. The techniques commonly used to extract knowledge from ANNs can be classified as pedagogical, decompositional, eclectic or compositional [1,22].

The **pedagogical techniques** see a trained network as a "black box". Techniques using this approach extract knowledge that characterise the output classes directly from the inputs. Some examples of this approach are: the technique developed by Saito and Nakano [15], which searches for combinations of input values which activate each output unit; the Gallant's technique [8], which is similar to Saito and Nakano's technique; the technique Validity Internal Analysis (VIA) [21], which uses linear programming to determine if a set of constraints placed on the network activation values is consistent; the technique EN [12,11], which permits a given input/output to be associated to the corresponding output/input; the ANN-DT algorithm [17] which uses a network to generate outputs for samples interpolated from the training data set and can extract rules from feedforward networks with continuous outputs; the technique developed by Tchoumatchenko and Ganascia [20], which extracts majority-vote rules (a list of literals that can be considered as either evidence for, or evidence against, a particular class) from trained networks; and the Trepan algorithm [5], which is used in this work. Given a trained ANN and the training set used for its training, the Trepan algorithm builds a decision tree. Trepan uses the trained ANN to label the training set and builds a decision tree on this dataset. Note that the class labels used by Trepan are not necessarily the true class labels, since the ANN classification may differ from the original class values. Trepan can also automatically generate artificial data and use the trained ANN to label them. Unlike most decision tree algorithms, which separate the instances of different classes by using a single attribute to partition the input space, Trepan uses *m*-

of-n expressions for its splits. A *m-of-n* expression is a Boolean expression which is satisfied when at least m (an integer threshold) of its n conditions (Boolean conditions) are satisfied.

Decompositional techniques extract rules from individual units. The network is decomposed in small networks (one unit network). The rules extracted from these small networks are combined to form a global relationship. Examples of this approach are: the KT technique proposed by Fu [7], which searches for combinations of weights that, when satisfied, guarantee that a given unit is active regardless of the state of the other inputs to the unit; the M-of-N technique [24], which searches, for each unit, sets of input connections whose summed weights exceed its bias, irrespective of the weights associated to the other input connections; the Hayashi's technique [9], which extracts rules that can present fuzzy conditions; a technique developed by Tan [19], which extracts rules from a particular network called Fuzzy ARTMAP [3]. This rule extracting process consists in directly translating parts of the networks architecture into rules.

Eclectic techniques combine the previous approaches. They analyse an ANN at the individual unit level but also extract rules at the global level. One example of this approach is the DEDEC technique [23], which extracts if-then rules from MLP networks trained with the backpropagation algorithm [14]. DEDEC combines the knowledge embedded on the network's weight and rules extracted by a symbolic algorithm.

Compositional approach was proposed to accommodate techniques that extract rules from ensembles of units. One example of this approach is the technique proposed by Schelllammer et al. [16]. The authors trained a recurrent ANN (Elman Networks and Recurrent Cascade Correlation) to learn sequences of word categories from a first-year primary school text. The knowledge extracted by this technique is a deterministic finite-state automata (DFA). This automata represents the grammar induced by the network.

3 Proposed Approach

The techniques for knowledge extraction mentioned in Section 2 suffer from some restrictions. Most of them can not be applied to any model of ANNs. Also, most of these techniques can only be applied to problems that have exclusively discrete-valued features and require special training algorithms and neural architectures. Moreover, some of these techniques do not scale well with the network size.

On the other hand, Trepan is a general algorithm that overcomes these limitations. It can be applied to any network model, independent of its architecture, training process, attribute values and size. Trepan builds a decision tree from a training set labelled by a trained ANN and moreover, it can use additional instances artificially generated. These artificial instances are labelled by the trained ANN and they can be used in the construction of the decision tree.

The main goal of this paper is the development of a general approach that, like Trepan algorithm, extracts symbolic representations from trained ANNs. For such, it investigates the use of symbolic learning algorithms, that are able to

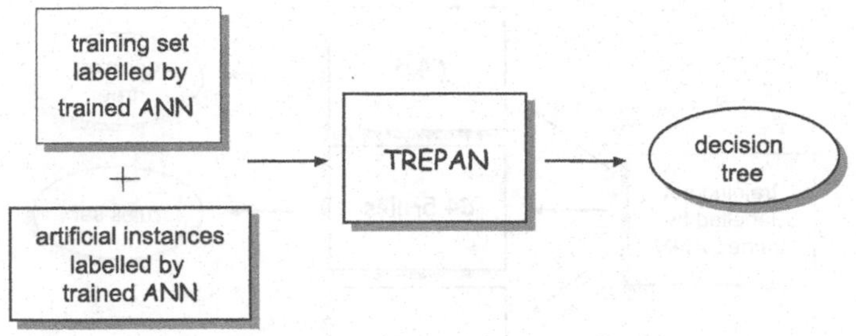

Fig. 1. General Schema of Trepan Algorithm.

learn concepts represented by propositional description, such as C4.5, C4.5rules [13] and CN2 [4], to extract symbolic representations from trained ANNs. The concepts learned by C4.5 are represented by a decision tree. A decision tree can be translated into a set of disjoint *if-then* rules. The concepts learned by CN2 and C4.5rules are represented by a set of *if-then* unordered rules. Decision trees and *if-then* rules are usually comprehensible and natural to humans.

The proposed approach in this paper, as well as the Trepan algorithm, does not suffer from the limitations previously described. It does not assume that the networks have any particular architecture, nor that they are trained in any special way. The induced symbolic representations are not directly affected by the network size. Furthermore, the proposed approach and Trepan can be used for application domain involving both real-value and discrete-value features.

Our approach, like Trepan algorithm, uses the trained ANN as a "black box" to classify the training set used for training of ANN. The training set labelled by the trained ANN is afterwards used as input to C4.5, C4.5rules and CN2. The hypotheses induced by the C4.5, C4.5rules and CN2 are then used to explain the behavior of the ANN.

However, unlike Trepan algorithm, the proposed approach does not use artificially generated instances. Figure 1 shows the general schema used by the Trepan algorithm. Similarly, Figure 2 shows the general schema of our approach using C4.5, C4.5rules and CN2 as symbolic learning algorithms.

4 Experiments

Several experiments were carried out in order to evaluate and compare the knowledge extracted from trained ANNs using the Trepan algorithm – Figure 1 – and the proposed approach – Figure 2. For such, two criteria were employed: fidelity to the ANNs from which the approaches of knowledge extraction were applied to and comprehensibility of the extracted knowledge.

Experiments were conducted on five datasets collected from the UCI repository [2]. These datasets, and their corresponding names, as shown in Table 1, are: *Heart Disease Databases (Cleveland Clinic Foundation)* (**heart**), used to diagnose heart disease; Wisconsin Breast Cancer Dataset (**breast**), used to pre-

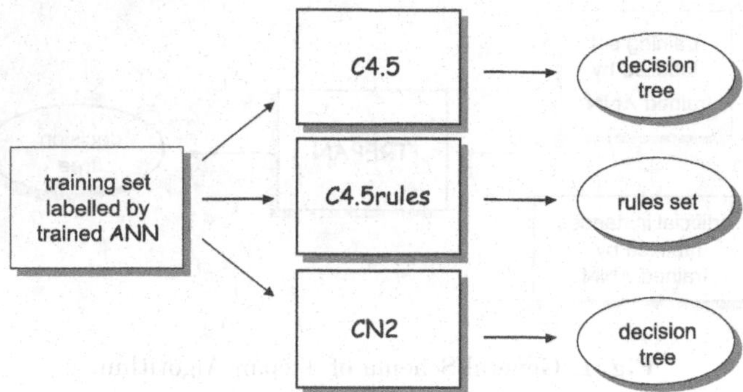

Fig. 2. General Schema of the Proposed Approach.

Table 1. Datasets Summary Description.

Dataset	#Instances	#Features (cont.,nom.)	Class	Class %	Majority Error	Missing Values
heart	303	13(6,7)	absence	54.13%	45.87%	yes
			presence	45.87%		
breast	699	9(9,0)	benign	65.52%	34.48%	yes
			malignant	34.48%		
votes	435	16(0,16)	republican	54.8%	45.2%	no
			democrat	45.2%		
pima	768	8(8,0)	0	65.02%	34.98%	no
			1	34.98%		
bupa	345	6(6,0)	1	42.03%	42.03%	no
			2	57.97%		

dict whether a tissue sample taken from a patient's breast is malign or benign; *1984 United States Congressional Voting Records Database* (**votes**), used to predict party affiliation; *Pima Indians Diabetes Database* (**pima**), used to predict whether a patient would test positive for diabetes according to the World Health Organization (WHO) criteria; *Bupa Liver Disorders* (**bupa**), used to predict liver disorders in male patients.

Table 1 summarizes these datasets. It shows, for each dataset, the number of instances (#Instances), number of continuous and nominal features (#Features), class distribution, majority error and if the dataset has missing values.

The experiments were conducted using the 10-fold cross validation methodology[1]. The fidelity and comprehensibility were measured on the examples in the test sets.

[1] A 10-fold cross-validation is performed by dividing the data into 10 mutually exclusive (folds) of cases of approximately equal size. The inducer is trained and tested 10 times; each time is tested on a fold and is trained on the dataset minus that fold. The cross-validation estimate of the accuracy is the average of the estimated accuracies from the 10 folds.

Table 2. ANN 10-Fold Cross Validation Error Rate (Mean and Standard Deviation).

heart	15.87 ± 3.02
breast	3.81 ± 0.77
votes	3.66 ± 0.85
pima	23.46 ± 1.65
bupa	35.93 ± 1.93

Fidelity is defined as the percentage of test-set examples where the classifications made by a tree or rule set agrees with those made by the associated ANN. This work uses the **infidelity rate** to measure fidelity, that is, the percentage of test-set examples where the classification made by a tree or rule set disagrees with those made by the associated ANN.

Comprehensibility is the facility which a human understands a learned hypothesis. The comprehensibility of extracted knowledge from ANNs is a very important measure for end users. Syntactic and semantic measures can be used to estimate comprehensibility. This work measures the syntactic comprehensibility, that is, the number of induced rules and the average number of condition per rule. To measure the number of rules, the decision trees induced by Trepan and C4.5 were translated to rule sets. To measure the average number of condition per rule when the decision tree uses *m-of-n* expression for its splits, the number of conditions of an *m-of-n* expression was counted as n conditions. For example, the Trepan expression $2 - of - \{x_1, \neg x_2, x_3\}$ has 3 conditions.

The ANNs used in the experiments were developed with the SNNS simulator [18]. The backpropagation with momentum algorithm [14] was used to train all the ANNs. A validation set is used to decide when the training should stop. The ANN architectures used in the experiments were chosen by trial and error from several tested architectures. The selected architectures were: **heart** (24-1-1), **breast** (9-3-1), **votes** (16-1), **pima** (8-2-1) and **bupa** (6-3-1). Table 2 shows the 10-fold cross validation error rate (the percentage of test-set examples that were not correctly classified) obtained by each ANN.

The C4.5, C4.5rules, CN2 and Trepan algorithms were used with default values assigned to their parameters. The **MinParameter** parameter of Trepan specifies the minimum number of instances (i.e. training instances plus artificial instances) to be considered before selecting each split. The default value is 1000, that is, Trepan uses 1000 instances at each node of the tree to make a decision about each split. If 1000 instances are not available in current node, Trepan generates $1000 - x$ instances (suppose x the number of available instances in current node). The **SplitTest** parameter defines if the splits at the internal nodes are *m-of-n* expressions or simple splits. The default value is *m-of-n* expression. It should be observed that C4.5 uses simple splits only.

To measure, for each dataset, the infidelity rate and comprehensibility between C4.5, C4.5rules and CN2 and the ANN, the whole dataset, after being classified by correspondent ANN (Trepan does this automatically, given the trained ANN), was feed to C4.5, C4.5rules and CN2. Thus, the class labels used for

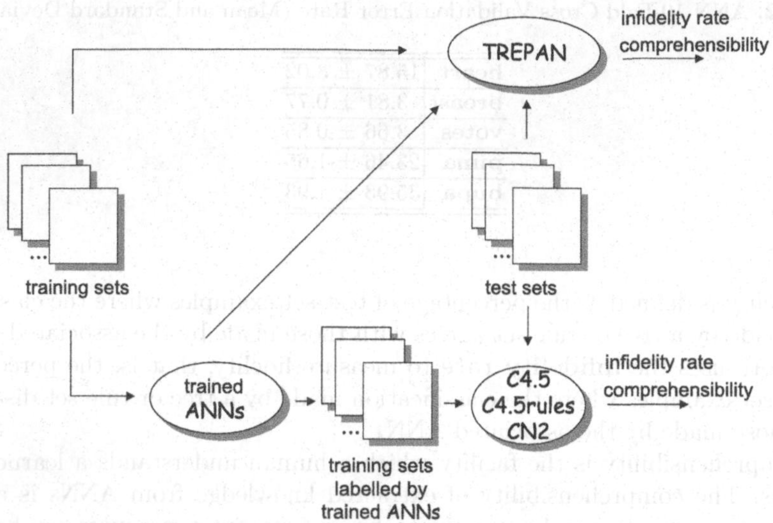

Fig. 3. Experiment Steps to Measure the Infidelity Rate and Comprehensibility.

Table 3. Infidelity Rate (Mean and Standard Deviation).

	C4.5	C4.5rules	CN2	Trepan
heart	14.51 ± 2.41	9.78 ± 1.28	11.78 ± 2.10	**6.39 ± 1.46**
breast	3.35 ± 0.49	**2.47 ± 0.48**	2.78 ± 0.83	4.38 ± 1.02
votes	1.82 ± 0.74	2.05 ± 0.71	**1.38 ± 0.61**	2.31 ± 0.77
pima	**7.04 ± 0.97**	7.17 ± 1.08	7.82 ± 1.13	8.60 ± 1.05
bupa	15.08 ± 3.45	15.36 ± 3.59	**12.74 ± 3.07**	12.99 ± 2.80

training the symbolic learning algorithms were determined by the classification provided by the ANNs for the dataset. Figure 3 shows the steps followed to measure the infidelity rate and comprehensibility.

Table 3 shows the infidelity rate obtained over the test sets. Table 4 shows the number of induced rules and Table 5 shows the average number of conditions per rule. Best average results are shown in boldface.

The *k-fold cross-validated paired t* test [6] with $k = 10$ was used to compare the infidelity rate and comprehensibility between the symbolic learning algorithms and Trepan. According to the *10-fold cross-validated paired t* test, the difference between two algorithms is statistically significant with 95% of confidence, if the result of this test is larger than 2.262 in absolute value.

Table 6 shows the results of the *10-fold cross-validated paired t* test. The symbol △ indicates that the symbolic learning algorithm (C4.5, C4.5rules or CN2) outperformed the Trepan algorithm while the symbol ▲ indicates that the outperform is at 95% confidence level. On the other hand, the symbol ▽ and ▼ indicate whenever Trepan outperforms the symbolic learning algorithms. It can be seen that although the infidelity rates associated to the symbolic learning

Table 4. Number of Induced Rules (Mean and Standard Deviation).

	C4.5	C4.5rules	CN2	Trepan
heart	18.80 ± 1.05	13.30 ± 0.73	17.70 ± 0.60	**9.10 ± 1.15**
breast	8.60 ± 0.64	7.80 ± 0.33	11.30 ± 0.47	**3.10 ± 0.67**
votes	8.00 ± 0.91	**5.50 ± 0.45**	11.70 ± 0.75	5.60 ± 0.43
pima	23.70 ± 0.78	**17.10 ± 1.06**	23.00 ± 1.13	25.00 ± 1.47
bupa	16.60 ± 3.50	**11.50 ± 2.29**	20.00 ± 3.68	21.40 ± 3.95

Table 5. Average Number of Condition per Rule (Mean and Standard Deviation).

	C4.5	C4.5rules	CN2	Trepan
heart	3.42 ± 0.08	**2.40 ± 0.04**	2.94 ± 0.11	10.23 ± 0.53
breast	3.34 ± 0.13	**2.25 ± 0.05**	2.48 ± 0.04	7.18 ± 0.38
votes	2.39 ± 0.25	**1.71 ± 0.09**	2.27 ± 0.08	7.51 ± 0.43
pima	5.40 ± 0.13	**2.77 ± 0.06**	2.86 ± 0.06	10.46 ± 0.50
bupa	4.21 ± 0.73	2.36 ± 0.40	**2.17 ± 0.38**	8.55 ± 1.47

Table 6. Results of *10-Fold Cross-Validated Paired t* Test.

	Infidelity rate			Number of induced rules			Average number of condition per rule		
	Trepan			Trepan			Trepan		
	C4.5	C4.5rules	CN2	C4.5	C4.5rules	CN2	C4.5	C4.5rules	CN2
heart	▼	▽	▽	▼	▼	▼	▲	▲	▲
breast	△	△	△	▼	▼	▼	▲	▲	▲
votes	△	△	△	▼	△	▼	▲	▲	▲
pima	△	△	△	△	▲	△	▲	▲	▲
bupa	▽	▽	△	▲	▲	△	▲	▲	▲

algorithms are usually better than those associated to Trepan, the difference is not statistically significant. The only situation where Trepan obtained a closer approximation to the ANN than the C4.5 algorithm with 95% of confidence for the **heart** dataset. As shown in Table 6, the symbolic learning algorithms obtained three statistically significant results on the number of induced rules. This seems uncommon since decision trees using *m-of-n* expressions in their splits are supposed to induce less rules than decision trees using simple splits. Regarding the average number of conditions per rule, the symbolic learning algorithms obtained superior statistically significant results than Trepan for all datasets. This was expected because decision trees with *m-of-n* expression usually induce less number of rules but having more conditions than conventional decision trees.

5 Conclusions

In this paper, a new approach to extract meaningful knowledge from trained ANNs was investigated. This approach considers the use of symbolic learning algorithms to induce comprehensible hypotheses from trained supervised ANNs in the following way: the already trained ANN is used as a "black box" to provide its own classification for the set of training instances; this newly classified set of training instances is afterwards used as input to any symbolic Machine Learning algorithm to induce its own hypothesis which is then used to explain the behavior of the ANN.

This approach is similar to the one used by the Trepan algorithm, although it does not generate new instances artificially as Trepan does.

The proposed approach was tested on five datasets using C4.5, C4.5rules and CN2 as symbolic learning algorithms. The infidelity rate and comprehensibility obtained by each algorithm were compared with Trepan. Although Trepan uses an additional set of artificial instance at each node of the tree, it obtained in only occasion a statistically superior fidelity rate compared with the symbolic algorithms (C4.5, for **heart** dataset). Regarding comprehensibility, the symbolic learning algorithms present better results than Trepan. These results indicate the potential of the C4.5, C4.5rules and CN2 algorithms to be used for extracting comprehensible knowledge from trained ANNs. Another advantage of the proposed approach is its generality. Like Trepan, it can be applied to all types of supervised ANNs, without restrictions.

In future works, the fidelity and comprehensibility of the proposed approach will be further investigated and validated on additional domains. Also, as the process of creation of artificial instances realized by Trepan does not take into consideration constraints of the domain, we plan to investigate Trepan behavior on artificial datasets.

Acknowledgments

The authors would like to thank Gustavo E. A. P. A. Batista for helpful suggestions and to CAPES for supporting this work.

References

1. R. Andrews, J. Diederich, and A. B. Tickle. A Survey and Critique of Techniques for Extracting Rules from Trained Artificial Neural Networks. *Knowledge-Based Systems*, 8(6):373–389, 1995.
2. C. Blake, E. Keogh, and C. J. Merz. UCI Repository of Machine Learning Datasets, 1998. http://www.ics.uci.edu/~mlearn/MLRepository.html.
3. G. A. Carpenter, S. Grossberg, N. Markuzon, J. H. Reynolds, and D. B. Rosen. A Neural Network Architecture for Incremental Supervised Learning of Analog Multidimensional Maps. *IEEE Transactions on Neural Networks*, 3:698–713, 1992.
4. P. Clark and T. Niblett. The CN2 Induction Algorithm. *Machine Learning*, 3(4):261–284, 1989.
5. M. W. Craven. *Extracting Comprehensible Models from Trained Neural Networks.* PhD thesis, University of Wisconsin - Madison, 1996.
6. T. G. Dietterich. Approximate Statistical Tests for Comparing Supervised Classification Learning Algorithms. *Neural Computation*, 10(7):1895–1924, 1997.

7. L. Fu. Rule Generation from Neural Networks. *IEEE Transactions on Systems, Man, and Cybernetics*, 24(8):1114–1124, 1994.
8. S. I. Gallant. *Neural Network Learning and Expert Systems.* MIT Press, 1993.
9. Y. Hayashi. A Neural Expert System with Automated Extraction of Fuzzy If-Then Rules. In *Advances in Neural Information Processing Systems*, volume 3, San Mateo, CA, 1991. Morgan Kaufmann.
10. C. R. Milaré and A. C. P. L. F. de Carvalho. Extracting Knowledge from Artificial Neural Networks using Symbolic Learning Algorithms. *Proceedings of Argentine Simposium on Artificial Inteligence - ASAI'2001*, 30:48–56, 2001.
11. M. C. Monard, C. R. Milaré, and G. E. A. P. A. Batista. A Tool to Explore Explanation Facilities in Neural Network. In *Proceedings of ACNN'98*, pages 128–132, 1998.
12. L. F. Pau and T. Götzche. Explanation Facility for Neural Networks. *Journal of Intelligent and Robotic Systems*, 5:193–206, 1992.
13. J. R. Quinlan. *C4.5 Programs for Machine Learning.* Morgan Kaufmann Publishers, CA, 1993.
14. D. Rumelhart, G. Hilton, and R. Williams. Learning Internal Representations by Error Propagation. In *Parallel Distributed Processing: Explorations in the Microstructure of Cognition. Volume 1: Foundations.* MIT Press, Cambridge, MA, 1986.
15. K. Saito and R. Nakano. Medical Diagnostic Expert System Based on PDP Model. In *Proceedings of the IEEE International Conference on Neural Networks*, pages 255–262, San Diego, CA, 1988. IEEE Press.
16. I. Schellharmmer, J. Diederich, M. Towsey, and C. Brugman. Knowledge Extraction and Recurrent Neural Networks: an Analysis of an Elman Network Trained on a Natural Language Learning Task. Technical Report 97-IS1, Queensland University of Technology, Australia, 1997.
17. G. P. J. Schmitz, C. Aldrich, and F. S. Gouws. ANN-DT: An Algorithm for Extraction of Decision Trees from Artificial Neural Networks. *IEEE Transactions on Neural Networks*, 10(6):1392–1401, November 1999.
18. SNNS. Stuttgart Neural Network Simulator, 1995. http://www.ra-informatik.uni-tuebingen.de/SNNS/.
19. A. H. Tan. Rule Learning and Extration with Self-Organizing Neural Network. In *Proceedings of the 1993 Connectionist Models Summer School*, pages 192–199, Hillsdale, NJ, 1994. Lawrence Erlbaum Associates.
20. I. Tchoumatchenko and J. G. Ganascia. A Bayesian Framework to Integrate Symbolic and Neural Learning. In *Proceedings of the Eleventh International Conference on Machine Learning*, pages 302–308, New Brunswick, NJ, 1994. Morgan Kaufmann.
21. S. Thrun. Extracting Rules from Artificial Neural Networks with Distributed Representations. In *Advances in Neural Information Processing Systems (Volume 7)*, Cambridge, MA, 1995. MIT Press.
22. A. B. Tickle, R. Andrews, M. Golea, and J. Diederich. The Truth will Come to Light: Directions and Challenges in Extracting the Knowledge Embedded within Trained Artificial Neural Networks. *IEEE Transactions on Neural Networks*, 9(6):1057–1068, 1998.
23. A. B. Tickle, M. Orlowski, and J. Diederich. DEDEC: Decision Detection by Rule Extraction from Neural Network. Technical report, QUT NRC, September 1994.
24. G. Towell and J. W. Shavlik. The Extraction of Refined Rules from Knowledge-Based Neural Networks. *Machine Learning*, 131:71–101, 1993.

Improving Pattern Recognition Using Several Feature Vectors

Patricia Rayón Villela[1] and Juan Humberto Sossa Azuela[2]

[1] Insituto Tecnológico y de Estudios Superiores de Monterrey-Campus Ciudad de México, Calle del Puente 222, Ejidos de Huipulco, México, D.F., 14380. México
prayon@campus.ccm.itesm.mx

[2] Centro de Investigación en Computación-IPN, Av. Juan de Dios Batíz, esquina con Miguel Otón de Mendizábal, México, D.F., 07738. México
hsossa@cic.ipn.mx

Abstract. Most pattern recognition systems use only one feature vector to describe the objects to be recognized. In this paper we suggest to use more than one feature vector to improve the classification results. The use of several feature vectors require a special neural network, a supervised ART2 NN is used [1]. The performance of a supervised or unsupervised ART2 NN depends on the appropriate selection of the vigilance threshold. If the value is near to zero, a lot of clusters will be generated, but if it is greater, then must clusters will be generated. A methodology to select this threshold was first proposed in [2]. The advantages to use several feature vectors instead of only one are shown on this work. We show some results in the case of character recognition using one and two feature vectors. We also compare the performance of our proposal with the multilayer perceptron.

Keywords: Pattern Recognition, Supervised ART2 Neural Network, Multilayer perceptron, Digit recognition.

1 Introduction

In general, pattern classification involves mapping a pattern correctly from the so-called feature space into a class-membership space [4]. The decision-making process in pattern classification can be thus summarized as follows. Consider a pattern represented as an n-dimensional feature vector.

$$X = [x_1, x_2, \ldots, x_n] \tag{1}$$

The task is to assign this vector to one of the K classes $C_1, C_2, \ldots, C_K$. Any supervised or unsupervised approach needs the description of the objects as a feature vector.

Supervised learning uses feature vectors with class labels, unsupervised learning uses feature vectors but without labels. The existence of a specific desired output for

C.A. Coello Coello et al. (Eds.): MICAI 2002, LNAI 2313, pp. 282–291, 2002.

each of the training set vector is what differentiates supervised from unsupervised learning [4].

The feed-forward multilayer perceptron is one of the most common neural networks with supervised learning, and it is normally trained by backpropagation [5]. ALOPEX is a stochastic parallel algorithm that treats the learning process in a neural network as an optimization problem [6]. The ART2-NN is an unsupervised classifier that accepts input vectors that are next classified according to the stored pattern they most resemble. The ART2 NN can adaptively create a new cluster corresponding to an input pattern if it is determined to be "sufficiently" different from the existing clusters. This is controlled by a vigilance threshold ρ [7]. Thus the ART2 NN allows the user to control the degree of similarity patterns placed in the same cluster. We use the same technique to select the threshold value, proposed on [2] is used.

In this paper we propose how to use de ART2 NN in a supervised way, using several feature vectors, instead of only one. Results for digit recognition are also presented.

2 Supervised ART2-NN

In this section the supervised version of the ART2 NN is briefly described. For the correct functioning of this supervised version, the following points are considered.

- An object is described by a set of sub-feature vectors, instead of only one feature vector, and
- For each sub-feature vector a vigilance threshold ρ is obtained.

Once these steps have finished, the supervised ART2-NN, can be used for training or recognition. The proposed NN is composed by several classifiers, each one with a standard ART2-NN connected to a memory map (MM), a set of logical AND gates that determine the operation mode: (0) training and (1) recognition. The outputs of the classifier are connected to a common adder and a set of comparators is used to select a reduced list of candidates. Each of the classifiers must be trained, and each MM should be constructed before the indexing stage can be used. All these stages are explained on the following sections.

2.1 Sub-feature Vectors

A supervised version of the ART2 is used in this paper. The advantage when using a supervised neural network is that we always know which features describe which object.

By using several feature vectors, classification is improved because the objects share common features. For example, the hair, the mouth, eyes, and so on can describe a person, and the features that describes each person, also belongs to another one.

The main advantages to describe an object by a set of feature vectors instead of only one are: 1) the information is distributed, 2) several feature vectors describe an object, 3) objects from different classes share common features and 4) variations among the different elements of one feature vector will be the same.

Once an object has been described by a set of sub-feature vectors, how can we use this information to get a classification using the supervised and unsupervised ART2 NN? At this point we have a set of sub-feature vectors (SFVs) for the different objects, but we do not know how many types of features we have, i.e., how many clusters for each SFV.

The problem is how to decide how many clusters should be generated. In a supervised problem, the number of clusters is given; the problem is that in most of the cases these are not known a priori. How to decide the number of clusters that are enough to any application is an open problem. To override this problem we propose to use the traditional supervised ART2 NN. The correct use of the ART2 needs for each SFV, the corresponding vigilance threshold ρ. The number of clusters obtained by the ART2 NN depends on this threshold values. The way to select this value is fully described in [2] and briefly described in Section 2.2. Thus the number of clusters for each SFV is given by the unsupervised ART2-NN.

Once the clusters have been generated, the information about to which objects these clusters belong is stored on a memory map, this step is considered in the supervised stage.

During the classification stage, the set of SFVs is given, and then the classification process gives a list of candidates that match these features. If the classifier does not let the features to be shared, then only one candidate is given.

2.2 Threshold Selection

The functioning of the ART2 NN is based on the selection of the vigilance threshold ρ. If a small value is selected, then similar features will be put in different clusters and then a lot of clusters will be generated. In the other hand, if a greater value is selected, then many clusters will be generated. This means that different features will be merged into the same cluster.

If a feature vector describes an object then just a threshold value should be selected, but if the object is described by several SFVs, then a threshold value for each SFV should be selected.

To select a suitable threshold, the following procedure is used with the aim to increase the intra-class distance and to decrease the inter-class distance.

If an object O_i belongs to class C_n, and an object O_j belongs to a different class C_m, then object O_i is differentiated from object O_j if they are classified into different classes, i.e.

$$O_i \in C_n \qquad O_j \in C_m \qquad \text{for } n \neq m$$

They get confused if they are clustered together.

$$O_i \in C_n \qquad O_j \in C_m \qquad \text{for } n = m$$

Now, if CD is the number of objects from different classes that can be differentiated, and CC the number of objects from the same class that are misclassified. The procedure to get the threshold value for supervised learning can be summarized as follows: select a value giving the greatest differentiation between objects belonging to different classes, giving at the same time the least confusion (misclassification) between objects belonging to the same class. The aim is to maximize *CD* and to minimize *CC*.

Let $v = CD\text{-}CC$. If $v=0$ then the threshold value does not differentiate, confusing thus among classes. If $v>0$ then the threshold value gets a better discrimination, giving a poor confusion among classes. If $v<0$ then the threshold value gets a greater confusion, giving a poor discrimination.

These three cases indicates that a positive value of v exhibits a better discrimination while a negative value shows a greater confusion; a value near to zero does not discriminate, neither it confuses. Considering these cases, we conclude that the criterion to be maximized should be positive and as greater as possible.

2.3 Training

For each SFV a classifier with its corresponding MM and ART2-NN as the one shown on Fig. 1 are used. The MM is a bi-dimensional array connected to the output of the ART2-NN with as many rows as clusters generated by the ART2, and as many columns as objects to recognize. The number of clusters generated by the ART2 depends on the vigilance threshold ρ [3]; it is during the training of each ART2, that each MM is constructed. The value on each cell of a particular MM represents the times a SFV is present on each object.

If we want to recognize, for example, 5 different objects with a SFV of 3 elements, the corresponding architecture for that SFV is shown on Fig. 1; in the example a SFV for object 3 is fed to the NN, this is classified into cluster 3, so cell (3,3) on the memory map is increased by 1. If a SFV is different from the existing ones, then a new cluster and a new row is created. Once the SFVs had been learned, the MM is weighted depending on the number of objects containing that SFV.

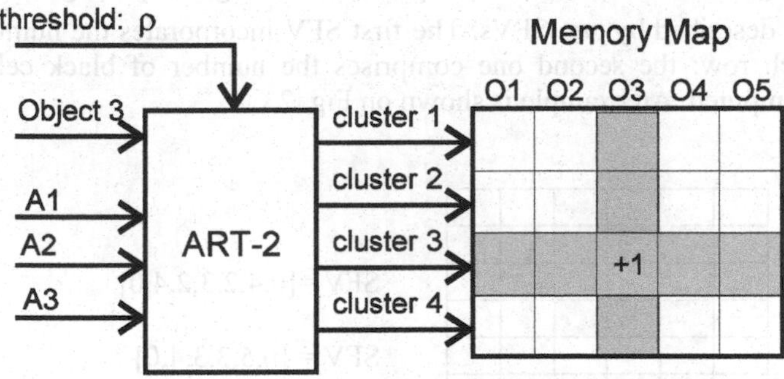

Fig. 1. Supervised ART2-NN during training

2.4 Indexing

During this stage the set of SVFs extracted from a test image are used to retrieve from the MM the objects that produced that SFVs giving as a result a list of candidate models. This list is finally reduced by means of a threshold mechanism. These two indexing steps are next explained in more detail.

2.4.1 Candidate Selection

During this step, each SFV in the test image is presented to the supervised ART2-NN. If this SFV is closed enough to one of the SFVs already learned by the NN then the corresponding NN's output would be turned on, selecting a row of the MM. Those objects for which their corresponding location values in this row are greater than 0 will receive the votes into the evidence-register. This process is repeated for each SFV in the test image. At the end of this process we will have as a result the set of hypotheses arranged as a histogram of votes. This histogram is obtained from the evidence-register.

2.4.2 Candidate Reduction

At the end of the candidate selection process we will have a histogram containing the number of votes that each model has received during this process. Intuitively, those objects with more votes are the best candidates. One way to decide which objects are present in the input image is by using a selection-threshold σ. This value is obtained considering the number of SFVs describing each object.

3 Digit Recognition

In this section the performance of the supervised ART2 NN and the multilayer perceptron is tested in the case of the digit recognition. Three different scenarios are considered:

1. Digit recognition with the supervised ART2 NN, using two SFVs.
2. Digit recognition with the supervised ART2-NN using one SFV.
3. Digit recognition with the multilayer perceptron using backpropagation.

Each digit is described by two SFVs. The first SFV incorporates the number of black cells for each row; the second one comprises the number of black cells for each column is computed. An example is shown on Fig. 2.

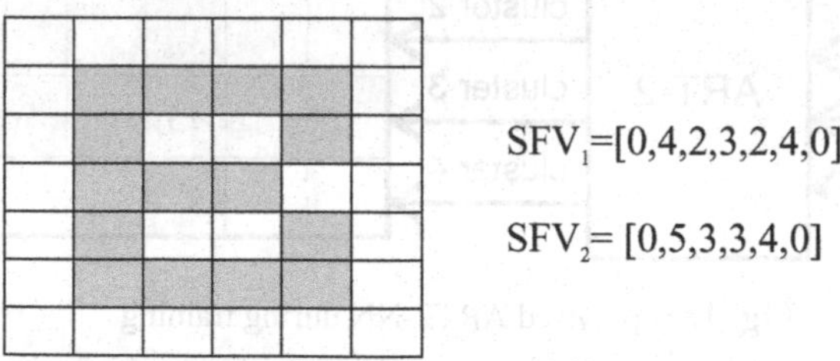

Fig. 2. Extraction for the SFV1 and SFV2

For each object on Fig. 3, the SFVs are obtained, and the procedure to select the vigilance threshold for each SFV described in Section 2.2 is applied.

For a given set of digits, these two features vectors are computed. In scenario 1, these two SFVs are used, each one with its corresponding supervised ART2-NN. In scenarios 2 and 3 we consider these two SFVs, but these are represented using just one SFV, for the example on Fig. 2, the SFV is given by [0,4,2,3,2,4,0,5,3,3,4,0]. For each digit, 4 different patterns were used during training, a total of 40 different patterns were used during training. Fig. 3 shows the training set.

Tables 1, 2 and 3 show the results obtained. The initial value for the threshold was selected according to column *thr*. This column has the threshold value that a specific class needs to classify all the objects (maximize CD). Then the average of these values is the initial threshold value. For each threshold value, and for each class (each digit), the CC and CD values are calculated. Finally the difference between CD and CC are shown on the last row. The smallest value is selected as the vigilance threshold. Table 1 shows the results for scenario 1, for SFV1 (1.72). The results for the SFV2 are shown on Tables 2 and 3.

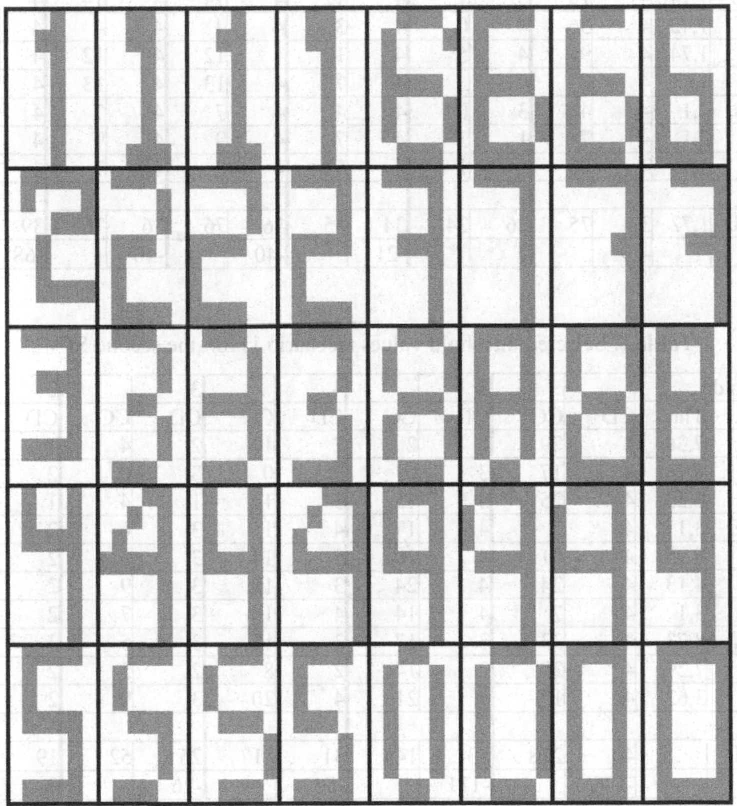

Fig. 3. Set used for training, 4 different patterns were used for each digit

As we can see on Table 2 the selected threshold value is 2, nevertheless to guarantee a good selection, the procedure is repeated. The results on Table 3 show that the recommended value for the SFV 2 should be chosen between 1.4 and 1.2. We choose 1.3 as the threshold value. For scenario 2, the suggested threshold is 1.7 (see Table 4).

Once the threshold values have been obtained, the ART2 NN is trained using their corresponding threshold values. During training the clusters are generated, and the information is stored. For each cluster generated by the ART2 NN, the column corresponding to the object is increased by one. In the case of scenario number 1, 14 different clusters were generated by the ART2 with the selected thresholds for the SFV1, and for the SFV2, 29 different clusters were generated.

Table 1. Selected threshold values (scenario 1) for the first SFV

Threshold				1,72		2,06		2,24		2,41		2,58	
	Thr	CD	CC	CD	CC	CD	CC	CD	CC	CD	CC	CD	CC
ZERO	1,41	4	1	3	0	3	4	3	6	3	12	3	12
ONE	2,25	4	0	0	0	3	0	4	0	4	0	4	1
TWO	2,26	4	9	3	5	3	5	4	10	4	10	4	13
THREE	1,74	4	10	3	7	4	12	4	14	4	14	4	16
FOUR	1,42	4	36	4	0	4	3	4	4	4	4	4	4
FIVE	1,74	4	9	4	5	4	12	4	12	4	12	4	13
SIX	1,1	4	0	4	3	4	7	4	13	4	13	4	16
SEVEN	2,1	4	4	3	0	4	4	4	7	4	7	4	10
EIGHT	2,1	4	7	1	3	4	7	4	9	4	9	4	14
NINE	1,1	4	0	4	1	4	5	4	7	4	7	4	8
TOTAL	1,72	36	75	26	24	34	55	36	76	36	76	39	107
V		-39		2		-21		-40		-40		-68	

Table 2. Selected threshold values (scenario 1) for the second SFV

Threshold				5		4		3		2	
	Thr	CD	CC	CD	CC	CD	CC	CD	CC	CD	CC
ZERO	7,36	4	29	2	2	2	10	2	4	1	1
ONE	8,73	4	17	3	0	3	0	3	0	2	0
TWO	6,25	4	25	3	15	3	10	1	4	1	2
THREE	3,1	4	7	4	17	4	15	3	6	2	2
FOUR	8,95	4	31	4	20	3	14	3	3	2	2
FIVE	4,13	4	24	4	24	3	18	3	9	2	3
SIX	3,1	4	7	4	14	4	10	3	7	2	1
SEVEN	8,73	4	33	3	17	3	12	3	5	3	2
EIGHT	7,29	4	28	2	14	2	8	2	5	2	1
NINE	3,62	4	17	4	21	4	20	3	9	2	2
TOTAL		40	218	33	144	31	117	26	52	19	16
V		-178		-111		-86		-26		3	

The number on each cell of the memory map tells us how many times a feature was selected for an object. The rows are the number of clusters generated by the ART2 NN and the columns are the objects that we want to recognize. As we mentioned, the number of clusters generated by the ART2 NN depends on the threshold value, for the SFV1 a value of 1.72 was used, and 1.3 for SFV2.

On the memory map the features of each object are stored, during the training stage. The MM let us get information about the features shared by some objects.

Table 3. Selected threshold values (scenario 1) for the second SFV

Threshold	1.8		1.6		1.4		1.2		1	
	CD	CC	CD	CC	CD	CC	CD	CC	CD	CC
ZERO	1	1	1	1	1	0	1	0	1	0
ONE	2	0	2	0	1	0	1	0	1	0
TWO	1	2	1	2	1	0	1	0	1	0
THREE	2	2	2	0	2	0	2	0	1	0
FOUR	2	2	2	2	2	0	2	0	1	0
FIVE	2	3	2	3	1	1	1	1	1	1
SIX	2	1	2	1	2	0	2	0	2	0
SEVEN	3	2	3	1	2	0	2	0	1	0
EIGHT	2	1	2	1	1	0	1	0	1	0
NINE	2	2	2	1	2	0	2	0	2	0
TOTAL	19	16	19	12	15	1	15	1	12	1
V	3		7		14		14		11	

Table 4. Selected threshold values (scenario 2) for the first SFV

Threshold	1.13		1.7		2.26		2.83		3.4		4.08	
	CD	CC	CD	CC	CD	CC	CD	CC	CD	CC	CD	CC
ZERO	1	0	1	1	1	2	2	4	2	9	2	10
ONE	1	0	2	0	3	0	3	0	3	0	3	0
TWO	1	0	1	2	1	3	1	4	2	7	3	10
THREE	2	0	1	1	3	2	3	6	4	9	4	15
FOUR	2	0	2	2	2	2	3	2	3	8	3	15
FIVE	1	1	2	3	3	6	3	9	3	15	3	20
SIX	2	0	2	1	2	4	3	7	4	8	4	10
SEVEN	2	0	3	1	3	4	3	5	3	9	3	12
EIGHT	1	0	2	1	2	3	2	5	2	8	2	8
NINE	2	0	2	1	2	4	2	10	2	17	4	20
TOTAL	15	1	18	13	22	30	25	52	28	90	31	120
V	14		5		-8		-27		-62		-89	

Once the information has been trained and stored, a new object can be classified. The supervised ART2 NN selects the cluster that most resemble an input, that cluster is then selected. All the objects sharing that feature receive the number of votes previously stored during the training stage. At the final stage a list of candidates is obtained during the classification process. One of the advantages to select a set of SFVs, instead of only one, is that each SFV selects the objects sharing that feature.

Once the NN was trained for the 3 scenarios, different objects from those used during training are used. Some classification results are shown on Table 5.

The same patterns used to train the supervised ART NN were used to train a multilayer perceptron using the backpropagation rule. The 3 different NNs were tested with different objects used during training. A set of these objects is shown on Fig. 4. The classification results are shown on Table 5. As we can see from this table, the supervised ART2 NN (in the cases of one and two features vectors) shows a better performance than the multilayer perceptron. As we can see from Fig. 4, for objects b and d, the output given by the multilayer perceptron was digit 1, with the supervised

ART2 NN; the given output was a most suitable digit than digit 1. In general the performance of the supervised ART2-NN was better than the multilayer perceptron.

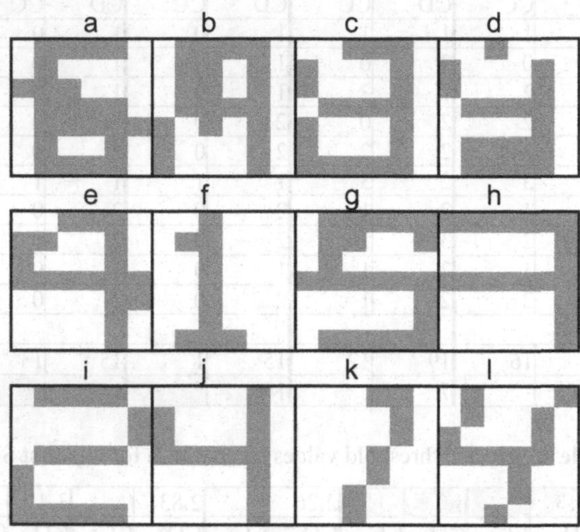

Fig. 4. Test set used for the 3 recognition cases

As we have mentioned, the supervised ART2-NN gives a list of candidates indicating the objects that most resembling the object at the input. Table 5 shows the results for the test patterns on Fig. 4. The number of votes for each digit, and the number that is recognized, is indicated on it. For example, for object (a) on Fig. 4, the output of the supervised ART2-NN using two SFVs was 4 votes for digit 6, and 2 votes for digit 8; and using one SFV, it was 2 votes for digit 6 and 2 votes for digit 8. As we can see, the advantage of using two SFVs is that the object most resembling the input pattern, gets more votes than the others.

4 Conclusions

In this paper we proposed to use a supervised ART2 NN using several feature vectors to recognize objects. The advantage to use several SFVs is that the information is distributed obtaining thus a better performance. Instead of having a candidate at the output, we get a list of ordered candidates in terms of the times they were indexed by each SFVs. This decreases misclassification. Another advantage is the using of a memory map. Here the information is stored and weighted. The information stored can be used to know where a given feature is found in an object. If it happens that different objects share a feature, the weight for this feature is proportional to the number of objects sharing it. On the other hand, if a feature belongs to just one object, then this feature is most relevant for that object.

Compared with the multilayer perceptron, the performance of the supervised ART2 NN was better. Table 5 shows the classification results. There were some cases where the output for the multilayer perceptron was near to zero; this was not the case for the supervised ART2-NN.

Table 5. Clasification results for the test objects on Fig. 4, for the three different cases

	scenario 1	scenario 2	scenario 3
a	6(4) 8(2)	6(2) 8(2)	8
b	8(2.5) 0 (1)	9(4) 8(1)	1
c	6(4) 8(2)	9(2)	8
d	0(2) 8(1.5)	3(1) 4(1)	1
e	4(4) 9(4)	9(4) 4(1)	4
f	1(4) 0(1)	1(3) 5(1)	1
g	2(1.5) 8(1)	8(2) 2(1)	----
h	9(4) 7(3)	4(1) 7(1)	4
i	2(1.5) 8(1)	2(1.5) 0(1)	----
j	4(4) 9(4)	4(3) 9(2)	4
k	1(4) 7(1)	7(2) 5(1.5)	3
l	4(4) 9(4)	5(1.5) 4(1)	4

Acknowledgments

We would like to thank the reviewers for their pertinent comments and the CONACYT, the ITESM and the CIC-IPN for their economical support for the development of this research.

References

1. H. Sossa, P. Rayón y J. Figueroa. Arquitectura basada en redes neuronales para el reconocimiento de rostros. Soluciones Avanzadas. Año 7, No. 63. Noviembre 1998.
2. P. Rayón and H. Sossa. A procedure to select the vigilance threshold for the ART2 for supervised and unsupervised training. LNAI 1793, pp. 389-400, Springer Verlag, 2000.
3. G.A. Carpenter and S. Grossberg, ART2: self-organizing of stable category recognition codes for analog input patterns. *Applied Optics*, 26, pp. 4919-4930, 1987.
4. R. Schalkoff, *Pattern Recognition: statistical, structural and neural approaches*. John Wiley & Sons, Inc., 1992.
5. J.A. Freeman and D. M. Skapura, *Neural Networks: algorithms, applications and programming techniques*. Addison Wesley, 1992.
6. A.S. Pandya and R. B. Macy, *Pattern Recognition with Neural Networks in C++*. IEEE Press, 1995.
7. G. Francis, The stability-plasticity dilemma in competitive learning. Department of Psychology Sciences. Purdue University. Technical Report No. 96-1, 1996.
8. C.G. Looney, *Pattern Recognition using Neural Networks*. Oxford University Press, 1999.

Learning Optimization in a MLP Neural Network Applied to OCR

Isis Bonet Cruz[1], Adolfo Díaz Sardiñas[1], Rafael Bello Pérez[1], and Yanetsy Sardiñas Oliva[2]

[1] Departamento de Ciencias de la Computación, Universidad Central de Las Villas, Carretera a Camajuaní Km 5½, Santa Clara, Villa Clara, Cuba, CP: 54830.
{isisb,adolfod, rbellop}@uclv.edu.cu

[2] Empresa de Servicios Informáticos, Circunvalación Norte, Ciego de Ávila, Cuba.
yanetsy@esica.co.cu

Abstract. This paper focuses on the possibilities of optimization of the training process of an MLP neural net using Backpropagation as a learning algorithm, employed as a classifier in an Optical Character Recognition (OCR) application. Also, the process for determination of a set of optimal parameters describing the characters that conform each class is described. The processing and analysis of the images in BMP, GIF, JPG and TIF format are included. A comparative study of the possibilities of improvement of the learning process of an MLP net employing heuristics for its design and training is made. As a fundamental result a substantial improvement of the net learning process is obtained and an OCR of great reliability is built.

1 Introduction

This project arises with as a necessity of transforming graphic documents into text, in order to facilitate the search on them. An OCR was implemented with the objective of being used in the office applications that are developed in the group AvilaSoft of the Empresa de Servicios Informáticos de Ciego de Ávila (ESICA).

For the Control of Documents that one of the office applications, a tool like this adds it bigger possibilities and efficiency in the search. It also helps to reduce the size of the files, because the scanned documents (TIFF) are files of great size, and to store them in text format diminishes it considerably.

An OCR is a software that allows characters recognizing. The method begins with an image of a text document, and through a series of modifications and processing, the image is finally translated to a text format.

Three processes are essential in the systems of characters recognition:

- Representation Process, where the scanned image of the document is treated in different ways to achieve a form of high level of the data. The image should be segmented to separate its elements, being obtained a group of small images as a result, where each one represents a character. The extraction of special characteristic and patterns of the image take the digitized data at a higher level. This is called extraction of features.

C.A. Coello Coello et al. (Eds.): MICAI 2002, LNAI 2313, pp. 292–300, 2002.

- Process of Generation of a Base of Knowledge. It contains a high level representation of all the well-known characters. This is the step where the system learns how to recognize the classes.
- Identification - Classification Process. Due to its high level representation and the information learned from the base of knowledge, it classifies the unknown character. There are different identification methods.

Among the formats of images it can be mentioned: BMP, GIF, JPG and TIF. Finally, to complete an OCR's functionality a first step is to read the files and to go analyzing them according to the description of the image format representing it, to take them to a common representation in form of a binary matrix, in which each element represents a pixel. Then, it corresponds the detection and extraction of the lines and later on the characters inside the line. In a second step, starting from the sub-matrix that describes the possible character a series of form parameters, distribution of white and black, position inside the line, etc. are calculated, allowing arrive to a detailed description of the portions of images. In a third step these constitute the entrances to a neuronal network (MLP topology) that is the one that finally makes the recognition and it returns the code of the element closest to the received description of the features of the minimum image. Once these codes are recognized and stored, they are taken to the output format text.

2 Image Processing

It should be kept in mind that the processing and the analysis of images are two different processes. The difference among them resides, fundamentally, in the extraction of information of the image. Images processing, as the processing of words, is the science of the reorganization. For example, the values of the pixels can be altered based on the shine and the established threshold or the shine of their neighbors, but the total quantity of pixels is unalterable. The analysis of the image, in contrast, tries to find the descriptive parameters that represent information of importance in the image. Of course, the steps of the processing are essential to carry out the analysis of the image.

For the processing of the image after the study of each of the formats that will be (BMP, JPG, GIF, TIF) it proceeded to transform them into a standard. These formats are transformed into a binary matrix, where each element contains the information of a pixel. The pixels with value 1 indicate that it is part of an object and with value 0 that belongs to the background.

The next step was the detection of components of the text, keeping in mind that a component is that element inside a binary matrix with logical sense, that is to say, lines, words, CharBoxs[1] and characters. Each component has a position and some dimensions inside the matrix.

This matrix, as the text that we commonly see, is composed of lines that would be sub-matrices separated by rows in white. As the matrix is binary, it is considered that a line is a minimum portion of the matrix that is defined by rows, where all the elements are zeros. For the detection of the lines we start with the beginning of the matrix, looking for the first row where at least one element is different from 0. It is

[1] Pixels matrix, which have a minimal with and the height of the line.

considered that there a line begins, and that all the rows that are in a serial way starting from this where some point 1 exists they will be part of the same one, until you arrive to a row where all the squares are 0, what would represent a complete white line in the image, and therefore a separation among components. Starting from that position, the same process continues until sweeping the whole matrix.

This same way each line is made up of words and these of characters. Once concluded the process of detection of lines, its necessary to check them, one to one, vertically to find in them the sub-matrices that delimits the objects. That is to say, those sub-matrices that are inside a line separated by pixels columns in white and with the same one high of the line, these were denominated CharBox (See Fig.1).

Results on the second line:

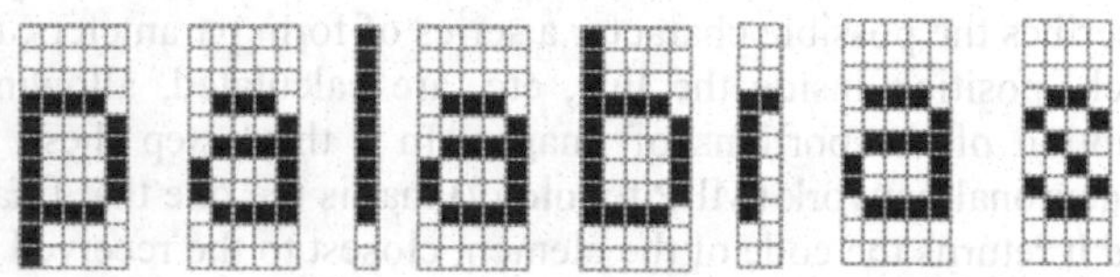

Fig. 1. Detection of the CharBoxs

These sub-matrices are not the smallest that can represent the characters because the line is defined on the upper part by the highest elements in the same one (l and b), and for the inferior one for the lowest (p), being in most of the cases white lines that don't constitute information of the object. So once again a purification process is made with those matrices, to eliminate those lines in white. These minimum sub-matrices that can be obtained of these CharBoxs contain what will be denominated character (to See Fig.2).

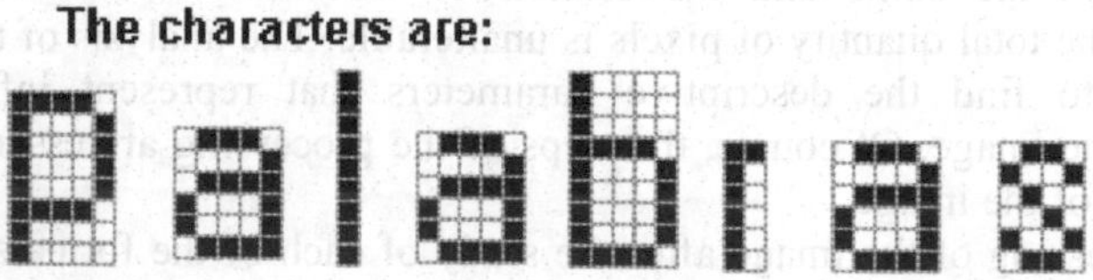

The characters are:

Fig. 2. Detection of the characters

The other elements of writing to be considered are the words. But really in the recognition process it doesn't influence at all. It would be important to keep them in mind when the exit, but as each object has associated its position in the matrix, it can be calculated when there is a change of word and to insert a space among them at the end. A word is (nothing but) a group of successive CharBoxs separated by a space.

3 Selection of Parameters to Describe the Characters

For a system of computing vision to carry out the "learning" it is needed the specification of a group of features or describers, from which each one of the objects studied is characterized. It is also necessary that this group of variables or features be sufficiently appropriate for the problem that is analyzed, in the sense of their discrimination. Only this property will facilitate that the system, during its learning be able to arrive to valid conclusions that allows it to carry out with success its future classification function.

The realization of these systems has a crucial step choosing the appropriate parameters to describe the objects. Once the required image processing has been done. In order to subdivide the image in its logical components up to the minimum component, the path to the image analysis is opened up. It is of usual interest to characterize the image for a group of describers, which should be insensitive to size variations, rotation, adjournment, etc. To the components of the image is applied size mensurations, position and form until establishing uniqueness, so that they can be differentiated through these measures.

For the implementation of the OCR there are several criterions to follow and variations for the definition of their entrances. One of them is for example, that the image of the character to classify, is segmented in a series of sub-matrix of NxN and that these constitute the entrances to the neural net and is compared directly with a filed representation. In this case, the net will take as many parameters as many pixels contained in the image matrix being analyzed. This brings the disadvantage that in order to achieve it, such matrix should complete restrictions of size, or at fewer of proportionality with the N that is taken like criterion for the dimensions of the same, and that when change the thickness of the letter or the size, could bring big difficulties because they modify certain criterions of relationship. Another pattern of classification is based on non-geometric characteristic as the density, or in the calculation of characteristics or complex mathematical transformations.

In this OCR, these matrix are not taken directly like entrances to the neural net, neither applies mathematical transformations of complexity to the function that describes the image but, that are proceeded to the definition and calculation of a series of parameters of form, distribution of black points, inclination, etc, that they describe such matrixes and that they complete the following basic conditions:

- Little variation inside of the class.
- Great separation of class.

That is to say, those elements of equal class have similar outputs in the group of analyzed parameters, as output of the classification. And that for cases of objects of different classes the outputs are very distant so as to distinguish that they don't coincide in the answer of the process of recognition.

In order to choose the parameters it was tried to search for the form in which the man can differentiate the characters for their characteristics, trying to reflect them in mathematical form. This way 42 describers were taken into account at first.

Multiple tests were made in order to know what minimal group of features was enough in order to describe the characters. In this study we found some that far of helping, hindered the recognition when the size of the character varied much. For example, a parameter of size that gave the relationship between the perimeter and the area didn't help to the recognition of the characters of different sizes.

After this exhaustive study it was decided the use of 21 parameters. Some of these measures were applied to the characters and others to the CharBoxs, because in some occasions the character didn't have all the necessary information. These parameters were based on statistical describers. Each one has a numeric value as a result. The used statistical describers can be divided in topological and geometric. The topological are those that have to do with the connection of the components and the holes inside character.

The calculated parameters are described as follows:

- *Euler number*: It is a topological parameter that describes the structure of the object, without keeping in mind its geometric form. As a typical topological describer, it makes mention to form properties that don't change with the size. The Euler number (E), or connectivity factor, is related to the number of connected components (Nc) and to the number of holes (Na) in each one. This can be defined as:

$$E = Nc - Na \tag{1}$$

This parameter is a local measure obtained as the sum of measures in local neighbors.

Separating the characters keeping in mind their quantity of components and their openings was an advanced step and allowed making groups of characters. The value of Euler could be 0, 1, 2, 3 and- 1. These values divide the characters into 5 sub-sets. The groups are divided into those that consists of an only simple component and no opening, a component simple and an hole, an only component and 2 holes, two components and no hole, and those that has three components.

Divided this way, the characters, in five groups, we proceed to analyze how to differentiate them within each one of these groups. Keeping in mind that the holes could be in different places within the character the Euler number for two parts of the character was calculated.

- *Euler number of the upper component*: It calculates the Euler number of the upper component, in case of existing this component; it allows to differentiate, for instance, stress of the ú from the diereses " ü ".
- *Euler number of the inferior component*: It calculates the Euler number of the inferior component, in case of existing this component; it allows to differentiate in the accented letters, a "á" of a " i ", since their Euler number is different.
- *Quantity of connected components*: This measure is also guided to look for connected components, but in this case those that are separated by horizontal lines, for example the " i " has two and the " l " one.
- *Form describer starting from the width and the high*: It gives the proportion of aspect of the image Width/High of the character.
- *Describer to differentiate the character height*: This parameter calculates the relationship between the quantity of rows in white above the character and below it, in order to know the position of the character inside the line, that is to say, if it is a high letter as the " l ", lower as the " p ", or central as the " a ".
- *Quantity of vertical lines*: It calculates the quantity of matrix regions that take its complete width and its positions. For example, this way " l " differs from " i ".
- *Quantity of horizontal lines*: It calculates the quantity of matrix regions that take its complete width and its positions. For example, it helps to differentiate the "E" from the "F"
- *Changes of white to black in the first row*: It calculates the quantity of contrast changes in the suitable row, for example, to differentiate the "n" from the " m " it is very useful. It is considered contrast change the step from 0 to 1, or vice versa.

- *Changes of white to black in the central row*: Idem to the previous one, but taking the central row.
- *Changes of white to black in the last row*: Idem to the previous one, but taking the last row.
- *Changes of white to black in the first column*: Idem to what was explained previously, but in this case for columns, taking like reference the first in this case.
- *Changes of white to black in the last column*: Idem to the previous one, but for the last column.
- *Relationship of the average of pixels of the object in the superior and inferior half of the character*: It calculates the relationship between the superior part of the element and the inferior part. A characteristic like this helps us to differ the characters that appear above or below the line. For example, the comma and the apostrophe, in form are very similar, but the apostrophe always appears in the superior part of the line and the comma in the inferior part.
- *Slope of the function that represents the character pixels*: The search of the linear function would facilitate the analysis of the characters that have linear form. In the other characters the slope of this straight line can be analyzed, this would indicate us in what direction is the biggest quantity in pixels that belong to the character.
- *Coordinates (x, y) of the center of gravity of the character*: It calculates the gravity center of the matrix according to the distribution of the elements of value 1. And it gives us the relationship of this point according to the dimensions of the matrix, so that if the size of the letter is changed for example, this relationship stays relatively constant.
- *Relationship between the superior quadrants*: It calculates the relationship between the quantity of black (1s) of the first and second quadrants.
- *Relationship between the inferior quadrants*: It calculates the relationship between the quantity of black (1s) of the third and quarter quadrants. These last two parameters help to differentiate characters. For example, "u" and "n", "b" and "d", etc. (keep in mind that the parameters are numerical results, and therefore, the differences that are remarkably visible are not it so much from the calculations point of view).
- *Eccentricity*: It gives the relationship between the axes of the ellipse that circumscribes the region of the character.
- *Orientation*: It gives the orientation of the character according to a relationship that involves the center of gravity of the image and the axes of the ellipse that circumscribes it.

4 Use of the Platform *SmartMLP* for the Design and Training of the Neuronal Network

The Multilayer Perceptron is a model of artificial neuronal network that simulates one of the countless functions of our nervous system: the classification. For this, it simulates structurally and functionally part of the nervous system. Exactly this was one of the causes for those that the MLP was chosen to solve the classification of the characters.

Because the complexity of the design work and implementation of the MLP and the slowness with which these processes were executed, software have been elaborated. This tools help to the designer of the network in these tasks and they implement algorithms of training that achieve equal results that the traditional, in smaller intervals of time. *SmartMLP* is an application developed in the Universidad Central de Las Villas (UCLV). This application allows, with facilities, to create and to train an MLP. It is difficult to define a priori the quantity of layers and neurons needed for a given problem. The use of this program helps to build different ANN and finally decide which to use.

The *SmartMLP* made some improvements to the algorithm of training Backpropagation, to achieve a bigger efficiency. Several changes and additions were carried out. The introduced improvements were the following:

- Use of a heuristic function for the calculation of the learning coefficient. This contributes to improve the convergence of the algorithm, accelerating its speed:

$$\eta = \sqrt{N_1^2 + N_2^2 + \ldots + N_n^2}\,, \tag{2}$$

- Where N_i is the quantity of examples of the learning set belonging to class l and n is total of classes
- Normalization of the entrances.
- Introduction of pedagogic techniques of example selection during the training. Specifically to Repeat Until Learning, which contributes to each updating of weight is made based on the examples that generate a bigger error, therefore the change in the weight is bigger and consequently the quantity of steps to give to reach the appropriate steps is smaller.
- Addition of an additional term to the function updating of weight -method of the Moment -, which causes that the network converge to maintain the address in the updating that took place. So that if the network is converging toward a minimum and it jumps it, acquiring with this a direction contrary to which it took, the inertia of the updating will make that the following steps are smaller, trying to attract again to the network toward the minimum.
- Inclusion of two approaches of stops that can contribute to eliminate unnecessary iterations of the algorithm of training.

Analyzing all these improvements that it introduces this application, it was decided their use for the construction of the MLP.

The neuronal network that is used in the OCR is an MLP with 21 inputs that belong together with the quantity of parameters defined in section 2, a layer of hidden neurons, and at the moment 100 classes of exits. Some symbols that are not common in the language were omitted. Approaches were taken for those letters where the capitals letters and case letters are the same or very similar.

Due to the great quantity of classes to be classified a set of training was needed sufficiently big so that the network could generalize. This set of training consists of examples that have 21 features. Each class has around 15 examples.

For the determination of the layers hidden, multiple tests with several nets were made utilizing 1 or 2 layers. According to the carried out tests the following conclusion was reached, for this case, with two nets, to local minimum you arrived very quick. Finally, you prove with a single layer they were made and a network of 35 neurons was obtained that has classified 92% of the set of training, as well as 91% of the control set.

Once the recognition of the possible characters is made by the MLP, to each character its code ASCII is associated, for its later writing. First the ambiguities that can be given are verified, for, in case of similar characters, these could be differentiated correctly.

The final objective of this work is to be able to make a OCR that can be used by any other system. For this an object COM was built that allowed reutilize this code.

5 Results

The development of tools for the Optical Characters Recognition is one of the slopes of intelligent recognition that are developed in the world, but its cost is extremely high, so its use is solely justified when used in big volumes of transactions.

Table 1. It shows the quantity of features used by the training of the network, the time of training and the learning percent

No. of features for example	Time of training	No. of training epoch	Learning rate	Learning percent
42	65:20:00h	150 000	0.375-1.025	62.00
31	52:00:00h	100 000	0.375-1.025	78.00
21	48:00:00h	100 000	0.375-1.025	91.00

In table 1, the obtained results of the training of the network are shown using the traditional Backpropagation algorithm, we can see that the correct reduction of the total of features influences directly in the speed-up of the learning as well as in its quality. This way, with the total of 21 features the best results are obtained as much in the speed as in the quality of the learning.

On the other hand in table 2 the comparative results of the training of the network are shown using 21 input features in their traditional variant, using alone the pedagogic heuristic for the training, using selection dynamic coefficient and lastly combining all methods mentioned in the previous section. It can be appreciated as the percent of correct classification is stable. For all the variants of used Backpropagation, however the reduction of the time of training is significant for all the employees' heuristic. Being the most significant the methods of presentation example to the learning and the use of the coefficient of dynamic learning those that achieved reductions of 33% and 25% respectively. However, the combination of all the methods shows the best results with a reduction of the time of learning of around 58%.

Table 2. It shows variants of MLP, time of training and learning percent

Used variant of Backpropagation	Time of training	Learning percent
Traditional	48:00:00h	91.00
Using Pedagogic Strategy of Training	32:30:00h	91.20
Using Coefficient of Dynamic Learning	36:50:00h	91.10
Combination of all the strategies of the section 4	20.20.00h	92.00

The application obtained has principal advantage concerning other applications in the literature, it is the minimal quantity of utilized features and their hind incidence in the acceleration of the learning process of the neural net. Normally, similar applications make use of examples with quantities of features that they vary from 60 until 120. In this case are demonstrated that with hardly 21 features are possible to carry out an efficient classification.
Another advantage is the utilization of heuristic during the training of the neural net, the one which allows to adapt this process to the evolution of the same. Achieving a greater speed and efficiency of the learning. This was possible for the employment of the SmartMLP platform that permits the use of this heuristics.

References

1. Díaz Sardiñas, Adolfo. "Heurísticas para el diseño de redes neuronales tipo Multilayer Perceptron (MLP) que utilizan Backpropagation (BP) como algoritmo de aprendizaje". UCLV. Master degree thesis.
2. Mollineda Cárdenas, Ramón Alberto.1997. "Sistema para el estudio de universos de objetos en imágenes". UCLV. Master degree thesis.
3. Bello Pauste, Carlos Enrique. "Uso de heurísticas y conjuntos borrosos en la implementación de un Multilayer Perceptron". UCLV.
4. Bello Pérez, Rafael. 1993. "Curso Introductorio a las Redes Neuronales Artificiales".UCLV.
5. Hilera Gonzáles, José Ramón. 1995. "Redes neuronales artificiales. Fundamentos, modelos y aplicaciones". Ed. Addison-Wesley Iberoamericana.
6. Russ, John C. "The Image Processing Handbook", 1991
7. Haralick R. A. y Shapiro L. Computer and Robot Vision, Volume I, Addison-wesley Publishing Company, USA, 1992.
8. Brend , J. Digital Image Processing. Springer - Verlag, Germany, 1993.
9. Smith, Steven W. The Scientist and Engineer's Guide to Digital Signal Processing.
10. Wallace, Gregory K. The JPEG Still Picture Compression Standard. IEEE in Transaction on Consumer Electronics. Massachusetts, 1991. http://www.cs.berkeley.edu/~tokuyasu/pubs/jvcir-new/node8.html.
11. Massey, Al. "Optical Character Recognition";
12. http://www.hal-pc.org/journal/APRIL98/REVIEWS/OCR/OCR.HTM.
13. Young, T. Gerbrands, J.J. Vliet, L.J. van. "Image Processing Fundamentals": http://www.ph.tn.tudelft.nl/Courses/FIP/noframes/fip.html.
14. "ISO IS-10918 - Understanding JPEG Image Compression". 1995: http://icib.igd.fhg.de/icib/it/iso/is_10918-1/pvrg-descript/chapter2.5.html.

Applications of a Collaborative Learning Ontology

B. Barros[1], M.F. Verdejo[1], T. Read[1], and R. Mizoguchi[2]

[1] Departamento de Lenguajes y Sistemas Informaticos
Escuela Técnica Superior de Ingenieros Industriales (U.N.E.D)
Ciudad Universitaria s/n, 28040 Madrid, Spain
{bbarros,felisa,tread}@lsi.uned.es
http://sensei.lsi.uned.es
[2] I.S.I.R., Osaka University
8-1 Mihogaoka, Ibaraki. Osaka, 567-0047 Japan
miz@ei.sanken.osaka-u.ac.jp
http://www.ei.sanken.osaka-u.ac.jp/index-e.html

Abstract. The objective of the research presented in this article is to find representational mechanisms for relating and integrating the collaborative learning elements present in real practical environments, create an integrated ontology that considers and relates these elements, and make use of it to define new collaborative learning scenarios. It is therefore necessary to identify the key ideas underlying the notion of ontology that will be essential in subsequent application development: a list of the basic elements that give rise to a common vocabulary for collaborative learning, and the relationship and dependencies between them. The Activity Theory framework is used as a theoretical foundation for organising the elements in the ontology. This ontology gives rise to the structured elements that form the conceptual structure for the definition and construction of CSCL environments, and the analysis and assessment of group collaboration.

Introduction

Collaborative learning is a kind of social activity involving a community of learners and teachers, where members share and acquire knowledge. As Vygotsky (1978) pointed out, "in a collaborative scenario, students interchange their ideas for coordinating when they working for reaching common goals. When dilemmas arise, the discussion process involves them in learning". When the learners work in groups they reflect upon their ideas (and those of their colleagues'), explain their opinions, consider and discuss those of others, and as a result, learn. In this way, each learner acquires individual knowledge from the collaborative interaction.

Collaborative learning systems are studied in the CSCL paradigm (Koschmann, 1996) which has been built upon a rich history of cognitive science research about how people work and learn. By combining the social and cognitive perspectives, it has the potential to help take important steps forward in understanding how learning might be achieved in real situations (Kolodner & Guzdial, 1997). As part of this social cognitive perspective, the socio-cultural theory proposes the Activity Theory (henceforth, AT) (Nardi, 1996) for representing the group activities where technology

C.A. Coello Coello et al. (Eds.): MICAI 2002, LNAI 2313, pp. 301–310, 2002.

plays a role as mediator. Within this theory, an analysis model was developed for identifying and representing the human and artificial elements involved in joint tasks (Engeström, 1987). This socio-cultural framework provides the concept of *activity* as a unit of analysis, with a rich internal structure necessary to make the context of a situation explicit, specifically the links between the individual and the social levels which stress the role of the tools as mediating artifacts.

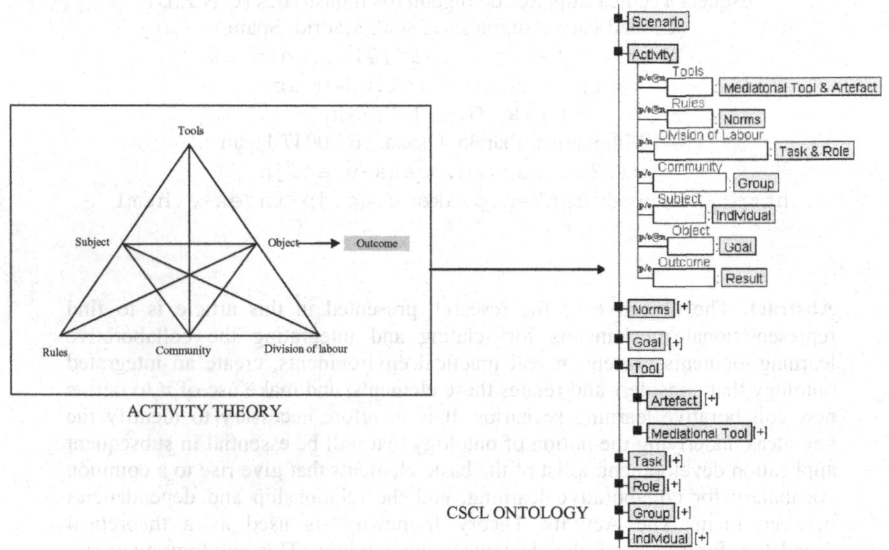

Fig. 1. The representation of the AT components in the ontology

In previous research, several different collaborative scenarios have been undertaken with university students using the DEGREE system (Verdejo & Barros, 2000) and AT (Verdejo & Barros, 1999). The results of this work show that collaborative learning scenarios are described in terms of people with learning goals, group structure, tools that are available, roles that take into account the tasks, and the restrictions of the use of the system (all within a particular context and domain). Furthermore, it was found that all these elements are included in the activity concept: the *community* involved and the *social norms* that govern it, the *division of labour* to be followed, the *tools* to be used, the *subject* and *object* of the activity, and finally, the *outcome* produced by the group. The natural extension of this work, is therefore, to develop a computational model rich enough to represent the interrelations between the aforementioned elements, in such a way as to be able to exploit them for designing new collaborative learning scenarios and tools. Ontologies are appropriate for this purpose because they offer a meta-model that is able to represent the basic collaborative learning concepts (that give rise to a common vocabulary (Mizoguchi & Bourdeau, 2000)), and the relationships and dependencies between them. In this sense, the ontology offers a higher conceptual knowledge level to describe collaborative learning.

This paper is organized as follows: an overview of a CSCL ontology is presented in the next section; subsequently, two applications of it for collaborative learning applications are presented, and finally, some conclusions are drawn.

CSCL Ontology

Proposals for CSCL ontologies have already been made with the emphasis placed on such aspects as: goals and communication models and problem-solving methods (Ikeda et. al., 1995), learning tasks (Mizoguchi & Sinitsa, 1996), learning goals and group formation (Inaba et. al., 2000). However, in real collaborative learning scenarios all these elements are interrelated and/or interdependent.

The ontology presented here draws together in an original way the different aspects of collaborative learning placing the emphasis upon the relationship between them. The underlined concepts in the ontology have drawn from the authors' experience of designing CSCL experiments. This ontology is defined within the AT framework (which underlines the importance of *relating* and *integrating* its components), and its nodes correspond to the main concepts in an AT activity: subject, rules, tools, community, division of labour, object (goal) and outcome (figure 1).

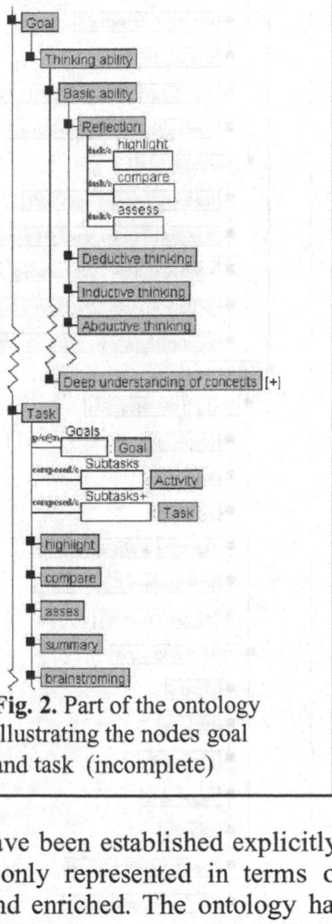

The structure and the knowledge represented in the previously mentioned ontologies have been refined to enable them to be incorporated under the corresponding nodes in this new ontology. Furthermore, the relationships and dependences between the concepts that make up this knowledge have been established explicitly. Therefore, most concepts in the ontology are not only represented in terms of declarative knowledge, but are also contextualized and enriched. The ontology has been developed in XML and Java. Furthermore, additional code has already been developed to facilitate its use in some applications, which opens up the possibilities for reuse in other educational enviroments.

Fig. 2. Part of the ontology illustrating the nodes goal and task (incomplete)

An example of part of the ontology can be seen in figure 2, where parts of the concepts "learning goals" and "learning tasks" are presented together with the way in which they are related. As can be seen, the node reflection is related to three tasks: highlight, compare, and assess, which in themselves are declared under the node task. The interdependencies (shown as labels in the figure) between the nodes represent the way in which concepts influence each other in collaborative learning scenarios.

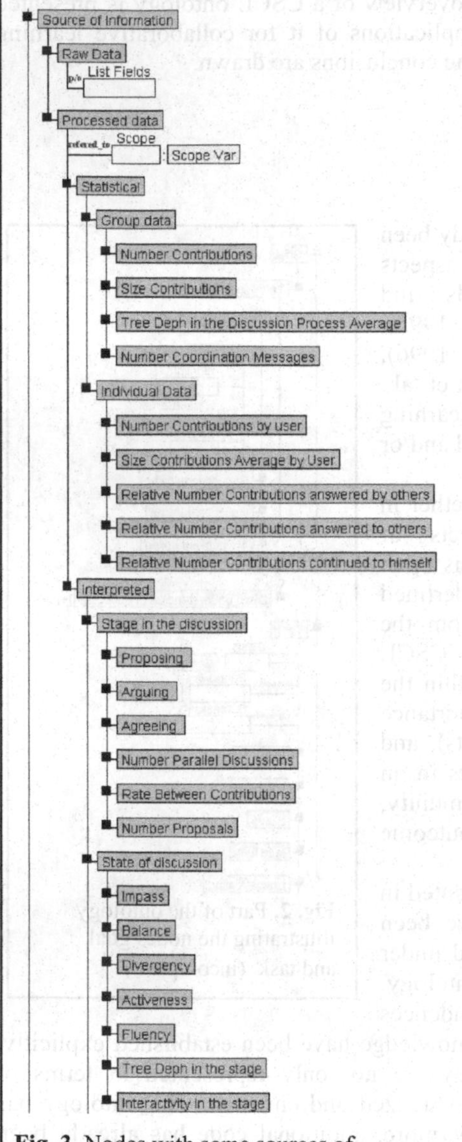

Fig. 3. Nodes with some sources of information for analysis of collaboration

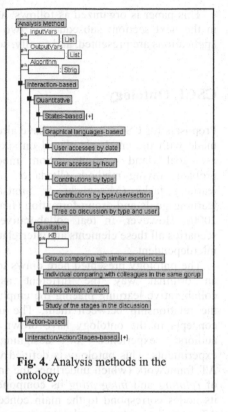

Fig. 4. Analysis methods in the ontology

Therefore, this ontology can be seen to be more than just a simple hierarchical tree, since it models the complex relationships between the concepts it contains.

Futhermore, the ontology also includes knowledge which is not explicitly represented in other collaborative learning ontologies, i.e., knowledge about the study and analysis of the learning process, since as Brown (1983) points out, the learning "process" is as important as the "result". For this reason, the ontology has been completed with the concepts necessary for analysis and collaboration: observed and interpreted data from the group process and the analysis methods. These concepts are expressed in two different nodes: Source of Information and Analysis method.

Firstly, the node Source of Information is needed to enable the representation of states of the learning processes and the participant attitudes, which is in itself divided into the following two nodes:

A Statistical node, whose contents are generated by interpreting the log of student activities in the scenario in terms of the elements that make up the collaborative environment. For example, given a scenario where a mediational tool has different categories, such as proposal, answer and question; and two roles that exist are writer and reader; a statistical variable could be "the number of contributions type-answer-made by a student with the role -writer-". These variables are explored in more detail in Barros & Verdejo (2000) and Barros, Mizoguchi &Verdejo (2001).

An Interpreted node, whose contents are inferred from the combination of the statistical data and a knowledge base composed of rules that relate statistical and process data. They represent the observed states of the learning processes and the participant attitudes, for example, the conversation flow can be defined to be based upon the user interactivity in the conversation, together with the average time between user contributions (both of which come from the statistical data).

Secondly, as can be seen in figure 4, the Analysis Method node contains three types of subnode in order to be able to represent three types of methods: Interaction-based, Action-based (Mulhembruck, 2001), Interaction-Action-Stage based. The first of which can be either quantative or qualitative. The qualitative methods are based upon inference techniques taken from artificial intelligence.

DEGREE, for example, uses fuzzy-inference as a qualitative analysis method for this purpose. Hence, in the ontology under the qualitative analysis node, there are several different approaches to performing qualitative analysis: group behaviour analysis, individual behaviour analysis, task summary, and study of the stages in the discussion (Barros & Verdejo, 2000).

CSCL Ontology Applications

Now that the structure of the ontology has been discussed it is possible to move on and consider some of its applications (figure 5). The ontology gives rise to the structured elements that make up the foundation necessary for the design and development of CSCL environments. Therefore, the development of such environments can be seen in terms of the selection of these elements, whose structure assists the design process. Furthermore, an analysis process can be undertaken of the students' activities together with the declarative knowledge present in task definitions, the elements that need to be observed, and the rules which relate them. Finally, the combination of all this declarative knowledge enables the creation of coaching processes that assist the students in the learning process. What follows is a description of the first two of these applications. Their development will help to refine the knowledge in the ontology.

Exploiting the Ontology for the Definition and Construction of CSCL

Collaborative learning scenarios need to be tailored to specific conditions. This is achieved by assigning particular values to a number of parameters, AT deals with most of them as we have described above. As has been previously presented, the ontology offers an explicitly structured list of usable values for those parameters. To define a collaborative learning case (a scenario or group of them) a designer should select the relevant concepts (nodes in the ontology) and, if necessary, adapt them to fit the case.

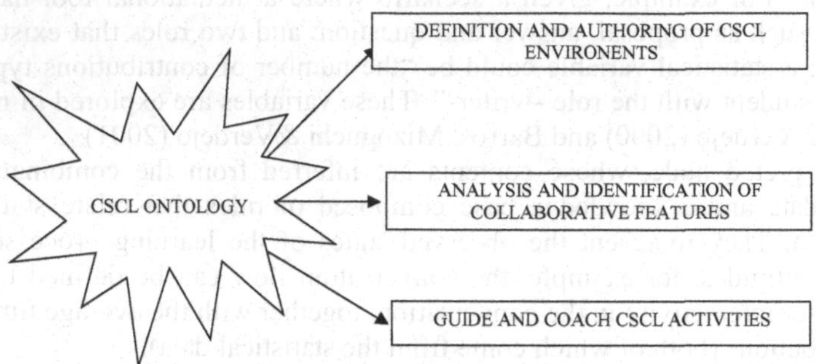

Fig. 5. Possible applications of the CSCL ontology

The first of the applications to be considered here is reengineered version of DEGREE (Barros & Verdejo, 2000), an asynchronous collaborative learning environment. The information handled is mainly textual, so a variety of editing tools and file management facilities are available. A shared workspace provides support for conversation in the form of semi-structured typed messages. When learners make their contributions they have to select a type from a predefined set which is referred to as a *conversational type*.

DEGREE has a configuration level aimed at defining the components used to support a collaborative scenario and installing a working environment for one or more groups. Workspaces are defined at this level by means of an authoring tool based on the CSCL ontology. The outcome of the configuration activity is a collaborative environment which enables the users to carry out the defined learning activities through asynchronous communication via Internet.

In this new version, the configuration level makes use of the ontology because it guides the designer in the process of specifying the collaborative learning scenarios due to its inherit structure.

When the designer selects a task, the configuration tool offers the most adequate mediational tools for the learning goals inherent in the task. The ontology includes the entry Mediational tool (as can be seen, on the left side of the figure 6), under the node Tool, having as one of its child nodes, Conversational structure, with the attribute "text" or "graphic" that indicates the type of representation that will be used in the collaborative environment. DEGREE works with textual information and its mediational tools will have this attribute set to "text". The Conversational structure node contains a number of graph types (such as experimental, constructive, or decision making among others). In this case, the conversational graph experimental is selected and subsequently used to create the scenario that can be seen in figure 6 (on the top-right).

Another example in which we are applying the ontology is a new collaborative learning tool that is currently been developed. It can be used both synchronously and asynchronously and makes use of visuals languages (Hoppe et. al, 2000) to function as a mediational tool. The tool enables the user to work with graphical spaces, whereby the user can identify areas of images and build an argumentative discussion around them based upon the types of visual components that have been previously configured. The user can directly manipulate different areas of a space and add different related concepts to them. The result is a conceptual map that represents the group discussion.

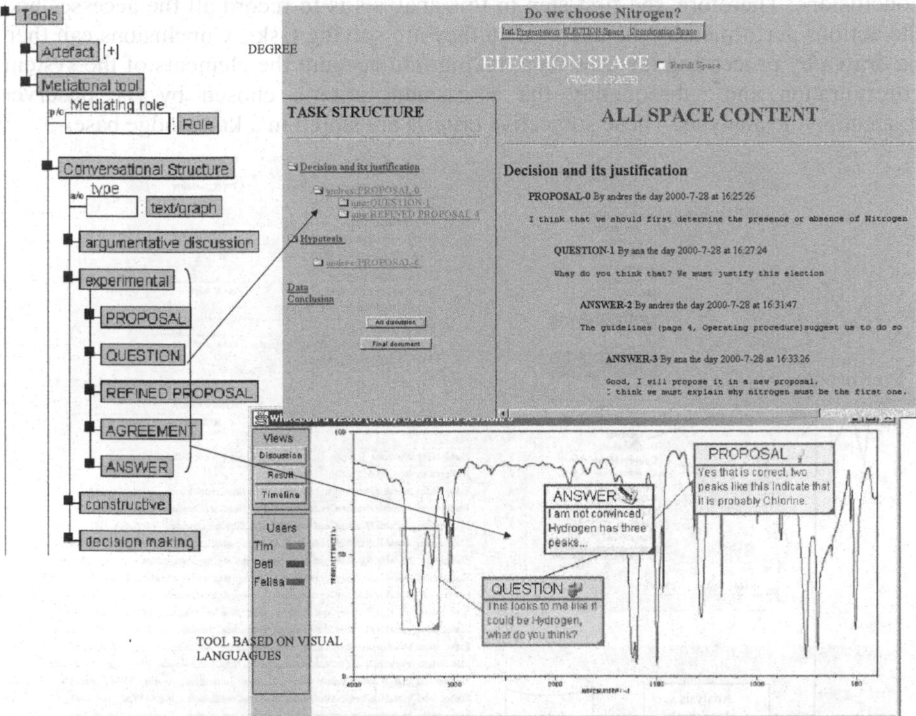

Fig. 6. An example of how the ontology represents the same concept about its mediatonal tool, in two collaborative systems: above a system that works with textual objects and below one that works with graphical objects

Both the underling technology in this new tool and the way in which it functions are different from DEGREE. However, they share the same conceptual foundation represented by the CSCL ontology. For example, even though DEGREE uses textual objects and the other graphical objects, both are based upon related semi-structured contributions. The difference between them lies in the way in which the contributions are displayed and manipulated by the tools, not in the underlying conceptual relationships. This can be clearly seen in figure 6 where the three contribution types contained in the section of the ontology (shown at the left of the figure), are presented in different ways in the two different tools (shown at the right of the figure).

Exploiting the Ontology for Analysis and the Assessment of Collaboration

"Collaborative learning research has paid close attention to the study of pupils interactions during peer-based work in order to analyse and identify the cognitive advantages of joint activity" (Dillenbourg, Baker, Blaye, & O'Malley, 1996). The aim of analysis, in general, is to understand and to interpret the collaborative process in order to be able to asses the conditions and elements for effective learning.

In the computational approach, analysing the collaboration consists of collecting data from the participants' actions and interactions and subsequently inferring conclusions. Therefore, the first step in this analysis is to record all the accesses and the actions performed by the users when they are solving tasks. Conclusions can then be drawn by processing this raw data, taking into account the elements of the system configuration and subsequently the assessment criteria chosen by the observer requesting the analysis. These subjective criteria are stored in a knowledge base.

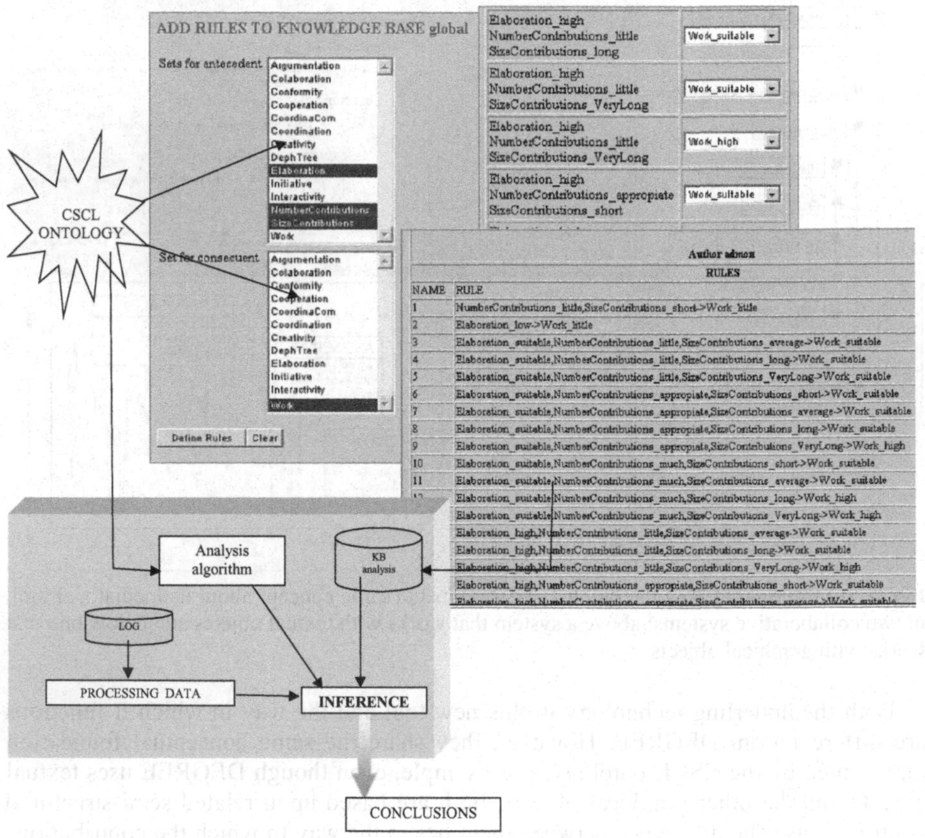

Fig. 7. Edition of the rules for the analysis, and the inference analysis methods

The designer of such knowledge bases needs to reflect on what kinds of data can be computed from the logged data, and how to express the relation between them as rules. How can an ontology help in this process? It can help by providing every element involved in the analysis: configuration elements, processing criteria (generic tasks aimed at computing the input values to the processing rules), and the antecedents and consequents of these rules. The rules themselves are not stored as part of the ontology but in a number of knowledge bases.

An external tool for editing these knowledge bases has been implemented. It takes a list of variables selected from those available in the ontology as its input, whose fuzzy values are calculated from the logged data. As can be seen in figure 4 they can be found in the ontology under the source of information node. Variables included in the ontology could be, for example, NumberContribution (whose values are defined to be: *little, appropriate* and *much*) or SizeContribution (with values: *short, average, long* and *very long*). Furthermore, the ontology also includes other variables that have been subjectively inferred from the processed data rather than directly extracted from the raw logged data. For example, Work (an assessment of the group's work quality) with values such as: *little*, *suitable* and *high* can be computed by taking into account: NumberContribution, SizeContribution, and Elaboration.

A tool that uses the ontology as input is provided for editing the rules in DEGREE. The rules are edited by selecting the variables (both antecedents and consequent) that the tool takes from the ontology. Subsequently, the tool automatically generates the complete set of rules for all possible combinations of the fuzzy values. Finally, for each rule generated, one possible value has to be chosen for the consequent, or NULL if the rule is not to be considered. Furthermore, rules can be generated by chaining together other rules, since the consequent of one rule can be the antecedents of subsequent ones. This process is summarised in figure 7. It also provides an environment that enables the selection of an analysis method (declared in the ontology under the Analysis method node, in figure 4), the knowledge base, and a log of a collaborative group; and then visualizes the conclusions of the analysis.

Conclusions

In this paper a computational model has been presented which interprets the Activity Theory in terms of a CSCL ontology. This ontology offers a conceptual knowledge level representation for collaborative learning. It is based upon the structure and the knowledge contained in previous ontologies together with knowledge which was not explicitly represented in other collaborative learning ontologies, i.e., knowledge about the study and analysis of the learning process. Furthermore, relationships and dependences between the concepts that make up this knowledge have been established explicitly.

This ontology has been designed to be reusable by different tools in many collaborative learning scenarios due to the combination of the theoretical AT framework with an underlying XML-based representation.

References

Barros, B. & Verdejo M.F (2000). "Analysing students interaction process for improving collaboration. The DEGREE approach", *International Journal of Artificial Intelligence in Education.*

Barros, B., Mizoguchi, R. & Verdejo M.F (2001). A Platform for Collaboration Analysis in CSCL: An ontological approach, Proc. AIED'2001, May 19-23, 2001.

Brown, J. S. (1983) "Process versus product: a perspective on tools for communal and informal electronic learning", *Report from the Learning: Education in the Electronic Age.*

Dillenbourg, P., Baker, H.P.M., Blaye, A. & O'Malley (1995) "The evolution of research on collaborative Learning" http://tecfa.unige.ch/tecfa/researchUlhm/ESF-Chap5.ps

Duffy, T.M., Lowyck, J. & Jonassen, D. (1992) *Designing Environments for Constructive Learning*, Sprinver-Verlag.

Engeström, Y. (1987) Learning by Expanding: An activity-Theoretical Approach to Developmental Research, Helsinki:Orienta-Konsultit Oy.

Hoppe,H.U., Gaßner, K., Muehlenbrock, M. & Tewissen, F. (2000) "Distributed Visual Language Environments for Cooperation and Learning: Applications and Intelligent Support", in *Group Decision and Negotiation* (Kluwer), Vol. 9, No.3, May 2000.

Ikeda, M., Hoppe, U.H. & Mizoguchi, R. (1995) "Ontological Issues of CSCL Systems Design", *Proc. AIED'95*, pp. 242-249, 1995.

Inaba, A., Supnithi, T., Ikeda, Mizoguchi, R. & Toyoda, J. (2000) "How Can We Form Effective Collaborative Learning Groups-Theoretical justification of Opportunistic Group Formation with ontological engineering" *ITS'2000*, pp.282-291.

Kolodner, J. & Guzdial, M. (1996) "Effects *with* and *of* CSCL: Tacking Learning in a New Paradigm", in (Koschmann, 1996), pp. 307-320.

Koschmann, T. (1996) (Editor) *CSCL: Theory and Practice of an emerging paradigm.* Lawrence Erlbaum Associates.

Kuutti, K. (1996) "Activity Theory as a Potential Framework for Human-Computer Interaction Research" in (Nardi, 1996), pp. 17-44.

Mizoguchi, R. & Bourdeau, J. (2000);"Using Ontological Engineering to Overcome Common AI-ED Problems", JAIED, 11, 107-121.

Mizoguchi, R. & Sinitsa, K.(1996) "Task Ontology Design for Intelligent Educational/Training Systems", *Proc. Workshop* on "Architectures and Methods for Designing Cost-Effective and Reusable ITSs", *ITS'96*, Montreal, pp. 1-21, 1996

Muehlenbrock, M., *Action-based Collaboration Analysis for Group Learning*, IOS Press, Amsterdam, 2001.

Nardi, B.A. (Editor) (1996) *Context and Consciousness. Activity Theory and Human-Computer Interaction*, MIT Press.

Verdejo, M.F. & Barros, B. (1999) "Combining User-Centered design and Activity concepts for developing computer-mediated collaborative learning environments: a Case Example" en ED-MEDIA'99. http://sensei.ieec.uned.es/~bbarros/edmedia99.html

Vygotsky, L.S. (1978) Mind in society: The development of higher psychological processes. Cambridge MA: Harvard University Press.

Automated Case Generation from Databases Using Similarity-Based Rough Approximation

Liqiang Geng and Christine W. Chan

Department of Computer Science
University of Regina
Regina, Sask, S4S 0A2, Canada
Telephone: 1-(306)-585-4071
Fax: 1-(306) 585-4745
chan@cs.uregina.ca

Abstract. Knowledge acquisition for a case-based reasoning system from domain experts is a bottleneck in the system development process. With the huge amounts of data that have become available, it would be useful to derive automatically representative cases from available databases rather than acquiring them from domain experts. This paper presents two algorithms using similarity-based rough set theory to derive cases automatically from available databases. The first algorithm SRS1 requires the user to decide the similarity thresholds for the objects in a database, while the second algorithm SRS2 can automatically select proper similarity thresholds. These algorithms require fewer parameters from domain experts than other case generation algorithms. Also they can tackle noise and inconsistent data in the database and select a reasonable number of the representative cases from the database. The experimental results were compared with those from well-known data mining systems, such as rule induction systems and neural network systems.

Keywords: case-based reasoning, rough sets, similarity measure, classification.

1 Introduction

Case-based reasoning (CBR) is a computerized method that attempts to study solutions that were used to solve problems in the past so as to solve current problems by analogy or association [Ketler, 1993]. The CBR approach has some advantages over the rule-based approach in unstructured and difficult-to- understand domains, such as diagnosis, planning and classification. Moreover, case bases are maintainable because new cases can be added and existing ones modified or deleted easily. However, it has been pointed out that knowledge acquisition for a CBR system is still a labor-intensive task. The classification accuracy of the developed CBR system is also dependent on the quality of the cases obtained from the domain experts [Chan et al, 2000].

Hence, automatically deriving high quality cases from an available database is one of the research directions for many CBR researchers. In this area, many issues have been and are being tackled, such as how to deal with noise and inconsistent data, how to reduce the number of the selected cases while maintaining classification accuracy,

C.A. Coello Coello et al. (Eds.): MICAI 2002, LNAI 2313, pp. 311–320, 2002.

how to make the case more compact, i.e. how to identify irrelevant features, and how to increase the classification accuracy of the derived case base.

In the late 1980s and early 1990s, many case base generation algorithms have been developed and successfully applied to a wide variety of learning tasks. Applications involve many areas, such as molecular biology [Cost et al, 1990] and speech recognition [Bradshaw, 1987]. However, these studies were all based on single domains and the algorithms developed might not perform as robustly on other domains.

Recently, many research works have been conducted on applying the soft computing method to case base generation. In [Cao et al, 2001] and [Pal et al, 2001], fuzzy set theory and rough set theory have been used to induce the representative cases. These algorithms first translate the numeric data into fuzzy linguistic terms and then derive the fuzzy rules from the database. The representative cases are then selected by applying the fuzzy rules. However, a disadvantage with these algorithms is that they did not tackle noise and inconsistent data explicitly, which is an important issue in practical problems. Furthermore, in using these algorithms many parameters and factors are required for the selection process. We believe that case generation should as much as possible rely only on the available data and not on information required from the domain experts. Therefore, our major focus is how to reduce the number of parameters that need to be defined by the experts or users. Our objective is to propose case generation algorithms that satisfy two requirements. First, the users need to specify a minimal number of parameters; secondly, the algorithms can tackle noise and inconsistent data explicitly.

In this paper, two case generation algorithms are proposed. A similarity-based rough set (SRS1) method and its variant (SRS2) are suggested to select a reasonable number of representative cases from an available data set. Section 2 discusses some basic concepts of similarity-based rough approximation. Sections 3 and 4 describe the proposed algorithms SRS1 and SRS2 respectively. In section 5, the algorithms are implemented and tested on some well-known data sets and the experimental results are presented. Section 6 gives the conclusion and some directions for future work.

2 Similarity-Based Rough Sets

Rough sets [Pawlak, 1991] is a mathematical tool used for dealing with vagueness and uncertainty in areas of artificial intelligence and cognitive sciences, such as data mining, decision making, and pattern recognition [Mrozek et al, 1998; Funakoshi , et al, 1998]. The concept of rough sets is based on the assumption that every object of the universe can be represented by some available information. Objects characterized by the same information are considered indiscernible. All the indiscernible objects form an elementary set, i.e., granule knowledge about the universe. If a given set of objects is a union of some elementary sets, it is referred as a crisp set; otherwise it is a rough set. A rough set can be represented by a pair of crisp sets, called the lower and the upper approximation that are the union of elementary sets. The lower approximation consists of all objects that surely belong to the set and the upper approximation contains objects that possibly belong to the set, with respect to the given knowledge.

However, indiscernibility relation-based standard rough sets can only deal with symbolic attributes in the decision table. Continuous attributes must be discretized into smaller intervals and then each interval translated into qualifiers before employing the rough set theory. The discretization methods adopted will greatly influence quality of the classification results. A CBR system usually involves continuous attributes; moreover, the similarity measures are usually used for retrieving the appropriate cases from the case base. Therefore, we adopted the similarity relation-based rough set approach for selecting representative cases. Similarity relation-based rough set is an extension of the standard rough set approach, which replaces the indiscernibility relation with a similarity relation in the approximation process [Slowinski et al 1997].

In some literature, relations that satisfy the reflexive property are called similarity relations, see for example [Slowinski et al, 1997]. In this paper, we define that similarity relations also have the property of symmetry. This property is incorporated to enhance computational efficiency, since processing symmetric similarity matrices require half the computational space and time as the asymmetric ones.

Suppose we are given a finite non-empty set U of objects, called the universe, a binary relation R defined on $U \times U$ is a similarity relation if and only if

1. aRa
2. $aRb \rightarrow bRa$

Where $a, b \in U$. From this definition, we can represent the relation R with an undirected graph. This allows us to define a similarity class for each object $x \in U$. The similarity class of x, denoted by $R(x)$ is the set of objects that are similar to x.

$$R(x)=\{y \in U / yRx\}$$

The rough approximation of a set $X \subseteq U$ is a pair of sets called lower and upper approximations of X, denoted by $R_*(X)$ and $R^*(X)$ respectively, where

$$R_*(X)=\{x \in X / R(x) \subseteq X\}$$

$$R^*(X)=\cup_{x \in X} R(x)$$

The lower approximation $R_*(X)$ of a set X is the set of objects whose similarity class belongs to X and the set consists of elements that can certainly be classified as elements of X, while the upper approximation $R^*(X)$ of X is the union of the similarity classes of objects in X and the elements in this set can possibly be classified as elements of X.

In order to make the approximation more robust and enable it to deal with noise in a database, we propose the extended lower approximation of a similarity-based rough set,

$$R_{*ext}(X)=\{x \in X / card(R'(x))/card(R(x)) >= ct\},$$

where $R'(x)=\{y / y \in R(x) \text{ and } d(y)=d(x)\}$ refers to the set of the objects that are similar to object x and have the same decision value as x. $ct \in [0, 1]$ is called the acceptable threshold of consistency, or consistency threshold in short, which defines the degree to which noisy data are tolerated. It is a parameter that needs to be specified by the domain experts in the proposed algorithms SRS1 and SRS2. $R_{*ext}(X)$ is the set of objects which are likely to be classified as elements of concept X at least with certainty ct according to the similarity relation R. If ct=1, $R_{*ext}(X)$ is identical to the standard similarity based lower approximation $R_*(X)$.

To conduct case generation, a source of data is represented as a decision table. The similarity relation is based on the objects in a decision table, from which the cases are derived. Let $A=(U, A\cup\{d\})$ be a decision table where U is the universe, A is a set of condition attributes and d is a decision attribute [Pawlak, 1991]. The condition attributes can be assumed to be continuous, ordinal, or nominal and the decision attribute is nominal. Let Va be a set of values of attributes of a, where $a\in A$, $r(d)$ be the number of decision values, d_i be the ith decision value, and $Yi=\{x\in U|d(x)=d_i\}$ be the set of objects that have the ith decision value in the decision table. $POS(R, \{d\})=\cup_{i=1}^{r(d)} R_{*ext}(Yi)$ is called the positive region of the partition $\{Yi|i=1,\ldots,r(d)\}$.

The coefficient $r(R, \{d\})=card(POS(R, \{d\}))/card(U)$ is called the quality of approximation of classification. It expresses the ratio of objects that can be correctly classified to all the objects in the table. The objects that cannot be classified are considered as inconsistent objects.

In order to obtain the similarity class for every object, first the similarity measure should be defined for each attribute. This definition depends on the type of attributes under study. The most widely used attribute types are interval-scaled attributes, ordinal attributes, and nominal attributes. Detailed discussion on the definition of similarity measures for these attributes can be found in [Han et al, 2000]. After obtaining the similarity measure for each attribute, we aggregate them to define the global similarity measure on the set of objects by taking their product or weighted sum. We say that object x is similar to object y if and only if the similarity measure between these two objects is greater than or equal to a similarity threshold st. st determines the granularity of classification; a higher st value indicates a more refined classification of the data into clusters of the representative cases. The value of st is usually set by the domain experts. In algorithm SRS1, this parameter should be specified by the user, while in SRS2, definition of this parameter is not required because the algorithm can automatically determine the similarity thresholds for each object.

3 SRS1 Algorithm

Based on the concept of similarity measure and rough set theory described above, we propose the following algorithm to find representative cases from a database. First, in addition to the similarity thresholds st and consistency threshold ct mentioned in Section 2, some variables used in the algorithm are defined as follows.

1. *SimilarNo(i)*: the number of objects similar to object i, including object i itself.
2. *SimilarClassNo(i)*: the number of objects similar to object i and having the same decision value as object i, including object i itself.
3. *Consistency(i)*: the ratio of the number of similar objects that have the same decision value as node i to the number of similar objects of node i, *Consistency(i)= SimilarClassNo(i)/SimilarNo(i)*. If *Consistency(i)* is less than ct, node i can be regarded as inconsistent.

The algorithm involves the following steps:

1. Given parameters *st* and *ct*, compute the similarity measures between objects and create a similarity relation graph.
2. For each node *i* in the relation graph, compute{
   SimilarNo(i), SimilarClassNo(i), and Consistency(i).
   }
3. Delete nodes that are considered inconsistent, which satisfy *Consistency(i)<ct*
4. While the node set is not empty{
   Select isolated nodes to case base.
   Select a node with the maximum value for *Consistency* and insert it into the case base. If there is a tie, select one with the maximum value for *SimilarClassNo*, if there is a tie again, randomly select one node.
   Delete all of the nodes connected to this node.
   }

First, according to the similarity measures and the similarity threshold *st*, we construct the similarity relation graph of the objects where each node represents an object in the data set. We then delete the inconsistent nodes according to the value of *Consistency* and threshold *ct*. Next we select the most representative node in terms of the consistency threshold *Consistency* and *SimilarClassNo* and delete all of its similar nodes. The process iterates until the node set is empty. Meanwhile we can obtain the ratio of the objects that can be classified correctly to the whole set of objects, *r(R, {d})*. If the ratio is too low, which means there are too many objects that cannot be classified, the threshold for similarity measure is increased to refine granularity of the clusters. Our experiments demonstrated that with a larger similarity threshold, more objects could be classified. But at the same time, the number of selected representative objects increases, which might give better classification accuracy.

4 SRS2: Automatic Determination of Similarity Threshold *st*

It is often difficult for users, even domain experts, to determine an appropriate value for the similarity threshold *st*. Therefore this threshold is usually obtained through trial and error. We propose that a more precise and robust definition of similarity can be inferred directly from the data sets. Krawiec et al, [1998] proposed a method to derive the discretization intervals for each conditional attribute in the decision rules. Their method is strongly local in that it computes the intervals for each conditional attribute independent of the rest of the conditional attributes. In our method, the entire set of conditional attributes is simultaneously considered. We only take into account the similarity measures between objects. The algorithm is as follows:

1. Compute the similarity measure between objects and create a similarity matrix.
2. For each object *i*, do{
3. Sort all the objects in descending order according to the similarity measure to object *i*
   SimilarNo(i)=0;
   SimilarClassNo(i)=0;
   SimilarSet(i)={};
   For each object *j* in the ordered list, do the following{
      SimilarNo(i)=*SimilarNo(i)*+1;

```
        SimilarSet(i)=SimilarSet(i)∪object j;
        If the decision value of object j =the decision value of object i
                SimilarClassNo(i)=SimilarClassNo(i)+1;
                Consistency(i)= SimilarClassNo/SimilarNo;
                If Consistency(i)<ct
                Break;
    }
    For each object j in SimilarSet(i), do the following in the descending order in terms
    of the similarity measure{
    SimilarSet(i)=SimilarSet(i)- object j;
    SimilarNo(i)=SimilarNo(i)-1;
    SimilarClassNo(i)=SimilarClassNo(i)-1;
    Consistency(i)= SimilarClassNo(i)/SimilarNo(i);
    If Consistency(i)>ct
        Break;
    }
    }
3. While the set of the objects is not empty{
    Select isolated nodes to case base.
    Select a node which has the maximum value for Consistency to the case base. If
    there is a tie, select one with the maximum value for SimilarClassNo, if there is a
    tie again, randomly select one node.
    Delete all of the nodes connected to this node.
    }
```

This algorithm assumes that similarity threshold for each object is unique and that these thresholds can be determined by the consistency threshold *ct* provided by the users or the domain experts. In this algorithm, we first compute the similarity matrix for the given set of objects. Then for each object we sort the other objects that are similar to it in descending order according to the similarity measures. For each object *i*, we denote the number of similar objects by *SimilarNo(i)* and the number of similar objects that have the same decision value as object x by *SimilarClassNo(i)*. The similarity threshold for object *i* should satisfy the consistency condition *SimilarClassNo(i)/SimilarNo(i)>ct.* Therefore, we select the similar objects in the ordered list one by one until the consistency condition is less than the given threshold *ct*. Finally we construct the similarity relation graph and obtain the representative cases with the same method of SRS1 described in section 3.

5 Experimental Results

These two algorithms were implemented in Java and the experiments were conducted on a Dell PC with 128Mb memory, 866MHz CPU speed. In the experiments, we applied the algorithms on three well-known data sets: iris (Fisher's Iris Plant Database), glass (Glass Identification Database) and pima (Pima Indians Diabetes Database). These are taken from the University of California Repository of Machine Learning Databases [Merz et al, 1996], widely used by the machine learning community for empirical analysis of algorithms. The Iris data set has four condition attributes, three decision values and 150 objects; the glass data set has nine condition attributes, six decision values and 214 objects; and the pima data set has eight condition attributes, two decision values and 768 objects.

Table 1. Experimental results of running SRS1 on Iris

ct\st	0.5	0.6	0.7	0.8	0.9
0.5	8, 88.7	13, 94.9	22, 95.3	47, 95.1	102, 95.8
0.6	8, 88.7	13, 94.9	22, 95.3	47, 95.1	102, 95.8
0.7	8, 88.7	13, 94.9	22, 95.3	47, 95.1	102, 95.8
0.8	5, 65.5	11, 92.1	22, 95.3	47, 95.1	102, 95.8
0.9	5, 65.5	7, 88.1	21, 96.1	46, 95.2	102, 95.8
1	5, 65.5	7, 88.1	15, 92.6	46, 95.2	102, 95.8

The classification accuracy of the derived case base is obtained in the following way: First, the user sets the similarity and consistency thresholds. The program is run and the set of selected representative cases is generated. The system then classifies the rest of the data according to the similarity-based case based reasoning algorithm. The experimental results of SRS1 on the Iris data set are shown in Table 1. The first number in each grid of the table represents the number of the selected cases, and the second number represents the classification accuracy of the derived case base. Experimental runs were conducted using SRS1 with different similarity and consistency thresholds. From the experiments, it was observed that when the similarity threshold *st* increases, the granularity of the classification becomes finer, the number of the selected objects increases, and the classification accuracy usually, but not always increases. When the consistency threshold *ct* increases, the system tolerates less noisy data and identifies more inconsistent data, therefore, the number of the selected case decreases, and the classification accuracy usually, but not necessarily, decreases also.

Table 2. Experimental results of SRS2 on three data sets

ct\data set	Iris	Glass	Pima
0.5	4, 88.4	17, 52.8	3, 34.6
0.6	4, 75.3	34, 62.2	3, 34.6
0.7	4, 94.5	41, 59.0	31, 67.7
0.8	6, 70.8	45, 56.2	55, 71.2
0.9	8, 94.3	50, 58.5	110, 67.8
1	14, 93.4	50, 62.1	157, 69.1

Table 2 presents the experimental results of SRS2 on the three data sets. Similar to Table 1, the first number in each grid represents the number of the selected cases, and the second number represents the classification accuracy of the derived case base. However for SRS2, only one parameter, the consistency threshold *ct,* requires definition. It is observed that when *ct* increases, the number of the selected cases increases. This is in contrast to the experiments with SRS1, in which when *ct* increases, the number of the selected cases decreases. This is because in SRS1, the similarity threshold and consistency threshold are given by the user and they have no inter-dependency, while in SRS2, the similarity threshold is determined directly by the consistency threshold. When the consistency threshold increases, the tolerance for noisy data decreases. Therefore, in the process of selection, the granularity of the clusters of cases becomes finer, and more objects are selected. In this experiment, no relationship between the consistent measure *ct* and the classification accuracy has been found.

Table 3. Comparison of the accuracy with other algorithms

Algorithms	Iris	Glass	Pima
C4.5	95.5	67.9	70.8
ANN	95.3	65	76.4
IBL3	96.7	65.4	68.2
LEM2	94	66.8	62
SRS1	95.3	66	72.2
SRS2	94.4	62.2	71.2

Table 3 compares the classification accuracy obtained using the SRS1 and SRS2 algorithms with those of four well known data mining systems: the tree induction algorithm C4.5 [Quinlan, 1988], layered Artificial Neural Network (ANN) [Rumelhart et al, 1986], Instance Based Learning 3 [Aha et al, 1991] and rule induction algorithm LEM2 [Grzymala-Busse, 1992]. From Table 3, it can be seen that the system classification accuracy for both SRS1 and SRS2 algorithms approximate the other well-known classification systems, provided the parameters are properly selected.

In addition to the three data sets shown in Table 3, more data sets from the University of California Repository of Machine Leaning Databases [Merz et al, 1996] have been tested. Each set of data was run with the *ct* and *st* values ranging from 0.5 to 1. The optimal classification accuracy for each data set is listed in Table 4. Comparison of the optimal classification accuracies for SRS1 and SRS2, shows that SRS2 has lower optimal classification accuracy than SRS1. But to increase the classification accuracy from 94.4 (for SRS2) to 95.3 (for SRS1) for example in the Iris data set, the number of selected cases increases substantially from 4 to 22. This increase in the number of selected cases happened for all the data sets tested, with the exception of the "balance-scale" data set. Hence it can be concluded that there is a tradeoff between the classification accuracy and the number of selected cases. The choice of the algorithms depends on a number of factors, including the ease with which the parameters of *ct* and *st* can be defined, the acceptable classification accuracy and number of selected cases generated by the algorithms, and the computational resources available for applications.

Table 4. Experimental results on seven data sets

Data sets	SRS1	SRS2
Iris	22, 95.3	4, 94.4
Glass	61, 66.0	34, 62.2
Pima	69, 72.2	55, 71.2
Wine	21, 97.5	12, 93.4
Car	312, 82.3	144, 76.3
Balance-scale	32, 87.0	44, 71.9
Zoo	54,95.7	8, 87.1

6 Conclusion

In this paper, we propose two similarity-based rough set algorithms SRS1 and SRS2 for selecting representative cases from data sets. These algorithms are elegant in that they need only one to two parameters to be specified before the selection process. SRS1 requires the user to input the consistency threshold and the similarity threshold. SRS2 only requires the consistency threshold from the user while it can automatically decide the optimal similarity threshold for each object and therefore reduces the testing time and generates fewer cases than SRS1. Both SRS1 and SRS2 algorithms can deal with noise and inconsistent data in a database. The selected cases are representative in that they can cover all of the data in the data set in terms of the similarity relation, and at the same time, these cases are not similar to each other. The experimental results indicate that the classification accuracy for both systems is comparable to the state-of-the-art data mining systems. In the future, we will incorporate the attribute reduct and weight assignment algorithms to make the generated cases more compact and increase the classification accuracy of the derived case base.

Acknowledgment

The authors are grateful for the generous support of Natural Sciences and Engineering Research Council (NSERC) of Canada.

References

[Aha et al, 1991] Aha, D.W., Kibler, D., Albert, M.K., Instance based learning algorithms. *Machine Learning* 6 37-66, 1991.

[Bradshaw, 1987] Bradshaw, G., Learning about speech sounds: The NEXUS project. *Proceedings of the Fourth International Workshop on Machine Learning* 1-11 1987

[Cao et al, 2001] Cao, G., Shiu, S., and Wang, X., A fuzzy-rough approach for case base maintenance. *Proceedings of the Forth International Conference on Case-Based Reasoning,* 118-130, 2001.

[Chan et al, 2000] Chan, C., Chen, L., and Geng, L. Knowledge engineering for an intelligent case-based system for help desk operations. *Expert System with Application*, 18, 125-132, 2000.

[Cost et al, 1990] Cost, S. and SalzBerg, S. (1990) A weighted nearest neighbor algorithm for learning with symbolic features. *Technical Report JHU-90/11.* Baltimore, MD: The Johns Hopkins University, Department of Computer Science.

[Funakoshi et al, 1998] Funakoshi, K. and Bao Ho, T. Rough set approach to information retrieval. *Rough Sets in Knowledge Discovery*, v2, Lech Polkowski, Andrzej Skowron (eds.). Heidelberg Publisher, New York : Physica-Verlag 166-177, 1998.

[Grzymala-Busse, 1992] Grzymala-Busse, J.W., LERS - a system for learning from examples based on rough sets. In Slowinski, R. (eds.), *Intelligent Decision Support, Kluwer Academic Publishers*, 3-18, 1992.

[Han et al, 2000] Han, J. and Kamber, K. *Data Mining: Concepts and Techniques.* Morgan Kaufmann Publishers, 2000.

[Ketler, 1993] Ketler, K. Case based reasoning: an introduction. *Expert System with Application*, 6, 3-8, 1993.

[Krawiec, et al, 1998] Krzysztof Krawiec, Roman Slowinski, and Daniel Vanderpooten, Learining Decision Rules from Similarity Based Rough Approximations 2: Applications, Case Studies and Software Systems. *Rough Sets in Knowledge Discovery*, v2, Lech Polkowski, Andrzej Skowron (eds.), Heidelberg ; New York : Physica-Verlag, 37-54, 1998.

[Merz et al, 1996] Merz, C.J., Murphy, P.M.,UCI Repository of machine learning databases. University of California, Department of Information and Computer Science, 1996.

[Mrozek et al, 1998] Mrozek, A. and Skabek, K. Rough sets in economic applications. *Rough Sets in Knowledge Discovery*, v2, Lech Polkowski, Andrzej Skowron (eds.). Heidelberg Publisher, New York : Physica-Verlag 238-271, 1998.

[Pal et al, 2001] Pal, S. K. and Mitra, P. Case generation: a rough-fuzzy approach. *Proceedings of Workshop Program at the 4th International Conference on Case-Based Reasoning*, 236-242, 2001.

[Pawlak, 1991] Pawalk, Z. *Rough Sets: Theoretical Aspects of Reasoning about Data*, Kluwer Academic Publishers, Dordrecht, 1991.

[Quinlan, 1988] Quinlan, J.R. *C4.5: Programs for Machine Learning*. Morgan Kaufmann Publishers, San Mateo CA, 1988.

[Rumelhart et al, 1986] Rumelhart, D.E., Hinton, G. E., Williams, R.J. Learning internal representations by error propagation. In: Rumelhart, D.E, McClelland, J.L. and the PDP Research Group (eds.), *Parallel distributed processing: Explorations in the microstructure of cognition*, MIT Press, Cambridge MA, 318-362, 1986.

[Slowinski et al, 1997] Slowinski, R and Vanderpoonten D. Similarity relation as a basis for rough approximations. *Advances in Machine Intelligence and Soft Computing* 4, 17-33, 1997.

On the Stability of Example-Driven Learning Systems: A Case Study in Multirelational Learning

Lourdes Peña Castillo and Stefan Wrobel

Otto-von-Guericke-University Magdeburg,
{pena,wrobel}@iws.cs.uni-magdeburg.de
http://kd.cs.uni-magdeburg.de

Abstract. A popular way of dealing with the complexity of learning from examples is to proceed in an *example-driven* fashion. In the past, several researchers have shown that using an example-driven approach, it is possible to learn even structurally complex generalizations which would have been difficult to find using other multirelational learning (ILP) algorithms. On the other hand, it is also well known that the quality of the learning results in example-driven learning may depend on the ordering of the examples; however, such stability issues have received almost no attention. In this paper, we present empirical results in several multirelational application domains to show that instability actually affects the performance of a well-known example-driven ILP system. At the same time, we examine one possible solution to the instability problem, presenting an algorithm which relies on stochastically selected examples and parallel search. We show that our algorithm almost eliminates the instability of example-driven search with limited additional effort.

1 Introduction

Within inductive learning, it is common to distinguish between *generate-then-test* and *example-driven* learning algorithms [6]. A generate-then-test learning algorithm, such as FOIL [12] or CN2 [1], starts with the most general hypothesis in its hypothesis space and then specializes this hypothesis based on heuristic measures that take all examples into account. An example-driven algorithm, on the other hand, takes individual examples as starting points and uses them to constrain the hypothesis space. AQ [5] and Progol [10], for instance, are example-driven algorithms. An important advantage of the example-driven strategy is that the individual examples can be used to guide the search for hypotheses. This is particularly evident in multirelational learning, where systems like FOIL often cannot deal successfully with problems requiring complex rules, while example-driven systems such as Progol have proven to be effective especially in structurally complex domains.

However, the additional power of the example-driven approach comes at a price. Since only one or a few individual examples are selected as a basis for

C.A. Coello Coello et al. (Eds.): MICAI 2002, LNAI 2313, pp. 321–330, 2002.

generalization in each round, the choice of examples can have a significant effect on the quality and contents of hypotheses that are learned. The user can not rely on obtaining identical, or at least identically performing results in each run: the learning system is *instable*. What is more, as pointed out in [6], example-driven algorithms are more easily misled by a few noisy examples and are hence less robust when the training data contains errors.

While it is well known that example-driven approaches potentially exhibit the kind of instability described above, such stability issues have not been considered in great detail in the literature. In this paper, we set about on a detailed empirical study on the stability of example-driven learning focusing on the area of multirelational learning (also known as inductive logic programming, ILP). We conduct experiments in five domains, and show that instability is not merely a theoretical possibility, but indeed affects the performance of Progol [10], a popular example-driven ILP learning system.

We also examine one possible solution to the problem, presenting an algorithm which relies on stochastically selected examples and parallel search. We show that our algorithm almost eliminates the instability of example-driven search with limited additional effort. Our approach also delivers a numerical characterization of the degree of instability of a particular application domain, providing additional insight about the behavior of several problems.

The paper is organized as follows. In the next section, we first recall the basics of example-driven learning algorithms and define what we mean by stability in this paper. In section 3, we discuss a new learning system called Mio which is designed to eliminate the problems of instability by relying on stochastically selecting multiple examples and parallel search. Section 4 describes our experiments. Related work is discussed in Section 5, and Section 6 concludes.

2 Example-Driven Learning and Stability

2.1 Multirelational Example-Driven Learning

Typically, a multirelational learning system takes as input background knowledge B, positive examples E^+ and negative examples E^-, and has to find a theory T such that T is complete and consistent ($\{T \mid (T \cup B \models E^+) \wedge (T \cup B \not\models E^-)\}$) [1] [11]. This theory T consists of a set of Horn clauses (rules) which will be used to classify new unseen examples $E^?$ as positive or negative.

A common approach used by ILP systems is the *sequential covering algorithm*, which means that the system learns one by one a set of rules that together cover the complete set of positive examples. The covering algorithm is used by example-driven and generate-then-test systems alike. The main difference between both approaches is how the system constructs a new clause C_{new} to be added to the final theory.

A generate-then-test system generates C_{new} based only on the hypothesis representation language and uses the training data to choose among candidate

[1] Note, however, that the condition of consistency is often relaxed and the systems actually try to minimize the classification error over the training data.

hypotheses. The candidates are typically evaluated using heuristic functions on their performance over all the positive and negative examples [6].

A system using the example-driven approach takes a positive example e (or few positive examples) not implied by the clauses constructed in earlier iterations as starting point to construct a clause C_{new} which is a generalization of e, i.e., together with the background knowledge explains e. In addition, C_{new} maximizes an evaluation function which typically takes into account the number of other positive examples covered compared with the negative examples also covered.

How e is generalized to obtain C_{new} is a specific feature of each example-driven system. As a typical instance of example-driven learning as described above, let us consider Progol, a state-of-the-art, example-driven, multirelational learner developed by Muggleton and described in [10] [9]. In each iteration, Progol takes a positive example e not covered by the clauses constructed in earlier iterations, and uses it to construct a minimal generalization sufficient to cover e, the so-called *bottom clause* C_{bot}, Progol then performs a general-to-specific search (A*-like) of the hypothesis space lower bounded by C_{bot} to find C_{new}. In other words, the most specific hypothesis is used as a lower bound of the hypothesis space searched when constructing C_{new} from e.

2.2 Stability

Since typically not every e that is selected leads to equally good generalizations C_{new}, the results obtained by many example-driven learning systems can be affected by the order in which the examples are taken by the system. This lack of stability might have negative consequences such as increasing the likelihood of obtaining sub-optimal results (ie. theories with lower prediction power), and getting different theories from the same set of training examples. We therefore define stability (after renaming variables) as follows.

Definition 1 (Stability). *A learning system is defined as* **stable** *(against reordering) when, given reordered but otherwise identical example sets,*

(a) *it obtains identical sets of clauses:* syntactic stability, *or*
(b) *if all different results have equal prediction power:* semantic stability.

This stability definition directs toward two possible measures of stability, or rather, instability: accuracy distance and syntactic distance.

Definition 2 (Accuracy Distance). *Let A and B be two theories obtained on reordered example sets, and let $\alpha_A \in [0,1]$ and $\alpha_B \in [0,1]$ be estimates of the true error of A and B. The* accuracy distance *between A and B is defined as*

$$\delta_{acc}(A,B) := |\alpha_A - \alpha_B|.$$

Definition 3 (Syntactic Distance). *Then consider A and B as sets of clauses, and $A_{bag} := bagOf(A \setminus (A \cap B))$ and $B_{bag} := bagOf(B \setminus (A \cap B))$ as bags of literals. The* syntactic distance *between A and B is defined as*

$$\delta_{syn}(A,B) = \begin{cases} \frac{|A_{bag} \setminus B_{bag}| + |B_{bag} \setminus A_{bag}|}{|A_{bag}| + |B_{bag}|} & \text{if} A \cap B \neq \emptyset, \\ 1 & \text{if} A \cap B = \emptyset \end{cases}$$

where $|(T)|$ *is the cardinality of* T.

Note that A_{bag} and B_{bag} contain the clauses' literals as single elements and might have duplicate literals. We define then the degree of stability of a learning system on a particular problem as follows.

Definition 4 (Instability Measures). *Let* E *be an example set from an application domain, and* L *an example-driven learning system. The* instability *of* L *on* E *can be measured as follows.*

Let $T_1, \ldots, T_n$ *be the theories obtained by running* L *on* n *random permutations of* E. *The* syntactic instability *of* L *on* E *(based on* n *permutations) is*

$$\frac{\sum_{i=1}^{n-1} \sum_{j=i+1}^{n} \delta_{syn}(T_i, T_j)}{n}.$$

The semantic instability *of* L *on* E *(based on* n *permutations) is*

$$\frac{\sum_{i=1}^{n-1} \sum_{j=i+1}^{n} \delta_{acc}(T_i, T_j)}{n}.$$

3 Enhancing the Stability of Example-Driven Learning

An obvious approach to enhance the stability of example-driven learning is to base the computation of C_{new} on more than one example in each round. One way to do this, as employed by the system *Golem* [8], is to pick a user-selected number of examples s each time and compare their respective clauses C_{new} to select the best one. In this section, we introduce the system Mio, which integrates the parallel stochastic search based on several examples with the outer covering loop of the algorithm, using previous solutions both to increase quality and to avoid unnecessary search through iterative deepening.

Mio is an example-driven learner that relates to Progol in two main aspects: 1) it uses a bottom clause constructed from the background knowledge and a positive example as a lower bound for the search-space, and 2) it defines the hypothesis representation language using mode declarations. However, contrary to Progol, Mio enforces type strictness, ie. it requires type definitions for all the arguments in the target predicate and the background knowledge predicates. These type definitions are used to constrain the instantiations of the arguments during the construction of the bottom clause.

At each iteration, Mio takes randomly a subset of positive examples of the same target predicate and creates an independent search agent[2] for each example in the subset to search its hypothesis space bounded by the bottom clause and the target predicate. Each agent performs an IDA* search and keeps a *transposition table*[3] during the search. The transposition table stores the clauses which cannot

[2] In this paper an agent can be seen as an independent process or a thread.

[3] Transposition table is a term used in game-playing that refers to a search enhancement. Basically, a transposition table is a large cache in which newly expanded states are stored.

be improved by adding a new literal, and is used to prune the search tree. A global best evaluation value (GBE-value) is used by the agents to stop searching when the GBE-value cannot be outperformed.

After every agent stops, all the agents' solutions are placed in a descending ordered list according to the evaluation function. Mio traverses this list and adds to the final theory (T) the solutions whose value is above an user-defined threshold. Every time a solution is added to T, all the examples covered by it are removed. Those examples which at the end do not provide a solution are added to a losers list. If an example in the losers list is selected again in a subset, no search is performed and its value is the initial value of the GBE-value.

The number of positive examples taken in each iteration is determined by two user-defined parameters. One parameter indicates which fraction of the remaining examples to be covered has to be taken, and the other is the minimum number of examples that Mio takes. These search parameters can be seen as another measure for the instability of a domain: the more examples necessary for stability, the less stable a domain is. We thus can measure stability of an application domain in a third way by determining the minimum percentage of examples required to achieve perfect stability (ie. $\forall A, B(\delta_{syn}(A, B) = 0)$).

Definition 5 (Instability Based on Required Parallelism). *Let E be an example set from an application domain, and L an example-driven learning system. Let $s \in [0, 1]$ be a parameter controlling the amount of parallel search performed by L. The* required parallelism *of L on E is the smallest number p such that the syntactic instability of L on E is 0 when using p as a value for s.*

4 Experiments

The goals of our experiments were:

1. to determine whether a well-known example-driven system is affected by instability and if so, to which degree;
2. to find out whether the level of stability obtained depends on the specific properties of an application domain; and
3. to explore the suitability of stochastic example selection and parallel search as a solution to the instability problem.

With these questions in mind, we performed experiments on five datasets in three real application domains (games, biochemistry and bioinformatics) and in the artificial problem of the eastbound trains proposed by Ryszard Michalski. A brief description of each dataset follows below.

- **Chess Moves.** The learning goal is to determine the set of valid moves for five pieces (king, queen, bishop, knight and rook)[4].

[4] The positive examples of this dataset are contained in the distribution package of CProgol 4.4.

– **Minesweeper.** It is a common one–person game where the learner has to identify tiles without a mine, and has been proved to be NP-Complete [3][5].
– **Eastbound Trains.** One has to classify trains based on their attributes[6].
– **Biochemistry.** The mutagenesis problem deals with the prediction of the mutagenic activity of small, heterogeneous molecules. For this experiment, we use the dataset $B3$ with 188 compounds described in [13].
– **KDD Cup 2001: Protein Function Prediction.** The task in this domain is to predict one specific function of the proteins encoded by the genes[7].

For the experiments, the set of positive examples from each dataset was arranged in various random permutations and both systems, Progol and Mio, were run on the same permutations. The results were compared using the syntactic distance defined in Section 2.2. Table 1 shows for each dataset the number of random permutations used, the total number of positive and negative examples contained, and the percentage of the remaining positive examples randomly selected by Mio for parallelization. The last column refers the reader to the Table with the description of the results obtained by both systems on each dataset.

Table 1. Description of the five datasets

Dataset	Num. Rand. Perm.	Training Data E^+	Training Data E^-	Test Data E^+	Test Data E^-	% of Uncovered E^+ Selected for Parallelization	See Table
Chess Moves	7	160	17	20	0	2%	2
Minesweeper	6	43	704	5	70	33%	3
Eastbound Trains	8	38	17	4	2	20%	4
Mutagenesis	5	111	58	14	5	30%	5
KDD Cup 2001	5	275	587	117	264	10%	6

The percentage of the uncovered positive examples taken by Mio for parallelization was gradually increased to try to determine the minimum percentage required to obtain perfect stability. This minimum percentage indicates the degree of instability intrinsic to every dataset (Definition 5). Also, for the first three datasets, Mio took a minimum of 4 examples for the parallel search. For the last two datasets, mutagenesis and gene function prediction, the minimum number of examples taken for parallelization was set to 20 and 15, respectively.

In the tables with the results, the column *Average Distance to Other Theories (Avg. Dist.)* is calculated for a given Theory T_i as $\frac{\sum_{j=1}^{n} \delta_{syn}(T_i,T_j)}{n-1}$.

[5] It is important to comment that the theories learned by both systems are not sufficient to win a minesweeper game.

[6] To generate the examples we used the Random Train Generator available at http://www-users.cs.york.ac.uk/~stephen/progol.html

[7] This task is part of task 2 from the KDD Cup 2001. In the KDD Cup 2001, the complete task 2 was to predict n of thirteen gene functions (http://www.cs.wisc.edu/~dpage/kddcup2001/).

Table 2. Theories about chess moves obtained by Progol (up) and Mio (bottom)

Theory T_i	Total Num. of Clauses	Total Num. of Literals	Times Obtained	Accuracy	Avg. Dist.	Run-time (sec)
Progol						
T1	11	23	4	100 %	0.285	9.01
T2	15	35	2	95 %	0.145	11.76
T3	16	36	1	95 %	0.150	8.63
Avg.	14	31.33	2.33	96.67 ± 2.36	0.193	9.80
Mio						
T1	11	23	7	100 %	0	5.75

Table 3. Minesweeper theories obtained by Progol (up) and Mio (bottom)

Theory T_i	Total Num. of Clauses	Total Num. of Literals	Times Obtained	Accuracy	Avg. Dist.	Run-time (hrs)
Progol						
T1	1	6	3	100 %	0.40	0.885
T2	4	14	3	100 %	0.40	2.310
Avg.	2.5	10	3	100 %	0.40	1.598
Mio						
T1	4	14	6	100 %	0	1.21

Table 4. Eastbound trains theories obtained by Progol (up) and Mio (bottom)

Theory T_i	Total Num. of Clauses	Total Num. of Literals	Times Obtained	Accuracy	Avg. Dist.	Run-time (min)
Progol						
T1	7	17	1	83.33 %	0.39	1.01
T2	7	13	6	66.67 %	0.29	1.18
T3	7	15	1	83.33 %	0.24	1.25
Avg.	7	15	2.7	77.78 ± 6.43	0.30	1.15
Mio						
T1	5	13	8	83.33 %	0	2.11

Table 7 shows a summary of the results obtained by Progol and Mio in the five domains. Run-time penalty is the factor in which the run-time of Mio increases compared with a version of Mio taking one example for each iteration. We have an increase in run-time because the parallelization is actually done sequentially (see Future Work). With our empirical results, we have shown that a state-of-the-art example-driven system is severely affected by syntactic instability; that parallel search based on randomly selected examples reduces the effects caused by reordering of the examples; and, that the minimum amount of parallelization required seems to be related to some intrinsic features of each dataset. In addition, Mio obtains in average compacter theories than Progol.

Table 5. Mutagenesis theories obtained by Progol (up) and Mio (bottom)

Theory T_i	Total Num. of Clauses	Total Num. of Literals	Times Obtained	Accuracy	Avg. Dist.	Run-time (hrs)
			Progol			
T1	22	41	1	89.47 %	0.40	1.46
T2	24	42	1	100 %	0.34	1.03
T3	22	35	1	89.47 %	0.33	1.09
T4	24	42	1	94.74 %	0.47	1.14
T5	23	40	1	89.47 %	0.33	1.16
Avg.	23	40	1	93.23 ± 4.26	0.37	1.18
			Mio			
T1	18	30	1	84.21 %	0.30	16.32
T2	20	29	1	89.47 %	0.24	14.12
T3	22	32	1	89.47 %	0.24	13.53
T4	20	33	1	84.21 %	0.37	15.03
T5	18	30	1	89.47 %	0.30	17.23
Avg.	19.6	30.8	1	87.37 ± 2.58	0.29	15.25

Table 6. Gene function theories obtained by Progol (up) and Mio (bottom)

Theory T_i	Total Num. of Clauses	Total Num. of Literals	Times Obtained	Accuracy	Avg. Dist.	Run-time (hrs)
			Progol			
T1	107	243	1	82.15 %	0.165	2.77
T2	114	253	1	79.79 %	0.130	2.14
T3	124	285	1	78.74 %	0.155	2.58
T4	115	257	1	81.10 %	0.133	2.20
T5	130	290	1	80.58 %	0.153	3.08
Avg.	118	265.6	1	80.47 ± 1.15	0.147	2.55
			Mio			
T1	114	120	1	84.51 %	0.060	3.51
T2	107	116	1	84.78 %	0.093	3.16
T3	114	123	1	83.99 %	0.073	3.28
T4	111	117	1	85.04 %	0.085	3.79
T5	116	123	1	83.99 %	0.095	3.22
Avg.	112.4	119.8	1	84.46 ± 0.42	0.081	3.39

Table 7. Summary of results obtained by Progol and Mio for each dataset

Dataset	Progol Avg. δ_{syn}	Progol Avg. δ_{acc}	Mio Avg. δ_{syn}	Mio Avg. δ_{acc}	Run-time Penalty
Chess	0.19	0.033	0	0.0	1.16
Minesweeper	0.40	0.0	0	0.0	5.60
Trains	0.30	0.22	0	0.0	2.69
Mutagenesis	0.37	0.056	0.29	0.032	4.53
Gene function	0.15	0.014	0.08	0.006	1.15

5 Related Work

Each single search agent in Mio uses the general approach of any example-driven covering learning system. The example-driven covering approach was first introduced in the sixties with the AQ system [5]. Other well-known example-driven systems are Cigol [7] and Golem [8]. Golem enhances the stability of example-driven learning by taking a user-selected number of examples s each time, and comparing their respective clauses C_{new} to select the best one. The example-driven covering system to which Mio relates the most is Progol [10]. Mio uses a declaration language to define the hypothesis language similar to the one that Progol uses, and every search agent in Mio computes the bottom clause in the same way as Progol does. However, Mio differs from Progol in the search strategy, in the heuristics used, and in the type strictness.

Some work has been done in parallel multirelational learning by Matsui *et al.* [4] and Fujita *et al.* [2]. Matsui *et al.* examine three parallelization approaches to speed up FOIL: partition of the search space, partition of the training examples, and partition of the background knowledge. The parallel approach of Mio can be seen as a partition of the training examples. Fujita *et al.* work in a parallel implementation of Progol. In [2] the design and a part of the implementation of parallel-Progol is discussed. However, in contrast with our work, the goal of these research groups is to speed-up the learning systems, and, additionally, they do not explore the stability of the results.

6 Conclusions and Future Work

In this paper a case-study about stability in multirelational learning was presented. Experimental results in five datasets show that a well-known example-driven system is affected by re-ordering of the examples, and that a viable solution to provide stability against reordering of the training data is stochastic selection of examples and parallel search. This approach is explored in Mio.

Mio is implemented in Java and SICStus Prolog. Since SICStus does not support multiple instances of the prolog emulator in the same Java process, all the calls to SICStus are synchronized, ie. performed sequentially. Thus, we do not obtain as much performance gain in terms of run-time with the parallelization as it could be expected. Fortunately, SICStus 3.9 to be released this year will solve this limitation[8]. We expect to get a significant improvement in the speed of the system by upgrading to SICStus 3.9.

The stability results presented in this paper are encouraging; however, some work needs to be done exploring the mutagenesis and KDD datasets. In both datasets, we were not able to obtain only one theory from all the random permutations (ie. reach perfect stability); however, Mio obtained more stable results than Progol in both domains. We suspect it is possible to increase the stability in these domains by taking more uncovered positive examples after the first iteration. It is part of the future work to explore this hypothesis in the datasets

[8] http://www.sics.se/isl/sicstuswww/site/comingfeatures.html

already mentioned and in data from new application domains. Also, we should explore the effects of noisy domains in Mio and the stability measures.

Acknowledgments

The authors would like to thank Susanne Hoche and Oscar Meruvia for revising previous versions of this paper, and Mark–A. Krogel for providing a preprocessed version of the KDD data. This work was partially supported by a scholarship of the federal state Sachsen-Anhalt, Germany, and by DFG (German Science Foundation), project FOR345/1-1TP6.

References

1. Peter Clark and Tim Niblett. The CN2 induction algorithm. *Machine Learning*, 3(4):261–283, 1989.
2. Hiroshi Fujita, Naoki Yagi, Tomonobu Ozaki, and Koichi Furukawa. A new design and implementation of Progol by bottom-up computation. In S. Muggleton, editor, *Inductive Logic Programming*, volume 1314 of *Lecture Notes in Artificial Intelligence*, pages 163–174. Springer-Verlag, 1996.
3. Richard Kaye. Minesweeper is NP-complete. *The Mathematical Intelligencer*, 22(2):9–15, Spring 2000.
4. Tohgoroh Matsui, Nobuhiro Inuzuka, Hirohisa Seki, and Hidenori Itoh. Comparison of three parallel implementations of an induction algorithm. In *Proceedings of 8th International Parallel Computing Workshop*, pages 181–188, Singapore, 1998.
5. Ryszard S. Michalski. On the quasi-minimal solution of the general covering problem. In *Proceedings of the V International Symposium on Information Processing (FCIP 69)*, volume A3 (Switching Circuits), pages 125–128, Yugoslavia, Bled, 1969.
6. Tom M. Mitchell. *Machine Learning*. McGraw Hill, first edition, 1997.
7. Stephen Muggleton and Wray L. Buntine. Machine invention of first-order predicates by inverting resolution. In J. Laird, editor, *Proceedings of the 5th Conference on Machine Learning*, pages 339–352, San Mateo, CA, 1988. Morgan Kaufmann.
8. Stephen Muggleton and Cao Feng. Efficient induction of logic programs. In Stephen Muggleton, editor, *Inductive Logic Programming*, volume 38 of *APIC Series*, pages 281–298. Academic Press, London, 1992.
9. Stephen Muggleton and John Firth. Relational rule induction with CProgol4.4: a tutorial introduction. In Sašo Džeroski and Nada Lavrac, editors, *Relational Data Mining*, pages 160–187. Springer-Verlag, 2001.
10. Stephen Muggleton. Inverse entailment and Progol. *New Generation Computing Journal*, 13:245–286, 1995.
11. Shan-Hwei Nienhuys-Cheng and Ronald de Wolf. *Foundations of Inductive Logic Programming*, volume 1228 of *Lecture Notes in Artificial Intelligence*. Springer-Verlag, Berlin, first edition, February 1997.
12. J.Ross Quinlan and R. Michael Cameron-Jones. Introduction of logic programs: FOIL and related systems. *New Generation Computing, Special issue on Inductive Logic Programming*, 13(3-4):287–312, 1995.
13. Ashwin Srinivasan, Ross D. King, and Stephen Muggleton. The role of background knowledge: using a problem from chemistry to examine the performance of an ILP program. *Transactions on Knowledge and Data Engineering*, 1999. under review.

Sharpe Ratio-Oriented Active Trading: A Learning Approach

Yang Liu[1], Xiaohui Yu[2], and Jiqing Han[1]

[1] Department of Computer Science and Engineering
Harbin Institute of Technology
Harbin, 150001, China
liuyang@hope.hit.edu.cn

[2] Department of Computer Science and Engineering
Chinese University of Hong Kong
Shatin, N.T., Hong Kong, China
xhyu@cse.cuhk.edu.hk

Abstract. Portfolio offers an effective way for managing investment risk through diversification. The key issue in portfolio management is how to determine the weight (portion) of each asset in the portfolio, so as to achieve high profit with low risk over a certain period of trading. We propose a learning-based trading strategy for portfolio management, which aims at maximizing the Sharpe Ratio by actively reallocating wealth among assets. The trading decision is formulated as a non-linear function of the latest realized asset returns, and the function can be approximated by a neural-network. Two methods based on supervised learning to train the network are proposed. Experiments show that the proposed trading strategy outperforms the static Sharpe Ratio trading method.

1 Introduction

Portfolio is an effective way of increasing returns while decreasing risk when investing in financial market. The study in portfolio management (or more specifically, portfolio selection) problems began with Markowitz's seminal paper [9], and there has been considerable attention to optimal portfolio selection strategies in the financial and statistics literature [11,4,1,3,5].

The basic issue in portfolio selection is how to diversify the investment to achieve high profit with low risk. However, it is not a goal that can be easily obtained. There is a fundamental relationship between return and risk: the higher the expected profit, the greater the risk and similarly, the lower the expected profit, the smaller the risk. Thus, a reasonable way to invest is not to only pursue high profit, but to pursue high risk-adjusted performance. Over the past several decades, various such performance measures have been proposed based on Markowitz's *mean-variance* paradigm, such as the *Sharpe Ratio* (the focus of this paper) [12,13], the *Jensen Alpha* and the *Treynor Ratio* [6].

The Sharpe Ratio is defined as

$$SR = \frac{\text{Average Return}}{\text{Standard Deviation of Return}} \tag{1}$$

C.A. Coello Coello et al. (Eds.): MICAI 2002, LNAI 2313, pp. 331–339, 2002.

Sharpe Ratio analysis has been widely adopted in Wall Street. However, like most current models based on Markowitz's paradigm, it is used for single-period investment, i.e., once the decision is made, the portfolio is supposed to be used for the whole investment period [8]. Such method is known as the *Static Sharpe Ratio Approach*. It cannot trace the changes in market and thus lacks the capability to adjust its decision adaptively.

On the other hand, in statistical learning and neural network community, little attention has been paid to the mean-variance analysis. Early trading systems just try to predict the financial time series (e.g., price series) and then make a decision based on the prediction in hope of maximizing the return. Such method has two deficiencies. First, As indicated by Bengio [2], Weigend [7], Moody [10] and Xu [14], global optimization of trading systems consisting of separate forecasting and trading modules provides better results than separately minimizing the MSE of the prediction module and subsequently reaching a decision based on a specified trading strategy. Second, using maximum profit as objective often leads to unsatisfactory performance due to its ignorance of risk.

Kang *et al* [7] first proposed a trading system that directly optimizes the Sharpe Ratio and compared its performance with an alternative method that just optimizes the profit. However, the system they proposed does not directly optimize the trading system parameters which determine when to buy or sell and does not explicitly depict the functional relationship between the realized return and the decision to be made. Moreover, though the system proposed does work for a simple two-asset case, it can not be trivially generalized to multiple-asset cases.

In this paper, we investigate the portfolio management problem from a new perspective and propose a new trading strategy which explicitly regards the decision for the next trading period as a non-linear function of the latest realized return. This system can also directly optimize the system parameters.

This paper is organized as follows. In Section 2, we present a Sharpe-Ratio-Oriented portfolio trading strategy. In Section 3, a two-step supervised learning approach is proposed to train the trading system. In Section 4, we propose a more sophisticated method which seeks to directly optimize the objective function in one-step. Section 5 describes the experiment and results. Section 6 concludes this paper and points out some problems to be addressed in the future.

2 Sharpe-Ratio-Oriented Active Trading (SROAT)

Consider the problem of investing on a portfolio of N assets. The goal of our trading system is to decide how to allocate the investment at each period to obtain maximum Sharpe Ratio. For simplicity of language, we assume that we have daily data. Define p_t^i to be the price of the asset i on day t, and x_t^i to be the *relative price return* on day t

$$x_t^i = \ln(p_t^i) - \ln(p_{t-1}^i) \simeq \frac{p_t^i - p_{t-1}^i}{p_{t-1}^i} \quad (2)$$

The investment allocation on day t is represented by the vector $\mathbf{w}_t = (w_t^1, \ldots, w_t^N)$, where $w_t^i \geq 0$ and $\sum_{i=1}^N w_t^i = 1$, where w_t^i represents the proportion of wealth invested in the ith asset.

The *portfolio return* on day t is defined to be

$$z_t = \mathbf{w}_t^T \mathbf{x}_t = \sum_{i=1}^{N} w_t^i x_t^i \tag{3}$$

The *cumulative profit* on investment, R, over T days is the product of the daily portfolio returns

$$P_T = \prod_{t=1}^{T} \mathbf{w}_t^T \mathbf{x}_t \tag{4}$$

Now let us take a look at $\mathbf{w}_t$. We expect that our system can dynamically decide $\mathbf{w}_t$ based on past and current observations. Since the market is nearly efficient, we can just take the last realized return into consideration. The system can decide $\mathbf{w}_t$ based on $\mathbf{x}_{t-1}$. Thus, we may establish a function mapping from the series $\mathbf{x}$ to $\mathbf{w}$

$$\mathbf{w}_t = \mathbf{f}(\mathbf{x}_{t-1}; \Theta) \tag{5}$$

In general, the function is non-linear and can be represented by a three-layer feed-forward neural network with $\mathbf{x}_{t-1}$ as input and $\mathbf{w}_t$ as output. Note that since the $\mathbf{w}_t$ is constrained by $w_t^i \geq 0$ and $\sum_{i=1}^N w_t^i = 1$, the output layer should use the *softmax* function as its transfer function.

With such formulation, the problem now is how to train the network to maximize the following objective function:

$$SR_T(\Theta) = \frac{\bar{z}}{\sqrt{var(z)}} = \frac{\frac{1}{T}\sum_{t=1}^T z_t}{\sqrt{\frac{1}{T-1}\sum_{t=1}^T (z_t - \frac{1}{T}\sum_{t=1}^T z_t)^2}} \tag{6}$$

where

$$z_t = \mathbf{w}_t^T \mathbf{x}_t = \mathbf{f}(\mathbf{x}_{t-1}; \Theta)^T \mathbf{x}_t \tag{7}$$

Since all decisions and return series are included in the objective function, and no specific target values for each input $\mathbf{x}_t$, we can not train the network directly with a standard supervised learning method. In sections 3 to 5, we will show several methods to train the network.

The trading system using the strategy mentioned above will actively reallocate the investment every day seeking to maximize the Sharpe Ratio. So we call it a *Sharpe-Ratio-Oriented Active Trading* (SROAT) method.

3 A Two-Step Supervised Learning Approach

As indicated in the previous section, the reason why supervised learning method cannot be used directly is that there are no corresponding target values for each

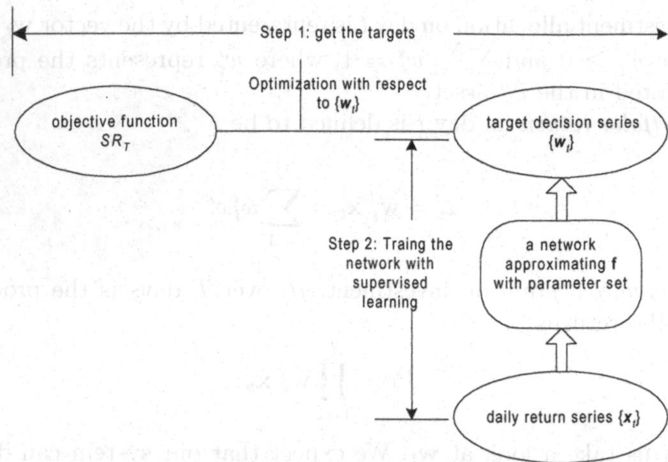

Fig. 1. The Two-Step Supervised Learning Approach

input pattern. However, the problem can be solved by decomposing the training process into two steps. In the first step, a sequence of desired target portfolio weights used for training the system is determined. Then the network is trained using those target values with standard supervised learning method. The details are as follows:

Step 1: Obtaining Target Weights

If we consider the objective function eq. (6) as a function of $N \times T$ independent variables $\{w_t^i\}(i = 1, \ldots, N; t = 1, \ldots, T)$, then $\{w_t^i\}$ can be obtained by

$$\{w_t^i\} = argmax_{\{w\}} \frac{\frac{1}{T}\sum_{t=1}^{T} \mathbf{w}_t^T \mathbf{x}_t}{\sqrt{\frac{1}{T-1}\sum_{t=1}^{T}(\mathbf{w}_t^T \mathbf{x}_t - \frac{1}{T}\sum_{t=1}^{T} \mathbf{w}_t^T \mathbf{x}_t)^2}} \tag{8}$$

Note that the standard gradient ascent method can not be directly used to find $\{w_t^i\}$, because $\{w_t^i\}$ are subject to the constraint $w_t^i \geq 0$ and $\sum_{i=1}^{N} w_t^i = 1$. Instead, by doing the following softmax substitution:

$$w_t^i = \frac{\exp(a_t^i)}{\sum_{j=1}^{N} \exp(a_t^j)} \tag{9}$$

we can perform the maximization with respect to $\{a_t^i\}$ directly using gradient ascent method. In case that T and N are large, some techniques, such as simulated annealing, must be employed to avoid the possible problem of local minimum.

Step 2: Training the Network via Supervised Learning

Having the target weights in hand, the network can be trained via standard supervised learning approach such as back-propagation. One thing to note is that we should not use MSE or SSE as the error function. That is because the output of the network are non-negative values that sum up to 1. They can be interpreted as the probability that the input pattern belongs to a certain class. So the logarithmic or cross-entropy error function

$$E_{log} = \sum_t \sum_i w_t^i \ln y_t^i + (1 - w_t^i) \ln(1 - y_t^i) \tag{10}$$

where y_t^i is the output of the network.

Though the experiments show that the performance of the two step method is appreciable (as will be shown in Section 5), it is likely to result in a suboptimal network, because the ultimate measure of performance $SR_T(\Theta)$ is not used to optimize Θ directly, and it is more liable to suffer from local-minimum problem. So, we should further develop a method that can directly optimize $SR_T(\Theta)$ in a single step.

4 Direct Optimization of Performance with Batch-Way Training

Given a trading system with objective function $SR_T(\Theta)$, the goal is to adjust the parameters Θ in order to maximize $SR_T(\Theta)$. The gradient of SR_T with respect to parameters Θ of the system after a sequence of T trades is

$$\frac{\mathrm{d}SR_T(\Theta)}{\mathrm{d}\Theta} = \sum_{t=1}^{T} \frac{\partial SR_T}{\partial z_t} \frac{\mathrm{d}z_t}{\mathrm{d}\mathbf{w}_t} \frac{\mathrm{d}\mathbf{w}_t}{\mathrm{d}\Theta} \tag{11}$$

where

$$\frac{\partial SR_T}{\partial z_t} = \frac{\frac{1}{T} var(z) - \frac{1}{T-1} \bar{z}(z_t - \bar{z})}{var(z)^{3/2}} \tag{12}$$

$$\frac{\mathrm{d}z_t}{\mathrm{d}\mathbf{w}_t} = \mathbf{x}_t \tag{13}$$

With this expression, The parameters Θ can be updated in a manner similar to the Widrow-Hoff rule (Widrow and Hoff 1960) used in standard back-propagation network. The only difference here is that the objective is not to minimize the error function such as MSE or SSE, but to maximize the function $SR_T(\Theta)$. The algorithm is summarized as follows:

1. Calculate the all weights, $\{\mathbf{w}_t\}$, in response to all input patterns $\{\mathbf{x}_t\}$ (Note there is time lap between $\mathbf{x}$ and $\mathbf{w}$, i.e., $\mathbf{w}_t$ corresponds to $\mathbf{x}_t$.) by making a feed-forward pass through the network.
2. Calculate all portfolio returns $\{z_t\}$, and $\bar{z}$, $var(z)$.

3. Calculate the delta value for all output nodes and hidden nodes with respect to each output. For the output unit, it miscalculated as
$$\delta_{it} = \frac{\partial SR_T}{\partial z_t}\frac{\mathrm{d}z_t}{\mathrm{d}w_t^i}g_i' = \frac{\frac{1}{T}var(z) - \frac{1}{T-1}\bar{z}(z_t - \bar{z})}{var(z)^{3/2}}x_t^i g_i' \tag{14}$$
where g_i' is the derivative of the activation function of the output unit i (As indicated before, it is a softmax function).
The delta values for hidden units can be calculated in a similar way.
4. Using these delta values to get the total derivative and update the network parameters by
$$\Theta^{\mathrm{new}} = \Theta^{\mathrm{old}} - \eta\frac{\mathrm{d}SR_T}{\mathrm{d}\Theta^{\mathrm{old}}} \tag{15}$$
where η is a small learning rate.
5. Repeat until the network converges.

The above two methods are both based on batch-way learning. They are useful, but in practice, we hope the network can have the ability to adapt itself to just available information (such as returns). The batch-way manner of the above method will hinder achieving this goal because each time it requires to train the network from the very beginning and thus is too computation intensive. So it is of interest to devise an on-line learning approach which is more computation efficient and can easily adapt to recent information.

5 Experiment

SROAT has been implemented using the two-step supervised learning approach proposed in Section 3 and tested on real-world stock indices. The experiment results and analysis are shown below.

We perform experiments of investing in a portfolio of three stock indices:

1. CAC 40 Index (France)
2. S&P 500 Index (USA)
3. Hang Seng Index (Hong Kong)

The data used are from January 4, 1999 to March 31, 2000, consisting of totally 326 day's closing prices. The first 200 data points (from January 4, 1999 to October 7, 1999) are used for training while the remaining 126 data points are used in the testing stage.

SROAT is tested and compared with other trading strategies in the experiment, including the Static Sharpe Ratio approach (SSR), and the simple investment strategy that puts all the wealth on one asset only. The transaction costs are assumed to be zero.

The experimental results are shown in Figure 1, 2 and Table 1. Figure 1 suggests that SROAT outperforms all other trading strategies. While SROAT does not beat others on each day, its performance does appear to be more stable

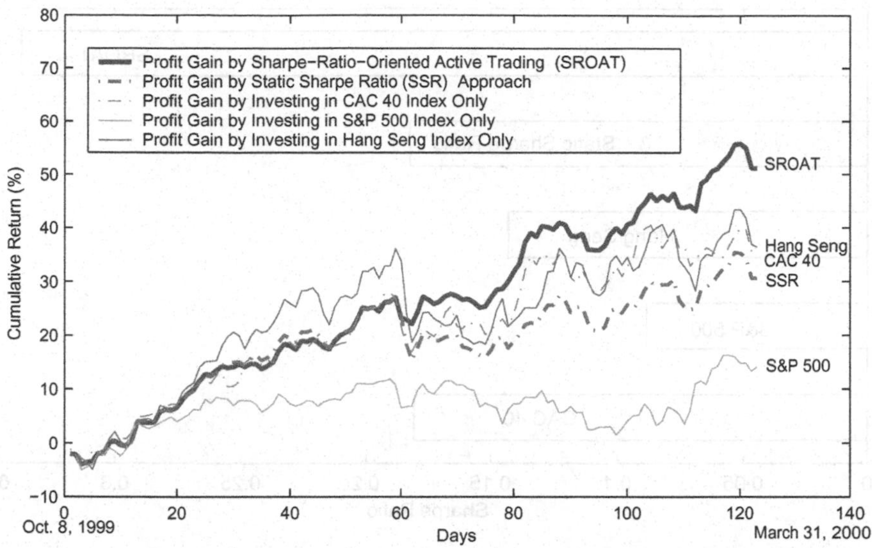

Fig. 2. Comparison of cumulative profit obtained by SROAT and other trading strategies

Table 1. Statistics of experimental comparison of SROAT with other trading strategies.

	SROAT	SSR	CAC 40	S&P 500	Hang Seng
mean of daily return	0.0036	0.0022	0.2537	0.1160	0.2707
standard deviation of daily return	0.0108	0.0123	1.4070	1.3085	1.8918
Sharpe Ratio	0.3375	0.1821	0.1803	0.0886	0.1431

and the risk is lower. Note the sudden price drop that happened around the 60th testing day. While all other trading strategies suffered from the sudden drop, SROAT successfully reallocated the investment and thus reduced the loss.

Table 1 compares the statistics of the experimental results of SROAT and other trading strategies. One may notice that the daily return of SROAT is lower than others. However, the standard deviation is also much lower than others and thus results in a greater Sharpe Ratio. This result reveals the essence the Sharpe-Ratio-based trading strategy, i.e., getting a good trade-off between return and risk, rather than purely pursuing higher return and ignoring risk.

6 Conclusion and Future Work

In this paper, we proposed a trading strategy SROAT for portfolio management that aims at maximizing the Sharpe Ratio by actively reallocating wealth among assets. The trading decision is regarded as a function of the latest realized returns of assets in the portfolio. Two different methods are proposed to train the

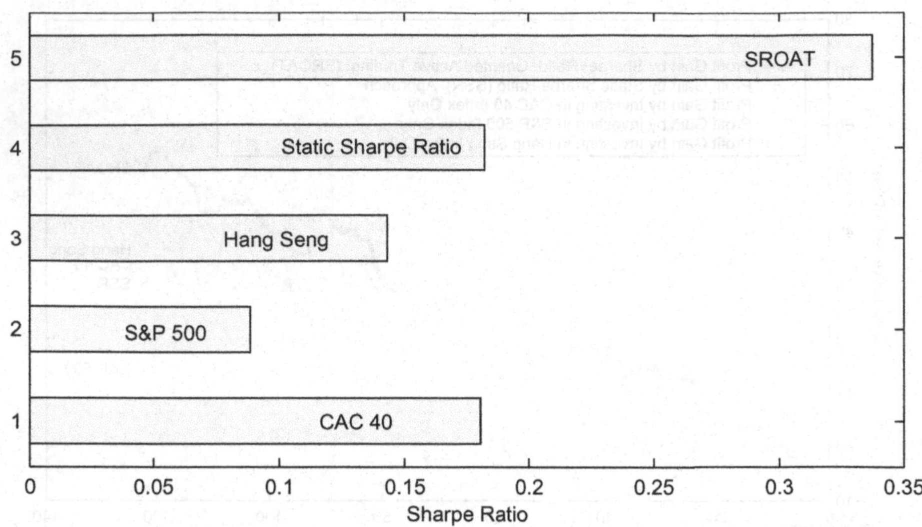

Fig. 3. Comparison of Sharpe Ratio over the testing period for SROAT and other trading strategies

neural network that seeks to approximate the function. The two-step supervised learning method is easy to implement. However, it does not directly use the objective function and thus may lead to suboptimal results. We further proposed a method which can directly optimize the network to achieve the performance goal. Experiments have shown that SROAT are sensitive to the price changes in market and outperforms all other trading strategies compared.

At the present stage, the transaction cost is not taken into consideration. However, transaction cost is a very crucial issue that must be considered in real-world trading. We will investigate how to incorporated it into SROAT. A potential problem is that when transaction cost is considered, the decision $\mathbf{w}_t$will not only depend on the latest returns $\mathbf{x}_{t-1}$, but also on previous decision $\mathbf{w}_{t-1}$. We may have to resort to the recurrent architecture instead of the simple feed-forward one employed in this paper.

Another issue to work on in the future, is how to use reinforcement learning algorithms to obtain more adaptivity.

References

1. P.H. Algoet and T.M. Cover. Asymptotic optimality and asymptotic equipartition properties of log-optimum investment. *The Annals of Probability*, 16(2):876–898, 1988.
2. Y. Bengio. Training a neural network with a financial criterion rather than a prediction criterion. In Y. Abu-Mostafa, A.N. Refenes, and A. Weigend, editors, *Decision Technology for Financial Engineering*. World Scientific, London, 1997.
3. T. Cover. Universal portfolios. *Mathematical Finance*, 1(1):1–29, 1991.

4. T.M. Cover and D.H. Gluss. Empirical bayes stock market portfolios. *Advances in Applied Mathematics*, 7:170–181, 1986.
5. T. Goll and J. Kallsen. Optimal portfolios for logarithmic utility, 2000.
6. D.A. Hammer. *Dynamic Asset Allocation: Strategies for the Stock, Bond, and Money Markets.* John Wiley and Sons, New York, 1991.
7. J. Kang, M. Choey, and A.S. Weigend. Nonlinear trading models and asset allocation based on sharpe ratio. In Y. Abu-Mostafa, A.N. Refenes, and A. Weigend, editors, *Decision Technology for Financial Engineering.* World Scientific, London, 1997.
8. R. Korn. *Optimal Portfolios: stochastic models for optimal investment and risk management in continuous time*, pages 11–13. World Scientific Publishing, 1997.
9. H.M. Markowitz. Portfolio Selection. *Journal of Finance*, March 1952.
10. J. Moody and L. Wu. Optimization of trading systems and portfolios. In Y. Abu-Mostafa, A.N. Refenes, and A. Weigend, editors, *Decision Technology for Financial Engineering.* World Scientific, London, 1997.
11. P. Samuelson. Lifetime Portfolio selection by dynamic stochastic programming, 1969.
12. W.F. Sharpe. Capital Asset Prices: A Theory of Market Equilibrium Under Conditions of Risk. *Journal of Finance*, September 1964.
13. W.F. Sharpe. The Sharpe Ratio – properly used, it tan improve investment. *The Journal of Portfolio Management*, pages 49–58, 1994.
14. L. Xu and Y.M. Cheung. Adaptive Supervised Learning Decision Networks for Traders and Portfolios. *Journal of Computational Intelligcnte in Finance*, 5(6):11–15, 1997.

A Framework for Social Agents' Interaction Based on Communicative Action Theory and Dynamic Deontic Logic

Amal El Fallah-Seghrouchni[1] and Christian Lemaître[2]

[1] Laboratoire d'Informatique de Paris Nord, LIPN, UPRES-A CNRS- 7030, France
elfallah@lipn.univ-paris13.fr
[2] Laboratorio Nacional de Informática Avanzada, LANIA, Mexico
cll@xalapa.lania.mx

Abstract. We propose an integrated approach through key concepts about social agents and multiagent systems. We start with the general concept of agent society as an entity structured by institution*s* and organization*s*, in the sense proposed by D. North. Agent interactions are presented within the theory based on communicative action theory introduced by J. Habermas. Among the three domains of discourse proposed by J. Habermas, the objective, the subjective and the social domains, we focus in this paper on the social domain of discourse to develop a new semantics based on dynamic deontic logic where we introduce the notion of complex object of the norms as proposed by P. Bailhache.

1 Introduction

In recent years, an important work has been done in MAS community around key concepts of social agents, social interactions [4], normative agent systems [5], [14], Institutions [12], and organizations [3]. In spite of all this work until now there has been no integration of those different, but complementary, views of agents' society.

Many potential applications of MAS to every day life have to do with helping humans in their daily work and with their different types of interaction through Internet or the Intranet of the company where they work. Those human assistant agents will be inserted in the social life of users, and as well as humans, agents behavior will need to comply with different types of laws, legal norms and rules.

We are interested to design systems that will be able to deal with situations like the following. Suppose that the chief executive officer of a company -or his electronic assistant- during a meeting with the planning workgroup, gives the order that the "final plan report should be finished in one week". What is the meaning of this order? Is it an order for one person of the workgroup, for all members of the workgroup, or for a subset of the members of the workgroup?

Most of the work done in MAS literature around agent interaction is about single agents interaction, or about group of agents treated as a single agent. Real applications are more complicated than that, our claim is that a new theoretical framework is needed to deal with issues like complex agents that should comply to different norms. Our aim is to contribute to this task, presenting an integrated framework for social agent interaction.

C.A. Coello Coello et al. (Eds.): MICAI 2002, LNAI 2313, pp. 340–350, 2002.

In order to do that, we present an integration of most of those concepts around the idea of a society of agents structured by institutions and organizations, in the sense proposed by D. North [13]. Agent interactions are presented within an extended framework of traditional speech act theory based on communicative action theory introduced by J. Habermas [6]. In this new framework, the content of natural language utterances is divided in three different domains of discourse: 1) the domain or world of objective facts *W*; 2) the internal or subjective domain of the sender *I*; and 3) the social relational domain of sender and receiver So.

Each domain has its own validity criteria and semantics. In [8] we have introduced an appropriate interaction formalism based on this communicative action theory.

In this paper we focus our attention on the social relational domain *So*, defining a new semantics based on an extension of dynamic deontic logic provided by [11]. This extension aims to improve the dynamic deontic logic by introducing deontic operators applied to complex agents in order to deal with social norms. As it is the case in deontic logic, the subject of a norm represents the agent who has the authority to enforce the norm, while the object of a norm is the agent who is supposed to comply it. Several variants of dynamic deontic logics have been proposed in the literature [10, 14]. Nevertheless, at our knowledge, the plurality of the norm subjects and objects has been scarcely, if ever, studied in MAS. In [2] some logical aspects of deontic logic including this plurality has been studied but the author focuses on the *"ought-to-be"* perspective, while specific features of agents (such as actions, communications, etc.) requires to take into consideration the *"ought-to-do"* perspective.

The remainder of this paper is structured as follows. In section 2 we introduce the general concepts of agent society and institutions based on D. North's economics theory as well as the basic types of agent we would deal with in the rest of the paper. In section 3 we recall the basic concepts of the communicative action agent interaction formalism we have discuss elsewhere. In section 4 we present the formal specification of communicative action for normative agents based on our dynamic deontic logic model; while in section 5 we discuss the main extensions of our formalism to complex agents. Finally, our main conclusions are stated in section 6.

2 Agent Society, Institutions and Agents

Activities of agents in agent society are governed by social rules, in the same way that human activities are ruled and enforced in human society. Following the work of D. North[13], and applying it to agent society, we introduce the notions of agent institution and agent organization as two basic concepts.

For us, agent institution is the framework within which agent interactions take place defining their interaction constraints. We will call these agents, social agents. Hence an agent institution defines not only the rules of the game in an agent society but also the players, who are the subjects of the norms, i.e., those who are in charge to enforce them, and who are the objects of the norms, those who must follow the norms.

From the pragmatic point of view, we introduced two different roles for social agents, the subject and the object agents, i.e., the one who has the authority to enforce the norm, and the one who is supposed to comply it. From interaction point of view we will distinguish two types of agent: atomic and complex agents. The fact that if a complex agent is a group of agents will introduce no difference in the dynamic of interactions which will cover three general cases: one to one, one to many, and many to many.

We are interested to study in this work the social interactions involving norms, i.e., those interactions covered by one or several institutions and applied to groups of agents. A norm is meaningful if it is shared by or is applied to a "group of agents" [2].

Some examples of human interactions that we are interested to manage in their *agent version,* where we substitute the human user by his agent assistant, are the following:

- Interaction among two or more companies
- Interaction among the chief executive officer and all his employees
- Interaction among the members of a working group
- Interaction between two employees of the same company.

For instance, we are interested to provide a precise meaning to the sentence: "The chief executive officer orders to his company Y to do action z". What does it mean : "every employee in Y must perform z", "at least one of them must do z" or at least a "sub-group" of employees in Y must perform z"?

In order to deal with this type of issues, we need to build a rich enough formalism able to deal with different cases of interaction among groups of agents. For instance, in the case of obligation we need to be able to distinguish among different types of obligation: "strong" obligation (every agent is obliged to do an action), "weak" obligation (an individual agent is obliged to do an action) and what we call "flexible" obligation (at least *a significant but sufficient* sub-group of agents is obliged to do an action). In section 4 we present the formal specification of the different types of norms for the deontic concepts of obligation, permission and prohibition.

3 Communication Action Formalism

In [8] and [9] we have presented a new agent interaction formalism based on Habermas/Bühler communication action theory. This formalism includes the three layer validity domains of this theory, as well as the focus of attention shift to the receiver point of view. Interaction among agents implies complex patterns of speech act interchanges. If these message interchanges are to be fruitful, interlocutors must be able to decide if each message they receive is or is not acceptable for them. If they think a message is not valid they must reject it, with a criticism or a reason why they do not accept it. If the receiver R accepts the message he can then interpret it and act accordingly.

We claim that what is needed at present stage of MAS real applications in open domains is a formal theory helping to control meaningful speech act interchanges among agents. We need a theory of meaning based on the receiver of the speech act, the one who can accept or reject it as valid or invalid. With this shift in our focus, looking at the receiver instead of the sender, we can assure real control of agent interactions.

A second issue in our theory is to go beyond the classical formal semantics. Following Habermas we claim that the content of natural language utterances are about three main topics: the domain or world of objective facts *(W)*, the internal or subjective domain of the sender *(I)*, and the social relational domain of sender and receiver *(So)*. The key point here is that each domain has different validity criteria. We assume the following validity criteria: For *W* we assume the classical True/False semantics; for *I* we assume a Truthful/Untruthful semantics; and for *So* we assume a Right/Not-right semantics. Any utterance might be criticized from the three points of view, although, there is always a more natural criticism for each type of speech acts.

3.1 Validity Claim Procedures

True/False validity: This procedure implies that a third person can verify the truth or untruthfulness of the fact. The receiver, R, can accept an assertoric sentence if he knows what kind of reasons the sender, S, would have to cite in order to convince him his assertion is true. If R has some doubts about the reasons S may have, he can reject the utterance or ask for more arguments about the validity of the assertion.

Truthful/Untruthful validity: This procedure implies that R can decide if he trusts S or not according what S has said as well as on his past experience with S, i.e., on his truthfulness model of S. If the truthfulness of S is not good enough, R may: 1) refuse S´s utterance because he does not trust him; or 2) try to ensure some commitment of S that gives him some confidence that the intention expressed by S will become a social commitment. In this case, R will shift the domain of discourse from *I* to *So*.

Right/Not Right validity: In So-domain, R must analyze if S is violating (or not) a social norm of any sort, or a social commitment between S and himself. This implies the existence of shared norms between S and R, as well as the existence of a third agent who can eventually enforce the norm compliance. We include social commitment in the sense of Castelfranchi and co-workers [4] but we exclude the non-social commitment, since there is no third party who can enforce the commitment and thus can be treated in the I domain. Social context for So-domain, is defined in terms of institutions or the set of norms (general social and legal norms, specific commercial norms, internal organization norms, individual contracts, social commitments, etc.). Besides the domain and the functional role of each agent related to a specific utterance –sender or receiver- we need to know the social relationship of each agent in the institution or set of institutions involved by the utterance: are they, subject agents or object agents?

In [8] we present an utterance validation procedure for this new approach. In the following sections we will focus on interactions among social agents in So domain of discourse, and present a model and a formalism for such kind of interactions based on a model of dynamic deontic logic.

4 Formal Specification of Communicative Actions for Normative Agents

4.1 Overview of Normative Statements

It is well established that deontic logic is suitable to deal with social norms and to sketch the lines that underline the (not)acceptable actions or states of affairs according to deontic considerations. It concerns normative concepts such as *obligation, permission, prohibition* that can be applied, both, to actions and states of affairs. As it has been discussed in several papers [5, 14] deontic logic can capture the concept of *"Ought-to-be"* but captures hardly the one of *"Ought-to-do"* since it introduces several well known paradoxes [11].

Nevertheless, from MAS perspective, where agents share organizations and norms, the *"Ought-to-do"* concept plays a central role especially when norm sentences involve actions. To capture this concept, an alternative logic has been proposed in several essays. Following [5,11], we agree that a deontic logic based on a logic of actions [7] like Dynamic Deontic Logic (DDL) is suitable to express normative concepts about actions. The main features of DDL can be summarized as follows:

- The underlying logic of actions allows to express norms about actions. For instance *"it is obligatory, permitted, prohibited, etc., to perform an action x"*.
- DDL is free of the main classical paradoxes as demonstrated in [11].

4.2 A Language of Actions Based on Dynamic Deontic Logic

The language we will use is based on PDL (Propositional Dynamic Logic) and is close to the one defined in [11].

Syntactical Aspects of the Language of Actions. To define the language of actions for our social agents, let us assume that an action is done by an agent/human and not considered as a program as usually in standard PDL. The formal language of PDL as a language of actions will be called PDL (L_{action}).) and built up from two sets of primitive symbols Act and Fml where:

- *Act* is a countable set of atomic actions. An action is performed by an agent and its execution leads to a new state of the world. The set of all actions satisfies the following conditions:
  if x and y are actions then:
  - (x ; y) , a sequence of actions (perform x then perform y);
  - (x ∪ y), non-deterministic choice of actions (perform either x or y);
  - -x, (omit x which is different from doing the negation of x);
  - and x* : iteration (perform x finitely many times),

  are actions.
- *Fml* is a the set of formulae defined as the least set which contains all atomic formulae satisfying that if A, B are formulae and x an action then:
  - ¬A, the negation of A
  - (A∧ B) , the conjunction of A and B;
  - and [x]A, where [x]A means that after the performance of x, A necessarily holds;

  are also formulae.

Model of Action. An action model is defined as a tree-like structure M=(W, R, V) where W, R, and V are as in the basic logic of action defined by :

- W, is a non-empty set of formulae representing the set of all the states of the world.

- R is a function that assigns to every action x a binary relation R(x) on W. R(x) is the transition relation associated with the action x. (s, t)$\in$R(x) means that "if the action x is performed at the state s, then the state t is reached". If the action x is not performed, then no transition occurs (no state t is reached).
- V is a valuation function that assigns to each atomic formula P a sub-set V(p) of W. V(p) is the set of states satisfying P (where p is true).

  As demonstrated in [13] the function R satisfies the following conditions: for all x, y $\in$ Act
  - $R(x ; y) = R(x) ; R(y)$
  - $R(x \cup y) = R(x) \cup R(y)$
  - $R(-x) \cap R(x) = \emptyset$
  - $R(--x) = R(x)$
  - $R(x^*) = (R(x))^*$
  - $(W, \cup\{R(x) : x \in Act\})$ is a tree-like graph.

Semantical Aspects of the Language of Actions. The formal semantics of our language is out of the scope of this paper, and can be defined as usual. It is defined as usual (more details such as semantics and axiomatization are available in [11]). Let us recall the main aspects of this semantics.

For all formula A in Fml, a relation $M,s \models A$ is defined as:

- $M,s \models P$ iff $s \in V(P)$ for any atomic formula P
- $M,s \models \neg A$ iff $M,s \not\models A$
- $M,s \models A \vee B$ iff $M,s \models A$ or $M,s \models B$
- $M,s \models [x]A$ iff for all $t \in W$, $(s, t) \in R(x)$ implies $M,s \models A$

4.3 Deontic Operators

Let us give a brief and informal overview on the main standard deontic operators and their thruth conditions. As said before, deontic logic concerns deontic norms (or normative constraints) governing a given organization. The main feature of the deontic norms is that they can be violated. When a violation holds, a sanction should be applied. Several deontic logics have been proposed as variants of dynamic logic [7] to specify deontic constraints [5, 10, 14]. The central definition is: $F(x) = [x]V$, which means that an action x is forbidden if it leads to a state where a violation V holds. This definition is quite similar to the "sanction predicate" S used by Anderson's reduction of deontic logic [1].

In this paper, we will adopt the sanction formula S, since we are interested by "what happens and who/whom is/are concerned" when a violation occurs. The sanction depends on the object of the norm and the institution as we will see later. The standard deontic operators (obligation, permission and prohibition, etc.) are usually defined as:

D1. $O_x =_{def} [-x]\, S$ (x is obligatory, i.e. not doing x leads to a sanction S)
D2. $P_x =_{def} [x]\neg S$ (x is permitted, i.e. no sanction holds if x is done)
D3. $F_x =_{def} [x]\, S$ (x is prohibited, i.e. doing x leads to a sanction)

Different interactions between these operators can be defined, such as:

I1. $F_x = O_{-x}$ (if an action is prohibited then its omission -i.e. not doing x- is obligatory and vice versa)

I2. $P_x = \neg F_x$ (if an action is permitted then it is not prohibited and vice versa)

I3. $O_x \supset P_x$ (if an action is obligatory then it is permitted)

I4. $P_x = \neg O_{-x}$ (if an action is permitted then it is not obligatory to omit it and vice versa).

Let us remark that I4. can be deduced from I1 and I2.

4.4 MAS Requirements for Social Agents

Several variants of dynamic deontic logics have been proposed in the literature. Nevertheless, at our knowledge, the plurality of the norm subjects and objects has been weakly considered in MAS field. To meet the requirements of MAS populated by normative agents, it is necessary to extend the deontic norms in several ways. In fact, the relationship between the subject of norm and its object influences the interpretation of normative sentences according to the organizational aspects of agents (the domain So in our communicative action theory, see utterance acceptance in section 3).

In addition, the presence of several organizations in the same system needs to consider several norm-systems or institutions. While considering social agents, it is necessary to be able to express sentences such as: "*According to an organization O, governed by a given institution I_k, it is permitted for an agent a* (atomic or complex) *to do the action x*". Hence the main requirements for social agents as defined in section 1, include:

- The norms should concern both states of affairs and actions.
- The objects of norms should be both atomic and complex agents. Let us note that the extension of the subjects of norm will not be presented here due to space restriction.
- A rich enough formalism is needed to interpret normative sentences considering individual, collective, and individually collective norms, as the one we will present in section 5.
- A unified framework to manage communicative actions involving norms.

Example: Suppose that an advisor *A* orders to the group of his *PhD* students *G "you have to propose a paper before march 23"*. We would like to distinguish three possible interpretations:

- Every PhD student must propose a paper before march 23;
- The group of PhD student as a whole must propose a paper before march 23 ;
- Only some students in the group must propose a paper before march 23.

From the communicative point of view, the order corresponds to an obligation towards the advisor and can be expressed using a directive communication act as defined by Dignum et al.[6]: DI*R (A, G, O_x)* where x is: *propose a paper before march 23.*The advisor order (or obligation) will be accepted or not according to the relationship between the advisor and his students -i.e., has he the right or not ?- as defined in the utterance acceptance of the communicative act and more precisely w.r.t. the right/not right procedure defined in section 3.

This simple example emphasizes an important ambiguity in the norm interpretation, since standard deontic operators cannot deal with the qualification of the norm object, especially when we have to address both atomic and complex agents. To remove such ambiguity, we introduce 3 variants for each standard norm as we will see in the next section (Section. 6.1):

- Individual norms applied to atomic agents (as in the case of standard norms).
- Collective norms applied to a complex agent.
- Individually collective norms applied to all the agents belonging to the complex agents.

The sanction issue must be refined according to the new kinds of norms. This issue will be discussed in the next section when deontic operators will be defined.

5 Extension of Norms to Complex Agents

The norms considered in this section are obligation, permission and prohibition applied to both atomic and complex agents.

5.1 Logical Foundations

Let us consider a complex agent $\alpha = \{$ a, b, c..$\}$ as a set of agents, each of them could be atomic or complex. Let A, B, ..etc., denote the sub-sets of α such that $A \subset \alpha$ and $B \subset \alpha$ etc. We will distinguish the case where a, b, c .. are atomic and the case where they are complex. Let us start with the most simple case, i.e. a, b, c ... are atomic.

First Case: α is a complex agent composed by a set of atomic agents.

What does it mean that the agent α is obliged towards an other agent S_b (the subject of the obligation) to do some action x? Intuitively, common sense implies that x is obligatory for some group if it is obligatory for everybody in the group (here α). So, we will call it "a strong obligation" denoted by O_{ICO} and said *"individually collective obligation"*.

Definition of O_{ICO}: $O_{ICO}(S_b, \alpha, x) =_{def} \forall a \in \alpha, [-a(x)]\, S(S_b, a)$

The question now is which permission corresponds to O_{ICO}?

Knowing that $P_x = \neg O_{-x}$; i.e. x is permitted if omit x (–x) is not obligatory (see I4. in section 5.3), we can deduce the corresponding permission as: $\exists a \in \alpha, P(S_b, a, x)$.

This permission may be interpreted as a kind of individual permission. We can remark that this permission is different from the usual permission. Hence, we name it a "weak permission" denoted by P_I and said *"individual permission"*.

Definition of P_I: $P_I(S_b, \alpha, x) =_{def} \exists a \in \alpha, [a(x)]\, \neg S(S_b, a)$

What we need now is to express a permission as it is usually interpreted for a group, society, company, etc. In other words, some action is permitted for a group if it is permitted for every one in this group. This kind of permission corresponds to what we call "a strong permission", denoted P_{ICO} and said *"individually collective permission"*.

Definition of P_{ICO}: $P_{ICO}(S_b, \alpha, x) =_{def} \forall a \in \alpha, [a(x)] \neg S(S_b, a)$

Reciprocally, it is necessary to look for the corresponding obligation. We use again the interaction I4 ($P_x = \neg O_{-x}$) as defined in section 5.3, which leads to a "weak obligation", denoted O_I and said "individual obligation".

Definition of O_I: $O_I(S_b, \alpha, x) =_{def} \exists a \in \alpha, [-a(x)] S(S_b, a)$

Second Case: α is a complex agent composed by a set of complex agents (a complex agent may be defined recursively).

Let us examine the case of a complex agent himself composed by a set of complex agents. Obviously, an atomic agent is a trivial case of complex agent. Consider again the original strong obligation: $O_{ICO}(S_b, \alpha, x) =_{def} \forall a \in \alpha, [-a(x)] S(S_b, a)$, but now we will generalize a to any kind of agent: atomic or complex, i.e. any subset A.

In this case the objects of obligation will be universally quantified. So, it is possible to define norms to be applied to sub-sets of objects. A Strong obligation can be refined on two ways.

The first one keeps the name of strong obligation (since it generalizes the first strong obligation), although we will write it as O_{IC}.

Definition of O_{IC}: $O_{IC}(S_b, \alpha, x) =_{def} \forall A \subset \alpha, [-A(x)] S(S_b, \alpha)$

This obligation should be interpreted henceforth as for every sub-group (atomic or complex agent) of α it is obligatory to do x. If x is not done, α as a whole is sanctioned.

The second one is called "flexible obligation" (the particular case is when A coincides with an atomic agent), denoted O_C and defined as follows.

Definition of O_C: $O_C(S_b, \alpha, x) =_{def} \exists A \subset \alpha, [-A(x)] S(S_b, A)$,

This obligation should be interpreted as for some sub-group A of α, it is obligatory to do x. The Sanction S should be applied to A if x is not done.

Now, we can easily define their dual permissions as follows:

Definition of Strong Permission P_{IC}: $P_{IC}(S_b, \alpha, x) =_{def} \forall A \subset \alpha, [A(x)] \neg S(S_b, A)$

This permission should be interpreted as for every sub-group of α it is permitted to do x; i.e., no A will be sanctioned if he does x.

Definition of Flexible Permission P_C: $P_C(S_b, \alpha, x) =_{def} \exists A \subset \alpha, [A(x)] \neg S(S_b, A)$

This permission should be interpreted as for some sub-group A of α, it is permitted to do x ; i.e. A will not be sanctioned if he do x.

Finally, we obtain three variants for each norm:

Obligation	Dual Permission
Weak Obligation $O_I(S_b, \alpha, x) =_{def} \exists a \in \alpha, [-a(x)] S(S_b, a)$	Weak Permission $P_I(S_b, \alpha, x) =_{def} \exists a \in \alpha, [a(x)] \neg S(S_b, a)$
Flexible Obligation $O_C(S_b, \alpha, x) =_{def} \exists A \subset \alpha, [-A(x)] S(S_b, A)$	Strong Permission $P_{IC}(S_b, \alpha, x) =_{def} \forall A \subset \alpha, [A(x)] \neg S(S_b, A)$
Strong obligation $O_{IC}(S_b, \alpha, x) =_{def} \forall A \subset \alpha, [-A(x)] S(S_b, \alpha)$	Flexible Permission $P_C(S_b, \alpha, x) =_{def} \exists A \subset \alpha, [A(x)] \neg S(S_b, A)$

5.2 Remarks

Keeping in mind that:

- the negation of universal quantifier $(\forall x, p \equiv \neg(\exists x\, \neg p))$
- the duality between permission and obligation ($P_x = \neg O_{\neg x}$),

and the inclusion rules :

- $A \subseteq B \Rightarrow O_{IC}(S_b, B, x) \supset O_{IC}(S_b, A, x)$;
- $A \subseteq B \Rightarrow O_C(S_b, A, x)) \supset O_C(S_b, B, x)$

one can easily verify that :

- A strong norm implies a flexible norm which implies a weak norm (the universal quantifier implies the existential one).
- Also, some other interesting implications such as O_{IC} implies P_C ;O_C implies P_{IC}, etc.

Examples:

- By the law, it is permitted for a president of party pp to propose a candidate (case of atomic agent).
  P_I (Law, pp, "propose a candidate").
- By the law it is permitted for each party p to present a candidate (case of every complex agent).
  P_{IC} (Law, p , "present a candidate").
- By the law it is permitted for the Liberal Party to participate to a meeting, it is not the case for all the parties (case of some complex agents).
  Pc (Government, Liberal Party , "participate to the meeting").

In a similar way, we can re-define other norms such as prohibition.

Prohibition (F for forbidden)

Weak Prohibition: $F_I(S_b, \alpha, x) =_{def} \exists\, a \in \alpha, [a\,(x)]\, S(S_b, a)$

Flexible Prohibition: $F_C(S_b, \alpha, x) =_{def} \exists\, A \subset \alpha, [A\,(x)]\, S(S_b, A)$

Strong Prohibition: $F_{IC}(S_b, \alpha, x) =_{def} \forall A \subset \alpha, [A\,(x)]\, S(S_b, \alpha)$

Examples:

- It is prohibited for the president P to present more than one candidate. Otherwise, he will be sanctioned.
  F_I (Law, P, "present more than one candidate ").
- It is prohibited for some parties (small parties for instance) Sp to participate in presidential election.). The prohibition concerns some but not all the parties . Any small party concerned by the prohibition will be sanctioned if does it.
  Fc (Law, Sp, "participate in presidential election").
- It is prohibited for each party Py to present more than one list of candidates. Each party will be sanctioned if he does it.
  F_{IC} (Law, Py, "present more than one list of candidates").

6 Conclusion and Future Work

The primary contribution of this paper is the integration for the first time, in a coherent framework of important concepts of social agency that have been treated separately in the literature, such as North's concepts of institutions and organizations, Habermas communicative theory, dynamic deontic logic treated by Dignum et al. and Ngoc Duc and object extension to complex agents treated by Bailhache.

Several extensions of this work should be conceivable. Among the most promising we can note the following three: 1) the extension of our DDL semantics to complex subjects of the norm ; 2) the refinement of the sanction concept according to the institutional context ; and 3) the definition of more appropriate semantics for subjective domain I, where the BDI semantics based on perlocutionary effects on the receiver can not be of much help since our shift to the receiver point of view needs a new formalism based on the notions of Truthful and Untruthful.

Acknowledgements

Partial research support has being provided by 31827-A grant from Mexico's National Council of Science and Technology, CONACYT.

References

1. A.R. Anderson. "The Formal analysis of normative systems." In Rescher, N. (ed.), The logic of decision and action, U. Pittsburgh Press, 1956.
2. P. Bailhache. *"Essai de Logique Déontique"*. Librairie Phil. J.Vrin. Paris, 1991.
3. K.M. Carley, L. Gasser. *" Computational Organization Theory"*. In G. Weiss (ed.), Multiagent Systems. MIT Press, 1999.
4. C. Castelfranchi. *"Modeling social action for AI agents"*. In Art. Intelligence 103, Elsevier, 1998
5. F. Dignum, J.Ch. Meyer and R. Wieringa. *"A dynamic logic for reasoning about sub-ideal states"*. In J. Breuker, (ed.), ECAI workshop on Artificial Normative Reasoning, 1994.
6. J.Habermas. *"Postmetaphysical Thinking"*. The MIT Pres. Cambridge, 1996.
7. D. Harel. *"First Order Dynamic Logic"*. LNCS 68 Springer. 1979.
8. C. Lemaître, A. El Fallah Seghrouchni. *"A Multi-Agent Systems Theory of Meaning Based on Habermas/Bühler Communicative Action Theory"*. In Lecture Notes in Artificial Intelligence 1952, Advances in Artificial Intelligence, M. Monard, J. Sichman (eds.). Springer. 2000.
9. C. Lemaître, A. El Fallah Seghrouchni. *"A Comprehensive Theory of meaning for communication acts in Multi-Agent Systems"*. In the proceedings of ICMAS-2000.
10. J.Ch.Meyer, R.J.Wieringa (eds.). *"Deontic Logic in Computer Science, Normative System Specification"*. John Wiley, 1993.
11. H.Ngoc Duc. *"Semantical Investigations in the Logic of Actions and Norms"*. PhD. Thesis, Institut für Logik und Wissenschaftstheorie, 1995.
12. P. Noriega. *"Agent-Mediated Auctions: The Fishmarket Metaphor"*. PhD. Thesis, Universitat Autónoma de Barcelona, 1998.
13. D. C. North. *"Institutions, Institutional Change and Economic Performance"*. Cambridge U. Press, 1990.
14. R.J. Wieringa, Weigand H., J.- J.Ch. Meyer, and F. Dignum. *"The inheritance of dynamic and deontic integrity constraints"*. In annals of mathematics and artificial intelligence 3. 1991.

Autonomous Agents for Ubiquitous Collaborative Environments

Jesús Favela[1], Manuel Alba[2], and Marcela Rodríguez[1,3]

[1] Departamento de Ciencias de la Computación, CICESE, Ensenada, México
favela@cicese.mx

[2] TheBrain Technologies Corp., Santa Monica, CA, USA
malba@thebrain.com

[3] Facultad de Ingeniería, Universidad Autónoma de Baja California, Mexicali, México
marcerod@cicese.mx

Abstract. The proliferation of different computing devices such as handhelds and wall-size whiteboards, as well as Internet-based distributed information systems are creating ubiquitous computing environments that provide constant access to information regardless of the user's location. Handheld computers are being transformed from personal electronic agendas into mobile communication devices with intermittent network connectivity. Thus, these devices are becoming a natural medium to tap into an ubiquitous computing infrastructure. Not only do they store much of the user's personal information (contacts list, meeting schedule, to-do list, etc.), but they are always at hand, in sharp contrast with desktop computers. Handhelds, however, most often operate disconnected from the network thus reducing the opportunities for computer-mediated collaboration with other peers or computational resources. In this paper we present an extension to the COMAL handheld collaborative development framework to support autonomous agents that can act on behalf of the user. We discuss scenarios that take advantage of such platform and the design decisions that were made to implement it. The use of the framework is illustrated with the development of an agent that recommends talks within a conference, based on the context and the user's profile.

1 Introduction

The number of users of handheld computers around the world grows at an impressive rate. Personal Digital Assistants (PDAs), smart cell phones and similar electronic devices are now part of our daily lives. As new services and more powerful devices reach the market this tendency will certainly continue in the near future.

Due to the personal nature of handheld computers, most of its applications today are oriented to single users and require limited or no connectivity at all. However, the users of these devices work in collaborative environments in which the need to exchange information and share ideas with others is very clear. Additionally, the information stored in handheld computers: dates of meeting and events, contacts information, to-do lists, and e-mail messages, plays a central role in a large number of collaborative applications. Thus, as these devices become more pervasive and support network connectivity, we expect them to become major players in future ubiquitous collaborative environments [5, 9].

C.A. Coello Coello et al. (Eds.): MICAI 2002, LNAI 2313, pp. 351–360, 2002.

Handheld collaborative applications developed to this date, have been mostly exploratory in nature, and it is not yet clear what will be the role that such devices will play in an ubiquitous computing environment, enriched by context-sensitive information sources. Addressing these issues will necessarily require the development of robust prototypes to be tested under realistic conditions.

Ubiquitous computing environments provide natural interfaces to interact with a variety of devices (handhelds, laptops, electronic whiteboards, etc.) which provide almost constant access to information and processing resources [12]. Furthermore, the interconnected infrastructure as a whole should be able to sense the context in which a specific situation is taking place and adapt to it according to its location of use, the people and objects that are around, and changes of those entities over time [3].

Increasingly, handhelds provide alternatives for network connectivity, yet they are often inactive and even when in use they are most of the time disconnected from the network, which severely limits their use for ubiquitous collaboration. Even if there were no technological or economical considerations to disconnect from the network, social issues might prevent users from doing so, as exemplified by cellular phone users that go off-line when they don't want to be disturbed.

In these circumstances, autonomous agents that act on behalf of the user and reside on a desktop computer or trusted server, might be able to maintain a limited user presence and execute actions on his behalf while he is disconnected or inactive.

To explore the potential of such an approach, we have extended COMAL [2], a handheld collaborative development framework, to support the development of autonomous agents in ubiquitous collaborative environments. Before we present the extended framework, we first discuss three use scenarios and the requirements of the software infrastructure that we have identified from them. We finish the paper presenting a sample application and discuss our conclusions and future work.

2 Use of Agents in Ubiquitous Collaborative Applications

In order to lay the foundation of the proposed framework, we first analyzed a set of possible utilization scenarios for the use of autonomous agents in ubiquitous collaborative applications. This analysis helped us determine key issues to be addressed in the development of the framework we are presenting. The applications analyzed and their associated use scenarios are described next.

2.1 Conference Scheduling Agent

A user attends a conference with multiple simultaneous tracks. On her handheld device she fills a form in which she specifies her main interest within the scope of the conference. While she registers at the conference she connects her handheld to a point of presence to send her profile, which launches an agent that will communicate with another agent in the conference server to build for her a personalized recommended schedule given her preferences. Once the schedule is generated it will be stored in the server and downloaded to the handheld the next time it is connected to the network. The data will be integrated in the calendar application in the handheld.

As the conference progresses users could add notes or grade the talks they attend. If these notes are marked as being public they will be downloaded to the server when the user connects to a point of presence in the conference. Public notes from other users will be transmitted to the connected user, as will updates to the schedule based on recommendations made by other users with similar profiles [10]. Users could also exchange notes and recommendations using their handheld computers without requiring a connection to the network.

2.2 An Agent That Deals with Shared Resources

A user is co-authoring a research paper with a couple of colleagues and he needs to incorporate his final contributions and send the paper today. However, the latest version of the paper is currently locked in a shared repository by one of his co-authors who has left town to attend a conference for the week. The user sends a message to his co-author's agent who will decide, based on the context and the trust he has to the author making the request, whether or not to liberate the resource.

In [7], Moran et al. describe a tool named Doc2U that could be the basis for supporting this scenario. With Doc2U shared resources are added to the roster of an instant messaging and presence awareness application. A user then can be aware of the state of resources, such as a document being locked. An instant message can be sent directly to a co-author or to a resource in the form of a command. In this case the decision to unlock a resource is left to the user, but he could have configured an agent to act on his behalf when he is disconnected or inactive. An agent can be seen in the roster of a handheld-based instant messaging application, such as Doc2U, as another user to which one can send messages or commands such as "launch". When the device has no access to the network, all events generated are stored by the handheld and later sent, when access to the network is provided or a synchronization process is performed. A similar approach is used for information flowing from the application server to the mobile device, if the device is not accessible, all messages and other events are blocked until the exchange of data is possible.

2.3 Meeting Assistant

In this scenario people attending a meeting have personal mobile devices and the meeting place provides desktop computers to aid in group collaboration. At least one of the computers should serve as a data distribution point between mobile devices and the desktop computers inside the room. This scenario is frequently seen at electronic meeting rooms and intelligent environments as the ones described in [11].

Each meeting participant is then able to share personal information, send messages, data, and even presentations to other participants. The distribution of the information could be performed user to user, directly using the mobile devices, or user to desktop computers, allowing asynchronous communication. Meeting information could then be transferred from a public screen to the mobile device to be updated, and from the mobile device to the public screen, to make changes public as described in [4].

When the meeting ends, users could then leave the room with a copy of agreements reached and other important information generated during the session in their mobile devices. This information could be displayed later for modification, review, or distribution among users not present during the meeting.

Users that are not able to attend a meeting or need to leave early could leave behind an agent with limited competence to represent them by either raising issues when certain topics are discussed, or voting on their behalf. Software that helps in meeting coordination as is the case in Electronic Meeting-room Systems or that provide intelligent support for meeting in electronic whiteboards as in the case of the Tivoli project [8], could integrate these agents with certain ease. Alternatively, an agent could record certain aspects of the meeting and present a brief to the user. To automate the capture of live experiences and provide flexible access to them has been identified as one of the main research issues in ubiquitous computing [1]

3 Requirements for the Development Framework

Based on the scenarios just presented we have identified the following requirements for an application development framework that can be used to build autonomous agents for ubiquitous collaborative applications:

1. Disconnected mode of operation. Network access was not always present in the application scenarios discussed earlier. In fact, the presence of this resource was minimal. Applications and agents should be able to store outgoing information until data exchange is possible.
2. Consistent development API. The libraries used in the framework provide a set of consistent functions to be used in both the handheld application and its desktop counterpart. This API acts as a basis on top of which handheld collaborative applications can be built following a predefined structure.
3. Different communication modes. Support for exchanging information is provided through data synchronization (between handheld devices and desktop computers) and point-to-point connections (to access networked resources, when possible).
4. Users should be able to launch agents explicitly or they could be launched automatically when certain conditions are met.
5. Agents should be able to communicate with its user and with other agents in other desktops or a server. Additionally, agents should be able to read and write to the repository where the user's personal information is stored.

The first three requirements are satisfied by COMAL (Collaborative Mobile Application Library), an architecture and a set of application libraries designed to build Shared Objets for Portable Environments, or SOPE applications, as described in the next section. To satisfy requirements four and five, we have extended COMAL with SALSA (Simple Agent Library for Sope Applications). This extension, described in Section 5, allows users to implement simple agents on top of SOPE's to act on behalf of the user while he is disconnected. Developers using this framework can then concentrate more on building the ubiquitous collaborative solution itself, rather than doing low level programming.

4 COMAL's Development Framework

COMAL's architecture includes the following main components [2].

1. Application servers. These servers store application information across the network, this data may even be distributed among several servers and databases on different sites or replicated to increase availability.

2. A terminal or desktop computer that acts as an access point. This computer is used to access both networked information and the handheld device.
3. A handheld application. This is the mobile device used while the user is away from his desktop. The application is also used to collaborate with people carrying similar devices, or with the surrounding environment. COMAL currently supports the Palm Computing Platform and its operating system PalmOS.

Another important component, always present when collaboration takes place, is the communication channels between the previously listed items. COMAL currently supports TCP/IP over IrDA or a serial connection. The COMAL libraries reside only in the desktop and handheld computers, the rest of the handheld collaborative application is not different from most collaborative systems.

4.1 COMAL's Software Architecture

The software architecture used in the COMAL development framework is illustrated in Figure 1. The dotted rectangle encapsulating the three applications represents a handheld collaborative application, named SOPE.

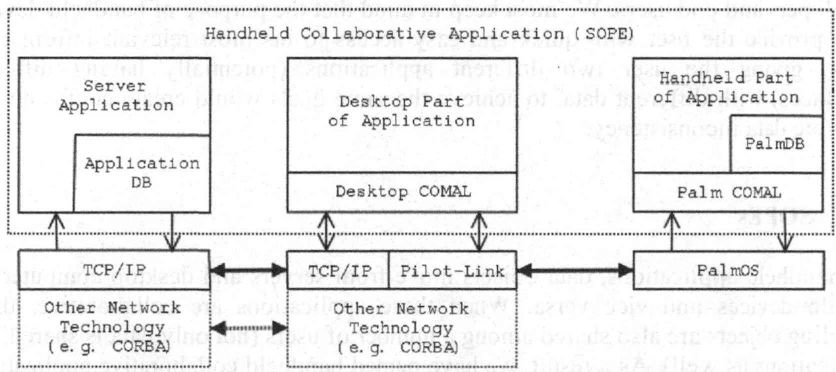

Fig. 1. Software architecture of the COMAL development framework

The PalmOS layer under the handheld application contains methods to exchange data with desktop computers, and allows direct TCP/IP connections with the server application using Palm's implementation of this protocol. Next we describe the two libraries defined by COMAL.

4.2 COMAL Libraries

The COMAL desktop library provides function calls to send, receive and synchronize data to and from Palm devices. This library has mechanisms to receive requests for information from the Palm device, process the transaction and store the result until the handheld device becomes available. The library can also receive information having the handheld device as its final destination and, again, store it until delivery is possible. The desktop portion of COMAL is developed on top of pilot-link, a set of

UNIX libraries built to access databases and store and retrieve information to and from Palm devices.

The library implemented on the Palm handheld is primarily made of wrappers around standard system calls of the PalmOS libraries. These wrappers allow the exchange of data such as user lists, messages and events, objects commonly used in typical collaborative systems. Using these extensions, developers are no longer limited to exchange standard data types and Palm's built-in databases, now they also can send and receive application specific information to be used in the desired handheld application.

Besides allowing data exchange, the Palm library provides support for disconnected mode transactions through a collaborative events database in the Palm device. When no network connection is available, outgoing events are stored temporarily in the database and sent once access to the required resource is granted.

Some of the data types used in collaboration are already present as standard data types or databases on the Palm computing platform (e.g. short text notes and dates of events). When this is the case, instead of providing our own versions of such formats, we take advantage of data types and applications already available. This allows for a seamless integration of existing Palm software with handheld collaborative applications being developed, while reducing application complexity for both developers and end users. We most keep in mind that the purpose of handheld devices is to provide the user with quick and easy access to his most relevant information. Thus, giving the user two different applications (potentially having different interfaces) with different data, to achieve the same goals would create confusion and promote data inconsistency.

4.3 SOPEs

On handheld applications, data objects move from servers and desktop computers to mobile devices and vice versa. When these applications are collaborative, these traveling objects are also shared among a number of users (not only data is shared, but applications as well). As a result, we have named handheld collaborative applications built on top of the COMAL development framework SOPEs (Shared Objects for Portable Environments).

According to the framework's architecture, SOPEs use the COMAL libraries as the communication infrastructure to exchange information between them and with other external applications, allowing its integration into existing collaborative applications.

It may appear that a SOPE is just the handheld component of a handheld collaborative application, since the rest of the application is equal to most common desktop oriented groupware systems and the COMAL development framework deals mainly with issues of desktop to handheld and handheld to handheld communication. However, the ability of the COMAL desktop library to access resources available in remote locations extends the SOPE beyond the desktop computer. See how in Figure 1 we describe the SOPE as the entire handheld collaborative application, because of this remote accessibility.

5 Extending COMAL to Support Autonomous Agents

Agents are computer programs that have goals and methods to achieve these goals. They are implemented to assist a user in accomplishing a task. An agent can be used to search for information, schedule a meeting or perform actions on behalf of the user. Agents exhibit autonomous behavior in the sense that they use internal mechanisms to make decisions as to how to reach their goals.

Pattie Maes identified two issues to be dealt with in designing and implementing autonomous agents: competence and trust [6]. Competence related to the mechanisms used by the agent to acquire knowledge and make decisions. Agents normally acquire competence by observing and imitating the user and receiving feedback from it, thus adapting their behavior to conform to the user's expectations. The issue of trust relates to the confidence that the user has on the agent to delegate work on him. Trust is build over time based on the agent's response to the tasks assigned to it.

To implement autonomous agents on top of COMAL we designed an agent library named SALSA (Simple Agent Library for Sope Applications). SALSA is located on top of the Desktop COMAL library extension of COMAL (see Figure 1). An agent programmed using SALSA includes components for perception, action and reasoning as illustrated in Figure 2. The perception module accesses the Application Database, and feeds the reasoning subsystem, which governs the actions, including deciding what to perceive next. The application database is a component of the COMAL framework and includes information synchronized with the handheld. The actions that can be triggered by an agent include sending a message to the user or another agent, or creating a new agent with a predefined subgoal that can be automatically launched or sent to the user for him to decide whether and when to execute it. The reasoning component can be implemented as a simple action/perception rule or with a more sophisticated algorithm. This is left to the user based on his application's logic.

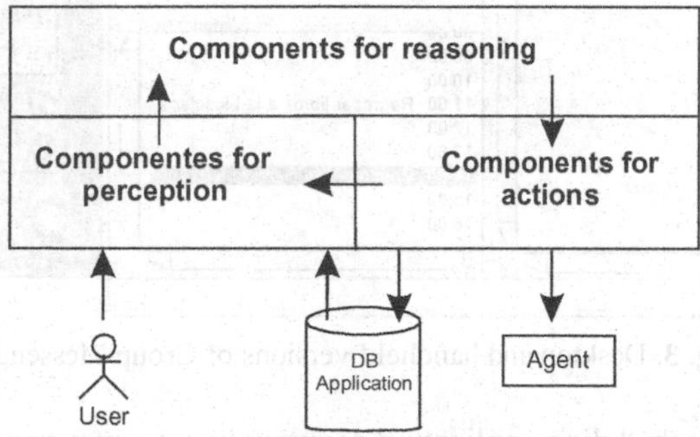

Fig. 2. SALSA's agent architecture

To implement an agent, SALSA defines an abstract **Agent** class, which controls the life cycle of an agent. The library provides a set of primitives through which the desktop application can **create** and **kill** an agent. An agent can **communicate** with other agents residing on another desktop or a trusted server to **evaluate** the user's interests and decide of what actions to take. Next we describe how an agent can be implemented to enhance an application developed by COMAL.

6 Extending a SOPE Application with an Autonomous Agent

To illustrate the extension to the COMAL framework proposed in the previous section, we describe an agent that extends the functionality of the Group Messenger SOPE described in [2], to provide the functionality of the first use scenario suggested earlier. Group Messenger is an instant messaging and calendar application, with clients for a desktop and a Palm. User information is stored in the server, allowing users to access this data from different devices. The information in the handheld is synchronized with the server every time the device is connected to a point of access.

As seen on Figure 3, the interface of Group Messenger displays other users inside a panel. To the right of each user's name, a label is displayed with the connection status of users in the list, and the connection status of the current user is displayed in the bottom of the window. This is the interface of the application installed on the desktop side of the system. Clicking on one of this buttons displays a dialog box to send a message to the corresponding user. The frame to the right shows the calendar that is synchronized with the one in the handheld computer. User status in the application can be one of the following: On Line, Off Line, Busy, or Around, this last one, when the user is in transit from one place to another using his handheld computer, and may establish a network connection shortly. In the handheld device the dates and events are handled through the Date Book application and the events manager bundled with PalmOS. The figure shows the instant messaging part of the application.

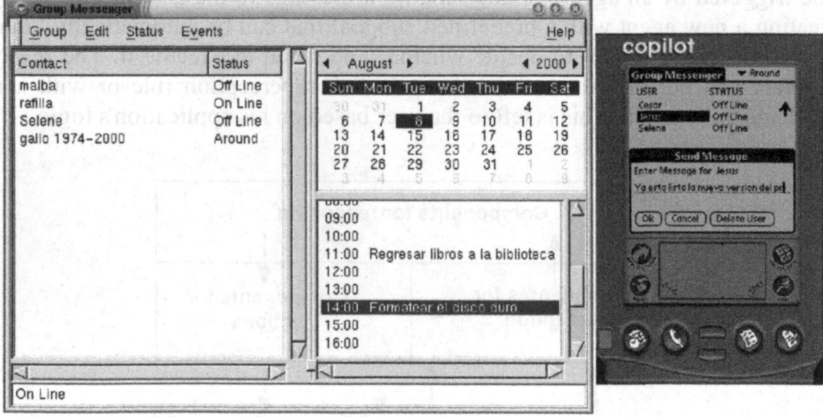

Fig. 3. Desktop and handheld versions of Group Messenger

The conference scheduling application requires two agents, one that represents the user and stores his profile, and a second one in the server which is in charge of creating new conference schedules based on a given profile and recommendations from other conference attendees. Figure 4 illustrates how the conference scheduling agent interacts with Group Messenger. The messages shown in bold correspond to the agent library while the others are part of COMAL. To activate the agent the user sends his profile, the user's agent will simply pass this information to the conference's agent. Once a schedule is generated it will be sent back to the user's agent who will store it in the application database using the COMAL API. The user's calendar will be updated the next time the handheld is synchronized using a point of access.

If an agent needs to communicate with the user it can do so by sending a message using the COMAL primitives. The user will visualize an agent as another user in the roster of the Group Messenger application. In Figure 3, the application shows the presence of the agent "gallo 1974-2000", which is "around", which means that the agent is alive and currently deactivated. Using this interface the user could communicate directly with the agent by sending it meaningful commands.

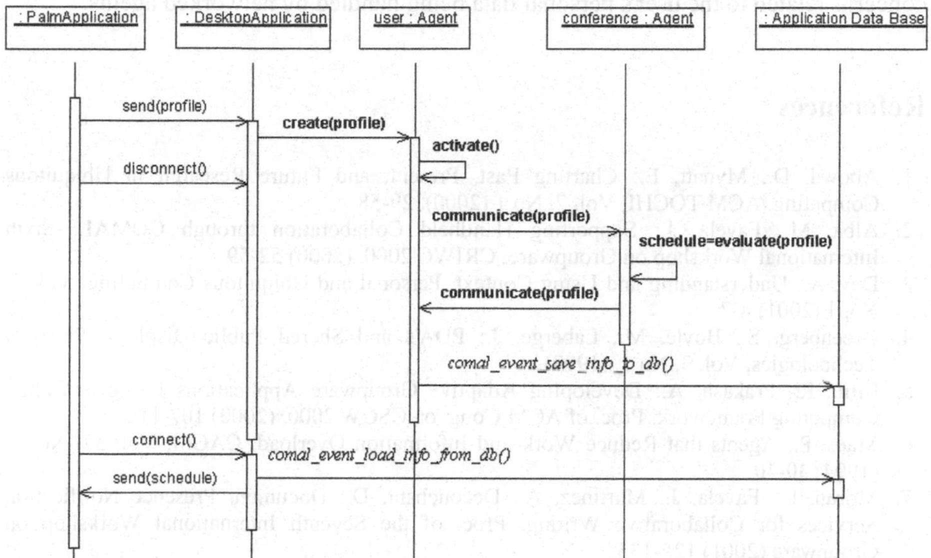

Fig. 4. Behavior of the conference scheduling agent for Group Messager

7 Conclusions and Future Work

Handheld devices will play a major role in the future of ubiquitous collaborative applications. They combine the advantages of portability, low cost, wide market acceptance, and wireless communication. Today, a large number of PDA users store personal information, relevant to most groupware applications, in these devices. Furthermore, new services and technologies are now reaching the market to provide these devices with access to popular network applications such as e-mail and web access. However, due to the nature of PDA's, this connectivity will be intermittent.

Even when there is a marked tendency to provide uninterrupted network access to handheld computers there will always be scenarios in which handhelds are disconnected, for example, to minimize network failures, and to provide users with location specific information. Additionally, users might decide to disconnect (or simulate being disconnected) for privacy concerns.

To satisfy the requirement for constant access to ubiquitous applications we have proposed the use of autonomous agents to which a user delegates responsibilities while disconnected from the network. To facilitate the development of such agents we have extended the COMAL framework with an agent library we have called SALSA. With SALSA developers can extend ubiquitous collaborative applications to account for intermittent connectivity even when the application requires constant access to the user. We have illustrated the use of SALSA with the extension of a COMAL application to support the creation of a conference schedule by social filtering.

None of the scenarios considered here require agents to change location, yet, it is clear that agent mobility might be required to support certain scenarios. We plan to extend our work to account for such behavior. Additional, we plan to address security concerns related to the user's personal data being handled by networked agents.

References

1. Abowd, D., Mynatt, E.: Charting Past, Present, and Future Research in Ubiquitous Computing. ACM TOCHI, Vol. 7, No 1 (2000), 29-58
2. Alba, M., Favela, J.: Supporting Handheld Collaboration through COMAL. Sixth International Workshop on Groupware, CRIWG'2000. (2000) 52-59
3. Dey, A.: Understanding and Using Context. Personal and Ubiquitous Computing. Vol. 5, No. 1 (2001) 4-7
4. Greenberg, S., Boyle, M., Laberge. J.: PDA's and Shared Public Displays. Personal Technologies, Vol. 3, No 1, (1999)
5. Litiu, R., Prakash, A.: Developing Adaptive Groupware Applications Using a Mobile Computing Framework. Proc. of ACM Cong. on CSCW'2000. (2000) 107-116
6. Maes, P.: Agents that Reduce Work and Information Overload. CACM, Vol. 37, No. 7, (1994) 30-40
7. Moran, L., Favela, J., Martinez, A., Decouchant, D.: Document Presence Notification Services for Collaborative Writing. Proc. of the Seventh International Workshop on Groupware (2001) 125-133
8. Moran, T., Melle, W., Chiu, P.: Tailoring Domain Objects as Meeting Tools for an Electronic Whiteboard. Proc. of ACM CSCW 98. (1998) 295-304
9. Myers, B.A., Stiel, H., Gargiulo, R.: Collaboration Using Multiple Pdas Connected to a PC. Proc. of ACM CSCW 98. (1998) 285-294
10. Sarwar, B et al.: Using Filtering Agents to Improve Prediction and Quality in the GroupLens Research Collaborative Filtering System. Proc. of ACM Conf. on CSCW'98 (1998) 345-354
11. Streitz, N.A., et al.: i-land: An Interactive Landscape for Creativity and Innovation. Proc. of the ACM CHI'99. (1999) 120-127
12. Weiser, M.: Some computer science issues in ubiquitous computing. CACM, Vol. 36, No. 7, (1993) 75-84

A Framework for Agent Based Network Management Systems

Alberto Caballero[1] and Ronny Alfonso[2]

[1] Facultad de Ingeniería Industrial, ISPJAE.
albe_cu@yahoo.com
[2] Centro de Estudios de Ingeniría de Sistemas, ISPJAE.
ralfonso@ceis.ispjae.edu.cu

Abstract. This article discusses the use of intelligent and mobile agents in some tasks of network management: modeling network and fault management. So, presents a framework for agent based network management systems and describes the principal types of the agents in this architecture and its integration functionality. Finally, the paper lists a number of benefits that the use of an agent-based architecture reports.

1 Introduction

Nowadays, the networks move a big amount of information around the world. One error on the network functionality is fatal because the user of today's network expects the increasing reliability and quality of service. In this way, Management Network must guarantee, for instance, the network integrity, it must provide the most recently information about the network structure, the status of the network services and the occurred faults.

The problem with information flooding a network in the case of malfunction is particularly severe if we take into account that a solution has to be found quickly. The fault has to be diagnosed quickly and fixed automatically or a human operator needs to be informed and advised as to the proper course of action. In large networks, operators have to interact remotely with many devices from the managing workstation. To accommodate the diversity of network components, management applications incorporate large numbers of interfaces and tools. Network management systems are usually huge monoliths that are difficult to maintain [1].

Instead of one centralized and usually very large application that encodes the complete intelligence of the system, a number of relatively small systems, or agents, are involved in a cooperative effort to resolve a problem. This does not imply that the large system is merely divided into smaller pieces. For example, several centralized applications, each capable of addressing a certain aspect of a problem, can be tied together by a communication system. It would allow for exchange of their viewpoints and coming up with strategies to make progress or to combine the results into a solution. Each of the cooperating systems may be considered an agent and the system, a Multi-Agent System (MAS).

Although an agent-based system can be implement with any client/server technology, it differs from classical client/server systems because there is no clear distinction between a client and a server.

C.A. Coello Coello et al. (Eds.): MICAI 2002, LNAI 2313, pp. 361–366, 2002.

In the section 2, this paper describes some of the principal ideas of the use of agents in network management according to the OSI Management Functional Areas. It shows potential applications such as network modeling and fault detection tasks. In the next section (section number 3), it examines the foundations of the network management multi-agent system architecture, defines the types of the agents that present some interests for this architecture and describes this framework according to the agent types functionality. In the fourth section, the benefits of using this systems architecture are presented and compared with the traditional paradigms. Concluding remarks are shown in the last section.

2 Network Management

The studies in the network management has been moved by the searching of some autonomous techniques that assure the well-running of the network [1]. Anyone of these tools should provide a reliable support for all tasks that are contemplated in the OSI Management Functional Areas. Following, we describe some of the principal ideas of the use of intelligent agents in network management and show potential applications in network modeling and fault detection.

2.1 Network Modeling

One of the principal areas in the network management is the network configuration, in which the automatic discovery is one of the fundamental functions. Discovery might target many goals, from the simplest case, finding the devices of the network that is of our interest, to the most complex, where it is concerned with the construction of more detailed views of the network situation. Those views may include, for example, available services on a device or devices that satisfy certain constraints. If in this case, the constraints are functions of device status, then the discovery complexity grows, and it is very hard to implement using classical client/server approaches. For this reason, mobile code and intelligent behavior are very important thing to perform discovery tasks [2].

The network modeling process through discovery tasks may be develop by a mobile agent that, for example, can be created with a sole goal of sending the identifier of a visited (managed) node to the manager node. The view of the network is obtained when this agent travels through the entire network and returns to the manager node.

The termination of the task can be determined heuristically inside the agent, for example, by counting the hops or an average number of visits of a particular node [1].

According to the constraints that are incorporated in the discovery agent, we can obtain different partial network models [3]. For example, if it is considered one device's type then it is obtained a network model consisting only of devices of this type. In other case, if the constraint is on the utilization of a node, then we may obtain a model that shows over-utilization problems. These network models can be created dynamically.

2.2 Fault Management

Following the same principles that in network modeling, it is considered that fault discovery is the process that constructs a specialized model of the network that shows device with the same criteria: 'it has problems'. In other words, the network diagnostic is similar to the modeling network.

For example, an agent performing selective discovery of nodes with utilization level exceeds a certain threshold, builds a model of over-utilized nodes. If the conditional on discovery establishes violations of what is considered normal behavior of network device, then the agents perform a fault detection function. Others might try to collect additional information, perform enhanced tests or execute a recovery routine, and it's not necessary to be confined to a single network device. They may implement complex and correlation algorithms for fault detection [4].

It is possible that a single agent does not perform this task. In this case, where the problem's solution depends on more than one isolates agent, we may have societies of small and relatively simple agents that need to cooperate in this way. Several types of the intelligent agents interact for diagnosing network faults; each of them addresses one aspect of the problem, and solves it by reinforcing the given hypothesis by the observations of a large number of the same agents. The solution to the problem emerges through the integration of the hypotheses of each species [5, 6].

These agents can be used to address problems autonomously leading to an immediate recovery if such an action is possible. The network manager will either be informed about the event or will be alerted if an automatic recovery is not possible or requires human involvement. A number of such specialized network-repair agents might provide a high degree of network immunity to a wide range of problems.

3 Network Management Multi-agent System Architecture

According to the preliminary solutions seen above we noted that the behavior of agents in its environment depends on some basic characteristics:

- Autonomy
- Adaptability
- Mobility
- Flexibility
- Activity / Proactivity
- Communication / Collaboration

On the other hand, as an agent is a little part of a MAS, the last characteristic is more than a simple capability of mutual and environmental interactions. In these cases:

- The system has a global task
- There is not agent in system that controls another one in order to obtain the global task
- Any agent is able to evaluate it's own behavior according to local criteria.

In this way, this architecture considers the agent as an entity that consist on beliefs, skills, interaction language and cooperative social attitude. All agents must have its own identity and must be able to determine what other agents are executing in its same location and what message other agents accept and send.

3.1 Agent Types

The problem's solutions are the result of the interaction of the several atomic agents. In this way, we define four (4) types of mobile agents that perform the basic task of the systems:

1. Modeling Agent
2. Configuration Agent
3. Diagnostic Agent
4. Repairmen Agent

The agents (of any type) are sent or received by Agent Host's (AH). The AH is another agent type that must allow multiple agents to coexist and execute simultaneously, to communicate with each other and the AH and they must prevent agents from directly interfering with each other. An AH controls creation, suppression and migrations of the other agents which are placed in it. They skills and beliefs change in the time and are the skills and beliefs of their other agents that exist in it. They know the others AH's which they exchange information. This exchange is carried out by messages passing. The inter-communication of AH's in the network take place by the movement of one or more mobile agents that exist in it.

For each considered device in management network systems, exists one AH. An AH has the capability to help other agents and modify the specified itinerary of a coexisting or an arrival agent, especially when it's not the relevant itinerary for the current task.

A Modeling Agent (MA) is an intelligent and mobile agent. It travels to the network device and takes the important characteristics to the network management. A MA has beliefs in the beliefs and skills of the other MA's which are in the same AH. They communicate by exchanging the device's information, between MA's or between the MA and the AH.

When the MA is created, the human manager puts in its body some constraints. According to this constraints they produce different network models. For example, the constraint may be the device type and the result is the network schema with all device of this type.

The MA suppression takes place when the own agent decides it, it occurs when it supposes that visited all designed nodes.

Other architecture's agent type is the Configuration Agent (CA). A CA is a small entity that has a set of values to configure the network device according to the manager criteria or the other agent's beliefs. CA senses the beliefs of other agent through the communication mechanisms. Autonomously, the CA actives its functionality when notes that is necessary to configure some devices.

A Diagnostic Agent (DA) is capable to detect malfunctions in the network device. It may do several types of test to the device status: from the simplest parameter evaluation to the most complex communication with other agent.

First, a single DA verifies that the device characteristic value is in the correct range. If the answer is affirmative then the DA interacts with other DA's to look for the other erroneous situations.

Each DA is specialized in the detection of specific problem, and only the integration among all DA's in the MAS allow complex fault detection that concern to more that one device.

Sometimes, the fault detection may encode complex algorithms and it success depends on the agent ability to interchange messages about the device status information.

Often, DA can use, as a starting point, the models that produce the CA's when they are showing the over-utilization nodes.

A Repairmen Agent (RA) is another type of intelligent and mobile agent. It decides the procedure to solve the specific problem that the DA identifies. If the RA determines the problem solutions then if must interact with some CA to set the new status values of the managed devices.

In case that is not possible, the RA has the mechanism to alert the human and a DA generates the reports to the manager node.

As we see below, the success of the task in Network Management Multi-Agent Based Systems Architecture depends on the agent's integration and the communication mechanism's effectiveness.

4 Benefit Analysis

The use of mobile agents may have several advantages over other implementations of network management systems. For example, the CPU and network resources consumption is limited. A mobile agent with a unique and well-defined task executes in only one node at a time. Other devices in the network do not run an agent until needed. So, mobile agents carry the functionality with them and it does not have to be duplicated at every location.

The classic network management systems transfer a great amount of device's information to a single node. The presented solution reduces the network traffic, because the transfer of agent to every device (and run there) creates less traffic than moving the data.

In other way, if we consider the interaction of all agents then the system reports the following advantages over a single agent or centralized approach:

- Provide an autonomous solution to the network management, the human manager does not act if it's not needed.
- Distribute computational resources and capabilities across a network of interconnected agents. Whereas resource limitations, performance bottlenecks, or critical failures may plague a centralized system, these systems do not suffer from the single point of failure problem associated with centralized systems.
- The network management agents model the problems in terms of autonomous interacting component-agents, providing a more natural way of representing task solution and integration of the different part of the systems
- Efficiently retrieve, filter, and globally coordinate information from the network nodes spatially distributed.
- Enhances overall system performance, spatially along the dimensions of computational efficiency, reliability, extensibility, robustness, maintainability, responsiveness, flexibility and reuse.

5 Summary

In this paper we identify an agent-based solution for the network management problems. A framework for an agent based architecture was proposed, in order to satisfy the requirements of some task of network management systems: modeling network and fault management. The technical approach in this proposal is to implement an agent based Network Management System, by using intelligent agent technologies, as the technological means for all Network Manager – Network Device interactions.

References

1. Bieszczad, A., Pagurek, B. and White, T., Mobile agents for network management. IEEE Communications Surveys, vol.1, no.1, Four Quarter 1998.
2. Schramm, C., Bieszczad, A. and Pagurek, B., Application-Oriented Network Modeling with Mobile Agents. *Proc. of the IEEE/IFIP Network Operations and Management Symposium (NOMS '98),* New Orleans, Louisiana, Feb. 1998.
3. White T. et al., Intelligent Network Management using Mobile Agents, *Proc. of the 2nd Canadian Conf. on Broadband Research (CCBR '98),* June 21-24, 1998, Ottawa, Canada.
4. El-Darieby, M., Intelligent Mobile Agents for Network Fault Management, Technical Report SCE-98-13, System and Computer Engineering, Carleton University, 1998.
5. White, T. and Pagurek, B., Towards Multi-Swarm Problem Solving in Networks. In *Proc. of the 3rd Int'l Conf. on Multi-Agent Systems (ICMAS '98),* July 1998.
6. White T., Bieszczad A., Pagurek B., Distributed Fault Location in Networks Using Mobile Agents, *Proc. of the Int'l Workshop on Agents in Telecommunications Applications IATA'98, (AgentWorld '98),* Paris, France, July 4-7, 1998.

A Multi-agent Cooperative Intelligent Tutoring System: The Case of Musical Harmony Domain*

Evandro de Barros Costa[1], Hyggo Oliveira de Almeida[1],
Emerson Ferreira de Araújo Lima[1], Ricardo Rubens Gomes Nunes Filho[1],
Klebson dos Santos Silva[1], and Fernando Maia Assunção[2]

[1] Departamento de Tecnologia da Informação
Universidade Federal de Alagoas
Campus A.C. Simões, Tab. do Martins, Maceió -AL – Brazil, Phone: +55 82 214-1401
ebc@fapeal.br

[2] Departamento de Sistemas e Computação - UFPB, Campina Grande-PB
fernando@dsc.ufpb.br

Abstract. This paper presents a cooperative intelligent tutoring system which adopts a multiagent approach, here applied to Musical Harmony domain. This system integrates an ITS with a Web hypermedia component resulting in a Web-based distance educational system. The essential idea in our research is to define and develop an environment that provides effective means to involve human learners, tutoring system and human teachers, in productive cooperative interactions based on problem solving situations. The system architecture consists of eight main entities: Learner, Teacher, Human Expert System, Set of artificial tutoring agents, Hypermedia Component, as well as, three interfaces modules to assure interactions between theses entities. Here we give an overview of the system, emphasising the multi-agent system and the main interactions between human and artificial agents. We also bring out particular aspects related to domain knowledge modelling and its consequences in the multiagent design, learner modelling, and a mechanism from the tutoring system to supporting adaptive navigation on the teaching material.

Keywords: Intelligent Tutoring System, Multiagent Systems, Adaptive Hypermedia, Distance Learning

1 Introduction

Cooperation notion has been assumed by education community as an important mechanism to achieve an effective learning [SLAV 85, 90]. In particular, this mechanism has been used in some Intelligent Tutoring System (ITS) research and more recently in computer-based distance learning. One approach on this direction is to provide ITS with a pedagogical approach combining learning by doing and learning by instruction [COST 95]. On the other hand, a big part of researching in Cooperative ITS deals with questions related to: (i) model of learners which allow a

* This Project is partially supported by the Brazilian Government within the CNPq Program.

C.A. Coello Coello et al. (Eds.): MICAI 2002, LNAI 2313, pp. 367–376, 2002.

Tutoring System to provide individualised actions and adaptive interactions which focuses on building open and inspectable learner model [BULL 95], [PAIV 95]. This leads to the possibility of learners to inspect the learner model which the system has made of him, having the opportunity to discuss and change the results from this model. Other important question in ITS claims to (ii) multiple representation of domain knowledge [CUMM 91] and (iii) multiple pedagogical strategies [GIRA 99]. Also, there is research on (iv) how to integrate ITS with adaptive hypermedia systems [BRUS 98].

In this perspective, we have addressed the questions above in the context of a big project aiming a cooperative educational system model for promoting presencial and distance learning that is named MathNet [COST 00]. This effort is the result of a special way to integrate interesting characteristics of a Multi-agent Intelligent Tutoring System model named MATHEMA [COST 95, 96, 98] with a CSCL environment SHIECC[LABI 98].

This paper, in particular, presents a cooperative intelligent tutoring system in the domain of Musical Harmony on the basis of MathNet model. This system integrates an ITS with a Web hypermedia component resulting in a Web-based distance educational system. The essential idea in our research is to define and develop an environment that provides effective means to involve human learners, tutoring system, and human teachers in productive cooperative interactions. In reality, this system is already implemented as a prototype on the Web*. Here we give an overview of the system, emphasizing the multi-agent system and the main interactions between human and artificial agents. We also bring out particular aspects related to solutions to the questions (i), (ii), and (iv) mentioned before.

The remainder of this paper has been organised as follows. In Section 2 we present conceptual architecture of the proposed system. In Section 3 we present our approach to model domain knowledge and its consequence in building a society of tutoring agents. Also, we define the tutoring agent structure. The specification of the interactions in the environment is discussed in Section 4. In Section 5 we present in more details the tutoring system and its architecture. In Section 6 a functional view of Tutoring System is presented.. Finally, the conclusions are presented in Section 7.

2 Conceptual Architecture of the System

We define and developed a system that corresponds to a computer-based cooperative interactive learning environment for distance education via Web which adopts a multi-agent approach [COST01]. The architecture of this system is illustrated in Figure 1 and consists of eight main entities: Learner, Teacher, Human Expert System, Set of artificial tutoring agents, Hypermedia Component, as well as, three interfaces modules to assure interactions between theses entities: Learner Interface, Teacher Interface, HES Interface.

Learner: an active human agent who is interested in learning about a certain domain knowledge. In this case, the domain of traditional harmony.

---

* http://www.shartweb.tci.ufal.br

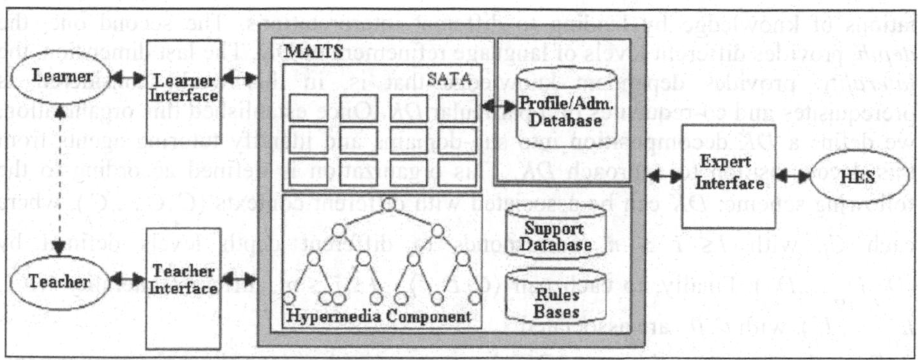

Fig. 1. Conceptual Architecture of the System

Teacher: a human agent responsible for playing a facilitator role for promoting assistance to the learner and interacts directly with him.

MAITS *(Multi-Agent Intelligent Tutoring System)*: Responsible for assuring productive interactions with Learner/Teacher. It contains four modules: **SATA**, hypermedia component, support database and rules bases.

HES *(Human Experts Society)*: works as sources of knowledge to the SATA, being responsible for building and maintaining the tutoring agents from SATA.

Learner Interface: this interface allow the communication between the learner and the system. All interactions are achieved through a browser.

Teacher Interface: Allow communication between the teacher and the system, and as well as the learner interface, it is accomplished through a Web browser.

Expert Interface: Responsible for communication between HES and MAITS.

3 SATA

3.1 From Domain Knowledge Model to Multiagent System

Considering the need for improvement and effectiveness in the interaction process between the learner and the system, considering productive and adaptive interactions, we have addressed some quality requirements towards the design of a good learning environment. These quality requirements include searching for good qualities in domain knowledge and other questions mentioned in Section 1. Based on these requirements, we have primarily worked on the improvement of the domain knowledge (DK), taking into account a trade-off between richness and structure [COST96].

We propose a particular way to consider multiple views on *DK* and then providing it with a suitable organization in terms of computational structure. Then, a particular *DK* is viewed as a set of interrelated sub-domains. Considering a goal-oriented approach, in a teaching/learning situation, we define three dimensions for *DK*: *context*, *depth*, and *laterality*. The first one, the *context* provides multiple representations of knowledge by leading to different interpretations. The second one, the *depth*, provides different levels of language refinement of DK. The last dimension, the *laterality*, provides dependent knowledge that is, in this work, considered as prerequisites and co-requisites of a particular *DK*. Once established this organization, we define a *DK* decomposition into sub-domains and identify tutoring agents from this decomposition to approach *DK*. This organization is defined according to the following scheme: *DK* can be associated with different contexts $(C_1, C_2 \ldots, C_n)$, where each C_i, with $1 \le i \le n$, corresponds to different depth levels defined by $(D_{11}, D_{12}, \ldots, D_{mi})$. Finally, to each pair $\langle C_i, D_{ij} \rangle$, $1 \le j \le m$, different laterality $(L_{111}, L_{112}, \ldots, L_{ijt})$, with $t \ge 0$, are associated.

From the dimensional view of *DK* plus some considerations about the requirements mentioned above, it is necessary to manage a big complexity in the involved knowledge. To deal with this complexity and its consequences in the co-operative interaction process, we have adopted multiagent approach. This approach seems to be natural to that end by offering various benefits from knowledge engineering. Also, it offers suitable techniques apparatus and methods from the field of Distributed Artificial Intelligence.

Then, we define a *DK* decomposition into various sub-domains *d* via the following criteria: from each C_i we define m sub-domains by the following pairs: $\langle C_i, D_{i1} \rangle$, $\langle C_i, D_{i2} \rangle, \ldots, \langle C_i, D_{in} \rangle$, with $1 \le i \le n$, and to each one of them we associate various support sub-domains d_{ijk}, $0 \le k \le t$, responsible for the laterality dimension. Therefore, we have defined two kinds of sub-domains: (i) from $\langle C_i, D_{ij} \rangle$ view we define the sub-domain d_{ij} and (ii) from the lateralities identified to each $\langle C_i, D_{ij} \rangle$ view, we define *L* support domains d_{ijt}. Then, we can identify the multiagent system through the following criteria: to each sub-domain d_{ij} we define an agent Ag_{ij} endowed with knowledge on this subdomain, and to each lateral support domain d_{ijt}, we define a lateral support *agent* Ag_{ijt} having specific knowledge on this domain. These agents are connected by means of dependency relations. These relations allow the identification of different interactions among agents [COST98].

3.2 Knowledge and Agents in Musical Harmony

We have identified two contexts in Musical Harmony: C_1 = Traditional harmony and C_2= Functional harmony. To C_1 we define several levels of depths: D_{11} = Voice in a basic level, D_{12} = Chords (Position), D_{13} = Melodic Intervals, D_{14} = Harmonic Intervals, D_{15} = Connection of Chords. Considering a pair $\langle C_1, D_{11} \rangle$, we can identify the following lateralities: L_{111} = *Notes* , L_{112} = Ciphers. From a view connected with the pair $\langle C_1, D_{11} \rangle$ we define the sub-domain d_{11} to study of Traditional harmony focused on Voice study in a basic level. A curriculum connected to this sub-domain includes the following topics: Extension (Soprano, Alto, Tenor, Bass), Distance, Distribution, Types of movement. Then, we define a tutoring agent on this sub-domain. The same procedure must be done to every sub-domain and tutoring agent. More details about agent definition are presented in the next sections.

3.3 The Society of Agents

The society is an open multi-agent system. It is made up of a collection of tutoring agents that may, through established protocols, co-operate among themselves to achieve the teaching/learning activity to promote the learning of a certain human learner. This society is designed to be open and dynamic in the sense that it allows maintenance operations such as the entry and the exit of agents, besides eventual modifications in the knowledge and in the inference mechanisms of an agent [COST98].

Each one of the agents is an ITS in some domain, having the necessary knowledge to achieve pedagogical tasks in this domain. These agents are cognitives and possess properties like autonomy, goal-oriented, social ability [FRAN 96].

3.4 Agent Structure

DEFINITION 1: Let *TA* be a tutoring agent. Then, the basic structure of *TA* is defined as follows: $TA = \langle TS, SS, DS \rangle$, where *TS* denotes a Tutoring System, *SS* denotes a Social System, and *DS* is a Distribution System, where $TS = \langle Expert, Tutor, learner\ modeller, Knowledge\ Base \rangle$, $SS = \langle SK, SM, AL, Coord, Coop, Maint \rangle$, and $DS = \langle Control, Communication \rangle$.

The tutoring system (*TS*) is responsible for the cooperative interactions between a tutoring agent and a human learner/teacher, in learning activities. The social system (*SS*) is responsible for the co-ordination of co-operative activities, reflecting the social behaviour of the agent. The distribution system (*DS*) executes the sending/receiving of messages through the communication environment. More details on Social and Distribution systems can be found in [COST 96, COST 97].

4 Specification of the Interactions

This section illustrates two types of interactions: (1) the interaction that occur between the human learner and the SATA through a tutoring agent at each time; (2) the interaction among tutoring agents.

4.1 Between a Human Learner and the SATA

The cooperative interactions between a learner and an agent in the SATA take place in a problem-solving situation. The idea is that from a problem-solving activity various pedagogical functions can be accomplished by the agent in order to support an adaptive interaction process. These interactions can be seen through a process of message exchange in which a TA sends a certain message whose content is **X** to the learner and the learner answer it with a message whose content is **Y**. The content of **X** may be a problem, an explanation, a diagnosis, a criticise, a help, a hint, etc. On the other hand, the content of **Y** based in general on **X**, may be a solution, a query, an argumentation, ask, etc. This interaction process is monitored by the mediator module. In so doing, the mediator module provides means to achieve adequate interventions during problem solving.

4.2 Interaction among Agents

In this interaction type, we focus the discussion on a particular issue: how agents decide to achieve a certain goal together. We define that this process occurs as follows. First of all, an agent tries to solve a task by itself. In the case that the agent can perform alone all the actions needed in the task solution, it does so. Otherwise, it activates its social mechanisms to select one or more agents that can perform the needed action(s) in order to solve a task which it cannot perform. Once this selection has been done, the agent starts an interaction protocol.

5 Microview of Tutoring System

In this section, we describe the Tutoring System from a Tutoring Agent in more detail by emphasising their main modules and their sub-modules.

5.1 Tutor Module

This module is responsible for directly interacting with the Learner by selecting pedagogical resources from a curriculum structure defined over the domain. For accomplish their functionalities it is divided into sub-modules, described below.

Mediator: Responsible for interaction with the Learner. It is based on a graphical interface.

Hypermedia Guide: Responsible for adaptive navigation. It guides the learner through HTML document. This document is generated by the Pedagogical Task Manager.

Pedagogical Tasks Manager: Manages the pedagogical knowledge stored in the database, generating HTML documents with the resources (concepts, examples, exercises, etc) needed to the learning of a certain learner.

Answers Evaluator: Responsible for evaluate the learner answers.

Pedagogical Knowledge: Database where is stored the pedagogical knowledge (concepts, examples, exercises, etc).

5.2 Learner Modelling Module

This module is responsible for acquiring, maintaining, and representing informations about individual learners. These informations are useful in order to tutor module makes pedagogical decisions. This module implements a solution to open and inspectable learner model according to question mentioned in Section 1. Also, it may implement a distributed diagnosis mechanism based on the multiagent platform available. For achieve their goals, it is divided in submodules, described below.

Remediator: Responsible for choose the next action of the system according to the learner cognitive diagnostic.

Historical Manager: Responsible for organization of all pedagogical knowledge viewed by the learner.

Profile Manager: Responsible for updating the learner level, considering the new resources and his performance in problem solving.

Cognitive Diagnostic: Responsible for inferring the learner knowledge about a specific domain previously taught for the system.

Inspection: Responsible for inspection mode. In other words, if the learner disagree about his profile (controlled by the Profile Manager), then the system have to show those exercises whose learner answers were wrong, and ask for the resolution of similar problems.

Learner Model: Data repository about historical and profile of the learner.

5.3 Expert Module

This module is responsible for problem solving and explanations of the solutions. The functionalities provided by the this module are played by the following sub-modules.

Inference Engine: responsible for reasoning on two knowledge bases: Correct Rules Base and Mal-Formed Rules Base (which contains rules about some kind of misunderstanding of the domain).

6 Example of Learner-Tutoring System Interactions

We now examine a particular interaction situation involving Learner-Tutoring System, illustrating functionalities provided by the Tutoring system, according to Figure 2.

1 – Let us consider a scenario where the Tutoring System be with the interaction control. Once the Learner is connected to the system, the Tutor module starts an interaction session with him by assuring his login.
2 – The **Tutor Module** through the **Pedagogical Tasks Manager (PTM)** requests **Learner Modeling Module (LMM)** the next sequence of pedagogical resources to be showed to the Learner.
3 – The **LMM** through the **Profile Manager (PM)** recovers information from the **Learner Model (LM)**.
4 – The **PM** sends the informations to the **Historical Manager (HM)**. Then HM check whether the Learner covered, in the last pedagogical session, all the resources contents established.
5 – Case the content has not been covered as a whole, **HM** returns the sequence of resources remaining to the **PTM**. Also, it returns a list of resources already presented to the Learner in order to **PTM** can generate the review content.

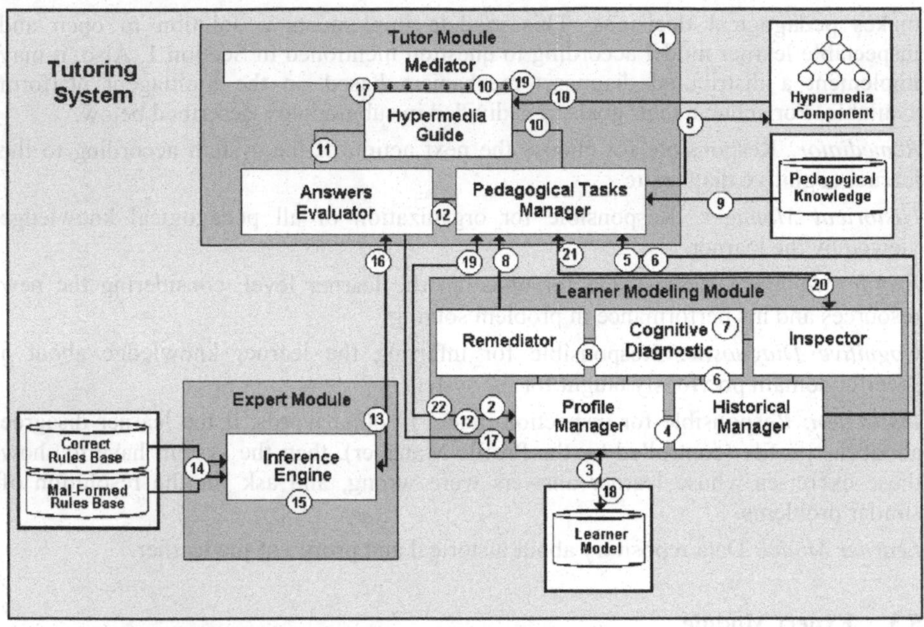

Fig. 2. Functional view of Tutoring System

6 – Case there is not incomplete sequence of resources already presented to the Learner, **HM** sends the profile informations to the **Cognitive Diagnostic** and returns to **PTM** a list of resources before presented to the Learner, generating review content.
7 – The **Cognitive Diagnostic** processes the informations based on a set of rules defined by the expert, obtaining the current learning level from Learner.
8 – Following the sequence, **Cognitive Diagnostic** send this learning level to **Remediator**. Finally, Remediator sends back to **PTM** the sequence of resources to be presented from now on to the Learner.
9 – Having these sequence of resources, **PTM** generates HTML documents (**Hypermedia Component**) needed to be presented new resources from databases (**Pedagogical Knowledge**). Case the Learner requests a review, the HTML documents to review are generated.
10 – The **Hypermedia Guide** guides the Learner to target document through the **Mediator**. Then, the Learner interacts with the **Mediator** according to the type of resource. Case the resource be a problem, the Learner must answer this problem.
11 – Once this problem is solved, the solution will be send to **Answers Evaluator**.
12 – If the problem is based on multiple choice, the **Answers Evaluator** finds the correct answer in the **PTM**, comparing it with the Learner answer. The result will be send to **Profile Manager** from **Learner Modeling Module**.
13 – If the problem is an open question, the **Answers Evaluator** sends to the **Expert Module** the informations about the problem and learner solution.
14 – The **Expert Module** by means of the **Inference Engine** works on **Correct Knowledge Base e Incorrect Knowledge Base** in order to trie validate the solution.

15 – Case the current agent do not be sufficient to validate the solution in a isolated way, it tries to cooperate with other tutoring agents. This is done by the **Inference Engine** requesting **Social Layer** to searching for agents in SATA.
16 – Once the solution is validated, the **Inference Engine** returns to **Answers Evaluator** both learner performance and the path of prove followed by the system.
17 – The **Answers Evaluator** sends to **Profile Manager** the performance obtained in the evaluation process. It also sends to the **Mediator,** by means of **Hypermedia Guide,** performance and path by which traced during the prove which identified the performance.
18 – The **Profile Manager** updates the **Learner Model**.
19 – At the end of each sequence of resources, the **Profile Manager** requests **Pedagogical Tasks Manager** to show the Learner his current learning level and performance concerning the sequence of resources worked. At this moment, the Learner may discuss and change (by a negotiation mechanism through try again to solution a given problem) the learner model.
20 – In case of learner disagreement, the **Pedagogical Tasks Manager** requests inspection to the **Learner Modeling Module**. This module, will verify through the **Inspector** whether the learner had some problem during problem solving over similar problems.
21 – Case the **Inspector** find some occurrence of these problems, a new sequence of resources is sending to **Pedagogical Tasks Manager** to be presented to the learner as a second opportunity in problem solving process (similar problems).
22 – In case agreement by the learner regarding to the Learner Model result, a new sequence is requested to the **Learner Modeling Module.** (goto step 2)

7 Conclusions

In this paper we have presented the design and development of a multi-agent cooperative intelligent tutoring system which has been applied to Musical Harmony domain. We have mainly emphasised the modelling of domain knowledge and its consequences towards a society of agents via a multi-agent approach. Regards to this society we have defined the agent structure and the co-operation model among them. Also, we have mainly focused on the interactions learner-tutoring system, during problem solving activities and their consequences. Here, we have focused on learning modelling and its influence on the mechanism to support adaptive navigation on the teaching material organized as a hypermedia document over the Web structure.

We are currently developing musical editor in order to provide more interesting resources in the manipulation of musical graphic objects. Also, we have been defining improvements to better accomplish the process of distributed learner modelling considering the multi-agent system defined.

References

[BRUS 98] Brusilovsky, P. “Methods and techniques of adaptive hypermedia. In: Brusilovsky, Peter et al. (Ed.). Adaptive Hypertext and Hypermedia, Netherlands, 1998. P. 1-43.

[COST 95] Costa, E.B.; Lopes, M.A.; Ferneda, E. MATHEMA: A Learning Environment Based on a Multi-Agent Architecture. In J. Wainer and A. Carvalho, editors, Proc. of 12th Brazilian Symposium on Artificial Intelligence, Volume 991 of Lecture Notes in Artificial Intelligence, pages 141-150. Springer-Verlag, Campinas, Brazil, October 1995.

[COST 96] Costa, E.B., Perkusich, A. Modelling the Cooperative Interactions in a Teaching/ Learning Situation. In Proceedings of Third International Conference on Intelligent Tutoring Systems - ITS'96, Montreal, Canada, June, 1996.

[COST 98] Costa, E.B.; Perkusich, A.; Ferneda, E. From a Tridimensional view of Domain Knowledge to Multi-agent Tutoring System. In F. M. De Oliveira, editor, Proc. of 14th Brazilian Symposium on Artificial Intelligence, Volume 991 of Lecture Notes in Artificial Intelligence, LNAI 1515, pages 61-72. Springer-Verlag, Porto Alegre, RS, Brazil, November 1998.

[COST 01] Costa, E.B.; Almeida, H.O.; Lima E.F.A.; Nunes, R.R.G.; Silva, K. S.; Assunção, F. M. Shart-web – Um sistema tutor multiagentes em harmonia na web. In Third Workshop Agent-Based Learning Environment on Brazilian Symposium in Computer Education, Vitória, ES, Brazil, November 2001.

[CUMM 91] Cumming, G.; Self, J. Learner Modelling in Collaborative Intelligent Educational Systems. In: Proceedings of the IEEE International Conference Frontiers in Education (FIE'98), Tempe, Arizona, November, 1998.

[LABI 98] Labidi, S., Ferreira, J. Technology-Assisted Instruction Applied to Cooperative Learning. In: Peter Goodyear (ed.), Teaching Knowledge and Intelligent Tutoring, Norwood, N.J.: Ablex, 1991

[PAIV 95] Paiva, A., Self, J., Hartley, R., Externalising Learner Models. In: Proceedings of AI-ED 95 - World Conference on Artificial Intelligence in Education, Washington, DC; August 16-19, 1995, pp. 509-516.

[SLAV 85] Slavin, R. et al. Learning to cooperate, cooperating to learn. NY: Plenum, 1985.

[SLAV 90] Slavin, R. E. Cooperative: Theory, Research and Practice. Prentice Hall, 1990.

Reacting to Unexpected Events and Communicating in Spite of Mixed Ontologies

Adolfo Guzmán, Carmen Domínguez, and Jesús Olivares

Centro de Investigación en Computación, Instituto Politécnico Nacional,
Av. J. Bátiz esq. Miguel Othón, C. P. 07738, Mexico City.
aguzman@cic.ipn.mx,
http://www.cic.ipn.mx

Abstract. We describe our experiences in building agents (and their environment) that could solve important problems in agent to agent communication, in manners that are not pre-programmed or reactive: *(1) Two agents may have different ontologies.* We do not assume that agents share the same classification of concepts: they have each one its own ontology or concept categorization. Agents can not exchange concepts: they have to exchange symbols (words of natural language), which the receiving agent has to map to the intended concept, for interaction to be meaningful. *(2) The model for interaction.* Our agents interact through scripts or frames having roles, resources and prerequisites. Agents select which roles in what scripts to play, in order to satisfy their purposes. *(3) Unexpected events happen* and throw the agents out of their current plan or execution. *(4) Planning* is needed in this changing world.

Key words: Ontology, unexpected events, concept tree, script, multiple threads.

1 Introduction

The project seeks to produce a theory, model and environment populated with agents that follow useful behavior (such as "go and sell these apricots") derived from purposes that take into account resources. These agents interact with agents written elsewhere, thus differing in their intentions, models, vocabulary, and messages.

Agents engage in "orchestrated interactions" or scripts. An agent must obey not only its own rules (behaviors, algorithms): it must also adopt the rules imposed to it by the scripts on which it takes part. For instance, if it goes into a restaurant in the role `customer` (to eat something), it must obey (most of) the rules that the script `at_a_restaurant` impose on the `customer`. In this way, an agent acquires additional obligations (additional threads to execute) on top of those initially owned.

Different ontologies do exist. Most agents are not built by us, but by somebody else. Thus, our agents will interact mostly with "unknown and never seen before" agents from all over the planet. These will express their wishes or purposes uttering different messages coming from their different knowledge structures. Hence, mechanisms to exchange knowledge among heterogeneous systems are needed.

C.A. Coello Coello et al. (Eds.): MICAI 2002, LNAI 2313, pp. 377–386, 2002.

The need for multiple threads. For versatility, an agent may have several behaviors: algorithms or threads that pursue some purpose (`how_to_be_rich`, `how_to_cross_the_street`, `how_to_bargain...`) and may be simultaneously executing several of them, and thus pursue several purposes concurrently.

Unanticipated events will happen. An agent was `selling_a_car`, when the `buyer` ran away. What to do? An agent can not have a specific program to handle every possible exception (the "frame problem" of John McCarthy); it must have more general rules. Unexpected events are words in the second tape of an Interaction Machine [16].

2 Related Works

Languages for agent execution. KQML [2], a declarative language, is a message format and a message handling protocol to enable agents to interoperate and share knowledge in run time without any concern about the contents of the messages. TCL [5] is a high-level scripting language that enables a user to define mobile agents. TeleScript is also an important recent development in the area. Java is multi-threaded. Creating LIA (Language for Interacting Agents) facilitates easier coding and study of desired features. It differs from KQML in the sense that KQML is not concerned with the content of the message and therefore makes no changes nor equivalence among ontologies. LIA differs from TCL in that LIA agents communicate even if they have different ontologies. TCL and KQML are not concurrent.

Interaction Machines. They are defined [16] as extensions to the Turing Machine model to enable it to deal with models that are incompletely specified and that can be completed interactively; they are concerned with the incompleteness of Godel's theorem. An Interaction Machine is a Turing Machine extended with an additional tape that contains an infinite number of (infinite types of) strings written with letters of an (infinite) alphabet. Interaction Machines enable us to model open systems: those exposed to external events, such as unplanned events. Our work on these events is inspired by this model, which postulates an infinite number of *types* of external events, with an *infinite alphabet.* It is thus impossible to write a program to handle even each *type* of event (there is an infinite number of them). To overcome this difficulty, we organize the (infinite) collection of "unanticipated" strings into a tree of unforeseen events (Figure 1), following the lines of CYC [6] and Clasitex [9].

Ontologies. The first author worked in the CYC Project [13], which tried to construct the common knowledge tree in order to solve big problems in Artificial Intelligence. CYC shows that it is possible to form taxonomies of specialized knowledge areas (which is what we intend to do here, see Table 1), in addition to classifying the common knowledge (goal that, due to its extension –between one and ten million concepts– was not achieved by that project). Trees of specialized knowledge, where the tree takes the form of a data dictionary, were used by the first author [7-9].

Similar scenarios. [11, 12] describe a scenario similar to the one we propose, but with single-threaded code and a common ontology, outlining how a set of autonomous agents cooperate to coherent management of information in environments where there are diverse information sources.

Our current and previous related work. This paper is based on our theses [1] and [15]. [10] describes earlier work. [7] uses a common ontology to map (manually) the data dictionaries of an otherwise strange data base, thus making its tables, fields and values understandable to the casual user. Written in db manager Progress. [9] relates words to concepts; it finds the main topics in an article written in Spanish. It does not work on key words, but on concepts. It uses a concept tree. For this reason, it can find an article talking about shoes, even if the article does not contain such word, but it contains instead boot, moccasin, sandals..., even if these words may refer to other contexts or concepts: moccasin is also a tribe of American Indians... [3, 4] extend [9] by using weights for selecting concepts.

2.1 Status

A *theory* has not been developed, except a simple one for unforeseen events. A *model and a working environment* have been developed. An *imperative language*, LIA, and its programming environment has been constructed (in C and Java, for a PC), and used for simple examples. We wrote a *compiler* from LIA to p-code, which is then interpreted. This provides for easy change of LIA syntax and semantics. Once LIA is frozen, we will probably build a compiler from it to Java. Now, the environment assumes that all agents work inside the same computer; later, the agents should be set free to run on different nodes of the Web. For this, we plan to make it FIPA-complaint. MEI, the *Machine of Unexpected Events*, which contains a simple micro planner (Section 5.1), as well as COM, the *Ontology Comparator*, are working. There is a *parallel planner* [15]. COM now works with fixed relations (verbs); we will relax this later, through the use of nodes in the ontologies representing *the relations.* We propose work on automatic handling and *recovery of e-errors in e-commerce*, based on MEI. *Applications* in LIA are scanty, due to its youth.

3 Model for Agent Interaction in Our Work

This is an overview; the next sections provide more detail.

3.1 Agents Are Multi-threaded, Have Resources and Purposes

Scripts (`renting_a_house, at_vacation, at_an_auction`) describe the intercourse between several *roles* (`cooker, student, owner...`), following R. Schank and Marvin Minsky [14]. Each role can be instantiated later by an agent. Each role is a program (a thread) in LIA, having requirements (prerequisites for its instantiator agent), resources consumed, purposes achieved and resources produced at the end of the interaction. Scripts are not active, they do not run until its roles are instantiated by agents. A role interacts (exchanges information) with another role via LIA commands *accept* and *out* [15].

Agents are autonomous, proactive units (individuals; software packages) that initially possess several threads (for instance, `how_to_swim`, `how_to_be_honest`), purposes (Ex: to sell these apricots, to buy a piano...)[1] and resources (apricots, $10,000, a VW car, knows how to cook...). Each agent decides which of its threads to activate, in view of purposes and resources. Often, to achieve a purpose, it must engage in interactions via scripts with other agents. It does so by voluntarily acquiring (obeying, following, instantiating) some *role* in some *script* (those that best match[2] its abilities and resource limitations). An agent may engage in several *scripts* simultaneously.

An agent may replan its purposes in view of achievements, closeness to purposes, and resource status.[3] A fortuitous event (Section 5) may alter the plan of the agent and reaction threads may be used to deal with it. This forces them to micro planning, and macro planning [15].[4]

3.2 There Is an Environment, and a Language for Enacting These Agents

The environment provides: (a) an editor in which to write LIA threads, define agents and scripts; (b) a P-compiler for LIA; (c) an execution machine, that executes the P-code; (d) MEI; (e) the ontology comparator; (f) global and regional variables for the agents; (g) a matcher of agent purposes to resources produced by each role of a script[2]; (h) a (macro) planner.[3, 4] The LIA world contains resources, global variables (time, temperature...), regional variables,[5] agents, scripts, and unexpected events. Agents and scripts are constructed using LIA [15].

Differentiating features of our work: (a) it handles unforeseen events; (b) agents can communicate even if they use different knowledge organizations/structures.

3.3 They Communicate Using Each One Its Own Ontology

Unless agents are written by the same person, they can not be sure that they exchange *words* that are universally understood by everybody.[6] Thus, they have to exchange

---

[1] A *purpose* is a proposition that, when it becomes True, it is considered fulfilled.

[2] This matching is not described here, but it also uses COM and the planner.

[3] At the moment, this replanning is "automatic," instead of being agent-requested.

[4] Planning occurs not only because unforeseen happenings, but also due to resource depletion, failure or forfeit in a given interaction (the `buyer` ran away; I could not sell my car).

[5] Regional variables are used ("seen") only by agents and roles which declare them.

[6] There are some words or symbols that are unambiguous (map to a unique meaning or concept): 7, π, London, Ludwig van Beethoven, Fourier Transform... Most words (mole, star...) are ambiguous. A concept is usually represented by more than one word: the concept that I have in my mind of a certain cereal, written *maiz* in Spanish, is also mapped into by words such as elote, pozol (Spanish), maize, corn (English),...

ambiguous words or descriptions of what they want or mean. Since we want our agents to communicate with *your, his* and *her* agents, we do not assume that all agents use the same interpretation for a natural language word, or that they share the same concepts or the same concept organization. Instead, agents have to face the problem of how to make sure that what I hear is what you mean; i. e., to be reasonably sure that my mapping of *your* words to my concept is probably what *you* had in mind. If in doubt, our agents ask clarifying questions or queries to the other agent, until an acceptable meaning (concept) is transmitted.

Table 1. Two similar but not identical ontologies or trees of concepts. Concepts appear in bold: **Grain,** meaning a seed of a plant used for eating. Words appear in italics: *grain,* which may mean **Grain** (seed of plant), **Small particle** (*bit, pellet, grain, speck, fragment*), or **Texture** (*texture, grain, nap, striation*)

Ontology of Agent A		Ontology of Agent B	
Fruit	*fruit, fruits*	**Seed**	*seed, grain*
Grain	*grain, seed, seeds*	**Sorghum**	*Sorghum*
Bean	*bean, frijol*	**Oat**	*oats, oat, grits*
Soya bean	*soya bean*	**Bean**	*bean, kidney bean*
Black bean	*black beans*	**Black bean**	*black bean, frijol negro*
Cereal	*cereal*	**Soya bean**	*soya bean, soybean*
Wheat	*trigo, wheat*	**Corn**	*maize, maiz, maíz*
Corn	*corn*	**Wheat**	*Trigo*
Sorghum	*sorghum*	**Peanut**	*Peanut, maní, cacahuate*
Citric	*citric, citrics*	**Fruit**	*Fruit*
Orange	*naranja, orange*	**Tangerine**	*Tangerine*
Lemon	*lemon, limón,*	**Lemon**	*Lemon*
Apricot	*apricot*	**Avocado**	*Avocado*
Pineapple	*piña, pineapple*	**Pineapple**	*Pineapple*
Avocado	*avocado, avocados*	**Orange**	*Orange*
		Prune	*Prune*

4 Communication between Agents That Use Different Ontologies

This section presents our approach (others exist) on how agents using different dialects or concept hierarchies (trees of concepts) communicate meaningfully.

Matching words arising from concepts in different ontologies. We describe here COM which, when two agents interact, has to map words to concepts. When an agent (A, say) utters a word (*corn,* in "I want to sell *corn*") to B (the listening agent), several cases arise:

(1) B knows word *corn* (not the example in Table 1) and maps into the same concept which has the same father in B. Thus, *corn* in A maps to **Corn** son of **Seed**; in B also into **Corn** son of **Seed.** We can say that A has transmitted **Corn** through *corn* to B.

(2) B has no knowledge of word *corn* (Refer to Table 1). In this case, B guesses and asks A (all this intercourse is done by COM, automatically, without explicit calls from A or B, so that –if COM is successful– they appear to be transmitting concepts among themselves, when in fact they are exchanging words): *"Is it a kind of a fruit?"*. A answers with **Cereal**, the father of **Corn**, and transmits *"it is a cereal"*, which makes a recursive call to COM. In our example, word *cereal* is also not understood by B. Then A tries **Grain,** the father of **Cereal,** and transmits *"it is a grain or seed or seeds"*. B has these words and thus knows that A is talking about **Seed**. [We went up in the ontology trees, looking for some common concept. If one or two steps upwards do not produce a match, perhaps their ontologies are incomparable, and further communication is impossible.] Now, we want to go down; A must convey **Corn** to B, not just **Grain.** Thus A sends B all the sons and grandsons of **Grain,** together with their properties: *(bean size 1cm, skin smooth...), (trigo size 1mm, skin smooth, shape elliptical...)...*, which B must match against the sons and grandsons of its **Seed.** This matching is a recursive call to COM, since what is *skin* for one is *peel* or *epidermis* for the other, what is *pale orange* for A is just *orange* for B, and one expresses sizes in centimeters, but the other in inches... [7]

(3) B knows *corn* as **Corn** but its father is **Seed,** while in A, the father of **Corn** is **Cereal,** and the father of **Cereal** is indeed **Seed** (not the example in Table 1), thus:
A: **Seed – Cereal – Corn** B: **Seed – Corn**
In this case, a match is obtained, although **Corn** has in A a grandfather that matches just the father (not the grandfather) of **Corn** in B.

(4) when *corn* arrives to B, it may have many possible matches. (Think of you wanting to buy a screwdriver, and talking to a hardware store clerk that sells 25 classes of screwdrivers). A: **Screwdriver** *screwdriver* B: **Screwdriver – Phillips screwdriver, Flat screwdriver, Z-shaped screwdriver...**
In this case, a match has been found by COM, and further disambiguation is not possible by using the ontology tree of A (its **Screwdriver** has no leaf nodes), but by resorting to use, price... intended ["For what do you want the screwdriver?" "How large?". This extension is beyond current COM].

(5) More cases exist [15], but the reader gets the idea.

How big can a given tree of concepts be? CYC [13] assumes that there are between one and ten million common concepts (common sense concepts, that everybody shares). From this tree, an agent is interested only in a few hundred: seeds and their properties, say. A common tree for concept disambiguation is not needed, but it may help.

5 Handling Unexpected Events

Autonomous agents, as well as human beings, must face the fact that the world is unpredictable, due to incomplete information, uncertain environment, unknown proc-

[7] The concepts in an ontology have properties (attributes) and values, not shown in Table 1.

esses, acts of other agents, or just Murphy's Law. An unexpected event, when sensed by an agent, modifies its participation in *scripts*, forcing it to execute contingency or emergency roles (called reaction threads), to postpone or cancel some current scripts in which it is engaged, and later, to do replanning.[3] Non perceived events are ignored, although that may lead to catastrophe.

Unexpected events are handled by MEI, a machine placed outside the interaction environment, which (1) produces unexpected events at random times; (2) locates each agent capable of perceiving an event,[8] when it occurs; (3) for each of these agents, MEI interrupts its threads, (4) selects and starts some reaction thread in response to the event; (5) activates some of the interrupted threads; (6) detects the end of the event; (7) activates some more of the interrupted threads, and (8) stops (usually) the reaction thread. In this manner our agents react to unexpected events. We will later incorporate into each agent calls to functions (2) to (8), to make them more autonomous.

5.1 How to React to an Infinite Number of Unexpected Events

There is an infinite number of fortuitous events, but an agent can only have a small number of predefined reaction threads: it can know how to react to "winning the lottery" (reaction depends if it has no savings, owns its home...), but not how to react to "finding some money". How can it survive? With the help of the tree of unexpected events. This tree (Fig. 1) is infinite in principle, and each node contains an event and the names of the possible reaction threads for that event; see also Fig. 2. More general events appear near the root. The branches denote the relation "subset". Reaction threads often have preconditions for they to be useful: "must have umbrella", "must have raincoat", "must be near a shade"... are some preconditions for certain reaction threads for event "rain".

When one of the infinite number of unexpected events occurs, a perceiving agent uses the tree of unexpected events to select, from the reaction threads it owns, the most specific one pertaining to the event. In this manner (4) above gets executed.

Every agent owns at least one reaction thread: the most general one.

To know which of the normal threads stopped in (3) are continued in (5), in spite of the unexpected event, the agent uses an *incompatibility* algorithm (not described here) to detect which threads can not run simultaneously with the reaction thread (4).

The reaction thread started in (4) is ended (8) when its *purpose* has been achieved, usually because the unexpected event stops. At this moment, the incompatibility algorithm restarts (7) some more of the threads that were not restarted in (5), due to incompatibility with the unexpected event. Finally, some of the threads stopped in (3) are never restarted, due to lack of resources. Replanning[4] (not discussed here) may be needed. Execution of (2) to (8) is called microplanning. [15] shows applications.

[8] An agent perceives (detects its beginning and end times, as well as its other features: intensity...) an event if it has a reaction behavior for that event or for an specialization of it.

unexpected_event: `still; astonished.`
  natural_event: `cry; run.`
    rain: `open_umbrella; wear_raincoat; run; get_wet.`
    earthquake: `faint; freeze; help_people; hide.`
    fire: `call_fireman; run; tell_others.`
    ...
  life_threatening_event: `cry; pray.`
    assault: `cry; call_police; call_family.`
    accident: `call_ambulance; call_police; get_scared.`
    sickness: `call_doctor; tell_others.`
      sick_pilot: `replace_pilot.`
    ...
  lucky_event: `be_happy.`
    won_lottery: `save_money; buy_house; buy_car.`
    bumped_into_old_friend: `go_to_the_restaurant; greetings.`
    ...
  offers_event: `accept_proposal; be_happy.`
    offer_job: `begin_work.`
    offer_gift: `accept_gift.`
    ...
  lack_event: `ask_help, stay_suspended.`
    things_lack: `replace_for_newOne.`
      airplane_lack: `cancel_fligh; delay_flight.`
      money_lack: `request_to_the_Bank.`
    defect: `repair_defect.`
      fail_airplane: `move_passengers.`
      product_defect: `replace_for_newOne.`
    ...
  ... (many_other_events):...

Fig. 1. Tree of unexpected events. In **bold** are the events; in `Courier font` are the possible reaction threads to that event. Every agent is born with a finite number of reaction threads. The tree may be infinite, since it contains *all* possible reaction threads

```
Role open_umbrella()
{ requisite  { umbrella ;  }
local     { int x ;     }
print(" Open the umbrella");  //no further
atomic actions
```

Fig 2. Reaction thread, written in LIA. This role sits in some agents, those that are able to perceive rain and know that one way to react to rain is `open_umbrella`. An agent may have other reaction threads for rain, for instance `run, wear_raincoat`. These are the reactions known to the agent for unexpected event rain. Which one to execute depends on the resources available to the agent at the time of the rain

6 Conclusions

Communication of concepts among unfamiliar agents must be through symbols or words of a natural language. The receiving agent must map the symbols or words it receives, into the right concept in its *own* ontology; hence, the paper gives a useful solution to the problem of mapping a concept in one ontology to the closest concept in another.

Unforeseen events are handled using the background of Interaction Machines.

Acknowledgements

We are grateful to IPN authorities for their wisdom in founding (1997) CIC and its Agents Laboratory. We thank Prof. Michael N. Huhns and his group at University of South Carolina for advice and help during fruitful conversations. Work was partially supported by grants Conacyt-28026, NSF-Conacyt-32973, and CGEPI-980744. The second author acknowledges CONACYT and IPN-COFAA research assistantships.

References

(•) In Spanish. Authors' papers can be read and copied, freely, full text, from CIC's Digital Library, through http: //www.cic.ipn.mx/~aguzman

1. Dominguez, C.: Handling Infinite Unexpected Events in Agents Interactions. M. Sc. thesis in Computer Science, CIC-IPN Mexico City (2002) •
2. Finnin, T.; Weber, J.; Widerhold, G., et al. Specification of the KQML Agent Communication Language (draft). The DARPA Knowledge Sharing Initiative External Interfaces Working Group (1993)
3. Gelbukh, A, Sidorov, G., and Guzman, A.: A Method Describing Document Contents through Topic Selection. Lecture notes in Workshop on String Processing and Information Retrieval, (IEEE Computer Society, Los Alamitos, CA) Cancun, Mexico (1999) 73-80
4. Gelbukh, A, Sidorov, G., and Guzman, A.: Document Comparison with a Weighted Topic Hierarchy. DEXA-99. Lecture Notes in 10-th International Conference on Database and Expert System Applications, Workshop on Document Analysis and Understanding for Document Databases, (IEEE Computer Society, Los Alamitos, CA) Florence, Italy (1999) 566-570
5. Gray, Robert S.: Agent Tcl. In Dr. Dobb's Journal, March (1997)
6. Guha, R.V. and Lenat, D.: Enabling Agents to Work Together *CACM*, No. 37 (1994) 7
7. Guzman, A.: Project "Access to Unfamiliar Data Bases." Final Report, IDASA, Mexico City. (1994) •
8. Guzman, A.: ANASIN, Intelligent Analyser and Synthesiser of Information. Technical Report: User Manual. IDASA. Mexico City (1994b) •
9. Guzman, A.: Finding the Main Themes in a Spanish Document. Journal Expert Systems with Applications, Vol. 14, No. 1, 2, (1998) 139-148

10. Guzman, A., Olivares, J., Demetrio, A., and Dominguez, C.: Interaction of Purposeful Agents that Use Different Ontologies. In: Osvaldo Cairo, Enrique Sucar, Francisco J. Cantu (eds.): Lecture Notes in Artificial Intelligence 1793, MICAI 2000: Advances in A. I. Springer Verlag, Heidelberg (2000) 557-573.
11. Huhns, M. N.; Singh, M. P. and Ksiezyk T.: Global Information Management Via Local Autonomous Agents. In: M. N. Huhns, Munindar P. Singh, (eds.): Readings in Agents, Morgan Kauffmann Publishers, Inc. San Francisco, CA (1997)
12. Huhns, M. and Singh, M.: Managing Heterogeneous Transaction Workflows with Cooperating Agents. In: Nicholas R. Jennings and Michael J. Wooldridge, (eds.): Agent Technology: Foundations, Applications and Markets, Springer-Verlag, Heidelberg (1998) 219-240
13. Lenat, D. and Guha, R.: Building Large Knowledge-Based Systems. Reading, MA: Addison Wesley., Reading, MA. (1989)
14. Minsky, Marvin: The Society of Mind. Simon & Schuster Inc. (1985)
15. Olivares, Jesus: An Interaction Model between Purposeful Agents with E-Commerce Examples. In Ph. D. Thesis. Defended in November 2001. CIC-IPN, Mexico City. (2002) •
16. Wegner, Peter: In Tutorial Notes: Models and Paradigms of Interaction, Department of Computer Science, Brown University, USA, September (1995)

Logic of Interaction for Multiagent Systems

Matías Alvarado[1,2], Leonid Sheremetov[1,2], Ernesto Germán[1], and Erick Alva[1]

[1] Center for Computing Research of the National Technical University, (CIC-IPN), Mexico
Av. Juan de Dios Batiz esq. Othon de Mendizabal s/n. Col. Nueva Industrial Vallejo, México, D.F., C.P. 07738

[2] Instituto Mexicano del Petróleo, Programa de Matemáticas Aplicadas y Computación, Eje Central Lázaro Cárdenas 152, CP. 07730 México DF.

{matias,sher}@cic.ipn.mx

Abstract. The purpose of this paper is to develop a modal logic of interaction based on roles that each agent can play within a scenario. A role is defined as a set of beliefs, goals and actions. The agent looks for the realization of his goals according to those goals of the scenario in which it participates playing a role. The same agent can play different roles in different scenarios. A common model of communicative and physical interactions is proposed for its formalization as a modal logic of interaction. It is argued that different interaction types, as collaboration, negotiation and competence can be considered as particular cases of this model. The proposed model is illustrated using the well-known example of multiagent exploration of a distant planet.

1 Introduction

Agent-based computing has the potential to significantly improve the theory and the practice of modeling, designing, and implementing complex computer systems. Software systems of that type to be robust and scalable require autonomous agents that can complete their objectives while situated in a dynamic and uncertain environment, that can engage in rich, high-level social interactions, and that can operate within flexible organizational structures. High-level interaction within an organizational context is considered as essential property of agent-based computing [1, 2]. This article is about a model of interactions in multiagent systems (MAS).

One area of much interest in MAS research is the use of mathematical logic for specifying the properties of agents and multi-agent systems. One of the first works in this field was the Cohen-Levesque theory of intention [3], where the authors developed a quantified multi-modal logic, with modalities for representing beliefs and goals, and an apparatus for representing actions that was loosely based on dynamic logic [4]; beliefs and goals were characterized using possible worlds semantics [5]. Building largely on this work, attempts have been made to use similar logics to capture various other properties of BDI agents [6, 7] and multi-agent systems [8].

Recently, more emphasis has been made upon the aspects of group behaviour of agents than to single-agent models. This change of focus implies the necessity to consider the notions of joint mental attitudes and actions. The main difference between single and group modalities of these concepts is the role that interactions

C.A. Coello Coello et al. (Eds.): MICAI 2002, LNAI 2313, pp. 387–400, 2002.

play in their planning and execution. We can speak about "interacting mental attitudes" constituting a state of a MAS and "interacting actions" as well. Different aspects of this type of behavior are studied in dialogue theories as communicative interactions and in planning approaches as concurrent interacting actions of agents committed to a common goal [9, 10, 11, 12,13].

The approach proposed in this article is based on a common model of interactions for BDI agents acting and interacting according to their role within a certain organizational context. Though a special emphasis has recently been made on the importance of the role modeling especially while developing software engineering methodologies for MAS programming [14, 15, 16], there is a gap between these attempts of agent programming and the BDI theory itself (even in the case of the authors of the BDI theory [14]). One of the reasons of that gap, to our concern, is the absence of a concept of interaction in this theory. So, the purpose of this paper is to develop a concept model of a MAS as the basis for a modal logic of interaction and mutual actions based on the BDI abstraction and role modeling.

2 Conceptual Framework

The proposed model is based on a concept of interaction. As it has been already mentioned, a concept of *interaction* between agents is central to model and understand behavior of a MAS. We claim that these interactions can be divided into two groups, which we call *communicative interactions* and *physical interactions*. *Communicative interactions* are those that have effect mainly on the mental states of agents. This type of interactions is well studied in the speech act theory and has effects in a number of communication languages in agents community using principles of the above mentioned theory [17, 18]. *Physical interactions*, on the other hand, have effects on the state of external domain or environment. They take place while agents perform physical actions, let us call them "multi-agent or interacting concurrent actions", which have mutual effects. The purpose of this section is to propose a common model for interactions of both types and to further formalize it as a modal logic of interaction.

Let us begin with the basic definitions, these can be divided into the following groups: defining agent mental state (Belief, Goal, Action - atomic and compound -, and Possible world), defining organizational context of multiagent system (Scenario, Role, Plan, State, Agent), and, finally defining aspects of interaction between agents within a given organizational context (Negotiation, Collaboration and Competition). Each set of formulas are combined in the classical manner through logical connectives $\neg$, $\wedge$, $\vee$, $\rightarrow$, $\leftrightarrow$; the logic closures of three sets are joined to obtain the object language $\mathcal{L}$. Modal operators to model beliefs B, goals G, actions *do* and the action possibility *could* are introduced, so that the agent's beliefs, goals and actions are modeled through the modal formulas $B_i\varphi$, $G_i\ \varphi$, $[do_i\ \alpha]\ \varphi$ and $[could_i\alpha]\varphi$, meaning "*agent* i *believes* φ", "*agent* i *has the goal* φ" and "*to achieve* φ *the agent i does action* α" and "*if agent i could execute action* α *it would achieve goal* φ". In addition, the temporal operator Next($[do_i\alpha]\varphi$) for "*at the next time agent i executes action* α *to achieve the goal* φ", Next($[could_i\alpha]\varphi$) for "*at the next time agent i could execute action α and would get goal* φ" and ◊φ for "*is possible* φ". Resulting modal language is a subset of the closure of language $\mathcal{L}$ joined with the modal operators.

We define a Kripke structure $M = \langle W,\pi,D,\Im,M\rangle$, where W is the set of possible worlds or states, π is the assigning function from W to the set of interpretations, D is the function that encodes the dynamic of actions execution between states, ℑ is the function that encodes the agent's beliefs over subsets of W, and analogously, M is the mapping encoding the agent's goals over subsets of W.

2.1 Semantics

Let Ag = {1, 2,…, n} be a set of symbols to denote *agents* and i, j ∈ Ag. The formula φ is an i *belief* $B_i\varphi$ in the world s_0, if and only if it is true in all the possible worlds from s_0 by means of the partial relationship $R^{Bi} \subseteq W\times W$; Let the set of time points $T = \{t_1, \ldots, t_m\}$ be, t, t' ∈ T and ∝ a partial order over T such that t ∝ t' if and only if time t' is later to t. Satisfaction definition of $B_i\varphi$ is as follows:

$$M, s_0, t \models B_i\varphi \text{ iff } \quad M,s,t' \models \varphi \text{ such that } (s_0, s) \in R^{Bi} \text{ and } t \propto t'. \quad (1)$$

The set of beliefs of agent *i* is denoted $B_i = \{B_i\varphi\text{: } \varphi \text{ is propositional formula}\}$. Partial relation of accessibility R^{Bi} is with respect to agent i, so that different agents have different possible worlds and so different beliefs and goals. Important remark is that the partial relation of accessibility avoids problems of logic omniscience and ideal reasoning [19] for each agent. In a similar way definitions for *goals* and *actions* are introduced. Let $R^{Gi} \subseteq W\times W$ be a partial relation of accessibility between worlds concerning the agent i goals:

$$M,s_0,t \models G_i\, \varphi \text{ iff } \quad M,s,t' \models \varphi \text{ such that } (s_0, s) \in R^{Gi} \text{ and } t \propto t'. \quad (2)$$

In order to introduce the modal action operator *do* some previous definitions are required. Let $A = \{a_1, \ldots, a_m\}$ be the set of atomic actions. A compound action $\alpha = (a_1, \ldots, a_n)$ is such that $\alpha \in A^{xn}$ the n-cartesian product of A with n = |α| the length of action α. The execution of α is over W^{xn}, the n-cartesian product of W , so that $D^i_\alpha \in W^{xn}$ is the relation of accessibility between states by realization of α by agent i. For atomic actions *a* D^i_a is an accessibility relation between worlds, either reflexive or asymmetric; Thus, definition of modal operator for atomic action *a* is as follows:

$$M,s_0,t \models [do_i\ a]\varphi \text{ iff } M,s_0,t \models G_i\varphi,\ M,s,t' \models \varphi \text{ such that } (s_0, s) \in D^i_a \text{ and } t \propto t'. \quad (3)$$

In this case the accessibility is in one step so that possible worlds are directly accessed from s_0. For compound actions,

$$M,s_0,t \models [do_i\ \alpha]\varphi \text{ iff } M,s_0,t \models G_i\varphi,\ M,s,t' \models \varphi \text{ such that } (s_0, s) \in D^i_\alpha \text{ and } t \propto t'. \quad (4)$$

Now, D^i_α is the accessibility relation reflexive, asymmetric and transitive between worlds. Furthermore, D^i_α is the composition of D^i_{aj}, with a_j the atomic action in the j-th place of α. The map D encoding the dynamic of structure *M* is D = { D^i_α : α is an action, n ≥ 1}. The operator *could* [1] is introduced; it captures that agent i has the possibility to perform action α in order to get φ but α is not being performed yet,

$$M,s_0,t \models [could_i\alpha]\varphi \text{ iff } M,s_0,t \models G_i\varphi \text{ and } M,s,t' \models [do_i\alpha]\varphi \text{ with } (s_0,s) \in D^i_\alpha \text{ and } t \propto t'. \quad (5)$$

A temporal operator *Next* is also introduced for both cases as follows:

$$M,s_0,t \models Next([do_i\alpha]\varphi) \text{ iff } M,s,t' \models \varphi \wedge B_i\varphi, \quad (6)$$

with $(s_0, s) \in D^i_\alpha$, $t \propto t'$ and does not exist $t'' \in T$ with $t \propto t'' \propto t'$.

$$M,s,t \models Next([could_i\alpha]\varphi) \text{ iff } M,s',t' \models [do_i\alpha]\varphi \wedge \Diamond B_i\varphi, \quad (7)$$

with $(s_0, s) \in D^i_\alpha$, $t \propto t'$ and does not exist $t'' \in T$ with $t \propto t'' \propto t'$.

An agent *i* is defined by a 3-tuple $i = (B_i, G_i, X_i)$, where B_i are the beliefs (pre-conditions), G_i are the goals (beliefs to achieve or post-conditions) and X_i are the actions. The mental state of an agent is the 2-tuple of beliefs and goals (B_i, G_i). The state *s* of a scenario is a 2-tuple s = (B, G), where B and G are the union of the beliefs and goals respectively of the roles of the scenario that pass through that state, and they form the pre-conditions and post-conditions of the state. Rules of agent reasoning concerning beliefs are:

Table 1. Reasoning rules for beliefs

Axiom		Name
$M, s, t \models (B\varphi \wedge B(\varphi \rightarrow \psi)) \rightarrow B\psi$	K	Modus Ponens (Distributivity)
$M, s, t \models B\varphi \rightarrow \varphi$	T	Knowledge
$M, s, t \models B\varphi \rightarrow B(B\varphi)$	4	Positive Introspection
$M, s, t \models \neg B\varphi \rightarrow B(\neg B\varphi)$	5	Negative Introspection

In this paper the accessibility relation of belief is reflexive and it explains that the so called *Knowledge* axiom T should be satisfied. Concerning goals the same axioms are satisfied. We have the following notation for common beliefs (and goals):

$$M, s, t \models B_{i,j}\varphi \text{ iff } M, s, t \models B_i\varphi \wedge B_j\varphi \quad (8)$$

for agents i and j, and in general for n agents, let $Ag' \subseteq Ag$ be a subset of agents having the common belief φ, then:

$$M, s, t \models B_{A'}\varphi \text{ iff } M, s, t \models \wedge_{i \in A'} B_i\varphi. \quad (9)$$

For nested beliefs (and goals) we have:

$$M, s, t \models B_i(B_j)\varphi \text{ for } i, j \in A, \text{ and in general, } M, s, t \models B_i(\wedge_{j \in A'} B_j\varphi_j) \quad (10)$$

[1] The notion of *Could,* introduced in this article differs from the similar notions of *Capability, Practical Possibility* and *Can* operators as they are defined in [20], that is why another notion is used.

In this paper, we define the set of beliefs and goals modal formulas with the nesting operation over modal operators B and G as a Noetherian structure. It means that we have a finite nesting of modal operators; this way the infinite nesting is avoided.

3 Scenario for Roles Interaction

The key notion of the model is that defins a role. Roles can be played by individual or multiple agents and their purpose is to define the achievable objectives, to indicate the ensuing organizational relationships between the participants, to set the channels through which interaction should occur, and to dictate the patterns of interchange that are appropriate. The change of the agent's state is the realization of an action that belongs to the agent's role in search of reaching its goal defined in the role. This implies the balance between the mechanism for revision of beliefs and the derived effects from the execution of the actions. Accompanying the role definitions are the organization rules that define the concomitant procedures or the emergent norms in which role enactment takes place. Thus, the rules specify, among other things, which agents can adopt what kind of roles and under what terms and conditions, what should happen if roles are updated/modified and how conflicts between roles should be handled. The organizational context is captured by a scenario concept. The *scenario* is a n-tuple:

$$E = \langle St, Ag, R, K, B, \mathcal{S}, I, P, G_f, T \rangle, \tag{3}$$

where St is the set of states of the scenario, Ag - the set of agents, R - the set of roles that the agent can take in E, K is the relation of role assignment, B is the set of general beliefs of E, S is the hierarchical structure among the roles of the scenario, I is the set of interactions among the roles of the scenario, G_f is the scenario's goal, and P is the plan of the scenario, conformed by a structured set of interactions such that G_f is the final goal of the plan.

Follows the definitions of each element of a scenario. $R = \{r_1,...,r_m\}$ is the set of symbols to denote roles. A *role* r is a 3-tuple $r = \langle B_r, G_r, X_r \rangle$, where B_r, G_r and X_r are beliefs, goals and actions respectively of a role. An agent i is a set of roles: i = {r : r es rol} = $\{r : r = \langle B_r, G_r, X_r \rangle\}$. These roles are assigned to agents by means of the $K \subseteq AxR$ relation. The same role can be played by different agents and one agent can play a set of roles. The set of beliefs B of the scenario can be defined in one of the following ways:

1. $B = \cup^n_{i=1} B_i$. To denote the union of all beliefs of the agents that form the scenario. This approach can generate inconsistencies if in the same state an agent believes φ and another agent believes $\neg\varphi$ if the access relationship is reflexive.
2. $B = \cap^n_{i=1} B_i$. To denote the intersection of all beliefs of the agents that form the scenario. This model solves the problem of inconsistency of the beliefs. But, in turn, it allows the set of beliefs occasionally to be empty. This set is the base to define the common or shared beliefs.
3. $B = Cn(\cap^n_{i=1} B_i)$. To denote the deductive closure of the agent's beliefs starting from the intersection of the beliefs of the agents.

4. $B = Cn(B')$ con $B' \subseteq \cup^{n}_{i=1} B_i$. To denote consistent maximal subset of the union. In this approach the set B' of beliefs is not unique[2].

In a similar way, the set of goals $\Psi = \{\psi_i : \psi_i$ is formula of first order} of the scenario can be defined. The *structure S* of the scenario refers to the preeminence or prevalence relationships that are settled down on a role with regard to another one within the scenario. We base on the lattice definition of the set of roles R to define the structure. Being $S = (R \times R, \leq)$, that is to say, S is the Cartesian product on R, partially ordered by means of ≤. Given $r_1, r_2 \in R$, if $r_1 \leq r_2$ it is said that r_2 prevails on r_1 in E. The relationship of prevailing allows to model diverse organizational relationships among the roles, such as a superior and a subordinate in a hierarchical structure, the fact that a player has the control of the ball in a ball game, that an individual has the word in a dialogue, a role which coordinates the other ones in the execution of a coordinated action, etc.

Let $Ac = \{\alpha_1,.., \alpha_n\}$ be the set of actions that can be executed in the scenario. The interactions I are settled down among the roles, each one carrying out an action at time and state. Let $I = (RxAcxTxG))^{xn})$, so that the set of interactions I is defined by means of $I = (I \times I) \times W$, that is to say, given $\iota_i = (r_i, \alpha, t, \omega)$, $\iota_j = (r_j, \beta, t', \chi) \in I$, $((\iota_i, \iota_j),s)$ denotes the interaction of the role r_i that executes the action α in the time t to obtain ω with the rol r_j that executes the action β in time t' to achieve χ, in the world (state) $s \in W$. It can be seen that given $\iota = (r, \alpha, t, \omega) \in I$, we have the elements which use the action operators, *do* and *could*: $[do_r^t\ \alpha]\ \omega$ as well as $[could_r^t\ \alpha]\ \omega$.

The *plan P* of the scenario is defined as P = (I x I, ″), a partially ordered set of interactions, where the partial order ″ establishes the branched sequence of realization of interactions among the roles through which the plan P is carried out. G_f is the element in P that defines the last interaction in the scenario. From the formal point of view, plan execution is modeled according to usual logical connectives composition of modal formulas, and application of *modus ponens* supports the dynamics of action execution. In the next section, a general formalization of interaction in a scenario is given and different types of interaction are characterized, that is: collaboration, negotiation, and competition.

4 Interaction Framework

Intuitively, collaboration is the plan of actions executed in such a way that the internal goals of the plan interact necessarily in the concurrent fashion. Collaboration is a possible result of negotiation (sometimes this negotiation is implicit, when agents revise their conflicting goals without direct communication). Competition can be considered as a particular case of cooperation (when the agents compete obeying the same organizational rules) or as the impossibility of cooperation. Formally it can be defined as follows. Given $\iota_i = (r_i, \alpha, t, \omega)$, $\iota_j = (r_j, \beta, t', \chi) \in I$, the interaction $((\iota_i, \iota_j),s) \in I$ of the role r_i that executes the action α in the time t to achieve ω with the role r_j that executes the action β in the time t' to achieve χ, in the world (state) $s \in W$. In

[2] In this case, the functions F_B y F_G that map the sets of beliefs in the maximal B' and chosen G', respectively, must be included.

terms of execution of the actions, the state s is such that $M,s \models G_i\,\varphi \wedge G_j\,\psi \wedge G_{i,j}(\gamma)$. The general definition of interaction INT can be written in the following way using the modal operator *Could*:

$$M,s \models ([Could^{t}_{ri}\alpha]\varphi \quad INT \quad [Could^{t'}_{rj}\beta]\psi) \wedge G_{i,j}(\gamma) \rightarrow \gamma \tag{4}$$

if and only if there are states M,s', M,s" and M, $\bar{s}$, such that

$$M,s' \models \varphi \wedge B_{i,}\varphi, \quad M,s" \models \psi \wedge B_{i,}\psi \text{ and } M, \bar{s} \models \gamma \wedge B_{i,j}\gamma \wedge B_{i,j}(B_{j,i}\gamma), \tag{5}$$

where sDs', sDs" s'D $\bar{s}$ and s"D $\bar{s}$. D is the accessibility relationship among the states by means of the execution of the corresponding action. In addition, the set of agents beliefs is $B_{i,j} \subseteq B_i \cap B_j$ consistent and maximal (is not unique) such that $Cn(B_{i,j}) \vdash \gamma$. General, preconditions for INT are that roles of interaction should be elements of the structure S and they should pertain to set of interactions: $(r_i,r_j) \in S$ and $((r_i,\alpha,t,\gamma),(r_j\beta,t',\gamma), s) \in I$. This couple of conditions applies to every type of interaction that follows.

In the case a conflict exists between the beliefs or goals of agents that interact to achieve a common goal, the *negotiation* type of interaction can be considered. This conflict is given among the belief of one agent with regard to the set of another agent's beliefs, or vice versa. It means that $\varphi \wedge \psi = \bot$, where obtaining a subset of B implies the process of belief revision [21]. Formally:

$$M, s, t \models (([do_{ri}\alpha]\varphi \text{ NEG } [do_{rj}\beta]\psi) \wedge G_{i,j}\,\gamma) \rightarrow \gamma \tag{6}$$

iff M, $\bar{s}$, t $\models \gamma \wedge B_{i,j}\,\gamma$ is satisfied for some state $\bar{s}$.

Preconditions for the negotiation:

$$\begin{aligned} &M,s \not\models \gamma \\ &M,s \models \varphi \wedge B_i\varphi \text{ and } B_i \cup \{\psi\} \vdash \phi \\ &M,s \models \psi \wedge B_j\psi \text{ and } B_j \cup \{\varphi\} \vdash \phi \end{aligned} \tag{7}$$

Then, being B'_i= revision($B_{i,}\ \psi$) such that $B'_i \vdash \gamma$, and B'_j= revision($B_{j,}\varphi$) such that $B'_j \vdash \gamma$

$$M,s_1 \models \varphi,\ M,s_2 \models \psi,\ sRs_1,\ sRs_2. \tag{8}$$

The negotiation can result in collaboration (consensus is achieved) or competition (in the opposite case). The *collaboration* is formalized in the following way. Let Bi |- φ and Bj |- ψ. The agents i, j collaborate to achieve the goal γ iff γ is deducible from the consistent intersection of Bi and Bj.

$$M, s, t \models (([do_{ri}\alpha]\varphi \text{ COL } [do_{rj}\beta]\psi) \wedge G_{i,j}\,\gamma) \rightarrow \gamma \tag{9}$$

iff M, $\bar{s}$, t' $\models \gamma \wedge B_{i,j}\,\gamma$ is satisfied for some state $\bar{s}$ iff

$M,s \models \varphi \wedge B_i\varphi$, $M,s \models \psi \wedge B_j\,\psi$ and $\exists B'_i \subseteq B_i$ y $\exists B'_j \subseteq B_j$ such that B'i ∩ B'j is consistent and Cn(B'i ∩ B'j)|- γ.

During the *competition* interaction, the participating agents seek to achieve the same goal. The impossibility of consensus means that only one of them can achieve it and the rest of agents can not. The later is reflected in the beliefs of the agents in the final state in which the goal is achieved. At the beginning of the competition, each agent has a goal to achieve γ as long as the rest of the agents don't achieve it.

$$M, s, t \models (([do_{ri}\alpha]\varphi \text{ COMP } [do_{rj}\beta]\psi) \wedge G_{i,j}\, \gamma) \rightarrow \gamma \quad \text{iff} \tag{10}$$

$M, \bar{s}, t' \models \gamma \wedge B_i\, \gamma \wedge B_j\, \neg\gamma \wedge B_j(B_i\, \gamma) \wedge B_i(B_j \neg\, \gamma)$ is satisfied for some state $\bar{s}$ and $t \leq t'$.

It means that

$$M, s, t \models (G_i\gamma \wedge G_i(B_j{\sim}\gamma)) \wedge (G_j\gamma \wedge G_j(B_i{\sim}\gamma)) \tag{11}$$

Different models of interaction discussed above are illustrated in fig. 1.

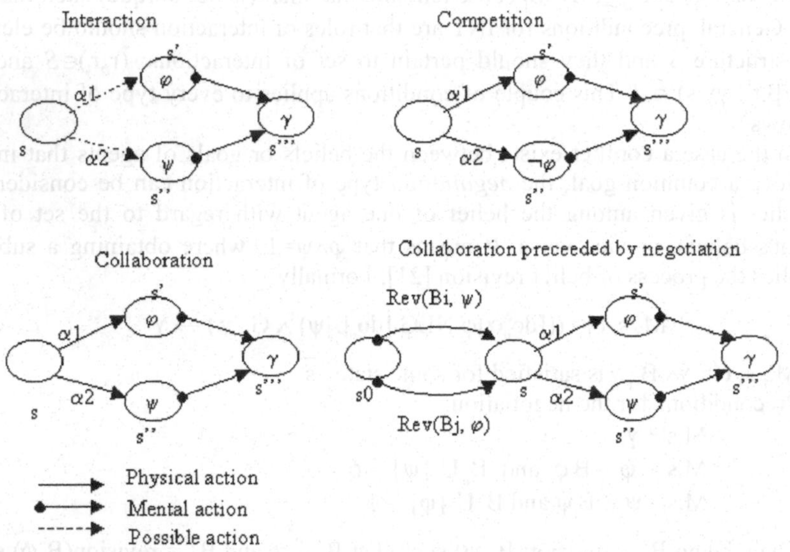

Fig. 1. Models of interaction

5 Example

To illustrate how this model works in more details, we will show how agents can be built for the scenario, adapted from [22, 23]. This scenario is well known as the most suitable for reactive agents with subsumption architecture. Steels even argues that logic-based agents are "entirely unrealistic" for this problem [23].

The *objective is to explore a distant planet, more concretely, to collect samples of a particular type of precious rock.* The *location of the rock samples is not known in advance, but they are typically clustered in certain spots. A number of autonomous vehicles are available that can drive around the planet collecting samples and later re-enter a mothership spacecraft to go back to earth. There is no detailed map of the planet available, although it is known that the terrain is full of obstacles-hills, valleys, etc. - which makes it difficult for vehicles to exchanging communications.* The problem we are faced with is about building an agent control architecture for each vehicle, so that they will cooperate to collect rock samples from the planet surface as efficiently as possible.

To simplify the example we'll consider a planet divided grid-like into a number of equally sized squares corresponding to the unit of movement of the agent (actually it looks like a cooperative vacuum world). We also will assume the following:

- A vehicle can move forward or turn left or right,
- Two vehicles can't occupy the same square at the same time,
- Clusters of samples occupy one square,
- Each time a vehicle works only with one cluster and can carry only one sample,
- A vehicle is equipped with a sensor that detects obstacles within a distance of two squares,
- Vehicles can communicate with each other within a distance of two squares: if another vehicle is detected, the current belief set is communicated to it.

The scenario E = <St, A, R, K, B, Σ, I, P, G_f, T > is defined as follows:

A={{vehicle}, mothership}

R={transport, stock, quest, clamper}

We define four generic roles for exploring, transportation, accumulation and camping/resetting activities. These roles are assigned to two scenario agents as follows:

VehicleR(transport, quest, clamper)

MothershipR(stock)

Let us assume that the final goal of the scenario is to collect all the samples: Gf =~sample().

To avoid deadlocks (when a conflict between two vehicles to occupy a square occurs) all the transport and quest roles are ordered Σ=(i, j, ≤).

As an example, we show a fragment of a *vehicle i* mental state definition as follows (Table 2):

Table 2. Initial beliefs, goals and actions of the *vehicle* agent

Beliefs:

B_i(has(sample))
B_i (position(x, y, d))
B_i (cluster(x, y))
B_i (B_m(position(x, y)))

Actions (atomic):

a_1 - receive(i, φ)
a_2 - detect(o, x, y), where *o* is any object, can be an obstacle, a sample or another vehicle.
a_3 - move(x, y, d), where *d* is direction
a_4 - inform(j, φ)

Goals:

G_i (avoid(obstacle))
G_i(sample(x_m, y_m)), where (x_m, y_m) are coordinates of the mothership.

Actions (composite):

α_1 - explore
α_2 = receive PAR (move SEQ detect(sample, x, y)[3]

[3] The formalization of action is beyond the scope of this article.

In a general case, this scenario can be considered as a collaborative one because of the following:

$$M,s,t \models ([Could_i\alpha]\varphi \wedge [Could_j\alpha]\varphi \wedge G_i\gamma \wedge G_j\gamma) \rightarrow \gamma, \tag{12}$$

where $\varphi = G_i(sample(x_m, y_m))$, a goal of the *transport* role, $\gamma = \sim sample()$, a goal of a scenario.

Some example rules follows:

$$Gi(position(x_m, y_{m,}\_)) \wedge Gi(has(sample)) \rightarrow Gi(sample(x_m, y_m)) \wedge Gi(\sim has(sample)), \tag{13}$$

defining the goal of the transport role to bring the sample to the mothership.

$$Gi(\sim has(sample)) \wedge Gi(position(x, y_,\_)) \wedge Gi(detect(sample)) \rightarrow Gi(cluster(x, y)) \wedge Gi(has(sample)), \tag{14}$$

denoting the fact that to pick up a sample, a clamper must be located in the relevant square containing samples; etc.

A fragment of a plan $P=(I^n, \leq)$ composed of interactions can then be defined as follows.

$$\begin{aligned} P=\{&((i^{:quest}, explore, t, G_i(cluster(x,y))), (j^{:quest}, explore, t, G_j(cluster(x,y))), s), \\ &((i^{:trans}, move, t, G_i(position(x,y,\_))), (j^{:trans}, move, t, G_j(position(x,y,\_))), s'), \\ &((i^{:clamp}, collect, t, G_i(has(sample()))), (j^{:clamp}, collect, t, G_j(has(sample()))), s''), \\ &\quad((i^{:trans}, inform, t, G_j(cluster(x,y) \vee B_j(\sim cluster(x,y))), \\ &\quad(j^{:trans}, receive, t, G_j(cluster(x,y) \vee B_j(\sim cluster(x,y))), s'''), \ldots\} \end{aligned} \tag{15}$$

Interactions relate agent goals with actions. Playing the roles of a scenario and to achieve their goals, all agents execute their compound actions in interaction (direct or indirect) with other agents. These interactions take place at the level of atomic actions. For example, any pair of agents playing role of a *quest* interact interchanging the information about a cluster or preventing accidents. In the later case, a typical conflict situation of competence occurs when any two vehicles try to occupy the same square:

$$\begin{aligned} &M,s,t \models G_i\ (position(x,y,\_)), \\ &M,s,t \models G_j\ (position(x,y,\_)) \end{aligned} \tag{16}$$

It can be solved as follows:

$$M,s,t \models Next([do_i\alpha]\varphi) \wedge Next([do_j\alpha]\varphi) \wedge \leq(i,j) \rightarrow [do_i\alpha]\varphi \wedge \sim[do_j\alpha]\varphi \tag{17}$$

such that $M,s',t' \models \varphi \wedge Bi\varphi \wedge Bj(\neg\varphi) \wedge Bi(Bj(\neg\varphi))$, $sR^{Next}s'$, where $\varphi = position(x,y,\_)$, $\alpha = move(x,y,d)$.

The example has been implemented using Java, Prolog and VRML. The NEG, COM and COMP predicates are implemented as Prolog clauses. The scenario, structure and plan are sets of clauses (some of them are constraints) as well as the pre-conditions that allow the execution of actions, which in turn set post-condition clauses. Agents' beliefs and goals are Prolog facts that should be eventually revised or updated.

6 Related Works and Conclusions

A number of attempts have been made by researchers within DAI to develop formal models of real agents and multi-agent systems. In this article, a conceptualization of a model of interaction based on the role modeling is presented. A major advantage of using roles is that they can be updated without having to update the actions for every agent on an individual basis. Roles are defined as standardised patterns of behaviour. In our framework multiple roles played by an agent are also allowed.

Roles and role-based interactions are also considered within the other frameworks [24, 25]. In the model of electronic organisations (electronic institutions), they are composed of a vast amount of heterogeneous (human and software) agents playing different roles. A concept of a dialogic institution is introduced in that model where agents interact through illocutions. These interactions are articulated through agent group meetings, which are called scenes, which define a generic pattern of conversation protocol between roles. The concept of a scene is similar to the scenario concept in our model. Obviously, the main difference with our approach is that only dialogic actions are associated to roles.

In addition to the role definition, the concept of interaction is a fundamental issue for modelling open MAS. The so called algorithmic interactions hold well defined computational processes implemented through Turing Machines. This type of interaction is implemented by the OOP, more precisely, objects *were developed just to interact algorithmically.* On the other hand, first deployments modelling non-algorithmic interaction, inherent to alive, dynamic and open systems were introduced few years ago by P. Wegner and R. Goldin. *Interaction Machines* [26] deal with any kind of interactive event not restricted to the agent interaction well determined ad hoc. This type of interaction is one of the major goals of MAS research both in the development of formal methods and programming techniques.

Another important point of concern is the possibility to model deontological properties (laws, norms, obligations, etc) governing the group behaviour. Quite a few authors have argued that such concepts are an important tool to "glue" autonomous agents together in a multi-agent system [27, 28, 29]. In [27] some general comments about the formalization of norms and obligations are given using an extension of PDL for multiple modalities, where the authors argue that desires, obligations and norms can be based on preference orderings directing the choice of future actions. Being in general out of the scope of this article due to space limits, in our model these modalities are partially covered by the structure (S) element of the model where partial order is also used for preference ordering.

Our approach is based mainly on the use of modal temporal logic. The main reasons for this choice are the model based on mental states of agents and the concurrent nature of the actions. Modal temporal logic for modeling the behavior of MAS was used first in Concurrent MetateM language [30]. Another approach was developed by Wooldridge [31], where the logic that extends classical first-order logic with the introduction of modalities for representing beliefs, intentions, and actions of agents, as well as temporal modal connectives for representing the time-varying properties was used. An integrated approach to reasoning about concurrent actions using PDL logic and CTL logic in a Processes Algebra formal account is reported in [32].

Important point of concern is the long-standing gap between the BDI logical model and practical agent implementations. It might seem that the BDI model is becoming less important, due to the looseness of its connection to practical systems, and because of its failure to guide research into implementation directions in any obviously useful way. One of the possible ways for the implementation is the use of declarative languages based on the first-order logic. In ConGolog, concurrent actions are sets of actions jointly executed such that the Prolog implementation is a list of atomic predicates [33]. The ConGolog implementation of an agent would be an argument of the predicate denoting the actions being performed without explicit ConGolog implementation of agent's beliefs and goals. Our experience implementing the described model shows us it would be convenient to work with hybrid systems such that the procedural concurrent aspects of actions and interactions are implemented with non-declarative languages (like Java or C++), whereas the BDI aspects dealing with the inferential processes being implemented with declarative languages (as Prolog or Golog).

Formalization of different aspects of this model is under development. In the current work we are trying to consider the concept of obligation in a more explicit way, because of its vital importance for the development of the agents behavior in organizational context. A fair application domain of our logic is the modeling of robots interaction such that shared action execution do not necessarily require explicit messages interchange.

Acknowledgements

Partial support for this research work has been provided by the CONACyT, Mexico within the project 31851-A "Models and Tools for Agent Interaction in Cooperative MAS", as well as the 31991-A “Multi Agent Systems for the modeling of objects using information of their appearance”, and by the National Technical University, Mexico, within the project CGEPI980739. The authors thank Gustavo Núñez (UAEH, México), Ulises Cortés (UPC, Spain), Frank Dignum (UU, The Netherlands), and José Arrazola (BUAP, México) for their ideas and comments of the work reported in this article.

References

1. Jennings, N. R. On agent-based software engineering. Artificial Intelligence, 2000, 117:277-296.
2. Ferber, J. Multi-Agent Systems, Addison-Wesley, MA, 1999.
3. P. R. Cohen and H. J. Levesque. Intention is choice with commitment. Artificial Intelligence, 42:213--261, 1990.
4. D. Harel. Dynamic logic. In D. Gabbay and F. Guenther, editors, Handbook of Philosophical Logic Volume II --- Extensions of Classical Logic, pages 497--604. D. Reidel Publishing Company: Dordrecht, The Netherlands, 1984. (Synthese library Volume 164).
5. J. Y. Halpern and Y. Moses. A guide to completeness and complexity for modal logics of knowledge and belief. Artificial Intelligence, 54:319--379, 1992.
6. A. S. Rao and M. P. Georgeff. Modeling rational agents within a BDI-architecture. In R. Fikes and E. Sandewall, editors, Proceedings of Knowledge Representation and Reasoning (KR&R-91), pages 473--484. Morgan Kaufmann Publishers: San Mateo, CA, April 1991.

7. Chainbi, W. A belief-goal-role logic for a single-agent system. Proceedings of the 16th ACM SAC2001 Symposium on Applied Computing March 11 - 14, 2001, Las Vegas, NV USA.
8. M. Wooldridge. Coherent social action. In Proceedings of the Eleventh European Conference on Artificial Intelligence (ECAI-94), Amsterdam, The Netherlands, 1994, pp. 279--283.
9. Traum, D. Speech Acts for Dialogue Agents. M. Wooldgridge and A.Rao. Foundations of Rational Agency, Kluwer Academic Publishers, 1999, pp. 172-201.
10. L. Cavedon, A. Rao, L. Sonenberg and G. Tidhar, Teamwork via team plans in intelligent autonomous agent systems, International Conference on WorldWide Computing and its Applications, Tsukuba, Japan. Lecture Notes in Computer Science 1274, Springer (1997).
11. M. Tambe. Towards Flexible Teamwork. Journal of AI Research, 7(1997), 83-124.
12. Grosz, B. & Kraus S. Collaborative Plans for complex group action. AI, 86(2):269-357, 1996.
13. Boutilier, C. & R.I. Brafman. Planning with concurrent interacting actions. Proc. Of the 14th National Conf. On AI (AAAI97), 1997.
14. Kinny D., Georgeff, M., & Rao, A. A Methodology and Modelling Technique for Systems of BDI Agents. Technical Note, 58. Australian Artificial Intelligence Institute, 1996.
15. Nwana, H. S., Ndumu, D. T., and Lee, L. C, ZEUS: An Advanced Tool Kit for Engineering Distributed Multi Agent Systems, *Prac. App. Agent Multi- agent Systems (PAAM),* (March, 1998), 377 - 391.
16. Michael Wooldridge, Nicholas R Jennings and David Kinny. The Gaia Methodology for Agent-Oriented Analysis and Design. *Autonomous Agents and Multiagent Systems*, 3, 285-312, 2000.
17. Finin, T., Labrou, Ya., & Mayfield J. (1997) KQML as an agent communication language, in J. Bradshaw, ed., Software Agents, AAAI/MIT Press, 1997.
18. FIPA Agent Communication Language, Foundation for Intelligent Physical Agents, URL: http://www.fipa.org.
19. M. Alvarado, An approach to Knowledge and Belief based on Kleene Three-Valued Logic, Ph D Thesis, Technical University of Catalonia, Spain, 1998.
20. W. Van Der Hoek, B. Van Linder and J-J.Ch. Meyer, An integrated modal approach to rational agents. In Michael Wooldridge and Anand Rao, Foundations of Rational Agency, pages 133--167, Kluwer Academic Publishers: 1999.
21. Nir Friedman and Joseph Y. Halpern. Modeling Belief in Dynamic Systems, Part II: Revision and Update. Journal of Artificial Intelligence Research 10 (1999) 117-167
22. L. Steels. Cooperation between distributed agents through self organization. In Y. Demazeau and J.-P. Müller, editors, *Decentralized Al - Proceedings of the First European Workshop on Modelling Autonomous Agents in a Multi-Agent World (MAAMAW-89),* pages 175-196. Elsevier Science Publishers B.V.: Amsterdam, The Netherlands, 1990.
23. G. Weiss (Ed.) Multiagent systems: a Modern Approach to Distributed Artificial Intelligence. The MIT Press Cambridge, Mass. 1999.
24. C. Castelfranchi and R. Falcone (1997). From Task Delegation to Role Delegation. In *Proceedings of the AI*IA* 97: *Advances in Artificial Intelligence Congress.* LNAI: 1321, pp. 278-289.
25. 25 M. Esteva, J. A. Rodríguez-Aguilar, J. L. Arcos, C. Sierra, and P. Garcia. Institutionalising open multi-agent systems. A formal approach. Technical report, Artificial Intelligence Research Institute. Spanish Council for Scientific Research. IIIA Research Report 2000-01 (http://www.iiia.csic.es/Publications/Reports/2000), 2000.
26. 26.Wegner, P. and Goldin D., Mathematical Models of Interactive Computing, URL: http://www.cs.brown.edu/people/pw/home.html 1999.

27. 27. F. Dignum, D. Kinny, L. Sonenberg. Motivational Attitudes of Agents: On Desires, Obligations and Norms. *In Proc of the Second International Workshop of Central and Eastern Europe on Multi-Agent Systems, CEEMAS'01*, Cracow, Poland, September, 2001, pp. 61-70.
28. 28. C. Castelfranchi, F. Dignum, C.Jonker and J. Treur. Deliberate Normative Agents: Principles and Architectures, In *Proceedings of ATAL-99,* Orlando, 1999. pp 206-220.
29. 29. L. Cavedon and L. Sonenberg. On social commitments, roles and preferred goals, In *Proceedings of ICMAS'98,* Paris, July 1998, (ed) Y. Demazeau, pp 80-87.
30. 30. M. Fisher. Towards a semantics for Concurrent METATEM. In M. Fisher and R. Owens, editors, Executable Modal and Temporal Logics. Springer-Verlag: Heidelberg, Germany, 1995.
31. 31. M. Wooldridge. This is MyWorld: The Logic of an Agent-Oriented DAI Testbed. In M. Wooldridge and N. R. Jennings, editors, Intelligent Agents: Proceedings of the 1994 Workshop on Agent Theories, Architectures, and Languages, Springer-Verlag, 1995.
32. 32. Chen, Xiao & De Giacomo Giuseppe, Reasoning about Nondeterministic and Concurrent Actions: A Process Algebra Approach, Short version in 30th AAAI Conference, 1996.
33. 33. Raymond Reiter, Knowledge in Action: Logical Foundations for Specifying and Implementing Dynamical Systems. MIT Press, 2001.

Towards a Model for an Immune System

Rosa Saab[1], Raúl Monroy[1], and Fernando Godínez[2,*]

[1] Tecnológico de Monterrey, Campus Estado de México
Carretera al Lago de Guadalupe Km. 3.5, Atizapán, 52926, Mexico
00471599@academ01.cem.itesm.mx, raulm@campus.cem.itesm.mx
[2] Tecnológico de Monterrey, Campus Monterrey
Av. Eugenio Garza Sada 2501 Sur, Monterrey, 64849, Mexico
a1444909@mail.mty.itesm.mx

Abstract. Immune systems of life forms have been a rich source of inspiration to computer scientists. Problem solving strategies, borrowing ideas from the immune system analogy, have been successfully applied to challenging problems of modern computing. However, no formal model of a typical immune system has so far been proposed. This paper reports on an experiment towards modelling an immune system using process algebra. Our model of the immune system separates individual components. Each element is specified in terms of its observable behaviour. This paper also provides a formal specification of some properties of an immune system, including robustness and self-stabilisation. It outlines the sort of mechanisms that are required to formally verify the resulting model.

Keywords: Multi-agent systems, Computer Immunology, Process Calculi.

1 Introduction

Immune systems of life forms have been a rich source of inspiration to computer scientists. They suggest problem solving strategies that have been successfully applied to challenging problems of modern computing. Apart from effectiveness, immune systems portray properties that are highly desirable in computer programs, e.g. robustness, and reliability. Above all, however, simplicity is what makes immune systems so attractive: they are made out of a number of simple, coordinated cells, each of which carries out but a small part of a task. The simplicity of the individual, together with the striking effect of the collection, drives research aimed at building an analogous computer program. Yet, research seems to proceed without a formal model of an immune system.

This paper reports on an experiment towards modelling an immune system. The model provided is intended to be employed both by biologists, as a controlled laboratory, and by computer scientists, as a reference for developing – and hopefully discovering – problem solving strategies inspired in biology. The

* This research was supported by two CONACYT grants: i) REDII and ii) 33337-A.

C.A. Coello Coello et al. (Eds.): MICAI 2002, LNAI 2313, pp. 401–410, 2002.

model comprehends only aspects of behaviour[1], as presented in [11,8]. To specify it, we have used a process algebra.

Process algebras are suitable for modelling, analysing and building complex communicating systems out of simpler ones. Communicating systems, called *agents*, are circumscribed by their entire capabilities of interaction, called *actions*. Process calculi are well established in both industry and academia and have been successfully applied to formal system development. Rather than using an existing process algebra, e.g. CCSand CSPwe suggest to use a combination thereof. This is because modelling the immune system requires uniting results found through many years of research. In particular, our model involves aspects about duration of actions, probabilistic quantification for non-determinism and multiple communication.

Also this paper provides a formal specification of some properties associated with an immune system. This includes effectiveness, self-stabilisation and robustness. The model, unfortunately, is not suitable for formal analysis yet. We outline directions to indicate what sort of toolbox is required to formally analyse our model.

Paper Overview. The rest of the paper is organised as follows: We first motivate the sort of formalism required to model the behavioural aspects of an immune system (§2). Then we argue that these informal requirements can be captured using a particular process algebra, which is then presented (§3). Then, using the algebra, we specify the behaviour of some immune system components (§4). We next outline how to conduct formal model analysis, as well as providing guidelines towards mechanical analysis (§5). Finally, related work is contrasted (§6) and conclusions drawn from our experiments presented (§7).

2 Modelling an Immune System

The aim of this section is twofold: i) to motivate the sort of apparatus required to model a system as complex as the immune one; and ii) to introduce the process algebra we have chosen to attempt such an enterprise, as well as its limitations.

2.1 Immune Systems: General Features

An immune system consists of a number of cells, each of which performs a small, specific task. Cells are independent but they coordinate one another, coping with individual limitations. The system is thus highly distributed. Its overall behaviour is assumed to be a product of both the number and the kind of interactions that happen amongst individual cells. Cell behaviour is simple and so in principle amenable to modelling and verification.

[1] For a physical, chemical model of the immune system, the reader is referred to [4] as well as [11].

An immune system is diverse: cells of the same kind vary from one to other. This involves non-self detection. So what is distinguishable to one cell goes unnoticed to others. Yet, an immune system is highly robust. To improve the level of success, lymphocytes complement their recognition abilities by travelling the body through the blood stream and the lymphatic system [7]. Mobility is hence crucial to immune system performance.

An immune system is highly dynamic. Cell population, as well as the structure of such population, changes with time and according to circumstances. Some cells last a few days but some others last a few years. Non-cell components, such as antigens, last as long as the body does. Cells therefore obey to a sort of universal clock, they are programmed to die – *apoptosis.* To compensate for short-lived cells, the body is continuously producing immune system components. Yet the population self-stabilises. Population increase amounts to detection of invading microorganisms. It is usually followed by the corresponding decrease after disease elimination.

Learning and memory are key to body protection. If the immune system detects an unknown invader, not only will it battle the invader, but it will also attempt to learn the invader structure. As a result, the immune system will evolve a collection of components (antibodies, MHC, etc.), specially designed to detect and protect the body against the invader.

While travelling through the blood stream, a group of immune system's components may coincide and form a chain, *clustering.* Together, the chain is able to provide a sophisticated defence, which is stronger than that given by each cell in isolation.

2.2 Process Calculi: General Features

Process calculi have been successfully applied to formal development of communicating systems. This section aims to show process calculi provide a means for expressing central aspects associated with immune system behaviour.

There are aspects of an immune system that can be modelled directly using a suitable process algebra. Cell diversity, for example, can be appropriately modelled by providing the associated agent an affinity set. With it, an agent is capable of recognising others if, through interaction, it receives a datum belonging to its own affinity set. Both because we want to model memory, and because our agents communicate values, the intended process algebra ought to be message-passing [6].

Immune system actions cannot be assumed to be instantaneous. While specifying the duration of each action may not be realistic, it can prove to be useful if certain properties need to be verified. Markovian process algebras, such as PEPA [5], extend a classical process algebra with stochastic timing information. The duration of each action is specified with a distributed random variable, yielding a Markov process. The Markov process may then be used to compute performance measures.

Similarly, immune system choices cannot be assumed to be non-deterministic. For example, while interacting, a component of the immune system may show specific preferences to do one thing over other. Probabilistic process calculi extend classical ones by adding a probabilistic quantification for non-determinism. Probabilistic processes can also be realised as Markov, stochastic process and, hence, existing theories within such framework can be used to prove properties about these processes. WSCCS [12] is an example probabilistic process algebra, where choices are quantified with *weights* and, thus, probabilistic specification amounts to *relative frequency*. The heavier an action's weight of an action the more chances for it to happen.

Mobility can be captured using a higher-order process calculus, e.g. the π-calculus [9]. Then action names, as well as processes themselves, are communicated allowing the specification of dynamic reconfiguration of the process linkage. This sort of apparatus is indeed required for producing a precise account for an immune system. However, the model is far more complex and so here we constrain ourselves to a more modest, limited but intuitive model, which involves only a single site.

Given that we constrain ourselves to a singled-site system, our model does not include clustering either. Clustering requires specifying coordination and competence protocols, which increases the complexity of the model. In what follows, we briefly describe a standard process algebra which allows for multiple process communication, quantification of choice, duration of action and for the communication of values of any kind. The calculus is assumed to come in a synchronous or asynchronous version. If synchronous, action duration is irrelevant, as expected. Otherwise, the activity rate of each action is considered to evaluate system performance.

3 A Process Algebra

We assume value expressions, e, built from value variables $x, y, \ldots$, value constants $v_1, v_2, \ldots$ and any other operators, e.g., $+, \times, \ldots$. We also assume boolean expressions, b, with similar properties except that they are closed under the logical connectives. The set of actions, $\mathcal{A}ct$, contains the set of input actions, the set of output actions and the unobservable action τ, which denotes an internal, unknown activity. Input actions are of the form $a?x$. Respectively, output actions are of the form $a!e$. Actions, input or output, may take no parameters at all. In that case, we simply write $a?, a!, \ldots$ [2].

The set of *agent expressions*, $\mathcal{E}$, is defined as the smallest set that contains the agent expressions below:

- $a?x.E$, $a!e.E$, $\tau.E$, *prefixes* (a an action name, x an input variable, e an output expression);
- $w_1 \colon E_1 + w_2 \colon E_2$ *choice* (w_1 and w_2 weights);
- $E_1 \{\!|L|\!\} E_2$, a *composition* (L a set of action names);
- $E \setminus L$, a *restriction* ($L \subseteq \mathcal{L}$); and
- E/L, a *hiding* (L a set of action names).

[2] Strictly speaking, we should annotate the actions with their associated activity rate. However we omit such information for the sake of readability.

where E, E_i are already in $\mathcal{E}$. Informally, the meaning of the *combinators* is as follows: prefix, (.), is used to convey the discrete actions an agent may perform. For example, $a.E$ denotes an agent capable of executing the action a, and then evolving into E. $a?x.$ accepts any input value, binding the value variable x, whereas $a!e.$ sends e to the outside world.

Choice, +, disjoins the capabilities of the agents that are either side of it; as soon as one performs any action, the others are dismissed. Choices are quantified: $w_1\colon E_1 + w_2\colon E_2$ means that we shall see w_1 occurrences of E_1 for each w_2 of E_2. We shall use $\sum_{i \in I} w_i : E_i$ for the summation of all processes E_i, $i \in I$.

Parallel composition, ($|\{L\}|$), is used to express concurrency. Let L be a set of action names, then $E_1|\{L\}|E_2$ denotes an agent where E_1 and E_2 proceed independently, interacting one another only via some action name in L. When L is empty, we simply write $|||$. We shall use $\prod_{i \in I} E_i$ for the composition of all processes E_i, $i \in I$.

Restriction, (\ ), is used to enforce communication as well as binding the scope of actions: $E \setminus L$ behaves like E, except that it cannot execute any action a that uses a name in L. Finally, hiding, /, is used for internalising actions: E/L is as E except that any one time it is about to perform an action in L, it will produce τ instead.

We are now ready to present our model of an immune system. Due to space constrains, we necessarily leave out some components, including some types of lymphocyte, antigens, antibodies and infected cells.

4 A Behavioural Model for an Immune System

This section presents part of our behavioural model for an immune system. In the model, each component is idealised: It cannot spontaneously die as time goes by. The corresponding real component or faulty agent, C^r, can be specified by simply making the idealised agent, C, work with its own individual clock, `Clock`:

$$C^r \stackrel{\text{def}}{=} C|\{\mathcal{L}(C)\}|\texttt{Clock}(\mathcal{L}(C))$$

$$\texttt{Clock}(K) \stackrel{\text{def}}{=} m\colon \sum_{a \in K} a.\texttt{Clock}(K) + 1\colon \tau.\mathbf{0}$$

Where $\mathbf{0}$ denotes the *deadlock* process, capable of doing nothing whatsoever, and where $\mathcal{L}(C)$ denotes the syntactic sort of C [3]. As expected, after m ticks, C is likely to die.

4.1 The Natural Killer

A *Natural Killer*, *NK*, plays a major role in the protection of the body against disease. It may get engaged in either of three main activities: i) recognise the

[3] The *syntactic sort* of a process P is a set containing the names of the actions that P may take ever.

presence of antigens or infected cells; ii) having identified it, attack the non-self until possibly extinguishing it; and iii) regulate the immune response. These activities are all a form of interaction.

On cell recognition, the interaction may be direct, in the case of an infected cell, or indirect, in the case of an antigen, via an specific antibody. On cell attack, the interaction takes the form of toxin injection from the NK into the non-self and is usually lethal. On response regulation, the interaction amounts to cytosine injection from the NK into the blood stream. This either suppresses or stimulates the development of T lymphocytes, each of which may inherit different features. Also on response regulation, an NK may proliferate.

Initially, an NK is ready to detect the presence of either an antibody or an infected cell. If an antibody is detected, `encrust`, the NK will absorb it and then specialise itself as a terminator of the specific antibody's antigen. This process, called *affinity maturation*, we model simply using memorisation. Here is the associated model:

$$
\begin{aligned}
\mathtt{NK}(R,A) &\stackrel{\text{def}}{=} 1\colon \mathtt{encrust}?x.\mathtt{NK}(R, A\cup\{x\})\\
&\quad + 1\colon \mathtt{bind}?y.\,(\,\mathbf{if}\,(y\in R\cup A)\,\mathbf{then}\,\mathtt{NK}'(R,A)\,\mathbf{else}\,\mathtt{NK}(R,A))
\end{aligned}
$$

where $\mathtt{NK}(R,A)$ models the behaviour of an NK, assuming some reception capabilities, R, and an antibody population, A (initially empty).

Upon non-self detection, `bind`, the cell will either attempt to kill it, `txn`, or react according to the immune stimulus, `cts`. While attacking it, an NK may successfully get rid of the antigen, `die`, or may get exhausted, τ, dying immediately afterwards. If it injects cytosine into the blood stream, an NK will either extinguish its own response, $\downarrow$, or proliferate, $\uparrow$. α is an oracle which returns how many cells ought to be left upon proliferation:

$$
\begin{aligned}
\mathtt{NK}'(R,A) &\stackrel{\text{def}}{=} 1\colon \mathtt{txn}!.\mathtt{NK}''(R,A) + 1\colon \mathtt{cts}!\uparrow.\mathtt{NK}'''(R,A)\\
\mathtt{NK}''(R,A) &\stackrel{\text{def}}{=} w_0\colon \mathtt{die}?.\mathtt{NK}(R,A) + w_1\colon \mathtt{txn}!.\mathtt{NK}''(R,A) + w_2\colon \tau.\mathbf{0}\\
&\qquad (w_0 \gg w_1 \gg w_2)\\
\mathtt{NK}'''(R,A) &\stackrel{\text{def}}{=} \mathtt{cts}?x.\mathtt{NK}'''(R,A,x)\\
\mathtt{NK}'''(R,A,x) &\stackrel{\text{def}}{=} \mathbf{if}\,(x=\downarrow)\,\mathbf{then}\,\mathtt{NK}(R,A)\\
&\quad + \mathbf{if}\,(x=\uparrow)\,\mathbf{then}\,\mathtt{NK}'(R,A) \,\Big\|\, \prod_{i=1}^{\alpha}\mathtt{NK}'(R,\emptyset)
\end{aligned}
$$

4.2 The Monocyte Cell

Monocytes aim to engulf non-self, either active or inert (*debris*), and thereby getting rid of it. They also help other immune system components recognise the presence of invading microorganisms. In particular, monocytes have the capability of functioning as an *antigen presenting cell*, APC, for which they first require to interact with antibodies, `apc`. Here is our model of a monocyte:

$$\begin{aligned}
\mathtt{M}(R,I) \stackrel{\text{def}}{=} & w_0 : \mathtt{bind}?x.\mathtt{M}'(R,I,x) \\
& + w_1 : \mathtt{cts}?y.\,(\,\textbf{if}\,(y = \uparrow)\,\textbf{then}\,(1 : \mathtt{cts}!\uparrow.\mathtt{M}(R,I) + 1 : \mathtt{bind}?x.\mathtt{M}'(R,I,x)) \\
& \qquad \textbf{else}\,\mathtt{M}(R,I)) \\
& + w_2 : \mathtt{apc}?.(\,\textbf{if}\,(I \neq \emptyset)\,\textbf{then}\,\mathtt{apc}!(x \in I).\mathtt{M}(R, I - \{x\})\,\textbf{else}\,\mathtt{fail}!.\mathtt{M}(R,I)) \\
& + w_3 : \tau.\mathtt{Macrophage} \\
& \quad w_0 > w_1 > w_2 > w_3
\end{aligned}$$

As indicated by the model, to bind and then absorb a non-self, monocytes require a stimulus, cytosine. Upon detection, they absorb as much non-self as possible but may die if go beyond their digest capability. Sometimes, monocytes move from the blood stream into the muscular tissue, hence, differentiating into a macrophage. Macrophages, not included herein, are just as monocytes except that they are bigger and may swell an infected area. The definitions below complete the model:

$$\begin{aligned}
\mathtt{M}'(R,I,x) & \stackrel{\text{def}}{=} \textbf{if}\,(x \in R)\,\textbf{then}\,\mathtt{M_p}(R,I,x)\,\textbf{else}\,\mathtt{M}(R,I) \\
\mathtt{M_p}(R,I,x) & \stackrel{\text{def}}{=} w_0 : \mathtt{engulf!.die?.M'_p}(R,I,x) + w_1 : \tau.\mathbf{0} \\
& \quad w_0 = DC \times w_1 \\
\mathtt{M'_p}(R,I,x) & \stackrel{\text{def}}{=} \mathtt{bind}?y.\,(\,\textbf{if}\,(x = y)\,\textbf{then}\,\mathtt{M_p}(R,I,x)\,\textbf{else}\,\mathtt{M}(R, I \cup \{x\}))
\end{aligned}$$

Here DC amounts to the digestion capability of an standard monocyte. If any one monocyte engulfs beyond DC, it may die.

4.3 The B Lymphocyte

B cells play a chief role at yielding the *acquired immune response*. They are concerned with 4 main activities: i) getting rid of the non-self; ii) learning from past attacking activities; iii) providing a repository for documenting experienced attacks; and iv) tuning the cell reception capabilities, via either antibody encrustation or through incoming cytosine.

$\mathtt{B}(R,A,I)$ represents a B cell with reception capabilities R, population of antibody encrustation A and repository of previous attacks I:

$$\begin{aligned}
\mathtt{B}(R,A,I) \stackrel{\text{def}}{=} & w_0 : \mathtt{cts}?y.\mathtt{B}(R \cup \{y\}, A, I) \\
& + w_0 : \mathtt{encrust}?x.\mathtt{B}(R, A \cup \{x\}, I) \\
& + w_1 : \mathtt{endocyte}?z.\mathtt{B}(R, A, \sigma(I)) \\
& + w_1 : (\,\textbf{if}\,(I \neq \emptyset)\,\textbf{then}\,\textbf{query}!(u \in I).\mathtt{B}(R,A,I)) \\
& + w_0 : \mathtt{bind}?v.\mathtt{B}(R,A,I,v) \\
& \quad w_0 \gg w_1 \\
\mathtt{B}(R,A,I,v) \stackrel{\text{def}}{=} & \textbf{if}\,(v \in R \cup A)\,\textbf{then}\,\mathtt{engulf!.die?.P}(R,A,I,v) \\
& \textbf{else}\,\mathtt{B}(R,A,I) \Big| \prod_{i=1}^{\alpha} \mathtt{AB}(\epsilon)
\end{aligned}$$

As indicated by the model, once the antibody-antigen complex has been formed, a B cell may engulf it and then endocyte it, endocyte, hence, modifying the repository of known attacks, $\sigma(I)$. The information in the repository, I, can be consulted any other time, query. The size of the repository increases monotonically, upon endocytosis.

When its receptors bind to an specific antigen, bind, a B cell differentiates into plasma cell, $\mathtt{P}(R, A, I, x)$. Then, the plasm cell will immediately yield a fixed but arbitrary number of antibodies, AB, specific to the detected antigen, ending up as a *B memory cell*, Bm:

$$\mathtt{P}(R,A,I,y) \stackrel{\text{def}}{=} \tau.\mathtt{Bm}(R,A,I,y) \{\!|\mathtt{cts},\mathtt{encrust}|\!\} \prod_{i=1}^{\alpha_0} \mathtt{AB}(y)$$

$$\begin{aligned}\mathtt{Bm}(R,A,I,y) \stackrel{\text{def}}{=} {} & w_0 \colon \mathtt{cts?}.\left(\prod_{i=1}^{\alpha_1} P(R,A,I,y) + \mathtt{Bm}'(R,A,I,y)\right) \\ & + w_1 \colon \mathtt{endocyte?}z.\mathtt{Bm}(R,A,I,\sigma(I)) \\ & + \textbf{if } (I \neq \emptyset) \textbf{ then } w_1 \colon \mathtt{query!}(u \in I).\mathtt{Bm}(R,A,I) \\ & \quad w_0 \gg w_1\end{aligned}$$

$$\mathtt{Bm}'(R,A,I,z) \stackrel{\text{def}}{=} 1 \colon \mathtt{cts!}\!\uparrow.\mathtt{Bm}'(R,A,I,z) + 1 \colon \mathtt{cts!}\!\downarrow.\mathtt{Bm}(R,A,I,z)$$

The behaviour of a B memory cell is pretty similar to that of a B cell. The main difference being that the B memory cell is involved in the regulation of the immune response. After the reception of cytosines, a B memory will, in turn, inject cytosines into the blood stream. This will result in a number of interactions whereby the cell may either proliferate or suppress the immune activity. Notice that once differentiated, a B memory cell will never go back to its original, B cell state.

The Complete Model. To complete our model for the immune system, we need only to compose the elements and then properly link them. To approach composition, we first look into main components:

$$\mathtt{NS}\{\!|bind, txn, engulf, die|\!\}\mathtt{ISC}\{\!|cts|\!\}\mathtt{BloodStram}$$

where NS stands for non-self components, antigens and infected cells, and ISC for immune system components, lymphocytes, monocytes and antibodies, properly linked.

The initial population of each agent type will be different and so should be set according to standard literature. We specify an immune system at an idle state by omitting antigens and infected cells. Clearly, agent population and links can be set according to the type of analysis to be conducted. With this, we complete the description of our model of the immune system. We now give attention to formally specifying its associated properties.

5 Immune System Formal Analysis

An immune system aims to protect the body against invading microorganisms. It portrays a number of properties one would like to have in a contemporary computer system application, for instance effectiveness, reliability, robustness, adaptability and self-stabilisation – to mention a few –. This section aims to provide a formal specification about some of these properties. It also outlines the sorts of mechanisms that are required to prove the proposed model enjoys them.

To specify properties, we use predicates over the external structure of a system, called a *configuration*. Action execution, which yields changes on a system configuration, is taken as a language generator. So each process is given meaning via the language it generates, represented by a set containing all its possible configurations. Given an initial, non-empty population of non-selves, *effectiveness* is achieved when the system gets rid of all of them, becoming idle. This property can be formally verified using methods borrowed from probabilistic process calculi: a system is effective if the expected value of non-self population tends to zero.

Self-stabilisation is achieved if, after activity, the immune system goes back to a configuration similar to the initial one. Put differently, an idle system does not evolve. Thus, the expected size of the configuration of an infected immune system should tend to the size of that configuration after eliminating the non-self. *Robustness* is achieved if, no matter the population of a particular component, the system does not loose effectiveness. Thus, the expected value of non-self population should tend to zero, even though we omit part of the immune system population from the initial configuration. There are of course properties that cannot be even specified within our model. For example, adaptability involves learning, an aspect that we deliberately left out.

To formally analyse our system, we need not other than existing proof methods. However, these methods ought to be re-implemented so that they can be used to analyse partial system behaviour. This is because, prior to verification, existing methods first compute the entire system behaviour but this is not always possible, especially when the system space is infinite. The space associated with our immune system is essentially infinite and so is the language it generates. This is because, the configuration evolves dynamically. Accordingly, we need to do our observations along a predefined number of transitions, ticks of a universal clock.

6 Related Work

Hofmeyr and Forrest have invented ARTIS, an architecture for immune computer systems [7]. While ARTIS involves the basic ingredients of an immune system, the authors do not develop the underlying model. Rather they include only operational ideas associated with immunology – attack detection, learning and rejection –.

Artificial Immune System, AIS [1], portrays a collection of mechanisms that combine characteristics found in some elements of a natural immune system (cells and proteins). The mechanisms are used to address intrusion detection, so the underlying model does not consider the entire variety of system elements. A similar argument applies to both [3] and [2, pages 242-261]. Other applications of immune system phenomena can be found in [10].

7 Conclusions

We have presented a model for an immune system based in process algebra. Our model involves only aspects of behaviour, ignoring other important subtleties, such as learning and detection. Our model can be used to analyse immune system's expected population, with which we can address properties like effectiveness, robustness and self-stabilisation. To conduct formal analysis of our system, however, we need to extend existing techniques so as to incorporate the analysis of partially developed infinite-state systems. While this development is time consuming, the associated payoffs are worthwhile. We reckon the resulting tool could be used as a controlled laboratory by biologists.

References

1. R. Belew and S. Forrest. Learning classifier systems, from foundations to applications. In P. L. Lanzi, W. Stolzmann, and W. Wilson S, editors, *IWLCS'99*, volume 1813 of *Lecture Notes in Computer Science*. Springer, 2000.
2. D. Dasgupta. *Artificial Immune System and Their Applications*. Springer, U.S.A., 1998.
3. P. DeHaeseleer, S. Forrest, and P. Helman. A immunological approach to change detection: Algorithms analisis and implications. In *Proceedings of the 1996 IEEE Symposium on Research in Security and Privacy*, pages 110–119. IEEE Computer Society Press, 1996.
4. M. Ferencík. *Handbook of Immunochemistry*. Chapman & Hall, 1st edition, 1993.
5. S. Gilmore, J. Hillston, and M. Ribaudo. An efficient algorithm for aggregating PEPA models. *IEEE Transactions on Software Engineering*, 27(5):449–464, May 2001.
6. M. Hennessy and H. Lin. Proof systems for message passing process algebras. *Formal Aspects of Computing*, 8(4):379–407, 1996. Also available from Sussex as Computing Science Technical Report 3/93.
7. S. Hofmeyr and S. Forrest. Architecture for an artificial immune system. *Evolutionary Computation Journal*, 8(4):443–473, 2000.
8. R. López, F. Díaz, and S. Arias. *Biología Celular*. Editorial Iberoamérica, México, 1991.
9. R. Milner. *Communicating and Mobile Systems : the π-Calculus*. Cambridge University Press, England, 1999.
10. L. A. Segel and I. R. Cohen. *Design Principles for the Immune System and Other Distributed Autonomous Systems*. Oxford University Press, New York, U.S.A., 2000.
11. D. Stites and T. Abba. *Medical Immunology*. McGraw-Hill, 1997.
12. C. Tofts. Processes with probablities, priority and time. *Formal Aspects of Computing*, 6(5):536–564, 1994.

A New Measure for the Accuracy of a Bayesian Network

Alexandros Pappas and Duncan F. Gillies

Department of Computing, Imperial College of Science, Technology and Medicine,
180 Queen's Gate, London SW7 2BZ, United Kingdom
{ap297,dfg}@doc.ic.ac.uk

Abstract. A Bayesian Network is a construct that is used to model a given joint probability distribution. In order to assess the quality of an inference, or to choose between competing networks modelling the same data, we need methods to estimate the accuracy of a Bayesian network. Although the accuracy of a Bayesian network can be easily defined in theory, it is rarely possible to compute it in practice for real-world applications due to the size of the space representing the variables. Instead, alternative characteristics of a Bayesian network, which relate to and reflect the accuracy, are used. A popular formalism that adopts such methods is the Minimum Description Length (MDL). It models the accuracy of a Bayesian network as the probability of the Bayesian network given the data set that it models. However in the context of Bayesian Networks, the MDL formalism is flawed, exhibiting several shortcomings. In its place, we propose a new framework for Bayesian Networks. We specify a measure, which models the accuracy of a Bayesian network as the accuracy of the conditional independencies implied by its structure. Experiments have been conducted, using real-world data sets, to compare MDL and the new measure. The experimental results demonstrate that the new measure is much better correlated to the actual accuracy than the MDL measure. These results support the theoretical claims, and confirm the significance of the proposed framework.

1 Introduction

A Bayesian network is a construct that is used to model a given joint probability distribution. In effect, a Bayesian network represents the relationships between a set of variables [8, 10]. A Bayesian network does not necessarily represent causation between a set of variables. For example, the parents of a node should not necessarily be considered causes of the node, although they can be interpreted as such in certain cases; instead, they should be viewed as shields against other influences.

A principal feature of a Bayesian network is the conditional independencies between the variables implied by the structure of the network. The absence of an arc (direct connection) between two nodes of a Bayesian network implies certain conditional independencies regarding these nodes. However, the structure of a Bayesian network does not imply dependencies between the variables of the joint probability distribution that it represents. The existence of an arc (direct connection) between two nodes of a Bayesian network does not imply dependence regarding these nodes. All independencies implied by the structure of a Bayesian network are

C.A. Coello Coello et al. (Eds.): MICAI 2002, LNAI 2313, pp. 411–419, 2002.

considered conditional; an unconditional independence can be viewed as a conditional independence given the empty set.

In this paper, we make three assumptions about the Bayesian network, which limit the scope of the research. Firstly, the Bayesian network models a data set. We are only concerned with the accuracy of a Bayesian network with respect to the joint probability distribution described by a data set, independently of the method used to build the network. Secondly, we assume that the data set is complete, and lastly that the variables of the data set are finite.

2 The Accuracy of a Bayesian Network

We will start with an intuitively appealing definition of the accuracy of a Bayesian network. A Bayesian network (*BN*) is accurate with respect to a data set (*D*), if and only if, the joint probability distribution represented by the Bayesian network (P_{BN}) matches the joint probability distribution described by the data set (P_D).

Both the joint probability distribution represented by the Bayesian network and the joint probability distribution described by the data set can be represented as *n*-dimensional matrices of $states_1 * \ldots * states_n$ elements, assuming the data set has *n* variables, and each variable v_i has $states_i$ states. Since a matrix of *n* elements can be represented geometrically as a point in the $\Re^n$ space, then both the joint probability distribution represented by the Bayesian network and the joint probability distribution described by the data set can be represented geometrically as points in the $\Re^{states_1 * \ldots * states_n}$ space. In view of the geometrical representation, the degree to which the joint probability distribution represented by the Bayesian network matches the joint probability distribution described by the data set is reflected by how close the corresponding points are.

The degree of accuracy of a Bayesian network is inversely related to the distance between the point corresponding to the joint probability distribution represented by the Bayesian network and the point corresponding to the joint probability distribution described by the data set.

Correspondingly, the degree of inaccuracy of a Bayesian network, with respect to a data set, is defined as the geometrical distance between the point corresponding to the joint probability distribution represented by the Bayesian network and the point corresponding to the joint probability distribution described by the data set.

$$inaccuracy(BN) = inaccuracy(BN, D) = distance(P_{BN}, P_D) \tag{1}$$

The Euclidean distance is used as a distance measure to derive one of the possible definitions for the inaccuracy of a Bayesian network; alternative measures of distance between joint probability distributions could be used, such as the Kullback-Liebler distance.

$$inaccuracy(BN) = \sqrt{\sum_{v_1=1}^{states_1} \cdots \sum_{v_n=1}^{states_n} (P_{BN}(v_1, \ldots, v_n) - P_D(v_1, \ldots, v_n))^2} \tag{2}$$

The joint probability distribution described by the data set is determined directly from the data set, while the joint probability distribution represented by the Bayesian network is determined indirectly from the data set. The range of values for the degree of inaccuracy of a Bayesian network is $[0,\sqrt{2}]$.

Unfortunately, although the accuracy of a Bayesian network is well defined in theory, and an appropriate measure of inaccuracy is specified, it is rarely possible to determine the degree of inaccuracy of a Bayesian network in practice for real-world applications. This is due to the fact that in most cases it is computationally unfeasible to determine and use the joint probability distribution described by the data set, because of both processing and storage limitations. For example, for the Hepatitis C data set, which was used for our experimentation, the matrix of the joint probability distribution described by the data set is 9 dimensional containing 14,696,640 elements. So, it is not only computationally unfeasible to determine the matrix, but also virtually impossible to use the matrix in practice. This is principally the reason why a Bayesian network is used to model the joint probability distribution described by the data set, instead of the joint probability distribution itself.

3 Minimum Description Length (MDL)

We noted in the previous section that it is rarely possible to determine directly the degree of accuracy of a Bayesian network due to computational complexity. For real-world applications, alternative characteristics of a Bayesian network, which relate to and reflect the accuracy, are used to model and examine the accuracy of a Bayesian network. A formalism commonly used for this purpose is the Minimum Description Length (MDL) [11] (see also [4]). The MDL formalism evaluates a model of a data set based on the length of the description of the data set. This is the sum of the length of the description of the model and the length of the description of the data set given the model. The length of the description of the model reflects the model size and complexity, while the length of the description of the data set given the model is interpreted as the model accuracy.

In the context of the Communication domain, the MDL formalism is employed in data compression, in order to identify the model that provides the shortest description of the data set. In this case, the length of the description of the data set is the number of bits required to encode the data set. This is the sum of the number of bits required to describe the model and the number of bits required to encode the data set given the model.

In the context of Bayesian Networks, the length of the description of the data set given the Bayesian network is the negation of the log likelihood of the Bayesian network given the data set, which is interpreted as the degree of inaccuracy of the Bayesian network. In effect, the MDL formalism models the accuracy of a Bayesian network with respect to a data set as the likelihood of the Bayesian network given the data set. The complexity term of the MDL measure is missing, since the complexity of the structure of the Bayesian network is not taken into account when evaluating the accuracy of the network.

$$accuracy(BN) = accuracy(BN, D) = \log_2(P(BN \mid D)) \tag{3}$$

The likelihood of a Bayesian network given the data set is equivalent to the likelihood of the data set given the Bayesian network.

$$\begin{aligned}
&\max_{BN\in B}\{accuracy(BN,D)\} \overset{MDL}{=} \max_{BN\in B}\{P(BN \mid D)\} = \\
&\max_{BN\in B}\{\frac{P(D \mid BN)P(BN)}{P(D)}\} = \max_{BN\in B}\{P(D \mid BN)P(BN)\} = \\
&\max_{BN\in B}\{P(D \mid BN)\} \\
&\text{since } \forall BN \in B, P(D) \text{ is constant, and } P(BN) \text{ is uniform}
\end{aligned} \tag{4}$$

The range of values for the degree of accuracy of a Bayesian network, with respect to any data set, is (-∞,0].

Since the MDL formalism evaluates the likelihood of a Bayesian network given a particular data set, the specific range of values for the degree of accuracy of a Bayesian network, with respect to a given data set, depends on the nature of the data set. As a result, it is not possible to determine the degree of accuracy of a Bayesian network unless the nature of the data set is examined. The degree of accuracy of a Bayesian network, with respect to a data set, is affected directly by the size of the data set [3]. Consequently, the MDL formalism can only be used to compare "relative" degrees of accuracy for a set of Bayesian networks and for a particular data set. Any results acquired and any conclusions drawn are valid for the Bayesian networks, only in view of the particular data set.

Although the MDL formalism is being used in the field of Bayesian Networks, it was initially developed for the Communication domain where the focus is the transmission of a message. In the field of Bayesian Networks, the focus is the construction of a network that models the joint probability distribution in a given data set. Evidently, the semantics of these two fields are different, and thus the MDL formalism, which has been developed for the communication domain, is being taken out of context when used in the field of Bayesian Networks.

The MDL formalism examines the accuracy of a Bayesian network with respect to the data entries of the data set, and not with respect to the joint probability distribution represented by the data set.

Other formalisms that have been developed to evaluate the characteristics of a Bayesian network are the Akaike Information Criterion (AIC) [1] and the Bayesian Information Criteria (BIC) [14]. However, both of these formalisms are identical to the MDL formalism with regards to the evaluation of the accuracy of a Bayesian network. Bayesian Network learning algorithms, such as the Maximum Weight Spanning Tree (MWST) algorithm [2], provide some sort of an evaluation scheme for a Bayesian network. However, each algorithm is based on its own heuristic methods, which do not specify clearly what the characteristics of a Bayesian network are, and how these are evaluated.

4 A New Definition of Accuracy in Bayesian Networks

We have developed a formal framework for describing the accuracy of Bayesian Networks. Full details can be found in [9], but for now we state just the central theorem of the framework.

Given:

- A data set (D) representing a joint probability distribution (P) over variables (V)
  $P_D = P(V)$
  $\alpha(v) = V - (descendants(v) \cup \{v\})$
- A Bayesian network (BN) of nodes (N), arcs (A), distribution (P')
  $BN = (N, A, P')$
  $P_{BN} = P'(N)$

Provided:

- The nodes of the Bayesian network are the variables of the joint probability distribution represented by the data set
  $N \equiv V$
  $\forall i, n_i \in N, v_i \in V : n_i \equiv v_i$
- The probabilities of the Bayesian network reflect the corresponding probabilities of the joint probability distribution represented by the data set
  $\forall i, n_i \in N : P'(n_i \mid parents(n_i)) = P(n_i \mid parents(n_i))$

Then:

➢ The Bayesian network is accurate with respect to the data set, if and only if, the conditional independencies implied by the structure of the Bayesian network are conditional independencies of the joint probability distribution represented by the data set
  $P_{BN} = P_D \Leftrightarrow \forall i, v_i \in V, \forall W, W \subseteq a(v_i) : P(v_i \mid W \cup parents(v_i)) = P(v_i \mid parents(v_i))$

We refer to the set of conditional independencies implied by the structure of a Bayesian network as the Network Conditional Independencies (NCI) set. The NCI set contains only those conditional independencies implied by the structure of the network that are derived directly from the definition of a Bayesian network, as presented in [9] (see also [8]). Additional conditional independencies implied by the structure of the network that are derived using d-separation are not included in the NCI set.

Our framework introduces the NCI Soundness theorem and the NCI Incompleteness theorem, which are remarkably significant for the field of Bayesian Networks.

The NCI Soundness theorem indicates that given a data set there exists a Bayesian network whose NCI is sound, that is the network conditional independencies also belong to the data conditional independencies. It guarantees that given any data set it is possible to construct an accurate Bayesian network.

The NCI Incompleteness Theorem indicates that there exists at least one data set for which there exist no Bayesian networks whose NCI is complete. Thus given any data set it might be impossible to construct a Bayesian network whose structure implies all the conditional independencies of the joint probability distribution represented by the data set.

Computationally it is feasible to measure the inaccuracy of each conditional independence implied by the network, using a dependency measure such as Mutual Information. The conditional dependency measure (DM) for variables A and B given variable C is the conditional Mutual Information (MI) for variables A and B given variable C.

$$DM(A,B \mid C) = MI(A,B \mid C) = \sum_A \sum_B \sum_C P(A,B,C) \log_2 \frac{P(A,B \mid C)}{P(A \mid C) P(B \mid C)} \quad (5)$$

By setting $C = \varnothing$ we obtain an unconditional dependency measure. Using the framework theorems and the definition of Mutual Information, it is possible to derive the following definition for the inaccuracy of a Bayesian Network.

$$\begin{aligned} &inaccuracy(BN) = inaccuracy(NCI) \\ &inaccuracy(NCI) = \begin{cases} \sum_i inaccuracy(NCI_i) & NCI \neq \varnothing, NCI_i \in NCI \\ 0 & NCI = \varnothing \end{cases} \\ &inaccuracy(NCI_i) = DM(NCI_i) \\ &DM(NCI_i) = MI(NCI_i) \end{aligned} \quad (6)$$

We call this measure the Network Conditional Independencies Mutual Information (NCIMI) measure.

The framework facilitates the comparison of individual Bayesian networks with regards to their characteristics, and provides the theoretical means to justify when and why a particular Bayesian network is more accurate than another Bayesian network. The framework can clarify the procedure of the addition and deletion of arcs and nodes from the structure of a Bayesian network [13], and provide the means to illustrate and explain the effects of such actions on the characteristics of a Bayesian network. The framework can supply a theoretical rationale to the process of the introduction of a hidden node within the structure of a Bayesian network [7] and the effects of such an action. The framework can be employed to develop Bayesian Network construction (learning) algorithms [15] as tree search algorithms that examine the accuracy of a Bayesian network and use the degree of inaccuracy as the evaluation function of the tree nodes.

5 Experimental Results

Several experiments were conducted using real-world problems. One data set that was used represents information concerning Hepatitis C patients, while a second data set provides information about morphological development of neurons [6]. The Hepatitis C data set has 1672 data entries, each being an individual Hepatitis C patient characterised by 9 distinct variables. The neurons data set has 44 data entries, each about an individual neuron, characterised by 6 distinct variables. At any time, only three variables of the given data set were used to carry out the experiments and collect experimental results. This limited approach was adopted, so that it was computationally feasible to calculate the joint probability distribution represented by the data set. The experiments were conducted for a collection of different data sets, created by randomly selecting the set of variables. For a given data set, all possible tree structured Bayesian networks that can model the given data were used to carry out the experiments and collect experimental results.

For a given data set and a given Bayesian network, the experiments determine the accuracy of the Bayesian network with respect to the data set. Three quantities were computed. First, the actual degree of inaccuracy of the Bayesian network, computed as the Euclidean distance between the data distribution and the joint probability distribution of the network. Secondly, the degree of inaccuracy of the Bayesian network according to the Minimum Description Length formalism, and thirdly the degree of inaccuracy of the Bayesian network according to our new measure.

The experimental results are presented below in a tabular and graphical form. The graphs are scatterplots of the actual degree of inaccuracy of the Bayesian network, against either the degree of inaccuracy measured by the MDL, or our NCIMI measure. Trendlines are drawn and their corresponding R^2 value computed. The closer the R^2 value of the trendline is to 1, the more reliable the trendline is, and the better it fits the points of the graph. The best trendline for the points of a graph is associated with the correlation of the variables represented in the graph. A low correlation coefficient indicates that the variables are unrelated.

According to the MDL formalism, the degree of inaccuracy of a Bayesian network, with respect to a data set, is affected directly by the size of the data set [3]. For the data sets of the Hepatitis C domain, the average degree of inaccuracy of the Bayesian networks examined is 7858.3; for the data sets of the Neurons domain, the average degree of inaccuracy of the Bayesian networks examined is 245.26. Thus, the average degree of inaccuracy of the Bayesian networks for the data sets of the Hepatitis C domain is 32.04 times greater than the average degree of inaccuracy of the Bayesian networks for the data sets of the Neurons domain. This result is not only of the same magnitude but also very close to the size ratio of the Hepatitis C data set and the Neurons data set, which is 38. The experimental results point to a linear correlation between the degree of inaccuracy of a Bayesian network, with respect to a data set, and the size of the data set, which agrees with what is predicted in theory.

The NCIMI measure does not exhibit the shortcomings of the MDL formalism. It provides a proper error norm so that the inaccuracy of the networks for the different data sets can be compared. It will be seen both visually and by the statistical measures, that it reflects the true accuracy of the network much better than MDL.

	Correlation (Hepatitis C)	**Correlation (Neurons)**	**R^2 value (Hepatitis C)**	**R^2 value (Neurons)**
MDL	0.31	0.14	0.09	0.02
NCIMI	0.97	0.73	0.94	0.53

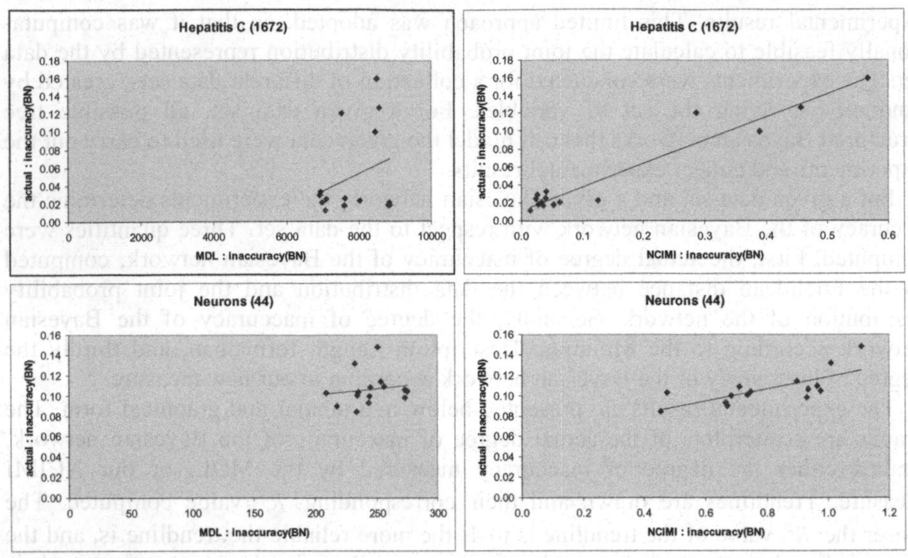

6 Conclusion

We have proposed a framework for Bayesian Networks, in order to examine the accuracy of a Bayesian network. The framework has subtle similarities with research by Pearl [10], Neapolitan [8], and Chow & Liu [2]. Further investigation is required to identify these similarities, and to amalgamate these seemingly different methodologies into a unified framework. Using the framework, we have proposed a new accuracy measure for Bayesian networks called the NCIMI measure, which is based on assessing conditional independencies implied by the structure of the Bayesian network. The framework is formally established, with several definitions and theorems, and well-defined semantics. Applying our measure to real-world problems we have demonstrated that it is more closely correlated with the actual accuracy than the popular MDL measure, which was defined for a different application within a different formal system and with a different set of assumptions.

The data sets employed for the experiments are data sets of just three variables. Supplementary experiments are in hand, employing larger data sets with more than three variables. However, the data sets have to remain relatively small so that the experiments are computationally feasible. The refinement and the extension of the framework will result in an even greater understanding of Bayesian Networks, while the supplementary experiments will offer further insight, and additional evidence in support of the proposed framework.

References

1. Akaike H. “A new look at the statistical identification model”, IEEE Transactions on Automatic Control, 19:716-723, 1974
2. Chow C.K., Liu C.N. “Approximating discrete probability distributions with dependence trees” IEEE Transactions on Information Theory, 14:462-467, 1968

3. Friedman N., Yakhini Z. "On the sample complexity of learning Bayesian networks" Proceedings of the 12th Annual Conference on Uncertainty in Artificial Intelligence, 1996
4. Friedman N., Geiger D., Goldszmidt M. "Bayesian network classifiers" Machine Learning, 1997
5. Jensen F.V. "An introduction to Bayesian networks" UCL Press, 1996
6. Kim J., Gillies D.F. "Automatic Morphometric Analysis of Neural Cells" Machine Graphics and Vision 7(4), 1998
7. Kwoh C.K., Gillies D.F. "Using Hidden Nodes in Bayesian Networks" Artificial Intelligence 88:1-38, 1996
8. Neapolitan R.E. "Probabilistic reasoning in expert systems: theory and algorithms" Wiley-Interscience, 1990
9. Pappas A., Gillies D. "The Accuracy of a Bayesian Network" Technical Report, Imperial College, 2002 (www.doc.ic.ac.uk)
10. Pearl J. "Probabilistic reasoning in intelligent systems: networks of plausible inference" Morgan Kaufmann, 1988 (4th printing, 1997)
11. Rissanen J. "Modelling by shortest data description" Automatica, 14:465-471, 1978
12. Russell S., Norvig P. "Artificial Intelligence: a modern approach" Prentice Hall International, 1995
13. Sucar L.E., Gillies D.F., Gillies D.A. "Uncertainty Management in Expert Systems" Artificial Intelligence 61:187-208, 1993
14. Schwarz G. "Estimate the dimension of a model" The Annals of Statistics, 6(2):461-464, 1978
15. Tahseen T. "A new approach to learning Bayesian network classifiers" Ph.D. Thesis, Imperial College, 1998

FINDS: A Training Package to Assess Forensic Fibre Evidence

Roberto O. Puch and Jim Q. Smith

University of Warwick, Coventry CV4 7AL, United Kingdom,
R.O.Puch@stats.warwick.ac.uk, J.Q.Smith@warwick.ac.uk

Abstract. In this paper we present FINDS a training system for new forensic scientists and a prototype of a knowledge base system. This system is for pre-assessment and assessment of fibre evidence. The pre-assessment and assessment involves uncertain reasoning through a Bayesian network for fibre transfer, persistence and retrieval. FINDS also provides support in the training of new forensic scientists on decision making under uncertainty. This training is required when a forensic scientist needs to decide whether a forensic fibre analysis is cost-effective for clients such as the police and law firms.

1 Introduction

Recently there have been significant developments in how inference should be conducted in a judicial setting [6, 5, 4]. There is now a growing consensus that such inferences should be made on the basis of a likelihood ratio: the probability of evidence given the prosecution case is true divided by the probability of the evidence given the defence case is true. Unfortunately many of those who are winning the intellectual argument for doing this are finding it difficult to get these methodologies to be used directly by juries although this has been tried [3]. This paper reports on recent advances in the UK which attempt to rectify this situation. In work sponsored by the Home Office of the UK statisticians have developed software which is designed to train forensic scientists to present an accurate and compelling account to a jury of the strength of their evidence. It also acts as a prototype of decision support software for these scientists to use in routine cases. Inferences are thus made to the court by the scientist, aided by the statistician through the training software (FINDS: Forensic Inference Networks for Decision Support) outlined and illustrated in this paper. In this way some of the difficulties of educating juries directly are sidestepped.

Forensic scientists, professionally trained in evidence acquisition, are easier to train in the weighing of the forensic evidence than are juries or judges. Even so, for software that purports to train and support such inferences to be credible, it must have various features. Firstly it must be user-friendly. In particular it must be customised so that the required inputs and outputs are familiar to the forensic scientist, that is following the protocols proposed by forensic scientist [1]. Forensic scientists learn about a particular case through an incident report. Training software therefore needs to be designed so that the inputs describing the case are requested in a format mirroring as far as possible the structure of

C.A. Coello Coello et al. (Eds.): MICAI 2002, LNAI 2313, pp. 420–429, 2002.

these reports. Similarly it must be apparent that outputs of the software answer directly not only the sorts of questions that might be asked by the counsel before the case is heard but also helps the scientist appreciate how to weigh evidence in analogous case reports she might need to write and cross examinations to which she might be subjected. Furthermore technical details of the working of the software need to be suppressed except when they are essential to a proper understanding of the inferences being made.

Second it is most helpful to centre this training on those cases which the scientist will encounter most frequently; namely volume crimes like burglaries and robberies and the sort of forensic evidence collected in such cases. Such incidents need to be categorised by type. We argue here that one of the best ways of doing this is through a Bayesian network. Hereafter we abbreviate Bayesian networks to BN, and its plural to BNs. BNs have now been established as an important modeling tool and have recently been used as a framework within which to express certain, albeit as yet rather restrictive judicial hypotheses [5]. Within our software we have built a library of such networks to support our particular interest of volume crime cases. In this paper for simplicity we discuss the weighing of fibre evidence in a robbery case, but our software is able to train in more complicated tasks, like the weighing of combinations of evidence both in type and location and in a range of type of incident.

Third it must be transparent to the trainee that the inferences supported by the software are able to incorporate the latest relevant experimental data and expert judgements. Inevitably some of the expert judgements will have a degree of uncertainty associated with them and sometimes there will be a question as to the relevance of certain experimental data to the case being explored. However the software allows a sensitivity analysis of the data to be carried out. By playing with the settings in the program the forensic scientist can come to a good understanding of the extent to which different aspects of the evidence and modeling hypotheses influence the balance she will report of the evidence for and against the prosecution case.

Recently in the UK it has become necessary to balance the analysis of forensic evidence against costs. A further novel feature of this software is that it supports the forensic scientist in advising her client, either the defence or prosecution counsel, of the promise that a costly forensic analysis will produce strong enough evidence for that counsel to win his case.

In Section 2 we present a BN for fibre transfer, persistence and retrieval. We describe how to learn this BN from the physics of transfer and persistence and how to compute a marginal probability distribution in the network. In Section 3 we describe FINDS through a case study.

2 A Bayesian Network for Fibre Transfer, Persistence and Retrieval

The forensic scientist compares through the likelihood ratio the probability of evidence given the prosecution proposition $Pr(Ev|C)$ against the probability of

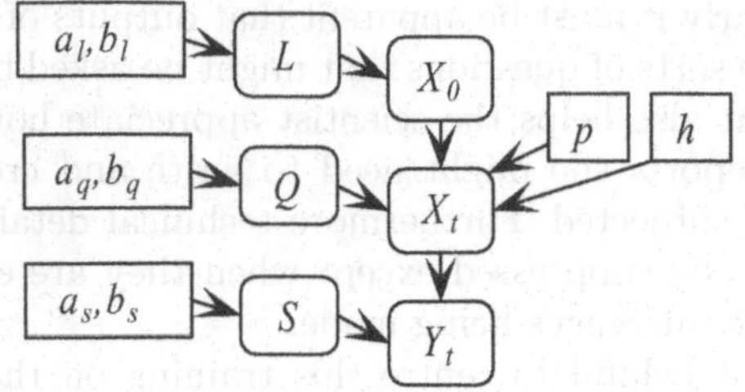

Fig. 1. *A BN for fibre transfer, persistence and retrieval*

evidence given the defence proposition $Pr(Ev|\overline{C})$. In the case study presented in Section 3 the evidence takes the form of the number of retrieved fibres. The prosecution proposition is "C: Mr U wore the mask found at the crime scene at the time when the crime took place". Thus the evidence conditional on C becomes the number of fibres retrieved from the offender coming from the offender environment by chance and from the mask. In this section we present a network for computing a distribution for the number Y_t of fibres retrieved from the suspect's head hair that were originally transferred from the mask.

In the case study presented in Section 3, for the sake of brevity, we describe the defence proposition "$\overline{C}$: the suspect has never worn the mask", which does not use the BN described in this section. However the second defence proposition that FINDS supports "the suspect owns a mask like the one one collected by the police, but he has not worn it for t hour" does use this BN.

2.1 Learning the Structure of a Bayesian Network

A BN provides semantic tool to represent the joint probability distribution of several random variables. Once the BN is learnt, it provides an efficient tool to compute marginal distributions on the variables of interest, see [7]. Figure 1 shows a BN for fibre transfer, persistence and retrieval.

The physical process may be seen in three phases: transfer, persistence and retrieval. In the transfer phase the loose fibres on the mask are transferred to the offender's hair. This process occurs mainly when the offender puts the mask on and removes it. The factors that affects the transfer are mask sheddability and the recipient hair type. Mask sheddability is the propensity of the mask to shed fibres and depends on the mask wear and material, e.g. a mask with high cotton content sheds more fibres than one with high nylon content. Transfer reception is the propensity of the head hair to receive fibres from the mask and comprises hair length and hair style, e.g. a person with long curly hair typically receives more fibres than a person with short straight hair.

The variables L and X_0 model transfer. The distributional assumptions for L and X_0 are: $L \sim Gam(a_l, b_l)$ and $X_0|L \sim Pois(L)$. L models the average number of fibres that are transferred to the offender's head hair and X_0 models the actual number of transferred fibres.

The parameters a_l and b_l are chosen based on mask sheddability and transfer reception which are both categorised to take the values: very low, low, medium, high, very high. Transfer experimental data are classified into these categories and for each category a_l and b_l are computed. The computed a_l's and b_l's are recorded into a look-up table which FINDS then uses to determine the Gamma distribution that is displayed to the forensic scientist.

In the persistence phase, the fibres are gradually removed from the offender's hair as time passes by: as a person moves, the fibres drop. This process is accelerated if the person is jogging or running and more dramatically when the offender combs, brush or wash his hair. Thus the factors that affect persistence are the time between crime commission and fibre retrieval, the recipient hair type, the physical and head disturbance, e.g. fibres drop at a faster rate from straight hair than curly hair. Physical disturbance refers to activities comprising sitting, jogging and running, and hair disturbance refers to combing, brushing and washing.

The variables X_0, Q and X_t model persistence. The distributional assumptions are: $Q \sim Beta(a_q, b_q)$ and $X_t \sim Bin(X_0, pdQ)$. The variable Q models the proportion of fibres that persisted in the offenders head up to time t without considering physical and head disturbance. The variable X_t counts the number of fibres that persisted with success rate pdQ from the initially transferred fibres X_0. The parameters a_q and b_q are computed based on experimental data classified according to the time t between crime commission and fibre retrieval and persistence recipient but without considering any disturbances. The parameters p and q are computed from experimental data as well which are recorded, together with the values of a_q and b_q in a look-up table.

In the retrieval phase the fibres that persisted on the offender's head hair are removed. Once a suspect is arrested the police retrieves the fibres on his hair by either combing or taping. The comb or tape is placed in a plastic bag and sent to the forensic laboratory for analysis. The factors that affect fibre retrieval are the retrieval method and the recipient hair type. Retrieval method refers to whether a standard comb, a primed comb or a tape is used. A standard comb is any comb with a very small gap between its teeth. A primed comb is a standard comb that have been treated to maximise the proportion of fibres retrieve. The tape is any transparent tape. Hair type affects retrieval, for example, a comb is not an efficient retrieval tool when the suspect has tightly curly hair; in this case tape is a more efficient tool.

The variables X_t, S and Y_t model fibre retrieval. The distributional assumptions are: $S \sim Beta(a_s, b_s)$ and $Y_t \sim Bin(X_t, S)$. S models the proportion of fibres that are retrieved in the laboratory. The variable Y_t counts the number of fibres that are actually retrieved from the suspects hair given that the proportion of recoverable fibres is S and that the number of fibres on the offender's hair is X_t. The parameters a_s and b_s are computed based on experimental data classified through retrieval method and recipient hair type and stored in look-up table.

2.2 Computing the Marginal Distribution of Y_t

A BN represents a recursive factorisation of the joint distribution, that is, the factors are given by the conditional distributions of the random variables given its parents (or predecessors in the graph). In our BN the factorisation given by the BN is

$$P(L, X_0, Q, X_t, S, Y_t) = P(L)P(X_0|L)P(Q)P(X_t|X_0, Q)P(S)P(Y_t|X_t, S).$$

Now that we have the BN, which includes the choice of parameters and discount factors, we can compute the marginal distribution of Y_t. This is done in two stages. In the first stage conjugate Bayesian pairs of distributions on variables in the network are used to simplify the analysis. Once all conjugacy has been exploited, the resulting network is discretised. In the analytic simplification stage we use the Poisson-Binomial and Gamma-Poisson relationships, computed as shown is Figure 2. The resulting simplified BN is given in Figure 3.

$$\left.\begin{array}{r} X_0 \sim Pois(L) \\ X_t|X_0, Q \sim Bin(X_0, pdQ) \end{array}\right\} \Rightarrow X_t|L, Q \sim Pois(pdQL);$$

$$\left.\begin{array}{r} X_t|L, Q \sim Pois(pdQL) \\ Y_t|X_t, S \sim Bin(X_t, S) \end{array}\right\} \Rightarrow Y_t|L, Q, S \sim Pois(pdQLS);$$

$$\left.\begin{array}{r} L \sim Gam(a_l, b_l) \\ Y_t|L, Q, S \sim Pois(pdQLS) \end{array}\right\} \Rightarrow Y_t|Q, S \sim NegBin(a_l, 1/(1 + pdQb_lS)).$$

Fig. 2. The analytic simplification of the BN

We need to compute the marginal distribution of Y_t in the BN in Figure 3, in which no further conjugacy can be exploited. To perform this computation we discretise the Beta variables Q and S which allows the calculation of an approximate probability table of the joint distribution of Q, S and Y_t. The last step is then to compute the marginal of Y_t by summing over the discrete values of Q and S.

3 Case Study: A Robbery Case

In this section we describe FINDS through a case study, which is simplification of a case study currently used by the British forensic science service. The case study is presented below.

Two masked men, armed with guns, burst into a post office and threaten the counter staff. The takings for the day were handed over and the men left.

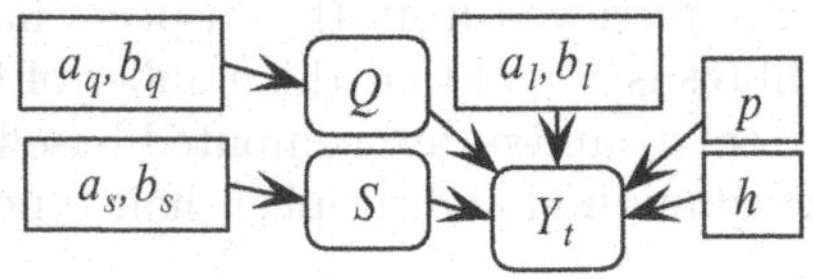

Fig. 3. *The simplified BN*

Witnesses inside the shop said that one of the men was wearing a dark green balaclava mask. Witnesses outside said that the two men were driven away from the scene at high speed in a car driven by a third man. The witnesses saw articles being discarded from the car as it drove away and a later search by police officers led to the recovery of a dark green balaclava. From the registration number taken by a witness, the police identified the vehicle as having been stolen the previous night. The police said that a burn-out vehicle found 10 miles away is the stolen vehicle, nothing apart from the shell of the vehicle remains.

Following a tip-off, Mr U was arrested the following day. He denied all knowledge of the incident. Samples of his head hair, blood and combings from his head hair were taken. He has a large number of clothing items and the police did not have a good idea of what he may have been wearing at the time. There was no submission of these items. Thus all the available forensic evidence resided in the mask.

The forensic scientist would receive information about the incident through a case report from the police. Additional information that she might need to have to supplement this, together with updates on any new information about the case relevant to the forensic investigation, would be communicated to the scientist by the police.

We start with the Case Information screen, displayed in Figure 4. The forensic scientist enters into this screen the information from the case report and interview which is relevant to the computation of the likelihood ratio. The prosecution proposition is "$C =$ The suspect wore the mask at the time of robbery". In the top section of the screen the forensic scientist chooses the defence proposition that she would like to assess. The choices are "The suspect has never worn the mask" and "The suspect owns the mask; mask not worn for time t". In our case study the suspect denied all knowledge of the incident and so the defence proposition is "$\overline{C} =$ The suspect has never worn the mask".

In the middle left section of the screen the the forensic scientist enters information relevant to fibre transfer. The transfer factors are: mask sheddability and transfer reception. Mask sheddability refers to the propensity of the mask to shed fibres which comprises mask wear and material. The choices are: very low, high, medium, low and very low. Transfer reception refers to hair propensity to receive fibres and comprises hair type and length. In the case study the dark green balaclava is made of cotton, material that is know to shed large numbers of fibres, thus the mask sheddability is high. The suspect was described by the officer as having short straight hair. Experimental data [8, 2] suggests that this type of hair is a "medium" transfer recipient.

In the middle right section of the screen the forensic scientist enters the factors that affect fibre persistence: time from crime commission to hair combing, persistence recipient, head and physical disturbance. Persistence recipient refers to the hair ability to retain fibres over time and comprises hair type and length. The choices for this factor are: very low, high, medium, low and very low. Experimental data [8, 2] suggests that a person with short straight hair is a "low" persistence recipient. The head disturbance choices are: none, combed and

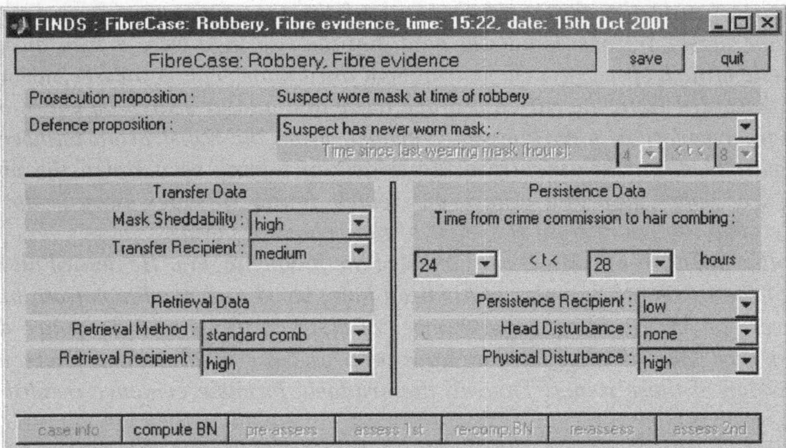

Fig. 4. *The Case Information screen*

washed. The police reported to the forensic scientist that the suspect appear not to have taken a shower at least for a day and his hair look messy suggesting that his hair was not comb, so there was no head disturbance. Physical disturbance comprises activities such as sitting, jogging, running and their combinations. The forensic scientist decides on one of the choices: low, medium and high. The police reported to the forensic scientist that when the suspect was confronted by the police he tried to escape by later was capture, thus physical activity is high.

In the bottom left section of the screen the forensic scientist enters the retrieval factors: retrieval method and retrieval recipient. Retrieval methods are: standard comb, primed comb and tape. The comb submitted by the police is a standard comb. Retrieval recipient refers to whether the hair type facilitates the retrieval and the choices are: very low, high, medium, low and very low. Experimental data [8, 2] suggests that a person with short straight hair is a "high" retrieval recipient when a comb is used.

The second screen is the ComputeBN screen, displayed in Figure 5, and has a two-fold aim: it displays the distributions and static parameters h and p that FINDS computes for the BN from the Case Information screen, and allows the forensic scientist to modify these values. These computations are done for the prosecution proposition, labeled as numerator, and for the defence proposition, labeled as denominator. In our example the defence proposition does not involve fibre transfer and therefore there are no push buttons for the denominator.

The parameters h and p can be modified by typing them into the corresponding text boxes. The distributions are modified through a fitting facility, in the bottom left section of the screen. The distribution for L is displayed by pushing the button "LS". Then the forensic scientist move the vertical lines with the mouse to her chosen values. Then she chooses the certainty of her chosen interval through the slide bar on top of the plot. Pressing the "Fit" button makes

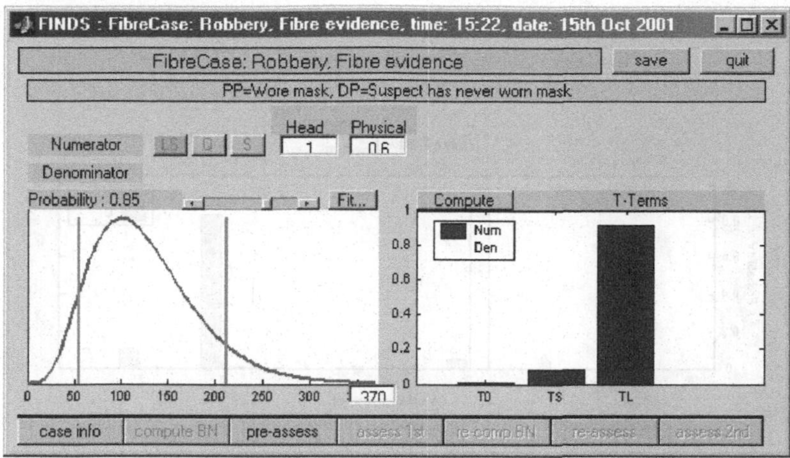

Fig. 5. *The ComputeBN screen*

FINDS to compute a distribution whose area under its density function is equal to the chosen uncertainty. Once the forensic scientist is content with her choices of distribution, then she presses the "Compute" button to compute the marginal distribution on the number of fibres retrieved from the suspect's head hair that were originally transferred from the mask.

In a training session the trainee can load the a case from the knowledge base for the same case study but assessed by a senior scientist. Then she can compare whether her choices of distributions and discount factors with the senior scientist's choices. She can also load similar cases to learn how changes in the scenario affects the input of this screen.

The third screen is the pre-assessment screen whose purpose is to provide support to the forensic scientist to decide whether a forensic analysis of the collected fibres is cost effective. Her decision is based on two probability distribution, one conditional on the prosecution C and the other conditional on the defence proposition $\overline{C}$, on the possible likelihood ratios transformed into seventh categories. These categories are worded as, 1: strong support for the defence, 2: support for the defence, 3: weak support for the defence, 4: no support, 5: weak support for the prosecution, 6: support for the prosecution and 7: strong support for the prosecution. Notice that in the pre-assessment screen in Figure 6 the label $C - bar$ refers to the defence proposition $\overline{C}$. The computation of the likelihood ratios incorporate the probability distribution on the number of fibres Y_t retrieved from the suspect's hair and the uncertainty on the presence of fibres in people's head hair by chance, taking into account fibre rarity.

The forensic scientist uses this screen to decide whether commissioning a forensic analysis is cost effective by observing at the probability distribution of the likelihood ratios given her client's proposition. In our example the prosecution is the client and thus if the probabilities for categories 5, 6 and 7 are high

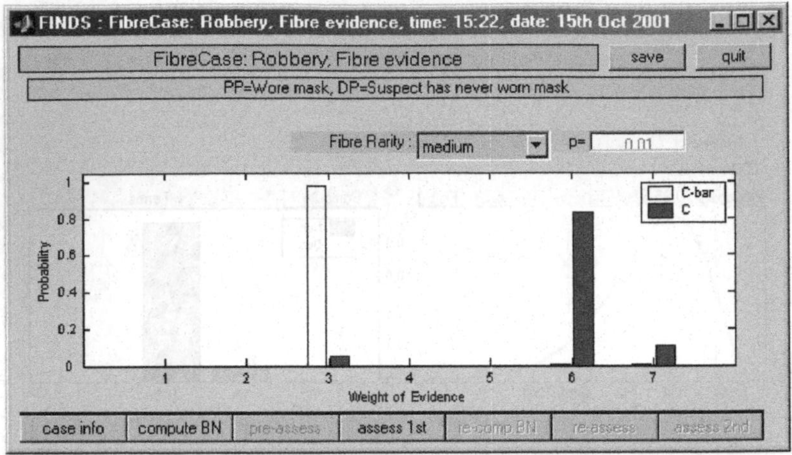

Fig. 6. *The pre-assessment screen*

then she will be confident that an analysis is very likely to support the prosecution proposition, provided it is true. In the screen in Figure 6 the forensic scientist would advice the prosecution to go ahead with the forensic analysis of the retrieve fibres to determine whether they came from the mask collected close to the crime scene.

The fourth screen, displayed in Figure 7, is the assessment screen and its purpose is to compute the likelihood ratio given the results of the forensic examination of the fibres retrieved from the suspect's head hair and the mask collected close to the crime scene. The results of the forensic analysis provides more detail information which is then used to compute the likelihood ratio that will be reported in court. These detail information are the rarity of the fibre, number of fibres that match the mask fibres and the number of groups that do not match the mask fibres. The rarity is entered by comparing it with the rarity of fibres such as cotton and acrylic whose rarity has been previously studied.

The case is completed with the information on this screen. The case is then recorded in the knowledge base. Later this case can be loaded and the pre-assessment can be compared with the actual results in the assessment for calibration.

4 Conclusions

In this article we presented FINDS, a training package for the pre-assessment and assessment of fibre evidence. We have shown that FINDS can provide support for the training of new forensic scientist on uncertain reasoning and decision making. We showed how FINDS can direct the trainee to systematically reason, through a BN, on uncertainties arising from fibre transfer, persistence and retrieval. We described how FINDS can guide the trainee to decide on whether a forensic

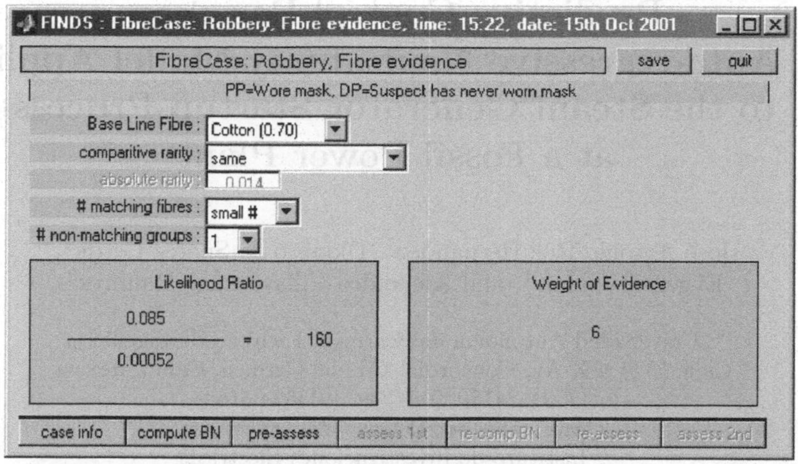

Fig. 7. *The assessment screen*

analysis on a particular case is cost-effective. FINDS is currently used by the British forensic science service.

FINDS was also designed to be a prototype for an operational knowledge base system for case pre-assessment and assessment. The transition to an operational system has prompted the need of higher resolution experimental data and extra features such as a facility to identify cases as similar. These issues are currently being addressed.

References

1. Cook, R, IW Evett, G Jackson, PG Jones and JA Lambert (1998)"A model for case assessment and interpretation", Science and Justice; 36(2): 226-231.
2. Cook R, MT Webb-Salter, L Marshall (1997) "The significance of fibres found in head hair", Forensic Science International; 87:155-160.
3. Dawid AP (2001) "Bayes theorem and weighing evidence by juries", Research Report No. 219, Department of statistical science, University Colledge London, London, UK.
4. Dawid AP (1998) "Modelling issues in forensic inference", In 1997 ASA proceedings, section on Bayesian statistics, 182-186.
5. Dawid AP and IW Evett (1997) "Using a graphical method to assist the evaluation of complicated patterns of evidence", J Forensic Sci; 42(2): 226-231
6. Dawid AP, J Mortera (1996) "Coherent analysis of forensic identification evidence", J Royal Statistical Society Series B; 58:425-443.
7. Jensen FV (2001) "Bayesian networks and decision graphs", Springer-Verlag, New York.
8. Salter MT, R Cook (1996) "Transfer of fibres to head hair, their persistence and retrieval ", Forensic Science International; 81:211-221.

Predictive Control Based on an Auto-regressive Neuro-fuzzy Model Applied to the Steam Generator Startup Process at a Fossil Power Plant

José Antonio Ruz Hernández[1], Dionisio A. Suárez Cerda[2], Evgen Shelomov[1], and Alejandro Villavicencio Ramírez[2]

[1] Universidad Autónoma del Carmen, Facultad de Ingenieria
Calle 56 # 4 X Av. Concordia, Cd. del Carmen, Cam., Mexico
C.P. 24180, Tel/Fax: (9)382-6516
{jruz,eshelomov}@pampano.unacar.mx

[2] Instituto de Investigaciones Eléctricas
Av. Reforma No. 113, Col. Palmira
62490 Temixco, Morelos, Mexico
{suarez,avilla}@iie.org.mx

Abstract. This paper presents an application of artificial intelligence techniques to the improvement of the operation of a thermoelectric unit. The capacity for empirical learning gained from artificial intelligence systems was utilized in the development of the strategy. A neuro-fuzzy model for the steam generator startup process is obtained from experimental data. Ultimately, the neuro- fuzzy model is combined with a predictive control algorithm to produce a control strategy for the heating stage of the steam generator. This provides the operators at the fossil power plant with the necessary information to efficiently accomplish the heating process. The information gained from the control strategy is not directly applied to an automatic control scheme; it is presented to the operator who then decides on its application. Therefore, in this way the information is used to develop a strategy that takes into consideration the personal capacity and the working routine of the operator. The simulation tests that were carried out demonstrated the feasibility and the beneficial results that can be obtained from the application of any of the three variants of predictive control proposed in this paper.

1 Introduction

Improvement of the operations at the fossil power plants is a constant concern of all instances involved in the process of power generation because increase in production means increased financial benefits and general well-being. Essentially, the heating process of the steam generator at a fossil power plant is a problem of control. Traditionally this problem is solved manually by experienced operators. The main technical difficulty for an automatic control at the startup stage at these power plants is the presence of a significant transport delay which can

C.A. Coello Coello et al. (Eds.): MICAI 2002, LNAI 2313, pp. 430–439, 2002.

cause instability and problems in maintaining the temperature gradients within controlled stages of change.

The conventional predictive control uses lineal prediction models to estimate future output values in the process [1,2]. In general, lineal models are not sufficiently representative of the process in the case of non-lineal plants because non-lineal models based on the physical principles of conservation are too complicated to be used in predictive control schemes and involve high costs in computerization and time. On the other hand, recent developments in artificial intelligence such as fuzzy logic and neural networks offer alternatives for models for non-lineal processes. The fuzzy inference systems [4,6,7], as well as the neural networks [11,12], have been demonstrated as being universal approximators and therefore they can be used for non- lineal input-output mapping with arbitrary approximation. In this way, the fuzzy inference systems and the neural networks can be used as process models with more acceptable computational costs [3]. A variety of control schemes use this kind of model, such as inverse control, the internal model control and the predictive control based on models [4,12,13]. In this paper we develop a variant based on the last scheme, which we have called "predictive control based on an auto-regressive neuro-fuzzy model" [5,14], because the model corresponds to a Fuzzy Inference System based on an Adaptable Network (ANFIS) [6,7] which is capable of auto-regressive execution.

2 Problem Description

During most of the steam generator startup process, the operator must not exceed certain limits in the gradient of the temperature[1] in the downcomers [8]. The actions at the disposal of the operator to control the heating of the fluid in the steam generator concern the quantity of fuel that is consumed as well as the aperture of the steam drains located along the length of the steam pipes. However, for operative reasons these drains are handled with caution because they are subject to a gradual closure program and preferably should not be used as controls.

There are further restrictions at another heating and pressurization stage at the steam generator. These no longer apply to the temperature in the downcomers, but to the difference between the temperature of the main steam and the temperature of saturation in the drum. However, the control is carried out in the same way, by simply diminishing the gradient reference value to a level that, by experience, is known to be within the limits set by the design. After a certain period of heating, positive pressure readings are registered in the pressure of the main steam. This is another variable which should be considered. There are no real, absolute restrictions on the evolution of this process, but an increase must always be guaranteed. This variable is affected by the position of the drains as well as by the usage of the steam in the heating of the steam pipes and the turbine metals. Figure 1 shows the curves for heating and pressurization in the steam generator startup process.

[1] Temperature gradient is the temperature change rate

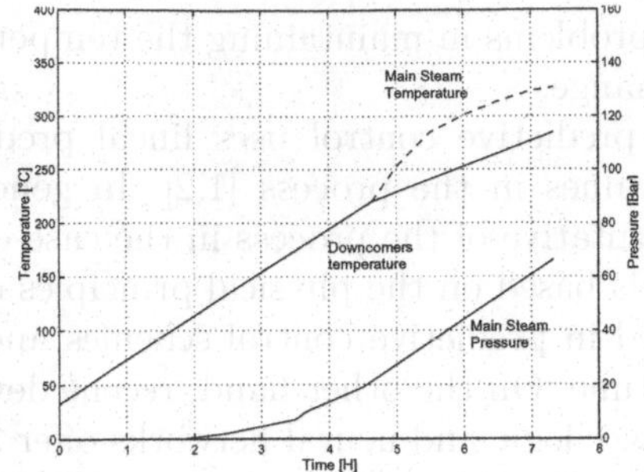

Fig. 1. Curves for Heating and Pressurization in the Steam Generator.

In the first instance, the problem to be solved can be seen as the control of the internal temperature of the downcomers. The maximum limit of the gradient is an important factor in this variable. If the temperature is greatly reduced or if there are regularly prolonged periods of time in the startup of the steam generator, operation costs are increased due to a higher consumption of fuel, demineralized water and energy from the National Electrical Network. Therefore the faster the heating in the startup process, the lower the consumption of the resources mentioned, but at the same time there is an increase in the thermal stress on the steam generator and, as a consequence, the premature ageing of the pipes.

With reference to the previous description, the problem that is solved in this investigation is the design and the simulation testing of the feasibility of a control mechanism which allows the estimation of the optimal fuel flow required, taking into consideration the conditions described for this process.

3 Development of a Control Algorithm

In order to solve the problem presented, a predictive control algorithm based on an auto- regressive neuro-fuzzy model was developed. The scheme is shown in Figure 2 and involves the use of neuro-fuzzy identification to obtain an auto-regressive model from empirical data on temperature and fuel flow involved in the startup process of the steam generator. The predictive model will be used in an optimal control strategy to link the problem of numerical optimization with the operational limitations of the technical problem explained above.

3.1 Development of the Model

In our case, the neuro-fuzzy identification was obtained by using an ANFIS type system with a dimension 2 regressor; 5 membership functions of the Gaussian type for each input; and 25 rules of the Takagi-Sugeno type [9], which requires the estimation of 30 antecedent parameters and 75 consequent. For this purpose, several tests were run using a table with experimental data obtained at 10-second

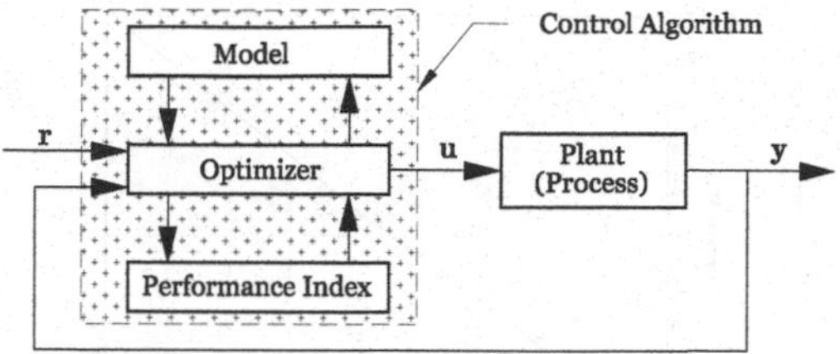

Fig. 2. Strategy for Predictive Control Based on an Auto-Regressive Neuro-Fuzzy Model.

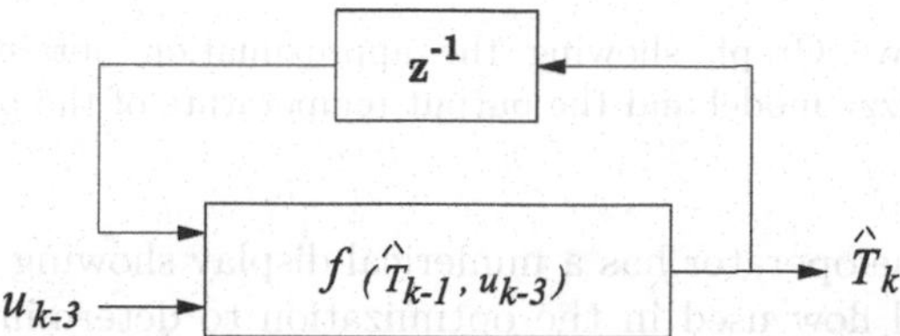

Fig. 3. Auto-regressive neuro-fuzzy model for 10-second sampling periods.

intervals, initiating at the startup of a fossil power plant. This data was based on the use of a series-parallel scheme with different candidate inputs with antecedent and consequent parameters synchronized according to the Algorithm of Hybrid Learning which combines the Back Propagation Rule and the Least Squares Estimator to finally select those that give the least test error after 10 epochs. This selection criterion for the inputs is simple and produced satisfactory results [10]. The function that defines the network which achieved the best reproduction of the data corresponding to the plant output was:

$$\hat{T}_k \approx f(T_{k-1}, u_{k-3}) \tag{1}$$

where:

T_{k-1}: Value for the temperature in ^oC at the sampling instant $k-1$
u_{k-3}: Value for the fuel flow in M^3/H in the sampling interval $k-3$

The total quadratic error in the exercise was 0.115. To accept an auto-regressive model it, is necessary to test it in a feedback scheme, as shown in Figure 3.

The comparison between the data on the temperatures at the plant and the approximations with the auto-regressive model are shown in Figure 4 by continuous and broken lines, where it can be observed that both are almost superimposed.

3.2 Numerical Optimization Applied to the Process

Concerning the problem of numerical optimization, the following principal points were taken into consideration:

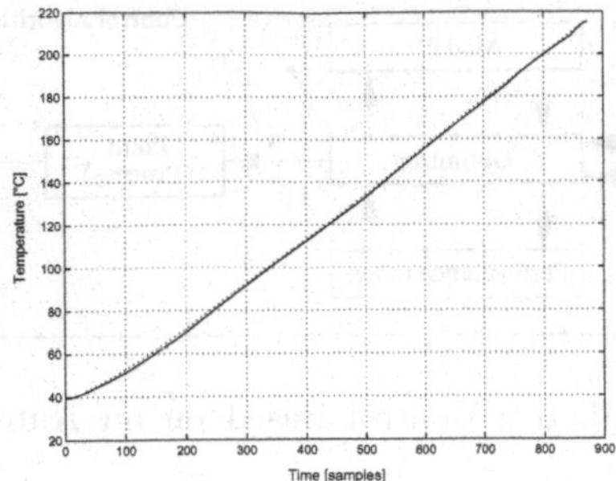

Fig. 4. Comparative Graph showing the approximation obtained from the auto-regressive neuro-fuzzy model and the output temperature of the plant in ^oC.

- Given that the operator has a numerical display showing precision to a decimal, the fuel flow used in the optimization to determine the optimal fuel flow is given as:

$$\Delta = 0.1M^3/H \tag{2}$$

- the interval from which the values for the variable of volume fuel flow are taken is:

$$0 \leq u_k \leq 10M^3/H \tag{3}$$

- there is no existing mathematical model for the process to be controlled, neither are the derivatives known and therefore the properties are unknown. We only have experimental data on the subject;
- an auto-regressive neuro-fuzzy model for the process to be controlled is available.

We also need to consider the following existing operative conditions in order to develop the control algorithm that can be applied to any fossil power plant with similar characteristics to those we have identified:

- The control signal u_k will remain constant for 10 minutes;
- every ten minutes the operator will take a reading of the temperature of the plant;
- the control signal will be updated every 10 minutes;
- the operator will close the control loop every 10 minutes.

Three operational variants were tested for numerical optimization and are described below.

3.3 First Optimization Variant

This involves determining the optimum fuel flow u_k without restrictions, to minimize the following performance index:

$$J(u_k) = \alpha_k(\hat{T}_{k+1} - T^r_{k+1})^2 + \beta_k(u_k - u_{k-1})^2 \tag{4}$$

where:

$\hat{T}_{k+1}$: Predicted temperature in ^oC corresponding to the following ten minutes

T^r_{k+1}: Temperature reference in ^oC corresponding to the following ten minutes

u_k: Optimal fuel flow in M^3/H to be used in the following ten minutes

u_{k-1}: Fuel flow applied in the process during the previous ten minute period

α_k: Scalar corresponding to the weight of the quadratic error of the temperature

β_k: Scalar corresponding to the weight of the control effort

The equation (4) is unconventional because the optimization has been adapted to the actual operating conditions at the fossil power plants and because, in our application, the control signal will be updated every 10 minutes.

In order to minimize the previous performance index, a search is carried out to determine the optimal fuel flow. This is achieved using a procedure of varying the fuel flow according to the equation (2) in the interval given in (3) and evaluating it in the performance index in such a way that, by comparing each evaluation, the fuel flow necessary to minimize the equation (4) can be determined. It is necessary to make *dli* predictions[2] because in the case of (4) we need to find out T_{k+1}, whereby evaluating the auto-regressive neuro-fuzzy model. The initial $d-1$ predictions involve the known fuel flow from the previous period $k-1$, where d is the delay corresponding to the combustion flow signal in the neuro-fuzzy model[3]:

$$\begin{aligned} \hat{T}^2_k &= f(T^1_k, u_{k-1}) \\ &\vdots \\ \hat{T}^d_k &= f(\hat{T}^{d-1}_k, u_{k-1}) \end{aligned} \tag{5}$$

where:

T^1_k: is the temperature for the period k.

Once the initial predictions have been carried out, we must calculate those in which the optimal fuel flow to be applied during the period should be determined according to the optimization procedure:

$$\begin{aligned} \hat{T}^{d+1}_k &= f(\hat{T}^d_k, u_k) \\ &\vdots \\ \hat{T}^{dli}_k &= f(\hat{T}^{dli-1}_k, u_k) \\ \hat{T}_{k+1} &= f(\hat{T}^{dli}_k, u_k) \end{aligned} \tag{6}$$

Note that the optimum combustion flow to be determined is stated as u_k because the quantity of fuel used during the first predictions is known, being based on the delay d used in the model. These predictions should be done iteratively for

[2] In this case 60 since the model is based on 10-second sampling period

[3] 3 samples of 10 seconds in this case

each variation in the combustion flow and in each k period of 10 minutes during the generator startup process.

3.4 Second Optimization Variant

This consists in using the first function objective of variant 1, given in the equation (4), but the restriction of finding the minimum usage of fuel u_k- that maintains the controlled temperature below the given reference, has been added. It is possible that there is no minimum for this situation however, if this should be the case, the fuel required will be calculated on the basis of the first variant, although the controlled output will be reasonably above the reference at a minimum distance. We will denote the fuel needed in these cases as u_k+. The restrictions can be written in the following way:

$$u_{k-} \cup u_{k+} = u_k, \qquad u_{k-} \cap u_{k+} = \emptyset \tag{7}$$

where $\emptyset$ is the empty set, and

$$u_{k-} = \{u_k \mid T^r_{k+1} - \hat{T}_{k+1} \geq 0\} \tag{8}$$

$$u_{k+} = \{u_k \mid T^r_{k+1} - \hat{T}_{k+1} < 0\} \tag{9}$$

Accordingly, once the function objective has been minimalized, the optimal fuel to be used will be calculated in the following way:

$$u_k \in \mathrm{I\!R} = \left\{ \begin{matrix} u_k - |u_k - \neq \emptyset \\ u_k + |u_k - = \emptyset \end{matrix} \right\} \tag{10}$$

3.5 Third Optimization Variant

The two previous variants minimize a function of cost that does not involve temperature deviations corresponding to intermediate samples at 10 seconds in each period of 10 minutes. Therefore we will now use the following:

$$J(u_k) = \frac{\alpha_k}{60} \sum_{j=d}^{dli+d-1} [\hat{T}^{j+1} - T^r(60(k-1)+j+1)]^2 + \beta_k(u_{k-1} - u_k)^2 \tag{11}$$

where:

$$\hat{T}^{j+1} = f(\hat{T}^j, u_k) \tag{12}$$

Note that here this performance index corresponds to an average of $69-d+1$ evaluations of the permormance index (4) at the sampling instants. The samples $j = 1, \ldots, d-1$ have not been considered, because the fuel usage for determining u_k is not included here, as this information is available from the previous period u_{k-1}.

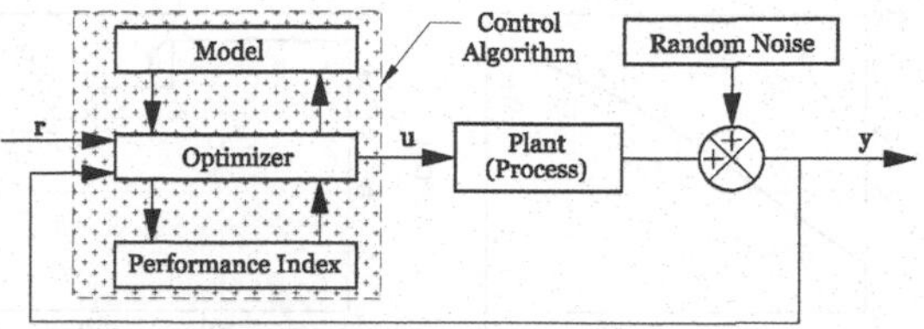

Fig. 5. Proposed Scheme to Test Robustness.

4 Simulation Results

This section contains the results obtained from the simulation of the predictive control scheme shown in Figure 2 and for the different variants of the optimization procedure described in the previous section, using the auto-regressive neuro-fuzzy model as a predictor as well as a plant in the scheme.

The value of α_k in the three optimization variants is 1. The value of 0.1 is assigned to β_k, except in the third variant where the value of 0.01 was used.

In all cases, the simulation tests were carried out by programming the control algorithm in MATLAB for a startup with a reference signal of the conventional temperature shown in Figure 6. With this reference an initial startup gradient of $91^oC/H$, descending to $75^oC/H$, down to $60^oC/H$ is sought after.

The results obtained with the three variants are similar. The temperature tracking curves, in all cases, almost overlap with the temperature reference. At the changes in gradient reference, we can observe slight increases in the tracking error. The fuel consumption is similar in all cases. In the some way, the curves representing the behavior of the gradient show a clear tendency to be the same as those of the gradient reference, with slight deviations within acceptable operational limits.

5 Robustness Tests

Random noise was added to the original predictive control scheme shown in the previous section, with the aim of simulating errors in the measurements of temperatures taken in the plant, see Figure 5.

Given that the control algorithm is based on an auto-regressive neuro-fuzzy model that provides temperature predictions, the random noise is propagated through the same channels. This procedure serves as a test for the robustness of the constructed algorithm because the optimization routines that were used will determine the fuel flow at each updating stage. In the case of the previous simulations, the robustness test demostrate the same tendencies observed in the three variantes, as can be seen in Figure 6, which correspond to the control algorithm for variant 3.

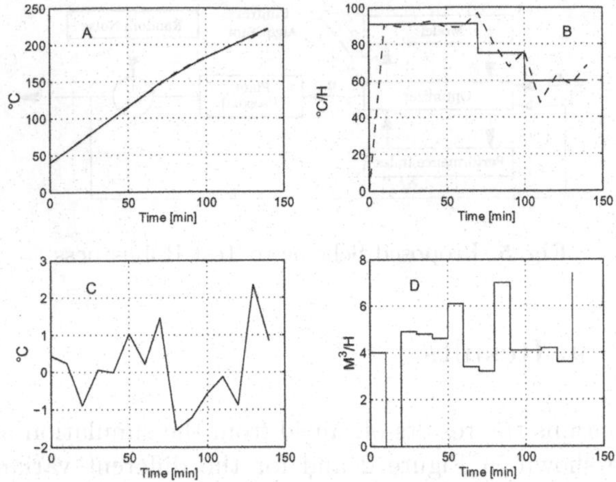

Fig. 6. A) Tracking of the temperature reference; B) Behavior of the gradient; C) Tracking error; D)Fuel flow suggested to the operator.

6 Analysis of the Results

According to the previous graphs the tracking of the temperature reference is adequate in all the variants, even when random noise is added to the measurements. We can see that the temperature tracking error increases when the change rate in temperature descends to $60^oC/H$, which causes transient instability in the behavior of the gradient. In the case of the proposed optimization variants it was observed that the control algorithm provides us with the fuel flow to be used by the operator for each period. This achieves a temperature tracking reference with a very small quadratic deviation. The robustness test applied to each of the variants showed that in some fuel update periods the error increases but in small degrees, and that they consequently have little effect on the temperature tracking. This indicates that the temperature control of the fluid transported in the downcomers is adequate.

7 Conclusions

From these results we can observe that the control algorithm that has been developed fulfills the principal design requirements to solve the problem and furthermore it can be applied to the different fossil power plants in the country. The neuro-fuzzy identification demonstrated the efficiency of this type of technique to easily obtain from the data reliable models of the process, and that they are useful as predictors in control predictive schemes based on the model. It is possible to improve the behavior of the temperature gradient by adding a third term which participates in the performance index to be minimized. A control scheme based on an auto-regressive neuro-fuzzy model is provided and this represents an improvement in the operation of the fossil power plants.

References

1. Clarke, D.W., Mohtadi, C., Tuffs, P.S., Generalized Predictive Control. Automatica, Vol. 23, No. 2, (1987) 137–160
2. Sousa, J.M., Babuška, R., Bruijn, P., Verbruggen, H.B., Comparison of Convencional and Fuzzy Predictive Control, Proceedings of the IEEE, (1996)
3. Babuška, R., An Overview of Fuzzy Modeling and Model–Based Fuzzy Control, World Scientific Series in Robotics and Intelligent Systems– Vol. 23, Fuzzy Logic Control Advances in Applications, Part I: Tutorials pp. 3–36, World Scientific Publishing Co. Pte. Ltd., (1999)
4. Babuška, R., Verbruggen, H.B., An Overview of Fuzzy Modeling for Control, Control Eng. Practice, Vol. 4 No. 11, pp. 1593–1606, (1996)
5. Ruz, J.A., Sintonización Optima de un Controlador Difuso para el Calentamiento y Presurización del Generador de Vapor de una Unidad Termoeléctrica, Tesis de Maestria, Univ. Autónoma del Carmen, México, (2001)
6. Jang, J.-S.,R. ANFIS: Adaptive-Network-based Fuzzy Inference System, IEEE Transactions on Systems, Man and Cybernetics, Vol. 23, No. 3, May/June (1993)
7. Jang, J.-S.,R., Sun, Ch.-T., Neuro Fuzzy Modeling and Control, Proceedings of the IEEE, Vol. 83, No.3, March. (1995)
8. Comisión Federal de Electricidad, Procedimiento de Operación General, Centro de Adiestramiento de Operadores Ixtapantongo
9. Takagi, T., and Sugeno, M., Fuzzy Identification of systems and its applications to modeling and control, IEEE Trans. Syst., Man, Cybern., Vol 15, pp. 116–132, (1985)
10. Jang, J.-S.,R., Input Selection for ANFIS learning, Proceedings of the Fifth IEEE International Conference on Fuzzy Systems, Vol. 2, pp. 1493-1499, (1996)
11. Haykin, S., Neural Networks, Prentice-Hall, Inc., N.J., 2nd ed., (1999)
12. Nϕrgaard, M., Ravn, O., Poulsen, N.K., and Hansen, L.K., Neural Networks for Modelling and Control of Dynamic Systems, Springer-Verlag London Limited (2000)
13. Narendra, K.S., and Parthasarath, K., Identification and Control of Dynamical Systems Using Neural Networks, IEEE Trans. On Neural Networks, Vol. 1, No. 1, (1990)
14. Ruz H., J.A., Suárez, D.A. Shelomov, E., Control Predictivo basado en un modelo neurodifuso auto-regresivo aplicado al proceso de arranque del generador de vapor de una unidad termoeléctrica, VIII Seminario Anual de Automática, Electrónica Industrial e Instrumentación SAAEI' 2001, Matanzas Cuba, 17–19 Sept. (2001)

Modeling Dynamical Causal Interactions with Fuzzy Temporal Networks for Process Operation Support Systems

Gustavo Arroyo-Figueroa and Raúl Herrera-Avelar

Gerencia de Sistemas Informáticos, Instituto de Investigaciones Eléctricas,
Av. Reforma 113, Col. Palmira, 62490 Temixco Morelos Mexico
garroyo@iie.org.mx
http://www.iie.org.mx

Abstract. Fossil Power Plants are faced with ever-increasing requirements for better quality, higher production profits, safer operation and stringent environment regulation. New technologies are required to reduce the operator's cognitive load and to achieve more consistent operations. The research described in this work intended to develop an efficient reasoning methodology for operation support systems. The proposed approach is based on a novel fuzzy reasoning to deal uncertainty and time, know as Fuzzy Temporal Network (FTN). A FTN is a formal and systematic structure (DAG), used to model dynamical causal interactions between the occurrence of events. The mechanism of possibility propagation is based on Mamdani inference method (fuzzy logic control methodology). The proposed approach is applied to fossil power plant diagnosis through a case study: the diagnosis and prediction of events in the drum level system.

1 Introduction

Computer systems and information technology have been extensively used in power plant process operation. This trend is motivated by increasing requirements for higher productions profits, safer operation and stringent environment regulation. Distributed control systems (DCS) and management information systems have been playing an important role in increase this requirements. However, in nonroutine operations such as fault diagnosis, human operators have to rely on their own experience. During disturbances, the operator must determine the best recovery action according to the type and sequence of the signals received. In a major upset, the operator may be confronted with a large number of alarms, but very limited help from the system, concerning the underlying plant condition. Faced with vast amount of raw process data, human operators find it hard to contribute a timely and effective solutions. The power plants require new technologies to reduce the cognitive load placed upon operators.

Analytical solution methods exist for many power operation and control problems. However, the mathematical formulations of real-word processes are obtained under certain restrictive assumptions, and even with these assumptions the resolution of

C.A. Coello Coello et al. (Eds.): MICAI 2002, LNAI 2313, pp. 440–449, 2002.

power-plant problems is not trivial. On the other hand, there are many uncertainties in the process, because power plants are large, complex and influenced by unexpected events and the evolution of time. Intelligent operational systems were born for this industrial need and deal with the uncertainties. As an effort towards the development of an intelligent operation support system for power plant [1,2,3], the knowledge representation and the reasoning mechanism used for efficient problem solving are being investigated.

Fuzzy logic has shown its ability to handle this kind of uncertain in industrial automation, such as diagnostic systems [4, 5]; fuzzy classification [6]; and decision support systems [7]; this indicates its potential role in solving power-plant problems. In this study, the dealing of uncertainty and time are covered through a fuzzy temporal net. Using fuzzy logic each linguistic causal-temporal sentence can be defined by a possibility distribution. We propose building a events network that facilitates temporal representation and reasoning with uncertainty and time. The temporal model is called "Fuzzy Temporal Network". In this directed acyclic graph model, each temporal node represents an event or state change of a variable and the arcs represent causal – temporal relationships between the nodes. The proposed approach is applied to fossil power plant operation for prediction task.

2 Fuzzy Temporal Reasoning

2.1 Temporal expressions

In the context of industrial process, the knowledge is described in an imprecise and vague path using ill-defined linguistic terms such as "about 3 minutes". Each of such linguistic terms can be described by a possibility distribution, for instance: "when the speed of the feedwater pump increase, there is increase in the feedwater flow "about 3 minutes after the increase of the speed". Figure 1 shows the triangular possibility distribution that represent the temporal representation of the event "about 3 minutes".

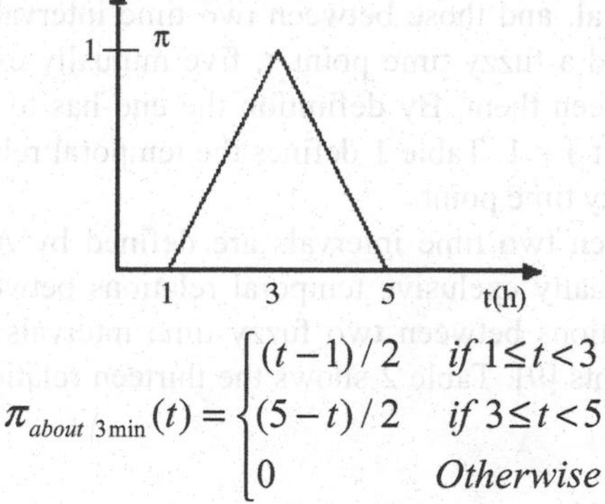

$$\pi_{about\ 3\min}(t) = \begin{cases} (t-1)/2 & if\ 1 \le t < 3 \\ (5-t)/2 & if\ 3 \le t < 5 \\ 0 & Otherwise \end{cases}$$

Fig. 1. Temporal triangular possibility distribution for a event occurrence

2.2 Temporal Relationships

Allen's interval algebra and its thirteen relations provide the temporal basis of the temporal systems [8]. Each event has an associated interval denoted [a,b], where "a" is the starting time point and "b" is the ending point. A fuzzy time point can be represented by a normalized possibility distribution associated with each punctual event. Hence, a time interval is a representation of two fuzzy time points, there are three kinds of temporal relationships between points and intervals: those between two points, those between a point and interval, and those between two intervals.

Defined the temporal elements (points and intervals) as normalized possibility distribution, the relationship between two temporal elements is measured by the possibility and necessity, which are two principal measures in possibility theory [9]. The relations between two fuzzy time points are defined by the conditional possibility. There are three possible relationships between two fuzzy time points: before, at the same time, and after. The possibility of the relation ® between any couple of fuzzy time points τ_1 y τ_2 is given by:

$$\Pi(®(\tau_1, \tau_2)=\max\{\min[\pi_{\tau_1}(\tau_1), \pi_{\tau_2}(\tau_2)]\} \quad \begin{matrix} \tau_1 \in S_{\tau_1} \\ \tau_2 \in S_{\tau_2} \\ \tau_1 ® \tau_2 \end{matrix}$$

The necessity measure is computed by the definition of necessity:

$$N(p) = 1 - \Pi(\sim p)$$

$$N\,(®(\tau_1, \tau_2)=1- \max\{\min[\pi_{\tau_1}(\tau_1), \pi_{\tau_2}(\tau_2)]\} \quad \begin{matrix} \tau_1 \in S_{\tau_1} \\ \tau_2 \in S_{\tau_2} \\ \tau_1 (\sim ®)\, \tau_2 \end{matrix}$$

where ~® is the complement of ®.

As a fuzzy time interval can be defined by a couple of fuzzy time points, temporal relations between intervals can therefore be defined based on those between fuzzy time points. There are two kinds of relations between intervals: those between a time point and a time interval, and those between two time intervals. Given a fuzzy time interval $i = \{\tau_{id}, \tau_{if}\}$ and a fuzzy time point τ, five mutually exclusive temporal relations are possible between them. By definition the end has to be after its beginning: $\Pi(\tau_{id} < \tau_{if}) = 1$; $N(\tau_{id} < \tau_{if}) = 1$. Table 1 defines the temporal relations between a fuzzy time interval and a fuzzy time point.

The relations between two time intervals are defined by Allen' interval algebra. There are thirteen mutually exclusive temporal relations between two intervals. The definition of each relations between two fuzzy time intervals can be made by their respective extreme points [9]. Table 2 shows the thirteen relations between two fuzzy time intervals.

Table 1. Temporal relations between a fuzzy time interval and a fuzzy time point

τ before I i after τ	$\tau < i$ $i > \tau$	$N(\tau<i) = N(i>\tau)$ $= N(\tau_{id} > \tau)$
τ after I i before τ	$\tau > i$ $i < \tau$	$N(\tau>i) = N(i<\tau)$ $= N(\tau_{if} < \tau)$
τ start i i started by τ	τ s i i s' τ	$N(\tau\ s\ i) = N(i\ s'\ \tau)$ $= N(\tau_{id} = \tau)$
τ during i i contained τ	τ d i i d' τ	$N(\tau\ d\ i) = N(I\ d'\ \tau)$ $= \min(N((\tau_{id} < \tau), N(\tau_{if} > \tau))$
τ finish i i finished by τ	τ f i i f' τ	$N(\tau\ f\ i) = N(i\ f'\ \tau)$ $= N(\tau_{if} = \tau)$

Table 2. Temporal relations between two fuzzy time intervals

i before j j after I	$i < j$ $j > i$	$N(I < j) = N(j > i)$ $= N(\tau_{id} > \tau_{jf})$
i met by j j meet i	i m j j m' i	$N(i\ m\ j) = N(j\ m'\ i)$ $= N(\tau_{id} = \tau_{jf})$
i overlap j j overlapped i	i o j j o' i	$N(i\ o\ j) = N(j\ o'\ i)$ $= \min(N((\tau_{id} < \tau_{jd}), N(\tau_{if} > \tau_{jf}))$
i start j j started by i	i s j j s' i	$N(I\ s\ j) = N(j\ s'\ i)$ $= \min(N((\tau_{id} = \tau_{jd}), N(\tau_{if} > \tau_{jf}))$
i contained j j during i	i d j j d' i	$N(i\ d\ j) = N(j\ d'\ i)$ $= \min(N((\tau_{id} > \tau_{jd}), N(\tau_{if} < \tau_{jf}))$
i finish j j finished i	i f j j f' i	$N(I\ f\ j) = N(j\ f'\ i)$ $= \min(N((\tau_{id} < \tau_{jd}), N(\tau_{if} = \tau_{jf}))$
i equal j	j e i	$N(I\ e\ j) = N(j\ e'\ i)$ $= \min(N((\tau_{id} = \tau_{jd}), N(\tau_{if} = \tau_{jf}))$

2.3 Temporal Distance

The temporal distance between two events can be seen as the time delay between their time occurrence. The temporal distance defines the quantitative aspects over the delay between two events.

Given τ_1 and τ_2 two fuzzy time points represented respectively by two possibility distributions $\pi_{\tau_1}(\tau_1)$ and $\pi_{\tau_2}(\tau_2)$ with their respective supports S_{τ_1} and S_{τ_2}. The possibility measure for the temporal distance between τ_1 and τ_2 can be computed:

$$\delta_{21}(\mathbf{l}) = \max(\min(\pi_{\tau_1}(\tau_1), \pi_{\tau_2}(\tau_2))) \text{ if } \mathbf{l} \in \delta_{21}$$
$$\tau_1 \in S_{\tau_1}$$
$$\tau_2 \in S_{\tau_2}$$
$$\tau_1 - \tau_2 = \mathbf{l}$$
$$\delta_{21}(\mathbf{l}) = 0 \qquad \text{otherwise}$$

where $S_{\delta_{21}}$ is the support of the distance function which can be obtained from S_{τ_1} and S_{τ_2}:

$$S_{\delta_{21}} = \{\mathbf{l} \mid \exists\, \tau_1 \in S_{\tau_1}, \tau_2 \in S_{\tau_2}, \tau_2 - \tau_1 = \mathbf{l}\}$$

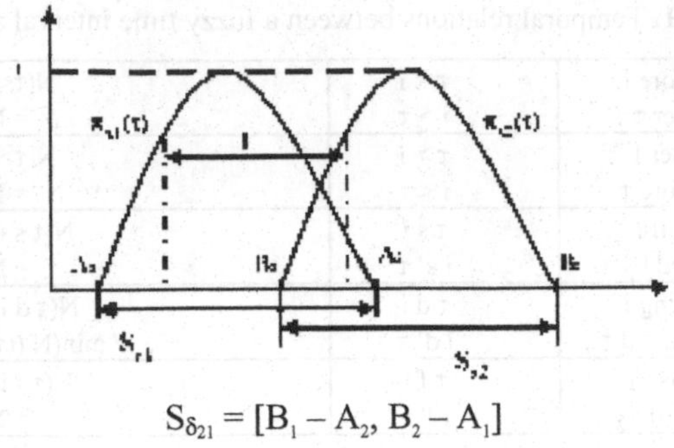

Fig. 2. Temporal distance computation between two fuzzy time points

3 Fuzzy Temporal Network

3.1 Definition

A Fuzzy Temporal Network is a formal and systematic structure used to model the temporal evolution of a process with uncertainty. A FTN is a directed acyclic graph (DAG). In the net a node describes an event (fact) and an arc describes a causal and temporal numerical relation between two nodes (events). The principal characteristic of the FTN is its capacity to handle temporal linguistic expressions about the occurrence of events, like "some minutes" or "about 5 minutes". These linguistic expressions are represented by using possibility distributions. To construct an FTN the knowledge engineer should specify the parameters associated with each node, and the possibility distributions associated with each arc [4].

Figure 3 shows an example of a small FTN and Table 3 presents the variable definitions of the FTN. The network represents the knowledge process of the drum system, obtained from an expert operator of a power plant. The drum is a subsystem of a fossil power plant that provides steam to the superheater and liquid water to the water wall of a steam generator. The drum is a tank with a steam water valve on the top and feedwater pumps, to provide water. One of the main problems in the drum is maintaining a safe operation level. There are many disturbances that affect the operation of the drum level. The following text describes the events (bold), the linguistic terms (underlined) and the variables (italic) related to an increment in the feedwater flow.

"The dynamic of the FW pump (FWP) is faster than the dynamics of the FW valve (FWV). When a *FW pump* current **augmentation** occurs, the *FW flow* **increase** (FWF) is detected about 1 min later and when a *FW valve* opening **increase** occurs the *FW flow* **increase** (FWF) is detected about 3:00 min later. And the *drum level* **high** condition (DRL) is detected about 1:30 min after the FW flow **increase** detection."

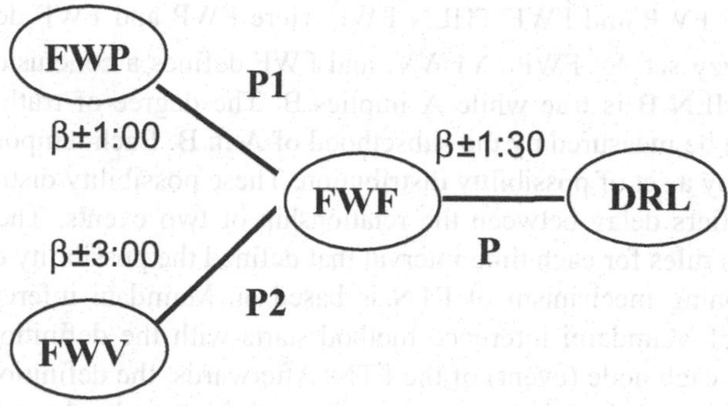

Fig. 3. Fuzzy temporal network for the drum-level example

Table 3. Definition of the FTN of the drum-level system

Temporal Range = 0.30-6:30 min Temporal Unit = minute

VARIABLES:

a) Process variables:

FWP augmentation in the feedwater pump
FWV opening the feedwater valve
FWF increase of the feedwater flow
DRL increase in the level in the drum

b) Causal variables:

P_1=[FWP → FWF]
P_2=[FWV → FWF]
P_3=[FWF → DRL]

c) Temporal variables

$\beta(P_1)$ = about1:1:00 min, $\beta(P_2)$ = about 3:00 min $\beta(P_3)$ = about 1:30 min

3.2 Reasoning Using Temporal Fuzzy Networks

Fuzzy Logic techniques have been through extensive practical implementations in industry in the form of intelligent control. A fuzzy logic scheme is commonly described by a set of fuzzy rules. With these rules, the interconnected relationships between variables can be expressed. Fuzzy rules are like ordinary IF ... THEN ... rules, except for two important differences: the premises and conclusions of fuzzy rules contain linguistic variables, and the inference procedure with fuzzy rules is different from that with conventional rules.

The design parameters of a fuzzy logic mechanism consist of three parts: the fuzzification interface, the fuzzy rule base and inference, and the defuzzification interface. The fuzzification interface converts the numerical values of the input variables into linguistic variables. The fuzzy rule and inference mechanism provides the definition of linguistic rules and includes the decision-making logic, which infers fuzzy actions employing fuzzy implication and the inference rules mentioned. The defuzzificacion converts the inferred action, which interpolates between rules that are fired simultaneously, to a numerical values.

A fuzzy net can be seen a set of rules where the fuzzy rules takes the form: "IF A THEN B". This defines a fuzzy relation from fuzzy set A to conclusion fuzzy set B, where A is the event cause and B is the event consequence. In the example, the rule is defined as IF FWP and FWF THEN FWF. Here FWP and FWF define a composite condition fuzzy set A= FWP ∩ FWV, and FWF defines a conclusion fuzzy set B. A rule IF A THEN B is true while A implies B. The degree of truth of the rule IF A THEN B can be measured by the subsethood of A in B. Each temporal linguistic term is described by a set of possibility distribution. These possibility distributions show the fuzzy quantifiers delay between the relationship of two events. The fuzzy rule database contains rules for each time interval that defined the possibility distribution [10].

The reasoning mechanism of FTN is based on Mamdani inference method [11]. The design of Mamdani inference method starts with the definition of membership functions for each node (event) of the FTN. Afterwards, the definition of the rule's set for each time interval of the events parent and child must be done. These rules show the temporal causal relationship between two events. Finally, a defuzzification method is applied to obtain a time of occurrence of the past or future event(s), see Figure 4. The possibility degree of the past or future event is obtained by the membership function of the linguistic term for the all time interval.

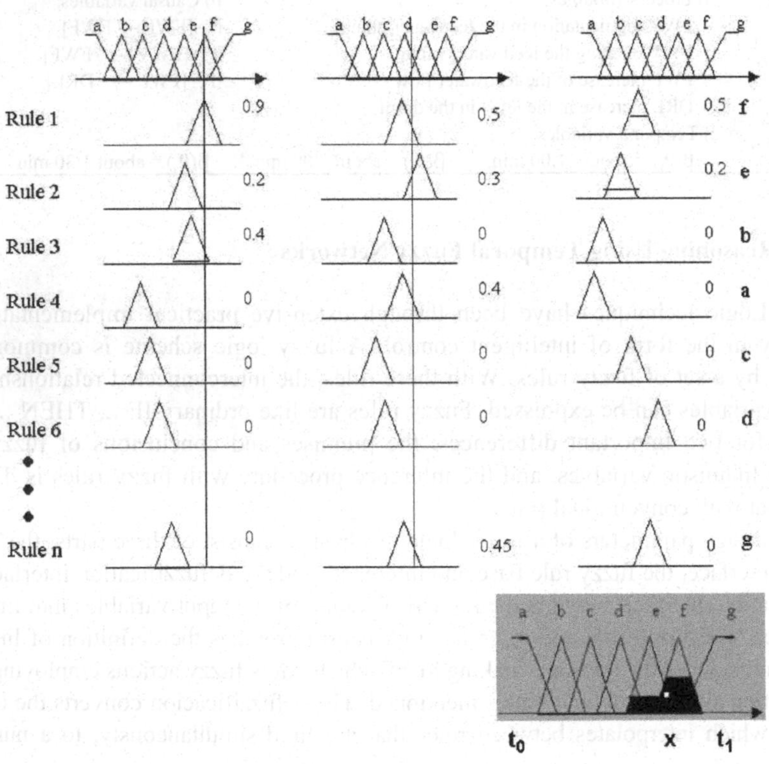

Fig. 4. Mamdani inference of the Fuzzy Temporal Network

4 Experiments and Results

The modeling of dynamical causal relationships with FTN was evaluated while tested in a fossil power plant training simulator. The definition of the event time intervals and possibility degree of truth for each rule was obtained based on knowledge about the process combined with data from failure simulation tests. For the relationship between FWP – FWF. Figure 5 shows the time interval defined [25-114 seconds]. The fuzzy rule's set for this time interval definition between FWP-FWF was 49 rules.

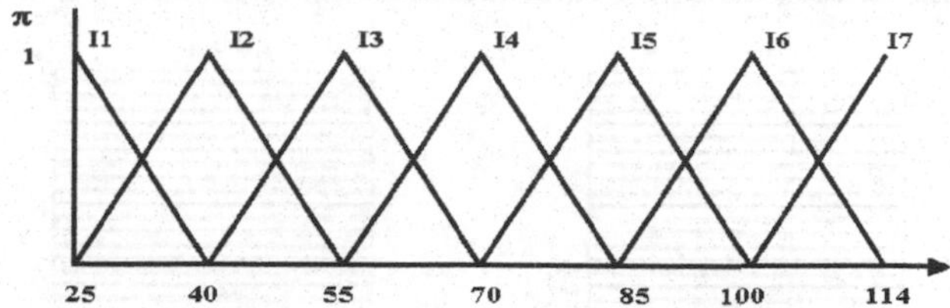

Fig. 5. Possibility distribution for causal-temporal relation between FWP-FWF

First experiment (prediction task). An increment of the speed of the pump of the feedwater (FWP) is detected at time 15 seconds. This timing occurs in the first and second time interval and the rules 1 to 14 are actived. The disjunction of 3 fuzzy sets generate the area of fuzzification for the FWF. To obtain a crisp value, the output fuzzy set must be defuzzified. With the Mamdani inference scheme, the center of gravity defuzzification method is often used. This method computes the "time occurrence" of the center of gravity of the fuzzification area under the fuzzy set for FWF. The application of defuzzification method gives a time of 70.6 seconds, this time corresponds to the subinterval two, with a possibility degree of Π=0.94, see Figure 6.

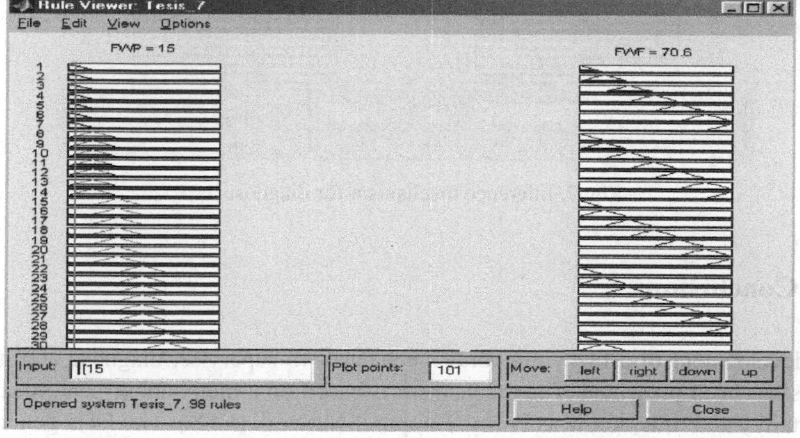

Fig. 6. Inference mechanism for prediction task

Second experiment (diagnosis task). An increment in the feedwater flow (FWF) is detected at time 110 seconds. For the relationship FWF – FWP, this time corresponds to the fifth and sixth time intervals and the rules 29 to 42 were actived. The application of defuzzification gives a time of 88.1 seconds with a possibility degree of occurrence of Π= 0.51 into the time interval 25 to 114 seconds. For the relationship FWF – FWV, this time corresponds to the fifth and sixth time intervals and the rules 29 to 42 are actived. The application of defuzzification gives a time of 214 seconds with a possibility degree of Π= 0.89 into the time interval 104 to 248 seconds, see Figure 7.

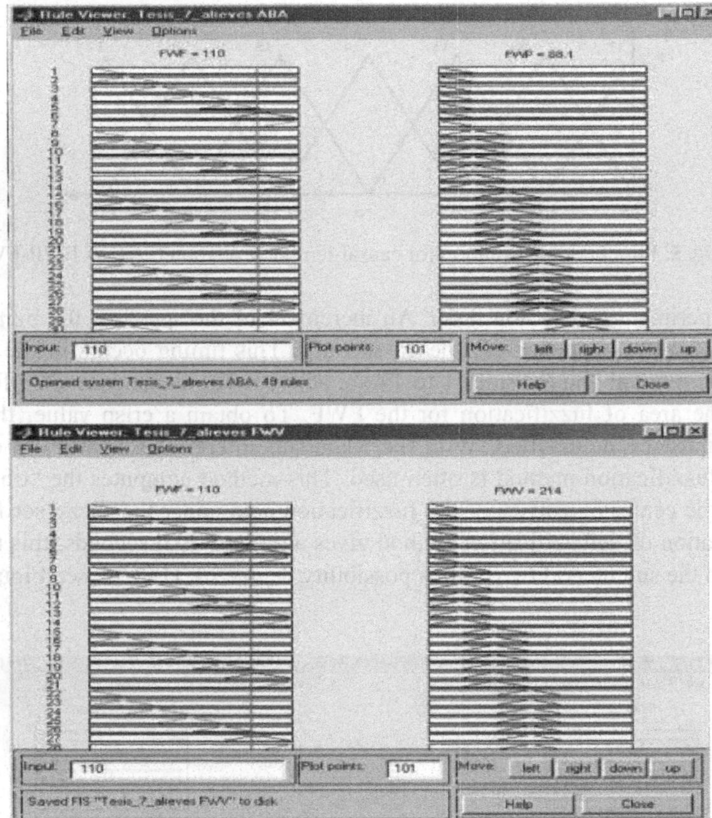

Fig. 7. Inference mechanism for diagnosis task

5 Conclusions

The development of a fuzzy temporal mechanism to supervise, diagnose and predict events has been presented. The mechanism is based on a methodology onto deal with uncertainty and time, know as Fuzzy Temporal Network (FTN). The FTN generates a formal and systematic structure, used to model the temporal evolution of a process under uncertainty. The FTN's inference mechanism is based on classic Mamdani inference method utilized in the design of fuzzy logic controllers. The inference mechanism gives the time interval of occurrence and achieves the diagnosis and prediction tasks. The current trend will be focused on developing and integrating our approach in a intelligent system for process operation in fossil power plants.

References

1. Falinower C. & Mari B. SACSO: An Expert System for Fossil-Fuel Power Plant Operations. *Technical Report HI21/94-006*, Electricité de France, Paris, France. (1994)
2. Tsou J. HEATXPRT Heat Rate Improvement Advisor Prototype Version. *User Manual Electric Power Research Institute,* Palo Alto, California, (1995)
3. Lerner U., Parr R., Koller D., and Biswas G. Bayesian fault detection and diagnostic in dynamic systems. In *Proc. of the 17th National Conference on AI 2000*, Austin, TX, August 2000, pp. 531-537
4. G. Arroyo-Figueroa G., L. E. Sucar., E. Solis E., and A. Villavicencio: SADEP – a fuzzy diagnostic system shell – an application to fossil power plant operation. *Expert Systems with Applications*, **14** (1/2), (1998), 43-52
5. Chen Ziang: Fuzzy temporal reasoning for process supervision, *Expert Systems*, **12** (2), (1995), 123-137
6. Yuan Yufei, and Shaw Michael J.: Induction of fuzzy decision trees. *Fuzzy Sets and Systems*, **69**, (1995), 125-139
7. Qijun Xia and Ming Rao.; Dynamic case-based reasoning for process operation support systems, *Engineering Applications of Artificial Intelligence*, **12**, (1999), 343-361
8. Allen James F.: Maintaining Knowledge about Temporal Intervals. *Communications of the ACM*, **26**-11, (1983), 832-843
9. Didier Dubois and Henri Prade: Fundamentals of Fuzzy Sets, Kluwer Academic Publishers, The Netherlands, (2000)
10. Jerry R. Mendel: Uncertain Rule-Based Fuzzy Logic Systems: Introduction and New Directions, Prentice Hall, (2000)
11. Verbruggen Henk B. and Babuska Robert, ed: Fuzzy Logic Control Advances in Applications, World Scientific, Series in Robotics and Intelligent Systems (1999)

Resection Simulation with Local Tissue Deformations for Computer Assisted Surgery of the Prostate

Miguel A. Padilla Castañeda and Fernando Arámbula Cosío

Laboratorio de Imágenes y Visión (LIV),
Centro de Instrumentos,
Universidad Nacional Autónoma de México,
México, D.F., 04510
{padillac,arambula}@aleph.cinstrum.unam.mx

Abstract. We present a three-dimensional anatomical and deformable model of the prostate for prostatectomy simulation. The model was build from a set of ultrasound images with the prostate contour, automatically annotated, with a technique based on a genetic algorithm and principal components analysis. The model simulates resection operations and local tissue deformations during virtual resectoscope interaction. A mass-spring method is used to model tissue deformation due to surgical tool interaction. Through 3D mesh modification and updating of the nodes of the mesh, the model is able to show in real time, resections and local tissue deformations produced by the user. The anatomical model is designed to assist the surgeon (in conjunction with an optical tracker) to perform Transurethral Resections of the Prostate (TURP) by showing in real time the position of the resectoscope inside the body of the patient and the deformation of the prostate shape during resection.

1 Introduction

Minimally invasive surgical procedures offer significant advantages over traditional open surgery techniques, however these procedures restrict surgeon movements, the visibility, and difficult the spatial orientation inside the operation site, resulting in increased training periods for each surgeon and relatively slow surgical procedures. An interesting alternative is to develop computer aided surgery (CAS) systems, that assists the surgeon during a real surgery, or training systems that help the residents to get the skills in shorter periods of time. In both cases, systems must simulate the physical behaviour of living tissues. Approaches like those reported in [4,6,12,13] face the problem of modelling in real time, realistic tissue deformations for surgery simulation at the contact with virtual surgical tools.

Realistic simulation of tissue cutting is another important research topic in surgery simulation [2,3,8]. Bro-Nielsen [5] reported an approach for surgery simulation based on a finite element method for real time deformations with biophysical realism. Unfortunately this method is too low for tissue cutting operations even in simple mesh modifications.

Bielser and Gross [3] reported an interactive simulation technique for surgical cuts that simulates cutting operations using a virtual scalpel. The cuts in their approach are

C.A. Coello Coello et al. (Eds.): MICAI 2002, LNAI 2313, pp. 450–459, 2002.

made in a line like way, and focus on the problem of refining the mesh along the cut line to produce continuous dissections. They use the mass-spring model to simulate real time deformations based on the scalpel friction.

In this work is reported a technique for resection simulation which incorporates local tissue deformation for prostatectomy simulation. The prostate model was build from a set of ultrasound images with the prostate contour, automatically annotated with a technique based on a genetic algorithm and a principal components analysis.

The elastic behaviour of the prostate is modelled with the mass-spring method for deformable bodies, which provides good visual realism for a training system. Resections are modelled through the removal of nodes and geometrical elements from the volumetric mesh. The deformation is produced by the pressure acting on the surrounding tissue of the resected zone, derived from the volume change. The results show that the model is able to simulate resections performed by the user.

Although we use a set of well known approaches, such as the mass-spring method and the finite element meshes, the conjunction of these techniques for the construction of a prostate model for surgery simulation is an original application. This model is intended to be used in a computer assisted prostate surgery system, like the one that we are developing at the *Lab. Imágenes y Visión*, which would be able to show the surgeon, the prostate shape and the position of the cutting instrument during a simulation of a transurethral resection of the prostate (TURP). According to what we know, this system is one the few that nowadays are being developed for prostatectomy simulation. Gomes *et al.* [10] report a similar system for prostatectomy, that focus on specifying and modelling a training and monitoring system for TURP, but which does not include a prostate model that simulates real time physical behaviour.

2 Volumetric Model of the Prostate

Construction of the geometric model of the organ is an important task for surgery simulation. The complexity of the 3D mesh structure is a point to be considered, resulting in a trade-off between realism and interaction. A more complex mesh corresponds to a higher time response of the system. For this reason, an adaptive finite element mesh generation method is needed to find the equilibrium between realism and time response. The main idea of the method is to approximate the continuous prostate domain Ω to a discrete domain Ω^*, where Ω^* consists of a 3D mesh formed by a set of volumetric finite elements of smaller size and regular form.

2.1 Sampling of the Ultrasound Images of the Prostate

To reconstruct an approximation of the three-dimensional shape of the prostate, we use a set of transversal ultrasound images, separated by intervals of *5mm* along the main axis of the prostate. For every ultrasound image, the prostate contour was automatically annotated (Fig. 1), using a technique based on a genetic algorithm [1]. The algorithm optimises the parameters of a point distribution model of the prostate, that was build by the application of a principal components analysis over a training set of images originally annotated by a human expert in ultrasound.

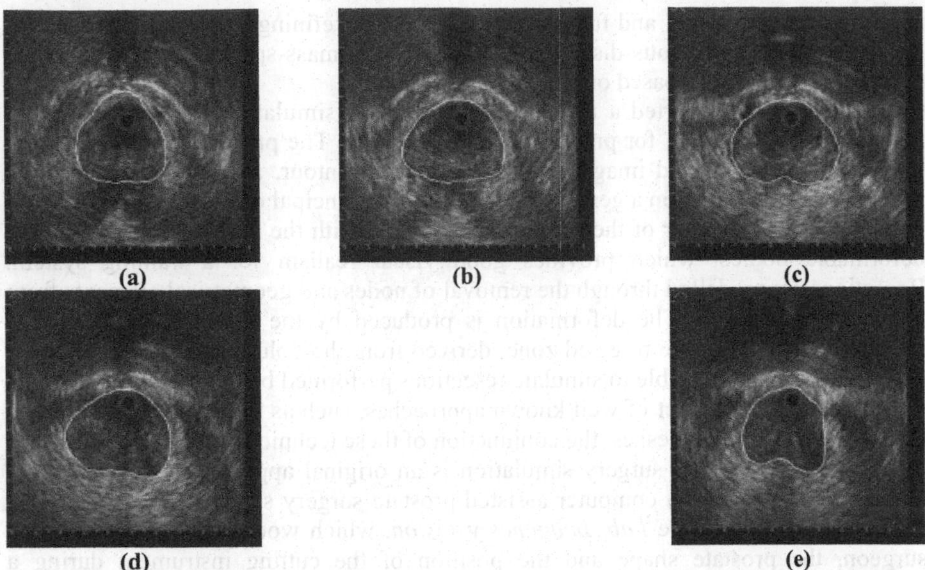

Fig. 1. Transversal ultrasound images with the prostate contours automatically annotated. **(a)** At *5mm* from the bladder neck. **(b)** At *10mm*. **(c)** At *15mm*. **(d)** At *20mm*. **(e)** At *25mm*

Then, each of the five cross-section of the prostate was sampled in a radial manner, taking as a sampling center the main axis of the ultrasound transducer. With these sampled and aligned cross-sections and the new contours calculated using cubic spline interpolation, the 3D shape of the prostate was build (Fig. 2). Both the angle α in the radial sampling and the number c of points in the cubic spline interpolation can be adjusted, in order to get a prostate 3D mesh with enough visual realism and acceptable time response.

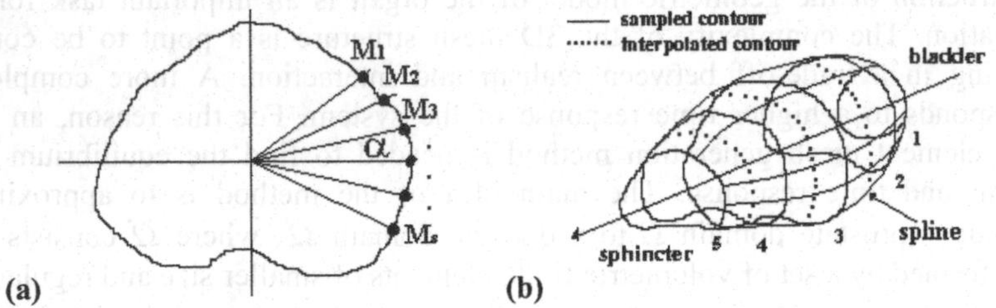

Fig. 2. Prostate shape. **(a)** Radial sampling of a prostate cross-section with sampling angle α and s samples ($s=360/\alpha$). **(b)** 3D model of the prostate surface build from the ultrasound images

To model the prostate as a solid body, and to propagate the deformations through its structure, we build, from the shape obtained, a volumetric finite element mesh of the prostate. Because of the irregularity of the prostate shape, to get the internal 3D mesh, some layers from the prostate capsule (external surface) to the prostate urethra (internal surface) were used. We used an artificially created prostate urethra. Like the values of α and c, the number l of internal layers is also adjustable (Fig. 3).

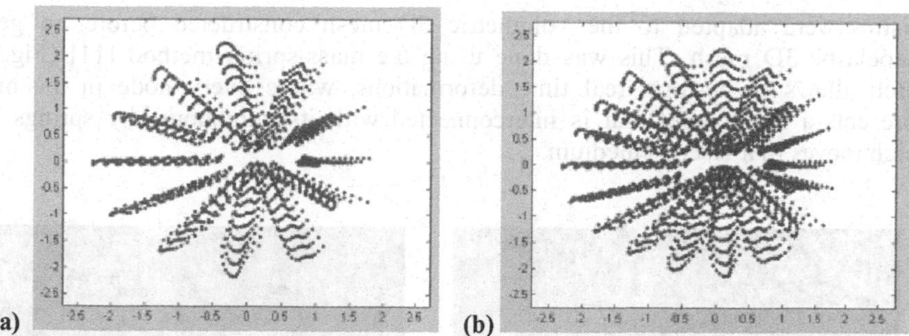

Fig. 3. Samples of prostate cross-sections, sampled in radial manner and interpolated with cubic spline. Each sampled prostate was interpolated at *15* contours at radial axis and divided in *10* layers from the capsule to the urethra. **(a)** Sampled at *30°*. **(b)** Sampled at *20°*. The *x* and *y* axis shows the real size in millimeters

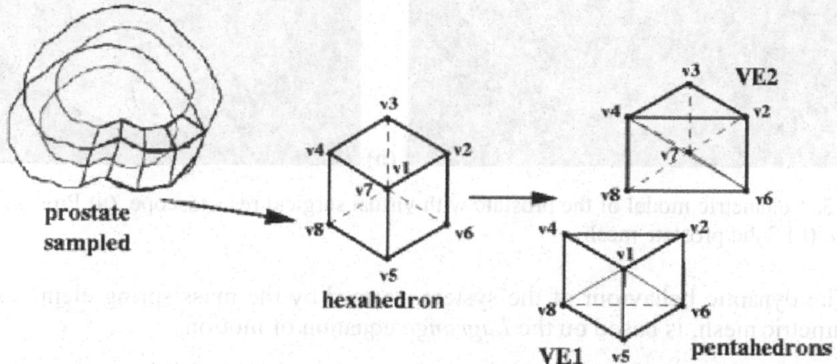

Fig. 4. Construction of the finite elements VE_1 and VE_2 of the volumetric 3D mesh of the prostate, from the prostate sampled points to the triangulation of pentahedrons VE_1 and VE_2.

2.2 Finite Element Mesh of the Prostate Volume

After sampling the 3D shape of the prostate, a graphical finite element model was build from the points extracted from the sampling process (Fig. 4).

The first step was to generate a set H of hexahedrons from the previous prostate sampled points. Then, every hexahedron was divided in two pentahedrons VE_1 and VE_2. A triangulation process was applied over the pentahedrons VE_1 and VE_2, resulting in eight triangles for every finite element VE_1 and VE_2.

In figure 5 can be observed a 3D finite element mesh of the volume of the prostate build with the method described. The figure also shows the solid representation of the prostate mesh.

3 Physical Model of the Prostate

The prostate physical behaviour is modelled as a deformable body with physical characteristics like mass, stiffness and damping coefficients. These physical characteristics were adapted to the volumetric 3D mesh constructed before, to get a viscoelastic 3D mesh. This was done using the mass-spring method [11] (Fig. 6), which allows to perform real time deformations, where every node in the mesh represents a mass point that is interconnected with its neighbours by springs and which moves in a viscous medium.

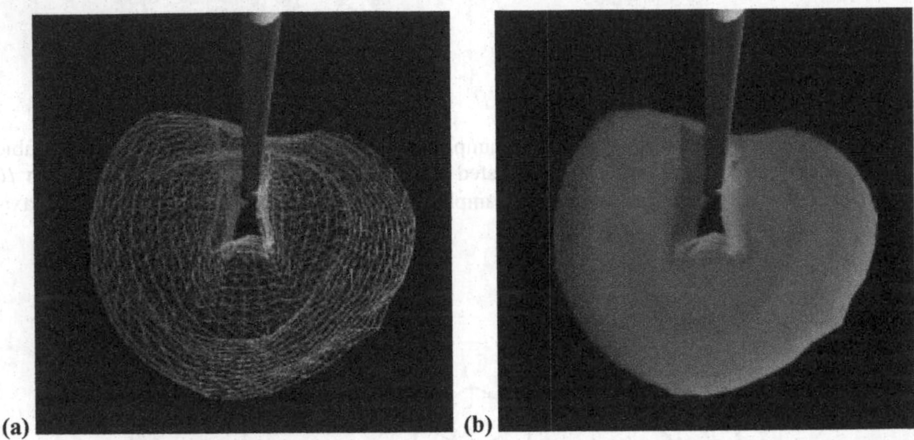

Fig. 5. Volumetric model of the prostate with virtual surgical resectoscope. **(a)** Prostate surface mesh. **(b)** Solid prostate mesh

The dynamic behaviour of the system, formed by the mass-spring elements in the volumetric mesh, is based on the *Lagrange* equation of motion.

$$m_i \frac{d^2\mathbf{x_i}}{dt^2} + \gamma_i \frac{d\ \mathbf{x_i}}{dt} + \mathbf{g_i}(t, \mathbf{x_i}) = \mathbf{f}_i(t, \mathbf{x_i}) \tag{1}$$

Where m_i is the mass of the node N_i in the mesh, at *Cartesian* coordinates $\mathbf{x}_i$; γ_i is the damping coefficient of the node (viscosity of the medium); $\mathbf{g}_i$ is the internal elastic force and $\mathbf{f}_i$ all the external forces acting on the node.

In this approach the internal elastic forces acting on the node *i* are given by the following linear equation:

$$g_i = \sum_{j \in N(i)} \mu_{i,j} \frac{\left(\|x_i - x_j\| - l^0_{i,j}\right)(x_i - x_j)}{\|x_i - x_j\|} \tag{2}$$

Where $\mu_{i,j}$ is the stiffness coefficient of spring connecting node N_i and N_j for all the neighbours in *N(i)* and $l^0_{i,j}$ is the spring length at rest position. In this manner, the deformations occur as a result of the elastic inner energy change, produced by the spring elongation.

Due to the computational speed needed and for simplicity in the programming, we have used the *Newton-Euler* integration method to resolve the dynamic system equation (1).

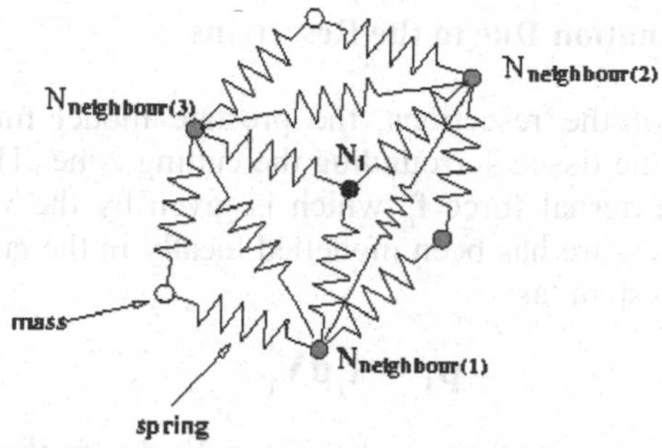

Fig. 6. A mass node element N_i connected with three neighbours by spring elements

4 Tissue Resection

Tissue resection simulation requires that resection emulates the real cuts that are performed in a real TURP procedure. For this reason, the cuts must look continuous and must expose the internal material of the prostate body. Initially, in this approach the problem of refining the mesh around the cut zone has been ignored, but we have focused on modelling the deformation that the prostate suffers after every cut is made.

4.1 Modification of the Geometrical Model

For cutting simulation, when a collision between the prostate and the resectoscope body is detected, the contact vertex v_c in the mesh is calculated. Then, the geometrical elements (pentahedrons and triangles) and mechanical elements (springs) that surround the vertex N_i are removed from the mesh. Finally the vertex N_i is also removed from the mesh (Fig. 7).

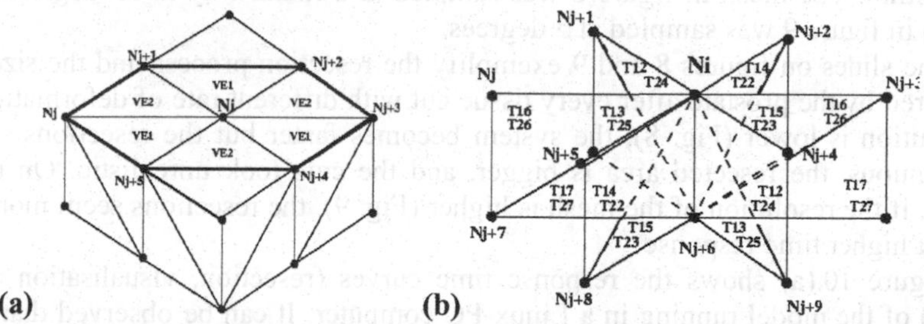

Fig. 7. Geometrical elements that are adjacents to the contact vertex N_i to be removed from the mesh at every cutting operation, where N_j is the j neighbour vertex of N_i. **(a)** Cutting zone adjacent to N_i. **(b)** Elements to remove, where every T_{ij} is the j triangle of the pentahedron VE_i

In order to visualise the inner tissue exposed after the resection (after removing the adjacent elements of the vertex N_i), the elements corresponding to the tissue exposed are added to the surface mesh, which is the visible layer.

4.2 Tissue Deformation Due to the Resections

As a consequence of the resections, the prostate model must deform due to the pressure exerted by the tissue surrounding the cutting zone. This pressure acts on the equation (1) as an external force $\mathbf{f}_i$, which is given by the volume variation in the cutting zone. The pressure has been modelled locally in the cutting zone, in a similar way as a hydraulic system, as:

$$\mathbf{p}_i = k_i \mathbf{dV}_i \tag{3}$$

Where $\mathbf{p}_i$ is the pressure acting in the vertex N_i, due to the cutting of surrounding tissue; k_i is the hydraulic resistance of the vertex N_i; $\mathbf{dV}_i$ is the volume variation around the vertex N_i. The volume variation $\mathbf{dV}_i$ is defined as:

$$\mathbf{p}_i = \mathbf{c}_i \sum_{j \in VA(N_i)} \frac{V_j^c}{V_j^0} \tag{4}$$

Where V_j^c is the volume of the pentahedron v_j adjacent to the vertex N_i ($\forall v_j \in VA$, where VA is the set of adjacent pentahedron to the vertex N_i to remove); V_j^c is the initial volume of all the pentahedrons adjacent to the vertex N_i, that has not been removed in the resection; $\mathbf{c}_i$ are the *Cartesian* coordinates of the cut zone center.

5 Results

In figures 8 and 9 are shown some views of the prostate model, that have been build with the method of finite element mesh generation described in this paper. The figures correspond to a prostate mesh with different resolution level (different number of nodes in the mesh), which are obtained by varying the control parameters of the algorithm. The mesh in figure 8 was sampled in a radial way at *15* degrees, and the mesh in figure 9 was sampled at *5* degrees.

The slides on figures 8 and 9 exemplify the resection process and the size change suffered by the prostate after every tissue cut with different rate of deformation. If the resolution is lower (Fig. 8), the system becomes faster but the resections seem less continuous, the resected area is bigger, and the cuts look unrealistic. On the other hand, if the resolution of the mesh is higher (Fig. 9), the resections seem more natural but at higher time response.

Figure 10.(a) shows the response time curves (resection, visualisation and total time) of the model running in a Linux-PC computer. It can be observed that the time response grows linearly as the mesh resolution is higher. On the other hand, figure 10.(b) shows that the percentage volume variation of the prostate after some resections, grows with a constant rate. Both curves could help to choose the resolution mesh which best corresponds with the prostate volume change in a real surgery, but keeping the system under an acceptable bandwidth for real time visualisation (20-60 hz) [7].

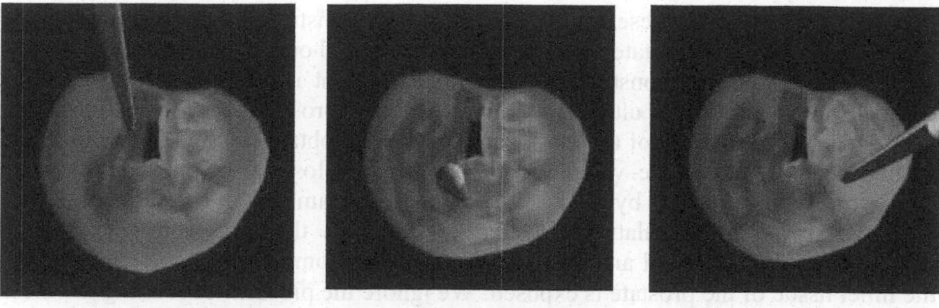

Fig. 8. Resections in a prostate model of 3600 nodes in the mesh (*α=15, c=15, l=10*)

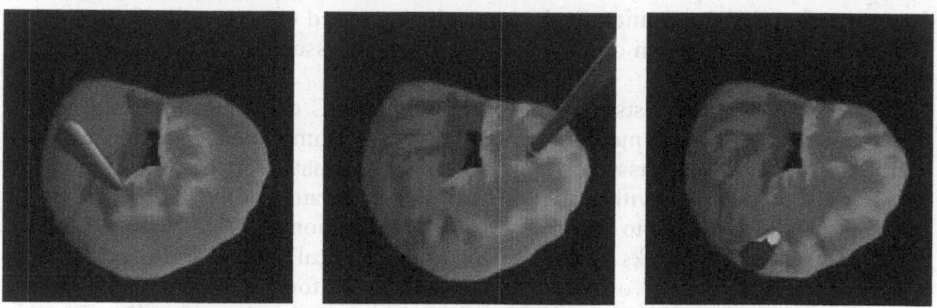

Fig. 9. Resections is a prostate model of 10800 nodes in the mesh (*α=5, c=15, l=10*)

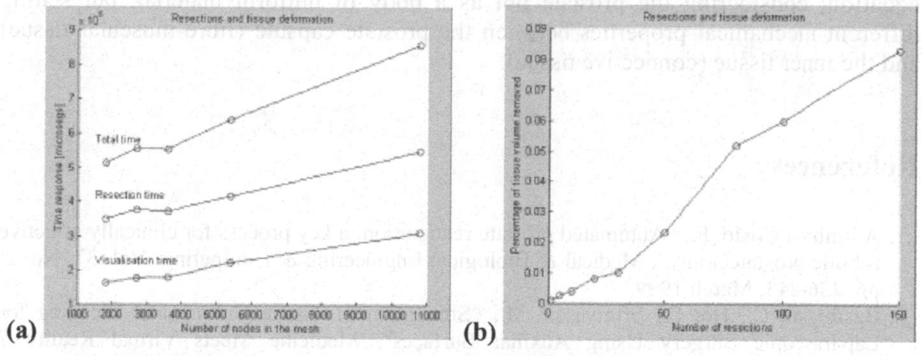

Fig. 10. (a) Time response of the model with different mesh resolution (number of nodes). **(b)** Percentage volume variation of a model with 5400 nodes in the mesh

6 Conclusion

Techniques like finite elements meshes and mass-spring method for deformable objects, in conjunction with techniques for automatic object recognition in a set of ultrasound images, allow for the construction of organ models for surgery simulation, like the prostate model presented in this paper. The construction of a prostate model for computer assisted prostatectomy is an interesting and original application.

First we present the construction of a finite element mesh of the volume of the prostate. We used a set of ultrasound images with the prostate contour, automatically annotated. The resolution of the mesh can be varied to obtain more visual realism and with a percentage volume variation of the prostate closer to a real surgery, with appropriate time response, by modifying the control parameters of the method.

During resection simulation, when collision with the virtual resectoscope is detected, some mechanical and geometrical elements from the mesh are removed and the inner tissue of the prostate is exposed. We ignore the problem of refining the mesh along the resected zone, but we focus on the tissue deformation after every resection. We consider, at the moment, that having a 3D model with a high resolution is good enough for producing cuts with visual realism without having to refine the mesh. However, the mesh generation method must be improved to reduce the size variation between finite elements, in order to produce uniform tissue cut operations inside the whole soft body.

Considering that the tests were made on a Linux-PC computer, the results show that the dynamic physical model is well suited for real time interactions for resection simulation, that involves tissue cutting and tissue deformation. In this sense, having a more robust workstation with graphics hardware accelerators will drastically improve the time response in order to get an acceptable visualisation bandwidth.

In the short term, it looks difficult to get biomechanical studies of the prostate that allow physical validation of the model. Fortunately, for a prostatectomy training system, a model that visually behaves well is enough in the short term [7]. For this reason, we are planning to collaborate with an urologist to determine the right mechanical properties, which provide visual realism. At this point, possible improvements to the mechanical model are: to incorporate a non-linear elasticity equation; considering the prostate not as a body of uniform material, but setting different mechanical properties between the prostate capsule (fibro-muscular tissue) and the inner tissue (connective tissue).

References

1. Arámbula Cosío, F., "Automated prostate recognition: a key process for clinically effective robotic prostatectomy", Medical & Biological Engineering & Computing. Vol. 37, No. 2, pp. 236-243, March 1999.
2. Basdogan, C., Ho, C., Srinivasan, M., "Simulation of Tissue Cutting and Bleeding for Laparascopic Surgery Using Auxiliar Surfaces", Medicine Meets Virtual Reality 7 (MMVR-7), San Fransisco, California, pp. 38-44, IOS Press, 1999
3. Bielser, D., Gross, M., "Interactive Simulation of surgical Cuts", Computer Graphics and Applications. Proceedings of the IEEE on The Eighth Pacific Conference, pp. 116 –442, 2000
4. Boux de Cason, F., Laugier, C., "Modelling the Dynamics of a Human Liver for a Minimally Invasive Surgery Simulator", Second International Conference on Medical Image Computing and Computer-Assisted Intervention MICCAI, pp. 1156-1165, 1999.
5. Bro-Nielsen, M., "Finite Element Modeling in Surgery Simulation", Proceedings of the IEEE, Vol. 86, No. 3, pp. 490-503, March 1998.

6. Cotin, S., Delingette, H., Ayache, N., "Real Time Volumetric Deformable Models for Surgery Simulation", IEEE Transactions on Visualization and Computer Graphics, Vol. 5, No. 1, pp. 62-73, January-March 1999.
7. Delingette H., "Toward Realistic Soft Tissue Modeling in Medical Simulation", Proceedings of the IEEE, vol.86, No.3, pp.512-523, March 1998.
8. Frisken-Gibson, S., "Using Linked Volumes to Model Object Collisions, Deformation, Cutting, Carving, and Joining", IEEE Transactions on Visualization and Computer Graphics, Vol. 5, No. 4, pp. 333-348, October-December 1999.
9. Fung, Y. C., "Biomechanics-Mechanical Properties of Living Tissues", 2ed. Berlin: Springer-Verlag, 1993.
10. Gomes, M.P.S.F., Barret, A.R.W., Timoney, A.G., Davies, B.L., "A Computer Assisted Training/Monitoring System for TURP Structure and Design", IEEE Trans. On Information Technology in Biomed., Vol. 3, No. 4, pp. 242-250, 1999.
11. Güdükbay, U., Özgüç, B., Tokad, Y., "A spring force formulation for elastically deformable models", Computers & Graphics, Vol. 21, No. 3, pp. 335-346, 1997.
12. Kühnapfel, U., Cakmak H.K., MaaB, H., "Endoscopic surgery training using virtual reality and deformable tissue simulation", Computers and Graphics, 24, pp. 671-682, 2000.
13. Padilla, C.M.A, Arambula C. F., "Deformable Model of the Prostate for Computer Assisted Surgery", VI Taller Iberoamericano de Reconocimiento de Patrones TIARP 2001, México, D.F, Noviembre 12 y 13, 2001.

Biometrics and Data Mining: Comparison of Data Mining-Based Keystroke Dynamics Methods for Identity Verification

Francisco J. Gutiérrez[1], Margarita M. Lerma-Rascón[1], Luis R. Salgado-Garza[2], and Francisco J. Cantú[1]

[1] Center for Artificial Intelligence, ITESM, Campus Monterrey
Ave. E. Garza Sada #2501 Sur, Monterrey, Nuevo León, C.P. 64849, México
Corresponding author: Francisco Gutiérrez, francisc@alumni.caltech.edu
[2] Computer Science Department, ITESM, Campus Monterrey

Abstract. Biometrics is the field that differentiates among various people based on their unique biological and physiological patterns such as retina, finger prints, DNA and keyboard typing patterns to name a few. Keystroke Dynamics is a physiological biometric that measures the unique typing rhythm and cadence of a computer keyboard user. This paper presents a Data Mining-based Keystroke Dynamics application for identity verification, and it reports the results of experiments comparing different approaches to Keystroke Dynamics. The methods compared were Decision Trees, a Naïve Bayesian Classifier, Memory Based Learning, and statistics-based Keystroke Dynamics.

1 Introduction

With the proliferation of online computer systems and the increased use of these systems for day-to-day operations and business transactions, security today is more important than ever. Security measurements currently involve a variety of approaches that go beyond the typical typed password identification, these include such methods as finger print recognition, retina scanning, and DNA testing to name a few. Each of these approaches is known as a biometric method, each of the characteristics these methods measure is known as a biometric, and the field that studies all these methods is known as Biometrics. To avoid confusion, in this paper the word Biometrics is capitalized when referring to the field as a whole, but it is not capitalized when referring to a method or a measurement.

Biometric methods measure biological and physiological characteristics to uniquely identify individuals. The main drawback of most biometric methods is that they are expensive to implement, because most of them require specialized hardware. Keystroke Dynamics is a biometric method that measures the unique typing pattern of individuals, and therefore does not require more hardware than a keyboard, making it an attractive option over other biometric techniques. The key assumption behind Keystroke Dynamics is that every keyboard user has a unique pattern in his typing timing for different letters and letter combinations

C.A. Coello Coello et al. (Eds.): MICAI 2002, LNAI 2313, pp. 460–469, 2002.

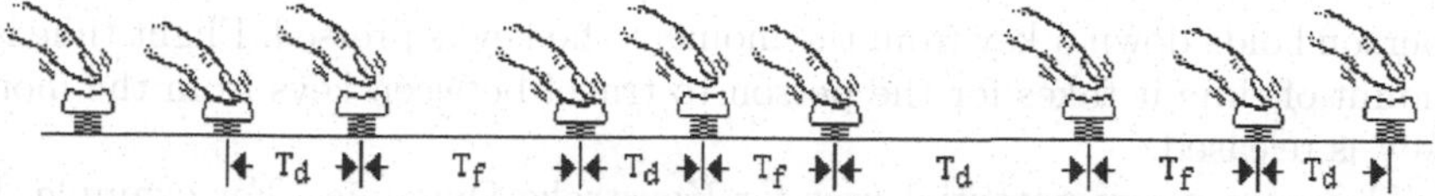

Fig. 1. Keystroke Dynamics variables: dwell time and flight time.

[4]; hence, the task of a Keystroke Dynamics application is to discover these patterns.

Data Mining is a set of techniques derived from research in Artificial Intelligence and Machine Learning that have been extensively used to extract patterns from data in a wide variety of contexts, so it is reasonable to assume that a Keystroke Dynamics application can be built using Data Mining techniques. In this paper we show that this is in fact the case, specifically, we present a Keystroke Dynamics application developed using Decision Trees, Clustering, and a Naïve Bayesian Classifier; all of which are Data Mining techniques. In addition we compare the performance of these techniques with Instance Based Learning and with the statistics-based approach to Keystroke Dynamics. The rest of this paper is organized as follows; First we introduce Keystroke Dynamics and the Data Mining techniques used in this application, later we describe the software tools developed, and finally we describe the experiments performed and the results obtained.

2 Keystroke Dynamics

Keystroke Dynamics is a biometric method that tries to identify unique patterns in the typing of different keyboard users. The history of Keystroke Dynamics dates back to World War II, when the United States Army Signal Core discovered that an individual keying rhythm on a telegraph transmission was unique. This was corroborated in the early 80's when the National Science Foundation and the National Bureau of Standards in the U.S. conducted a study, which concluded that typing patterns have unique characteristics that can be identified. Later on, SRI International (Stanford Research Institute) developed a technology for Keystroke Dynamics applications based on statistical techniques. Their Keystroke technology learned the user's typing rhythm by having the user fill-out a registration page, and it could subsequently remember that pattern and use it to identify a user as he was typing. Today, NetNannie Software, Inc. uses a commercial version of the technology developed by SRI international to restrict the access of children to websites with content that their parents consider inappropriate [1].

In order to recognize different users, a Keystroke Dynamics application must observe each user while typing, and learn the user's unique pattern from the variables observed. Each person has different typing characteristics, such as keystroke duration, how long it takes to press and let go of a key, error frequency, etc. Keystroke Dynamics concentrates on two of these characteristics, dwell time and flight time as seen in Figure 1 . Dwell time is the amount of time a person holds down a key from the moment the key is pressed. Flight time is the amount of time it takes for the person to travel between keys from the moment a key is released.

There are many potential uses for Keystroke Dynamics. For example, Keystroke Dynamics could make password sharing a useless fraud technique. Application Service Provider (ASP) companies sell access to their data and give access to their clients via a password, but sometimes the customer willingly gives the password to other people (non-customers). Using Keystroke Dynamics, ASPs could prevent unauthorized users from logging-on since their keystroke patterns would not match those of a legitimate customer. As another example, credit card companies could integrate Keystroke Dynamics as an added security measure when the client makes a major purchase by having the client identify himself typing either a password or a Personal Identification Number. This way, only the cardholder would be able to use the credit card since the PIN or password without the correct keystroke pattern would not work.

Most Keystroke Dynamics work to date has been done using statistical techniques, although other approaches have also been used. Monrose and Rubin report recent work using a Bayesian Classifier and cite work using neural networks [4]. However, to the best of our knowledge, there have been no applications of Decision Trees to Keystroke Dynamics prior to the work reported in this paper.

3 Data Mining

Data Mining is the process of learning a predictive model from a database using any of an assortment of techniques derived from Artificial Intelligence and Machine Learning research. These techniques include Decision Trees, Bayesian Networks, Neural Networks, Genetic Algorithms, Instance Based Learning, and Cluster Analysis. Although technically statistics-based techniques such as regression can be classified as Data Mining, historically statistics was the first to tackle pattern recognition problems, and the rest of the techniques came much later as challengers and complement to statistics, so statistics is usually viewed as separate from Data Mining. One of the main differences between statistics and Data Mining is that most statistical techniques assume a certain *a priori* distribution of the data, whereas Data Mining does not assume anything about the data. Another difference is that statistical regression models have difficulty dealing with non-linearity, but other Data Mining techniques do not have this problem.

In general, the Data Mining process, independently of the technique used, first learns a classification or prediction model from historical data, and then subsequently uses this model to classify a new observation, or to predict the outcome of a new trial. The Data Mining techniques used for this application were Decision Trees, a Naïve Bayesian Classifier, Clustering, and Instance Based Learning.

A Decision Tree is a way of representing a set of rules to predict the value of an unknown variable from a set of known variables. These variables are arranged in the form of a tree where the leaf nodes represent possible values of the unknown variable, the branch nodes represent the known variables, and the branches emerging from a branch node represent all the possible values of that node. Decision Trees can be learned from a set of past data with a Decision Tree induction algorithm. The main Decision Tree induction algorithms are the entropy algorithm with the Max Gain and the Max Gain Ratio criteria[7], the GINI algorithm, and the χ^2 algorithm.

A Naïve Bayesian Classifier is another way to predict the value of an unknown variable from a set of known variables [6]. However, unlike Decision Trees, a Bayesian Classifier outputs a probability distribution over the possible values of the goal variable instead of giving a definite answer. A Naïve Bayesian Classifier is just a Bayesian Network based on the assumption that the values of the known variables are independent of each other given the goal variable. The independence assumption might not fully correspond to the actual causal relationship between variables, this is why this type of Bayesian Classifier is called Naïve, but in practice it produces classifications comparable in accuracy with those of a Decision Tree.

Instance Based Learning is another technique to learn the value of an unknown variable when the other variables are known. This technique is based in a distance measure between observations. The value of the unknown variable is determined by the K nearest neighbors of the observation using a simple majority function or a weighted average [8].

Clustering is a data mining technique used to discover patterns in data and to find the intrinsic structure of a data set. This is also known as unsupervised learning because there is no variable to classify, Clustering just groups the information into sections of attributes that are close to each other using a distance measure. Clustering can be useful to discretize a continuous set of data. There are many Clustering techniques, the interested reader is referred to Duda and Hart [2]. The techniques used for this application are K-means and Fuzzy C-Means Clustering, the algorithms for these can be found in Wang [10].

4 Data Mining vs. Statistics for Keystroke Dynamics

SRI International implemented the first commercially successful application using a statistical approach. The Data Mining-based Keystroke Dynamics application described in this paper was implemented using Decision Trees, Clustering, and a Naïve Bayesian Classifier. In order to compare all the approaches directly with each other we also built a statistical model and an Instance Based Learning model in a spreadsheet in addition to the software application. We used the same data with all the approaches.

In the statistical approach the dwell and flight times are measured a number of times for each letter for each user, their mean and standard deviation are calculated, and a statistical model for each user is built based on these parameters. The hypothesis that a user is who he claims to be, is accepted or rejected in a given observation based on the likelihood of the observation given the model for that user. For the Data Mining based approach, the dwell and flight time for each letter are discretized over a set of observations using a Clustering algorithm. These discrete observations are used to build a Decision Tree or a Bayesian Classifier. The goal variable is taken to be a "yes" when the observation comes from the user whose model is being built, and it is taken to be a "no" when the observation comes from any of the other users.

The key differences between the statistical and the Data Mining approaches have to do with the information they consider in building a user model. The Data Mining method discretizes the inputs whereas the statistical method does not, so it loses information not lost in the statistical method. However, the Data Mining method includes information from all observations in the creation of an individual model, whereas the statistical method uses only information from the particular user. A Decision Tree induction algorithm and a Naïve Bayesian Classifier take into account not only the similarities between the patterns of the same user, but also the differences of this pattern with all the other patterns observed in building the model. Therefore, the Data Mining approaches take into account the whole context, and they fine-tune their models for each user whenever a new observation is added into the system. In contrast, the statistical model can only improve the model on a user whenever a new observation from that particular user is added.

5 Software Developed

In order to conduct this research, we developed Bonsai, a Data Mining tool, and BonsaiBouncer, a Keystroke Dynamics tool based on Bonsai. Both Bonsai and BonsaiBouncer were developed in Java and can be obtained by contacting the authors of this paper.

Bonsai is a general purpose Data Mining tool that can do both supervised and unsupervised learning, which means that it can be used to predict a goal variable, or it can be used to find patterns in data where no explicit goal variable is given. To do supervised learning Bonsai can learn Decision Trees and a Naïve Bayesian Classifier. For unsupervised learning Bonsai can do K-Means and fuzzy C-Means cluster analysis. A screenshot of Bonsai is shown in Figure 2.

To learn Decision Trees, Bonsai can use the entropy algorithm with the *Max Gain* criterion, the entropy algorithm with the *Max Gain Ratio* criterion, and the GINI algorithm. To prune the trees, Bonsai uses the χ^2 method as described in Russell and Norvig [5]. Bonsai can also draw pictures of the trees it generates. All Decision Trees pictured in this paper were generated and drawn with Bonsai (Figures 2 and 3). Once a Decision Tree is grown, Bonsai translates the tree into a set of rules, and it can also produce a lift chart like the one shown in Figure 2 to measure the performance of the decision tree with test data.

Bonsai takes data as input in a text format separated by tabs, attributes have to be discrete for supervised learning, but they can be continuous for cluster analysis, so both capabilities can be used in tandem to discretize data first, and then do supervised learning.

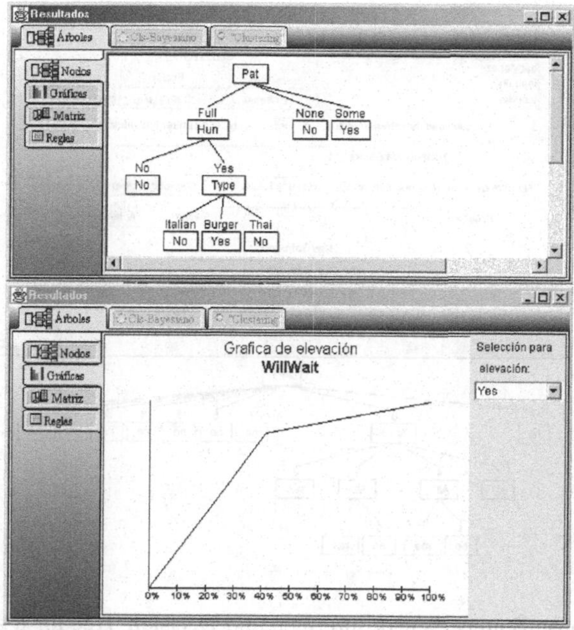

Fig. 2. Decision Tree and Lift Chart Generated by Bonsai.

Bonsai can also suggest a good number of clusters in K-means and fuzzy C-means Clustering (a good K, or C). We found empirically that this can be accomplished by minimizing the sum of square distances from the centroid of each cluster to each data point plus the sum of square distances from the center of mass of the complete data set to each cluster centroid.

BonsaiBouncer is the Keystroke Dynamics tool built using Bonsai's Data Mining algorithms, it uses a Naïve Bayesian Classifier, and the three different Decision Trees supported by Bonsai. BonsaiBouncer has a data gathering mode, an offline batch mode, and an online mode.

In the data gathering mode, the user types a string of characters, several times. BonsaiBouncer then measures the flight and dwell times in milliseconds for each of the keys typed and stores these in a data file. If the user makes a mistake, BonsaiBouncer ignores that observation, clears the field, and the user needs to type again the complete string.

The batch and online mode can only be used after an observation database has been created using the data gathering mode. To operate in the online mode the user identifies himself and types the same string used to create the observations database. BonsaiBouncer then discretizes all data, and each of the four BonsaiBouncer algorithms generates a user model from the observations database. Each of these models outputs a veredict as to whether the user is who he claims to be, the Decision Tree based models can only output a"yes" or a "no", but the Bayesian Classifier based model outputs a number between 0 and 1 representing the probability of "yes".

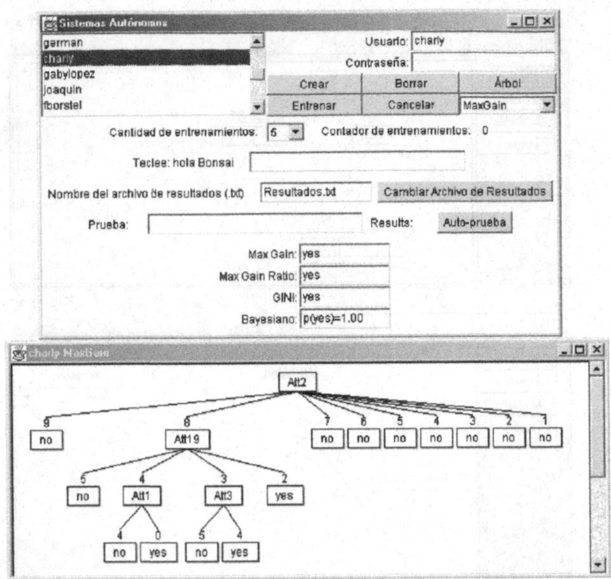

Fig. 3. BonsaiBouncer's user interface and Decision Tree for a specific user.

In the offline batch mode, BonsaiBouncer reads in previously recorded observations, and treats each one of these exactly as if it was the input from a user of the online mode. BonsaiBouncer then outputs to a file the results from each of the four user models for each observation.

A screenshot of BonsaiBouncer's user interface and a Decision Tree generated for a specific user is shown in Figure 3.

6 Experimental Results

We performed several experiments with BonsaiBouncer to test the effectiveness of Decision Trees in Keystroke Dynamics, and to compare different methods with each other. In addition to the Decision Tree and the Naïve Bayesian Classifier models used by BonsaiBouncer, we created a statistical model and an Instance Based Learning model in a spreadsheet. The statistical model was simply a deviation threshold rejection test, if the measured time for any of the keystrokes went beyond a variance threshold from the training data mean the user was rejected, and otherwise the user was accepted. The Instance Based Learning method we used was the 5-Nearest neighbors approach using an unweighted majority function, and the closest distance as the tie braker. If a user was classified as the same person he claimed to be he was accepted, otherwise he was rejected.

To collect data and build the observation database used in all the experiments, we asked 21 students to type the string "hola Bonsai" 20 times, discarding the first two observations of each user as "warm-ups", and randomly selecting 3

Table 1. BonsaiBouncer performance, comparision among several Decision Tree algorithms, the Naïve Bayesian Classifier, the statistical method, and Instance-Based Learning.

Method	Genuine User False Neg. (%)	Internal Imp. False Pos. (%)	External Imp. False Pos. (%)
D.T. Max Gain	42.9%	0.0%	4.8%
D.T. Max Gain Ratio	36.5%	3.2%	4.8%
D.T. GINI	42.9%	3.2%	3.2%
Bayes Classifier I	25.4%	3.2%	1.6%
Statistics I	44.4%	3.2%	1.6%
Bayes Classifier II	14.3%	4.8%	1.6%
Statistics II	39.7%	4.8%	1.6%
I. B. Learning	28.6%	4.8%	4.8%

observations per user to serve as test data, so we ended up with 15 observations per user in the model database. We then generated 3 test data sets; a set of "genuine users" who tried to login as themselves, a set of "internal impostors" whose data was in the model but tried to login as somebody else, and a set of "external impostors" whose data was not in the model at all and tried to login as somebody in the model. To collect the last data set we asked 8 more people to "train" the model without letting them know that their data was going to be used differently to that of the other users.

To test the different methods and report the results we ran all the models with the 3 test data sets, and measured the percentage of false negatives and false positives, that is, the percentage of genuine users that are erroneously prevented from logging in, and the percentage of impostors that are erroneously allowed to log in. We generated Receiver Operating Characteristic(ROC) curves for the Naïve Bayesian Classifier, and for the statistical method, but we only used a table for the Decision Tree and the Instance Based Learning methods. This was because the first two methods use a threshold that can be tuned to trade false positives for false negatives, so at different threshold levels the results are different, but the last two methods do not have that flexibility and produce only one result. To facilitate the comparison we included in the table two results from each of the threshold-based methods in the same range as the single-result methods.

To generate the decision tree and Bayesian classifier models we needed to discretize the data. We used Bonsai's K-Means Clustering capabilities to discretize in all the dwell and flight times of all the observations and to find a good number of discretization intervals. Bonsai found 8 clusters in the data and we used these as discretization intervals, with the midpoints between cluster centroids as interval boundaries. Once discretized, we used BonsaiBouncer to generate Decision Tree and Bayesian Classifier models to evaluate the 3 test data sets. The results of all the models are summarized in Table 1, and in the ROC curves for the Bayesian Classifier (Figure 4), and the statistic method (Figure 5).

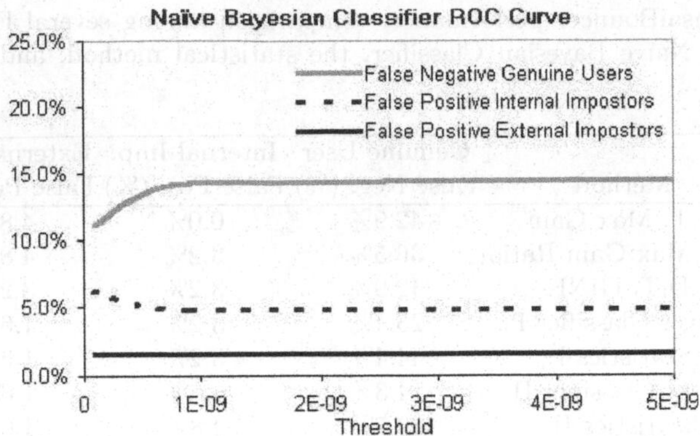

Fig. 4. ROC curve for the Naïve Bayesian Classifier.

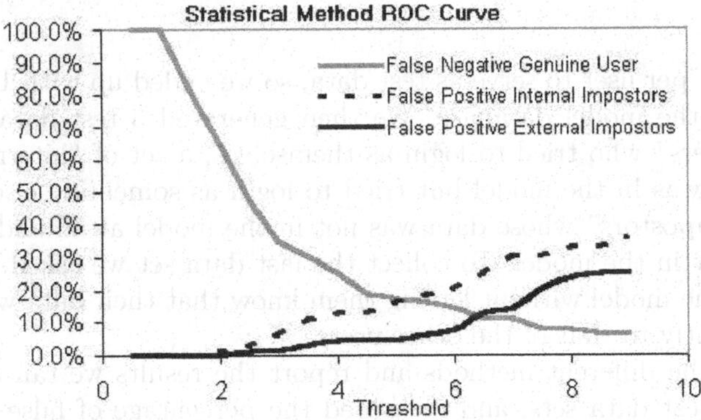

Fig. 5. ROC curve for statistics-based Keystroke Dynamics.

7 Conclusions and Future Work

From the experiment results we can see that the best performing method overall was the Bayesian Classifier. The variations between all the other methods are not large enough to warrant a distinction, and more data would have to be collected in order to observe a clear pattern of superiority from one method over the others. In particular we can see that the Decision Tree based methods are in the same range as the statistical method, but they do not have the flexibility of a threshold that the statistical method has. However, we can observe that the Decision Tree based methods tend to be more succesful at rejecting inside users than the statistical method. This result makes sense because Decision Tree algorithms try to differentiate between all the users in the training data, and actively exploit the differences between users as well as the similarities. This result suggests that statistics based approaches could benefit from integrating a Decision Tree approach in their calculations in order to prevent fraud from inside impostors.

For future work, we plan to integrate the statistics based approach and memory based learning into BonsaiBouncer and test the application with a larger data set. It would also be interesting to use all these techniques simultaneously with the goal of creating a system that performs better than any of the single techniques individually.

References

1. Biopassword: BioPassword Keystroke Dynamics. A white paper. Retrieved January 14th, 2002, from http://www.biopassword.com/home/technology
2. Duda, R., Hart, P.: Pattern Classification and Scene Analysis. John Wiley & Sons, Inc. (1973)
3. Gonick, L., *et al* : The Cartoon Guide to Statistics. HarperCollins Publishers (1993)
4. Monrose, F., Rubin, A.: Keystroke Dynamics as a Biometric for Authentication. (March 1999).
5. Norvig, P, Russell, S.: Artificial Intelligence: A Modern Approach. Prentice Hall, New Jersey (1995)
6. Poole, D., Mackworth, A., Goebel, R.: Computational Intelligence: A Logical Approach. Oxford University Press (1998)
7. Quinlan, J.R., Quinlan, R.R.: C4.5: Programs for Machine Learning. Morgan Kaufmann Publishers (1992)
8. Schmidt, C.(2000): KDD Instance Based Learning. Retrieved January 14th, 2002, from http://www.kddresearch.org/Groups/AI-CBR/IBL.ppt.
9. U. K. Government and Biometrics Working Group (2000): Best Practices in Testing and Reporting Biometric Device Performance, version 1.0 Retrieved January 14th, 2002, from http://www.afb.org.uk/bwg/bestprac10.pdf
10. Wang, Li-Xin: A Course in Fuzzy Systems and Control. Prentice Hall (1997)

Qualitative Systems Identification for Linear Time Invariant Dynamic Systems

Juan J. Flores and Nelio Pastor

División de Estudios de Postgrado
Facultad de Ingeniería Eléctrica
Universidad Michoacana de San Nicolás de Hidalgo
Morelia, México
{juanf,npastor}@zeus.umich.mx

Abstract. The problem of Systems Identification starts with a time-series of observed data and tries to determine the simplest model capable of exhibiting the observed behavior. This optimization problem searches the model from a space of possible models. In traditional methods, the search space is the set of numerical values to be assigned to parameters. In our approach we are constrained, and therefore limit the search space, to Linear Time-Invariant models. In this paper, we present the theory and algorithms to perform Qualitative Systems Identification for Linear Time Invariant Dynamic Systems. The methods described here are based on successive elimination of the components of the system's response. Sinusoidals of high frequencies are eliminated first, then their carrying waves. We continue with the process until we obtain a non-oscillatory carrier. At that point, we determine the order of the carrier. This procedure allows us to determine how many sinusoidal components, and how many exponential components are found in the impulse response of the system under study. The number of components determines the order of the system. The paper is composed of two important parts, the statement of some mathematical properties of the responses of Linear Time Invariant Dynamic Systems, and the proposal of a set of filters that allows us to implement the recognition algorithm.

1 Introduction

The problem of Systems Identification starts with a time-series of observed data and tries to determine the simplest model capable of exhibiting the observed behavior. This optimization problem searches the model from a space of possible models. In traditional methods, the search space is the set of numerical values to be assigned to parameters. In our approach we are constrained, and therefore limit the search space, to Linear Time-Invariant models.

The Systems Identification process can be decomposed in two steps: the first step called structural (or qualitative) identification, involves determining the qualitative features of the mechanism; once we know the nature of the mechanism, in the second step we proceed to determine the numerical value of the parameters of the model determined in the first step.

C.A. Coello Coello et al. (Eds.): MICAI 2002, LNAI 2313, pp. 470–477, 2002.

The problem we are assessing in this paper is that of Qualitative Systems Identification for Linear Time Invariant Dynamic Systems. This kind of systems can be represented by Linear ordinary Differential Equations with Constant Coefficients. Although this problem may seem over-constrained, there are many important problems in engineering and physics that can be expressed in mathematical terms by this kind of differential equations. We could even assess time-varying or even non-linear systems, if we consider them as piece-wise decomposed by linear approximations of the original systems. So, this is a limited yet interesting domain to start with.

We can roughly decompose the problem of Systems identification in two stages: qualitative and quantitative identification. The first part tries to determine the *shape* of the identified system. That is, the qualitative form of the system inside the black box. In the second part, given that we know the kind of system we are dealing with, we try to determine the numerical value of its parameters. This second part can be done by any optimization process (e.g. minimum square error [8,9], genetic algorithms [4,5,6,10,11], etc.). Some algorithms use an optimization process to determine both faces at the same time (e.g. genetic algorithms [2,7]).

Section 2 describes some properties of Linear Time-Invariant Dynamic Systems. These properties will be used in section 3 to define an algorithm capable of determining the structure of such a system. The process of determination of the structure of a system is performed by repeated elimination of components of the impulse response of the system. Finally, in section 4, we conclude our work and present the limitations and future work.

2 Linear Time-Invariant Dynamic Systems

As mentioned before, linear ODEs with constant coefficients are the most studied kind of differential equations; they have complete analytical solutions. Also, there is a good number of problems that can be described by this kind of equation, and more complicated cases can be reduced to one or several of these equations.

In this section, the theory of solution of linear ODEs with constant coefficients, and a qualitative interpretation is presented. The facts presented in this section are the basis for the framework developed and presented in the next section.

Consider the homogeneous nth-order ODE given in equation 1.

$$a_0 \frac{d^n x(t)}{dt^n} + a_1 \frac{d^{n-1} x(t)}{dt^{n-1}} + \cdots + a_{n-1} \frac{dx(t)}{dt} + a_n x(t) = 0 \tag{1}$$

where $a_0, \ldots, a_n$ are real constants.

The solution represents the behavior of the system in response to the forcing function and initial conditions $X(0), X'(0), ..., X^{(n)}(0)$.

It is quite natural to think of an exponential function as a candidate solution to that equation. Substituting $x = e^{rt}$ in equation 1 and factoring e^{rt} yields equation 2.

$$e^{rt}(a_0 r^n + a_1 r^{n-1} + \cdots + a_{n-1} r + a_n) = e^{rt} Z(r) \tag{2}$$

$x(t)$ is a solution of equation 2, for those values of r that satisfy the characteristic equation. i.e. the roots of polynomial $Z(r)$. The general solution of equation 1 is of the form:

$$x(t) = c_1 e^{r_1 t} + \cdots + c_n e^{r_n t} \tag{3}$$

We can see that the natural response of an nth-order system, is the sum of n exponential terms. One for each root of the characteristic equation of the ODE. If it has positive roots, the system is unstable, otherwise, it is stable. If the roots of the characteristic equation of the ODE are all real, the system's response is non-cyclic. If the characteristic equation has complex roots, they come in conjugate pairs, in which case, the general solution is still of the form of equation 3, only that each pair of complex roots $(r \pm i\omega)$ becomes an exponential sinusoidal function. This property is known as Euler's identity.

$$C_1 e^{(r+i\omega)t} + C_2 e^{(r-i\omega)t} = e^{rt}(A_1 \cos \omega t + A_2 \sin \omega t) \tag{4}$$

So, if we restrict the kind of systems we are to analyze to those that can be expressed by an nth-order ordinary differential equation with constant coefficients, we know the kind of responses we are to get. We can express the behavior of a system in terms of the exponential and sinusoidal components in the response. We define

$$E_n(t) = \sum_{1 \le i \le n} a_i e^{r_i t} \tag{5}$$

as a summation with at most n exponential terms, and

$$ES_n(t) = \sum_{1 \le i \le n} a_i e^{r_i t} \sin \omega_i t \tag{6}$$

as a summation of exponentially decreasing sinusoidal functions. Note that we are not interested in giving analytical solutions to the differential equation, but a qualitative description of its behaviors. That is, all possible different qualitative forms of the solution to equation 1.

Theorem 1 *Given a system of order n, the response can be expressed as in equation 7.*

$$X(t) = E_{n_1}(t) + ES_{n_2}(t) \tag{7}$$

where $n_1 + 2n_2 = n$. This result is evident from equation 3, equation 4, and the definitions of equations 5 and 6.

We see that if the second term of equation 7 does not exist, the response will be acyclic. Otherwise, it is a sinusoidal wave, where $E_{n_1}(t)$ represents its axis or attractor, and $ES_{n_2}(t)$ its sinusoidal components.

Note that if we include a forcing function, the system's response would be decomposed into Natural (the solution to the homogeneous equation) and Forced responses. If we restrict the forcing functions to be of the form $e^{\alpha t} \sin \beta t$ (i.e. constant, exponential, or sinusoidal), the forced response always has the same qualitative form as the forcing function [1]. This would preserve the qualitative form of the response, and only add one more exponential or sinusoidal term to the response.

Let us analyze the qualitative form of the responses, as expressed by eq. 7. This qualitative form can be derived from the qualitative form of its exponential and sinusoidal components. The qualitative behavior of the exponential part of the response is characterized by Theorem 2.

Theorem 2 $X(t) = E_n(t) = \sum_{1 \le i \le n} a_i e^{r_i t}$ *exhibits at most n extrema (maxima or minima), including the one when* $t \to \infty$.

We will assume, without loss of generality, that $r_1 > r_2 > \ldots > r_n$. Theorem 2 is equivalent to saying that the derivative $X'(t)$ has at most n different zeroes. That is,

$$\begin{aligned} X'(t) &= -c_1 a_1 e^{-r_1 t} - \ldots - c_n a_n e^{-r_n t} = 0 \\ &= c_1 a_1 e^{-r_1 t} + \ldots + c_n a_n e^{-r_n t} = 0 \end{aligned} \tag{8}$$

Case 1. Considering all a_i are positive integers, we perform the following variable change, $z = e^{-t}$, so equation 8 becomes

$$-X'(t) = c_1 a_1 z^{r_1} + \ldots + c_n a_n z^{r_n} = 0 \tag{9}$$

Equation 9 is a polynomial in z of degree r_1, which has at most $n = (r_1 - r_n)$ non-zero roots, plus one zero root. For the $z_i (i = 1, \ldots, r_1)$ non-zero roots of polynomial 9, satisfy equation 10

$$z_i = e^{-t_i} \Rightarrow t_i = -\ln z_i \tag{10}$$

From those n possible roots, we are interested in those that make $t_i \geq 0$, that is, $0 \leq z_i \leq 1$. In this particular case, the proposition is satisfied.

Case 2. Considering the r_i's are rational numbers with a common denominator d, that is, $r_i = \frac{i}{d}$. In this case, we can perform the variable change $z = e^{-t/d}$, so,

$$\begin{aligned} -X'(t) &= c_1 a_1 z^{k_1} + \ldots + c_n a_n z^{k_n} = 0 \\ &= c_1 k_1 z^{k_1} + \ldots + c_n k_n z^{k_n} = 0 \end{aligned} \tag{11}$$

Using the same reasoning procedure, we have at most $(k_1 - k_n + 1) = n$ real roots $z_i = e^{-t_i/d} \Rightarrow t_i = -d \ln zi$. Again, we are only interested in those roots that make $t_i \geq 0$, that is, $0 \leq z_i \leq 1$. Same result as in previous case.

Case 3. A similar reasoning procedure can be applied for the case where the a_i's are non-rational numbers.

As mentioned in [3], if the frequencies of the sinusoidal components of equation 7 are equal, their shapes are reduced to one. If their frequencies are different, they can be seen as the fastest sinusoidal mounted on the slowest one. If two frequencies of the sinusoidal components are very close together, the resulting wave beats.

The results presented in this section fully characterizes all possible responses of a LTI Dynamic System. In the next section we will describe how to use these results to produce a framework for performing Systems Identification at the qualitative level.

3 Identification Algorithm

The identification algorithm presented in this section is based on the fact (see equation 7) that the response of a LTI system can be decomposed in a sumation of exponential terms. If some of those exponential terms are complex, in which case they are conjugate complex pairs, each pair forms a sinusoidal. If we can think of an algorithm capable of separating the terms of Equation 7 we can determine the structure or qualitative form of the system exhibiting the observed behavior. Separating the terms of the system's response can be performed by a filtering process.

Assume the observation of the system includes a number of samples large and frequent enough to show all details of the system's behavior. If this assumption does not hold, we can miss important events that would not let us identify the system properly.

Also, assume the terms of equation 7 are sorted in order of increasing frequencies (i.e. $w_0 < w_1 < \ldots < w_n$), where the first n_1 of those terms are non-oscillatory exponentials, and are equivalent to a sinusoid of zero frequency. The filtering process eliminates each component at a time, starting by the component with the highest frequency. Each time we eliminate one sinusoidal component, the remainder contains the summation of all the previous components except the eliminated one.

$$X^*(t) = E_{n_1-1}(t) \tag{12}$$

The elimination of components continues until the rest of the signal is non-oscillatory.

The filtering process is based mainly in the evaluation of the derivative at each time point of the observed signal (i.e. the system's response). The points where the derivative is zero is where the extreme points are located. Once we locate the extreme points, we can approximate the attractor or carrier signal by finding the middle points between adjacent extrema. All computed middle points constitute the remainder of the signal. A spline approximation is used to smoothen the form of the carrier and has proven to provide better results than the bare filtered data. Figure 1 illustrates the procedure. Extremes are marked with plus signs and the computed middle points with asteriscs. The signal formed by the middle points constitutes the carrier of the original wave.

The algorithm is recursively applied until the remainder is non-oscillatory. In that case, it must be a summation of exponential terms, and we proceed to determine the degree of that summation (i.e. number of terms).

The algorithm in figure 2 uses the basic principle illustrated in figure 1 to implement the recursive filter. Figure 3 shows the successive application of the filtering procedure on a signal $x(t)$.

The current status on implementation is the following. The Systems Identification algorithm, including filters have been implemented using Matlab. In our implementation, the input is the observed signal, and the output is the structure of the black-box system.

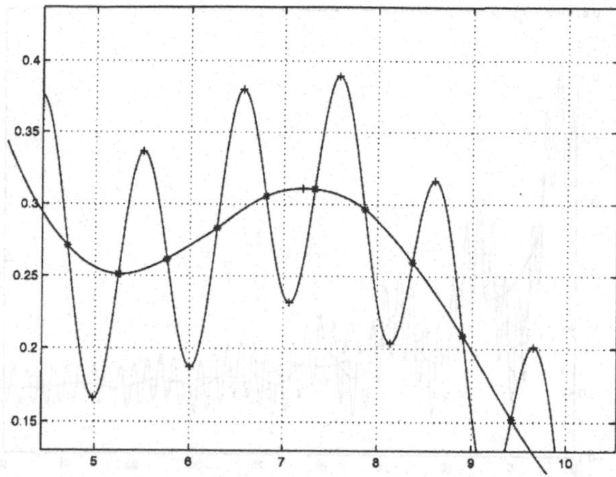

Fig. 1. Average Filtering

Filtering Algorithm

Determine maxima and minima of the signal
Compute the middle points between adjacent extrema
Trace the carrier wave (i.e. $x^*(t)$) by joining adjacent middle points
If the signal remainder is oscillatory, repeat the process
Otherwise, finish

Fig. 2. Filtering Algorithm

4 Conclusions

We have presented the analysis, algorithms, and implementation of a framework to perform Qualitative Systems Identification for Linear Time-Invariant Systems.

Once identified the structure of the system we send it to a parametric identification module to complete the identification process. The parametric identification part has been implemented using genetic algorithms, which have proven to be efficient.

The system has been successful in determining the sinusoidal components of different test systems we have fed it with. Nonetheless, the filters still need some work on the detection of non-oscillatory components. Since the middle points of a damped sinusoidal do not exactly match the carrier, when we join them, they present small oscillations even when we have removed all the oscilatory components. This fact has lead us to higher the order of the system by two in some cases.

An expression for the time complexity is also needed. We need to compare how our algorithm behaves with respect to traditional approaches.

Acknowlegements

This research has been supported by Conacyt grant No.31857A, and CIC-UMSNH grant No. 9.3

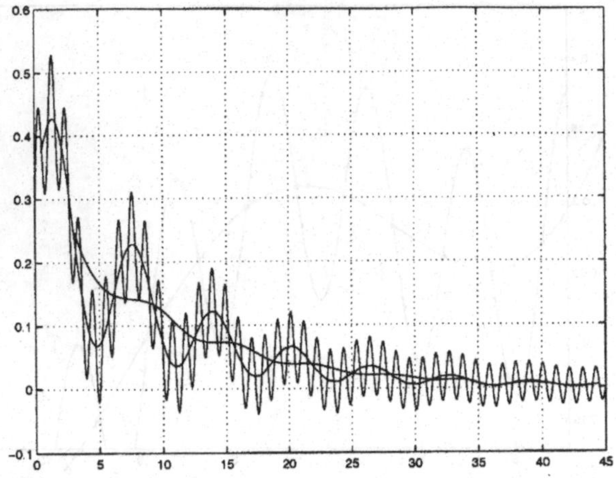

Fig. 3. Component Elimination Process

References

1. W.E. Boyce and R.C. DiPrima. *Elementary Differential Equations.* John Wiley, New York, second edition, 1969.
2. C.J. Downing, B. Byrne, K. Coveney, and W.P. Marnane. Controller optimisation and system identification using genetic algorithms. Technical report, Dept. of Electrical Engineering University College Cork., 1996.
3. Juan J. Flores and Art M. Farley. Reasoning about constant coefficient dynamic systems. In *Proc. 9th Int. Workshop on Qualitative Reasoning About Physical Systems,* Amsterdam, The Netherlands, May, 1995.
4. David E. Goldberg. *Genetic Algorithms in Search, Optimization, and Machine Learning.* Addison Wesley, Boston, 1998.
5. Randy L. Haupt and Sue Ellen Haupt. *Practical Genetic Algorithms.* Wiley Interscience, New York, 1998.
6. K.J. Hunt. Black-box and partially known system identification with genetic algorithms. In *European Control Conference*, Savoy Place, London WC2R 0BL, UK, 1993.
7. K. Kristinsson and G.A. Dumont. System identification and control using genetic algorithms. *IEEE Trans. Syst. Man Cybern.*, 22(5):1033–1046, 1992.
8. Lenart Ljung. *System Identification: Theory for the user.* Prentice-Hall, Englewood Cliffs, NJ, 1987.
9. Soderstrom T. Stoica P. *System Identification.* Prentice Hall, USA, 1989.
10. Nelio Pastor. Identificacion de sistemas dinamicos utilizando algoritmos geneticos. Master's thesis, School of Electrical Engineering, University of Michoacan, Morelia, Mexico, 2000.
11. Fazel Naghdy Zang Zibo. *Application of Genetic Algorithms to System Identification.* Departament of Electrical and Computer Engineering University of Wollogong, Australia, 1987.

Monitoring the Execution of an Intelligent Planning System

José Guillermo Valdéz and Pablo H. Ibargüengoytia

Instituto de Investigaciones Eléctricas
Av. Reforma 113, Palmira
Temixco, Mor., 62490, México
valdez_pepe@hotmail.com, pibar@iie.org.mx

Abstract. Applying intelligent planning in most real applications requires the separation between a plan generator agent and an execution agent. This paper presents the development of an execution monitoring agent for a dynamic planner that has been developed for assistance of an operator in a power plant. A brief description of the dynamic planner is presented together with a description of the representation language utilized. This language is inspired in the SRI's ACT formalism. The execution agent receives a plan and notifies the operator the actions required for a given state of the process and certain given goals. The main contribution of the paper is the conversion from the ACT formalism to a Petri net for robust and efficient monitoring.

1 Introduction

Intelligent planning is one area of artificial intelligence (AI) that has been influenced by the increasing demand of applications in real problems. Historically, different planning programs have been developed for different scenarios according to the target problem and the assumptions taken [1].

The scenario considered in this work takes into account the context of the world, where changes are dynamic and continuous. In this kind of planning, called continual planning systems, the separation of the generator and executor agent is necessary. Here, a plan generation is continuously made and if faults or deviations from the expected behavior are detected, a new plan is designed. This kind of planers requires a knowledge representation in several layers of abstraction in order to produce short-term plans continuously. The plans are issued and the monitoring agent supervises if the expected effects of the suggested actions are meet.

This paper discusses the design of the monitoring agent (MA) as part of an intelligent planning system for a real and continuous application, namely the assistance to the operator during special maneuvers of the operation of a power plant [4]. These maneuvers include for example, the start up phase, the programmed stop, or changes in the load. The maneuvers are composed by several actions that the operator executes, e.g., closing valves, starting pumps, opening switches, etc. The state of the process is obtained utilizing sensors and other sources of information like personnel reports.

C.A. Coello Coello et al. (Eds.): MICAI 2002, LNAI 2313, pp. 477–485, 2002.

The plan generating agent provides a plan. The MA accesses the state of the plant so it can generate messages for a graphical user interface (GUI) in order to display the commands advised to the operator.

The following section briefly reviews some related work in the international community. Next, section 3 describes the representation language selected in this project. Section 4 introduces the Petri nets mechanism utilized in the implementation of the MA. Section 5 describes the proposed monitoring agent and presents the conversion between plots and Petri nets. Section 6 describes an application example and section 7 concludes the paper.

2 Related Work

There are several international communities working in the intelligent planning area. Some are specially working in representation languages that can be used in the description of different procedures. Other groups are working in dynamic and continuous planning systems for real world applications.

In the representation language area, the Process Specification Language (PSL) [6] represents a great effort in the design of a language for express process information. PSL is an interchange format designed to help exchange process information automatically among a wide variety of manufacturing and business applications such as process modeling, process planning, scheduling, simulation and project management. However, the domain application tackled in this project requires the description of very specific actions and procedures in the continuous and dynamic processes in the power generation industry.

Several intelligent planning systems have been developed for real applications. The interest in this project are the distributed and continuous planning systems [1]. One example is the work carried out in the NASA's Jet Propulsion Laboratory [5]. One of their applications is the assistance of an operator for tracking antennas for deep space communication [2] and other NASA's space operations [3]. An important contribution of this group is its actions representation language. This language expresses temporal relations restricted between different activities in the corresponding process. Addiitionally, different hierarchy levels can be used in the expression of the activities. Also for NASA, Williams and Nayak [11] developed a reactive planner for a model-based executive. This is a hybrid system that combines a classical planner and a model-based mechanism that provides an appropriate capability to generate responses to anomalous situations.

The Stanford Research Institute (SRI) focuses its work in distributed and continuous planning, where several agents generate and execute their plans following a common goal. They are the developers of the ACT formalism [7], i.e., a framework and representation language capable of exchange knowledge between the plan generating agent and the plan execution agent. Their main application is in the military operations planning where the plan is generated by the automatic system, the actions are commanded by human agents and the execution is carried out by machines [8].

```
(TG1G
  (environment
    (cue (achieve(turbine1 generating)))
    (preconditions (test(turbine1 stand-by))))
  (plot
    (tg1gi (type conditional)
     (orderings (next tg1g1)))
    (tg1g1 (type conditional)
     (achieve (switch-generator-tg1 closed))
     (orderings (next tg1gf))
    (tg1gf (type conditional))))
```

Fig. 1. An example of an ACT.

3 Representation Language

After the revision of the work in the international community, the *ACT* formalism developed at the Stanford Research Institute (SRI) was chosen as the representational language [7]. By definition, an ACT describes a set of actions that can be executed in order to achieve an established purpose in certain conditions. The following example shows how a typical piece of expert knowledge can be represented in one ACT.

> The conversion between a gas turbine in rotating mode to the turbine in generating mode can be obtained closing the field generator switch.

Here, the purpose is to get the gas turbine in the generating mode. This can be achieved if the environment conditions include the gas turbine in the rotating mode. The action that is executed consists in closing the field generator switch. In general, the actions are all those atomic operations than can be executed in the plant by the operator or his/her personnel, e.g., close a switch. The purpose is the condition that will be present in the process when the actions have been executed. The conditions refer to the state of the process that must be present before the actions can be executed.

Syntactically, an ACT is formed by the following three elements:

name: a unique ID for the ACT,

environment: a set of goal expressions that define the environment conditions that hold before and after an ACT is executed,

plot: a network of activities where the nodes represent the atomic activities that need to be executed to complete the ACT goal. The arcs of the network represent temporal relations between the different activities.

The plot can be seen as the lowest level of abstraction of the activities carried out in the control of the plant. An example of an ACT is shown in the Fig. 1.

The elements of the *plot* section are the representation of a network. The syntax of the nodes includes a name, a type, the action, the ordering and other elements. The type can be *conditional* or *parallel*. In the parallel node, all the

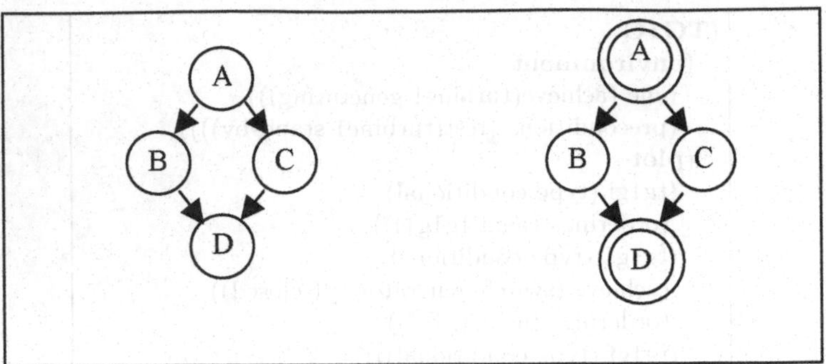

Fig. 2. Graphical representation of two ACTs' plots.

trajectories that include that node must be executed, while in the conditional node, just one of the paths can be executed. The *orderings* field indicates the temporal order in which the action must be executed. In the example of Fig. 1, there is an arc from node *tg1gi* to the node *tg1g1*. The conditional nodes are usually represented by a single circle and the parallel nodes by double circles. Figure 2 shows two simple representation of the plot section in two different ACTs. In the left plot, after executing the conditional node A, either node B or node C can be executed and finally node D. Thus, two different sequences can be followed: **A-B-D** or **A-C-D**. In the right plot, after executing the parallel node A, both B and C nodes must be executed. Later, when both nodes finish, then the node D is executed. The activities corresponding to node D cannot start until activities of nodes B and C are finished. Activities corresponding to nodes B and C can be executed in parallel or in any order. For more information about this formalism, consult [7].

A complete plan consists in the concatenation of the plot section of all the ACTs in the plan. This concatenation is called the **intention graph**.

4 Petri Nets

Given the intention graph formed by the concatenation of the plot nodes of the selected ACTs, a mechanism to schedule the set of actions is required. The Petri nets (PN) are considered a natural mechanism to model the structure and behavior of a dynamic process. The PN were defined by Karl Adam Petri in 1962 [9]. Compared with other graphic approaches to model dynamic behavior, like finite states machines, the PN allow expressing processes that require synchrony, concurrency, decisions and exclusion. Besides, the PN represent a mathematical formalism that is utilized in the analysis of the dynamic behavior of the system.

The PN are directed graphs formed by the tuple $PN = \{P, T, Pre, Post\}$ where $P = \{p_1, \ldots, p_n\}$ is a non-empty, finite set of node elements called *places*. A place represents a state that the system may be in. $T = \{t_1, \ldots, t_n\}$ is a non-empty, finite set of elements called transitions. Each transition has zero or more input arcs, coming from its input places, and zero or more output arcs, going

- Take the first node in the plot and create the first node in the PN
- For every node n in the plot:
  - if the node n is parallel:
    * generate a transition t such that $Pre(t) = \{n\}$,
    * make $Post(t) = \{all\ children\ nodes\ of\ n\}$,
    * form a unique transition t_n from all the transitions whose *Post* function is n.
  - if the node n is conditional:
    * generate a transition t for every child node of n,
    * make $Post(t) = \{all\ children\ nodes\ of\ n\}$,

Fig. 3. An example of an ACT.

to its output places. *Pre* is a function that represents the input arcs and *Post* represent the output arcs of the transitions. A *token* is the dynamic element in the PN. The number of tokens can vary between the nodes and they determine the situation of the network at a given time. The tokens reside in the nodes and move between them.

The graphic representation of the PN can be seen at the right side of Fig. 4. Nodes are circles and transitions are rectangles. The *Pre* and *Post* functions are represented by the input or output arrows in or from transitions. The tokens are represented by dots in the nodes (not shown in Fig. 4). For example, the complete description of the PN shown in Fig. 4 is the following:

$$
\begin{aligned}
P &= \{p_1, p_2, p_3, p_4, p_5, p_6, p_7\} \\
T &= \{t_1, t_2, t_3, t_4\} \\
Pre(t_1) &= \{p_1\},\ Pre(t_2) = \{p_2\},\ Pre(t_3) = \{p_3\},\ Pre(t_4) = \{p_3\} \\
Post(t_1) &= \{p_2, p_3, p_4\},\ Post(t_2) = \{p_5\},\ Post(t_3) = \{p_6\},\ Post(t_4) = \{p_7\}
\end{aligned}
$$

The number and distribution of the tokens present in the network control the execution of a PN. A PN is activated when a transition is triggered. A transition is triggered when it is sensitized, i.e., there exist at least the same number of tokens in the input nodes than input arcs to the transition. The transition trigger consists in the creation of tokens in the output nodes of the transition and the removal of tokens from the input nodes to that transition.

5 Monitoring Agent

The MA carries out two main functions. First, the conversion between the intention graph to a PN. Second, the navigation of the resulting network [10].

Structurally, the plot network and a PN are similar. A conversion from every plot network in a PN will allow controlling the execution of all the tasks presented, in the sequence defined by the knowledge engineer. The algorithm proposed for this conversion is shown in Fig. 3.

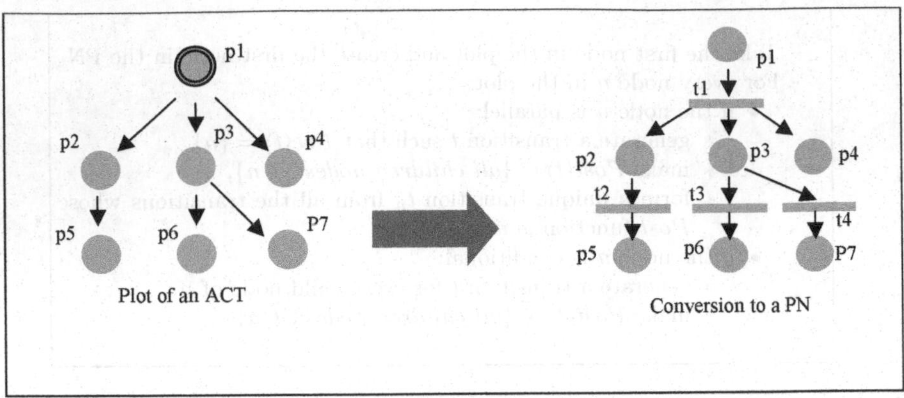

Fig. 4. Example of the conversion from plot to Petri net.

Figure 4 shows the conversion between a plot and the resultant PN. Notice that $p1$ is a parallel node that creates transition $t1$. The $Post(t1)$ are the nodes $p2$, $p3$, and $p4$.

The PN is executed following the next procedure.

- The MA marks the first node in the PN and creates a Java thread for each marked node.
- The thread assigned to each node has three main functions:
  1. issues a message to the operator (through the GUI) with the corresponding action,
  2. assesses the effects of that action, and
  3. verifies for the maximum execution time of that action. The knowledge engineer gives the execution time at ACT edition time.

Figure 5 shows a data flow diagram of the execution of the MA.

The MA constantly verifies the state of all the transitions in the PN. When all its input nodes finish their execution, then the transition is triggered and the marks of the input nodes are removed, and the output nodes (if any) are marked and executed. This operation is made cyclically until all the nodes in the intention graph have been executed, or an error is detected. In case of an error, then the MA solicits a new plan to the generating agent and the process starts again.

6 Application Example

The system was developed in a first prototype, and was tested with a simple case. This is, the configuration of the equipment of a combined cycle power plant that the operator must establish given a specific load.

A combined cycle power plant consists mainly in four equipments: the gas turbine, the heat recovery steam generator (HRSG), the steam turbine and the

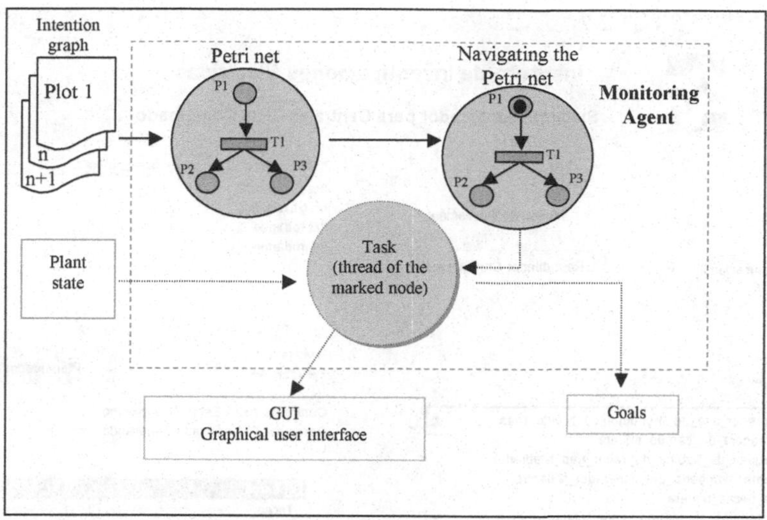

Fig. 5. Data flow diagram for the MA.

generators. There is usually one generator per turbine. The gas turbine receives air and gas in a specific proportion to produce high pressure gases at high temperature. These gases produce the rotation that moves the generator corresponding to this turbine. After producing mechanical work, the gases are still at very high temperature, so that energy can still be exploited. The gases are introduced to the heat recovery that, sometimes with the assistance of extra burners called after burners, produces steam from the feed-water system. After the steam is superheated, it is introduced to the steam turbine to convert the energy carried out by the steam in work and finally, in electricity through the corresponding steam generator. This plant is called combined cycle since there are two types of generators combined to produce the complete unit power. All these equipments can be in different working modes: cold, hot stand by, running and generating. To reach a specific goal, the operator must set to certain mode certain equipment in the plant. For example, to reach a load of 100 %, the unit must have their two gas turbines in generating mode, the two HRSG with their burners operating and the steam turbine also in the generating mode. The plan provided to the operator is the activities that he/she must execute to pass all equipment to the generating mode in the correct sequence. It is not possible to start the HRSG before the gas turbines for example. However, to reach 60 % of load, the operator can have two gas turbines and one steam turbine without after burners, or this load can also be reached with two gas turbines alone.

Figure 6 shows one view of the system's screen when the prototype is working (in Spanish).

In the left side there is a window with the configuration that the user of the prototype can establish, i.e., the value of the main variables. In the right part of the screen, there is a window with the current state of the plant. Next, the user

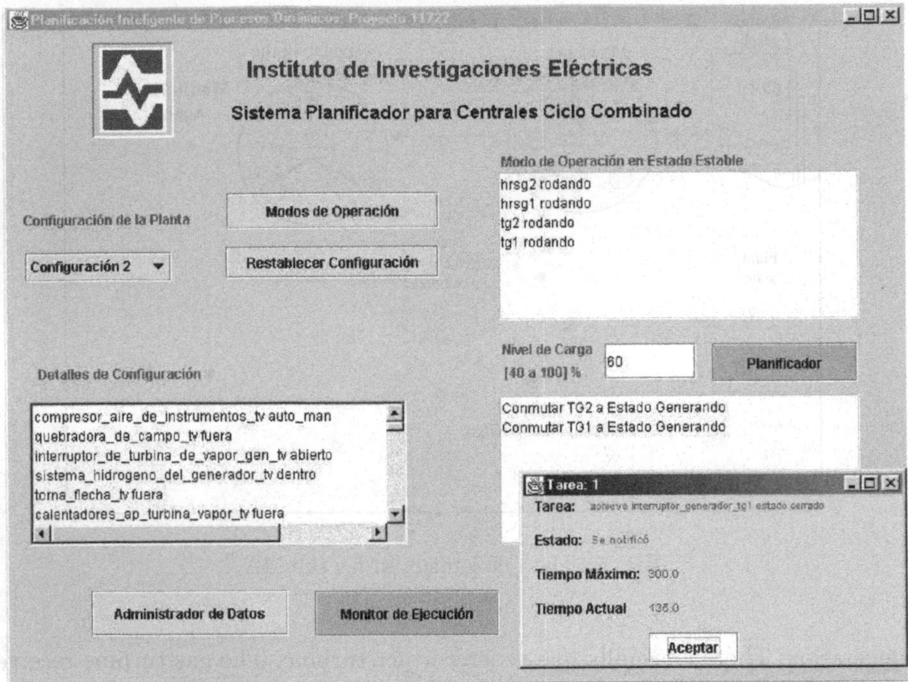

Fig. 6. Example of the operator interface to the system.

can set the required goal as a percentage of the base load of the plant. Thus, with all this information, a plan is generated. This plan is shown as a list of the identifiers of the ACTs that have to be executed. Finally, a small window at the lower right shows the concurrent thread that the monitor just created when an action has to be executed by the operator. This thread window shows the advised action, the current time and the maximum time allowed for the execution of this action.

Experiments were carried out in this simple domain combining different goals under different initial configurations of the plant. Also, additional experiments with simulated intention graphs, with more complex structures have been implemented. The results have shown that the Petri net navigation corresponds exactly to the monitoring function in an intelligent planning system. The system was written in Java under windows 2000 work station.

7 Conclusions

This paper has presented the design of a monitoring agent in a dynamic planning system. The system is being utilized for the support of an operator of a thermoelectric power plant. The system helps an operator in the decisions that he/she has to take in response to special maneuvers in the process of generating energy. The monitoring agent receives a plan from a planning generating agent and converts it to a Petri net in order to control the execution of the plan. Petri nets have proved to be an appropriate mechanism to control the behavior of dynamic real time systems. The conversion between the plot and the PN is carried out at the parser time, when the knowledge is captured in the ACT formalism.

Two main aspects form the contribution of the monitoring agent for plan execution. First, an algorithm to convert the plot in a Petri net has been presented. Second, a procedure to navigating the PN has been used to schedule the execution of the plan [10].

Acknowledgments

This research work is supported by the IIE, infrastructure project 11984, and the grant 35082-A from CONACYT.

References

1. M.E. desJardins, C.L. Ortiz E.H. Durfee, and M.J. Welverton. A survey research in distributed, continual planning. *AI Magazine*, 20(4):13–22, 1999.
2. F. Fisher, T. Estlin, D. Mutz, and S. Chien. Using artificial intelligence planning to generate antenna tracking plans. In *Proc. 11 Annual Conference on Innovative Applications of Artificial Intelligence (IAAI-99)*, Orlando, Fl., U.S.A., 1999. IAAI.
3. A.S. Fukunaga, G. Rabideau, S. Chien, and D. Yan. Aspen: A framework for automated planning and schedulling of spacecraft control and operations. In *Proc. International Symposium on AI, Robotics and Automation in Space (i-SAIRAS)*, Tokio, Japan, 1997.
4. Pablo H. Ibargüengoytia and Alberto Reyes. Continuous planning for the Operation of power plants. In P. Noriega C. Zozaya, M. Mejía and A. Sánchez, editors, *Proc. ENC-01 Encuentro Internacional de Ciencias de la Computación*, pages 199–208, Aguascalientes, Ags., México, 2001.
5. Russell Knight, Gregg Rabideau, Steve Chien, Barbara Engelhardt, and Rob Sherwood. Casper: Space exploration through continuous planning. *IEEE Inteligent Systems*, 16(5):70–75, 2001.
6. Amy Knutilla, Craig Schlenoff, Steven Ray, Stephen T. Polyak, Austin Tate, Shu Chiun Cheah, and Richard C. Anderson. Process specification language: An analysis of existing representations. Technical Report NISTIR 6160, National Institute of Standards and Technology, Gaithersburg, MD, USA, 1998.
7. K.L. Myers and D.E. Wilkins. The act formalism", version 2.2b. Technical report, SRI International Artificial Intelligence Center, 1997.
8. K.L. Myers. Cpef a continuous planning and execution framework. *AI Magazine*, 20(4):63–69, 1999.
9. C.A. Petri. Communication with automata. Technical Report RADC-TR-65-377, Rome Air Dev. Center, New York, NY, USA, 1966.
10. José G. Valdez. *Desarrollo de un monitor de ejecución para un planificador inteligente*. Tesis de licenciatura, Instituto Tecnológico de Tuxtla Gutiérrez, Chiapas, México, May 2001.
11. Brian C. Williams and P. Pandurang Nayak. A reactive planner for a model based executive. In *Proc. International Joint Conf. on Artificial Intelligence*. IJCAI, 1997.

A Structural Model of ECA Rules in Active Database

Xiaoou Li, Joselito Medina Marín, and Sergio V. Chapa

Sección de Computación, Departamento de Ingenieria Eléctrica, CINVESTAV-IPN, Av.IPN 2508, A.P. 14-740, Col. Zacatenco, México D.F., 07360, México
email: lixo@cs.cinvestav.mx

Abstract. Active database systems have been developed for applications needing an automatic reaction in response to certain conditions being satisfied or certain event occurring. The desired behavior is expressed by ECA-rules (event-condition-action rules). Generally, ECA rules and their execution are represented by rule language, for example, defining TRIGGERs in an active database. Then, database behavior prediction or analysis can be realized through other approaches such as algebraic approach, trigger graph methods, etc.. Therefore, in such active databases, rule representation and processing are separated. In this paper we propose a structural model which integrates rule representation and processing entirely, it is called Conditional Colored Petri Net (CCPN). CCPN can model both rules themselves and their complicated interacting relation in an graphical way. If the rule base of an active database is modeled by CCPN, then rule simulation can be done. An example is illustrated in the paper.

Keywords: active database, ECA rules, colored Petri net

1 Introduction

Traditional database management system (DBMS) stores data and information passively, and we just can perform actions implicit either by user programs or through interactive interfaces. In contrast, active database manager systems (ADBMS) have an active behavior. ADBMS not only stored data and information, also reacts to events and carry out actions according to these events (such as insert data, delete data, update data, etc.). Active database behavior is achieved through definition of *Event-Condition-Action* (ECA) rules as part of the database. Occurrence of events triggers the evaluation of a *condition* and if the condition evaluates to be true, then the *action* is executed [1], [2].

Active database systems are very powerful, but developing even small active rule applications can be a difficult task due to the unstructured and unpredictable nature of rule processing. During rule processing, rules can trigger and untrigger each other, and the intermediate and final states of the database can depend upon which rules are triggered and executed in which order. We say ECA rules execution is indeterministic, asynchronous, concurrent, parallel, etc. These features make it difficult to find a formal model for ECA rules execution and

C.A. Coello Coello et al. (Eds.): MICAI 2002, LNAI 2313, pp. 486–493, 2002.

analysis. For these reasons, rule languages or query languages are most widely adopted in existing ADBMSs.

In almost all ADBMSs, the description of rules refers to how rules themselves are normally expressed using a database programming language, a query language, or as objects in an object-oriented database. Furthermore, programmer support is of paramount importance if active rules are to be adopted as a mainstream implementation technology in business environments. Important facilities for supporting the developers of rule bases include the ability to query the rule base and to trace or in some other way monitor rule system behavior. This means that several different models are needed for rule representation and processing. These approaches have disadvantages like the existence of redundant rule data and the need for combining all models.

In this paper we develop an extended colored Petri net model in which rules can be represented, analyzed, and processed entirely. Furthermore, the model can be extended to be useful in temporal, object-oriented and other database systems. As to our knowledge, few researchers use Petri net theory in advanced database systems for rule processing [3],[4], [5],[6]. The most interesting one is [3]. The authors proposed an Action Rule Flow Petri Net (ARFPN) model, and a workflow management system was illustrated to verify the ARFPN model. However, their model has much redundant structure because of using many BEGIN OFs, END OFs to describe events, conditions and actions. In our approach this drawback will be overcome by using conditional transitions.

2 Active Database Systems

An active database management system integrates event-based rule processing with traditional database functionality. Generally, an *event-condition-action* rule has the following structure:

on event
if condition
then action 1
else action 2

When there are changes in the database an event occurs, then one or more rules may be triggered. Once a rule fires, the conditions of this rule are checked and if the conditions are satisfied, the actions of the rule are executed.

Active rule processing syntax includes two models: knowledge model and execution model. Knowledge model indicates what can be said about active rules in that system. Knowledge model essentially supports the description of active functionality, the features dealt with in this model often have a direct representation within the syntax of rule language.

Execution model specifies how a set of rules is treated at runtime. Although the execution model of a rule system is closely related to aspects of the underlying DBMS (e.g., data model, transaction manager), there are number of phases in rule evaluation, illustrated in Fig. 1, and are the follows [1]:

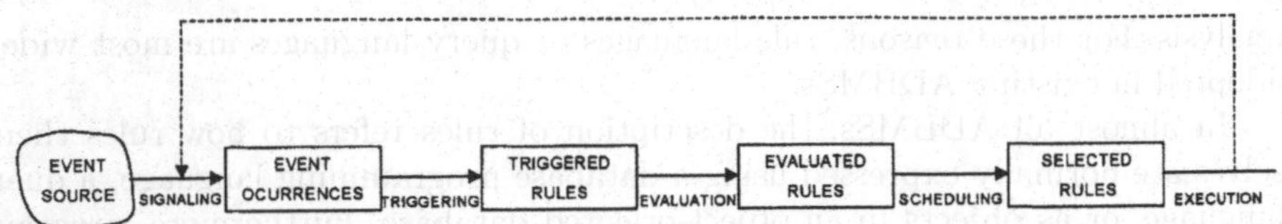

Fig. 1. Principal steps that take place during rule execution.

Signaling, it refers to the occurrence of an event caused by an event source.
Triggering, fires a rule when an event specified in this rule takes place.
Evaluation, verify the conditions of the triggered rules.
Scheduling, determines what happens when multiple rules are triggered at the same time.
Execution, carries out the actions of the triggered rule.

It is not easy to monitor ECA rules execution based on rule language. However, if a formal model is developed to represent all rules in the rule base and their relations, then the management of ADBMS could be abstracted to operations or processes based on this model. Therefore, the management complexity of an ADBMS system will be greatly reduced. The objective of our research is to develop such a model which can both describe all above three features and reveal the structural relation between ECA rules.

3 Conditional Colored Petri Net

Petri Nets are a graphical and mathematical tool for modeling concurrent, asynchronous, distributed, parallel, indeterministic, and/or stochastic systems. Petri net may be extended widely and applied in every area with logic relations. Colored Petri net is suitable for systems in which communication, synchronization and resource sharing are important. ECA rule can be modeled by colored Petri nets such as in [3]. However, there exists much redundant Petri net structure for using "begin of", "end of" events, conditions and actions.

In order to express clearly and exactly the three components of an ECA rule, we need to analyze ECA rule execution again. When an ECA rule is executed, event detection is a process to get a result 0 or 1 (represent the event is detected or not), therefore, it is more convenient to model it as a place of Petri net. If the detection result is 1, then a token is deposited into this place. On the other hand, an action of one rule maybe an event of another rule, i.e., The conjunction of the set of actions and events is not empty. Modeling actions as places also obey human cognition. The condition part of an ECA rule will be evaluated after event detection, so it should be expressed by a downstream of the place representing the event. We can use a conditional transition to model it. If there are tokens in each upstream place, then the condition attached on the transition will be evaluated, then the transition fires provided the condition is completed. Our idea may be represented by a simple Petri net like Fig. 2

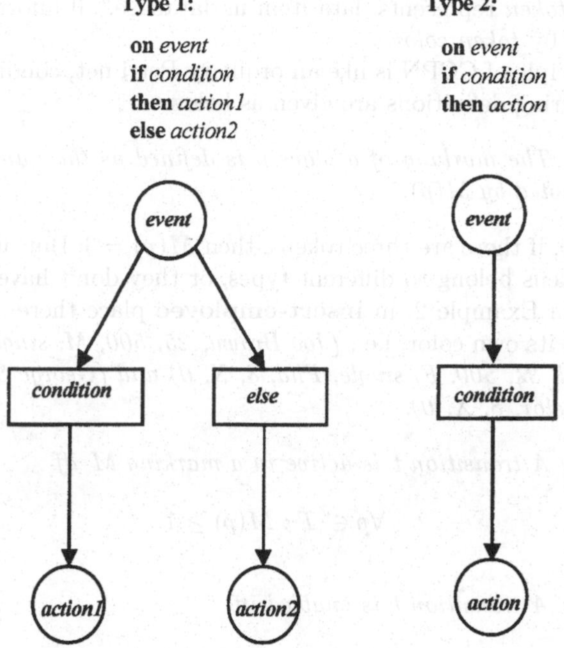

Fig. 2. A simple Peri net explaination of two types of ECA rules

Based on above analysis, we give formal definitions of Conditional Colored Petri Net model (CCPN).

Definition 1. *A conditional colored Petri net is a tuple*

$$CPN = \{\Sigma, P, T, A, N, C, Cond, E, I\}$$

where

Σ is a finite set of non-empty **types** or color sets.
P is a finite set of **places**.
T is a finite set of **transitions**.
A is a finite set of **arcs**, such that

$$P \cap T = P \cap A = T \cap A = \Phi.$$

N is a **node** function. It is defined from A into $P \times T \cup T \times P$.
C is a **color** function. It is defined from P into Σ.
Cond is a **condition** function. It is defined from T into expressions such that

$$\forall t \in T : Cond(t) = \mathbb{B}(Var(Con(t))).$$

I is an initialization function. It is defined from P into closed expressions such that

$$\forall p \in P : [Type(I(p)) = C(p)_{MS}].$$

In CCPN, *token* represents data item in database, all information of a data item is carried by *token color.*

Firing principle of CCPN is like an ordinary Petri net, conditional transition enabling and firing definitions are given as below.

Definition 2. *The marking of a place p is defined as the number of tokens in that place. denoted by $M(p)$.*

In a place p, if there are three tokens, then $M(p) = 3$. But, it is possible that these three tokens belong to different types, or they don't have the same color. For example, in Example 2, in **insert-employee** place there are three tokens, each token has its own color, i.e., *(Joe Brown, 25, 500, M, single, Master, 8, X, 0), (Susan Hill, 34, 500, F, single, Phd, 8, X, 0) and (George Star, 30, 500, M, married, Bachelor, 8, X, 0).*

Definition 3. *A transition t is active in a marking M iff*

$$\forall p \in^{\cdot} T : M(p) \geq 1.$$

Definition 4. *A transition t is enabled iff*

- t is active;
- $Cond(t) = 1$.

If t is enabled, token transition may be made. The token transition process is the same as in an ordinary Petri net, remove one token from each upstream place and add one token to each downstream place. However, the token color added to the downstream will correspond to the *action* in the rule. for example, in Fig.3, the transition **t1** is enabled for the token *(Susan Hill, 34, 500, F, single, Phd, 8, X, 0)* in place **p1**, after **t1** fires, the token *(Susan Hill, 34, 500, F, single, Phd, 8, X, 0)* will be removed from the place **p1**, a new token *(Susan Hill, 34, 750, F, single, Phd, 8, "A", 0)* will be added to the downstream place **p2**.

4 An Example

Example 1. There are 6 rules in an active database.

Rule 1

on insert employee
if e.degree = "Phd"
then modify e.status = "A" and e.salary = e.salary * 1.50

Rule 2

on insert employee
if e.degree = "Master"
then modify e.status = "B" and e.salary = e.salary * 1.25

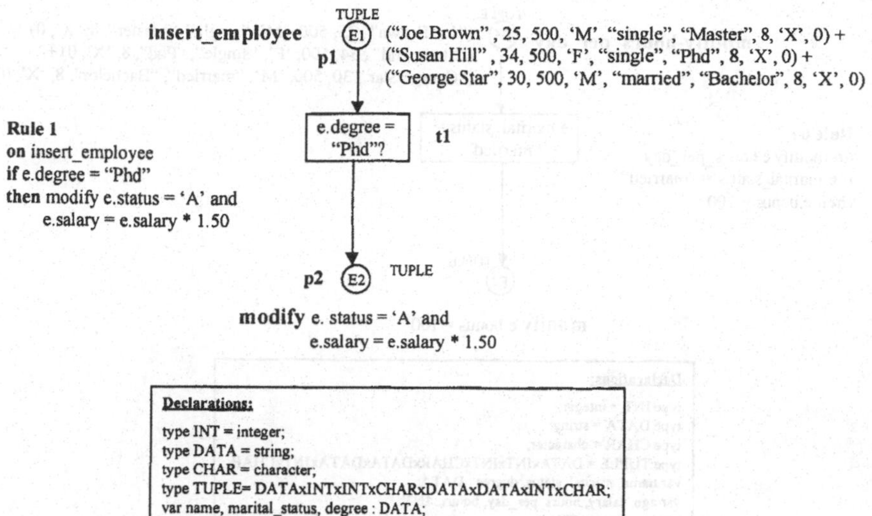
Tuple : (name, age, salary, sex, marital_status, degree, hours per day, status, bonus)
TUPLE
insert_employee
E1
p1
("Joe Brown" , 25, 500, 'M', "single", "Master", 8, 'X', 0) +
("Susan Hill" , 34, 500, 'F', "single", "Phd", 8, 'X', 0) +
("George Star", 30, 500, 'M', "married", "Bachelor", 8, 'X', 0)
Rule 1
on insert_employee
if e.degree = "Phd"
then modify e.status = 'A' and
e.salary = e.salary * 1.50
e.degree = "Phd"?
t1
p2
E2
TUPLE
modify e. status = 'A' and
e.salary = e.salary * 1.50
Declarations:
type INT = integer;
type DATA = string;
type CHAR = character;
type TUPLE= DATAxINTxINTxCHARxDATAxDATAxINTxCHAR;
var name, marital_status, degree : DATA;
var age, salary, hours_per_day, bonus : INT;
var sex, status : CHAR;

Fig. 3. CCPN model of Rule 1

Rule 3

on insert employee
if e.degree = "Bachelor"
then modify e.status ="C" and e.salary = e.salary * 1.10

Rule 4

on insert employee
if e.salary > manager.salary
then modify e.salary = manager.salary-100

Rule 5

on insert employee
if e.sex = "F"
then modify e.hours_per_day = e.hours_per_day - 2

Rule 6

on modify e.hours_per_day
if e.marital_status = "married"
then e.bonus = 100

Note that this example is constructed by the authors, such problems as inconsistence may exist. Here we just want to illustrate the developed CCPN model. In fact, such problems could be resolved by PN based analysis or other approaches, which is not the content of this paper.

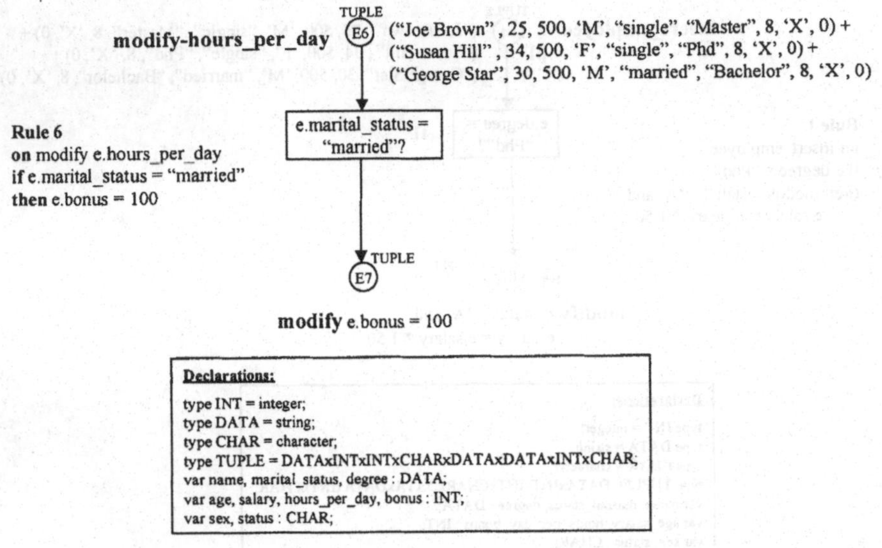
Tuple : (name, age, salary, sex, marital_status, degree, hours per day, status, bonus)
modify-hours_per_day
TUPLE
E6
("Joe Brown", 25, 500, 'M', "single", "Master", 8, 'X', 0) +
("Susan Hill", 34, 500, 'F', "single", "Phd", 8, 'X', 0) +
("George Star", 30, 500, 'M', "married", "Bachelor", 8, 'X', 0)
Rule 6
on modify e.hours_per_day
if e.marital_status = "married"
then e.bonus = 100
e.marital_status = "married"?
TUPLE
E7
modify e.bonus = 100
Declarations:
type INT = integer;
type DATA = string;
type CHAR = character;
type TUPLE = DATAxINTxINTxCHARxDATAxDATAxINTxCHAR;
var name, marital_status, degree : DATA;
var age, salary, hours_per_day, bonus : INT;
var sex, status : CHAR;

Fig. 4. CCPN model of Rule 6

CCPN models of Rule 1, 4 are shown as Fig. 3, 4. CCPN model of all the six rules is shown as Fig. 5.

5 Conclusion and Future Work

In this paper we propose a modified colored Petri net model Conditional Colored Petri Net (CCPN) model for ECA rules in active database. CCPN is a structural model for active rules rather than a rule language. In an active database, relation between rules is very important, CCPN can model both rules themselves and this complicated relation in an graphical way.

CCPN model development is the first step of our investigation on this direction. Based on this model, we will give methods to predict active rule behavior and analyze desired properties of active rules such as termination, confluence, etc.. A software platform on connecting our model and POSTGRES is being planned too.

References

1. Paton N.W., Diaz O., "Active Database Systems", *ACM Computing Surveys*, Vol. 31, No. 1,1999, pp. 64-103
2. Chakravarthy S., "Early Active Database Efforts: A Capsule Summary", *IEEE Transactions on Knowledge and Data Engineering*, Vol. 7, No. 6, 1995, pp. 1008-1010

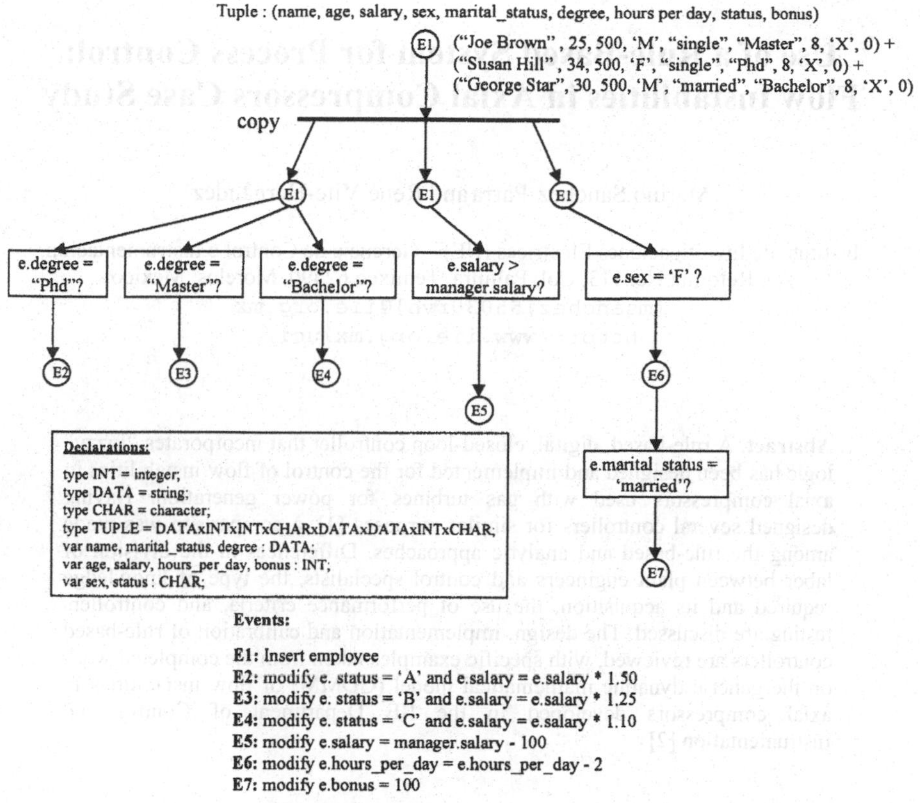
Tuple : (name, age, salary, sex, marital_status, degree, hours per day, status, bonus)
E1
("Joe Brown", 25, 500, 'M', "single", "Master", 8, 'X', 0) +
("Susan Hill", 34, 500, 'F', "single", "Phd", 8, 'X', 0) +
("George Star", 30, 500, 'M', "married", "Bachelor", 8, 'X', 0)
copy
E1
E1
E1
e.degree = "Phd"?
e.degree = "Master"?
e.degree = "Bachelor"?
e.salary > manager.salary?
e.sex = 'F' ?
E2
E3
E4
E5
E6
e.marital_status = 'married'?
E7
Declarations:
type INT = integer;
type DATA = string;
type CHAR = character;
type TUPLE = DATAxINTxINTxCHARxDATAxDATAxINTxCHAR;
var name, marital_status, degree : DATA;
var age, salary, hours_per_day, bonus : INT;
var sex, status : CHAR;
Events:
E1: Insert employee
E2: modify e. status = 'A' and e.salary = e.salary * 1.50
E3: modify e. status = 'B' and e.salary = e.salary * 1.25
E4: modify e. status = 'C' and e.salary = e.salary * 1.10
E5: modify e.salary = manager.salary - 100
E6: modify e.hours_per_day = e.hours_per_day - 2
E7: modify e.bonus = 100

Fig. 5. CCPN model of all rules

3. Schlesinger M. and Lörincze G., Rule modeling and simulation in ALFRED, *the 3rd International workshop on Rules in Database (RIDS'97) (or LNCS 1312)*, Skövde, Sweden, June, pp. 83-99, 1997
4. Guisheng Y., Qun L., Jianpei Z., Jie L., Daxin L., "Petri Based Analysis Method For Active Database Rules", *IEEE International Conference on Systems, Man and Cybernetics*, vol. 2, 1996, pp. 858-863
5. Li X. and Chapa S. V., Optimization of Deductive Database System by Adaptive Fuzzy Petri Net Approach, *IASTED International Conference on Artificial Intelligence and Soft Computing (ASC2001)*, Cancun, Mexico, May 21-24, 2001, pp. 6-11
6. Barkaoui K. and Maïzi Y., Efficient answer extraction of deductive database modeled by HLPN, *8th International Conference on Database and expert systems applications (DEXA'97), Toulouse, France, September 1-5, 1997 (also LNCS vol. 1308)*, pp. 324-336
7. Jensen K., "An Introduction to the Theoretical Aspects of Colored Petri Nets". *Lecture Notes in Computer Science: A Decade of Concurrency*, vol. 803, edited by J. W. de Bakker, W.-P. de Roever, G. Rozenberg, Springer-Verlag, 1994, pp. 230-272

Use of a Rule-Based System for Process Control: Flow Instabilities in Axial Compressors Case Study

Marino Sánchez-Parra and René Vite-Hernández

Instituto de Investigaciones Eléctricas (IIE) – Gerencia de Control e Instrumentación. Av. Reforma No. 113, Col. Palmira, Temixco 62490, Morelos, México.
{msanchez,55030rvh}@iie.org.mx
http://www.iie.org.mx/uci/

Abstract. A rule-based, digital, closed-loop controller that incorporates "fuzzy" logic has been designed and implemented for the control of flow instabilities in axial compressors used with gas turbines for power generation. Having designed several controllers for similar purposes [1], a comparison was made among the rule-based and analytic approaches. Differences in the division of labor between plant engineers and control specialists, the type of knowledge required and its acquisition, the use of performance criteria, and controllers testing are discussed. The design, implementation and calibration of rule-based controllers are reviewed, with specific examples taken from the completed work on the generic dynamic mathematical model (GDMM) of flow instabilities in axial compressors developed in the IIE Department of Control and Instrumentation [2].

1 Introduction

"Fuzzy" logic and "rule-based" techniques were originally advocated by Zadeh [3] and Mandani and Assilian [4], [5] as a means of both capturing human expertise and dealing with uncertainty. These concepts were soon applied to ill-defined industrial processes. Such systems are normally operated by experienced individuals who often achieve excellent results despite receiving information that is imprecise. The origin of this imprecision might be time delays between the application of a control signal and indication of its effect, nonlinearities in the system dynamics, or degraded sensors [6]. Processes to which the fuzzy, rule-based approach has been applied include automatic train operation and automatic crane operation [7], [8] and the control of cement kilns[9], control of wood pulp grinders, and sewage treatment plants [10]. The process industry and in particular the cement industry, was the first to apply the new technique to control large-scale process [9]. Since the successful implementation of this technology, there has become an even greater interest in the field of Power Industry and currently new applications are emerging every day [11], [17], [18], [21].

In many instances, the degree of control achieved using the fuzzy, rule-based approach was superior to that which had been attained using strictly manual methods. These successful applications and others recently reported [11] have shown that the technique is both practical and benefic for the control of ill-defined processes and to the operation of well-characterized systems.

C.A. Coello Coello et al. (Eds.): MICAI 2002, LNAI 2313, pp. 494–505, 2002.

This paper explores the construction and use of rule-based systems for process control. Specifically, the objective of the control methodology described herein is the automation of discrete control actions that are not, or can not be, undertaken by human operators on a reasonable time scale (e.g., second or milliseconds).

We report an application of rule-based intelligent control techniques to avoid a process disturbance in axial compressors that affects the continuity of operation and availability of gas turbine based generators frequently used in the power generation Industry. The paper is concerned with the use of a generic dynamic mathematical model (GDMM) of flow instabilities in axial compressors that was realized in a previous IIE project [2], to test and evaluate three fuzzy logic rule-based intelligent control strategies (ICS). The major objective was to control the so called *surge phenomena* [12], by means of the following procedure: First, three conventional PID controllers were implemented and evaluated with simulation tests and a carefully analysis of the results was made, afterwards the conventional controllers were substituted by Fuzzy Logic Controllers (FLCs) that are of nonlinear nature and more robust than the conventional control [4]. The next step was to compare the results between the automatic conventional control and the automatic rule-based control.

1.1 Fuzy Logic and Rule-Based Control

Zadeh [3], [13], introduced fuzzy logic to describe systems that are "too complex or too ill-defined to admit a precise mathematical analysis. Its major features are the use of linguistic rather than numerical variables and the characterization of relations between variables by fuzzy conditional statements. He foresaw the technique as having applications in fields such as economics, management, and medicine. Mandani and Assilian [5], recognizing that fuzzy logic provided a means of dealing with uncertainty, extended the concept to industrial process control in the expectation that it would be applied to systems for which precise measurements of the state variables could not be obtained. Fuzzy logic and rule-based systems are a means of dealing with imprecision, a method of modeling human behavior, and a means of achieving control of industrial systems that can not be modeled rigorously. Regarding process control, "The principal difference between the fuzzy, rule-based approach and conventional techniques is that the former uses qualitative information whereas the latter require rigid analytic relations to describe the process". However, for recent fuzzy logic control applications made in the IIE [1], the simulation tests results (between the mathematical dynamic models and the control algorithms) supplies a lot of information in the form of process data that are translated to graphs representatives of the process variables. Then we make use of the information contained in those graphs to get the control rules by means of a "mapping" of the control and operation concepts implicit in the graphs to qualitative actions that are evaluated by an inference machine.

In summary, the knowledge bases of the developed rule-based ICS reported in this paper were made synthesizing the information contained in graphs of the best simulations tests results previously obtained with the PID control strategies tested with the GDMM. In addition we applied the experience and process knowledge acquired with the intensive realization of simulation tests.

The GDMM was developed by the authors making use of a compressor mathematical model reported in the literature by Greitzer [14], [15]. As the original model reported was manufactured for simulation purpose and not for control purposes, Vite and Sanchez [2] added the elements necessary for use the model in surge control applications. The obtained GDMM reproduces the dynamics of flow instabilities in axial compressors. The validation tests made were compared with those in the literature.

The control strategies implemented use the compressor discharge pressure and the inlet air flow compressor variables, while the controlled variable is the air bleed flow, which is regulated by a generic bleed valve. These are real and economic instrumentation requirements joined with the rule-based ICS based on fuzzy logic. The main benefits in using fuzzy logic for control in place of conventional methods is that they are easier to design, easy to implement and generally more robust than conventional controllers [16].

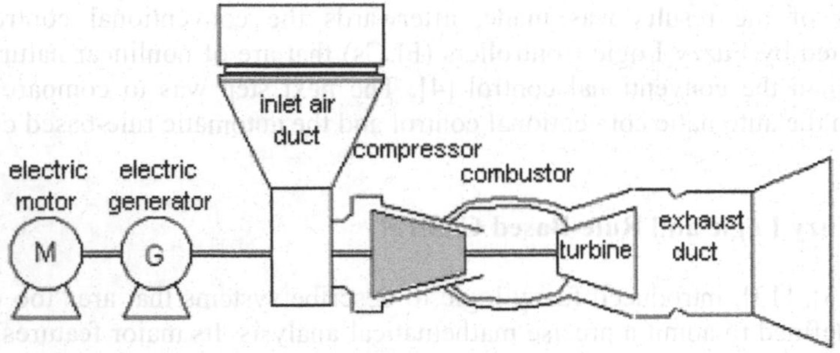

Fig. 1. Turbo Generator schematic

1.2 Process Description

Compressors are widely used for the pressurization of fluids. Applications involve air compression for use in Turbo Generators (TG) based in combustion turbines (CT) in Power Industry, likewise for the pressurization and transportation of gas in the process and chemical industries. This article focuses on a commonly used type of continuous flow compressors: the *axial compressor*, where the gaseous fluid is processed in a direction parallel to the rotational axis. In these machines, the entering fluid is pressurized by first accelerating it via the kinetic energy into potential energy by decelerating the fluid in diverging channels. Toward low mass flows, stable operation of axial compressors is constrained by two aerodynamic flow instabilities: rotating *stall* and *surge* [12], [19]. Compressor *surge* is an axisymmetric oscillation of the mass flow and pressure rise. Modeling and control of this oscillations is of considerable interest since *surge* limits the useful range of mass flows where the compressor operates stably. Large amplitude surge can also damage the compressor [19].

The axial flow compressor consists essentially of a stationary inlet casing, a rotating impeller with rotating blades which imparts a high velocity to the air, and a number of fixed diverging passages or stator blades, in which the air is decelerated with a consequent rise in static pressure. The later process is one of diffusion, and consequently, the part of the compressor containing the diverging passages is known as the diffuser [19]. Fig. 2 shows the internal construction of an axial compressor.

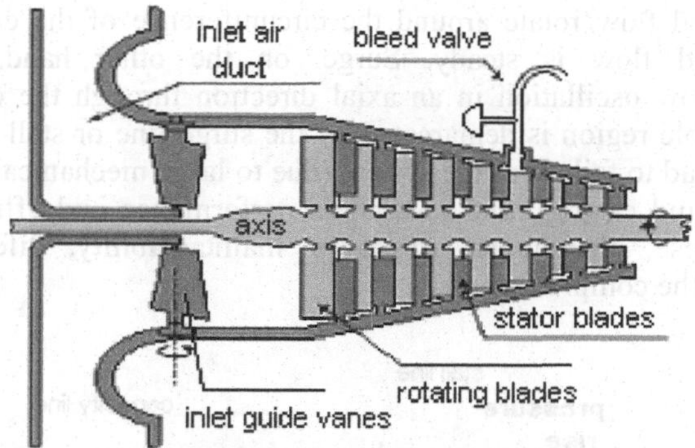

Fig. 2. Axial compressor schematic.

System Description: An idealized compression system is depicted in Fig. 3. In this idealized system, an incompressible fluid is pressurized in the compressor and is discharged into a closed tank that contains a compressible gas. This tank discharges via a throttle valve into another large reservoir. Essential elements in this system are the *compressor* that realizes the pressurization, the inertance of the incompressible fluid in the compressor and throttle ducts, the mass storage capacity of the system in the closed tank, which is often called the *plenum*, and the throttle, which represents the system pressure requirements (e.g., losses due to resistance in the piping or effects of subsystems). In a steady-state situation, the net mechanical energy provided by the compressor is dissipated by the throttle.

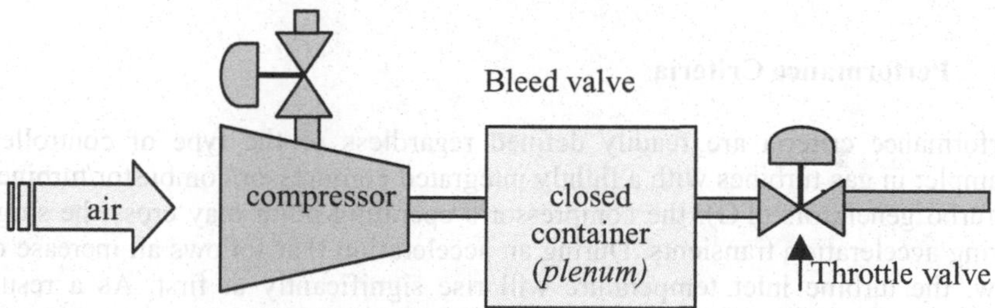

Fig. 3. Idealized compression system

The performance of a compressor is often specified in a compressor map by curves that relate the rotational speed, the pressure rise across the compressor, and the mass flow through the compressor, as shown in fig. 4. Steady-state operating points with constant rotational speed are indicated by speed lines (also called compressor characteristics), and the rotational speed increases in the direction of the arrow. The operating range of a compressor is bounded for high mass flow by the limited capacity of the compressor. For low flow regimes, the operating range is limited by the occurrence of aerodynamic flow instabilities: *rotating stall* and *surge*.

1.3 Aerodynamic Compressor Flow Instabilities: Rotating Stall and Surge

Both instabilities are perturbations of the steady state, axisymmetric flow under normal operating conditions. Rotating stall is a non- axisymmetric instability in which regions of stalled flow rotate around the circumference of the compressor, but the annulus-averaged flow is steady. Surge, on the other hand, is an unsteady, axisymmetric flow oscillation in an axial direction through the entire compression system. The stable region is demarcated by the surge line or stall line. Rotating stall and surge can lead to failure of the system (due to large mechanical and thermal loads in the blading and casing), and restrict its performance and efficiency. Therefore, suppressing these phenomena improves maintainability, life span, and the performance of the compressor.

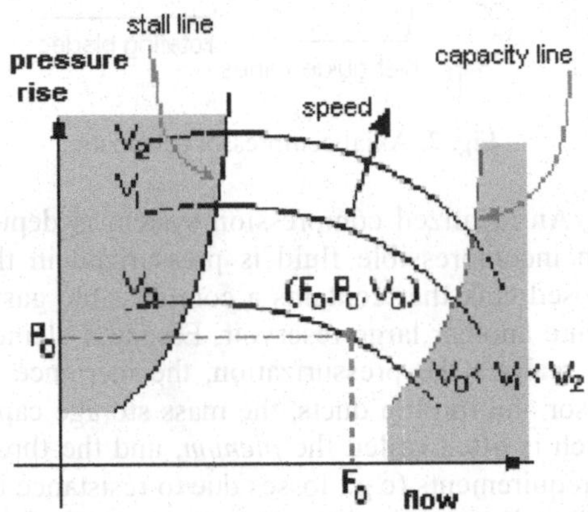

Fig. 4. A schematic representation of a compressor map

1.4 Performance Criteria

Performance criteria are readily defined regardless of the type of controller. For example: in gas turbines with a tightly integrated compressor/combustor/turbine, such as turbo generators (TG), the compressor's operating point may cross the surge line during acceleration transients. During an acceleration that follows an increase of fuel flow, the turbine inlet temperature will rise significantly at first. As a result, the compressor exit pressure may rise because of the increased back-pressure of the turbine. Also, the operating point may initially move toward the surge line because of the slow response time of the compressor speed and, thus, the air mass flow. In both cases, the system's response time to changing operation requirements is constrained by the permissible pressure rise and mass flow variations. Note hat the operation of gas turbines is also constrained by the allowable inlet turbine temperature resulting from metallurgical limitations.

Fig. 5 illustrates the oscillatory mass of air flow belonging to surge condition. It is possible to distinguish four *surge* categories: *mild surge, classic surge, modified surge y deep surge.* Due to he big mechanical and thermal strengths in blades and casing, surge can produce a total system failure and causes a severe damage with the TG unit out of service. In contrast, there is no direct way to utilize performance criteria in the design of rule-based systems.

The proposed automatic control strategy must include the detection of stall /surge to get the avoidance of such dynamic conditions and in the worst case, when surge is present, it shall be eliminated in a few milliseconds. Then the maintenance time will drop and the useful life of the TG will be extended without damage.

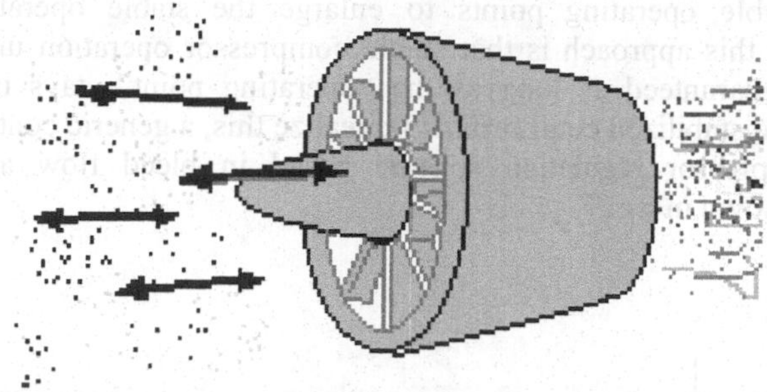

Fig. 5. Air flow through compressor is oscillatory when surge is present

2 Analytic Controller

A description of the control strategies for the prevention and avoidance of surge phenomena in axial flow compressors is presented. The proposed control algorithms are PI based and the differences between the algorithms are in the control variables manipulation and how to get the set point adjustment. Fig. 6 shows a generalized schematic controller diagram.

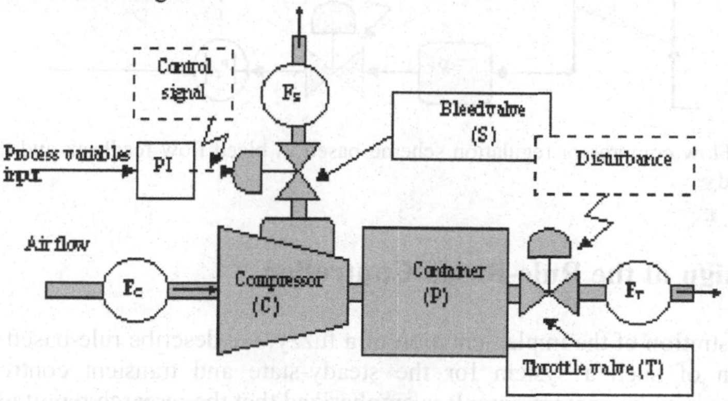

Fig. 6. Anti*surge* control strategy (generalized).

Next is a resume of the control actions to avoid the surge:

- The air flow compressor variable F_C is regulated and its value always must be greater than the minimum flow value (or surge value).
- The controller sets the control signal output to the compressor bleed valve. This is a corrective action
- The controller structure is proportional plus integral type (PI).
- The system disturbances are generated with the throttle valve, emulating the system mechanical load.
- Air flow compressor F_C, bleed flow F_S and the throttle flow F_T are measured.

The "first generation" of active controllers implemented in experimental setups has been based on stabilization by linear feedback. The objective of these controllers is to stabilize unstable operating points to enlarge the stable operating region. The motivation for this approach is that stable compressor operation under disturbances can only be guaranteed as long as the "operating point" stays in the domain of attraction of the stabilized equilibrium. To realize this, a generic control strategy is the PI Flow compressor regulation scheme based in bleed flow and throttle flow feedforward shown in fig. 7.

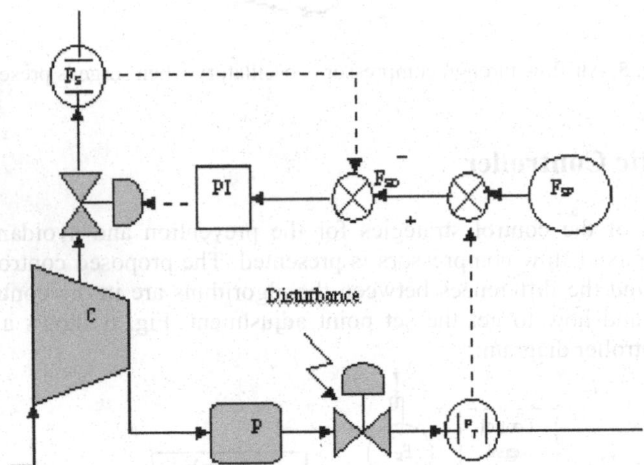

Fig. 7. PI Flow compressor regulation scheme based in bleed flow feedback and throttle flow feedforward

3 Design of the Rule-Based Controller

As an illustration of the implementation of a fuzzy, we describe rule-based controller, the design of such a system for the steady-state and transient control of flow instabilities in axial compressors. It is emphasized that the research reported here is an experimental evaluation of how a fuzzy, rule-based ICS might be used in process control. As reported by Bernard [6], the applied methodology is of general use. However, the subsets and rule base described herein are unique to the control of flow instabilities.

Knowledge acquisition is the essential task in the design of a rule-based controller. If this is not done in a through and rigorous manner, then the controller could not work properly. Relative to the design of a rule-based system for the control of flow instabilities in axial compressors, it was not possible either to observe operators actions nor to question them about the operation procedures, because the flow instabilities appear suddenly and nobody in a plant knows when it will be present and therefore operators do not have experiences about it.

The complete process of design considers the following tasks:

1st. task, for a careful review of the information about a surge (graphs of process variables) occurred in a gas turbine unit belonging to the Comision Federal de Electricidad (CFE) in Mexico, and to analyze the graphs (blade path temperature, speed path and compressor discharge pressure) with the engineering staff of the power plant. The conclusions obtained from the analysis were a valuable treasure of information.

2nd task, was a research job about the flow instabilities that included the study of some very useful papers [12],[14], [15], [19] to get a formal comprehension with the dynamic process.

3rd task, consisted in the implementation of Greitzer model [14] for flow instabilities in PC platform with LabWindows software programmed in C language. As the Greitzer model was done for emulating the process and we need a model for control purposes, we modified the original compressor model adding a bleed valve with its corresponding dynamic considerations. We named it as the "generic dynamic mathematical model" (GDMM). The results of the GDMM were compared with those in [14] and they showed to be reliable.

4th task, The implementation of six flow instabilities control strategies proposed in literature, based on PI controllers with feedback and feedforward paths, with simulation tests for each one. This task included the controllers tune process.

5th task, Selection of the best performance, only two, PI based flow instabilities control strategies with feedforward and feedback with the substitution of each PI controller for a Fuzzy Controller, assuming that a non-linear controller as a fuzzy, rule-based, controller, would give better control in a natural fashion.

6th task, Mapping of the collected data from the simulation tests (with PI control) for the air flow and compressor discharge pressure variables to graphs. With those graphs we identified the universe of discourse for each calculated linguistic variable, the error and the error derivative, and from a rigorous analysis we developed the control rules for three cases. Tables 1 to 3 show the rules tested for the controllers.

To get a relationship of the rule-based fuzzy controller performance with the selected number of membership functions (and consequently the number of control rules), three cases were proposed and implemented:

Case 1: Three membership functions for inputs and seven singleton for control output.
Case 2: Five membership functions for inputs and seven singleton for control output.
Case 3: Seven membership functions for inputs and eleven singleton for output.

The fuzzy control structure was designed as the usual methodology in [22], [23]. Fig. 8 shows the control strategy for the rule-based ICS.

Table 1. Case 1: 9 control rules

		ED		
		N	**Z**	**P**
E	**N**	CF	CM	CS
	Z	CS	MV	OS
	P	OS	OM	OF

Table 2. Case 2: 25 control rules

		ED				
		NB	**NS**	**Z**	**PS**	**PB**
E	**NB**	CF	CF	CF	CM	CM
	NS	CM	CM	CS	CS	CS
	Z	CS	CS	MV	OS	OS
	PS	OS	OS	OS	OM	OM
	PB	AM	AM	OF	OF	OF

Table 3. Case 3: 49 control rules

		ED						
		NB	**NM**	**NS**	**Z**	**PS**	**PM**	**PB**
E	**NB**	CF	CMF	CM	CMS	CS	MV	OS
	NM	CMF	CM	CMS	CS	MV	OS	OMS
	NS	CM	CMS	CS	MV	OS	OMS	OM
	Z	CM	CMS	CS	MV	OS	OMS	OM
	PS	CM	CMS	CS	MV	OS	OMS	OM
	PM	CMS	CS	MV	OS	OMS	AM	OMF
	PB	CS	MV	OS	OMS	OM	OMF	OF

For the antecedents:

N: Negative Z: Zero P: Positive
S: Small M: Medium N: Big

And for the consequents:

C: Close MV: Maintain Valve O: Open
F: Fast M: Moderate S: Slow

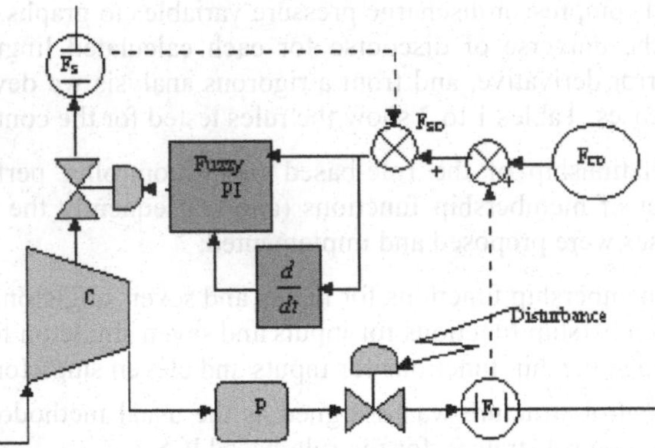

Fig. 8. Block diagram of the rule-based fuzzy control for compressor flow instabilities

4 Simulation Tests Results for the Avoidance Flow Instabilities Rule-Based Fuzzy Control

Objective: Avoidance of compressor flow instabilities
Characteristics: Bleed flow regulation
Control strategies: Bleed flow feedback and throttle flow feedforward

Two kinds of simulation tests were realized for the selected case.

1) Rule base change tests (3 cases).
2) Load change tests (4 cases).

4.1 Rule Base Change Tests

The selected rule-based control strategy was evaluated for the proposed control rules groups (9, 25 and 49 rules). Furthermore we included a test load condition that promotes de system instability.

4.2 Load Change Tests

For each test were made three load condition changes:

- Process Condition 1: 45% al 35% throttle valve position variation.
- Process Condition 2: 35% al 25% throttle valve position variation.
- Process Condition 3: 25% al 35% throttle valve position variation.
- Process Condition 3: 35% al 45% throttle valve position variation.

Fig 9 shows the avoidance flow instabilities rule-based fuzzy control

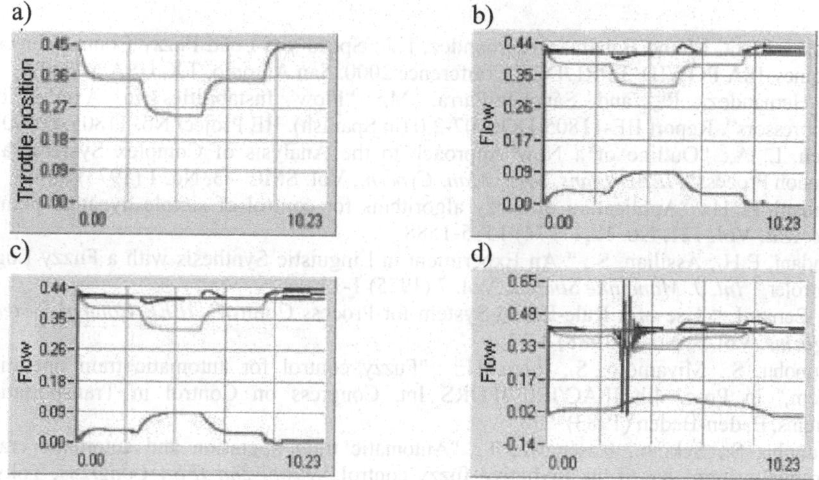

Fig. 9. a)Load change test under the conditions: 1, 2, 3 and 4. Flow variation in response to load change test for b) 9 control rules and c) 25 control rules and 49 control rules under the conditions: 1, 2, 3 and 4.

5 Conclusions

Rule-Based fuzzy control was presented as an alternative to solve the axial compressor flow instabilities due to *surge*. The rule-based fuzzy controller (R-B FC) presented was implemented in PC platform in C language, and it was inspired in a digital-PI conventional controller. However, rule-based control with fuzzy logic provided an algorithm that could convert the linguistic control strategy based on expert knowledge into an automatic control strategy, and using fuzzy inference, we could synthesize a nonlinear control surface obtained from an interpolation mechanism, generalizing the control surface of the conventional PI controller.

Simulation tests were made for three sets of control rules (9, 25, 49 rules) required for the selected number of membership functions for the universe of discourse (3, 5, 7 membership functions). The best experimental result of the R-B FC was with 25 rules. With 9 rules we had a non adequately well defined control surface and with 49 rules we had too much rules that made very difficult the manual tune controller task .

Then for the axial compressor flow instabilities problem the R-B FC showed to be more robust than the PI linear controller. Furthermore, in the R-B FC the plant engineer can define the control rules adequate or required for each process operation region of particular interest, enabling the controller robustness.

As we proved, with this new control technique the tune controllers process is dependent of the plant engineer or operators expertise but it could be a long and time consuming process. That's a good reason to continue the control effort developing automation techniques for the R-B FC that makes friendly and efficient the tune controller effort.

References

1. Sánchez-Parra, M and Bahamaca-Fernández, L.J.: Speed and Load Fuzzy Control for Gas Turbines. ISA POWID/ EPRI /DOE Conference 2000. San Antonio, TX, USA. (2000)
2. Vite-Hernández, R., and Sánchez-Parra, M.: "Flow Instabilities in Axial Flow Compressors". Report IIE-11805-DOC-07-2.0 (in Spanish). IIE Project No. 11805, (2000)
3. Zadeh, L. A.: "Outline of a New Approach to the Analysis of Complex Systems and Decision Process", *IEEE Trans. Syst., Man, Cybern.*, Vol. SMC – 3, No. 1 (1973) 28-44
4. Mandani, E. H.: "Application of fuzzy algorithms for control of simple dynamic plant", *Proc. IEE*, Vol. 121, No. 12, (1974) 1585-1588
5. Mandani, E.H., Assilian, S., " An Experiment in Linguistic Synthesis with a Fuzzy Logic Controler", *Int. J. Manchine Studies,* Vol. 7 (1975) 1-13
6. J.A. Bernard, " Use of a Rule-Based System for Process Control", *IEEE Control Systems Magazine*, Vol. 8, No. 5 (1988) 3-13
7. Yasunobu, S., Miyamoto, S., Ihara, H.: "Fuzzy control for automatic train operation system," in Proc. 4th IFAC/IFIP/IFORS Int. Congress on Control in Transportation Systems, Baden-Baden (1983)
8. Yasunobu, S., Sekino., Hasegawa, T.: "Automatic train operation and automatic crane operation systems based on predictive fuzzy control," *Proc. 2nd IFSA Congress*, Tokyo, Japan (1987) 835-838
9. Holmvlad, L. P., Ostergaard, J. J.: "Control of a cement kiln by fuzzy logic," in *Fuzzy Information and Decision Process*, M. M. Gupta and E Sanchez, Eds. Amstedam: North-Holland (1992) 389-399
10. Maiers, J., Sherif, Y.S.: "Application of Fuzzy Set Theory", *IEEE Trans. Syst., Man, Cybern.,* Vol. SMC – 15, No. 1 (1985) 175-189
11. Bonissone, P.P., Badami, V., Chiang, K.H., Khedkar, P.S., Marcelle, K.W., Schutten, M.J.: "Industrial Applications of Fuzzy Logic at General Electric". Proc. IEEE, Vol.83, No. 3, (1995). 450-465
12. Willems, F., De Jager, B.: "Modeling and Control of Compressor Flow Instabilities", *IEEE Control Systems*, vol. 19, no. 5 (1999) 8 – 18
13. Zadeh, L. A.: "Making Computers Think Like People", *IEEE Spectrum*, Vol. 21, No. 8 (1984) 26-32

14. Greitzer, E.M.: "Surge and Rotating Stall in Axial Compressors. Part I, Theoretical Compression System Model", *ASME J. Eng. Power*, Vol. 98, no 2 (1976) 191–198
15. Greitzer, E.M.: "Surge and Rotating Stall in Axial Compressors. Part II, "Experimental Results and Comparison With Theory", *ASME J. Eng. Power*, Vol. 98, no 2 (1976) 199–217
16. Mandani, E.H.: "Twenty Years of Fuzzy Control: Experiences Gained and Lessons Learned". Fuzzy Logic Technology and Applications, Robert Marks, Ed. IEEE Technical Activities Board (1994) 19-24
17. Tarabishy, M.N.: "An Application of Fuzzy Logic to Power Generation Control". *Proceedings of the 58th American Power Control*, Vol. 1, (1996) 315-319
18. Garduño,R., Sánchez,M.:"Control System Modernization: Turbogas Unit Case Study". *Proc. IFAC Control of Power Plants and Power Systems*. Vol. II, Power Plants (1995) 245-250
19. Gravdahl, J.T.: "Modeling and Control of Surge and Rotating Stall in Compressors". *IEEE Transactios On Control Systems Technology*, Vol. 7, no. 5 (1999) 567- 579,
20. Abdelnour, G.M., Chang, C.H., Huang, F.H. et al: "Design of a Fuzzy Controller Using Input and Output Mapping Factors". *IEEE Transactions on Systems, Man, and Cybernetics*, Vol. 21, No. 5 (1991) 952-959
21. Momoh, J.A., Tomsovic, K.: "Overview and Literature Survey of Fuzzy Set Theory in Power Systems", *IEEE Transactions on Power Systems*, Vol. 10, No. 3 (1995) 1676-1690
22. Wang, L.: A Course in Fuzzy Systems and Control, Prentice Hall, Inc. (1997)
23. Driankov, D., Hellendoorn, H., Reinfrank, M. An Introduction to Fuzzy Control. Springer – Verlag. (1993).

A Distributed Event Service for Adaptive Group Awareness

Dominique Decouchant[1], Ana María Martínez-Enríquez[2], Jesús Favela[3], Alberto L. Morán[1,4], Sonia Mendoza[1], and Samir Jafar[1]

[1] Laboratoire "Logiciels, Systèmes, Réseaux", Grenoble, France
{Dominique.Decouchant,Alberto.Moran,Sonia.Mendoza,Samir.Jafar}@imag.fr
[2] Depto de Ingeniería Eléctrica, CINVESTAV-IPN, D.F., México
ammartin@mail.cinvestav.mx
[3] Ciencias de la Computación, CICESE, Ensenada, B.C., México
favela@cicese.mx
[4] Facultad de Ciencias UABC, Ensenada, B.C., México

Abstract. This paper is directly focused on the design of middleware functions to support a distributed cooperative authoring environment on the World Wide Web. Using the advanced storage and access functions of the PIÑAS middleware, co-authors can produce fragmented and replicated documents in a structured, consistent and efficient way. However, despite it provides elaborated, concerted, secure and parameterizable cooperative editing support and mechanisms, this kind of applications requires a suited and efficient inter-application communication service to design and implement flexible, efficient, and adapted group awareness functionalities.

Thus, we developed a proof-of-concept implementation of a centralized version of a Distributed Event Management Service that allows to establish communication between cooperative applications, either in distributed or centralized mode. As an essential component for the development of cooperative environments, this Distributed Event Management Service allowed us to design an Adaptive Group Awareness Engine whose aim is to automatically deduce and adapt co-author's cooperative environments to allow them collaborate closer. Thus, this user associated inference engine captures the application events corresponding to author's actions, and uses its knowledge and rule bases, to detect co-author's complementary or related work, specialists, or beginners, etc. Its final goal is to propose modifications to the author working environments, application interfaces, communication or interaction ways, etc.

Keywords: Web cooperative authoring, distributed event management, DEMS, adaptive group awareness inference engine, AGAIE.

1 Introduction

Collaborative authoring is a complex activity; it needs that requirements from the production, coordination and communication spaces [2] be addressed. Based on this, several studies (e.g. [1]) have identified a set of design requirements that

C.A. Coello Coello et al. (Eds.): MICAI 2002, LNAI 2313, pp. 506–515, 2002.

collaborative authoring applications must support, including: enhanced communications, enhanced collaboration awareness [7] - focused and peripheral, and segmented document and version control. The PIÑAS platform [6] addresses these requirements by providing services for collaborative authoring on the Web. The most important PIÑAS features are 1) Seamless distributed cooperative authoring, 2) Full integration to the existing Web environment, 3) Flexible and reliable distributed cooperative architecture, 4) Document and resource naming based on URLs, 5) Document replication for high availability, 6) Elaborated distributed author management, 7) Automatic updating of replicated information, and 8) Session Management and Group Awareness.

However, other needs can be identified besides these ones considering the following scenario: Authors Domingo and Ana are writing a document, working in two of its fragments. This information is shown by the awareness capabilities of the platform (for instance, Radar View). Nevertheless, the first fragment is an image (currently under modification by Domingo) and the second fragment contains the related explanation or comments (currently under modification by Ana). The resulting state of the document will most probably result in semantic inconsistencies if both authors don't become aware of the impact of their changes.

At the fragmentation and permission level, the inconsistencies will pass without being noticed if both authors have the required permission to modify the requested fragments. However, the changes performed to each fragment will indirectly or directly affect the semantic consistency of the document. We highlight that semantic consistency of concurrent productions also constitute a required feature in a collaborative environment. Thus, we introduce the concept and the need of an adaptive and deductive group awareness function based on the capturing and treatment of the cooperating application events.

Inter-application Communication Mechanisms

Inter-applications communication mechanisms are a requirement of collaborative applications and a challenge for their developers. Several studies have addressed this issue and a generic model can be stated based on them: a producer element generates information that may be of interest to consumers. A dedicated mechanism allows the information being produced to be delivered to consumers. In point-to-point communications, the information is sent directly from the producer to the consumer, and a unique Id for each of them is used as the addresses for the communication (e.g. RPC) [10] and Java's RMI [11]). In multicast communications, the information is sent from a producer to a set of consumers (e.g. CORBA Event Service [8], and Java Message Service (JMS) [12]). Further classification can be achieved by considering message-based and event-based communication models.

We next present the Distributed Event Management Service (DEMS) designed for PIÑAS, its implementation, and then introduce the Adaptive Group Awareness Inference Engine (AGAIE) that we designed on top of the DEMS.

2 Design of a Distributed Event Management Service

In the scope of the PIÑAS platform, designed to support a Web cooperative authoring environment, we propose to develop specific mechanisms based on the definition of a dedicated but extensible Distributed Event Management Service (DEMS). Thus, the goal of this part of the work is to design the model and the structure of DEMS that will be in charge of the transmission, management and delivery of group awareness events among all applications (cooperative or not).

The DEMS receives events generated by the applications, manages them (ordering and storage), and transmits them to subscribed applications. Thus, the applications are independent of event transmission and of event diffusion. Moreover, the problem of distributed event transmission concerns only to DEMS, and so it's application transparent.

To be generic, the PIÑAS platform provides the DEMS that allows it to be used by different kinds of cooperative applications. This way, we plan to support multi-user applications capable of providing direct communications (synchronous or asynchronous) among users. All these applications will be combined to constitute a powerful cooperative environment.

From the conceptual point of view, the DEMS (see Fig. 1) is designed as a component to which applications may 1) subscribe to receive notifications (events), 2) perform special actions to configure both outgoing and incoming event flows, and 3) send typed and parametrized events.

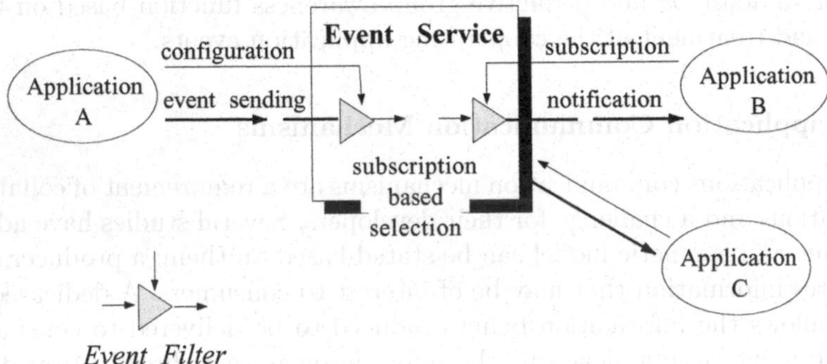

Fig. 1. Schematic Representation of the Distributed Event Management Service

By means of configuration, each application may restrict event diffusion, defining the targeted users and/or applications authorized to receive the events. In the same way, an application may define the kinds of events it is interested in receiving, and only events of these types will be delivered to it.

The event service is a component of the PIÑAS platform, and it transparently runs in both centralized and distributed environments. Thus, it provides support to each application to notify events to other local or remote applications.

2.1 Producer / Consumer Agents

The DEMS has two different sets of clients: 1) *"Producer Agents"* which produce events and transmit them to the service for diffusion, and 2) *"Consumer Agents"* which subscribe to the service in order to receive and consume events.

To be able to send events, a Producer Agent must register itself to the DEMS that returns to it a unique producer Id. Using this Id, the producer agent may perform some configuration actions (see Fig. 1) to extend or restrict the diffusion scope of its events. As an example, some users (i.e. A, B and C) who want to establish a private cooperative session must precise to only diffuse the events to their corresponding colleague's applications.

In a symmetrical way, to capture only certain events, Consumer Agents must provide some rules to filter event categories and/or sources (see Fig. 1).

2.2 Specification of the Distributed Event Management Service

An event is the information unit automatically produced each time an agent performs an action on a shared or private object. To a lesser degree, actions performed on private objects also are interesting to realize elaborated group awareness functions (e.g. expert and novice matching).

Thus, an event is defined as a set of actions executed by an agent on objects[1]:

```
Event = Agent + {Object} + {Action + [Parameters]}
```

Agents

The notion of *Agent* includes the information that allows to identify the nature of the entity that executes the actions on the objects. So, it is not sufficient to identify the active entity (the author), but also the source of these actions (the site and application Ids):

```
Agent = Author + Site + Application
```

This Agent naming principle is based on the PIÑAS author and site naming conventions (see [6]). It maintains and uses the author definition for controlling actions applied to shared resources (documents, images, author entities, etc), and defining sets of roles (e.g. manager, writer, reader, chairman, speaker, reviewer, etc) by which users can act. The role notion is essential to express the social organization of the group work, and constitutes the base for protecting objects from unauthorized actions.

Objects

An event is generated each time an object (usually shared) is accessed. The object's state is characterized by the values of its attributes. A document, a document fragment, an author, and an event are representative examples of

[1] The notation {entity} denotes the possibility to have more than one entity.

objects. The granularity of handled objects may change from one application to another or, more generally, the granularity of executed accesses on the same object varies from one action to another in the same application. For example, a document object is composed of objects of finer granularity such as fragments.

Actions

Actions provide information or represent the user's work: working focus (selection), type of action (cut, paste, copy, open, save), type of object (text, image, annotation), action dynamics (instant, frequency) and their specific attributes (color, bold, plan, importance).

2.3 Configuration and Control of Event Production / Consumption

An important problem to keep in mind is the problem of exporting the variables which compose the user's working environment [9]. To solve this problem, the DEMS provides configurable producer and consumer agents for controlling event production and consumption.

The needs of users and hence the configuration of their work environments evolve regularly in the course of time. These evolution requirements come from their interactions and cooperative processes with other users. For example, in a shared environment, collaborators might change their focus between individual and cooperative work: when collaborators focus on their individual work, they only need general information about the work of others. While they focus on the collaborative task, information must be more specific and more precise. In addition, by means of the shared environment interface, collaborators get familiar with a domain, a task and a group. For example, if a collaborator learns the way other colleagues work, then he can anticipate their actions, and adequate his own, based on the actions they have performed.

Following this principle, a producer agent can authorize, refuse or limit the publication of its events towards certain authorized consumers. Symmetrically, a consumer agent can choose the set of producers.

```
Production_Ctrl = Agent + {Object + Action + {Autorized_Consumer}}
Consumption_Ctrl = Agent + {Object + Action + {Autorized_Producer}}
```

2.4 Event Transmission: A Distributed Service

Cooperative environments typically include group awareness applications (or widgets) that are event producers and/or consumers. For example, cooperative editors like Alliance [3] or AllianceWeb [4] (see Fig. 2) are both producers and consumers of events produced by other co-author applications. Thus, a cooperative editor instance has to be aware of events generated by other co-author applications to reflect and integrate their productions in the author's working environment. In quasi real-time mode, the "radar view" application has to show the different author's working focuses in all working environments.

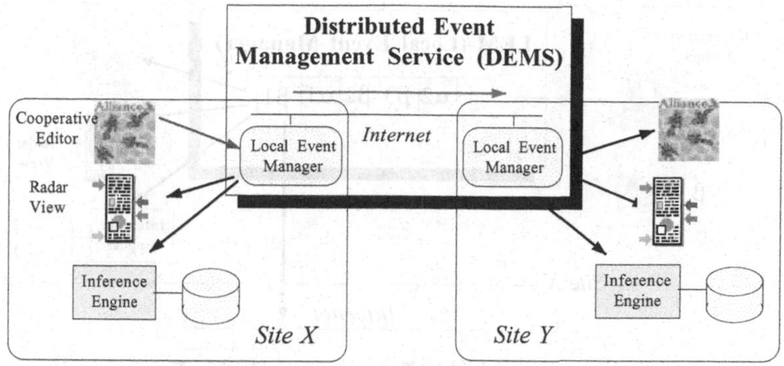

Fig. 2. Event Transmission between Distributed Cooperative Environments

So, considering two users working on two different sites (see Fig. 2) who are respectively using the AllianceWeb cooperative editor and the radar view application: each authoring event has to be diffused both to the local user's radar view and to the remote editor and radar view.

Thus, the DEMS is a distributed PIÑAS service: on each site a local server of this service acts as a concentrator of information (events) on the sender side and as a demultiplexer on the receiver side (site X in Fig. 2). On the sender side, the "Local Event Manager" (LEM) receives events generated by the local producer applications, and if necessary it dispatches them to the local consumers. On the receiver side (site Y in Fig. 2), the LEM instance will determine the applications that are registered as event consumers and distribute the events to them.

Thus, the AGAIE (see section 4) that first appears as a pure consumer of information will also act as an event producer generating/proposing quasi automatic updating of the user cooperative environment (adaptation of the author cooperative editing, proposition of new tools, co-authors, documents, resource and tool appearances).

3 First Implementation of the DEMS

The event management service is a distributed system composed by a set of Local Event Managers (LEM) that are connected together following the peer-to-peer principle. As shown in Fig. 3, each LEM receives the events generated by all local applications and stores them in a dedicated repository. In this event repository, events are classified following their arrival date in the system: it is important to note that no inter-event relation has been investigated and really doesn't appear necessary to establish within the event management system. In a first step, only the production order seems to be relevant.

Thus, the events generated by different applications are mixed within the manager's event repository. For example (see Fig. 3), events $\beta1$, $\beta2$ and $\beta3$ of the cooperative editor β are mixed with the events $\alpha1$ and $\alpha2$ of the cooperative editor α.

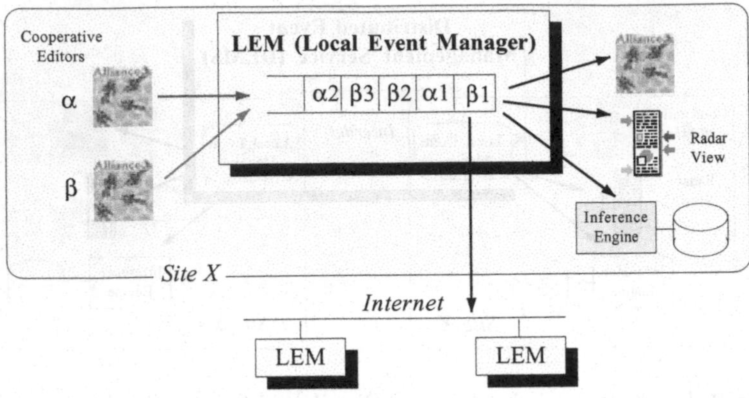

Fig. 3. Functional Principle of a Local Event Management Service

All events are stored in an ordered list implemented as a circular buffer. At the same time the events are stored in the local storage event base, they are also sent to other LEM that take part in the authors cooperative authoring sessions: these remote sites own a local copy of the shared document, and so, they are interested in obtaining all cooperative events related with this document. The LEM service is based on the following principles and constraints:

1. **Event Production** – Each author works with a cooperative authoring application that accesses the shared environment, and spontaneously generates events. The application event layer captures these actions and generates labeled (order ticket) events that are transmitted to the LEM.
2. **Event Consumption** – To obtain events, each client connected to the event manager has to use functions that handle a specific access descriptor. Using and updating specific state variables, this descriptor maintains the current state of event consumption.
3. **Non Blocking Production** – In all cases, this event distribution principle ensures that producers will never be blocked: each event producer must be able to produce new events even when the event storage area is full.
4. **Limited Event Storage Space / Missed Events** – If the limited event storage space becomes full, new elements replace the oldest ones. So, if some consumers (mainly observers) are slower than others, some events may be discarded and so missed.
5. **Dynamic Connection / Disconnection** – The producer and consumer applications may dynamically be connected or disconnected.

4 The Adaptive Group Awareness Inference Engine

One of the specific "group awareness" applications we targeted this study is the design and the implementation of the "Adaptive Group Awareness Inference Engine" (AGAIE) whose goal is to define an Adaptive and Deductive Cooperative environment [5].

Running on all co-author's site, the AGAIE is a consumer of all events generated by the co-author's applications (local and remote). Each AGAIE instance makes an "on-the-fly" analysis of the different events it receives. This analysis is performed in association with a knowledge base (rules and inferred data) that is regularly consulted and updated. The final goal of the AGAIE is to deduce information to propose modifications of the corresponding author environments.

The AGAIE functioning principle is organized following the three actions:

1. **The management of a knowledge base** – From the events managed (stored, replicated and/or distributed) by the DEMS, the AGAIE determines and analyzes the corresponding working actions, their sequence and frequencies, their scope of application, the focus and points of interests of the co-authors, and the working and storage author locations.
2. **The deduction of results on the base of pre-designed principles (Rule Base)** – A deductive system is assumed to work from past or known facts to infer or predict new facts. Known facts are the actions already performed by all cooperating authors during and/or out of the cooperative session. New facts are particular information deduced from the action analysis.
3. **The proposition of some new actions (inferred actions)** – that are proposed to be applied on the co-author environment(s).

Among many typical applications of the AGAIE principle (such as the development of the communication between co-authors, coordination support of authors, determination of common author interests, administration of user preferences, etc), the automatic detection of "expert" and "novice" users constitute a realistic and useful goal. Thus, it appears very useful to automatically detect the areas of expertise of some authors in order to help others who had been detected "in trouble" using some equivalent features.

Thus, based on the introduced DEMS, we are developing an AGAIE function able to detect and give marks to the authors in order to automatically determine both "specialists" and "novices/beginners" in the production of (for example) drawings. This Inference Engine is based on:

1. **Determining the focus and complexity of performed actions** – A knowledge base is constituted by the performed authoring actions. All events have to be analyzed to determine their action focus, and if the action is related to a drawing, it is first stored and then its semantics is evaluated. For example, the different actions may create, modify or delete a new graphical item, or modify one of its attributes or to apply some structuring actions (object group creation). During this phase, the point of interests of the author is evaluated as well as the complexity of the performed actions.
2. **Determining the user expertise level** – From the analyzed actions, we can add the temporal dimension: the actions are replaced in the temporal sequence of actions, and an appreciation of the efficiency and the ability of the author are produced. Thus, a user who generated many drawing editing

actions during a quite long time and who only produced a "quite" simple drawing, is classified as a "novice" or a user in trouble. In fact, the aim of this work is quite complex trying to express in rules the definition of an expert: "A drawing specialist is a user able to produce complex and high structured drawings in a quite short time". Of course, the problem is to well express the notion of "complex and high structured drawing", "poor or basic drawing", "short time", etc.

3. **Establishing "expert-beginner" relations** – Then, after determining some specialist and novice users, and regularly updating these evaluations, the AGAIE may propose to a beginner to take a glance, to observe or to analyze a specialist's work, i.e. to be "closer" to the specialist's working environment. Furthermore, the system may propose some special (synchronous or asynchronous) tools to the specialist and the beginner to establish a cooperative session where the specialist will be able to transfer his knowledge and his experience, or at least to give helpful advice to the beginner.

Thus, the AGAIE acts as an event producer whose aim is to propose modifications to cooperative applications. To do that, all event propositions are transmitted to other remote Inference Engine instances or LEMs (see Fig. 3). In this way, we have defined a distributed cooperative system in continuous movement that tries to help the co-authors to be more efficient in their group work.

5 Conclusion and Perspectives

In this work, we presented the design guidelines of a distributed event management service (DEMS) for the PIÑAS platform. This platform, initially designed to support distributed, cooperative and consistent production of documents on the WWW, has been extended to support a fully cooperative environment that includes both cooperative and non-cooperative applications. Currently provides a dedicated service which offers simple but efficient and ad-hoc inter-application notification and communication functions. To achieve this requirement, we designed and implemented a first centralized version of the DEMS that takes into account both the transmission and management of group awareness events among cooperative applications, which are essentially considered as producers and/or consumers of these events.

Also, we presented the example of AGAIE, an adaptive inference engine whose main goal is to capture all produced/exchanged events among cooperative applications. By analyzing these events on the fly using the inference rules of a database and based on the already deduced properties or actions, the AGAIE inference engine proposes actions to adapt co-author working environments in order to make their collaboration more efficient.

The PIÑAS platform is currently being validated by the development of the AllianceWeb cooperative Web browser/editor and a radar view application. These applications along with the AGAIE inference engine and other PIÑAS components, are being developed in parallel, to have them progressing in a concerted way.

Acknowledgements

This work is supported by the ECOS and ANUIES organizations (project M98M01), by CONACyT projects (29729-A and 33067-A), by CNRS-CONACyT projects (9018 / E130-505 and 10395 / E130-706), and by SEP-SESIC and UABC (grant P/PROMEP: UABC-2000-08), with the scholarship UABC-125 provided to Mr Alberto L. Morán.

References

1. R. Baecker, D. Nastos, I. Posner and K. L. Mawby, "The User-Centred Iterative Design of Collaborative Writing Software", *In Proc. of ACM/SIGCHI and IFIP Conference on Human Factors in Computing Systems (INTERCHI'93),* ACM Press, Amsterdam (Netherlands), pp. 399-405, 24-29 April 1993.
2. G. Calvary, J. Coutaz, and J. Nigay, "From Single User Architectural Design to PAC*, a Generic Software Architecture for CSCW", *In Proc. of the Conference on Human Factors in Computer Systems (CHI'97),* ACM Press, Atlanta, Georgia (USA), pp. 242-249, 22-27 March 1997.
3. D. Decouchant, V. Quint and M. Romero Salcedo, "Structured and Distributed Cooperative Editing in a Large Scale Network", *Groupware and Authoring (Chapter 13),* R. Rada, ed., Academic Press, London (Great Britain), pp. 265-295, May 1996.
4. D. Decouchant, A. M. Martínez and E. Martínez, "Documents for Web Cooperative Authoring", *In Proc. CRIWG'99, 5th International Workshop on Groupware,* IEEE Computer Society, Cancún (México), pp. 286-295, 15-18 September 1999.
5. D. Decouchant, A. M. Martínez, "A Cooperative, Deductive, and Self-Adaptive Web Authoring Environment", *In Proc. of the Mexican International Conference on Artificial Intelligence (MICAI'2000),* Lecture Notes in Artificial Intelligence, Springer Verlag, Acapulco (México), pp. 443-457, 11-14 April 2000.
6. D. Decouchant, J. Favela and A. M. Martínez-Enríquez, "PIÑAS: A Middleware for Web Distributed Cooperative Authoring", *In Proc. of the 2001 Symposium on Applications and the Internet (SAINT'2001),* IEEE Computer Society and IPJ Information Processing Society of Japan, San Diego, California (USA), pp. 187-194, 8-12 January 2001.
7. A. L. Morán, J. Favela, A. M. Martínez and D. Decouchant, "Document Presence Notification Services for Collaborative Writing", *In Proc. CRIWG'2001, 7th International Workshop on Groupware,* IEEE Computer Society, Darmstadt (Germany), pp. 125-133, 6-8 September 2001.
8. Object Management Group., *"CORBA Event Service Specification, Version 1.1"*, 2001, http://www.omg.org/technology/documents/formal/event_service.htm.
9. D. Salber, J. Coutaz, D. Decouchant and M. Riveill, "De l'observabilité et de l'honnêteté : les cas du contrôle d'accès dans la Communication Homme-Homme Médiatisée", *In Proc of the conference "Interface Homme-Machine" (IHM'95), CEPAD,* pp. 27-34, 1995 (In french).
10. Sun MicroSystems Inc., *"RFC 1050, RPC: Remote Procedure Call Protocol Specification"*, 1988, http://www.faqs.org/rfcs/rfc1050.html.
11. Sun MicroSystems Inc., *"Remote Method Invocation Specification Version 1.3.0"*, 1999, http://java.sun.com/j2se/1.3/docs/guide/rmi/spec/rmiTOC.html.
12. Sun MicroSystems Inc., *"Java Message Service Specification Version 1.0.2b"*, 2001, http://java.sun.com/products/jms/docs.html.

Mining Road Accidents

Eduardo F. Morales[1], Dulce Ma. Heredia[2], and Andrés F. Rodríguez[2]

[1] ITESM-Campus Cuernavaca, Paseo de la Reforma 182-A, 62589, Col. Lomas de Cuernavaca, Temixco, Morelos, Mexico
emorales@campus.mor.itesm.mx

[2] Instituto de Investigaciones Eléctricas
Paseo de la Reforma 113, 62240, Col. Palmira, Temixco, Morelos, Mexico
{dmhg,afrm}@iie.org.mx

Abstract. Knowledge Discovery in Data Bases has been established as a promising area for dealing with the increased stored data that is been generated in our times. Finding good patterns or relations between attributes and data is not an easy task and requires a long, and often painful, process. This article describes the process followed to discover useful patterns on a real data base of road accidents. This article has two main purposes: (i) to present a documented case of a data mining process followed on a real data base with useful hints and lessons learned during the process, and (ii) to present the main results of road accidents in Mexico.

1 Introduction

With the non-stopping increment of data, due to the increased automatization of processes, the inexpensive trend in costs of memory, and advances on data bases technology, finding patterns on data is one of the main challenges of this century. It has been estimated that the amount of data stored in the world's databases doubles every twenty months [11]. Knowledge discovery in databases (KDD) is a very active research area which aims to efficiently analyze data to discover useful patterns. In general, patterns explain something about the data and are used to take useful decisions in a highly competitive economy.

KDD is an interdisciplinary field involving database technology, machine learning, pattern recognition, statistics, high performance computing, and visualization techniques. KDD is defined as "the nontrivial process of identifying valid, novel, potentially useful, and ultimately understandable patterns in data" [4]. It is desirable for the patterns to be new and useful in the future and for taking decisions. It is also desirable for the patterns to lead to human insight.

KDD involves several steps in an iterative process, where as you uncover more "nuggets" in the data, you learn how to ask better questions to find better patterns. The whole process involves taking different decisions, starting from the selection and pre-process of the data, selection of algorithms and parameters, interpretations of results, and so on. All these decisions can produce different outcomes. One of the goals of this paper is to provide insights of the decisions

C.A. Coello Coello et al. (Eds.): MICAI 2002, LNAI 2313, pp. 516–525, 2002.

followed in this process and the lessons learned when dealing with a real data base which will hopefully benefit potential users of KDD technology.

The application domain is a data base of road accidents in Mexico. The attributes of this data base have changed over time and there are several missing and incorrect values. An adequate interpretation and mining of this data is important for the inclusion of preventive measures against accidents, specially targeted towards avoiding mortal accidents. The second goal of this article is to provide the main patterns found in this data base.

This paper is organized as follows. Section 2 describes the main characteristics of the road accidents data base. Section 3 presents the process that was followed and the main decisions taken for mining such data base. Section 4 has the main results of the process. Finally, section 5 gives conclusions and future research directions.

2 Road Accidents

CAPUFE[1] is the government institution which administers all the state-own roads in Mexico. Its Medical Service Department has a daily register of all the accidents that occur in the roads controlled by CAPUFE. This information has been mainly used as an historical account of the road accidents that occur in the main highways of Mexico and has not yet, to our knowledge, been exploited or sufficiently analyzed for supporting decisions that could be used, for instance, in the prevention of mortal accidents. The main motivation behind this research was to analyze road accidents data with different techniques to try to find useful patterns to prevent accidents.

We are not aware of any work for mining this type of data. An alternative approach to try to prevent accidents, has been the incorporation of intelligent systems within vehicles to help drivers during their trip [8].

We had access to data from 1995 until 1999. Each year has a different number of attributes which have changed even within a year. In total 35 different attributes have been captured during these years. These attributes register among other things, the name of the road where the accident occurred, the kilometer, time, date, day of the week, and weather conditions of the accident. They also register if the road was closed because of the accident and for how long, damages to the road, number of vehicles involved and their main characteristics, and the severity of the accident in terms of injured or dead people.

In the following section, a detailed description of the process followed for the extraction of useful patterns in this domain is given.

3 KDD Process

Figure 1 shows the typical process followed by KDD [4]. The following sections explain how we followed this process.

[1] Caminos y Puentes Federales de Ingresos y Servicios Conexos.

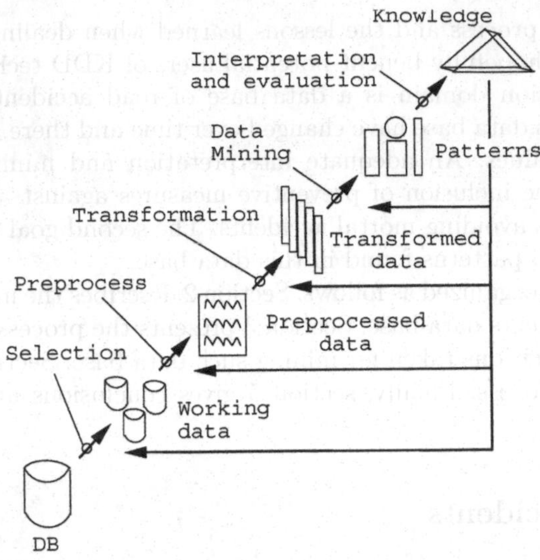

Fig. 1. KDD process.

3.1 Selection

Our first mayor decision was on which data to considered. Data from 1995 includes 33 attributes. The first half of 1996 has 22 attributes, and from then on, all the data bases have 17 attributes, 16 of which are common to all years.

We decided to work first on the data base with more attributes (from 1995). This data base has 4,380 registered accidents with 6,041 vehicles involved. Although considering the data base with larger number of attributes may sound like a natural thing to do, it can often be counterproductive. In general more attributes do not necessarily mean better results as different attributes produce different bias on the search for patterns (there are some good bias and some bad bias). We have experienced cases where increasing the number of attributes substantially degrades the results when mining a data base from the Mexican electricity utility [6]. Our decision intended to find if some attributes could be proved to be irrelevant with the analysis and if some attributes, not currently captured, are relevant for preventing road accidents. It is always possible to remove irrelevant attributes, whether adding new ones may turn out to be impossible.

Our next mayor decision was to decide whether include all the accidents in all the roads that are administered by CAPUFE or try to mine separately individual roads. We decided to follow both approaches. First to see if there are general patterns common to all roads, and then to see if there are particular patterns that are specific to particular roads. In general, mining selected coherent subsets can prove to be very useful. This can serve two purposes: (i) reduce the amount of data and (ii) focus the search with relevant-only data. If subsets are not "naturally" identifiable in the domain, a clustering technique can help to identify them. Although, we analyzed several of these roads, this paper describes only the results from the road Mexico-Cuernavaca, with roughly 600 records.

The final step involves the selection of the attributes. Some attributes were removed as they were considered irrelevant, such as the identity number of the report, number of the ambulance, and amount of time during which the sector was closed. When we considered mining information from all the roads, we eliminated the name of the road (to try to obtain general patterns regardless of a particular road) and we also eliminated the kilometer where the accident took place (since it depends on a particular road).

In the classification task, where the attribute class was chosen to be the severity of the accident, we eliminated two attributes which together were redundant with the class (the class was completely determined by them which were synonyms of the class).

Most data bases are not designed for analysis but mainly as an historical storage of information to be consulted. In many cases it is desirable to incorporate new information to the data base. In [6] the addition of new attributes derived from background knowledge proved to be useful in the discovery of more accurate and comprehensible patterns. We also decided to add new attributes which we thought were going to be useful for the analysis, such as, if the accident occurred during a holiday season, a particular festivity, or a particular season of the year.

Lesson 1: It is in general a good idea to keep as much attributes as possible as unexpected results may appear from apparently irrelevant attributes.

Corollary to lesson 1: There are nevertheless some attributes that should be removed as the number of attributes tend to degrade the performance of the algorithm. On the other hand, in many cases new attributes produce significantly better results. A careful selection of attributes is crucial for the following stages of the KDD progress and should always be given a careful thought.

3.2 Pre-processing

The pre-processing step involves cleaning the data, removing noise, if appropriate and necessary, and handling missing or unknown data. Upon closer analysis on the data, we encountered several inconsistencies in the data. Some instances have out of range or invalid values and most of them were replaced by unknown value. It is in general better to keep data with missing values than to eliminate it. In some cases, the right value was possible to deduce from other attributes (for instance, the day of the week considering the date of the accident). Other inconsistent values that were detected, for instance, between the brand of the vehicle and a particular model (e.g., Nissan and Topaz), were corrected giving preference to the model (e.g., replace Nissan with Ford). These attributes proved not to be relevant in the final results, although they may be of interest for car dealers. There were several typos in the data (e.g., Chirsler), which we were able to detect and correct.

There was a large number of missing values, whose proportion depended on the particular attribute. Most of them were less than 6%, however, some of them were around 50%, like the inclination of the road (ascending or descending), if the driver was using or not a seat belt or if he/she was drunk at the time of the accident (some statistics are given in table 1). These attributes were relevant for some of the discovered patterns.

Table 1. Percentage of some of the missing values in the data base of road accidents.

Attribute	ascending/ descending	damage to road	lane	straight/ curve	weather conditions	seat belt	drunk
Missing values (%)	55.96	18.49	2.83	6.23	2.53	46.10	45.74

Some attributes were discretize into more meaningful intervals, like the time of the accident, which was discretize into *dawn, sunset, day-light* and *night*.

The previously described steps and understanding of the domain, consumed most of our time.

Lesson 2: Be prepare to spend most of the time in the preparation and understanding of the data and the domain.

Corollary to Lesson 2: It pays off.

3.3 Definition of Methods, Goals and Transformation of Data

Our next step was to decide what to do. It is not always completely clear what type of analysis to perform on the data.

Our first step was to analyze single variables to obtain a general feeling of the domain (e.g., mean and standard deviation of particular attributes). We also plotted pairs of variables to get a basic "feeling" of the data. For instance, we plotted different attributes against the number of accidents. Without running any fancy algorithm, we were able to obtain the kilometers with the greatest number of accidents per road (e.g., the "infamous" curve called "la pera" in the road Mexico-Cuernavaca). Other interesting findings is that most of the accidents occur on straight roads, rather than curves. Most of the accidents involved grey cars and VWs. Some of these results need to be analyzed more carefully. For instance, finding that VWs are involved in more accidents does not necessarily mean that it is an unsafe brand, but it is most probably the case that it is the most popular brand in Mexico. With respect to the color, it may be the case, that it is a very popular color or that this color is more difficult to distinguished in roads than other colors. Although a more careful analysis needs to be performed, this initial analysis provided very valuable information.

Lesson 3: It is worth running as many basic analysis tools as possible, some of the most interesting findings can come from them. They help to understand the characteristics of the data and to clarify the data mining goals.

Corollary to Lesson 3: In many cases, most of this analysis has already been done.

3.4 Data Mining

There is a large number of public and commercially available algorithms for data mining. In general, the selection depends on the particular goals (classification, regression, segmentation, etc.) and the characteristics of the available data. In our case, we were specially interested in finding relations between the severity of the accidents with the rest of the attributes, but we were also interested in finding relations in general between attributes.

Considering the above goals, we decided to applied the following techniques (and particular tools):

- Bayesian network to analyze dependencies between attributes. There are very few available tools that induce Bayesian networks from data. In particular we use a commercially available tool called Bayesware [2].
- Association rules to characterize dependencies related with frequent co-occurrence between variables. We use a re-implementation of the Apriori algorithm [1] in Java which is part of the WEKA environment [11].
- Classification methods considering the severity of the accident as the class to predict. Here we used a Java re-implementation of C4.5 version 8, called j48, which is part of WEKA to induce decision trees, and CN2 [3], to induce classification rules.

The transformation process changes the data into the format required by each specific data mining algorithm. Since we used different algorithms, several transformations were performed (we are currently performing a more thorough analysis of the data with ADEX, an extendible data mining environment which can use several data formats and has a large set of data mining algorithms [9]). All of these methods were applied to all the data and to data of particular roads.

The decision of which tools/algorithms to use over the data directly affects the obtained patterns. Only a few years ago, the decision was mostly determined by the tools available to the user. With the amount of public domain and commercially available software, it is now possible to have a large variety of tools/algorithms from which to choose. In general, it is preferred to use tools which provide different algorithms. There has been some recent progress on automatically suggesting which algorithm to use given a particular data base (e.g., [7]), but these are still very preliminary and they tend to consider only a particular subset of algorithms.

Lesson 4: Do not make a decision on the algorithms to use until you have a clear idea of the goals and some insight of the general characteristics of the data (see Lesson 3).

Corollary to Lesson 4: Run as many algorithms as possible, given a particular goal; they often produce complimentary results.

3.5 Data Mining Process

For the classification task, our class attribute was severity of the injures, with four type of values: (i) no severe injuries, (ii) severe injuries, (iii) dead, and (iv) dead and severe injuries.

Our first trial with decision trees produced very large detailed models. A careful analysis of the results showed that we had several discrete attributes with a very large number of possible values. We decided to declare such attributes as continuous which gave much simpler results. One of such trees is shown in figure 2.

```
weather cond. <= 0
|   accident type <= 17: 1 (2180.0/45.0)
|   accident type > 17
|   |   accident type <= 19: 3 (70.0/5.0)
|   |   accident type > 19: 1 (5.0)
weather cond. > 0: 2 (954.0/61.0)
```

Fig. 2. Pruned tree obtained by j48 on the road accidents.

The pruned tree can be interpreted as follows:

If the weather conditions are not registered
  and the type of accident is a general type of collision
Then the accident is with no severe injuries
  (which covers 2,180 cases with a misclassification of 45).
If in the accident a car is flipped over, veers off, or a person is run over,
Then it is a mortal accident
If the weather conditions are registered
Then most of the accidents are with severe injuries

The above tree has an accuracy of 96.6% using a ten-fold stratified cross-validation test on the training data. The weather conditions are normally registered when there are relevant (e.g., rain, haze, fog).

If we remove the accident type, then *the severity of the accident is mainly determined by the weather conditions.*

Applying CN2 produced a very large number of rules with few conditions and small coverage. We eliminated some attributes, such as day of the month. After that, CN2 produced a more compact and meaningful set of results. Some of them are described below:

IF the accident type is a normal collision
  AND the weather condition is rain, fog or haze
THEN class = injured [169 0 0 4]
IF there is a multiple collision
  AND a vehicle veers off
  AND the weather conditions were not registered
THEN class = no severe injuries [0 638 5 0]
IF a car is flipped over, veers off or a person is run over,
  AND it is a two way road
  AND weather conditions are not registered

THEN class = mortal accident [0 2.33 51 0]
IF a car is flipped over, veers off or a person is run over,
AND weather conditions are reported
THEN class = mortal accident or severely injured [269 0 0 25]

The numbers between square brackets of the first rule mean that the rule cover 169 cases of class 1 (injured) and 4 cases of class 4 (mortal accidents). As can be seen, the rules are quite similar to the results obtained with the decision trees with some subtle differences.

We also tried to find relations among different variables. For them, we learned Bayesian networks and association rules.

From the Bayesian network, some of the results showed that *the data relating dates*, such as day of the week, month, year, season, festivity, etc., *are independent of the severity of the accident* and the conditions of such accident. This is important, since all the attributes related with holidays that we added turn out to be irrelevant, at least on the overall picture.

Also the tool found a *strong dependency between the inclination of the road, the lane where the vehicles were circulating and the severity of the accident.*

With the association rules we obtained many patterns, some of them with irrelevant and trivial associations, like "if July then summer". Some of the more interesting rules are shown below:

- (18%) if the accident involves one vehicle which veers off, then it is on straight roads (with 99% of confidence).
- (10%) if the accident involves one vehicle which veers off, was circulating on the slow lane of a two lane road, then the accident is without injuries (with 100% of confidence).

From the rules we were able to deduce that *45% of the accidents occur on straight roads with two lanes.* Some other associations were that accidents where a car veers off are without injuries, and most of them occur during the summer.

There were also some very specific pattern obtained from the road Mexico-Cuernavaca:

- Most of the severe injured accidents and mortal accidents involved multiple collisions, after kilometer 78.5, at night and a car was flipped over or a person was run over.

Lesson 5: The real relevant attributes are revealed only after doing several tests.

Lesson 6: The interpretation part is crucial and normally triggers the reinitialization of the whole process. Based on partial results, we repeated the experiments several times considering different attributes and running the algorithms with different parameters.

Corollary to Lesson 6: Most of the patterns turn out to be irrelevant, there are some interesting patterns, some already known, and very few are really new and useful to experts. Finding irrelevant patterns help us to get a better understanding of the data and the domain and direct us to ask better questions.

3.6 Main Results

Some obvious results are the correlation between number of deaths and not using a safety belt. There are other less intuitive, like grey color cars tend to have more accidents or that there are more bus accidents during the winter season that need more careful analysis.

It was found that particular climate conditions increase the number of accidents on particular areas. A preventive action could be to place a patrol in that area during such weather conditions and increase the warning signals.

After testing all the previously described algorithms under different conditions, here are some of the main results that were found:

- The attribute that tells whether the road is ascending or descending is directly related with the severity of the accident, the number of vehicles involved and the weather conditions.
- The causes of the accidents depends on the particular road.
- Most of the accidents occur on straight roads with two lanes and cars veering off.
- There are more accidents in the afternoon or dawn.
- If the vehicle was on the high speed lane there is a large probability that it will be a mortal accident.
- If the driver was drunk the accident is more severe.

For the Mexico-Cuernavaca road:

- Deaths depends on the inclination of the road and the lane where the vehicle was circulating.
- The seat belt affects the number of injure people and if the driver was wearing a safety belt (it appears as if drunk people tend not to use their seat belts!).
- Rain, wet carpet and fog is one of the mayor causes of accidents.
- Many accidents occur on descending sectors of the road and in open curves.
- Accidents depend on the kilometer, month and day of the week.
- There are more accident during summer.

Most of what we considered relevant results, came from the data mining tools.

The uncovered patterns should be used to take preventive actions. Some patterns need to be more carefully analyzed, interpreted and discussed with experts. A more detailed account of the patterns can be consulted in [5].

Lesson 7: The experts advice is crucial for the evaluation of patterns and recommendations of actions.

4 Conclusions and Future Work

This paper summarizes our experience in mining a real data base of road accidents. It illustrates part of what to expect when mining a real data base. We have included some hints and suggestions that we hope will be useful to other researchers using KDD technology.

Although, we think that new patterns can still be obtained from the data base, our preliminary finding gave us some very interesting patterns from the data, that can be directly applied.

Lesson 8: It is always possible to uncover new patterns.

References

1. Agrawal, R., Srikant, R. (1994). Fast algorithms for mining association rules in large databases (1994). In Bocca, J.M. Jarje, and C. Zaniolo (eds.), Proc. International Conference on Very Large Data Bases, Morgan Kaufmann, pp. 478-499.
2. Bayesware Limited (2000). Bayesware Discoverer 1.0 Professional Edition, http://bayesware.com/.
3. Clark, P. and Niblett, T. (1989). The CN2 induction algorithm. *Machine Learning Journal*, **3**(4):261-283.
4. Fayyad, U., Piatesky-Shapiro, G., Smyth, P. The KDD process for extracting useful knowledge from volumes of data. Comm. of the ACM, Nov. 95 Vol. 39, no. 11.
5. Heredia, D.M. (2001). Descubrimiento de Conocimiento en Datos de Accidentes Carreteros. Tesis de Maestría en Tecnologías de Información. ITESM - Cuernavaca.
6. Hernández, V., Morales, E. SIDEC: an attribute-based discovery system with background knowledge. *Congreso Iberoamericano de Inteligencia Artificial*, pp. 300-309, 1996.
7. Korb, K.B., Hope, L.R., and Hughes, M.J. (2001). The evaluation of predictive learners: some theoretical and empirical results. In *Lecture Notes in Artificial Intelligence 2167, 12th. European Conference on Machine Learning* (ECML-01). Luc de Raedt, Peter Flach (eds.), Springer Verlag, pp. 276-287.
8. Lobaco, J.F. (2000). Sistemas inteligentes de transporte aplicados para la prevención de accidentes. In *Primer Congreso Nacional de Prevención de Accidentes en Carreteras y Vialidades.*
9. Morales, E., Gómez, G., Sucar, L.E. (2001). ADEX: Ambiente de Descubrimiento EXtendible. In *Tercer Taller Internacional de Minería de Datos* (to be published).
10. Rulequest Research: data mining tools. C5.0 1.14 http://www.rulequest.com/see5-info.html
11. Witten, I.H. and Frank, E. (2000). Data Mining: practical machine learning tools with Java implementations. Morgan Kaufmann.

An Inference Engine for Web Adaptive Cooperative Work

Ana María Martínez-Enríquez[1], Aslam Muhammad[1],
Dominique Decouchant[2], and Jesús Favela[3]

[1] Depto de Ingeniería Eléctrica, CINVESTAV-IPN, D. F., México
ammartin@mail.cinvestav.mx, muhammad@computacion.cs.cinvestav.mx
[2] Laboratoire "Logiciels, Systèmes, Réseaux", Grenoble, France
Dominique.Decouchant@imag.fr
[3] Ciencias de la Computacíon, CICESE, Ensenada, México
favela@cicese.mx

Abstract. This paper describes the principle of an inference engine that analyzes useful information of actions, performed by cooperating users, to propose modifications of the states and/or the presentation of the shared objects. Using cooperative groupware applications, a group of people may work on the same task while other users may pursue their individual goals using various other applications (cooperative or non-cooperative) with different roles. In such environment, consistency, group awareness and security have essential significance. The work of each user can be observed by capturing their actions and then analyzing them in relation to the history of previous actions. The proposed Adaptive Inference Engine (AIE) behaves as a consumer of application events which analyzes this information on the basis of some predefined rules and then proposes some actions that may be applied within the cooperative environment. In all cases, the user controls the execution of the proposed group awareness actions in his working environment. A prototype of the AIE is developed using the Amaya Web Authoring Toolkit and the PIÑAS collaborative authoring middleware.

Keywords: Deductive and Adaptive User Environment, Inference Engine, AIE, Events, Producers and Consumers.

1 Introduction

In a cooperative environment, while sharing and cooperatively modifying shared resources, team members need to communicate and coordinate their actions. Especially in a distributed environment, co-presence notification and more generally group awareness [8] facilities are major features of groupware systems where collaborators are working 1) from different locations and 2) on different parts of the shared environment. It is also very difficult for a member to easily follow the contributions of others while he is producing a document. Additionally, if a user has limited skills in a specific subject, and an expert in this field is currently available, it will be convenient to make them aware of this fact. Hence we

C.A. Coello Coello et al. (Eds.): MICAI 2002, LNAI 2313, pp. 526–535, 2002.

propose to address these issues by: 1) establishing effective communication and coordination mechanisms, 2) integrating cooperative tools, 3) enhancing group awareness, 4) automatically detecting proximity of users work.

Our research concerns the cooperative production of complex XHTML/XML [1] documents on the Web. Thus, to achieve the above stated goals, we deal with the editing and cooperative actions within the cooperative environment on shared documents:

Applied actions on the document – document creation, naming, opening, saving, moving back and forward, but also:

- Editing actions: undo and redo of some actions, cut, copy and paste of some document parts, text search and spell checking,
- Formating: text alignment, justification, character and font style,
- Annotation: selection, add, post, delete or load annotation, move to selection or move to X-pointer and annotation configurating.

Coordination of the cooperative production – Document fragmentation and role assignment to co-authors

Applied actions to other shared objects – Definition and recognition of author, document resources (Metadata, pictures, video, etc), starting some tools, etc.

All of the above mentioned actions generate events which, when registered, will guide us to interpret the succession of the author actions on the shared resources using cooperative or non-cooperative applications. The event tracking is performed both on the local site and on the remote sites.

The storage and organization of events is done by the Event Manager or EM (section 3) which provides functions to allow the applications to capture both local and remote events in the same way. The Adaptive Inference Engine or AIE (section 4) constitutes a typical event consumer application for which we propose to develop innovative design principles and suited solutions to provide tools to realize a powerful Web distributed cooperative authoring environment. This research work is developed as part of the PIÑAS project (see section 2).

2 The PIÑAS / AllianceWeb Project

The PIÑAS / AllianceWeb project aims to determine the specific requirements and the dedicated techniques to support Web cooperative authoring environments, in order to enable distributed users to produce shared documents in a consistent and controlled way [3][4]. The AllianceWeb cooperative editor is being developed on top of PIÑAS (Platform for Interaction, Naming And Storage)[5] that provides means for supporting Web cooperative authoring (see Fig. 1).

To overcome WebDAV's [9] limitations and deficiencies [4], PIÑAS proposes support for cooperative authoring [7] based on document fragmentation, and so introduces several interesting distributed features: author identification, document and resource naming, document replication, consistency of the concurrent

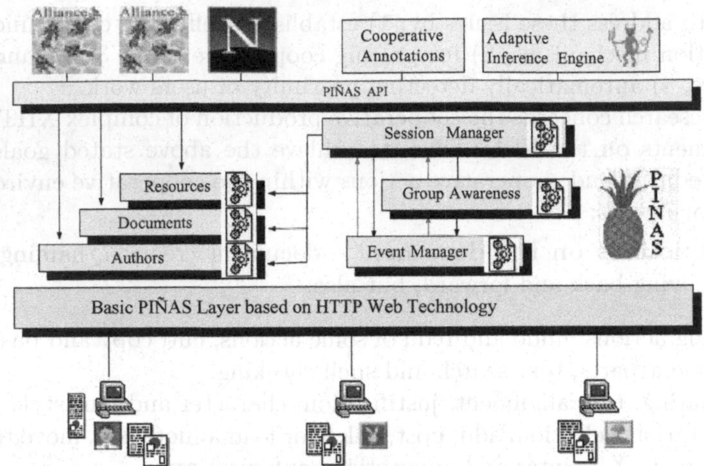

Fig. 1. The PIÑAS / AllianceWeb Architecture

(distributed) production, and an ad-hoc distributed document storage system. These features are based on the definition of basic concepts needed in a cooperative environment: users, documents, resources, and services.

PIÑAS provides a dedicated service (see Fig. 1) which offers simple but efficient and suited inter-application notification and communication functions. Over this platform, we have designed and implemented a Distributed Event Management Service that takes into account both the transmission and management of events between cooperative applications. An application (cooperative or not) is then essentially considered as producer and/or consumer of events.

3 The Distributed Event Manager

The middleware infrastructure Service is designed to allow easy communication and coordination between cooperative, non-cooperative and/or distributed application systems. Dedicated mechanisms are then provided to (possibly heterogeneous) applications to allow them to exchange data and to deliver pertinent information to the right place, in time, and in a useful format.

Thus, the PIÑAS middleware includes a Distributed Event Management Service (DEMS) whose aim is to capture the actions performed by users and their applications to store them as events, and distribute them to some (possibly remote) consumer applications interested in their treatment or analysis. The design principle of the DEMS function (see Fig. 2) includes the following characteristics:

1. It includes dedicated mechanisms for capturing and submitting events to the DEMS service that follows a three-step "connect-put-disconnect" (CPD) protocol. The producer have 1) to connect to the service, 2) send all its events, and 3) close the connection. Disconnection is typically performed when the application exits. Consumer applications follow a similar consumption protocol "connect-get-disconnect" (CGD).

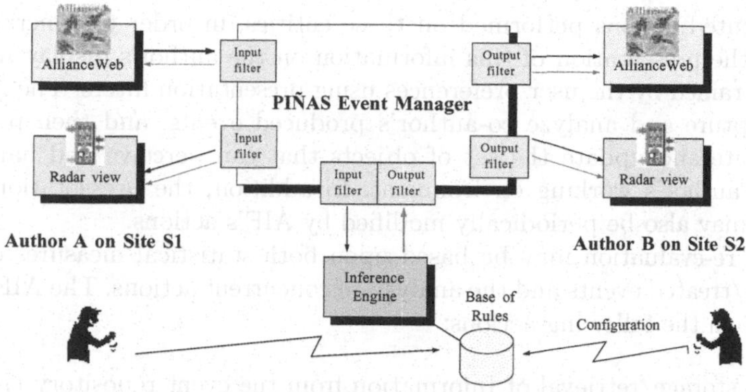

Fig. 2. Event Producers / Consumers and the Inference Engine

2. It offers input and output filtering functions. The DEMS function allows producer and consumer application to respectively initialize and modify filters to respectively control the exporting and the importing of events.
3. The DEMS manages a storage space where events are memorized in a circular buffer. This event storage space is limited, and if it becomes exhausted, new elements replace older ones. So, if some consumers are a bit slow, some events may be discarded and so missed. In a first step, we admit this limitation is acceptable because consumers are mainly observers that are tolerant to event loses.
4. Despite the fact that the EM service is distributed, the producers and consumers are well identified with a unique Id. Thus, each event generated by a particular producer is identified and delivered to interested (possibly remote) consumers in a reliable way.

The types of applications that are considered as producers and consumers of events are different. Basically the producers are cooperative or mono-user applications running the user's cooperative workspace that implements a service (authoring and/or browsing, communication facilities, document formatting, etc). These applications produce events that directly show user's actions. Consumer applications are especially designed to analyze all or part of the produced events to support group awareness functions [6], like a Radar view, co-presence tools and Inference Engine. However, it is important to remark that the Inference Engine is both a consumer and a producer of events (see section 4).

Producers and consumers can dynamically connect to the DEMS when they want to send/get some events to/from the event repository.

4 The Adaptive Inference Engine

The Adaptive Inference Engine (AIE) aims to make the cooperative authoring environments more flexible, adaptive and efficient. The AIE determines the manipulated entities (e.g. shared documents, images, tables and co-authors) and the executed actions performed on these entities, in order to generate and/or modify the presentation of this information on the author's display which may be constrained by the user preferences using presentation filters. The AIE's goal is to capture and analyze co-author's produced events, and then periodically re-evaluate and update the set of objects that can perceive and handle them in each author's working environment. In addition, the presentation of these objects may also be periodically modified by AIE's actions.

This re-evaluation may be based upon both statistical measures of already received/treated events and the analysis of concurrent actions. The AIE principle is based on the following actions:

1. The storage/retrieval of Information from the event repository (Knowledge Based). This is an essential task of a deductive system to determine and analyze the cooperative working actions, their sequences, number and frequency, working and storage locations of each user, and with the help of this analysis, it can estimate the objectives and roles of each user. This information is first recovered and organized by the event manager (section Fig. 2).
2. The deduction of some results based on pre-designed principles (Rule Base). A deductive system is assumed to work from known facts to new facts. The known facts in cooperative work are the actions that have been performed by different co-authors during their working session and the new facts are the particular information that is deduced from the analysis of the actions.
3. The proposition of some new actions, which may be adapted within the cooperative environment.

Thus, the deduction of useful information depends upon the complexity or simplicity of the known facts as we will see next. The eventual study of activities allows us to design a deductive system which is able to make analysis and inject some adaptable actions within the cooperative work. In order to achieve them, we explain each goal of the AIE by writing a rule that follows the principles of AllianceWeb [2]:

- **Document partitioning.** A document is split into several fragments taking into account its logical structure.
- **Assignment of the roles.** Each fragment has associated an editing role for each author: [M-Manager, W-Writer, R-Reader, N-Null].
- **Mutually exclusive fragment authoring.** The role assignment is dynamic, and the writer role allows to modify a fragment in exclusive mode.
- **Management of group awareness.** The system notifies the contribution of each co-author to other co-authors.

4.1 Enhancing Effective Author Communication and Coordination

During a working session, the AIE takes into account the interests (expressed with filters) of the co-authors in order to resolve conflicts produced by communication among co-authors. For example, one author may have an interest to communicate with a coauthor while the second one may be busy and not interested in talking for the moment. Thus, the AIE informs the co-authors about the communication mode of each other and their availability concerning to certain constraints: time and place. This is tedious for one co-author but necessary to maintain privacy, confidentiality and concentration on work of his colleagues:

```
If author (document) = x
If author (document) = y
If Sync_Communication (x) = ''False"
Then
   Communication_Tool (x) ← TurnOff
   Announce (y) ← Author ''x" does not accept synchronous communication
Endif
```

By contrast, when a co-author prefers to communicate directly while he is inserting some particular object (image, figures, tables, etc), the rule is established as:

```
If author (document) = x
If role (x) = ''W"
If Sync_Communication (x) = ''True"
If author (document) = y
If role (y) = ''W"
Then
   Communication_Tool (y) ← TurnOn
   Announce (y) ← Synchronous communication with ''x" is authorized
Endif
```

Moreover if one user is strongly interested in communicating with another co-author and there is a conflict between filtering preferences of these two co-authors then, depending upon the strong interest of the first co-author, the AIE reaches a decision to modify the cooperative environment of one of the two co-authors. The system informs the degree of availability of all the users in the global cooperative environment. The process is explained by the following rule:

```
If author (document) = y
If Async_Communication (y) = ''True"
If author (document) = x
If Communication_Interest (x) = y
   (author ''x" has strong interest to communicate with ''y")
Then
   Announce (y) ← Modify preferences for communication
   (AIE sends message to ''y" to change his mode of communication
   depending upon strong interest of ''x")
Endif
```

The inference engine optimizes the communication and coordination among co-authors to allow them to establish an intensive and efficient cooperative work, using multimedia communication, annotation and negotiation tools, etc.

4.2 Automatically Detecting an Expert and a Novice

The AIE is designed to make decisions and to determine the activities of authors in which they have more expertise and can perform more efficiently, thus other co-authors who are not experts can benefit from his/her knowledge. The definition of expert (specialist) and novice (beginner) may vary, for example a math-expert is someone who can solve (complex or simple) mathematical problems efficiently. Whereas a beginner is someone who finds it difficult to do so. The AIE facilitates the detection of the experts and makes this information available, so beginners can contact them to ask for help to solve a simple/complex mathematical formula. These type of actions give some online help in the cooperative environment.

```
If nature (fragment_1) = ``MathematicalFormula"
If author (fragment_1) = x
If role (x) = ``W"
If classification (x) ≠ ``Mathematician"
If author (fragment_2) = y
If classification (y) = ``Mathematician"
Then
   Announce (x) ← MathBaseConsultation about the expert ``y" presence
   Announce (x) ← Open_Communication with ``y"
Endif
```

The author can declare himself as an expert in his configuration file. Otherwise the AIE can deduce this by means of statistics, each time the co-author writes a document. For example, to produce a mathematical formula in MathML, creation or modification events like those corresponding to <mrow> <mi> <mn> tags occur. The complexity and richness of the problem and solution should also be considered: e.g. the number of mathematical elements and their combination. The AIE deduces these facts from a large set of events captured periodically and compares them repeatedly with the previous results.

4.3 Helping the Co-authors with the Existing Shared Objects

During a particular session the cooperative authors manipulate shared objects that they utilize at various times and different locations. The AIE informs them about these type of objects that exist in the shared database as follows:

```
If author (document) = x
If role (x) = ``W"
If Editing_Action (x) = ``Insert_Image"
If DB_Shared_Objects = ``True"
   (the DB database of shared objects exists)
Then
  Announce(x) <- Consult the DB_shared_Objects
Endif
```

The shared objects database must be open to let the objects be shared by the co-authors. The database has the name of the shared objects, its type and storage location, who has the right to share this object, and how many co-authors had already shared this object. Some of various events generated during the insertion of an image in AllianceWeb based XHTML document are related to the following tags: <elem_new>, <elem_select>, <elem_pict>, <elemt_insert>.

By contrast, a co-author can add his self-prepared-object into the shared database, in order to be reused by his/her colleagues. The rule that establishes this situation is:

```
If author (document) = x
If role (x) = ‘‘W"
If DB_Shared_Objects = ‘‘True"
If Editing_Action (x) = ‘‘Create_Image"
If Shared_Object (x) = ‘‘Image_created"
   (an ‘‘Image" is created as a shared object by author ‘‘x")
If Pertain (DB_Shared_Objects) != ‘‘Image_created"
   (the ‘‘Image" does not exist in the DB database)
Then
   Integrate (DB_Shared_Objects) ← ‘‘Image_created"
   Announce (x) ← ‘‘Image_created" is available to be used by co-authors
Endif
```

4.4 Informing about Occurrence of Particular Events

An application or co-author may have interest in the occurrence of an special event for which they register their request to the AIE to be informed immediately when this particular event occurs. For example "x" has the interest to communicate with author "y", who has the right to annotate the document on which author "x" is writing. Then "x" enrolls his request to be informed immediately when "y" logs in. The rule can be described as:

```
If author (document) = x
If role (x) = ‘‘W"
If Sync_Communication (x) = ‘‘True"
If author (document) = y
If Annotation (y) = ‘‘True"
If session (y) = ‘‘Just_Login"
Then
   Announce (x) <- Author ‘‘y" has just logged on
   (a message is sent to ‘‘x" about ‘‘y" logging)
Endif
```

4.5 Well Administrating Author Preferences

Each co-author sets preferences to allow other co-authors to communicate or not with him, to control their accesses to his documents and resources, and to specify language and tools for negotiation. The AIE provides the information about the preferences of different co-authors. The document manager may have the right to see the preferences of the authors as follows:

```
If author (document) = x
If role (x) = ''M"
If author (document) = y
If query_action (x) = preferences_set (y)
Then
   announce (x) ← Display preferences of co-author ''y"
Endif
```

5 Conclusions and Perspectives

We proposed an event driven inference engine in the domain of middleware that works on top of an event repository, as a consumer of events received from the producer applications. The AIE receives events, analyzes them taking into consideration some predefined rules and principles and then proposes some actions which are injected within the cooperative environment for the progression of cooperative and non-cooperative applications. The DEMS and the AIE perform glue between producer and consumer applications. The actions performed by cooperating entities (co-authors and applications) are termed as events which are stored for reproduction of actions. The AIE consumes these events to achieve the following goals:

- To enhance communication, coordination, and awareness among co-authors. For example, the AIE informs immediately (synchronously or asynchronously) about the occurrence of the requested event.
- To integrate more functionalities to cooperative tools. The AIE informs co-authors of the existence of an object within the cooperative environment that can possibly be shared.
- To automatically detect expertise and users in trouble, as well as proximity of co-authors. From actions performed by the co-authors, determining interest and expertise and let these expertise be made available to beginners.

Other important actions in which the AIE will be centralized are: security regarding privacy and confidentiality, as well as recovery of lost data from the historical studies and analysis of cooperative environment. We may be able to determine which action caused loss of data and by reversal/recovery of that particular action we may recover some or the total contents of data.

Acknowledgements

This work is supported by ECOS and ANUIES organizations (project M98M01), by CONACyT projects (29729-A and 33067-A), and by CNRS-CONACyT cooperation projects (9018 / E130-505 and 10395 / E130-706).

Additional support is provided by Secretaría de Relaciones Exteriores de México, Dirección General de Cooperación Educativa Cultural, Dirección de Cooperación e Intercambio Económico (CED-III, 811.5/137).

References

1. N. Bradley, *The XML Companion,* First edition, Addison-Wesley Pub. Co., September 1998.
2. D. Decouchant, V. Quint and M. Romero Salcedo, "Structured and Distributed Cooperative Editing in a Large Scale Network", *Groupware and Authoring (Chapter 13),* R. Rada, ed., Academic Press, London (Great Britain), pp. 265-295, May 1996.
3. D. Decouchant, A. M. Martínez and E. Martínez, "Documents for Web Cooperative Authoring", *In Proc. CRIWG'99, 5th International Workshop on Groupware,* IEEE Computer Society, Cancun (México), 15-18 September 1999.
4. D. Decouchant, A. M. Martínez, "A Cooperative, Deductive, and Self-Adaptive Web Authoring Environment", *In Proc. of the Mexican International Conference on Artificial Intelligence (MICAI'2000),* Lecture Notes in Artificial Intelligence, Springer Verlag, Acapulco (México), pp. 443-457, 11-14 April 2000.
5. D. Decouchant, J. Favela and A. M. Martínez-Enríquez, "PIÑAS: A Middleware for Web Distributed Cooperative Authoring", *In Proc. of the 2001 Symposium on Applications and the Internet (SAINT'2001),* IEEE Computer Society and IPJ Information Processing Society of Japan, San Diego, California (USA), pp. 187-194, 8-12 January 2001.
6. P. Dourish and S. Bly, "Portholes: Supporting Awareness in a Distributed Work Group", *Proceedings of CHI'92 on Human Factors in Computing Systems,* P. Bauersfeld, J. Bennett and G. Lynch, ed., pp. 541-547, Monterey, California (USA), May 1992.
7. N. Streitz, J. Haake, J. Hannemann, A. Lemke, W. Schler, H. Schütt and M. Thüring, "SEPIA: A Cooperative Hypermedia Authoring Environment", *Proceedings of the European Conference on Hypertext and Hypermedia ECHT'92,* D. Lucarella, J. Nanard, M. Nanard, P. Paolini, ed., pp. 11-22, ACM Press, November 1992.
8. J. C. Lauwers and K. A. Lantz, "Collaboration Awareness in Support of Collaboration Transparency: Requirements for the Next Generation of Shared Window Systems", *Proceedings of CHI'90 on Human Factors in Computing Systems,* J. Carrasco Chew and J. Whiteside, ed., pp. 303-311, Seattle Washington, (USA), April 1990.
9. E. J. Whitehead Jr., M. Wiggins, "WEBDAV: IETF Standard for Collaborative Authoring on the Web", *IEEE Internet Computing,* pp. 34-40, September–October 1998.

Faults Diagnosis in Industrial Processes with a Hybrid Diagnostic System

Luis E. Garza[1], Francisco J. Cantú[1], and Salvador Acevedo[2]

Center for Artificial Intelligence[1], Department of Electrical Engineering[2]
Monterrey Institute of Technology
CETEC Tower, 5*th* floor, 2501 Garza Sada Avenue
Monterrey, NL, 64849, Mexico
Phone: (+52-8) 328-4197, Fax: (+52-8) 328-4189
{legarza,fcantu,sacevedo}@campus.mty.itesm.mx

Abstract. In this paper we present an approach to detect and diagnose multiple faults in industrial processes with a hybrid multiagent diagnostic system. We integrate artificial intelligence model-based diagnosis with control systems Fault Detection and Isolation (FDI) techniques. We adapt a probabilistic logic framework to perform fault detection and diagnosis tasks. The whole diagnosis task is performed by agents and is executed in two phases. In first phase, the Alarm Processor (AP) agent processes the discrete observations and alarms, and outputs a set of most likely faulted components. In second phase, Fault Detection (FD) agents discard the components not participating in the failure, by analyzing a set of continuous signals, that have a different behavior in normal and in faulty state. The FD agents include dynamic probabilistic models, able to deal with noise, nonlinear behavior and missing data. The output of the diagnostic system includes the components with abnormal behavior and the type of faults. We have tested our approach by diagnosing faults in a simulated electrical power network.

1 Introduction

With increasing process monitoring and ever-higher level of automation to achieve desired quality, industrial plants and technical processes have become more vulnerable to faults in instrumentation. The early detection of faults can help to avoid system shutdown, breakdown and even catastrophes involving human fatalities and material damage.

When unexpected downtimes caused by failures in process equipment occur, they should be minimized by the maintenance department, detecting and diagnosing the faults to repair them as soon as possible, even though this is not an easy task. Some of the fault scenarios are very complex, involve a large number of components, and have noisy and uncertain data.

Therefore, in order to increase the efficiency of the maintenance personnel when they attend failures, it is necessary to provide them with more powerful automated tools that help to speed up the process of diagnosis. Such a system

C.A. Coello Coello et al. (Eds.): MICAI 2002, LNAI 2313, pp. 536–545, 2002.

should be capable of handling large amounts of discrete as well as continuous valued signals. A diagnostic system able to deal with discrete and continuous signals, is what we called a *Hybrid Diagnostic System*.

In recent years much research has been devoted to the diagnosis of industrial processes, and results have been reported in [4]. Current hybrid diagnosis approaches, assume single fault scenarios [1,15], rely on physical causal models that are frequently not known in analytical form or are too complicated for calculations [12], or are not being scaled up to large systems with many discrete and continuos signals [6]. Another characteristic of these approaches, is that none of the above methods addresses the problem of missing data.

Typical industrial implementations of diagnostic systems include mathematical models and/or neural or fuzzy approaches. Mathematical models require precise mathematical relationships between process variables that most of the time are not known or are too complex to implement in real world processes. Neural networks are black-box models that do not provide more information, than the one that can be inferred from the output response, have problems with overfitting and poor performance in missing information scenarios [16]. In fuzzy systems applied to diagnosis the number of rules may grow exponentially even for small components or processes, and they can not deal in explicit form with missing inputs [5].

We propose a hybrid diagnosis methodology that integrates artificial intelligence model-based diagnosis and control systems fault detection and isolation techniques. This approach is adequate for the diagnosis of large industrial systems with discrete and continuous signals, and is able to deal with noise, missing data and nonlinearities in continuous signals.

2 Fault Detection and Diagnosis

The process of automated fault diagnosis can be viewed as a sequential process involving two steps: the fault detection, and the fault diagnosis task. Fault detection is concerned with the extraction of relevant features that indicate the existence of a fault. Fault diagnosis refers to the dimensional, spatial and temporal location and categorization of a fault or a set of faults in a given system.

Basic research on Fault Detection and Isolation (FDI) techniques, has gained increasing consideration world-wide. However, they are based on process models that attempt to construct a functional representation of a reference data set. When classical models (e.g. autoregressive moving average or ARMA models) are used, the investigators may sacrifice explicit knowledge of domain uncertainty for simplicity when they are forced to wrestle complex problems into parametric models [2]. Another disadvantage is that traditional models' performance degrades when confronted with missing information scenarios (e.g. partially corrupted sensor data).

In the other side, probabilistic models such as Dynamic Bayesian Networks (DBNs) [9] and Dynamic Network Models (DNMs) [2], are adequate tools for modeling and tracking, when the number of nodes and states is not large. However, these methods are disadvantageous due to space and computational requirements, to model a large quantity of subsystems or components, as those we can find in large industrial processes.

We propose a novel framework for fault detection that integrates discrete dynamic probabilistic models (DPMs) in an FDI observer scheme. The DPMs are learned from raw data, have simple inference structure and engine, and are able to deal with nonlinear behavior, noise, and missing inputs.

Diagnosis methods can be classified in two main approaches: The *empirical association-based* approach, and the *model-based* approach. The model-based approach is based on the fact that a component is faulty if its correct behavior is inconsistent with the observations. The empirical association-based approach takes great advantage of faulty models, that is, knowledge about failures given by experts. Model-based diagnosis is computationally efficient and has a well-developed set of inference algorithms with provable properties, such as soundness and completeness of diagnostics given the model, and they are becoming fairly successful tackling real-world applications. We use model-based diagnosis to process all discrete symptoms. Our probabilistic logic framework is able to deal with noise and missing data.

3 Description of the Approach

In the proposed methodology, the diagnostic system relies on the concept of agents. An agent implements a mapping from inputs history (sensor measurements or alarms) to outputs (diagnoses). In our approach, there are three types of agents: *Nature* is regarded as an agent that provides stochastic assumptions about components behavior. The *Alarm Processor* (AP) agent produces a set of explanations consistent with first observed symptoms. The AP agent is the basis of the first phase of diagnosis.

The second phase is based on *Fault Detection* (FD) agents associated to every component in the process. FD agents are modeled as dynamic agents specifying how streams of sensor data entail fault decisions. The output of the AP agent represents a partial diagnosis to be confirmed by FD agents. The FD agents are the main part of the second phase of diagnosis.

The diagnostic system architecture, shown in Figure 1, includes the following modules:

1. A *knowledge base* that stores the static model of the process under diagnosis. The model consists of a set of logic clauses and a set of probabilities about component states.
2. An *inference engine*, which processes the discrete and continuous symptoms to deliver a final diagnosis.
3. A *heuristics* module, that includes the strategies to select the most useful set of explanations, based on probabilities.
4. The *discretization* module, which converts the continuous signals measurements into a finite set of discrete states.

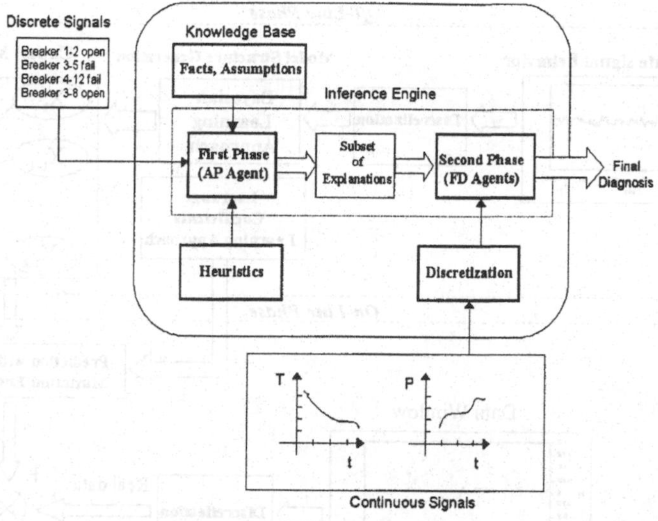

Fig. 1. Architecture of the DDICL system

The process model used by the diagnostic first phase includes the causal relationships between processes' components, observations or symptoms, and fault modes. In this step, reliability methods (such as Failure Mode and Effect Analysis or FMEA methods) or other approaches can be used to build the diagnostic model. We use Bayesian networks models, where cause-effect relationships and probabilities were extracted from expertise. The Bayesian network is translated to Horn clauses and then integrated to the probabilistic logic framework.

The first phase generates explanations consistent with the set of first observed symptoms. In large systems, with many symptoms coming from the process, many explanations can be generated. The fault probabilities computed by the diagnostic system and heuristics, are used to handle the combinatorial explosion in the number of explanations generated. The output of the first phase is a reduced set of explanations with the most likely components in a faulted state.

With noisy or unreliable information, it is possible that some of these components really did not participate in the failure scenario. To discard these components included in the reduced set of explanations, a second phase is introduced. This phase determines the real faulted components, based on the analysis made by the fault detection agents.

The second phase of diagnosis is a refining stage, where suspicious components given by the first phase, are analyzed by fault detection agents. The specification for a FD agent, makes use of probabilistic functions as a mean of modeling the steady-state dynamics of sensor measurements. The probabilistic functions are based on a statistical maximum entropy classifier [16]. The classifier has as input the sensor measurements previously discretized by using an adequate policy. The model represents the no-fault behavior of the associated component. The structure of the fault detection agent is shown in Figure 2.

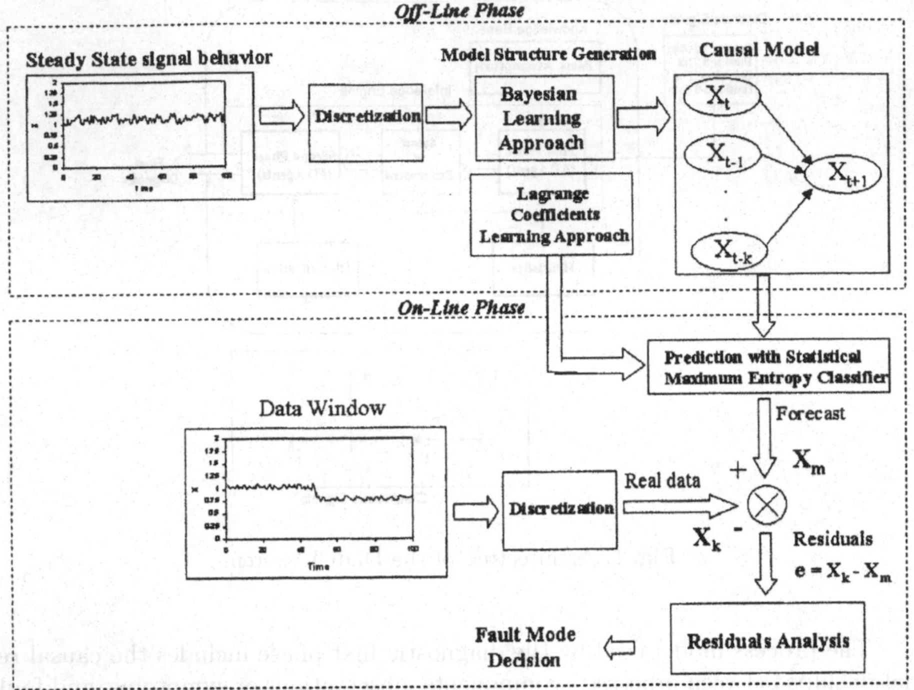

Fig. 2. Structure of a Fault Detection Agent

The offline phase involves the learning from time series data of the causal structure and the Lagrange coefficients for the probabilistic model. The online phase generates residuals by comparing the data under analysis and the steady state model, in order to determine the existence of a specific fault. The analysis of residuals determines the mode of operation of the device, and is achieved with the help of an Error Weighted Moving Average (EWMA) scheme, and suitable limit thresholds.

We use an extended Dynamic Independent Choice Logic (DICL) as the framework to develop the whole hybrid diagnostic system.

4 The Diagnostic Dynamic Independent Choice Logic

The Dynamic Independent Choice Logic is a logic for modeling multiple agents under uncertainty. DICL comprises a semantic framework that allows for independent choices made by various agents including Nature, and a logic program that gives the consequences of the choices. DICL relies on Bayesian inference, influence diagrams and decision theory to handle uncertainty.

The adapted DICL that supports the specification of the alarm processor agent and the fault detection agents, is what we called the Diagnostic Dynamic Independent Choice Logic (DDICL).

We assume a discrete time structure $\mathcal{T}$, that is totally ordered and has a metric over intervals. The logic programs representing the agents, are axiomatized in *phase space* [3].

A specialization of DICL used for diagnosis applications is defined as follows:

Definition 1.1. A diagnostic **Dynamic Independent Choice Logic theory** is a tuple $\langle \mathcal{A}, \mathcal{C}_0, \mathcal{F}_{AP}, \mathcal{P}_0, \mathcal{ASM}_a \rangle$, where

- $\mathcal{A}$ is a finite set of agents containing three types of agents: *Nature*, *Alarm Processor*, and *Fault Detection* agents,
- $\mathcal{C}_0$, agent *Nature*'s choice space, is a choice space with alternatives controlled by nature. These alternatives may correspond to possible states of a device,
- $\mathcal{F}_{AP}$, is the logic program specification for the alarm processor agent. This agent generates a set of explanations consistent with first observed symptoms.
- $\mathcal{P}_0$ is a function $\bigcup \mathcal{C}_0 \to [0,1]$ such that $\forall \chi \in \mathcal{C}_0 \quad \sum_{\alpha \in \chi} \mathcal{P}_0(\alpha) = 1$,
- $\mathcal{ASM}_a$ is a function such that $\mathcal{ASM}_a$ is an agent specification module for *Fault Detection* agent a.

We extend the definition for an *Agent Specification Module* (definition 2.1 given in [10]) with the notion of *probabilistic observation function*, to specify a *Fault Detection* agent:

Definition 1.2. An agent specification module for FD agent $a \neq \{0, AP\}$, written $\mathcal{ASM}_a$, is a tuple $\langle\ \mathcal{I}, \mathcal{O}, \mathcal{R}, \mathcal{L},\ \mathcal{F}_a,\ \phi\rangle$ where

- $\mathcal{I}$ is a set of fluents called the **inputs**. They specify what sensor values are available at various times. The range the input trace is the cross product of the ranges of the fluents in the inputs.
- $\mathcal{O}$, is a set of fluents called the **outputs**. An output is a propositional fluent that specifies a decision about the existence of a fault in a component at various times.
- $\mathcal{R}$, is a set of fluents called the **recallable** fluents. These are fluents whose previous values can be recalled.
- $\mathcal{L}$, is as set of fluents called the **local** fluents. These are fluents that are neither inputs, outputs nor recallable.
- $\mathcal{F}_a$ is an acyclic logic program. $\mathcal{F}_a$ specifies how the outputs are implied by the inputs, and perhaps previous values of the recallable fluents, local fluents, arithmetic constraints and other non-temporal relations as intermediaries.
- ϕ, is the **probabilistic observation function**, $\phi : Q \to \ \mathcal{P}_V$, mapping observation states Q into a distribution over predicted states $\mathcal{P}_V$. This function implements the dynamic probabilistic models.

5 Application

We illustrate the application of our approach in a simulated industrial-scale electrical power network. In case of power system disturbances, control center

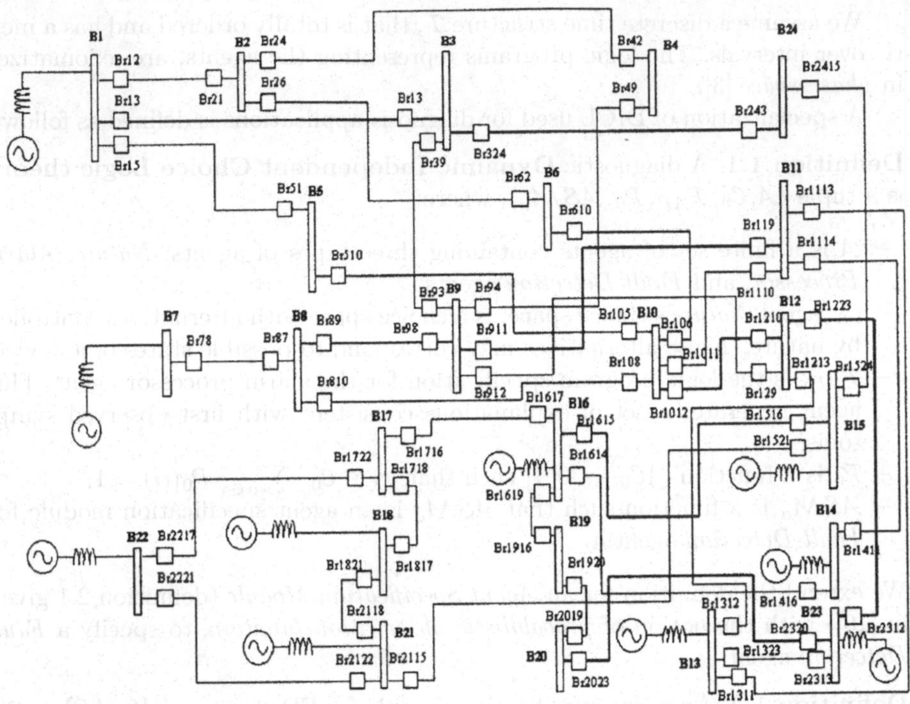

Fig. 3. IEEE reliability test system fault scenario

operators must use their judgement and experience to determine the possible faulted elements as the first step in the restoration procedures. The estimation of the fault location is difficult due to the possible presence of multiple faults, the overwhelming number of alarms generated, and the possibility of malfunction of protective devices. The type of faults include symmetrical faults (e.g. a three-phase to ground fault) and unsymmetrical faults (e.g. a line-to-ground fault).

The case study is the diagnosis of faults in a 24-node power transmission network described in [13] and shown in Fig. 3. The system consist of 24 nodes, 34 lines and 68 breakers. We run intensive simulations with single and multiple faults, multiple modes of failure, and load changes in the network. The Microtran software package [7] provided the voltage waveforms of the different scenarios. We simulate the missing data by deleting randomly 10 % of the original voltage data.

We describe one of the tested scenarios:

Inputs to phase 1

breakers opened:

(br3-1, br9-3, br9-4, br8-9, br9-11, br12-9, br10-6, br10-8, br11-10, br12-10, br16-14, br16-15, br16-17, br19-16)

breakers failed: (br3-9, br9-8, br9-12, br10-11, br10-12, br16-19)

Table 1. Evaluation by type of fault

Component State	*Correct*	*Wrong*	*% Accuracy*
A-B-C-GND	14	0	100.0
A-B-GND	10	0	100.0
A-GND	12	2	85.7
A-B	15	3	83.3
B-C	16	0	100.0
NO FAULT	17	7	70.8

Table 2. Evaluation by node

Node number	*Correct*	*Wrong*	*% Accuracy*
3	19	5	79.1
9	21	3	87.5
10	21	3	87.5
13	23	1	95.8

breakers with unknown status:
(br3-24, br9-3, br 10-5)

Output from phase 1
(*nodes: B3, B9, B10, B12, B16*)

Inputs to phase 2
(*nodes: B3, B9, B10, B12, B16*)
voltage measurements at nodes B3, B9, B10 ,B12, and B16

Output from phase 2
node B3 phase-A-to-B-to-GROUND Fault
node B9 phase A-to-B Fault
node B10 three-phase-to-GROUND Fault
node B16 phase-C-to-GROUND Fault

The diagnostic system accurately found the type of fault in the real faulted nodes B3, B9, B10 and B16. The output of the first phase of the diagnostic system was obtained by selecting the intersection of the most likely explanations with minimum probability threshold of 0.01.

Although node B12 is not a faulted node, it appears in the suspicious components because its associated breakers are present on the list of first symptoms. The voltage at node B12 is perturbed by the fault events at neighbor nodes. However, the FD agent for node B12 can determine the no-fault decision by analyzing the EWMA indices. In contrast, the analysis of other nodes voltages, like node B3 voltage, can confirm the type of fault by analyzing the EWMA indices. The overall performance evaluation of the system was achieved by randomly simulating different fault modes over a set of four randomly selected nodes. The summary of results are shown in Table 1 and 2.

6 Related Work

HybridDX [12] is a diagnostic system used in aeronautics, that include model-based diagnosis and continuous and discrete simulations of continuous processes. To model the dynamics in HybridDX, they use physical causal models that are frequently not known in analytical form or too complicated for calculations. In [6] a hybrid dynamic Bayesian network is used for monitoring and fault detection. We claim that using a tracking in similar fault scenarios as those we presented, is impractical and possibly unfeasible. In [15], Sampath presents a hybrid approach that incorporates the concept of virtual sensors and discrete events diagnosis. The analysis of sensor signals is performed by using different techniques, such as spectral analysis, principal components analysis, statistical discrimination, and practically any other technique. The approach by Sampath assumes single fault scenarios and does not address the problem of incomplete sensor data.

In [14] a hybrid algorithm for fault diagnosis in power networks is described. The algorithm includes hierarchical models that combine several reasoning methods such as heuristic, temporal, model-based diagnosis and neural networks. The system can handle multiple fault scenarios and multiple solutions, but can not discriminate between multiple mode faults (e.g. a three-phase-to ground fault from a line-to-line fault) as we do in our approach.

In [8] a diagnostic approach for electrical distribution systems is described. The system uses rule-based schemes together with neural networks. To discriminate between different mode faults, the system uses voltage magnitudes and phase angle of line currents, whereas in our approach we use just the voltage magnitudes to achieve the same function. As they implement the fault recognition task with neural networks, they can not deal with missing information scenarios. Their rule-based scheme is weaker than our approach in the way to handle uncertainty.

7 Conclusions

We have presented a methodology to diagnose hybrid systems for large and complex processes with discrete and continuous signals. Our approach integrates techniques from artificial intelligence model-based diagnosis and fault detection and isolation (FDI) approaches from control systems theory. We also have developed a novel probabilistic approach to model the dynamics of complex processes. The dynamic probabilistic models have a simple structure and inference engine and can deal with highly nonlinear behavior and missing data. We have shown a successful application in a simulated power network. The future work will focus on improving the percentage of identification of faults by exploiting more sophisticated techniques of residual analysis and the integration of fault models in first and second phase.

Acknowledgements

First author wish to thanks the support provided by the Mexican Consejo Nacional de Ciencia y Tecnologia.

References

1. Basseville M., Benveniste A., and Tromp L. 1998. Diagnosing Hybrid Dynamical Systems: Fault Graphs, statistical residuals and Viterbi Algorithms. In *Proc. of the 37th IEEE CDC*, Tampa, Fla. 1998, pp. 3757-3762.
2. Dagum P., Galper A., Horvitz E., and Seiver A. 1995. Uncertain Reasoning and Forecasting, Technical Report, Stanford University School of Medicine, Stanford, Cal. June 29.
3. Dean T., and Wellman M. 1991. *Planning and Control.* San Mateo, CA: Morgan Kaufmann.
4. Isermann R. and Ballé P. 1997. Trends in the Application of Model-Based Fault Detection and Diagnosis of Technical Processes. *Control Eng. Practice*, Vol. 5, No. 5, pp. 709-719.
5. Isermann R. 1997. On Fuzzy Logic Applications for Automatic Control, Supervision, and Fault Diagnosis. *IEEE Trans. on SMC-Part A: Systems and Humans*, Vol. 28, No. 2, pp. 221-235.
6. Lerner U., Parr R., Koller, D., and Biswas G. 2000. Bayesian Fault Detection and Diagnosis in Dynamic Systems. In *Proc. of the 17th National Conference on AI 2000*,Austin, TX, August 2000, pp. 531-537.
7. Microtran Power Systems Analysis Corporation. Microtran Reference Manual, Vancouver, BC Canada 1997.
8. Momoh J., Dias L., and Laird D. 1997. An Implementation of a Hybrid Intelligent Tool for Distribution System Fault Diagnosis. *IEEE Trans. on Power Delivery*, Vol. 12, No. 2, pp. 1035-1040.
9. Nicholson A. E., and Brady J. M. 1994. Dynamic Belief Networks for Discrete Monitoring. *IEEE Trans. On SMC* 24(11): 1593-1610.
10. Poole D., Logic programming for robot control. In *Proc. 14 th IJCAI, Montreal, August, 1995*, 150-157.
11. Poole D., The Independent Choice Logic for Modeling Multiple Agents under Uncertainty, *Artificial Intelligence*, Vol. 94, No. 1-2, special issue on economic principles of multi-agent systems, pp. 7-56, 1997.
12. Provan G. and Elsley D. 2000. Software Toolkit for Aerospace Systems Diagnostics. In*IEEE Aerospace Conf. Proc. 2000*, Vol. 6, pp. 327-335.
13. Reliability Test System Task Force, Application of Probability Methods Subcomitee. IEEE Reliability Test System. *IEEE Trans. on Power Apparatus and Systems*, Vol. 98, No. 6, pp. 2047-2054, 1979.
14. Rayudu R., Samarasinghe S., and Maharaj A., A Co-operative Hybrid Algorithm for Fault Diagnosis in Power Transmission, *IEEE Trans. on Power Delivery*, Vol. 12, No. 1, pp. 1939-1944, 2000.
15. Sampath M. 2001. A Hybrid Approach to Failure Diagnosis in Industrial Systems. In *Proc. of the ACC 2001*, pp. 2077-2082.
16. Yan L., and Miller D., General statistical inference for discrete and mixed spaces by an approximate application of the maximum entropy principle. *IEEE Trans. On Neural Networks*, **11** (3): 558-573.

Author Index

Lecture Notes in Artificial Intelligence (LNAI)

Vol. 2120: H.S. Delugach, G. Stumme (Eds.), Conceptual Structures: Broadening the Base. Proceedings, 2001. X, 377 pages. 2001.

Vol. 2123: P. Perner (Ed.), Machine Learning and Data Mining in Pattern Recognition. Proceedings, 2001. XI, 363 pages. 2001.

Vol. 2132: S.-T. Yuan, M. Yokoo (Eds.), Intelligent Agents: Specification, Modeling, and Application. Proceedings, 2001. X, 237 pages. 2001.

Vol. 2143: S. Benferhat, P. Besnard (Eds.), Symbolic and Quantitative Approaches to Reasoning with Uncertainty. Proceedings, 2001. XIV, 818 pages. 2001.

Vol. 2148: A. Nareyek (Ed.), Local Search for Planning and Scheduling. Proceedings, 2000. IX, 171 pages. 2001.

Vol. 2155: H. Bunt, R.-J. Beun (Eds.), Cooperative Multimodal Communication. Proceedings, 1998. VIII, 251 pages. 2001.

Vol. 2157: C. Rouveirol, M. Sebag (Eds.), Inductive Logic Programming. Proceedings, 2001. X, 261 pages. 2001.

Vol. 2159: J. Kelemen, P. Sosík (Eds.), Advances in Artificial Life. Proceedings, 2001. XIX, 724 pages. 2001.

Vol. 2160: R. Lu, S. Zhang, Automatic Generation of Computer Animation. XI, 380 pages. 2002.

Vol. 2166: V. Matoušek, P. Mautner, R. Mouček, K. Taušer (Eds.), Text, Speech and Dialogue. Proceedings, 2001. XIII, 542 pages. 2001.

Vol. 2167: L. De Raedt, P. Flach (Eds.), Machine Learning: ECML 2001. Proceedings, 2001. XVII, 618 pages. 2001.

Vol. 2168: L. De Raedt, A. Siebes (Eds.), Principles of Data Mining and Knowledge Discovery. Proceedings, 2001. XVII, 510 pages. 2001.

Vol. 2173: T. Eiter, W. Faber, M. Truszczynski (Eds.), Logic Programming and Nonmonotonic Reasoning. Proceedings, 2001. XI, 444 pages. 2001.

Vol. 2174: F. Baader, G. Brewka, T. Eiter (Eds.), KI 2001: Advances in Artificial Intelligence. Proceedings, 2001. XIII, 471 pages. 2001.

Vol. 2175: F. Esposito (Ed.), AI*IA 2001: Advances in Artificial Intelligence. Proceedings, 2001. XII, 396 pages. 2001.

Vol. 2182: M. Klusch, F. Zambonelli (Eds.), Cooperative Information Agents V. Proceedings, 2001. XII, 288 pages. 2001.

Vol. 2190: A. de Antonio, R. Aylett, D. Ballin (Eds.), Intelligent Virtual Agents. Proceedings, 2001. VIII, 245 pages. 2001.

Vol. 2198: N. Zhong, Y. Yao, J. Liu, S. Ohsuga (Eds.), Web Intelligence: Research and Development. Proceedings, 2001. XVI, 615 pages. 2001.

Vol. 2203: A. Omicini, P. Petta, R. Tolksdorf (Eds.), Engineering Societies in the Agents World II. Proceedings, 2001. XI, 195 pages. 2001.

Vol. 2225: N. Abe, R. Khardon, T. Zeugmann (Eds.), Algorithmic Learning Theory. Proceedings, 2001. XI, 379 pages. 2001.

Vol. 2226: K.P. Jantke, A. Shinohara (Eds.), Discovery Science. Proceedings, 2001. XII, 494 pages. 2001.

Vol. 2246: R. Falcone, M. Singh, Y.-H. Tan (Eds.), Trust in Cyber-societies. VIII, 195 pages. 2001.

Vol. 2250: R. Nieuwenhuis, A. Voronkov (Eds.), Logic for Programming, Artificial Intelligence, and Reasoning. Proceedings, 2001. XV, 738 pages. 2001.

Vol. 2253: T. Terano, T. Nishida, A. Namatame, S. Tsumoto, Y. Ohsawa, T. Washio (Eds.), New Frontiers in Artificial Intelligence. Proceedings, 2001. XXVII, 553 pages. 2001.

Vol. 2256: M. Stumptner, D. Corbett, M. Brooks (Eds.), AI 2001: Advances in Artificial Intelligence. Proceedings, 2001. XII, 666 pages. 2001.

Vol. 2258: P. Brazdil, A. Jorge (Eds.), Progress in Artificial Intelligence. Proceedings, 2001. XII, 418 pages. 2001.

Vol. 2275: N.R. Pal, M. Sugeno (Eds.), Advances in Soft Computing – AFSS 2002. Proceedings, 2002. XVI, 536 pages. 2002.

Vol. 2281: S. Arikawa, A. Shinohara (Eds.), Progress in Discovery Science. XIV, 684 pages. 2002.

Vol. 2293: J. Renz, Qualitative Spatial Reasoning with Topological Information. XVI, 207 pages. 2002.

Vol. 2296: B. Dunin-Kęplicz, E. Nawarecki (Eds.), From Theory to Practice in Multi-Agent Systems. Proceedings, 2001. IX, 341 pages. 2002.

Vol. 2302: C. Schulte, Programming Constraint Services. XII, 176 pages. 2002.

Vol. 2307: C. Zhang, S. Zhang, Association Rule Mining. XII, 238 pages. 2002.

Vol. 2308: I.P. Vlahavas, C.D. Spyropoulos (Eds.), Methods and Applications of Artificial Intelligence. Proceedings, 2002. XIV, 514 pages. 2002.

Vol. 2309: A. Armando (Ed.), Frontiers of Combining Systems. Proceedings, 2002. VIII, 255 pages. 2002.

Vol. 2313: C.A. Coello Coello, A. de Albornoz, L.E. Sucar, O.Cairó Battistutti (Eds.), MICAI 2002: Advances in Artificial Intelligence. Proceedings, 2002. XIII, 548 pages. 2002.

Vol. 2322: V. Mařík, O. Stěpánková, H. Krautwurmová, M. Luck (Eds.), Multi-Agent Systems and Applications II. Proceedings, 2001. XII, 377 pages. 2002.

Lecture Notes in Computer Science

Vol. 2279: S. Cagnoni, J. Gottlieb, E. Hart, M. Middendorf, G.R. Raidl (Eds.), Applications of Evolutionary Computing. Proceedings, 2002. XIII, 344 pages. 2002.

Vol. 2280: J.P. Katoen, P. Stevens (Eds.), Tools and Algorithms for the Construction and Analysis of Systems. Proceedings, 2002. XIII, 482 pages. 2002.

Vol. 2281: S. Arikawa, A. Shinohara (Eds.), Progress in Discovery Science. XIV, 684 pages. 2002. (Subseries LNAI).

Vol. 2282: D. Ursino, Extraction and Exploitation of Intensional Knowledge from Heterogeneous Information Sources. XXVI, 289 pages. 2002.

Vol. 2283: T. Nipkow, L.C. Paulson, M. Wenzel, Isabelle/HOL. XIII, 218 pages. 2002.

Vol. 2284: T. Eiter, K.-D. Schewe (Eds.), Foundations of Information and Knowledge Systems. Proceedings, 2002. X, 289 pages. 2002.

Vol. 2285: H. Alt, A. Ferreira (Eds.), STACS 2002. Proceedings, 2002. XIV, 660 pages. 2002.

Vol. 2286: S. Rajsbaum (Ed.), LATIN 2002: Theoretical Informatics. Proceedings, 2002. XIII, 630 pages. 2002.

Vol. 2287: C.S. Jensen, K.G. Jeffery, J. Pokorny, Saltenis, E. Bertino, K. Böhm, M. Jarke (Eds.), Advances in Database Technology – EDBT 2002. Proceedings, 2002. XVI, 776 pages. 2002.

Vol. 2288: K. Kim (Ed.), Information Security and Cryptology – ICISC 2001. Proceedings, 2001. XIII, 457 pages. 2002.

Vol. 2289: C.J. Tomlin, M.R. Greenstreet (Eds.), Hybrid Systems: Computation and Control. Proceedings, 2002. XIII, 480 pages. 2002.

Vol. 2291: F. Crestani, M. Girolami, C.J. van Rijsbergen (Eds.), Advances in Information Retrieval. Proceedings, 2002. XIII, 363 pages. 2002.

Vol. 2292: G.B. Khosrovshahi, A. Shokoufandeh, A. Shokrollahi (Eds.), Theoretical Aspects of Computer Science. IX, 221 pages. 2002.

Vol. 2293: J. Renz, Qualitative Spatial Reasoning with Topological Information. XVI, 207 pages. 2002. (Subseries LNAI).

Vol. 2295: W. Kuich, G. Rozenberg, A. Salomaa (Eds.), Developments in Language Theory. Proceedings, 2001. IX, 389 pages. 2002.

Vol. 2296: B. Dunin-Keplicz, E. Nawarecki (Eds.), From Theory to Practice in Multi-Agent Systems. Proceedings, 2001. IX, 341 pages. 2002. (Subseries LNAI).

Vol. 2299: H. Schmeck, T. Ungerer, L. Wolf (Eds.), Trends in Network and Pervasive Computing – ARCS 2002. Proceedings, 2002. XIV, 287 pages. 2002.

Vol. 2300: W. Brauer, H. Ehrig, J. Karhumäki, A. Salomaa (Eds.), Formal and Natural Computing. XXXVI, 431 pages. 2002.

Vol. 2301: A. Braquelaire, J.-O. Lachaud, A. Vialard (Eds.), Discrete Geometry for Computer Imagery. Proceedings, 2002. XI, 439 pages. 2002.

Vol. 2302: C. Schulte, Programming Constraint Services. XII, 176 pages. 2002. (Subseries LNAI).

Vol. 2303: M. Nielsen, U. Engberg (Eds.), Foundations of Software Science and Computation Structures. Proceedings, 2002. XIII, 435 pages. 2002.

Vol. 2304: R.N. Horspool (Ed.), Compiler Construction. Proceedings, 2002. XI, 343 pages. 2002.

Vol. 2305: D. Le Métayer (Ed.), Programming Languages and Systems. Proceedings, 2002. XII, 331 pages. 2002.

Vol. 2306: R.-D. Kutsche, H. Weber (Eds.), Fundamental Approaches to Software Engineering. Proceedings, 2002. XIII, 341 pages. 2002.

Vol. 2307: C. Zhang, S. Zhang, Association Rule Mining. XII, 238 pages. 2002. (Subseries LNAI).

Vol. 2308: I.P. Vlahavas, C.D. Spyropoulos (Eds.), Methods and Applications of Artificial Intelligence. Proceedings, 2002. XIV, 514 pages. 2002. (Subseries LNAI).

Vol. 2309: A. Armando (Ed.), Frontiers of Combining Systems. Proceedings, 2002. VIII, 255 pages. 2002. (Subseries LNAI).

Vol. 2310: P. Collet, C. Fonlupt, J.-K. Hao, E. Lutton, M. Schoenauer (Eds.), Artificial Evolution. Proceedings, 2001. XI, 375 pages. 2002.

Vol. 2311: D. Bustard, W. Liu, R. Sterritt (Eds.), Soft-Ware 2002: Computing in an Imperfect World. Proceedings, 2002. XI, 359 pages. 2002.

Vol. 2313: C.A. Coello Coello, A. de Albornoz, L.E. Sucar, O.Cairó Battistutti (Eds.), MICAI 2002: Advances in Artificial Intelligence. Proceedings, 2002. XIII, 548 pages. 2002. (Subseries LNAI).

Vol. 2314: S.-K. Chang, Z. Chen, S.-Y. Lee (Eds.), Recent Advances in Visual Information Systems. Proceedings, 2002. XI, 323 pages. 2002.

Vol. 2315: F. Arhab, C. Talcott (Eds.), Coordination Models and Languages. Proceedings, 2002. XI, 406 pages. 2002.

Vol. 2318: D. Bošnački, S. Leue (Eds.), Model Checking Software. Proceedings, 2002. X, 259 pages. 2002.

Vol. 2319: C. Gacek (Ed.), Software Reuse: Methods, Techniques, and Tools. Proceedings, 2002. XI, 353 pages. 2002.

Vol. 2322: V. Mařík, O. Štěpánková, H. Krautwurmová, M. Luck (Eds.), Multi-Agent Systems and Applications II. Proceedings, 2001. XII, 377 pages. 2002. (Subseries LNAI).